Ethnic and Native Canadian Literature

A BIBLIOGRAPHY

Ethnic and Native Canadian Literature

A BIBLIOGRAPHY

John Miska

UNIVERSITY OF TORONTO PRESS
Toronto Buffalo London

© University of Toronto Press 1990
Toronto Buffalo London
Printed in Canada
ISBN 0-8020-5852-3

Printed on acid-free paper

Canadian Cataloguing in Publication Data

Miska, John P., 1932–
Ethnic and native Canadian Literature

ISBN 0-8020-5852-3

1. Canadian literature – Minority authors –
Bibliography. 2. Canadian literature – History
and criticism – Bibliography. I. Title.

Z1376.E87M5 1990   016.8088′9971   C90-093936-2

*The publishers are grateful to Mr Miska for all his effort in
preparing this extensive bibliography for publication on his own
microcomputer.*

CONTENTS

PREFACE

Multiculturalism has become an integral part of present-day Canadian life. Subjects such as ethnicity, nativism, minority literatures and cultural pluralism constitute a significant portion of our school curricula and media output. Extensive studies are devoted to literatures in the non-official languages and to the image of the immigrant and native people in Canadian literature.

Owing to an ever-increasing demand for information on ethnic literatures expressed by educators, librarians and other information specialists, the Social Sciences and Humanities Research Council of Canada commissioned me to compile a research tool. The bibliography of close to 5,500 references to primary and secondary material from the earliest times to the present represents 65 nationality groups in more than 70 languages. Part of the material is derived from my preliminary bibliography entitled *Ethnic and Native Canadian Literature 1850-1979*, published in microform in 1979.

Criteria for inclusion

Inclusion in this bibliography was based on the following criteria: an author had to (1) publish books of poetry, fiction and drama in any language; (2) be born outside Canada and have settled in Canada as an adolescent or adult; (3) have written the work while residing in Canada; but (4) writers from France, the United States, Britain, Australia, and New Zealand were excluded. Within these general rules there are exceptions: (1) some Canadian-born authors were included (e.g. authors of German-Mennonite, Icelandic, Ukrainian descent) if their language of creation was other than English or French; and (2) native authors were included regardless of linguistic considerations. Part III includes several publications by French- or English-Canadian authors whose writings are related to ethnic and native people in Canada.

Sources of information

Citations for the bibliography have been gathered from major Canadian library resources and from relevant bibliographic sources such *Canadiana, Canadian Periodical Index, University of Toronto Quarterly, Canadian Ethnic Studies, Revue d'histoire littéraire du Québec et du Canada français*, as well as from the invaluable files of the Multiculturalism Sector of the Department of the Secretary of State. Research papers, review articles and book reviews were selected from periodicals, newspapers and individual bibliographies too numerous to be listed here. A systematic search has been conducted for primary materials and the location of Canadian university graduate theses by using a computer-based on-line literature search system offered by the National Library of Canada. The bulk of the material, however, was gathered by conventional methods through manual searches of library holdings, and by contacting individual authors of various nationality groups through telephone, correspondence or personal visits.

Organization of bibliographic data

The bibliography is organized into three main sections. Part I includes general reference tools such as bibliographies, monographic and research studies and collective works of a general nature. Part II, the major section of the book, represents the literary output of 65 nationality/language groups and writings about them. This section is arranged alphabetically by group, proceeding from the general to the specific, from the reference type of material to the individual authors, giving primary material first, followed by writings about them. Part III features publications relating to ethnic and native people in mainstream Canadian literature, with an indication of the individual nationality group(s) the writing is about. A list of periodical abbreviations is provided at the beginning and an author-subject index is given at the end of the compilation. The entries are numbered consecutively, each providing the following bibliographic information:

(1) Author(s); (2) title and source (e.g. periodical title, volume — issue number, if pagination is not consecutive throughout the volume — pagination), and date of publication; (3) in case of a monographic publication, place and publisher are also provided; (4) some of the reference material is followed by brief annotations.

Titles of publications, if written in a language other than English or French, are first given in the original, followed by the English translation set in brackets. Bibliographic information and biographical notes on authors whose creative language is French are given in the French language. Other information provided includes short biographical sketches of authors of poetry, fiction or drama, cross references and genre. An incomplete bibliographic entry is an indication that the citation was not available for consultation. Since the work on this volume has taken place over many years, some inconsistencies are bound to have occurred. I have done my best to correct them and any errors that remain are mine. The final version of the manuscript was prepared on a microcomputer and the data will be accessible to libraries on an on-line basis.

Acknowledgements

This bibliography received assistance in the form of suggestions and encouragement from several institutions and individuals. I am indebted to the National Library of Canada and to the libraries of the Universities of Ottawa, Toronto, Laval and Alberta for making their collections available to me. My gratitude is extended to professors Yar Slavutych, George Bisztray, Joseph Pivato, Michael Batts, Suwanda Sugunasiri, Nuzrat Yar Khan, Bogdan Czaykowski, Ronald Sutherland, Alexander Malycky, and many other subject, language and bibliographic experts for their generosity in providing additional information and advice. My thanks are also due to such language experts as Dr. Leo Niilo, Alecos Michaelides, Dr. Andrzej Bielanski, Elva Simundsson, George Payerle for their assistance in the specific sections and, above all, to Gerald Hallowell, of the University of Toronto Press, for providing expert editorial advice throughout the various stages of this publication. My sincere thanks to Judy Young and Barbara Preston, of the Multiculturalism Sector of the Department of the Secretary of State, for allowing me to consult institute files and records, and to the many individual authors for responding to the questionnaire and other requests for contribution to the bibliography. Special thanks go to my wife, Marulle, for her aptitude and resourcefulness in automating this project and for showing leadership in the organizational and administrative management of this extensive undertaking. Financial assistance received from the Social Sciences and Humanities Research Council of Canada, without which this project would not have materialized, is most gratefully acknowledged.

John Miska

ABBREVIATIONS

ACS NEWSL/ BULL AEC — *ACS Newsletter/Bulletin de l'AEC*
ACT BALT — *Acta Baltica*
ACT NAT — *L'Action nationale*
ALMAN Ó.S. THORGEIR — *Almanak Ó.S. Thorgeirssonar*
ALTA J EDUC RES — *Alberta Journal of Educational Research*
AMER-GERM REV — *The American-German Review*
AMER HUMAN IND — *The American Humanities Index*
AMER MAGY SZÉPM CZÉH NEGYED ÉRT — *Amerikai Magyar Szépmíves Czéh Negyedévi Értesítője*
AMER MAGY VIL — *Amerikai Magyar Világ*
AMER REV — *The American Review*
ANTIG REV — *The Antigonish Review*
APLA BULL — *Apla Bulletin*
ASPECTS FRANCE — *Aspects de la France*
AUST JEWISH FOR — *The Australian Jewish Forum*
AUST JEWISH HER — *The Australian Jewish Herald*
AUST LATV — *Australias Latvietis*
AUSZT MAGY — *Ausztráliai Magyarság*

BALTIM ÉRT — *Baltimorei Értesítő*
BETH NAPT — *Bethlen Naptár*
BKS ABR — *Books Abroad*
BKS CAN — *Books in Canada*
BLOOR W VILLAG — *Bloor West Villager*
BOOK REV IND — *The Book Review Index*
BORÉAL INT — *Boréal International*
BÖRSENBLATT DEUTSCH BHD — *Börsenblatt für den deutschen Buchhandel*
BULL ANALYT BIBLIO HELLÉN — *Bulletin analytique de bibliographie hellénique*
BULL CENTRE ÉTUD FRANCO-CAN OUEST — *Bulletin. Centre d'études franco-canadiennes de l'Ouest*

CAH BIBL LETTR QUÉB — *Cahiers de bibliographie des lettres québécoises*
CAHIERS HIBOU — *Les Cahiers du hibou*
CAL JEWISH VOICE — *The California Jewish Voice*
CAN-AMER REV HUNG STUD — *The Canadian-American Review of Hungarian Studies*
CAN AUTH BKMN — *Canadian Author and Bookman*
CAN BOOK REV ANN — *Canadian Book Review Annual*
CAN CHILDR LIT — *Canadian Children's Literature*
CAN ETH STUD — *Canadian Ethnic Studies/Études ethniques au Canada*
CAN FIC MAG — *Canadian Fiction Magazine*
CAN FORUM — *The Canadian Forum*
CAN FRANÇ — *Le Canada français*
CAN IND TIMES — *Canadian Indian Times*
CAN J FIC — *Canadian Journal of Fiction*
CAN JEWISH CONG — *Canadian Jewish Congress*
CAN JEWISH NEWS — *Canadian Jewish News*
CAN JEWISH OUTL — *Canadian Jewish Outlook*
CAN JEWISH Q — *Canadian Jewish Quarterly*
CAN JEWISH YEARB — *Canadian Jewish Yearbook*

CAN LIT	*Canadian Literature*
CAN MAG IND	*Canadian Magazine Index*
CAN NOTES QUERIES	*Canadian Notes and Queries/Questions et réponses canadiennes*
CAN POST	*Canada Posten*
CAN READER	*Canadian Reader*
CAN REV COMP LIT	*Canadian Review of Comparative Literature*
CAN SLAVON PAPERS	*Canadian Slavonic Papers*
CAN WOMAN STUD	*Canadian Woman Studies/Les Cahiers de la femme*
CAN WORLD FED	*Canadian World Federalist*
CAN ZION	*Canadian Zionist*
CHELSEA J	*Chelsea Journal*
CHRIST SCI MON	*Christian Science Monitor*
CHRON REV	*Chronicle Review*
CM	*Canadian Materials for Schools and Libraries*
COMBAT	*Combat, le journal de Paris*
CONG BIWEEKLY	*The Congress Biweekly, American Jewish Congress*
CONG BULL	*The Congress Bulletin*
CONG WEEKLY AMER JEWISH CONG	*The Congress Weekly, American Jewish Congress*
CONT VERSE II	*Contemporary Verse II (CVII)*
CORM DELF	*Cormorán y Delfín*
CORR ESP Q	*Correo Español de Quebec*
CRIT REV CAN LIT	*Critical Review of Canadian Literature*
CROSS-CAN WRIT Q	*Cross-Canadian Writers Quarterly*
CUAD LIT AZOR	*Cuadernos Literarios Azor*
CURRIC INQUIRY	*Curriculum Inquiry*
DAL REV	*Dalhousie Review*
DAUG VAN MÉN	*Daugavas Vanagu Ménesraksts*
DAY	*Day, The Jewish Journal*
DETR MAGY ÚJS	*Detroiti Magyar Újság*
DEUTSCHKAN JAHRB	*Deutschkanadisches Jahrbuch*
DZIEN POLSK ŠRODA LIT	*Dziennik Polski, Šroda Literacka*
ECHO MAG	*Echo Magazine*
ECHO TYG	*Echo Tygodonia*
EDMONT J	*The Edmonton Journal*
EEST HÄÄL	*Eesti Hääl*
EEST PÄEV	*Eesti Päevaleht*
EEST POST	*Eesti Post*
ÉLET IROD	*Élet és Irodalom*
ENG Q	*The English Quarterly*
ENG TODAY	*English Today*
ESP LIBR	*España Libre*
ESSAYS CAN WRIT	*Essays on Canadian Writing*
ÉTUD CAN/CAN STUD	*Études canadiennes/Canadian Studies*
EUROP IDEEN	*Europäische Ideen*
FEMME	*Femme, La-la Vie - le Monde*
FIGARO LITT	*Figaro Littéraire*
FIN POST MAG	*Financial Post Magazine*
FRENCH REV	*The French Review*
GERM CAN BUS REV	*German Canadian Business Review*

GERM LIFE LETTR	*German Life and Letters*
GLOBE MAIL	*Globe and Mail*
GŁOS POLSK	*Głos Polski*
GOLD KEYT	*Goldene Keyt*
HALIF CHRON HER	*Halifax Chronicle Herald*
HOLOS SPAS/RED VOICE	*Holos Spasytelia/The Redeemer's Voice*
HOMIN UKR	*Homin Ukraïny*
HUNG STUD REV	*Hungarian Studies Review*
ICELAND-CAN	*Icelandic-Canadian*
IMPRIM NEUE FOLGE	*Imprimatur Neue Folge*
INT FIC REV	*International Fiction Review*
IROD ÚJS	*Irodalmi Újság*
ITAL CAN	*Italian Canadiana*
J CAN CULT	*Journal of Canadian Culture*
J CAN FIC	*Journal of Canadian Fiction*
J CAN POETRY	*Journal of Canadian Poetry*
J CAN STUD	*Journal of Canadian Studies/Revue d'études canadiennes*
J COMMONW LIT	*The Journal of Commonwealth Literature*
J MENN STUD	*Journal of Mennonite Studies*
J POP CULT	*Journal of Popular Culture*
JAHRESB NEUE DEUT LIT	*Jahresbericht für neue deutsche Literatur*
JERUS POST MAG LIT SUPPL	*Jerusalem Post Magazine Literary Supplement*
JEU	*Jeu : Cahiers de théâtre*
JEÜD RUND MACC	*Jeüdische Rundschau Maccabi*
JEWISH BOOK ANN	*Jewish Book Annual*
JEWISH COMM NEWS	*Jewish Community News*
JEWISH CULT AFFAIRS, WORLD JEWISH CONG	*Jewish Cultural Affairs, World Jewish Congress*
JEWISH CURR	*Jewish Currents*
JEWISH DAILY FORW	*Jewish Daily Forward*
JEWISH FRONT	*Jewish Frontier*
JEWISH STAND	*Jewish Standard*
KALIF MAGY	*Kaliforniai Magyarság*
KAN FARM	*Kanadiïs'kyï Farmer*
KAN MAGY	*Kanadai Magyarság*
KAN MAGY ÚJS	*Kanadai Magyar Újság*
KAN MAGY ÚJS KÉPES NAGY NAPT	*Kanadai Magyar Újság Képes Nagy Naptára*
KAN UKR	*Kanadas'ka Ukraïna*
KAT MAGY VAS	*Katolikus Magyarok Vasárnapja*
KAT SZEM	*Katolikus Szemle*
KEN ADL	*Keneder Adler*
KÉPES MAGY VIL	*Képes Magyar Világhíradó*
KREŠT AKAD	*Kreštnske Akademie*
LAKEHEAD UNIV REV	*Lakehead University Review*
LATV AMER	*Latvija Amerika*
LAUR UNIV REV	*The Laurentian University Review*
LETH HERALD	*Lethbridge Herald*
LETS NAY	*Letste Nayes*

LETTR QUÉB	Lettres québécoises
LIET LIT SVET	Lietuvių Literatūra Svetur
LIT ALMAN	Literarny Almanak
LIT ECHO	Literarisches Echo
LIT HALF-YEARLY	Literary Half-Yearly
LIT MYST	Literatura i Mystetstvo
LIT VOL	Litopys Volyni
LIVR AUTR CAN	Livres et auteurs canadiens
LIVR AUTR QUÉB	Livres et auteurs québécois
LIVR D'ICI	Livre d'ici (Mensuel)
LOND AVĪZ	Londonas Avīze
LOND FREE PRESS	London Free Press
LOND GUARD	London Guardian
LYST PRYIAT	Lysty do Pryiateliv
MAGY ÉLET	Magyar Élet
MAGY HÍR	Magyar Hírek
MAGY HÍRLAP	Magyar Hírlap
MAGY MŰH	Magyar Műhely
MAGY NEMZET	Magyar Nemzet
MAGY ÚJS	Magyar Újság
MAL REV	The Malahat Review
MAN ARTS REV	The Manitoba Arts Review
MAN COUR NORD	Manitoba Courier - der Nordwesten
MAN SCHOOL J	Manitoba School Journal
MENN AUSL	Mennonitische Auslese
MENN LIFE	Mennonite Life
MENN MIRR	Mennonite Mirror
MENN REP	Mennonite Reporter
MENN RUND	Mennonitische Rundschau
MENN WART	Mennonitische Warte
MENN WELT	Mennonitische Welt
MÉS NOV ŽIV	Mésisnick Novy Život
MITT INST AUSL	Mitteilungen: Institut für Auslandsbeziehungen
MONT JEWISH LIFE	Montreal Jewish Life
MONT NACH	Montrealer Nachrichten
MONT STAR	The Montreal Star
MORG FREIH	Morgen-Freiheit
MORG J	Morgn-Journal
MUND ISR	Mundo Israelita
MYŚL POLSK	Myśl Polska
N DEUT RUND	Neue Deutsche Rundschau
NAROD GŁAS	Narodni Głasnik/National Herald
NASH ZHYTT	Nashe Zhyttia
NAT HERALD TRIB	The National Herald Tribune
NAY YIDD VORT	Naye Yiddishe Vort
NEDERL COUR	Nederlandse Courant
NEPR LIET	Nepriklausoma Lietuva
NEW CAN REV	New Canadian Review
NEW Q	The New Quarterly
N.Y. HERALD TRIB	The New York Herald Tribune
N.Y. TIMES	The New York Times
N.Y. TIMES BOOK REV	The New York Times Book Review

NOS LIVR	*Nos livres*
NOUV BARRE DU JOUR	*Nouvelle Barre du Jour*
NOUV REV FRANÇ	*La Nouvelle Revue française*
NOV SHLIAKH	*Novyĭ Shliakh*
NOWY DZIEN	*Nowy Dziennik*
NYELVÜNK KULTÚRÁNK	*Nyelvünk és Kultúránk*
NYUG MAGY	*Nyugati Magyarság*
NYUG MAGY ÉLET	*Nyugati Magyar Élet*
ONT LIB REV	*Ontario Library Review*
ONT REV	*Ontario Review*
OST WIAD	*Ostatnie Wiadomości*
OTTAWA CIT	*The Ottawa Citizen*
OTTAWA J	*The Ottawa Journal*
PERF ARTS CAN	*The Performing Arts in Canada*
PETIT J	*Le Petit Journal*
PIVN SIAĬV	*Pivnichne Siaĭvo*
POES HISP	*Poesia Hispanica*
POET CAN REV	*Poetry Canada Review*
POET CHIC	*Poetry (Chicago)*
PÕH TÄH	*Põhjala Tähistel*
POINT REP IND ANALYT ART	*Point de repère: index analytique d'articles de périodiques*
POL REV	*Polish Review*
PROBL COMMUN	*Problems of Communism*
PROC TRANS ROY SOC CAN	*Proceedings and Transactions of the Royal Society of Canada*
PRZEG HUMANIST	*Przegląd Humanistycny*
PRZEG TYG	*Przegląd Tygodniowy*
Q & Q	*Quill and Quire*
Q J LIB CONG	*Quarterly Journal of the Library of Congress*
QUÉB FRANÇ	*Québec français*
QUEEN'S Q	*Queen's Quarterly*
READ DIGEST	*Reader's Digest*
REF LAP	*Reformátusok Lapja*
REV HIST LITT QUÉ CAN FRANÇ	*Revue d'histoire littéraire du Québec et du Canada français*
REV UNIV COMP MADR	*Revista de la Universidad Complutense de Madrid*
REV UNIV MONCTON	*Revue de l'Université de Moncton*
SARNIA OBS	*Sarnia Observer*
SAT N	*Saturday Night*
SCAND STUD NOTES	*Scandinavian Studies and Notes*
SEATTLE POST-INT	*Seattle Post-Intelligencer*
SEMINAR J GERM STUD	*Seminar: Journal of Germanic Studies*
SEWANEE REV	*Sewanee Review*
SLAVON EAST EUR REV	*Slavonic and East European Review*
SLOVAK STUD	*Slovak Studies*
SLOVAK WORLD CONG BULL	*Slovak World Congress Bulletin*
ST CATH STAND	*St. Catharine's Standard*
STAND FREEH	*Standard Freeholder*
STOCK TID	*Stockholms Tidnigen*
STUD CAN LIT	*Studies in Canadian Literature*

STUD NOVEL	*Studies in the Novel*
TAM REV	*The Tamarack Review*
TĖV ŽIB	*Tėviškes Žiburai*
THIS MAG	*This Magazine*
TÍM ÞJOD ISL VEST	*Tímarit Þjodræknisfjelags Islendinga Vest*
TIMES LIT SUPPL	*The Times Literary Supplement*
TOR LIFE	*Toronto Life*
TOR SOUTH-ASIAN REV	*Toronto South-Asian Review*
TOR STAR	*Toronto Star*
TOR TEL	*Toronto Telegram*
TRANS ROY SOC CAN	*Transactions of the Royal Society of Canada*
TRIB GENÈVE	*Tribune de Genève*
TYD POLSK	*Tydzien Polski*
TYG POLSK	*Tygodnik Polski*
ÚJ EUR	*Új Európa*
ÚJ LÁTÓH	*Új Látóhatár*
ÚJ SYMP	*Új Symposion*
UKR CAN REV	*Ukrainian Canadian Review*
UKR DUM	*Ukraïns'ka Dumka*
UKR HOLOS	*Ukraïns'kyĭ Holos*
UKR KNYHA	*Ukraïns'ka knyha*
UKR PION	*Ukraïns'kyĭ Pionir*
UKR REV	*Ukrainian Review*
UKR ROD	*Ukraïns'ka Rodyna*
UKR SLOVO	*Ukraïns'ke Slovo*
UKR VISTI	*Ukraïns'ki Visti*
UKR WEEKLY	*Ukrainian Weekly*
UNIV TOR Q	*University of Toronto Quarterly*
UNIV WINDSOR REV	*The University of Windsor Review*
URDU CAN	*Urdu Canada*
URDU INT	*Urdu International*
UVAN	*Ukrains'ka Vil'na Akademiia Nauk v Kanada*
VABA EEST	*Vaba Eestlane*
VABA EEST SÕNA	*Vaba Eesti sõna*
VANC EGYH HÍR	*Vancouver Egyházi Híradó*
VANC SUN	*Vancouver Sun*
VICISS LUCHA	*Vicissitudes de la Lucha*
VIEWPOINTS	*Viewpoints: Canadian Jewish Quarterly*
VIL'N DUM	*Vil'na Dumka*
VIL'N SLOVO	*Vil'ne Slovo*
VIL'N SVIT	*Vil'nyĭ Svit*
VIST UKR	*Visti z Ukraïny*
VISTNYK	*Vistnyk/Herald*
VOIX IMAG	*Voix et images: études québécoises*
VYZV SHLIAKH	*Vyzvol'nyĭ SHliakh*
WASC REV	*Wascana Review*
WEST COAST REV	*West Coast Review*
WEST LIV	*Western Living*
WESTM EXAM	*Westminster Examiner*
WHIG STAND MAG	*Whig Standard Magazine*

WINN FREE PRESS	*Winnipeg Free Press*
WINN TRIB	*Winnipeg Tribune*
WORLD LIT TODAY	*World Literature Today*
WORLD LIT WRITT ENG	*World Literature Written in English*
YIDD TSAY	*Yiddishe Tsaytung*

I. REFERENCE WORKS

REFERENCE WORKS

BIBLIOGRAPHIES, DIRECTORIES

1   ANDERSON, W.W.
Caribbean Orientations: A Bibliography of Resource Material on the Caribbean Experience in Canada.   Toronto: Organization for Caribbean Canadian Initiatives and Williams-Wallace, 1985. xi, 238 pp.
[Includes more than 2000 titles relating to the Caribbean experience in Canada.]

2   ANDREWS, Christina Ann
"The Immigrant Experience in Canadian Children's Literature 1976 to 1985: An Annotated Bibliography." MLS non-thesis project, University of Alberta, 1986.   65 leaves.
[Contains more than 300 references.]

3   BANKS, Joyce M.
Books in Native Languages in the Rare Book Collections of the National Library of Canada/Livres en langues autochtones dans les collections des livres rares de la Bibliothèque nationale du Canada, rev., enl. ed. Ottawa: National Library of Canada, 1985.   xvii, 190 pp.
[Arranged chronologically by subject and language. Provides indices to translators, authors, editors, printers, publishers and titles. First edition was published in 1980.   93 pp.]

4   BONAVIA, George
Ethnic Publications in Canada: Newspapers, Periodicals, Magazines, Bulletins, Newsletters. Ottawa: International Productions, 1987.   xii, 158 pp.
[Arranged by subject, complete with bibliographic data and the occasional annotation.]

5   BONAVIA, George
Immigrants We Read About. Ottawa: International Productions, 1987.   228 pp.
[Includes chapters on immigrants and their experiences and their contributions to Canada; a list of books about immigrants and a section on biographical notes on noteworthy immigrants gathered from newspapers, periodicals and other sources.]

6   CANTIN, Pierre; HARRINGTON, Normand; HUDON, Jean-Paul
Bibliographie de la critique de la littérature québécoise dans les revues des XIXe et XXe siècles. Ottawa: C.R.C.C.F. (Université d'Ottawa), 1979.   5 v. (x, 1254 pp.) Ronéotypée.
[This compilation contains close to 19,000 references to secondary material on Québécois authors. It is light on minority authors.]

7   *Connections Two: Writers and the Land.*   Winnipeg: Manitoba School Library Audio-Visual Association, 1983.   123 pp. ports.
[Provides biographies of Manitoba authors and lists of their publications. Minority writers included are Kristjana Gunnars and James Tallosi. The first edition included Vera Lysenko and John Marlyn.]

8   DIONNE, René; CANTIN, Pierre
"Bibliographie de la critique." REV HIST LITT QUÉ CAN FRANÇ 2 (1982): 180-304.
[Includes 2250 references. Individual ethnic Canadian authors represented are Raymond Chassagne, Lilianne Dévieux Dehoux, Franck Fouché, Naïm Kattan, and Anthony Phelps.]

9   DIONNE, René; CANTIN, Pierre

"Bibliographie de la critique." REV HIST LITT QUÉ CAN FRANÇ 3 (1981-1982): 151-263.
[Individual authors included are Alexandre Amprimoz, Raymond Chassagne and Naïm Kattan.]

10   DIONNE, René; CANTIN, Pierre
"Bibliographie de la critique." REV HIST LITT QUÉ CAN FRANÇ 4 (1982): 119-234.
[Ethnic authors included are Alexandre Amprimoz and Jean Civil.]

11   DIONNE, René; CANTIN, Pierre
"Bibliographie de la critique." REV HIST LITT QUÉ CAN FRANÇ 5 (1983): 147-268.
[Includes bibliographic information on primary material, bibliographies, anthologies, research papers and monographs and review articles on individual authors. Ethnic Canadian authors writing in French included here are Alexandre Amprimoz, Jean Civil, Gérard Étienne, Naïm Kattan, Roland Morrisseau, Anthony Phelps and Alix Renaud.]

12   DIONNE, René; CANTIN, Pierre
"Bibliographie de la critique." REV HIST LITT QUÉ CAN FRANÇ 6 (1983): 99-232.
[A compilation of 2629 citations on books, essays, anthologies. Review articles on individual authors are provided (pp. 134-232). Some ethnic authors included are Alexandre Amprimoz, Jean Civil, Anthony Phelps, Naïm Kattan, Alix Renaud.]

13   DIONNE, René; CANTIN, Pierre
"Bibliographie de la critique." REV HIST LITT QUÉ CAN FRANÇ 9 (1985): 161-66.
[Major areas of coverage are bibliographies, anthologies, essays, monographs and books by individual authors.]

14   DIONNE, René; CANTIN, Pierre
"Bibliographie de la critique." REV HIST LITT QUÉ CAN FRANÇ 10 (1986): 131-275.
[Included are Alexandre Amprimoz, Naïm Kattan, Émile Ollivier and Anthony Phelps.]

15   DIONNE, René; CANTIN, Pierre
"Bibliographie de la critique." REV HIST LITT QUÉ CAN FRANÇ 14 (1987): 175-345.
[Includes Alexandre Amprimoz, Gérard Étienne, Émile Ollivier.]

16   EVANS, K., comp.
Masinahikan: Native Language Imprints in the Archives & Libraries of the Anglican Church of Canada. Toronto: Anglican Book Centre, 1985. xxiii, 357 pp.
[Includes references to 746 prints and 49 manuscripts in 44 languages published between 1780 and 1982.]

17   GABEL, Gernot U.
Canadian Literature: An Index to Theses Accepted by Canadian Universities 1925-1984. Köln: Edition Gemini, 1984.
[Includes references to theses on literature. Extensive indices are also provided.]

18   GNAROWSKI, Michael
A Concise Bibliography of English-Canadian Literature. Toronto: McClelland & Stewart, 1978. 145 pp.
[A select list of authors. Includes primary materials with major review articles about their writings. Ethnic authors represented are Frederick Philip Grove and Michael Ondaatje.]

19   GOLDSTEIN, Jay
"Bibliography." CAN ETH STUD 14, no. 3 (1982): 140-46.
[Covers history, immigration, education, assimilation, multiculturalism-bilingualism, and general

aspects of ethnicity.]

20 GREGOROVICH, Andrew S.
Canadian Ethnic Groups Bibliography. A Selected Bibliography of Ethno-cultural Groups in Canada and the Province of Ontario. Toronto: Ontario Department of Provincial Secretary and Citizenship, 1972. 208 pp.
[Provides names of groups, date of establishment, addresses, lists of officers. Arranged by nationality groups.]

21 HAMEL, Réginald; HARE, John; WYCZINSKI, Paul
Dictionnaire pratique des auteurs québécois. Montréal: Fides, 1976. 723 pp.
[Arranged alphabetically by author. Provides extensive biographies and references to publications by and about authors residing in Québec. Several immigrant poets and prose writers are listed. Also includes portraits of authors.]

22 HEATH, Jeffrey M., ed.
Profiles in Canadian Literature. Toronto/Charlottetown: Dundurn Press, 1980-1982. 4 vols. ports.
[Provides an essay on each author represented, along with chronology of major events, a list of publications by and about each author, and a list of criticisms. Volume 4 includes Austin Clarke.]

23 HROMADIUK, Bob
"Bibliography." CAN ETH STUD 17, no. 3 (1985): 168-203.
[The section under "Culture-Literature" includes 25 related entries.]

24 HROMADIUK, Bob
"Bibliography." CAN ETH STUD 19, no. 3 (1987): 187-219.
[Related subjects covered are: bibliography, culture, and literature of ethnic and native authors.]

25 JACQUES, Ruxl-Léonel
"Bibliographie/Bibliography." CAN ETH STUD 18, no. 2 (1986): 178-82.
[Includes 87 citations, mostly publications in French, relating to ethnic Canadian studies.]

26 JAWORSKY, S.J
"Newspapers and Periodicals of Slavic Groups in Canada During the Period of 1965-1969: An Annotated Bibliography." M.A. Thesis. University of Ottawa, 1971. 134 pp.
[A complete list of serials available in Canada. Individual language groups included are Russian, Ukrainian, Polish, Czech, Slovak, Croatian, Serbian, Macedonian. Newspapers published in the USA, but circulating in Canada, are also listed.]

27 KIRKCONNELL, Watson
"Lists of Publications, New Canadian." UNIV TOR Q 7 (1937-38): 590-600.
[A list of selected periodicals published in languages other than English or French. Similar compilations appeared in volumes 8, 9, and 10. Checklists of titles of ethnic publications are included annually from volume 12 on at the end of summaries on the subject.]

28 LACROIX, Jean-Michel
Anatomie de la presse ethnique au Canada. Bordeaux: Presses universitaires de Bordeaux, 1988. 493 pp. illus., photos.
[Includes references to 324 periodical and newspaper titles published in more than 50 languages. Provides the basic bibliographic data such as title, publisher, address of publisher, telephone, editor, frequency, format, nature, contents, language. Photos of title pages are also provided.]

29 *League of Canadian Poets.* [n.p.]: League of Canadian Poets, 1980. 180 pp. ports.

[The first edition appeared under the title *Catalogue of Members, The League of Canadian Poets,* 1976. Provides biographical notes, portraits, lists of publications and excerpts from review articles about each poet. Includes Rafael Barreto-Rivera, Hédi André Bouraoui, Cyril Dabydeen, Pier Giorgio Di Cicco, Mary di Michele, Lakshmi Gill, George Jónás, Tom Könyves, Suniti Namjoshi, Michael Ondaatje, S. Padmanab, Andreas Schroeder.]

30 LÉGARÉ, Yves
Dictionnaire des écrivains québécois contemporains 1970-1982. Montréal: Québec/Amerique, 1983. 399 pp.
[An alphabetical directory of contemporary authors residing in Québec. Includes biographical summaries and lists of publications. Ethnic authors included are Gérard Étienne, André Farkas, Paul Javor, Naïm Kattan, Alexis Klimov, Tom Könyves, Claudia Lapp, Maximilien Laroche, Serge Legagneur, Elizabeth Limet, Roland Morrisseau, Paul Ohl, Alice Parizeau, Thomas Pavel, Anthony Phelps, and Alix Renaud.]

31 LEMIRE, Maurice, ed.
Dictionnaire des œuvres littéraires du Québec, sous la direction de Maurice Lemire... Montréal: Fides, 1980. 4 vols.
[Tome 1: *Des origines à 1900*; Tome 2: *1900 à 1939*; Tome 3: *1940 à 1959*; Tome 4: *1960-1969.* Volume 4 covers novels, short stories, poetry and drama. Provides analytical papers on literary works, general bibliographies. Lists of new publications and compilations of review articles on Québécois authors are included. Several ethnic authors, e.g. Gérard Étienne, Anthony Phelps, Naïm Kattan, are represented.]

32 MAILHOT, Laurent; NEPVEU, Pierre, comp.
La Poésie québécoise: des origines à nos jours. Montréal: L'Hexagone, 1986. 642 pp.

33 MARTYNOWYCH, Orest T.
A Selective Preliminary Bibliography of Canadian Reference Materials Pertaining to Education within a Multicultural Context. Winnipeg: Manitoba Office of the Department of Secretary of State, 1979. 22 pp. Also includes: *A Preliminary List of Canadian Materials for Multicultural (Social Studies) Courses.* 23 pp.
[Provides bibliographic guides and monographic publications in print and non-print form.]

34 McLAREN, Duncan
Ontario Ethno-cultural Newspapers, 1835-1972: An Annotated Checklist. Toronto: University of Toronto Press, 1973. 234 pp.
[A basic reference tool, arranged by subject.]

35 MILTON, Norma
"Bibliography." CAN ETH STUD 15, no. 3 (1983): 140-50.
[Section "Literature, Art, Folklore" contains 41 related citations.]

36 MISKA, John
Canadian Prose Written in English 1883-1980: A Bibliography of Secondary Materials... Lethbridge: Microform Biblios, 1980. 292 pp. Microfiche.
[Includes 3370 references to books, monographs, graduate theses, research papers and other types of publications relating to such authors as Frederick P. Grove, Henry Kreisel, John Marlyn, Andreas Schroeder.]

37 MISKA, John
Ethnic and Native Canadian Literature 1850-1979: A Bibliography of Primary and Secondary Material. Lethbridge: Microform Biblios, 1980. 355 pp. Microfiche.
[This bibliography contains references to close to 3000 publications in 33 different languages.

Arranged by subject under nationality groups, each section provides citations on reference works, anthologies and individual authors under poetry, prose and drama.]

38 MORRISON, James H.
Common Heritage: An Annotated Bibliography of Ethnic Groups in Nova Scotia. Halifax: International Educational Centre, 1984. 130 pp.
[A compilation of 600 references on 16 ethnic groups.]

39 MUKHIN, J.S.
Slavic Collection of the University of Manitoba Libraries. Winnipeg: UVAN, 1972. 72 pp.
[A list compiled from the University of Manitoba library card catalogue.]

40 "Multicultural Literature and the Ethnic Press." COMMUNIQUÉ 3, no. 1 (1976): 54-60.
[A compilation of primary and secondary material.]

41 PLATNICK, Phyllis
Canadian Poetry Index to Criticism (1970-1979)/Poésie canadienne index de critiques (1970-1979).
Ottawa: Canadian Library Association, 1985. xxviii, 377 pp.
[Includes: Alexandre Amprimoz, Walter Bauer, Henry Beissel, Rienzi Crusz, Cyril Dabydeen, Pier Giorgio Di Cicco, Mary di Michele, George Faludy, André Farkas, Lakshmi Gill, Stephen Gill, George Jónás, Tom Könyves, Mary Melfi, Michael Ondaatje, George Swede, and Robert Zend.]

42 POYNTING, Jeremy
East Indians in the Caribbean: A Bibliography of Imaginative Literature in English. St. Augustine, Trinidad: University of West Indies, 1984. 34 pp.
[Includes references to Cyril Dabydeen.]

43 *Répertoire des écrivains franco-ontariens.* Sudbury, Ont.: Éditions Prise de Parole, 1987. 111 pp. illus.
[Includes Alexandre Amprimoz and Hédi Bouraoui.]

44 *Research on Immigrant Adjustment and Ethnic Groups. An Annual Bibliography, 1953-1954 -* Ottawa: Department of Citizenship and Immigration.
[Mimeographed lists of publications. Included are some papers on creative writing.]

45 RUSH, Stephan
Union List of Non-Canadian Newspapers Held by Canadian Libraries/Liste collective des journaux non-canadiens dans les bibliothèques du Canada. Ottawa: National Library of Canada, 1968. 69 pp.
[Contains 1075 titles arranged alphabetically by country. Provides cumulative title index.]

46 SAINT-JACQUES, Bernard
"The Languages of Immigrants: Sociolinguistic Aspects of Immigration in Canada." In *The Languages of Canada,* edited by J.K. Chambers. (Montréal: Didier, 1979) pp. 207-25.
[Provides an extensive bibliography: pp. 215-25.]

47 SALTMAN, Judith
Modern Canadian Children's Books. Toronto: Oxford University Press, 1987. 136 pp.

48 SENN, A.
"East European Languages and Literatures. American Bibliography, 1953." In *Modern Language Association of America,* 69, no. 2 (1954): 177-84.
[Includes references to ethnic Canadian authors.]

49 **STORY, Norah**
The Oxford Companion to Canadian History and Literature. Toronto: Oxford University Press, 1967. 935 pp.
[Biographical notes on Frederick P. Grove, Henry Kreisel and John Marlyn are provided, as well as sections on Indian and Inuit tales and legends.]

50 **TOUGAS, Gérard**
A Check List of Printed Materials Relating to French-Canadian Literature 1763-1968/Liste de référence d'imprimés relatifs à la littérature canadienne-française, 2nd ed. Vancouver: University of British Columbia Press, 1973. xv, 147 pp.
[First edition was published by same in 1958. 93 pp. Includes primary and secondary material. Individual minority authors included are Alice Parizeau, Anthony Phelps, etc.]

51 **TOYE, William,** ed.
The Oxford Companion to Canadian Literature. Toronto: Oxford University Press, 1983. 843 pp.
[Includes entries on Indian tales and legends (pp. 377-83); Indian literature (pp. 383-88); Inuit literature (pp. 390-91); Minority fiction (pp. 589-90). Includes biographies of the following authors: Walter Bauer, Austin C. Clarke, George Faludy, Frederick P. Grove, Wacław Iwaniuk, Pauline Johnson, George Jónás, Naïm Kattan, Rochl Korn, Henry Kreisel, Harold Sonny Ladoo, John Marlyn, Michael Ondaatje, Andreas Schroeder, George Škvor, Josef Škvorecký, Helen Weinzweig, Ludwig Zeller, and Robert Zend.]

52 **TOYE, William,** ed.
Supplement to the Oxford Companion to Canadian History and Literature. Toronto: Oxford University Press, 1973. 318 pp.
[Several entries on related subjects and authors are included.]

53 **VERRALL, Catherine,** comp.
Resource/Reading List 1987: An Annotated Bibliography of Resources by and about Native People. Toronto: Canadian Alliance in Solidarity with Native Peoples, 1987. 111 pp.

54 **WATTERS, Reginald Eyre**
A Checklist of Canadian Literature and Background Materials, 1628-1950, Being a Comprehensive List of the Books which Constitute Canadian Literature Written in English, Together with a Selective List of Other Books by Canadian Authors which Reveal the Backgrounds of that Literature, Compiled for the Humanities Research Council of Canada. Toronto: University of Toronto Press, 1959. 789 pp. 2nd ed. 1628-1960. 1972. xxiv, 1085 pp.
[Contents of the 2nd edition: Part I: Poetry, fiction, drama (pp. 3-451); Part II: Bibliography, essays, speeches, local history, religion, social history, scholarship, and travel (pp. 455-994). Includes some ethnic authors, e.g. Frederick P. Grove, Henry Kreisel and John Marlyn.]

55 **WATTERS, Reginald Eyre; BELL, Inglis Freeman**
On Canadian Literature, 1806-1960, A Check List of Articles, Books, and Theses on English-Canadian Literature, Its Authors, and Language. Toronto: University of Toronto Press, 1966. 165 pp.
[Includes secondary material, some of it relating to minority authors.]

56 *Who's Who in Canadian Literature 1983-1984.* Edited by Gordon Ripley and Anne V. Mercer. Toronto: Reference Press, 1983. 425 pp. 1985 ed. 399 pp. 1987 ed. 360 pp.
[Biographical notes on the following authors are included: Alexandre Amprimoz, Pier Giorgio Di Cicco, Mary di Michele, Jan Drabek, Lakshmi Gill, Stephen Gill, Kristjana Gunnars, Naïm Kattan, George Jónás, John Marlyn, Bharati Mukherjee, Henrikas Nagys, Suniti Namjoshi, Hannes Oja, Michael Ondaatje, F.G. Paci, Yar Slavutych, George Szanto, Gabriel Szohner, Stephen Vizinczey, Magda Zalán, and Robert Zend.]

57 *Who's Who in the League of Canadian Poets*, 3rd ed., edited by Stephen Scobie. Toronto: The League, 1988. 227 pp. ports.
[Includes more than twenty authors of ethnic origin, most of them listed in the previous editions.]

58 *Who's Who in the Writers' Union of Canada; A Directory of Members*. Toronto: The Writers' Union of Canada, 1988. 483 pp. photos.
[Includes biographical notes with portraits of authors, lists of their publications and addresses.]

59 WOYCENKO, Ol'ha
Slov'ıans'ki archivi v Kanadi: Kolekciï UVAN u Vinnipezi [Slavic Archives in Canada: UVAN Collections in Winnipeg] Winnipeg: UVAN, 1971. 24 pp. (Slavistica No. 71)
[A catalogue of monographic publications of Slavic literature held by libraries in Winnipeg.]

60 WRITERS' DEVELOPMENT TRUST. PRAIRIE GROUP
The Immigrant Experience. Toronto [n.d.] 43 pp.

BIBLIOGRAPHIC SOURCES

61 *The American Humanities Index.* Troy, N.Y.: Whitston, 1976- .
[Ethnic Canadian references are included.]

62 *Book Review Index*, edited by Barbara Beach and Beverly Anne Baer. Detroit: Gale, 1975- .
[Includes references to book reviews. Ethnic Canadian authors are represented.]

63 *Books in Canada.* March 1952 - Fall 1968. Toronto: Quill & Quire. 16 v. in 4.
[Known as the Quill & Quire Cumulative Catalogue; several ethnic authors are listed.]

64 *Cahiers bibliographiques des lettres québécoises.* Montréal: C.D.L.C.F. (Université de Montréal), 1966-
[Contains bibliographic data on books, research papers, primary and secondary material in English and French alike.]

65 *Canadian Book Review Annual*, edited by Dean Tudor, Nancy Tudor and Linda Biesenthal. Toronto: Peter Martin Assoc., 1975- .
[Arranged by subject, literature is subdivided into prose, poetry and drama. Includes ethnic Canadian authors.]

66 *Canadian Books in Print. Catalogue des livres canadiens en librairie.* 1967 - . Toronto: Canadian Books in Print Committee. Distributed by the University of Toronto Press and Le Conseil Supérieur du Livre, Montréal. From 1973 published by the University of Toronto Press. Edited by Rita Butterfield and Julia Richer (1967), Gerald Simoneau (1968-69), Harald Bohne (1970-73), Martha Pluscauskas (1974-78), Martha Pluscauskas and Marian Butler (1979-80), Marian Butler (1981-).

67 *Canadian Ethnic Studies/Études Ethniques du Canada.* Vol. I - 1969 - . Calgary: University of Calgary.
[Volumes I, no. 1, II, no. 1, and V, nos. 1-2 contain bibliographies of ethnic and native Canadian literature. General bibliographies are published in various issues from volume VI to date.]

68 *Canadian Magazine Index*, edited by Luci Lemieux. Vol. 1- (1985-).
[A reference guide to popular and special interest magazines, covering more than 200 periodicals. The index is published monthly with annual cumulations. Main part is arranged by subject,

followed by personal name index, alphabetically by author. Includes minority authors.]

69 *Canadiana.* January 15, 1951 -   . Ottawa: National Library of Canada.
[A national monthly catalogue of publications of Canadian interest. Supersedes *Canadian Catalogue of Books Published in Canada, about Canada, as well as Those Written by Canadians.* References relating to creative writings in the minority languages are listed under "Literature - Other Languages."]

70 *Contemporary Poets.* 2nd ed. With a preface by C. Day Lewis. Editor James Vinson. Associate editor D.L. Kirkpatrick. New York: St. Martin's Press, 1975. 1849 pp.
[The following minority poets are included: Henry Beissel, George Jónás, Andreas Schroeder. Provides biographical notes, lists of publications and excerpts from reviews and appraisals.]

71 *Current Book Review Citations.* Edited by Paula de Vaux. New York: Wilson, 1976 -
[Published annually, author/title arrangement, includes ethnic Canadian authors.]

72 *Livres et auteurs canadiens.* Montréal: Editions Jumonville, 1966 -   .
[Published annually, includes papers on fiction, poetry and drama. Bibliographies of current publications and portraits are included.]

73 *Point de repère: index analytique d'articles de périodiques québécois et étrangers.* Québec: Centrale des bibliothèques, Bibliothèque nationale du Québec. vol. 1 -   1984 -   .

74 *Revue d'histoire littéraire du Québec et du Canada français,* directeur René Dionne. Ottawa: Université d'Ottawa, 1980-   .
[Biennial publication, nos. 1-4 published by Bellarmin, Montreal. Each issue is devoted to a specific aspect of francophone literature. Includes research papers, book reviews and bibliographies. Ethnic Canadian authors are included.]

75 *Subject Guide to Canadian Books in Print.* 1973 -   . Edited by Harald Bohne and Martha Pluscauskas. Toronto: University of Toronto Press.

76 *University of Toronto Quarterly.* Toronto: University of Toronto Press, 1931 -   .
[The volumes published between 1938 and 1979 included annual lists of publications. Those written by authors of minority background are listed under "Other Languages."]

SURVEYS

77 ANDERSON, Alan B.; FRIDERES, James S.
Ethnicity in Canada: Theoretical Perspectives. Toronto: Butterworth, 1981. 334 pp.
[Provides a theoretical discussion on the term "ethnicity" in such related fields as sociology and social psychology.]

78 ATWOOD, Margaret
Survival: Thematic Guide to Canadian Literature. Toronto: Anansi Press, 1972. 287 pp.
[Chapters 4 and 7 are devoted to native and immigrant literature. Individual authors studied are Austin Clarke, Frederick P. Grove, John Marlyn, Michael Ondaatje, and Marika Robert.]

79 BALAN, Jars, ed.
Identifications: Ethnicity and the Writer in Canada. Edmonton: Canadian Institute of Ukrainian Studies, University of Alberta, 1982. 158 pp.
[A collection of papers presented to a conference held in Edmonton. Authors included are: Henry Kreisel: The Ethnic Writer in Canada (pp. 1-13); Yar Slavutych: Expectations and Reality: Early

Ukrainian Literature in Canada (pp. 14-21); George Bisztray: Canadian Hungarian Literature: Values Lost and Found (pp. 22-35); Jars Balan: A Word in Foreign Language: Ukrainian Influences in George Ryga's Work (pp. 36-52); David Arnason: Icelandic Canadian Literature (pp. 53-66); Danylo Struk: Emigré Ukrainian Literature in Canada (pp. 88-103); Judy Young: The Unheard Voices: Ideological or Literary Identification of Canada's Ethnic Writers (pp. 104-15); Seymour Levitan: An Introduction to Yiddish Writers (pp. 116-34); Panel discussions: Pier Giorgio Di Cicco, Maria Campbell, Andrew Suknaski, Rudy Wiebe (pp. 67-87), and Maara Haas, Myrna Kostash, George Ryga, and Yar Slavutych: Hyphenated Canadians: The Question of Consciousness (pp. 135-154). Individual annotations are included with papers under the appropriate nationality groups.]

80 BARBOUR, Douglas
Canadian Poetry Chronicle (1984): A Comprehensive Review of Canadian Poetry Books. With an appendix by Allan Brown. Kingston: Quarry Press, 1985. 101 pp.
[This is the first collection of Barbour's reviews in book form. Ethnic authors reviewed are William Bauer, Cathy Mátyás, Mary Melfi, and Michael Ondaatje.]

81 BLODGETT, E.D.
Configurations: Essays on the Canadian Literatures. Toronto: ECW Press, 1982. 223 pp.
[The paper "The Canadian Literatures as a Literary Problem" (pp. 13-38) provides a comparative study of the various dimensions of Canadian literature.]

82 BOURAOUI, Hédi André, ed.
The Canadian Alternative: Cultural Pluralism and the Canadian Unity. Downsview, Ont.: ECW Press, 1980. 110 pp.
[Includes papers presented to the conference held at Stong College, York University, Oct. 26-27, 1979.]

83 BOWLING, Joyce; HYKAWY, M.H., ed.
The Multilingual Press in Manitoba/La presse multilingue au Manitoba. Winnipeg: Canada Press Club, 1974. 248 pp.
[Contents: Part I: History, ideology, messages; Part II: Member publications, their past and present; Part III: Non-member publications, centennial projects and Winnipeg's International Centre.]

84 CAMPBELL, Douglas F., ed.
Banked Fires - The Ethnics of Nova Scotia. Port Credit, Ont.: Scribbler's Press, 1978. 249 pp.
[Chapter 10, written by D.F. Campbell, traces the ethnic literature in Nova Scotia.]

85 CANADA. CANADIAN CITIZENSHIP BRANCH
The Canadian Family Tree. Centennial edition 1867-1967. Ottawa: The Branch, 1967. 354 pp.
[The first publication in the series, *Notes on Canadian Family Tree,* 137 pp., was published in 1966. The third volume, *The Canadian Family Tree: Canada's Peoples,* was released in 1979. Each volume contains descriptions of ethnic literature.]

86 CANADA. ROYAL COMMISSION ON BILINGUALISM AND MULTICULTURALISM
Report. Vol. 4. Ottawa: Queen's Printer, 1969. 352 pp.
[Chapter VIII, "Arts and Letters," deals with ethnic literature, including Yiddish, Hebrew, Icelandic, Ukrainian.]

87 *Canadian Writers at Work: Interviews with Geoff Hancock.* Toronto: Oxford University Press, 1987. 312 pp.
[Includes interviews that originally appeared in *Canadian Fiction Magazine.* Two minority authors are also included: Bharati Mukherjee and Josef Škvorecký.]

88 *Caribbean Minority in Canada.* CAN LIT No. 95 (1982). Special issue.
[The entire issue is devoted to the Caribbean minority in Canada. Some of the relevant papers are: Stanley Atherton: The Tropical Traumas: Images of the Caribbean in Recent Canadian Fiction (pp. 8-14); Earl Birney: Meeting George Lemming in Jamaica (pp. 16-28); Austin Clarke: In the Semicolon of the North (pp. 30-37); Clement Wyke: Harold Ladoo's Alternate Worlds (pp. 39-49); Samuel Selvon: Sam Selvon Talking; A Conversation with Kenneth Ramchand (pp. 56-64); Elizabeth Sabiston: Hédi Bouraoui's Quest (pp. 67-83).]

89 **CENTRAL AND EAST EUROPEAN STUDIES ASSOCIATION OF CANADA (CEESAC)**
Banff Conferences on Central and East European Studies. Edited by Metro Gulutsan. Edmonton: CEESAC.
[The proceedings of two Banff Conferences were published by the Association, the first one in 1977, and the second in 1978, in 4 volumes each. Literary presentations included papers by A. Arnold, Ž.B. Juričić, Martin Kovács, A. Landsbergis, A. Levin, M. Lorbergs, John Miska, H.W. Panthel, M. Vasara, and Judy Young.]

90 **COMMUNIQUÉ** : *Canadian Studies.* Vol. 3, no. 1.
[This issue deals with multicultural studies. Contents: Multicultural studies in Canada (pp. 2-3); Bibliographies of ethnic groups (p. 4); Historical background (pp. 8-14); Interethnic relations, periodical literature, multicultural literature (pp. 15-65).]

91 **DABYDEEN, Cyril**
Asian-Canadian Writers: Bio-bibliographic Profile. Ottawa, 1984. 161 leaves. Manuscript.
[A survey conducted for the Multiculturalism Directorate. Includes studies on thematic and textual aspects of Chinese, Japanese, Indian, Sri Lankan and other national groups in Canada. Bio-bibliographic notes (pp. 92-145).]

92 **DAHLIE, Hallvard**
Varieties of Exile: The Canadian Experience. Vancouver: University of British Columbia Press, 1986. x, 216 pp.
[Describes the rich variety of Canadian literature considered to be an expression of exile. Several immigrant authors are represented from the earliest travellers' accounts to present-day writers, including Josef Škvorecký.]

93 **ELLIOTT, Lorris**
Literary Writing by Blacks in Canada: A Preliminary Survey, edited by Michael S. Batts. Ottawa: Multiculturalism, Department of the Secretary of State , 1986. 40 pp.
Prepared for the Multiculturalism Directorate as part of its series on ethnic Canadian literature. Contents: Introduction, bibliographies (pp. 3-11); Bio-bibliographical profiles (pp. 12-40).]

94 **GRABOWSKI, Yvonne; RAY, Riten, eds.**
Cultures and Writers; A Cultural Dialogue of Ethnic Writers; Proceedings of a Conference Sponsored by the Citizenship Development Branch of the Ontario Ministry of Citizenship and Culture, and Multiheritage Community Alliance of Toronto. Edited by Yvonne Grabowski. Consulting editor Riten Ray. Toronto: The Alliance, 1983. 51 pp.
[Includes 12 presentations on the role of ethnic Canadian authors in Canadian society. Speakers were George Ignatieff, Mavor Moore, Joy Kogawa, Sam Simchovitch, Aristides Yeroú, Yvonne Grabowski, Celestino de Iuliis, Thade Rachwal, Sive Stevanovic, Keith McLeod, and Valve André.]

95 **HARRISON, Dick**
Unnamed Country: The Struggle for a Canadian Prairie Fiction. Edmonton: University of Alberta Press, 1977. 250 pp.
[An analysis of the novels of Frederick P. Grove, Martha Ostenso and other prairie authors]

96   ISAJIW, Wsevolod, ed.
Identities: The Impact of Ethnicity on Canadian Society. Toronto: Peter Martin Associates, 1977. 221 pp.
[Includes a paper by Eli Mandel on ethnic influences on Canadian literature pp. 57-68.]

97   ITWARU, Arnold
The Invention of Canada: The Literary Production of Consciousness in Ten Immigrant Writers. Ottawa: National Library of Canada, 1984. 4 microfiches (370 fr.)

98   JOUBERT, Jean-Louis; LECARME, Jacques; TABONE, Éliane; VERCIER, Bruno
Les littératures francophones depuis 1945. Paris: Bordas, 1986. 383 pp. illus., photos.
[Arranged geographically under the general headings: Africa, Madagascar, Morocco, Mediterranian, Québec, etc. Includes references to Gérard Étienne, Naïm Kattan, Anthony Phelps and many other French-speaking ethnic authors residing in Canada.]

99   KIRKCONNELL, Watson
The Place of Slavic Studies in Canada. Winnipeg: Ukrainian Free Academy of Sciences. (*Slavistica* no. 31)

100   KLINCK, Carl, ed.
Literary History of Canada: Canadian Literature in English. Toronto: University of Toronto Press, 1965. 2nd ed. 1976. 3 vols. 550 pp., 410 pp., and 391 pp. respectively.
[Ethnic authors studied are: Frederick P. Grove, Henry Kreisel, Henry Beissel, George Jónás, Michael Ondaatje, Austin Clarke.]

101   KOVÁCS, Martin L., ed.
Ethnic Canadians: Culture and Education. Regina: Canadian Plains Research Center, 1978. 495 pp.
[Contains more than 30 papers presented to a conference held at the University of Regina, in October 1976. Theme: Culture, education and ethnic Canadians. Some of the papers (Linda Deutschmann) provide definitions of the term "ethnicity," which can be applied to creative writing in a pluralistic society.]

102   MACHALSKI, Andrew
Hispanic Writers in Canada: A Preliminary Survey of the Activities of Spanish and Latin-American Writers in Canada. edited by Michael S. Batts. Ottawa: Multiculturalism, Department of the Secretary of State, 1988. 51 pp.
[Prepared for the Multiculturalism Directorate as part of its series on ethnic Canadian literature. Part I provides an outline of the methods used in carrying out the survey, Part II gives bio-bibliographic profiles and lists of some publications of some 65 individual authors of Spanish-speaking background.]

103   MIGUS, Paul M., ed.
Sounds Canadian: Languages and Cultures in Multi-ethnic Society. Proceedings of the International Symposium Sponsored by the Canadian Ethnic Studies Association. Toronto: Peter Martin Associates, 1975. 261 pp. (Canadian Ethnic Studies Association Series, vol. 4)
[Selection of papers relating to culture, literature, and language.]

104   MORITZ, Albert; MORITZ, Theresa
The Oxford Illustrated Literary Guide to Canada. Toronto: Oxford University Press, 1987. 239 pp. illus.
[Arranged geographically east to west, includes several major minority authors.]

105   MOSS, John

A Reader's Guide to the Canadian Novel. Toronto: McClelland & Stewart, 1981. 399 pp.
[Ethnic authors included are Frederick P. Grove, Henry Kreisel and John Marlyn.]

106 MUKHERJEE, Arun P., ed.
Towards an Aesthetic of Opposition. Toronto: William-Wallace, 1987. 125 pp.
[This collection includes critical essays by South Asian writers living in Canada. The authors compare the writing style of Canadian-born Asian writers with that of immigrant Asian writers.]

107 *Multiculturalism for Canada; Report of a Conference Held at the University of Alberta, Edmonton, August 28-29, 1970.* Edmonton: University of Alberta and the Ukrainian Students' Club, 1970.

108 NEW, W.H., ed.
Canadian Writers since 1960. (Dictionary of Literary Biography, vol. 60). Second Series. Detroit: Gale, 1987. 470 pp. ports.
[Provides extensive studies on authors, along with lists of their publications and review articles about them. Ethnic authors included are Pier Giorgio Di Cicco, Bharati Mukherjee, Michael Ondaatje, and Alice Parizeau.]

109 O'BRYAN, K.G.; REITZ, J.G.; KUPLOWSKA, O.M.
Non-official Languages: A Study in Canadian Multiculturalism. Ottawa: Secretary of State, 1976. 274 pp.

110 PARAMESWARAN, Uma, ed.
The Commonwealth in Canada: Proceedings of the Second Triennial Conference of CACLALS. Part Two. University of Winnipeg, 1-4 October, 1981. Edited by Uma Parameswaran. Calcutta: Writers Workshop, 1983.
[Includes papers by Eli Mandel, John Wickham, J.J. Healy, Bharati Mukherjee Blaise, John Moss, Wendy Keitner, Perry Nodelman, and others. Excerpts from writers: Kristjana Gunnars, Reshard Gool, P.K. Page, Sam Selvon, Dorothy Livesay, Uma Parameswaran, etc. Also papers relating to Caribbean literature (John Wickham and J.J. Healy).]

111 *Slavs in Canada. Proceedings of National Conferences on Slavs.* Edmonton-Ottawa: Inter-University Committee on Canadian Slavs, 1965 (1st), 1967 (2nd).
[Contains papers on Slavic Canadian literature: vol. I (pp. 92-109); vol. II (pp. 235-46).]

112 SPROXTON, Birk, ed.
Trace: Prairie Writers on Writing. Saskatoon: Turnstone Press, 1986. 328 pp.
[Includes 30 essays and statements on prairie authors by Kristjana Gunnars, W.D. Valgardson, Henry Kreisel, Rudy Wiebe, Eli Mandel and others.]

113 STEARNS, Anna
New Canadians of Slavic Origin: A Problem in Creative Reorientation. Winnipeg: Ukrainian Free Academy of Sciences, 1960. 144 pp. (*Slavistica* 37-38)
[Contents: Part I: World affairs and the refugee (pp. 11-38); Part II: The newcomer's old and new world (pp. 39-54); Part III: The psychology of uprootedness (pp. 55-72); Case histories (pp. 73-133). Includes bibliography (pp. 135-41).]

114 SUGUNASIRI, H.J., ed.
The Search for Meaning: The Literature of Canadians of South Asian Origin, revised by Michael S. Batts. Ottawa: Multiculturalism, Secretary of State Department, 1988. 215 pp.
[Provides an overview of South Asian Canadian literature (pp. 5-25); Poetry (pp. 26-60); Short story in English (pp. 61-85); Novel in English (pp. 86-112); Punjabi literature (pp. 113-68); Gujarati literature (pp. 169-78); Bibliography (pp. 191-215). Individual papers contained in these sections are listed with annotations under their individual authors in section: Research Papers.]

115 SUTHERLAND, Ronald

No Longer a Family Affair: The Foreign-born Writers of French Canada. North Hatley, Que., 1986. 67 leaves.

[Prepared for the Multiculturalism Directorate. Contents: Introduction, methodology (pp. 1-9); Identification of authors (pp. 10-14); Bio-bibliographical profiles of Haitian (pp. 15-30), Egyptian (p. 31), Lebanese (p. 32), Italian (pp. 33-36), Jewish-Iraqi (pp. 36-37), German (p. 38), Russian-Belgian (pp. 39-40), Yugoslavian (pp. 40-42), Uruguayan (pp. 42-43), Other authors (pp. 44-47).]

116 VASSANJI, M.G., ed.

A Meeting of Streams: South Asian Literature. Toronto: Toronto South Asian Review, 1985. 145 pp.

[The essays and articles included provide an insight into the many aspects of South Asian literary activities in Canada. Arun Mukherjee: South Asian Poetry in Canada (pp. 7-25); Rajendra Singh: Remarks on Indo-Anglian Literature (pp. 27-31); Suwanda Sugunasiri: Reality and Symbolism in the Short Story (pp. 33-48); Frank Birbalsingh: South Asian Canadian Novels in English (pp. 49-61); M.G. Vassanji: The Postcolonial Writer: Myth Maker and Folk Historian (pp. 63-68); Ronald Sutherland: The Mainstream of Canadian Literature (pp. 69-77); Uma Parameswaran: Ganga in the Assiniboine: Prospects for Indo-Canadian Literature (pp. 79-93); Nuzrat Yar Khan: Urdu Language and Literature in Canada (pp. 95-108); Surjeet Kalsey: Canadian Panjabi Literature (pp. 109-19); Brenda E.F. Beck: Indo-Canadian Popular Culture: Should Writers Take the Lead in its Development? (pp. 121-32); Stella Sandahl: South Asian Literatures - A Linguistic Perspective (pp. 133-38).]

RESEARCH PAPERS, REVIEW ARTICLES

117 ANCTIL, Pierre

"Introduction : Le pluralisme au Québec/Ethnicity from Québec." CAN ETH STUD 18, no. 2 (1986): 1-6.

[The entire issue is devoted to ethnic studies in Canada. Individual nationality groups discussed are: Jewish, Chinese, Arabic groups, and Haitian.]

118 ANDRUSYSHEN, C.H.

"Publications in Other Languages." UNIV TOR Q 36 (1966-67): 545-46.

[A review of Ukrainian, Croatian, Slovak, and Polish Canadian creative writing. Further survey articles published in subsequent volumes of the *University of Toronto Quarterly* by the same author are as follows:

37 (1967-68): 589-609, introducing Stepan Semchuk, O. Prokopiv, V.O. Buyniak, Paul Yuzik, and other Ukrainian authors.

38 (1968-69): 486-95. A review of Stepan Semchuk's poetry and Joseph Kirschbaum's *Slovaks in Canada.*

39 (1969-70): 444-53. A summary of Slovak and Ukrainian literature in Canada.

40 (1970-71): 442-50; 41 (1971-72): 467-76. A review of L. Ukrainka, C.E. Petrowska, and Larysa Murovych.

42 (1972-73): 497-507. Reviewed are O. Kerch, H. Skvorodny, and Iâr Slavutych.

43 (1973-74): 447-58. L. Lysak, Illîa Kyriîâk, Ihor Shankovs'kyĭ, and M. Petrovs'kyĭ.

44 (1974-75): 447-58. A review of Ulas Samchuk and Stepan Semchuk.

45 (1975-76): 442-51. A summary of Ukrainian-Canadian works by Iâr Slavutych, Mykyta Mandryka, and M. Petrovs'kyĭ.]

119 APONIUK, Natalia

"Publications in Other Languages." UNIV TOR Q 47 (1977-78): 490-94.

[A review of the following anthologies: *Jubilee Collection of the Ukrainian Free Academy of Sciences; Ukraïns'ka Poeziîâ v Kanadi;* and *Antolohiîâ ukraïns'koiï poeziï v Kanadi.*]

13

120   AUGUST, R.
      "Babeling Beaver Hunts for Home Fire: The Place of Ethnic Literature in Canadian Culture." CAN
      FORUM 54, no. 643 (August 1974): 8-13.

121   BECK, Brenda E.F.
      "Indo-Canadian Popular Culture: Should Writers Take the Lead in Its Development?" In *A Meeting
      of Streams...*, edited by M.G. Vassanji. (Toronto: TOR SOUTH-ASIAN REV, 1985) pp. 121-32.
      [Items discussed are: What Indo-Canadian culture is not; Culture and identity; Canadian popular
      culture: an example; Popular culture: what it should be, and why it is significant.]

122   BIRBALSINGH, Frank
      "South Asian Canadian Novels in English." In *A Meeting of Streams...*, edited by M.G. Vassanji.
      (Toronto: TSAR, 1985) pp. 49-61.
      [This essay considers novels written in English by five South Asian Canadian authors: Harold
      Sonny Ladoo, Bharati Mukherjee, Saros Cowasjee, Stephen Gill, and Reshard Gool.]

123   BITTON, Janet Kay
      "The Canadian Ethnic Novel: The Protagonists' Search for Self-definition." M.A. Thesis, Université
      de Montréal, 1971.

124   BROWN, Lloyd. "The West Indian Novel in North America." J COMMONW LIT 9 (July 1970):
      89-103.

125   DABYDEEN, Cyril
      "A Compromise and Self-expression: Problems of the Third World Writer in Canada." In *Visible
      Minorities and Multiculturalism: Asians in Canada*, edited by K.V. Ujimoto and Gordon
      Hirabayashi. (Toronto: Butterworths, 1980) pp. 329-34.
      [Describes the presence of Indian, Chinese, Japanese, Caribbean, African authors in Canada.]

126   DEUTSCHMANN, Linda Bell
      "Decline of the WASP? Dominant Group Identity in the Ethnic Plural Society." In *Ethnic
      Canadians: Culture and Education*, edited by Martin L. Kovács. (Regina: Canadian Plains Research
      Center, 1978) pp. 411-18.
      [According to this author, British Canadians themselves are an ethnic group in a pluralistic
      society.]

127   DUKULÉ, Abdoul
      "Afrique-Québec: deux francophonies." PRÉSENCE FRANCOPHONE 26 (1985): 45-56.
      [La dépendance de la littérature africaine francophone à l'égard de la littérature française.]

128   ELLIOTT, Lorris
      "Literary Writings by Blacks in Canada." In *Canadian Black Studies*, edited by Bridglal Pachai.
      (Halifax: International Education Centre, Saint Mary's University, 1979) pp. 111-20.
      [An assertion of the importance of Black literary writing in Canada. Reference is made to Austin
      Clarke.]

129   "Ethnicity and Identity: The Question of One's Literary Passport." In *Identifications: Ethnicity and
      the Writer in Canada*, edited by Jars Balan. (Edmonton: The Canadian Institute of Ukrainian
      Studies, 1982) pp. 67-87.
      [A panel discussion with Pier Giorgio Di Cicco, Maria Campbell, Andrew Suknaski and Rudy
      Wiebe.]

130   GRABOWSKI, Yvonne

"Publications in Other Languages." UNIV TOR Q 47 (1977-78): 494-500.
[A review of Josef Škvorecký, L. Levchev (Bulgarian), and L'udo Bešeňovský (Slovak) authors.]

131   HATCH, Ronald B.
"Poetry." UNIV TOR Q 56 (1986-87): 29-45.
[Review of Rienzi Crusz: *Singing against the Wind*, Pier Giorgio Di Cicco: *Women We Never See Again* and *Post-sixties Nocturne*, George Faludy: *Selected Poems*, and Rachel Korn's works.]

132   HIRABAYASHI, Richard
"Ethnic Consciousness and an Analytical Framework for Culturally Sensitive Material." CAN CHILDR LIT 10, nos. 1-2 (1985-86): 81-89.

133   HUTCHEON, Linda
"Voices of Displacement." CAN FORUM (June/July 1985): 33-38.
[A survey article on current trends in immigrant Canadian poetry and fiction. Authors studied include Maria Jacobs, Jan Drabek, Henry Kreisel, John Marlyn, F.G. Paci, Maara Haas, Austin Clarke, Lorris Elliott, Harold Sonny Ladoo, Saros Cowasjee, Michael Cullen, Joy Kogawa, Joseph Pivato.]

134   "Hyphenated Canadians: The Questions of Consciousness." In *Identifications: Ethnicity and the Writer in Canada*, edited by Jars Balan. (Edmonton: The Canadian Institute of Ukrainian Studies, 1982) pp. 135-54.
[A panel discussion with Maara Haas, Myrna Kostash, George Ryga, and Yar Slavutych.]

135   JONES, Katie
"Dialect, Idiolect, Sociolect: Transformations of English in the Work of Raja Rao, Samuel Selvon, and Alice Walker." CHIMO No. 11 (1985): 4-13.

136   JOSEPH, Clifton
"Interviews from the 6th International Book Fair of Radical Black and Third World Books; Bradford, April 1987." FUSE 11, no. 1-2 (1987): 28-34.

137   KATTAN, Naïm
"L'escape dans la littérature canadienne; allocution." TRANS ROY SOC CAN 4th ser. 14 (1976) pp. 127-29.

138   KATTAN,   Naïm.
"Ten Years of Literature: A Writer at the Canada Council." In *The Human Element*, edited by David Helwig. (Toronto: Oberon Press, 1978) pp. 68-77.
[Describes own activities while with Canada Council.]

139   KIRKCONNELL, Watson
"The Literature of the New Canadians." In *Canadian Literature Today. From the Broadcasting Corporation.* (Toronto: University of Toronto Press, 1938) pp. 57-64.

140   KIRKCONNELL, Watson
"Literature, Other than English and French." In *Encyclopedia Canadiana* (1968). vol. 6 (Toronto: Grolier Society of Canada Ltd., 1968) pp. 179-82.
[A revised version of the same paper appeared in the 1977 edition, vol. 6 (pp. 180-82). Provides a summary of Gaelic, Icelandic, German, Ukrainian, Swedish, Jewish and Hungarian creative writing.]

141   KIRKCONNELL, Watson
"New-Canadian Letters." UNIV TOR Q 9 (1939-40): 320-23.

[A review article of Illia Kyriiak's *Syny Zemly*, A.I. Kmeta-IEfimovich's *The Hurricane*, Oleksander Luhovyĭ's *Za voliu Ukraïniĭ*, and Peter Johann Klassen's *Grossmutters Schatz.* Other articles by this author under the same heading published in subsequent volumes of UNIV TOR Q are:

10 (1940-41): 317-19. A summary of Icelandic, Polish, and Ukrainian letters.

11 (1941-42): 355-58. A review of Greeks in Canada, and W. Paluk: *Canadian Cossacks.*

14 (1944-45): 300-302. A summary of German, Icelandic, Polish, and Ukrainian letters.

15 (1945-46): 426-29. Introduces Aleksander Luhowyĭ: *Dark Clouds*, K.N. Julius: *Songs of Poems*, and Illia Kyriiak: *Syny Zemly.*

17 (1947-48): 425-29. A review of Icelandic, German, Ukrainian and Polish literature.

18 (1948-49): 396-401. Includes a checklist of titles. Individual authors discussed are G.J. Guttormsson and N.J. Gotlieb.

19 (1949-50): 433-40. A review of *Koop and Bua...*, and *Lost on the Steppe*, by Arnold Dyck, and *The Ballad of the Nocturnal Woods and Other Songs*, by Chava Rosenfarb.

20 (1950-51): Introduces two collections by Arnold Dyck: *My Trip to Germany* and *Verloren in der Steppe*, as well as R. Beck's *History of Icelandic Poets*, 1800-1940, and the accomplishments of Oleksa Haĭ-Holovko.

21 (1951-52): 423-27. A review of *Jewish Book*, by J.I. Segal, *Auschwitz*, by Joseph Rogel, *Verlorene Söhne*, by Peter J. Klassen, *De Opnaom*, by Arnold Dyck, and *In the Ukraine*, a 3-act drama, by Ivan Ukraïnetś.

22 (1952-53): 424-34. A review of Icelandic poetry (D. Bjornsson: *Rosvioir*), Jewish (I. Goldstick: *Poems of Yehoash*), German (A.J. Friesen: *Prost Mahlzeit*) writing in Canada.

23 (1953-54): 332-36. A review of Ukrainian, Icelandic, and Gaelic literature. The title of the section from this volume on has changed to: "Publications in Other Languages."

24 (1954-55): 334-40. A review of Jewish (Vera Black: *Poems*, Ida Massey: *My Children Grow*), Icelandic (P.S. Palsson: *A Search*), and Ukrainian writing.

25 (1955-56): 400-07. A review of Oleksa Luhovyĭ: *Zalizom i kroviu.*

26 (1956-57): 409-16. A review of Icelandic and German literature in Canada.

27 (1957-58): 567-80. A review of Hungarian (Tibor Baranyai: *Útszéli virágok*), Ukrainian (Mykyta Mandryka) and Icelandic (G.J. Guttormsson) poetry.

28 (1958-59): 482-92. A review of Icelandic and Ukrainian poetry.

29 (1959-60): Introduces poets Ferenc Fáy and Kálmán Bartha (Hungarian), Þ.Þ. Þorsteinsson (Icelandic), and Stanisław Michalski (Polish).

30 (1960-61): 508-19. A review of Pavel Javor's poetry.

31 (1961-62): 577-86. Authors reviewed are Mykyta Mandryka, András Korondi, Stanisław Michalski, IAr Slavutych, and some authors of belles lettres.

32 (1962-63): 522-36. A summary of Icelandic, Hungarian, Lithuanian, Polish, Byelorussian, and Ukrainian writing in Canada.

33 (1963-64): 499-507. Polish, Icelandic, Slovak, and Ukrainian authors are included.

35 (1965-66): 537-50. Review of the work of Stepan Semchuk, M. Sharyk, Mykyta Mandryka, Pavel Javor, and G.J. Guttormsson.

142 **KIRKCONNELL, Watson**

"Canada's Unseen Literature." In his *A Slice of Canada: Memoirs.* (Toronto: University of Toronto Press, 1967) pp. 75-82.

[A survey of German, Hungarian, Icelandic, Czech, Polish, and Ukrainian Canadian creative writing.]

143 **KOLESNIKOFF, Nina**

"Contemporary Doukhobor Poetry." CAN ETH STUD 14, no. 1 (1982): 62-73.

[Introduces four generations of poets, representing Peter Diachkoff, L.V. Rilkoff, I.F. Sysoev, I.P. Antifaeff, I.I. Rilkoff, P.P. Lezhebokoff, P.T. Stoochnoff, A.N. Shustova, I.K. Novakshonoff, and A.I. Plotnikoff.]

144   KREISEL, Henry
"The 'Ethnic' Writer in Canada." In *Identifications: Ethnicity and the Writer in Canada*, edited by Jars Balan. (Edmonton: The Canadian Institute of Ukrainian Studies, 1982) pp. 1-13.
[Describes the problems facing the ethnic author in linguistic and textual presentation of his/her experience. Most of the authors have managed to come to terms with these problems by studying the work of Joseph Conrad and A.M. Klein.]

145   KROETSCH, Robert
"The Grammar of Silence: Narrative Patterns in Ethnic Writing." CAN LIT No. 106 (1985): 65-74.

146   MANDEL, Eli
"The Ethnic Voice in Canadian Writing." In *Identities: The Impact of Ethnicity on Canadian Society*, edited by Wsevolod Isajiw. (Toronto: Peter Martin, 1977) pp. 57-68.
[The ethnic voice is examined through Jewish, German and Hungarian-Canadian writings. Individual authors analysed are Mordecai Richler, A.M. Klein, Irving Layton, John Marlyn, Robert Zend, Frederick Philip Grove, Rudy Wiebe and others.]

147   MANGUEL, Alberto
"A Place to Look at the World." OTTAWA CIT (Dec. 12, 1987) H1-2. ports.
[Presents the image of Canada as seen by immigrant authors Josef Škvorecký, George Faludy, Neil Bissoondath, and Rohinton Mistry.]

148   McANDREW, Marie
"Le traitement du racisme, de l'immigration et la réalité multi-ethnique dans les manuels scolaires francophones au Québec." CAN ETH STUD 18, no. 2 (1986): 130-42.
[A qualitative and quantitative analysis of immigration and multi-ethnic reality in French-Canadian textbooks.]

149   MELANÇON, Joseph
"La Figure de la metropole dans l'enseignement littéraire au Québec au XIXe siècle." ÉTUD CAN/CAN STUD 19 (1985): 149-156.

150   MITCHAM, Allison
"The Isolation of Protesting Individuals Who Belong to Minority Groups." WASC REV 7 (1972): 43-50.
[Relates to Jewish Canadian authors.]

151   MUKHERJEE, Arun P.
"South Asian Poetry in Canada: In Search of a Place." In *A Meeting of Streams*, edited by M.G. Vassanji. (Toronto: Toronto South-Asian Review, 1985) pp. 7-25.
[An analysis of the poetry of Michael Ondaatje, Himani Bannerji, K.S. Bhaggiyadatta, Rienzi Crusz, Cyril Dabydeen, Lakshmi Gill, Reshard Gool, Arnold Itwaru, Surjeet Kalsey, Suniti Namjoshi, S. Padmanab, Uma Parameswaran, and Asoka Weerasinghe.]

152   ORENSTEIN, Eugene
"Publications in Other Languages." UNIV TOR Q 46 (1976-77): 494-506.
[A review paper of the work of Jewish, Polish, and Ukrainian authors. For Jewish authors writing in Yiddish reviewed in this paper see entries relating to the individual poets and prose writers.]

153   PALMER, Tamara
"Ethnic Response to the Canadian Prairies, 1900-1950." PRAIRIE FORUM 12, no. 1 (1987): 49-73.

154   PALMER, Tamara J.; RASPORICH, Beverly J.

"Ethnic Literature." In *The Canadian Encyclopedia*. (Edmonton: Hurtig Publishers, 1985) vol. 1, pp. 595-98.
[A concise summary of sources, literary movements and individual language groups. Provides outlines of native literatures, as well as Acadian, Irish, Scottish and Welsh immigrant literatures, and some of the major ethnic-group literary accomplishments such as Ukrainian, German, Hungarian, Italian, Polish, Czech and Asiatic.]

155 PARAMESWARAN, Uma
"Ganga in the Assiniboine: Prospects for Indo-Canadian Literature." In *A Meeting of Streams...*, edited by M.G. Vassanji. (Toronto: Toronto South-Asian Review, 1985) pp. 79-93.
[Assimilation is being replaced by multiculturalism in Canadian life, a process depicted by such authors as Michael Ondaatje, Fred Wah, Surjeet Kalsey, Saros Cowasjee, and others.]

156 *Petit album des auteurs des cantons de l'est*. Saint-Élie d'Orford, Qué., 1980. 126 pp. ports.
[Provides biographies of authors and lists of their publications. Includes Agnès Bastin, Jean Civil, Francis Corpataux, Gilbert-Bernard Lathion, and Antoine Naaman.]

157 *Répertoire littéraire de l'ouest canadien*, edited by Edmond Cormier, Annette Saint-Pierre, Taïb Soufi, et Alexandre-L. Amprimoz. Winnipeg: Centre d'études franco-canadiennes de l'Ouest, 1984. 368 pp. ports.
[Gives biographies, lists of publications of individual authors and excerpts from their works. Ethnic and Métis authors represented are Alexandre Amprimoz, André Castelin, Donatien Frémont, Alfred Glauser, Alexandre de Laronde, Marguerite A. Primeau and Berthe de Trémaudan.]

158 SANDAHL, Stella
"South Asian Literatures - A Linguistic Perspective." In *A Meeting of Streams...*, edited by M.G. Vassanji. (Toronto: TSAR, 1985) pp. 133-38.
[An essay on the use of language as a determining factor in literary development.]

159 SCHAFER, Jurgen
"Building a National Literature: The Need for Emblems." J CAN CULT 1, no. 2 (1984): 67-76.

160 ŠKVORECKÝ, Josef
"Let's Have Less Ethnic Pork and More Ethic (sic) Print." BKS CAN 7, no. 3 (1978): 3-4.
[Offers a criticism of the way the Canadian government is handling multicultural activities.]

161 SLAVUTYCH, Îar
"Slavic Literatures in Canada: A Survey." In *Slavs in Canada; Proceedings of the First National Conference on Canadian Slavs*. Vol. 1. (Edmonton: Inter-University Committee on Canadian Slavs, 1966) pp. 92-109.
[A survey of the following Slavic language groups: Russian (pp. 92-93), Czech (pp. 93-94), Polish (pp. 94-95), Slovak (pp. 96-97), Ukrainian (pp. 98-109).]

162 SUGUNASIRI, Suwanda H.J.
"Emerging Themes in South Asian Canadian Literature." ASIANADIAN 5, no. 3 (1984): 26-28.

163 SUGUNASIRI, Suwanda H.J.
"Reality and Symbolism in the Short Story." In *A Meeting of Streams...*, edited by M.G. Vassanji. (Toronto: TSAR, 1985) pp. 33-48.
[South Asian short story in Canada is characterized by its emphasis upon realism. This paper describes the elements of folklore, village superstition, reality and symbolism in the work of Cyril Dabydeen, M.G. Vassanji, Surjeet Kalsey, Iqbal Ahmad, Stephen Gill, Lino Leitao, Saros Cowasjee, and Clyde Hosein.]

164 SUTHERLAND, Ronald
"The Imagination in Power." CAN FORUM 66, no. 774 (1987): 40-44.
[Review of *Invisible Fictions - Contemporary Stories from Québec*, edited by Geoff Hancock.]

165 SUTHERLAND, Ronald
"The Mainstream of Canadian Literature." In *A Meeting of Streams...*, edited by M.G. Vassanji. (Toronto: TSAR, 1985) pp. 69-77.
[Describes ethnic Canadian literature as the third category of comparative Canadian literature. Those mentioned include Jewish, Ukrainian, Gaelic, Czechoslovak, German, Hungarian, Japanese, Inuit, Indian, Italian, and South Asian literatures.]

166 TAXEL, Joel
"The Black Experience in Children's Fiction: Controversies Surrounding Award Winning Books." CURRIC INQUIRY 16 (1986): 245-81.

167 THACKER, Robert
"Foreigner: The Immigrant Voice in *The Sacrifice* and *Under the Ribs of Death*." CAN ETH STUD 14, no. 1 (1982): 25-35.
[A comprehensive study of the Hungarian and Jewish themes in Canadian literature.]

168 VASSANJI, M.G.
"The Postcolonial Writer: Myth Maker and Folk Historian." In *A Meeting of Streams...*, edited by M.G. Vassanji. (Toronto: TSAR, 1985) pp. 63-68.
[Describes V.S. Naipaul, Sam Selvon, Harold Sonny Ladoo, Cyril Dabydeen, and Clyde Hosein as preservers of the collective tradition, folk historians and myth makers.]

169 "The Verbal Mosaic." BKS CAN 7, no. 3 (1978): 3-15.
[Includes articles on literature in the non-official languages by Josef Škvorecký, Pier Giorgio Di Cicco, Ludwig Zeller, Irving Layton, Cecil Cloutier, Joy Kogawa, Robin Skelton, George Jónás. Also book reviews by Amilcare Iannucci, K.A. McLeod, C.D. Minni, Jack David, Michael Smith, and Duncan Meikle.]

170 WINKS, Robin W.
"The Sinister Oriental: Thriller Fiction and the Asia Scene." J POP CULT 19, no. 2 (1985): 49-61.

171 WONG-CHU, Jim
"Ten Years of Asian Literary Arts in Vancouver." ASIANADIAN 5, no. 3 (1984): 23-25.

172 YOUNG, Judy
" 'Amid the Alien Corn': An Unrecognized Dimension of Canadian Literature." In *Second Banff Conference of Central and East European Studies of Canada*, edited by Metro Gulutsan. (Edmonton: CEESAC, 1978) pp. 171-82.
[Describes some of the shortcomings experienced by authors in the non-official languages. These are: lack of readership, lack of feedback and recognition, as well as working in isolation. In spite of these, there is a clear testimony to the vitality of creative expression among writers of Central and East European background.]

173 YOUNG, Judy
"Canadian Literature in the Non-official Languages: A Review of Recent Publications and Work in Progress." CAN ETH STUD 14, no. 1 (1982): 138-49.
[A comprehensive survey of ethnic creative literature. Areas covered include poetry, fiction, anthologies and bibliographic sources.]

174 YOUNG, Judy

"Some Thoughts about the Present State of Bibliography in the Area of Canadian Ethnic Studies." In *Bibliography for Canadian Studies: Present Trends and Future Needs/Bibliographie pour les études canadiennes: situation actuelle et besoins futurs...*, edited by A.B. Piternick. (Willowdale, Ont.: Association for Canadian Studies, 1981) pp. 38-47.
[The past decade has witnessed dramatic developments in research on Canadian ethnic studies. The most notable improvements are in the fields of education, sociology, literature, political science and history. This paper provides a bibliographic survey of the resources that offer immediate access to the literature. At the end of the study a list of major bibliographies is given in the subject categories of general bibliographies, bibliographies by discipline and bibliographies by ethnic group.]

175   YOUNG, Judy
"The Unheard Voices: Ideological or Literary Identification of Canada's Ethnic Writers." In *Identifications: Ethnicity and the Writer in Canada.*, edited by Jars Balan. (Edmonton: The Canadian Institute of Ukrainian Studies, 1982) pp. 104-15.
[A bibliographic study of ethnic Canadian literature.]

ANTHOLOGIES

176   *The Asian-Canadian and the Arts.* WEST COAST REV, 16, no. 1, 1981. 85 pp.
[The whole issue is devoted to Asian-Canadian poetry and arts. Poets represented are Mabel Chiu, David Fujino, Lakshmi Gill, Kevin Irie, Roy Kiyooka, Joy Kogawa, Helen Koyama, Carol Matsui, Suniti Namjoshi, S. Padmanab, Gerry Shikatani, Jim Wong-Chu, and Paul Yee.]

177   *Canada in Us Now,* edited by Harold Head. Toronto: N.C. Press, 1976. 144 pp.
[Includes poems and short stories by Abbott Anderson, Dionne Brand, Vibert Cambridge, David Campbell, Austin Clarke, Liz Cromwell, Willis Cummins, Daryl Dean, Ron Gaskin, Harold Head, Harold Sonny Ladoo, Felizze Mortune, Malika Neru, Arthur Nortje, Charles Roach, Ven Thomas, Carol Tremain, Ann Wallace, Gloria Wesley.]

178   *Canadian Fiction Magazine; Trans1,* edited by Charles Lillard. Vancouver: Canadian Fiction Magazine, 1976. 216 pp.
[Short stories by Irma Grebdze, Walter Bauer, Yi-Chao Wen, Youssef El-Malh, Herbert Siebner, Arved Viirlaid, Éva Sárvári, Gabriel Szohner, J.A. MacLean, Robert Zend, Kristiina Aykroyd, Manuel Santos, Kamal Rostom, V. Tamulaitis, Pnina Granirer, Maria Green, Emmanuel Algizakis, Surjeet Kalsey, Ravinder Ravi, Yetvart Kedjian, Leroy Jensen, Tülin Erbas, Michele Pirone, Lini R. Grol, C.D. Minni, Gonzallo Millan, László Kemenes Géfin.]

179   *Canadian Fiction Magazine; Trans2,* edited by Geoffrey Hancock. Toronto: Canadian Fiction Magazine, 1980. 272 pp.
[This special issue, No. 36/37, is devoted to ethnic and native Canadian short story writers. Included are: Xavier Sutherland, Alootook Ipellie, Rita Joe, George Kenny, Joe MacNeil, Kristjana Gunnars, Solomon Ary, Chava Rosenfarb, Magda Zalán, Maria Ardizzi, Luciano Aconito, Wacław Iwaniuk, Richard Liu, Tonfang Po, Chen Jo-Hsi, Ulrich Schaffer, Surjeet Kalsey, Gianni Bartocci, Cyril Dabydeen, Juan C. Garcia, Ramon Supelveda, Jorge Etcheverry, Naín Nómez, Leandro Urbina, Pablo Urbanyi, Alex Domokos, Katchar der Mesrobian, Arved Viirlaid, Jaroslava Blazkova, Zděna Salivarová-Škvorecký, Josef Škvorecký, and Robert Zend.]

180   *Canadian Haiku Anthology,* edited by George Swede. Toronto: Three Trees, 1979. 104 pp.
[Includes poems by C.K. Harris, Eric Amann, Anna Vakar and others.]

181   *Canadian Overtones: An Anthology of Canadian Poetry Written Originally in Icelandic, Swedish, Norwegian, Hungarian, Italian, Greek, and Ukrainian, and Now Translated and Edited with Biographical, Historical, and Bibliographical Notes by Watson Kirkconnell.* Winnipeg, 1935. 104

pp.
[The following nationalities are represented: 15 Icelandic poets (pp. 16-48), 4 Swedish (pp. 50-61), 1 Norwegian (p. 62), 3 Hungarian (pp. 65-68), 15 Ukrainian (pp. 83-103) and some Greek and Italian poets.]

182 *Canadian Poetry Now: 20 Poets of the '80s* edited by Ken Norris. Toronto: Anansi Press, 1984.
[Ethnic authors included are Pier Giorgio Di Cicco, Mary di Michele, André Farkas, Raymond Filip, and Kristjana Gunnars.]

183 *Cross/Cut: Contemporary English Québec Poetry,* edited by Peter Van Toorn and Ken Norris. Montréal: Véhicule Press, 1982. 255 pp.
[The ethnic poets included are John Asfour, Henry Beissel, Béla Egyedi, Tom Könyves, Rochl Korn, Claudia Lapp, Mary Melfi, Filippo Salvatore, Peter Van Toorn. Biographical notes are also provided.]

184 *Cues and Entrances: Ten Canadian One-act Plays,* edited by Henry Beissel. Toronto: Gage, 1977. 185 pp.
[Includes ten plays and biographical sketches of authors. Ethnic writing included is a play by Henry Beissel: *For Crying Out Loud* (pp. 94-117).]

185 *The Dancing Sun: A Celebration of Canadian Children,* edited by Jan Andrews, illustrated by René Mansfield. Victoria/Toronto: Press Porcépic, 1981. 141 pp.
[A collection of short stories on themes of Japanese, Lebanese, Polish, Jewish, Chinese, Icelandic, Mennonite Canadian interest by Marjorie Holland, G. Joan Morris, Ann Rivkin, Irma Sanderson, Joyce C. Barkhouse, Sharon Drache, Mary Daem, R. Guttormsson, Susan Hiebert; poems by Alootook Ipellie, Cyril Dabydeen, Nancy Prasad, C.M. Buckaway, and Meguido Zola.]

186 *Dix poètes anglophones du Québec (Voix off),* présentés par Antonio D'Alfonso. Montréal: Guernica; Pantin, France: Castor astral, 1985. 175 pp.
[Bilingual edition. Includes the following authors: Louis Dudek, Daniel Sloate, Marco Fraticelli, André Farkas, Michael Harris, Mary Melfi, Ken Norris, Anne MacLean, Jane Dick and Antonio D'Alfonso.]

187 *Fiddlehead Greens: Short Stories from the Fiddlehead,* selected by Roger Ploude and Michael Taylor. Ottawa: Oberon Press, 1979. 210 pp.
[Includes short stories by Cyril Dabydeen, W.D. Valgardson and others.]

188 *Green Snow: Anthology of Canadian Poets of Asian Origin,* edited with an introduction by Stephen Gill. Cornwall, Ont.: Vista Publishers, 1976. 120 pp.
[Includes poems by K.V. Amembal, Rienzi Crusz, R.U. Gahun, Stephen Gill, Gurumel, A. Khan, Joy Kogawa, C. Lakshmi-Bai, Michael Ondaatje, S. Padmanab, M. Parakot, Uma Parameswaran, Gurcharan Rampuri, Ravinder Ravi, S. Sankaran, S. Sarkar, B.M. Sarup, W.A. Shaheen, 'Nadan' B.N. Sinha and A. Weerasinghe.]

189 *Gulls Flying in the Mist: Asian-Canadian Writing,* edited by Rienzi Crusz. Toronto: Williams-Wallace Publications, 1987.

190 *Inalienable Rice; A Chinese and Japanese Canadian Anthology,* edited by Garrick Chu. Vancouver: *Powell Street Review* and the Chinese Canadian Writers' Workshop, 1979.
[A collection of Chinese and Japanese Canadian poetry, fiction, illustrations and historical articles.]

191 *Invisible Fiction - Contemporary Stories from Quebec,* edited by Geoff Hancock. Toronto: Anansi, 1987. 437 pp.
[Minority authors included are Elisabeth Vonarburg, Alexis Klimov, Négovan Rajic, Thomas

Pavel.]

192 *Lakeshore Poets*, selected by Peter Van Toorn. Ste Anne de Bellevue, Que.: Muses' Company, 1982. 39 pp.
[Includes poems by Neil Henden, Ben Soo, Ruth Taylor, Stephen Brockwell, and Greg Lamontagne.]

193 *Literatura Hispano-Canadiense/Hispano-Canadian Literature/Littérature Hispano-canadienne; Cuentos/Poesía/Teatro*, edited by Diego Morín. Toronto: Alianza Cultural Hispano-Canadiense, 1984. 292 pp.
[Includes writings by Rubín Mendez, Luis Pérez Botero, Alfonso Rojo, Ricardo Serrano, Emilio Barón, Raúl Bartolomé, Manuel Betanzos Santos, Ilse Adriana Luraschi, Nubia Soda, José Luis Thénon, and Patricia Appleton.]

194 *Moans and Waves and other Poems by Stephen Gill, Bob Eadie, and Asoka Weerasinghe*. Cornwall, Ont.: Vesta, 1988. 90 pp.

195 *Mosaic in Media: Selected Works of Ethnic Journalists and Writers*, edited by Vera Ke and others. Toronto: Canadian Ethnic Journalists' and Writers' Club, 1986. 239 pp. photos.
[Includes writings by more than 90 authors, journalists, educators, and editors. Portraits and biographies are also provided.]

196 *Nothing but Stars: Leaves from the Immigrant Saga*, compiled by Magnus Einarsson. Ottawa: National Museums of Canada, 1984. 184 pp.
[A collection of 80 legends and anecdotes, 12 poems and a drama, representing more than twenty ethno-cultural groups.]

197 *One Out of Many: A Collection of Writings by 21 Black Women in Ontario*, edited by Liz Cromwell. Toronto: Wacro Productions, 1975. 72 pp.
[Contains poems by Lillian Allen, Marjorie Black, Dionne Brand, Vera Cudjoe, Simbo Mzuri Mdago-Hogan, Rachel McLean, Rrana Narayan, and some second-generation poets.]

198 *Other Channels: An Anthology of New Canadian Poetry*, edited by Shaunt Basmajian and Jones. Toronto: Associate Members, League of Canadian Poets, 1984. 68 pp.
[Represents 66 poets including Shaunt Basmajian, Antonio D'Alfonso, Stephen Gill, Steve Guerin, and Jiri Jirasek.]

199 *Other Voices: Writings by Blacks in Canada*, edited by Lorriss Elliott. Toronto: Williams-Wallace, 1985. 188 pp.
[Includes poems, short stories and plays by 43 authors such as Hopeton Anderson, Ayanna Black, Dionne Brand, Anthony Coker, Lorry Elliott, Arnold Itwaru, Harold Marshall, Enid D'Oyley, Charles Roach, Edward Watson, and others.]

200 *La Poésie québécoise: des origines à nos jours: Anthologie*, ed. Laurent Mailhot and Pierre Nepveu. Sillery, Qué.: Les Presses de l'Université du Québec, 1980. 714 pp. illus., ports.
[Arranged chronologically by authors' dates of birth, provides biographies, titles of publications, and poems by authors. Minority authors included are Monique Bosco (Austrian), Jean Baudot (Belgian), Alain Horic (Croatian), Serge Legagneur (Haïtian), Juan Garcia (Moroccan).]

201 *The Poets of Canada*, edited by John Robert Colombo. Edmonton: Hurtig, 1978. 303 pp.
[Includes poems by the following minority languages authors: Melech Ravitch, Rochl Korn, Walter Bauer, George Faludy, Wacław Iwaniuk, Yar (i.e ÎAr) Slavutych, Hannes Oja, Henrikas Nagys, Arved Viirlaid, Ludwig Zeller, Robert Zend, Henry Beissel, George Jónás, Michael Ondaatje, Andreas Schroeder, and Pier Giorgio Di Cicco.]

202 *Poets of the Capital*, edited by Frank M. Tierney and Stephen Gill. Ottawa: Borealis Press, [1973].
160 pp.
[Represents 46 poets, some of them (Stephen Gill, Rosemary Newcome) of ethnic origin.]

203 *Sad Dances in a Field of White*, edited by Charles C. Smith. Toronto: Is Five Press, 1985. 90 pp.
[A collection of Black poetry, representing Cyril Dabydeen, Gwen Hauser, Marlene Nourbese
Philip, J.M. Stevens, Krishantha Bhaggiyadatta, Claire Harris, and others.]

204 *Seaway Valley Poets (Anthology)*, edited by Stephen Gill and Roland C. Hamel. Cornwall, Ont.:
Vesta Publications, 1975. 127 pp.
[Includes poems by 26 poets residing in the Seaway Valley area. Of ethnic background are
Giancarlo Calicchia and Stephen Gill.]

205 *A Shapely Fire: Changing the Literary Landscape*, edited by Cyril Dabydeen. Oakville, Ont.:
Mosaic Press, 1987. 176 pp.
[Includes short stories and poems by authors of Caribbean descent: Austin Clarke, Max Dorsinville,
Gérard Étienne, Marlene Philip, Neil Bissoondath, Dionne Brand, Claire Harris, Daniel Caudeiron,
and Lillian Allen.]

206 *Sharing Through Poetry: A Multicultural Experience.* Toronto: University of Toronto Press for
the Ad Hoc Committee for "Sharing Through Poetry." [n.d.]
[Poets included are Pier Giorgio Di Cicco, Mary di Michele, João Lucio Monteiro, Jesús López-
Pacheco, George Stoubos, Anibal Trindade, Aristides Yerou, and Ludwig Zeller. Provides
biographical sketches.]

207 *Tales from Canada for Children Everywhere*, edited by Stephen Gill. Cornwall, Ont.: Vesta
Publications, 1979. 108 pp.
[Includes tales by Mary Melfi, Stephen Gill, Donna Gamache, Carolyn Kowalski, Roland C.
Hamel, and others.]

208 *This is My Best: Poems Selected by Ninety-one Poets.* Toronto: Coach House, 1976. 144 pp.
[Two ethnic poets are represented: Tom Könyves and Pier Giorgio Di Cicco.]

209 *Unfinished Anthology*, edited by Chris Faiers. Toronto: Unfinished Monument Press, 1984 -
[Includes poems by Shaunt Basmajian and several non-ethnic authors.]

210 *The Véhicule Poets.* Montreal: Maker Press, 1979.
[Poems by André Farkas and Tom Könyves.]

211 *Volvox: Poetry from the Unofficial Languages of Canada...In English Translation*, edited by
Michael Yates, Charles Lillard, and Ann J. West. Queen Charlotte Islands, B.C.: Sono Nis Press,
1971. 256 pp.
[Includes poems by T. Hiramatsu, George Faludy, Henrikas Nagys, Tülin Erbas, Nicholas Catanoy,
Bogdan Czaykowski, Jose Emilio Pacheco, Walter Bauer, Guttormur J. Guttormsson, Samar Attar,
Manuel Betanzos Santos, Rochl Korn, Robert Zend, Stephan G. Stephansson, Robert Brunner, J.I.
Segal, Hannes Oja, Luigi Romeo, Andreas Schroeder, Wacław Iwaniuk, Einar Pall Jonsson, Pavel
Javor, Walz Reinhard, Andrzej Busza, Arved Viirlaid, Ramon Mansoor, Yar (i.e. Íar) Slavutych,
and Takeo Nakano.]

212 *West Indian Stories*, compiled by Andrew Salkey. London: Faber & Faber, 1960. 224 pp.
[Of the 21 authors included, Samuel Selvon is represented by four short stories.]

213 WRIT 14: *Translation Issue: European Languages*, edited by Roger Greenwald. Toronto: WRIT,

1982. 167 pp.
[Includes four Canadian authors: Josef Škvorecký, Fedir Odrach, Yaacov Zipper, and Tamás Hajós.]

II. NATIONALITY/LANGUAGE GROUPS

ALGERIAN

INDIVIDUAL AUTHORS

CARDINAL, Marie (1929-   )
Neé à Alger, elle demeure maintenant à Montréal. Auteure de sept ouvrages. *The Words to Say It* a été traduit en 18 langues. Le film réalisé à partir de l'ouvrage a été visionné partout au Canada.

214   *The Words to Say It,* translated by Pat Goodheart.   Montréal: Véhicule Press, 1985. Autobiographical novel.

GHALEM, Nadia

215   *L'Oiseau de fer: cinq nouvelles.* Sherbrooke: Naaman, 1981. 68 pp. Nouvelles.

216   *Les Jardins de christal.* La Salle, Que.: Hurtubise HMH, 1981. 139 pp. Poèmes.

217   *Exil.* Montréal: The Author. Poèmes.

SARRAZIN, Claude-Gérard (1936-   )
Né à Alger, où il a obtenu un diplôme en éducation. Il est également détenteur d'un diplôme en musique. Il a douné des concerts comme pianiste au Canada et est l'auteur de plus de vingt ouvrages sur musique, l'éducation et la littérature.

218   *Phosphoros.* Montréal: Guérin, 1978. 191 pp. Roman.

219   *La Porte des dieux.* Montréal: Presses Sélect, 1980. 224 pp. Roman.

ARGENTINIAN

INDIVIDUAL AUTHORS

BALCARE, Alberto
Born in Argentina.

220   *A Long Night of Death.* Oakville, Ont.: Mosaic Press, 1986. 182 pp. Novel.

   Writings about:

221   Carey, Barbara. Review of *A Long Night of Death.* BKS CAN 16, no. 1 (1987): 25.

222   Curtis, D.A. Review of *A Long Night of Death.* CAN BOOK REV ANN 1986: 73.

MIBASHAN, David (1957-   )
Born in Buenos Aires, Argentina. Moved to Jerusalem for six years, before emigrating to Canada in 1982. He is a practising psychologist.

223 *Las Veultas a la Vida [Return to Life]*. Buenos Aires: Grupo Editor Latino-americano, 1985. 134 pp.

224 *Vida y Vuelta [Return Trip to Life]*. Buenos Aires: Grupo Editor Latino-americano, 1987.

URBANYI, Pablo (1939-   )
Born in a town in northern Hungary (now part of Czechoslovakia) and moved to Argentina with his parents in 1948, where he received his education. He moved to Canada in 1977, and teaches at Carleton University, Ottawa.

225 *Noche de Revolucionarios [Night of the Revolutionaries.]*.   Buenos Aires: Centro Editor, 1972. Short stories.

226 *Un revólver para Mack [A Revolver for Mack]*. Buenos Aires: Editorial Corregidor, 1974. Novel.

227 *The Nowhere Idea*, translated from the Spanish by Nigel Dennis. Toronto: Williams-Wallace, 1982. 169 pp. Novel.
[Based on his "En ninguna parte."]

228 *No Name.* Buenos Aires: Editorial Legasa, 1986. Novel.

AUSTRIAN

INDIVIDUAL AUTHORS

BOSCO, Monique (1927-   )
Romancière. Née à Vienne, Autriche. Éducation: Université de Montréal (B.A., M.A., Ph.D.). Emploi: Professeur à l'Université de Montréal. Prix littéraires: Prix du Gouverneur général (1970).

229   *Un amour maladroit.* Paris: Gallimard [1961] 213 pp. Roman.

230   *Les infusoires.* Montréal: Éditions HMH, 1965. 174 pp. Poèmes.

231   *La femme de Loth; roman.* Paris: R. Laffont; Montréal: HMH [1970] 281 pp. Roman.

232   *Jéricho: poèmes.* Montréal: HMH [1971] 63 pp. Poèmes.

233   *New Medea: roman.* Montréal: L'Actuelle, 1974. 149 pp. Roman.

234   *Lot's Wife,* translated from the French by John Glassco. Toronto: McClelland & Stewart, 1975. 149 pp. Novel.
[Translation of *La femme de Loth.*]

235   *Charles Lévy M.D.* Montréal: Quinze, 1978. 136 pp. Novel.

236   *Schabbat, 70-77.* Montréal: Quinze [1978] 100 pp. illus. Poèmes.

237   *Portrait de Zeus peint par Minerve.* LaSalle, Qué.: Hurtubise HMH, 1982. 179 pp. Roman.

238   *Sara sage: Roman.* LaSalle, Qué., 1986. 123 pp. Roman.

239   *Boomerang: nouvelles.* LaSalle, Qué.: Hurtubise HMH, 1987. 144 pp. Nouvelles.

Writings about:

240   Bonenfant, Joseph. "La poésie de Monique Bosco, une quête de justice." VOIX IMAG 9, no. 3 (1984): 13-21.

241   Brochu, André. "Portrait de Minerve peint par elle-même. Entrevue avec Monique Bosco." VOIX IMAG 9, no. 3 (1984): 5-12.

242   Drolet, Gilbert. Review of *Charles Lévy M.D.* Q & Q 44, no. 8 (1978): 48.

243   Escomel, Gloria. "Monique Bosco, l'iconoclaste." VOIX IMAG 9, no. 3 (1984): 47-54.

244   Escomel, Gloria. "Monique Bosco ou la Femme en quête de son double." LIBERTÉ 20, no. 2 (1978): 88-95.

245   Escomel, Gloria. "Monique Bosco ou le miroir brisé." NOUV BARRE DU JOUR 65 (1978)

246   Escomel, Gloria. "Œuvres de Monique Bosco." NOUV BARRE DU JOUR No. 65 (avril 1978): 90-97.

247 Gallays, François. "Les corps scellés. Analyse de trois romans de Monique Bosco." VOIX IMAG 9, no. 3 (1984): 35-45.

248 Gaulin, André. *Critique: Schabbat 70-71.* QUÉB FRANÇ No. 33 (1979): 10.

249 Gauvin, Lise. Review of *Charles Lévy M.D.* UNIV TOR Q 47 (1977-78): 341.

250 Goldin, Jeanne. "La Passion selon Monique Bosco." VOIX IMAG 9, no. 3 (1984): 23-33.

251 Lavallée-Huynh, Ginette. Critique: *Charles Lévy M.D.* NOS LIVR 9, no. 43 (1978)

252 Lepage, Yvan G. Critique: *Charles Lévy M.D.* LIVR AUTR QUÉB 1977: 49-50.

253 Michaud, Ginette. Critique: *Charles Lévy M.D.* LIVR AUTR QUÉB 1978: 96-97.

254 Ouellette-Michalska, Madeleine. Critique: *Charles Lévy M.D.* CHÂTELAINE 19, no. 2 (1978): 8.

255 Pavlovic, Myrianne. "Bibliographie de Monique Bosco." VOIX IMAG 9, no. 3 (1984): 55-82.

256 Simon, Sherry. "Bosco, Monique." In *The Oxford Companion to Canadian Literature*, edited by William Toye. (Toronto: Oxford University Press, 1983) p. 78.

257 Verduyn, Christl. "Looking Back to *Lot's Wife*." ATLANTIS 6, no. (1981): 38-40, 41.
[Review of *Lot's Wife*.]

KREISEL, Henry (1922-   )
Novelist, educator. Born in Vienna, Austria. He left his homeland for England in 1938 after the Nazi take-over. Sent to Canada by the British authorities in 1940. After an internment of eighteen months he attended Jarvis Collegiate and the University of Toronto, where he received his B.A. and M.A., followed by his Ph.D. from the University of London. He taught English literature at the University of Alberta and also served as Vice President Academic. Received the Sir Frederick Haultain Prize for Significant Achievement in the Fine Arts (1986).

258 *The Rich Man: A Novel.* Toronto: McClelland & Stewart, 1948. 263 pp. Novel.
[Also published by McClelland & Stewart in 1961. (New Canadian Library 24.).]

259 *The Betrayal.* [Toronto: McClelland & Stewart, 1964.] 218 pp. Novel.
[Also published by McClelland & Stewart in 1977, with an introduction by S. Warhaft. (New Canadian Library 77.) Reprinted in 1987.]

260 *The Almost Meeting and Other Stories.* Edmonton: NeWest Press, 1981. 148 pp. Short stories.

261 *Another Country: Writings by and About Henry Kreisel,* edited by Shirley Neuman. Edmonton: NeWest Press, 1986. 362 pp.
[This volume brings together Kreisel's unpublished writings. Includes stories and essays written over the decades. Contents: England and internment (pp. 13-72); Writings from internment (pp. 73-108); "Another country: Personal essays" (pp. 109-36); The writer's letters (pp. 137-69); Interviews (pp. 170-205); Includes bibliographies.]

Writings about:

262 Butovsky, Mervin. "Interview with Henry Kreisel." In *Another Country...* (Edmonton: NeWest Press, 1986) pp. 176-201.

263 Besner, Neil. "Across Broken Globes: *The Almost Meeting.*" In *Another Country...* (Edmonton: NeWest Press, 1986) pp. 334-37.

264 Cherniavsky, Felix. "Certain Worldly Experiences: An Interview with Henry Kreisel." SPHINX 2, no. 3 (1977): 10-22.

265 Greenstein, Michael. "Close Encounters: Henry Kreisel's Short Stories." In *Another Country...* (Edmonton: NeWest, 1986) pp. 338-42.

266 Greenstein, Michael. "The Language of the Holocaust in *The Rich Man.*" In *Another Country...* (Edmonton: NeWest, 1986) pp. 269-80. First published in ETUD CAN/ CAN STUD 4 (1978).

267 Greenstein, Michael. "Perceptives on the Holocaust in Henry Kreisel's *The Betrayal.*" In *Another Country...* (Edmonton: NeWest Press, 1986) pp. 285-92. First published in ESSAYS CAN WRIT 23 (1982).

268 Gürttler, Karin. "Henry Kreisel: A Canadian Exile Writer?" In *Another Country...* (Edmonton: NeWest Press, 1986) pp. 293-303. First appeared in *The Old World and the New: Literary Perspectives of German-Speaking Canadians*, edited by Walter E. Riedel. (Toronto: University of Toronto Press, 1984).

269 Hlus, Carol. "He Who Sells His Shadow." In *Another Country...* (Edmonton: NeWest Press, 1986) pp. 281-83. *He Who Sells His Shadow* is a radio drama.

270 Keith, W.J. "Almost Meeting." In *Another Country...* (Edmonton: NeWest, 1986) pp. 343-44.

271 Lecker, Robert. "States of Mind: Henry Kreisel's Novels." In *Another Country...* (Edmonton: NeWest, 1986) pp. 304-16. First appeared in CAN LIT No. 77 (1978).

272 Matheson, Gwen. Review of *The Rich Man.* CAN BOOK REV ANN 1975: 117.

273 McPherson, Hugo. "Betrayal, Desertion, Atonement." TAM REV 34 (1965): 106-11.

274 Owen, I.M. "Writers Out of Residence." BKS CAN 15, no. 4 (1986): 48-49.
[Review of *Another Country.*]

275 Robertson, George. "Guilt and Counter-guilt." CAN LIT No. 23 (1965): 72-74.

276 Scobie, Stephen. "On the Edge of Language." In *Another Country...* (Edmonton: NeWest Press, 1986) pp. 345-47.

277 Silvester, Reg. "Regionalism Tends to Obscure Writers." EDMONT J (May 7, 1979): C9.
[A panel discussion on regional literature.]

278 Stedmont, John. "Introduction." In *The Rich Man.* (Toronto: McClelland & Stewart, 1948) pp. v-viii.

279 Stephens, Donald. "Old Canadians Reviewed." CAN LIT No. 12 (1962): 83.
[Review of *The Rich Man.*]

280 Tausky, Thomas E. "Henry Kreisel." In *The Oxford Companion to Canadian Literature*, edited by William Toye. (Toronto: Oxford University Press, 1983) pp. 417-18.

281 Tausky, Thomas E. "Under Western Canadian Eyes: Conrad and *The Betrayal.*" In *Another Country...* (Edmonton: NeWest Press, 1986) pp. 317-33.

282 Warhaft, Sidney. "Introduction." In *The Betrayal.* (Toronto: McClelland and Stewart, 1971)

283 Watt, F.W. "Humane Vision." CAN LIT No 115 (1987): 202-03.
[Review of *Another Country.*]

284 Watt, F.W. "Letters in Canada: 1964 (Fiction)." UNIV TOR Q 34 (1964-65): 378.

285 Woodcock, George. "The Triumphant Exile." ESSAYS CAN WRIT No. 35 (1987): 82-87.
[Review of *Another Country.*]

WASSERMANN, Charles

Writing about:

286 Seliger, Helfried. "Charles Wassermann: Life and *Oeuvre* in the Service of Mutual Understanding." In *The Old World and the New...*, edited by Walter E. Riedel. (Toronto: University of Toronto Press, 1984) pp. 124-43.

WEISELBERGER, Carl (1900-1970)

287 *Der Rebbe mit der axt: dreissig geschichten [The Rabbi with the Ax: Thirty Stories],* edited by Herta Hartmanshenn and Frederick Kriegel. Victoria, B.C.: University of Victoria, 1973. 241 pp. Short stories.

288 *Eine Auswahl seiner Schriften [A Selection of His Writings],* edited by Peter Liddell and Walter Riedel. Toronto: German-Canadian Historical Association, 1981. Short stories.

Writing about:

289 Riedel, Walter E. "An Austrian in Ottawa: Carl Weiselberger's Canadian Experience." In *The Old World and the New...*, edited by Walter E. Riedel. (Toronto: University of Toronto Press, 1984) pp. 107-23.

BARBADIAN

INDIVIDUAL AUTHORS

CLARKE, Austin Chesterfield (1934-   )

Novelist, short story writer. Born in Barbados. Came to Canada in 1956. Attended Harrison College, Barbados (Oxford and Cambridge Higher Certificate), and the University of Toronto. Founding member of the Writers' Union of Canada and recipient of Canada Council Senior Arts fellowships (1968, 1974 and 1979), the University of Western Ontario President's Medal, Belmont Short Story Award, etc.

290   *Survivors of the Crossing.* Toronto: McClelland & Stewart, 1964. Short stories.

291   *Amongst Thistles and Thorns.* Toronto: McClelland & Stewart, 1965. 183 pp. Short stories.

292   *The Meeting Point: A Novel.*   Toronto: Macmillan/Boston: Little, Brown/London: Heinemann, 1967. 249 pp. Novel.
[The first volume of a trilogy.]

293   *When He Was Free and Young and He Used to Wear Silks: Stories.* Toronto: Anansi, 1971. 151 pp. Short stories.

294   *Storm of Fortune: A Novel.* Boston: Little, Brown, 1973. 312 pp. Novel.
[Second volume of a trilogy.]

295   *The Bigger Light: A Novel.* Toronto: McClelland & Stewart/London: Heinemann, 1975. 288 pp. Novel.

296   *The Prime Minister: A Novel.* Don Mills, Ont.: General Publishing, 1977. 191 pp. Novel.

297   *Growing Up Stupid Under the Union Jack: A Memoir.* Toronto: McClelland & Stewart, 1980. 192 pp. Autobiographical novel.

298   *Nine Men Who Laughed.* Markham, Ont.: Penguin, 1986. 225 pp. Short stories.

299   *Proud Empires.* London: Golancz, 1986 224 pp. Novel.

Writings about:

300   Atwood, Margaret. "Austin Clarke." In her *Survival: A Thematic Guide to Canadian Literature.* (Toronto: Anansi, 1972) pp. 151-52, 154.

301   Bannerman, James. "Black Child Views White Truth." MACLEAN'S 78 (Oct. 16, 1965): 68.
[Review of *Amongst Thistles and Thorns.*]

302   Baugh, Edward. "Prime Ministers Unlimited: West Indian Literary Report." QUEEN'S Q 87 (1980): 465-66.
[Review of *The Prime Minister.*]

303   Bessai, Diane. "West Indies: Here and There." CAN LIT No. 61 (1974): 106-09.
[Review of *Storm of Fortune.*]

304   Boxill, Anthony. "Novels of Austin C. Clarke: Review Article." FIDDLEHEAD 76 (1968): 69-72.

305   Boxill, Anthony. Review of *When He Was Free and Young...*. FIDDLEHEAD 95 (1972): 117-18.

306   Brown, Lloyd W. "Austin Clarke in Canadian Reviews." CAN LIT No. 38 (1968): 101-04.

307   Colter, Rob. Review of *The Prime Minister*. Q & Q 43, no. 14 (1977): 7.

308   Dabydeen, Cyril. Review of *Growing Up Stupid Under the Union Jack*. DAL REV 61 (1981): 156-57.

309   Dale, James. Review of *The Meeting Point*. CAN FORUM 48 (April. 1968): 19-20.

310   Dalt, Gary Michael. Review of *The Meeting Point*. TAM REV 45 (1967): 117, 120.

311   Dobbs, Kildare. "Caribbean Renaissance." SAT N 80 (November 1965): 59-60.
       [Review of *Amongst Thistles and Thorns.*]

312   D'Oyley, Vincent. "Adapting to the Metropolis." [Sound Recording] with Austin Clarke and Hunk Clarke. Toronto: Ontario Institute for Studies in Education, 1977.

313   Drolet, Gibbers. Review of *The Prime Minister*. Q & Q 44, no. 14 (1977): 7.

314   Garebian, Keith. "Lies and Grace." CAN LIT No. 90 (1981): 136-38.
       [Review of *Growing Up Stupid Under the Union Jack.*]

315   Hilts, Dan. "Little England Made Him." BKS CAN 9 no. 6 (1980): 23.
       [Review of *Growing Up Stupid Under the Union Jack.*]

316   Hlus, Carolyn. Review of *When Women Rule*. CAN BOOK REV ANN 1985: 207-08.

317   Hynan, Patrick. "Too Big for His Galoshes." BKS CAN 4, no. 6 (1975): 15.
       [Review of *The Bigger Light.*]

318   Marshall, Tom "Rum Mixers." BKS CAN 1, no. 4 (1971): 21.

319   Morgan, J. "Austin Clarke." MONTREALER 41 (September 1967): 32-33.

320   New, W.H. "Big Versus Small Playing Politics Colonial Way." OTTAWA CIT (Apr. 23, 1988): C3.
       [Review of *Proud Empires.*]

321   Pomer, B. Review of *Amongst Thistles and Thorns*. CAN FORUM 47 (August 1967): 118-19.

322   Powers, Gordon. Review of *Growing Up Stupid Under the Union Jack*. Q & Q 46, no. 6 (1980): 36.

323   Richler, M. "If Austin Clarke Doesn't Appear on Front Page Challenge, Does This Prove Prejudice?" SAT N 83, no. 11 (1968): 68, 70.

324   Sanders, Leslie. "Austin Clarke." In *Profiles in Canadian Literature*, edited by Jeffrey M. Heath. (Toronto/Charlottetown: Dundurn Press, 1982) pp. 93-100. port.

325   Scott, Chris. "Home is the 'Hoonta'." BKS CAN 6 (November 1977): 32, 34.

[Review of *The Prime Minister*.]

326 Slopen, B. "Caribbean Memoirs of Power and Privilege." Q & Q 46, no. 5 (1980): 23.

327 Sparshott, Francis. Review of *Amongst Thistles and Thorns*. ALPHABET 12 (August 1966): 93-96.

328 Stephens, Donald G. "The Bright New Day." CAN LIT No. 54 (1972): 84-86.
[Review of *When He Was Free and Young....*]

329 Stratford, Philip. "Six Ways to Escape the Canadian Winter." SAT N 80, no. 2 (1965): 26-27.
[Review of *The Survivors of the Crossing*. Also a review of Wallace Collins's *Jamaican Migrant*.]

330 Tyrwhitt, J. "Clarke Closes in." TAM REV 38 (1966): 89-91.

331 Waddington, Miriam. "No Meeting Points." CAN LIT No. 35 (1968): 74-75, 77-78.
[Review of *Meeting Point*. Cf. Lloyd W. Burns: "Austin Clarke in Canadian Reviews." CAN LIT No. 38 (1968): 101-04.

332 Wilson, Paul. Review of *Nine Men Who Laughed*. BKS CAN 17, no. 7 (1986): 20-21.

COLLINS, Wallace

333 *Jamaican Migrant*. Toronto: General Publishing, 1964. 122 pp. Autobiographical novel.

Writing about:

334 Stratford, Philip. "Six Ways to Escape the Canadian Winter." SAT N 80, no. 2 (1965): 26-27.
[Review of *Jamaican Migrant*.]

MARSHALL, Harold

Born in Barbados, former editor of the journal *Bim*. He came to Canada in 1965 and worked as a journalist in British Columbia and as a Communications Officer for the Winnipeg School Division. Several of his novels and short stories are still in manuscript form.

335 *Full Fathom Five*.

BELGIAN

INDIVIDUAL AUTHORS

BASTIN, Agnès (1938-   )

Née dans un petit village des Ardennes belges cerné de sapins sombres, repaires des sangliers, mêmée à la guerre de 40 par un milieu familial où l'héroïsme frôlait la témérité, Bastin habite Sherbrooke depuis 1971. Elle est licenciée en philosophie romane de l'Université Louvain, Belgique et poursuit actuellement ses études en maîtrise à la Faculté des arts à l'Université de Sherbrooke. Correctrice dans une maison d'édition de Sherbrooke depuis, Agnès Bastin a des scénarios de bandes dessinées ainsi que des articles dans les périodiques suivants: *Ellipse, Liberté, Présence francophone, La Presse, L'Écran, L'Estrie.*

336   *Où vers.* Sherbrooke, Qué.: Éditions Cosmos, 1972.   Poèmes.

337   *Poèmes,* dans *Ellipse,* no. 12, 1973.   Poèmes.

338   *Roséfine la Cristalline,* coauteur, Jacques Couture.   Sherbrooke, Qué.: Éditions Cosmos, 1973.

GUSBIN, Berthe

Naît en Belgique et vient au Manitoba avec sa sœur et son beau-frère. Elle s'installe avec eux à Le Pas, à trois cents milles au nord de Winnipeg où on y fait la coupe du bois et la trappe. Gusbin enseigne le violon de 1925 à 1939. Elle habite maintenant la ville de Victoria. Ses souvenirs de voyages et de vie au Canada sont consignés dans volume intitulé *Au nord du 53e.* Auparavant, elle avait publié *En vers et sur tout* ainsi que de nombreux poèmes et récits dans le journaux.

339   *En vers et sur tout.* Victoria: chez l'auteur, 1975.   70 pp.   Poèmes.

340   *Au nord du 53e.* Saint-Boniface, Man.: Éd. du Blé, 1982.   187 pp.

BYELORUSSIAN

BIBLIOGRAPHIES

341   HRYCUK, A.A.
"Byelorussian-Canadian Imprints, 1945-1970: A Preliminary Check List."   CAN ETH STUD 2, no. 1 (1970): 9-12.
[Includes references to books of poetry, short stories and novels.]

342   HRYCUK, A.A.; MALYCKY, Alexander
"Byelorussian-Canadian Publications: A Preliminary Check List."   CAN ETH STUD 2, no. 1 (1970): 5-7.
[Includes periodicals with complete publication data about the titles.]

GENERAL WORK

343   SADOUSKI, John
A History of the Byelorussians in Canada. Belleville, Ont.: Mika, 1981.
[Includes a chapter on Byelorussian press and literature in Canada, pp. 132-40. Bibliography: pp. 145-48. Authors discussed are Siarhei Khmara, Kanstantyn Akula and Mikola Viarba.]

INDIVIDUAL AUTHORS

AKULA, Kanstantyn (1925-   )
Novelist. Born in Western Byelorussia, graduated from secondary school in Vilna. He came to Canada in 1947 and settled in Toronto.

344 *Zmaharnyia darohi. apovests' [Combat Trails: Novel].* Toronto: The Author. 583 pp. Autobiographical novel.

345 *Haravatka: Dziarlivaia ptushka [Haravatka: The Bird of Prey].* Book 1. Toronto: Pahonya Publishers, 1965. 180 pp. Novel.

346 *Tomorrow Is Yesterday.* Toronto: Pahonya Publishers, 1968. 225 pp. Novel.

347 *Haravatka: Zakryvaulenae sontsa [Haravatka: The Red Sun].* Book 2. Toronto, 1974. Novel.

348 *Haravatka: Roman. [Haravatka: Novel].* Toronto: Pahonya Publishers, 1965-1981. 3 vol. Novel.

ARSENNAVA, Natalia

349 *Mizh berahami: Vybar paezii Natalli Arsennavai, 1921-1970 [Between the Shores: Natalia Arsennava's Poetry, 1921-1970].* Toronto: Belaruski Instytut Navuki i Mastatsva, 1979. xxxix, 350 pp. Poems.

CHILEAN

RESEARCH PAPERS

350 **ETCHEVERRY, Jorge**
"Chilean Poetry in Canada: Avant Garde, Nostalgia and Commitment." VICE VERSA (December 1984-January 1985)
[A study of the poetry of Manuel Aránguiz, Claudio Durán, Jorge Etcheverry, Naín Nómez, Erick Martínez, Gonzalo Millán and Ludwig Zeller.]

351 **FELICIANO, Margarita**
"Poetas chilenos en el exilio, el del Canada" [Chilean Poets in Exile: The Case of Canada]. NEW EUROPE 14, no. 48 (1985)
[Includes poems by Claudio Duran, Naín Nómez, Jorge Etcheverry and Gonzalo Millán. Short analysis of their work is also provided.]

352 **MANGUEL, Alberto**
"Laments of Chileans in Exile." OTTAWA CIT (Apr. 23, 1988) C2.
[Review of *Burning Bridges*, by Naín Nómez and *Lost Causes*, by José Leandro Urbina.]

353 **PERCIVAL, Anthony**
Review of *Chilean Literature in Canada*, edited by Naín Nómez and Pablo Urbanyi: *The Nowhere Idea*. UNIV TOR Q 52 (1982-83): 541-44.

354 **NÓMEZ, Naín**
Identidad y exilio: escritores Chilenos en Canadá [Identity and Exile: Chilean Writers in Canada]. Santiago de Chile: CENECA, 1986. 36 pp.
[A study of the writing of Leandro Urbina, Gonzalo Millán and Jorge Etcheverry. Published by Centro de Indagación y Expressión Cultural y Artística.]

ANTHOLOGIES

355 *Antología de Literatura Hispano-Canadiense/An Anthology of Hispano-Canadian Writing*, edited by José R. Varela and Richard A. Young, on behalf of APEDECHE. Edmonton: Association for the Development of Hispanic Culture in Edmonton.
[Includes poems and short stories by Naín Nómez, Lidia Ureta Sirandoni, Jorge Etcheverry, Constantino Tirado and Rollando Hugo Vergara.]

356 *Chilean Literature in Canada/Literatura Chilena en Canadá; A Bilingual Anthology*, edited by Naín Nómez. Ottawa: Ediciones Cordillera, 1982. xxiii, 247 pp.
[Contains poems and short stories by Manuel Aránguiz, Claudio Durán, Jorge Etcheverry, Erik Martínez, Gonzalo Millán, Naín Noméz, Ludwig Zeller, Juan Carlos Garcia, Manuel Jofré, Carlos Pastén, Ramón Sepulvéda and José Leandro Urbina.]

357 *Cruzando la Cordillera* [Crossing the Cordillera], edited by Juan Armando Epple. Mexico: Secretary of Public Education of Mexico, 1986.
[Includes short stories by Ramon Sepulveda and Jorge Etcheverry.]

358 *Poesía Chilena Contemporánea* [Contemporary Chilean Poetry]. Santiago: Andrés Bello, 1984. 358 pp.

[Includes some Chilean-Canadian authors: Claudio Durán, Jorge Etcheverry, Gonzalo Millán, Naín Nómez, Erick Martinez, and Ludwig Zeller.]

359   *Reembou*, edited by Basil Mogridge. Ottawa: Carleton University, 1979.
[A plurilingual poetry magazine, the first and only issue. Poems included by the following Chilean-Canadian authors: Gonzalo Millán, Gabriela Miralles, Luis Lama, Jorge Etcheverry, Jorge Fajardo, Jorge Cancino and José Leandro Urbina.]

360   *Revista Canadiense de Estudios Hispánicos.* 11, no. 1 (1984).
[Includes poems by Claudio Durán, Jorge Etcheverry and Naín Nómez.]

INDIVIDUAL AUTHORS

ALVARADO, Tito

361   *Ausencias [Absences].* Montreal: Edicions El Siglo, 1984. 69 pp. Poems.

362   *Geografia heroica [Heroic Geography].* Montreal: Editorial La Alborada, 1985. 54 pp. Poems.

ARANGUIZ, Manuel (1945-   )
Founder of the Maison Culturelle Québec-Amérique Latine, born in Santiago, Chile. He has worked as an actor, television script writer, dishwasher, teacher, translator. He has lived in Quebec since 1974.

363   *Cuerpo de silencio/Corps de silence.* Montreal: Maison Culturelle Québec-Amérique Latine, 1981. Poems.

CANCINO, Jorge (1930-   )

364   *Juglario.* Montreal: The Author, 1984. 92 pp. illus. Poems.
[In Spanish and French.]

DURÁN, Claudio

365   *Más tarde que los clientes habituales/After the Usual Clients Have Gone Home*, English translations by Rafael Barreto-Rivera. Toronto: Underwhich Editions, 1982. [30] pp. Poems.

ETCHEVERRY, Jorge (1945-   )
Poet. Born in Santiago, Chile. Studied Philosophy and Literature at the University of Chile and Carleton University, Ottawa. A member of the Santiago school of poetry, he has published in magazines in Latin America, Europe and North America. He is editor of *Ethnic Voices*, a literary supplement published in Ottawa, where he lives.

366   *El evasionista/The Escape Artist: Poems 1968-1980*, English translations by Christina Shantz. Ottawa: Ediciones Cordillera, 1981. 119 pp. Poems.
[Spanish text, parallel English translation.]

367   *La calle [The Street].* Santiago: Editorial Sinfronteras, 1986. 65 pp. Poems.

368   *The Witch*, English translations by Jorge Etcheverry and Paulette Turcotte. Ottawa: Split Quotation, 1986. 56 pp. Poems.
[Bilingual, Spanish and English text.]

GARCIA, Juan Carlos (1944-   )

Born in Santiago, Chile, studied at the Valdivia Normal School at the Southern University of Chile and at Queen's University in Kingston, Ont. He is currently completing his Ph. D. in Literature at the University of Toronto. He has published scholarly works and short stories in Chile, Canada and other countries.

369   *Historias del Poder [Stories of Power].* Santiegó Editorioal SinFronteros, 1986. 107 pp. Short stories.

KURAPEL, Alberto
Born in Chile, came to Canada and settled in Montreal. Singer and composer of Chilean songs, several of his chansons were recorded on phonodiscs with words in Spanish, French and English.

370   Correo de Exilio (poesia postal/Poésie postale). Montreal: Les Éditions du Trottoir, 1986. 65 pp. Poems.

LAVERGNE, Alfredo

371   *Cada fruto [Each Fruit].* Montreal: Éditions d'Orphée, 1985. 54 pp. Poems.

372   *Alas dispersas [Dispersed Wings].* Montreal: The Author,   52 pp. Poems.

MALLET, Marilu
Born in Chile, now a resident in Montreal. She wrote the script for *Il n'a a pas d'oubli* and published short stories in various periodicals.

373   *Les compagnons de l'horloge-pointeuse: nouvelles.* Montreal: Maison Culturelle Québec-Amérique Latine, 1981. Nouvelles.

374   *Voyage to the Other Extreme*, translated from Spanish by Alan Brown. Montreal: Véhicule Press, 1985. 105 pp. Short stories.

   Writing about:

375   Dansereau, Estelle. Review of *Voyage to the Other Extreme.* CAN ETH STUD 18, no. 3 (1986): 156-57.

MARTINEZ, Eric (1944-   )
A member of the Santiago School of poetry, he has published in several South American magazines. He studied at the University of Toronto and wrote his thesis "Altazor deVicente Huidobro: una aproximación analítica."

376   *Tequila Sunrise*, translated from Spanish by Christina Shantz and Alan Heatherington. Ottawa: Ediciones Cordillera, 1985. 95 pp. Poems.
       [Spanish and English text.]

MILLÁN, Gonzalo (1947-   )
Born in Santiago, Chile. Came to Canada in 1974. Received his M.A. from the University of New Brunswick. He lives in Montreal.

377   *La ciudad [The City].* Montreal: Maison Culturelle Québec-Amérique Latine, 1980. Poems.

378   *Vida 1968-1982 [Life 1968-1982].* Ottawa: Cordillera, 1984. Port. Poems.
       [Includes *Relación personal 1965-1967*, a Pedro de Oña award winning collection (1968) and *Vida: Antología* 1969-1982.]

NÓMEZ, Naín (1944-)
Poet, editor. Born in Talca, Chile. He taught Philosophy and Spanish at the University of Chile in Santiago, and did graduate work at the University of Toronto. He has published poems and short stories in the Americas and Europe.

379 *Historias del reino vigilado/Stories of a Guarded Kingdom: Poems. First Anthology 1965-1980,* English translations by Christina Shantz. Ottawa: Cordillera, 1981. 195 pp. Poems. [Text in Spanish and English.]

380 *Burning Bridges: Poems,* translated by Christina Shantz. Ottawa: Cormorant Books, 1988. 72 pp. Poems.

TRUJILLO, Renato
Born in Chile, published extensively prior to his coming to Canada. His poems are described as being free of political posturing and stagy effects.

381 *Behind the Orchestra.* Fredericton, N.B.: Fiddlehead Poetry Books/Goose Lane Editions, 1987. 67 pp. Poems.

URBINA, José Leandro (1949-)
Born in Chile. Studied Literature at the University of Chile and at Carleton University. He has published short stories in magazines in Latin America, Europe and the Americas. Recipient of a Canada Council grant in 1979 and a short term grant in 1980. His novel *Traveller of the Air* is in the process of being published. He has lived in Ottawa since 1976.

382 *Las malas juntas.* Ottawa: Cordillera, 1978. Short stories.

383 *Lost Causes: Stories,* translated by Christina Shantz. Ottawa: Cormorant Books, 1988. 92 pp. Stories.

VALLEJOS, Nelly Davis

384 *Ballade.* Montréal: The Author, 1984. Poèmes.

VIÑUELA de la VEGA, Eduardo Francisco (1944-)
Born in Valparaiso, Chile. Studied Law in his native land and published a novel there, *Después del tiempo* (1964), and a book of poems, *Palabras de Hombre* (1972). He lives in Montreal.

385 *Exil transitoire: poèmes/Exilio Transitorio: poemas,* French version translated by Johanne Garneau-Lassande. Montréal: Nouvelles Frontières, 1977. Poems.

386 *Nostalgia y presencia [Nostalgia and Presence].* Montreal: Editions d'Orphée, 1982. Poems. [In Spanish and French.]

ZELLER, Beatriz

387 *Poetisa con balcón y vista al mar,* illustrations by Ludwig Zeller. Oakville, Ont.: Oasis Publications, 1984. 26 pp. Poems.

ZELLER, Ludwig (1927-)
Born in Northern Chile. He has published several collections of surrealist poetry and has received awards for his artistic accomplishments. As a visual artist, he has worked in paper cutouts, calligrams and collage. Established his own publishing company, Oasis Publications, and has published more than twenty books of poetry. Works published in Canada include:

388 *Mujer en sueño/Woman in Dream.* Oakville, Ont.: Oasis Publications, 1975. Poem.
[A long poem also recorded in Spanish and English.]

389 *Cuando el animal de fondo sube la cabeza estalla/When the Animal Rises from the Deep the Head Explodes/Quand l'animal des propendeurs surgit la tête eclate.* English version of poems by John Robert Colombo, version française par Thérèse Dulac Guitérrez. Oakville, Ont.: Mosaic Press/Ottawa: Valley Editions, 1976. Poems.
[Trilingual work with 17 collages by Ludwig Zeller.]

390 *Circe's Mirrors,* translated from the Spanish by A.F. Moritz and Susana Wald. Toronto: Oasis, 1978. A poem.
[Translation of *Los espejos de circe.*]

391 *Los espejos de circe [Circe's Mirror].* Toronto: Oasis Publications, 1978. 18 pp. A poem.

392 *Nomades en la mandala/Wanderers in the Mandala,* translated from the Spanish by Susana Wald and A.F. Moritz. Toronto: Oasis Publications, 1978. 18 pp. A poem.

393 *Visiones y llagas/Visions and Wounds,* translated from the Spanish by Susana Wald. Toronto: Oasis Publications, 1978. 18 pp. A poem.

394 *In the Country of the Antipodes: Poems, 1964-1979.* Oakville, Ont.: Mosaic Press/Ottawa: Valley Editions, 1979. Poems.

395 *50 Collages.* Oakville, Ont.: Mosaic Press, 1981. Collages.

396 *Alphacollage.* 2nd ed. Erine, Ont.: Porcupine's Quill, 1982. Collages.

397 *La cabeza de mármol/The Marble Head,* English translation by A.F. Moritz and Beatriz Zeller. Toronto: Oasis Publications, 1984. 14 pp. A poem.

398 *Los escombos del alba/Rubble of Dawn,* English translation by A.F. Moritz and Beatriz Zeller. Toronto: Oasis Publications, 1984. 14 pp. A poem.

399 *Los ojos de la muerte/The Eyes of Death,* English translation by A.F. Moritz and Beatriz Zeller. Toronto: Oasis Publications, 1984. 18 pp. A poem.

400 *The Marble Head and Other Poems,* translated from the Spanish by A.F. Moritz and Beatriz Zeller. Oakville, Ont.: Mosaic Press, 1986. 95 pp. illus. Poems.

401 *A Celebration: The White Pheasant Flying in Multiple Languages and Visual Interpretations.* Oakville: Mosaic, 1987. 118 pp. Poems.

Writings about:

402 Lincoln, Robert. Review of *Cuando el animal...* CAN BOOK REV ANN 1976: 196.

403 Thomas, Alan. Review of *The Marble Head.* CAN BOOK REV ANN 1986: 114.

CHINESE

BOOKS, MONOGRAPHS

404   CHAN, Anthony B.
Gold Mountain: The Chinese in the New World. Vancouver: New Star Books, 1983.
[Chinese and Japanese creative writing in Canada didn't develop until quite recently. Under the influence of the Asian American literary movement, a school of writing began to emerge in the writing of such young authors as Paul Yee, Sky Lee, Jim Wong-Chu, Joy Kogawa, Rick Shiomi, Ron Tanaka and some other first and second-generation authors. Anthony Chan offers a study of these authors on pp. 187-197.]

405   *Coping with Racism: The Chinese Experience in Canada.* CAN ETH STUD 19, no. 3 (1987) Special issue.
[The entire issue is devoted to the Chinese in Canada. Includes papers on immigration, racism, discriminations. A paper on Chinese cultural traditions in Canada and on the Ethnic Hall exhibition at the Federal Museum authored by Ban Seng Hoe, pp. 148-62.]

406   LI, Peter S.
The Chinese in Canada. Toronto: Oxford University Press, Canada, 1988. 192 pp.
[This book focuses on the development of institutional racism against the Chinese as a racial minority from their first arrival in Canada in 1858 and its impact on the Chinese-Canadian community.]

ANTHOLOGY

407   *Inalienable Rice,* edited by Sean Gunn. Vancouver: Powell Street Review of Chinese Writers' Workshop, 1980.

INDIVIDUAL AUTHORS

CHEN JO-HSI, pseud. (Real name: TUANN, Lucy) (1938-   )
Born in Taiwan, received her education there and in the USA. Recipient of the Notable Book Award, issued by the American Literary Association. for *The Execution of Mayor Yin* (1978). Her writings have been translated into English, French, German, Japanese, Swedish and Norwegian.

408   [*Wonderful Clouds.*] Taipei: United Daily Press, 1962. Novel.
[In Chinese.]

409   *Spirit Calling.* Taipei: Heritage Press, 1962. Short stories.

410   [*Mayor Yin.*] Taipei: Yuanjing Press, 1976. Stories about the Cultural Revolution.

411   [*Selected Stories of Chen Ruoxi.*] Taipei: Lianjing Press, 1976. Short stories.

412   [*The Old Man.*] Taipei: Lianjing Press, 1978. Stories about the Cultural Revolution.

413 *The Execution of Mayor Yin and Other Stories from the Great Proletarian Revolution*, translated from the Chinese by Nancy Ing and Howard Goldblatt. Bloomington: Indiana University Press, 1978. xxviii, 220 pp. Stories.

414 [*The Repatriates.*] Taipei: Lianjing Press, 1978. Novel.
[In Chinese.]

415 [*Reminiscences of the Cultural Revolution Days.*] Taipei: Hungfan Press, 1979. Stories.
[In Chinese.]

416 [*Another Fortress Besieged.*] Taipei: Times Press Edition, 1981. Also: Hong Kong: Bafang Press, 1981. Stories.
[In Chinese.]

417 [*Random Notes.*] Taipei: Times Press, 1981. Stories.
[In Chinese.]

JANG, Charles (1927-)

Born in Hoi Pan, China, emigrated to Canada in 1950 via Hong Kong. After a brief stay with his father in Coaldale, Alberta, he returned to Hong Kong. In 1953 he came back to Canada and settled in Lethbridge, where he owns a grocery store. He has published several short stories in periodicals in Hong Kong. His novels, all written in Chinese, depict the life of Chinese people living in Canada.

418 [*Tears of Chinese Immigrants.*] Hong Kong: Lu Sen, 1959. 156 pp. Novel.

419 [*The Vagabonds.*] Hong Kong: Lu Sen, 1959. 61 pp. Short novel.

420 [*The Warm Flow of Love.*] Hong Kong: Lu Sen, 1960. 129 pp. Novel.

421 [*Foreign Offspring.*] Hong Kong: Lu Sen, 1962. 146 pp. Novel.

LITTLE, Jean (1932-)

Children's writer. Born in Taiwan, came to Canada at age of seven. Educated at the University of Toronto (B.A.) and the University of Utah. Recipient of the Vicky Metcalf Award (1974), Little, Brown Canadian Children's Book Award (1961), Children's Book of the Year, CLA, and the Ruth Schwartz Award (1985). She lives in Guelph, Ont.

422 *Mine for Keeps.* Toronto: Little, Brown and Co., 1962. Children's story.

423 *Home from Far.* Toronto: Little, Brown and Co., 1965. Children's story.

424 *Spring Begins in March.* Toronto: Little, Brown and Co., 1966. Children's story.

425 *When the Pie was Opened.* Toronto: Little, Brown and Co., 1968. Children's story.

426 *Take Wing.* Toronto: Little, Brown and Co., 1968 Children's story.

427 *One to Grow On.* Toronto: Little, Brown and Co., 1969. Children's story.

428 *Look Through My Window.* Don Mills, Ont.: Fitzhenry & Whiteside, 1970. Children's story.

429 *Kate.* Don Mills, Ont.: Fitzhenry & Whiteside, 1972. Children's story.

430 *From Anna.* Don Mills, Ont.: Fitzhenry & Whiteside, 1972. 201 pp. Novel.

431 *Stand in the Wind.* Don Mills, Ont.: Fitzhenry & Whiteside, 1975. Children's story.

432 *Listen for the Singing.* Toronto: Clarke, Irwin, 1977. Children's story.

433 *Mama's Going to Buy You a Mockingbird.* Markham, Ont.: Penguin, 1984. Children's story.

434 *Lost and Found.* Markham, Ont.: Penguin, 1985. Children's story.

435 *Different Dragons.* Markham, Ont.: Penguin, 1986. Children's story.

436 *Hey World! Here I Am.* Toronto: Kids Can Press, 1986. Children's story.

TONFANG PO, pseud. (Real name: LIN, Wender)
Born in Taipei, Taiwan, was educated there and at the University of Saskatchewan. He lives in Alberta, working as a Hydrologist.

437 [*The Dying Christian.*] 1968.

438 [*The Golden Dream.*] 1977. Short stories and essays.

439 [*Lake Louise.*] 1978. Novel.

WHEN ZHAO, pseud. (Real name: LIU, Richard) (1936-)

440 *Return of the Wild Goose.* Shanghai: Beijing People's Publishing House, 1980. Novel.

WONG-CHU, Jim (1949-)
Born in Hong Kong, came to Canada in 1953. Author of a photographic essay entitled "Pender Street East." Founding member of the Asian Canadian Writers Workshop. His poems have appeared in numerous periodicals.

441 *Chinatown Ghosts.* [Vancouver]: Pulp Press, 1986. 62 pp. Poems.

COLOMBIAN

INDIVIDUAL AUTHORS

ARANGO, Carolina McEwen de
Born in Colombia. She resides in Toronto, where she is active in the local Latin-American community.

442 *Fantasias [Fantasies].* Santiago/Toronto: Doblerrem, 1978. Poems.
[These poems are related to Bogotá, Medellin and Toronto.]

PÉREZ BOTERO, Luis A. (1922-)
Born in Colombia, moved to Canada in 1967. He is on the staff of the University of Saskatchewan, teaching Spanish. His novel *Spiritus Mundi* was finalist in the Concurso de Valladolid in 1978.

443 *Ulises en Sabanilla y utros cuentos [Ulyses in Sabanilla].* Madrid: Magisterio Español, 1978. 145 pp. Novel and short stories.

CROATIAN

BIBLIOGRAPHIES, DIRECTORIES

444 JURIČIĆ, Želimir B.
"Croatian-Canadian Creative Literature: A Preliminary Check List." CAN ETH STUD 5, no. 1-2 (1973): 27-29.
[Contains information on 40 names and pseudonyms.]

445 JURIČIĆ, Želimir B.; MALYCKY, Alexander
"Croatian-Canadian Periodical Publications: A Preliminary Check List." CAN ETH STUD 2, no. 1 (1970): 21-25.
[Includes 24 periodical titles with an index on geographical distribution of serial publications.]

446 MARKOTIĆ, Vladimir, comp. and ed.
Biographical Directory of Americans and Canadians of Croatian Descent with Institutions, Organizations, their Officers and Periodicals. 4th rev., enl. ed. Calgary: Research Centre for Canadian Ethnic Studies, 1973. xiii, 204 pp. (Occasional Monographs no. 1)
[Includes Croatian-Canadian authors and periodical titles.]

447 MARCOTIĆ, Vladimir
"Croatian Imprints of Canada: A Preliminary Check List." CAN ETH STUD 5, no. 1-2 (1973): 19-26.
[Comprises books and brochures published in Croatian or in other languages relating to Croatian-Canadians.]

448 PRPIĆ, George; PRPIĆ, Hilda
Hrvatske knjige knjižnice u iseljeništvu/Croatian Books and Booklets Written in Exile. Cleveland: The Authors in cooperation with the Institute for Soviet and European Studies, John Caroll University, 1973.
[Croatian-Canadian authors are included.]

Writing about:

449 Markotić, Vladimir. Review of *Hrvatske knjige i knjižnice u iseljeništvu.*. CAN ETH STUD 4, no. 1-2 (1972): 87-88.

RESEARCH PAPERS

450 JURIČIĆ, Želimir B.
"Ethnicity and their Ethnic Poets." In *Second Banff Conference on Central and East European Studies,* edited by Metro Gulutsan. (Edmonton: CEESA, 1978) pp. 22-40.
[An introductory paper on Yugoslav-Canadian authors of Croatian, Serb, Bosnian and Macedonian background. Includes some poems in the original with English translations.]

451 JURIČIĆ, Želimir B.
"Social Adjustment of Yugoslavs in Victoria: Methodical and Theoretical Problems." In *Canadian Slavonic Papers* 15, no. 1-2 (1973).

452 KESS, J.P.; JURIČIĆ, Želimir B.; KESS, C.A.
An Ethnic's View of Ethnicity: The Yugoslav Experience. In *Proceedings of PNCFL* 27, no. 2. 132-34.

ANTHOLOGIES

453 *Hrvatske pjesme [Croatian Poems],* edited by Božidar Vidov. Toronto: Mala Knjižnica Hrvata Izbjeglica, 1963. 32 pp.

454 *Zbirka lirike iz nove domovine [Lyric Poems from the New Country],* edited by Želimir B. Juričić. Toronto: Lirika, 1973.
[Includes poems by Mustafa Jahić, Ivan Bostjančić, Josip Gabre, Stanislav Pavlov, Šime Negro, Ruba Gverino, Ilija Ero Galić and Belka Živanović-Tarno. Provides biographical notes and portraits.]

Writing about:

455 Meheš, Mirko. Review of *Zbirka lirike iz nove domovine.* CAN ETH STUD 9, no. 2 (1977): 148-49.

INDIVIDUAL AUTHORS

HORIĆ, Alain

456 *Blessure au flanc du ciel.* Montréal, 1957. Poèmes.

JESIH, Pavao

457 *Crvena ruža na oltaru: Biografska pripovijest [Red Rose on the Altar: A Biographical Story].* Winnipeg: Peter Stanković, 1950. 334 pp. Novel.

KUTLEŠA, Jozo (1935-)

458 *The Mosaic of Life.* Toronto: F. Vedrina, 1970. 112 pp. Poems.

459 *The Sunrise of Joy and Love.* Toronto: Mystic Press, 1973. 124 pp. Short stories.

Writing about:

460 Rasporich, Beverly J.; Rasporich, Anthony W. Review of *The Sunrise of Joy and Love* and *The Mosaic of Life.* CAN ETH STUD 7, no. 2 (1975): 124-25.

MIDŽAN, Feri (1922-)
Born in Yugoslavia, came to Canada in 1964. Completed his education in accounting in Toronto and Montreal. He has an accounting company in Toronto.

461 *Sjećanja [Recollections].* Toronto, 1980. 79 pp. Short stories.

462 *Kikićev put u smrt; sjećanja druga [Kikić's Way to Death].* Toronto, 1980. 98 pp. Short stories.

NIKIĆ, Nana

463 *Novele iz nedavne hrvatske prošlosti [Short Stories from the Recent Past of Croatia],* in collaboration with Ana Katić. Toronto: Mala Knjižnica Hrvata Izbjeglica, 1963. 23 pp. Stories.

NIKOLIĆ, Rikard

464   *Blesci u sumrak: Roman [Flashes in the Sunset: Novel].* Winnipeg: Hrvatski Glas, 1953. 202 pp. Novel.

ŠOLA, Marijan Emil

465   *Još Hrvatska nij' propala: Rodoljubne pjesme [Croatia Has Not Perished Yet: Patriotic Poems].* Toronto: The Author, 1964. 120 pp. Poems.

CUBAN

INDIVIDUAL AUTHOR

ALOMA, René R. (1947-　)

A playwright and stage director in Toronto. Born in Santiago de Cuba. Studied fine arts at Wayne State University, Detroit and went on to earn an M.A. degree from the University of Windsor. His first play, *Once a Family*, won an honorary mention in the Clifford E. Lee Award competition in 1974. His children's plays have been widely produced in the United States and Canada.

466   *A Friend Is a Friend, or The Little Rag Doll that Wished to be a Star.* Toronto: Playwrights Union of Canada, 1979. 34 pp. Play.

467   *A Little Something to Ease the Pain.* Toronto: Playwrights Union of Canada, 1981. 81 pp. Children's play.

468   *Rosina in this Strange Land.* Toronto: Playwrights Union of Canada, 1988. Children's play.

CZECH

BIBLIOGRAPHIES

469 ŠKVOR, George J.
"Czech-Canadian Creative Literature: A Preliminary Check List of Authors and Pseudonyms." CAN ETH STUD 1, no. 1 (1969): 4.
[Includes 12 names compiled from the files of the author.]

470 ŠKVOR, George J.
"Czech-Canadian Periodical Publications: A Preliminary Check List." CAN ETH STUD 1, no. 1 (1969): 3.
[A list of 5 titles compiled from the samples available in the author's collection.]

471 ŽEKULIN, Nicholas G.A.
"Czech-Canadian Periodical Publications: First Supplement." CAN ETH STUD 5, no. 1-2 (1973): 31-34.
[Includes 16 titles with geographical index and index of non-Czech titles.]

RESEARCH PAPERS

472 "Czech Literature in Canada." In *The Canadian Family Tree*. (Ottawa: Canadian Citizenship Branch, 1967) p. 72.

473 GELLNER, John; SMEREK, John
""Czech and Slovak Literature in Canada." In their *Czechs and Slovaks in Canada*. (Toronto: University of Toronto Press, in association with the Masaryk Memorial Institute, 1968)
[The section on literature introduces Pavel Javor (i.e. Jiří Škvor), Jozef Dragoš-Alžbentinčan, L'udo Bešeňovsky, Jozef Zvonar-Tien and Ján Doranski.]

474 ŠKVORECKÝ, Josef.
"The Birth and Death of the Czech New Wave" TAKE ONE (Nov. 9, 1970)

475 ŠKVORECKÝ, Josef.
"Dobrý člověk v nedobré době" [A Good Man in Lousy Times]. LISTY 4 (1975)

476 ŠKVORECKÝ, Josef.
"At Home in Exile: Czech Writers in the West" BKS ABR 50 (1976): 308-13.

477 ŠKVORECKÝ, Josef.
"Některé normalizované kulturní výkony" [Some Establishments' Cultural Achievements]. LISTY 2 (1974): 20-23.

478 ŠKVORECKÝ, Josef.
"O Nových prózách v Literarním měsíčníku a jak to souvistí s jistým seznamen" [New Fiction in the Literary Monthly and how it Connects with a Certain List]. LISTY 5-6 (1973): 48-53.

479 ŠKVORECKÝ, Josef.
"Sémantika okolo spisovatelů" [Semantics in the Case of Authors]. LISTY 3 (1973): 23-27.

INDIVIDUAL AUTHORS

DRÁBEK, Jan (1935-   )
Born in Prague, educated at the American University, Washington, D.C., at the University of Mysore, India, and at the University of British Columbia. A former journalist, travel agent, refugee resettlement officer, high school teacher. He lives and writes in Vancouver.

480   *A co Václav? [Whatever Happened to Wenceslas?]* Toronto: Sixty-Eight Publishers, 1975. 260 pp. Novel.

481   *Whatever Happened to Wenceslas?* Toronto: Peter Martin Associates, 1975. 210 pp. Novel. [English version of *A co Václav?*]

482   *Melvin the Weathermoose.* Toronto: Holt, Rinehart and Winston, 1976. Juvenile story.

483   *Zpráva o smrti Róznkavalíra [Report on the Death of Rosenkavalier].* Toronto: Sixty-Eight Publishers, 1977. 240 pp. Novel.

484   *Report on the Death of Rosenkavalier.* Toronto: McClelland & Stewart, 1977. 224 pp. Novel. [English version of *Zpráva o smrti Róznkavalíra.*]

485   *The Lister Legacy.* Toronto: General Publishing, 1980. Novel.

486   *The Statement.* Toronto: Musson, 1982. 352 pp. Novel.

Writings about:

487   Ashby, Adele. Review of *Whatever Happened to Wenceslas?* CAN BOOK REV ANN 1975: 107.

488   Atwood, Margaret. "Courage and Passion." ESSAYS CAN WRIT No. 7/8 (1977): 97-100.

489   Bryans, John. "Punch Packing Czech." VANC SUN (Dec. 19, 1975): 34A. [Review of *Whatever Happened to Wenceslas?*]

490   Cleary, Val. "Drabek's Humane and Funny with Hair Trigger Sensitivity." GLOBE MAIL (Sept. 20, 1976) [Review of *Whatever Happened to Wenceslas?*]

491   "Compelling Novel on Enslavement of Czechoslovakia." ST. CATH STAND (Apr. 23, 1977): 20. [Review of *Report on the Death of Rosenkavalier.*]

492   Drolet, Gilbert. "Czechoslovakia: Magnificent Defiance." J CAN FIC 21 (1977/78): 138-40. [Review of *Report on the Death of Rosenkavalier* by Jan Drábek and The Bass Saxophone by Josef Škvorecký.]

493   French, William. "Action and Ideas, a Political Thriller, the Kind of Novel a Native Canadian would Find almost Impossible to Write." GLOBE MAIL (Apr. 9, 1977) [Review of *Report on the Death of Rosenkavalier.*]

494   Gauer, Stephen. Review of *The Statement.* Q & Q 48, no. 4 (1982): 28.

495   Keith, W.J. Review of *Report on the Death of Rosenkavalier.* CAN BOOK REV ANN 1977: 101-02.

496 "Memories Too Much." LOND FREE PRESS (May 14, 1977)
[Review of *Report on the Death of Rosenkavalier.*]

497 Oleson, Tom. "Seeing Ourselves as Others See Us - A Picture of Complacency." WINN FREE PRESS (May 14, 1977)
[Review of *Report on the Death of Rosenkavalier.*]

498 Quince, Peter. "Book Marks." WEST LIV (June 1977): 92.
[Review of *Report on the Death of Rosenkavalier.*]

499 Review of *Report on the Death of Rosenkavalier.* CHATELAINE (July 1977): 8.

JAVOR, Pavel, pseud. (Real name: ŠKVOR, Jiří [George]) (1916-1981)
Poet. Born in Martinice, Czechoslovakia, educated at Charles University, Prague. During the Second World War he served as a deputy member of the House of Commons. He came to Montreal in 1950 and took his doctoral degree in Slavic letters at the University of Montreal in 1960. Until his death he worked as an editor and broadcaster with Radio Canada International. He published six books of poems in Czechoslovakia. Some of his poems have been translated into other languages including English, French and German.

500 *Pozdrav domů [Greetings to Home].* New York: New-Yorske Listy, 1951. 35 pp. Poems.
[Winner of the first prize issued by the Christian Academy in Rome.]

501 *Chudá sklizeň /Récolte pauvre,* traduction Charles Černý. Paris: Éd. de la revue Rencontres, 1953. 33 pp. 2nd ed. 1965. Ibid. Poems.

502 *Daleký hlas: verše [Far-reaching Voice: Poems].* Toronto: Nový domov, 1953. 125 pp. Poems.

503 *Morgenwege: Gedichte Auswahl [Morning Roads: Selected Poems],* edited by Robert Vlach. Stockholm: Knižnice Lyriki, 1955. 24 pp. Poems.

504 *Nad plamenem píseň [Song Over Flames].* Stockholm: Czech Cultural Council Abroad, 1955. 60 pp. Poems.

505 *Hořké verše [Bitter Verses].* Toronto: Edice Naše Hlasy, 1958. 81 pp.

506 *Kouř z Ithaky: výbor z autorovy poesie [Smoke from Ithaca: Selected Poems].* New York: Universum Press, 1960. 90 pp. Poems.

507 *Kus života těžkého/Hardship of Life.* Toronto, 1967. 504 pp. Novel.

508 *Země křižovaná [Crucified Land].* Montreal: Concordia, 1970. 60 pp. 2nd ed. Haarlem, Netherlands: Czechoslovak Cultural Club.

509 *Chléb podaný [Bread for the Guest].* Stockholm: Sklizeň Svobodné Tvorby, 1975. 60 pp. Poems.

510 *Jediný domov [The Only Homeland].* Munich: Poezie Mimo Domov, 1977. 32 pp. Poems.

511 *Sa raison de vivre: roman,* traduction Anne Pierquet. Montréal: Presses Select, 1978. 292 pp. Roman.

512 *Krůpěje [Morning Dew].* Zurich: Confrontation, 1977. 80 pp. Also, Toronto: Sixty-Eight Publishers, 1977. 64 pp. Poems.

513 *Nápěvy [Melodies].* Toronto: Sixty-Eight Publishers, 1977. 64 pp. Poems.

514 *Far from You; Poems from the Czech*, translated by Ron D.K. Banerjee and Alfred French, with a profile of the poet by Maria Němcová Banerjee and a frontispiece by Jiří Lauda, edited by John Robert Colombo. Toronto: Hounslow Press, 1981. 78 pp. Poems.

515 *Plamen a píseň: Vybor versu [A Flame and a Song: Selected Poems]*, edited by Antonin Brousek. Toronto: Sixty-Eight Publishers, 1981. 131 pp. Poems.

Writings about:

516 Brešky, Dušan. "A Czech Poet in Canada: Pavel Javor's Life and Work." CAN ETH STUD 10, no. 1 (1978): 75.

517 Choulguine, Rostislav. "Pavel Javor." In *Circuit Fermé, Radio Canada*. (Ottawa, fev. 14, 1966) vol. 2.

518 Colombo, John Robert. "Škvor, George." In *The Oxford Companion to Canadian Literature*, edited by William Toye. (Toronto: Oxford University Press, 1983) pp. 760-61.

519 Den, Petr. "Slovo na Cestu" [A Word for the Journey]. In *Kouř z Ithaky*. (New York: Universum Press, 1960)

520 Dostál, Antonín. "Básnické dílo: Jiřího Škvora - Pavla Javora" [Poetic Work of Jiří Škvor - Pavel Javor]. PROMENY/METAPHORES 13, no. 3 (1976): 28-37.

521 Fuchsová, Jiřina. "Nad třemi sbírkami Pavla Javora" [Three Books of Poems by Pavel Javor]. PROMENY/METAPHORES 13, no. 4 (1976): 1-4.

522 Granjard, Henry. "A propos d'une traduction." In *Récolt pauvre*. (Paris: Ed. de la revue Rencontres, 1953) pp. 3-7.

523 Ještědský, Jan. "Daleký hlas" [Far-reaching Voice]. In *La litterature tchèque à l'étranger/Czech Literature Abroad*. (Stockholm: Czech Cultural Council Abroad, 1954).

524 Ještědský, Jan. Review of *Nedosněno, nedomilováno*. MĚS NOV ŽIV 17 (1965)

525 Jíra, Jaroslav. Review of *Horké verše*. SBORNIK (1958)

526 Kovář, Louis. Review of *Nedosněno, nedomilováno*. BKS ABR 40 (1966): 219.

527 Kratochvíl, Antonín. "Svědek našich snů" [Witness of Our Dreams]. KREŠT AKAD 4, no. 28 (1974): 587-89.

528 Měštan, Jaromír. Review of *Daleký hlas*. In *La littérature tchèque a l'etranger/Czech Literature Abroad*. (Stockholm: Czech Cultural Council Abroad, 1955)

529 Moritz, Albert. "World of Wanders." BKS CAN 11, no. 2 (1982): 22-23.
[Review of *Far from You.*]

530 "Pavel Javor." PEN IN EXILE (April 1960)

531 Radimský, Ladislav. "Czech Poets in Exile." In *Czechoslovakia: Past and Present. Anthology*. Vol. 1. (Haague, Netherlands: Mouton, 1969)

532   Review of *Pozdrav domů*. SKLIZEŇ (1952)

533   Valach, Robert. "Pavel Javor." In *La littérature tchèque à l'étranger/Czech Literature Abroad*. (Stockholm: Czech Cultural Council Abroad, 1955)

NEKOLA, Rudolf

534   *Noc v hoře Královské [Night on Mount Royal]*. Montreal: Robson Printers, 1943. 48 pp. Poems.

SALIVAROVÁ, Zdena   Josefa (1933-   )
Born in Prague, Czechoslovakia, where she was an actress. Wife of Josef Škvorecký. Came to Canada in 1968.

535   *Pánská jízda [Gentlemen's Ride]*. Prague: Československý Spisovatel, 1968. Novellas.
[A collection of three novellas:"Las Strada","Pánská jídza", and "Tma". German translation was published by Verlog und Welt, 1971.]

536   *Honzlová: Protest Song*.   Toronto: Sixty-Eight Publishers, 1972. 298 pp. Novel.

537   *Summer in Prague*, translated from the Czech by Marie Winn. New York: Harper and Row, 1973. 285 pp. Novel.
[Translation of *Honzlová*.]

538   *Nebe, peklo, ráj [Heaven, Hell, Paradise]*. Toronto: Sixty-Eight Publishers, 1976. 122 pp. Novel.
[Awarded the Egon Hostovský Memorial Prize for the best Czech fiction written in exile in 1976.]

539   *From Temporary Paradise*.

540   Ashes, Ashes, Fall Down. 1987.

Writings about:

541   Allen, Antonia. SAT N (1973)

542   Dollen, Charles. Review of *Summer in Prague*. BEST SELLERS (March 15, 1973)

543   Levin, Martin. "Novel." N.Y. TIMES BOOK REV (March 4, 1973)
[Review of *Summer in Prague*.]

544   Review of *Honzlová*. TIMES LIT SUPPL (June 2, 1973)

545   Steiner, George. "Under the Hammer." NEW YORKER (May 12, 1973)
[Review of *Summer in Prague*.]

ŠKVOR, George J. see JAVOR, Pavel

ŠKVORECKÝ, Josef (1924-   )
Born in Náchod, Czechoslovakia, attended Charles University in Prague, receiving his Ph.D. in Philosophy in 1951. He was a teacher, an editor's assistant, translator and scriptwriter. In 1968, after the Soviet invasion of Czechoslovakia, he immigrated to Canada and became a professor of English at the University of Toronto. As a novelist, essayist and publisher, he is one of the most accomplished authors in Canadian literature. An issue of *World Literature Today* (Autumn 1981) was devoted to Josef Škvorecký, who is a recipient of the Neustadt Prize for literature in 1980.

546   *The Cowards*, translated from the Czech by Jeanne Němcová. London: V. Gollanz, Harmondsworth: Penguin Books, 1970. 416 pp. Novel.
[Translation of *Zbabělci*.]

547   *Leoncino: Romanzo [The Lion Cubs: Novel]*. Milano: Garzanti, 1971. 337 pp. Novel.
[Italian translation of *Lvíče*.]

548   *Le lionenceau*, traduit du tchèque par F. Kérel. Paris: Gallimard, 1972. 358 pp. Roman.
[Translation of *Lvíče*.]

549   *Mirákl: politická detektivka [Miracle Game: A Political Detective Story]*. Toronto: Sixty-Eight Publishers, 1972. 2 v. 2nd ed. 1978. 575 pp. Novel.
[Transleted into Japanese (Hayakawa Shobo, 1976) and French (Gallimard, 1978).]

550   *Zbabělci [Cowards]*. Toronto: Sixty-Eight Publishers, 1972. 369 pp. Novel.
[First published in Prague, 1958. Translated into Danish (Hasselbalch, 1967), Hungarian (Tátra, 1968), German (Luchterhand, 1968), Italian (Rozzoli, 1969), English (Grove Press, 1970, Gollancz, 1970, Modern Classics, 1972), Polish (Slask, 1970), French (Gallimard, 1976), Swedish (Askild & Kärnekull, 1976), Serbian (Prosveta, 1967).

551   *Hříchy pro pátera Knoxe [Father Knoxe's Sins]*. Toronto: Sixty-Eight Publishers, 1973. 356 pp. (Klub čtenářů v zahranici) Novel.
[Translated into Swedish (Forlags AB Zetape, 1975).]

552   *Lvíče [The Lion Cub]*. Toronto: Sixty-Eight Publishers, 1974. 268 pp. Novel.
[Originally written in Czechoslovakia, this novel has been banned in that country since 1969. Translation published in German (Luchterhand), Italian (Garzanti, 1971), French (Gallimard, 1972), Slovenian (Založba Obzorja, 1973), Croatian (Stvarnost, 1973), Spanish (Dopesa, 1973), English (Grove Press, 1975, Bodley Head, 1976), Swedish (Norstedt, 1977).

553   *Miss Silver's Past*, translated from the Czech by Peter Kussi. New York: Grove Press, 1974. 297 pp. Novel.
[Translation of *Lvíče*.]

554   *Konec poručíka Borůvky: detektivní žalozpěv [The End of Lieutenant Borůvka: A Detective Psalm]*. Toronto: Sixty-Eight Publishers, 1975. 262 pp. Novel.

555   *Smutek poručíka Borůvky [The Mournful Demeanor of Lieutenant Borůvka]*. Toronto: Sixty-Eight Publishers, 1975. 277 pp. Novel.
[Originally published in Prague in 1966. Translated into Hungarian (Európa Press, 1968), Rumanian (Ed. Pentru Literatura Universala, 1969), Japanese (Hayakawa Shobo, 1976), Finnish (Werner Söderström, 1977).]

556   *The Bass Saxophone*, translated from the Czech by Káča Poláčková-Henley. Toronto: Anson-Cartwright Editions, 1977. 186 pp.; New York: A.A. Knopf, 1979, 208 pp.; London: Pan Books, 1980. 124 pp. Novel.
[Translation of *Legenda Emöke* and *Bassaxofon*.]

557   *Příběh inženýra lidských duší: entrtejnment na stará témata o životě, ženách, osudu, snění, ělnické třídě, fízlech, lásce a smrti [An Engineer of Human Souls: Entertainment on Old Themes of Life, Women, Bad Fortunes, Dreams, Labour Class, Guffaws, Love and Death]*. Toronto: Sixty-Eight Publishers, 1977. 2 vols. Novel.

558   *Príma sezóna [A Swell Season]*. Toronto: Sixty-Eight Publishers, 1977. 263 pp. Novel.

559   *Horkej svět [Boiling World].* Toronto: Sixty-Eight Publishers, 1978. Novel.

560   *Farářův konec. Podklad pro celovečerni tragikomedii. Naps Josef Škvorecký ve spolupráci s Evaldem Schormem [The End of a Priest. Written in Collaboration with Ewald Schorm].* [Hradec Králové] Nakladatelství Kruh, 1979. 154 pp. Novel.

561   *B ůh do domu [God Save Us!].* Toronto: Sixty-Eight Publishers, 1980. 122 pp. Play.

562   *Dívka z Chicaga [A Girl from Chicago].* Munich: Poczie mimo domov, 1980.

563   *Velká providka o Americe [A Tall Story of America].* Toronto: Sixty-Eight Publishers, 1980.

564   *Návrat porucíka Borůvky [The Return of Lieutenant Borůvka].* Toronto: Sixty-Eight Publishers, 1981. Novel.

565   *Dvě legendy [Two Legends].* Toronto: Sixty-Eight Publishers, 1981. 175 pp. Novel.

566   *Jiří Menzel and the History of Closely Watched Trains.* Boulder, Col.: University of Colorado Press, 1982.

567   *The Swell Season: A Text on the Most Important Things in Life.* London: Chatto & Windus, 1983. 226 pp. Novel.
[Translation of *Prima sezóna*, first published in English in Toronto: L. & O. Dennys, 1982.]

568   *Le saxophone basse et autres nouvelles.* Paris: Gallimard, 1983. 292 pp. Nouvelles.

569   *The Engineer of Human Souls: An Entertainment on the Old Themes of Life, Women, Fate, Dreams, the Working Class, Secret Agents, Love and Death.* Toronto: Lester & Orpen Dennys, 1984. 571 pp. Novel.
[Translation of *Příbéh inženýra lidských duši.*]

570   *Dvořák in Love,* translated from the Czech by Paul Wilson. Toronto: Lester & Orpen Dennys, 1986. 400 pp. Biographical novel.

571   *Sins of Father Knox.* Toronto: Lester & Orpen Dennys, 1988. Novel.
[Translation of Hvrichy pro patera Knoxe.]

Writings about:

Bibliography:

572   Kalish, Jana. *Josef Škvorecký: A Checklist.* Toronto: University of Toronto Library, 1986. iv, 232 pp.
[Includes primary and secondary material. The former, Part One, section is divided into eleven subsections such as First Editions of Fiction. Part Two: Secondary Sources contains critical and biographical material. Also includes a name index and a title index.]

Research Studies:

573   Abley, Mark. "An Epic of Humor and Honor." MACLEAN'S 97 (July 9, 1984): 47.
[Review of *The Engineer of Human Souls.]*

574   Abley, Mark. "New World Rhapsodies." MACLEAN'S 99 (Oct. 13, 1986): 69. port.

[Review of *Dvořák in Love.*]

575   Alexis, André. "Interview with Joseph Škvorecky." NOOVO MASHEEN - THE ACTIVE AREA No. 4 (1987): 35-41.

576   Blackburn, Christopher. "We Like it Hot, They Like it Not." BKS CAN 6 (December 1977): 21-22. [Review of *The Bass Saxophone.*]

577   Cairns, A.T.J. Review of *The Bass Saxophone.* CAN BOOK REV ANN 1977: 98-99.

578   Clark, Mathew. Review of *The Swell Season.* Q & Q 49, no. 1 (1983): 32.

579   Collins, Anne. "The Important Thing in Life." MACLEAN'S 95 (Nov. 15, 1982): 68-69. [Review of *The Swell Season.*]

580   Czarnecki, M. "Rebel Artist in Exile." MACLEAN'S 97 (July 9, 1984): 46.

581   Fraser, Keath. "Fox-Trot." CAN LIT No. 99 (1983): 174-76. [Review of *The Swell Season.*]

582   Freedman, Adele. "The Bass Saxophone: Explosive. A Bonfire on the Chilly Plains of CANLIT. The Bass Saxophonist Wrestling with..." GLOBE MAIL (July 30, 1977)

583   Fulford, Robert. "Another Country." SAT N 98, no. 1 (1983): 5-6.

584   Fulford, Robert. "Toronto Spring of Josef Škvorecký." SAT N 91, no. 5 (1976): 11.

585   Galt, George. "Lost in the Chorus." BKS CAN 15, no. 8 (1986): 17-18. [Review of *Dvořak in Love.*]

586   Goetz-Stankiewitcz, Marketa. "A Literary Scherzo." CAN FORUM 67, No. 771 (1987): 41-43.

587   Grabowski, Yvonne. "Publications in Other Languages." UNIV TOR Q 47 (1977/78): 494-96. [Review of *The Bass Saxophone.*]

588   Grabowski, Yvonne. "Publications in Other Languages." UNIV TOR Q 48 (1978/79): 490-93. [Review of *Le miracle* and *Přiběh inženyra.*]

589   Hancock, Geoff. "Interview with Josef Škvorecký." CAN FIC MAG No. 45/46 (1982-83): 63-96.

590   Hill, Douglas. "Fiction." UNIV TOR Q 52 (1982/83): 331-32. [Review of *The Swell Season.*]

591   Kertzer, Jon. Review of *The Bass Saxophone.* FIDDLEHEAD 116 (1978): 153-54.

592   Kundera, M. "1968: Prague, Paris and Josef Škvorecký." CAN FORUM 59 (August 1979): 6-9.

593   Levy, A. "A Couple Who Keep the Culture Alive." READ DIGEST (Can.) 123 (July 1983): 84-88.

594   Manguel, Alberto. "Lost in Translation." BKS CAN 16, no. 2 (1987): 13-14. [Review of *The Mournful Demeanor of Lieutenant. Borůvka.*]

595   Owen, I.M. "In the Mood." BKS CAN 12, no. 2 (1983): 13-14. [Review of *The Swell Season.*]

596 Owen, I.M. "Prague on the Humber." BKS CAN 13 (August 1984): 10-11.
[Review of *The Engineer of Human Souls.*]

597 Reeves, John. "Faith and Defiance - in Exile." TAM REV 72 (1977): 93-95.
[Review of *The Bass Saxophone.*]

598 Ricard, François. "Comment peut-on être tchèque?" LIBERTÉ 25 (oct. 1983): 122-24.
[Revue: *Le saxophone basse.*]

599 Sarner, Mark. "Portrait of a Political Exile: Why Josef Škvorecký, Czechoslovakia's Preeminent Novelist, is Very Much at Home in Cabbagetown." TOR LIFE (Agust 1977): 38, 84, 85.

600 Škvorecký, Josef. "An Artist's Fight for Freedom." PROBL COMMUN (September-October 1976)

601 Škvorecký, Josef. *Talkin' Moscow Blues: Essays about Literature, Politics, Movies, and Jazz,* edited by Sam Solecki. Toronto: Lester & Orpen Dennys, 1988. 367 pp.
[A collection of essays, interviews, biographical writing. Bibliography: pp. 365-67.]

602 Škvorecký, Josef. "Text pro případ že bych vypadl z okna nebo se zabil při autonehodě" [A Text in Case I Fall Out of a Window or Get Killed in a Car Accident]. LISTY 4 (1972): 17-25.

603 Škvorecký, Josef. "The Totalitarian Blues: A Toronto Writer's Extraordinary Memoir of Jazz Under the Third Reich." TOR LIFE (August 1977): 40, 41, 86, 89.

604 Solecki, Sam. "The Laughter and Pain of Remembering." CAN FORUM 64 (August-September 1984): 39-41.
[Review of *The Engineer of Human Souls.*]

605 Solecki, Sam. "Other Voices." CAN FORUM 59 (August 1979): 5.

606 Solecki, Sam. "Scherzo Capriccioso." CAN LIT No. 116 (1988): 175-77.
[Review of *Dvořak in Love.*]

607 Steinberg, Peter. Review of *The Bass Saxophone.* CAN FIC MAG No. 27 (1977): 137-38.

608 Stevens, Peter. "Imagination's Sources." CAN LIT No. 93 (1982): 131-33.
[Review of *The Bass Saxophone.*]

609 Stuewe, Paul. "Mark of the Exile." BKS CAN 10 (October 1981): 4-5.

610 Stuewe, Paul. "Prose Swings Hard, Hits High Notes." Q & Q (August 1977)
[Review of *The Bass Saxophone.*]

611 Such, Peter. "Czechoslovak Tales a Smashing Read." TOR STAR (July 26, 1977)
[Review of *The Bass Saxophone.*]

612 Thorpe, Michael. "Czech Elan Vital." CAN FORUM 62 (December 1982-January 1983): 40.
[Review of *The Swell Season.*]

613 Woodcock, George. "Farce as Truth." CAN FORUM 55 (November 1975): 35-37.
[Review of *Miss Silver's Past.*]

614 Woodcock, George. "Jazz as Subversion." CAN FORUM 57 (September-October 1977)

[Review of *The Bass Saxophone*.]

SNEPP, Ludek (1922-   )
Born in Czechoslovakia, came to Canada after World War II. He lives in London, Ont.

615   *Protichodci [Opponents]*. Plzeň: Západočeske Nakladelství, 1967.   287 pp.   Novel.

616   Pláňata [Wildings]. Plzeň: Západočeske Nakladelství, 1968.   243 pp.   Novel.

DANISH

BIBLIOGRAPHY

617   JENSEN, K.
      "Danish-Canadian Periodical Publications: A Preliminary Check List."   CAN ETH STUD 2, no. 1
      (1970): 27-29.
      [Compiled from McKin's *The Canadian Newspaper Directory*. Also includes indexes of non-Danish
      titles and geographic distribution.]

DOMINICAN (W.I.)

INDIVIDUAL AUTHOR

HARRIES, Amach
Born and educated in Dominica, W.I., where she founded the Little Theatre. Studied acting and dancing at the
University of West Indies. She emigrated to Canada in 1967 and continued her education at the Banff School
of Fine Arts and the University of Toronto. She taught drama, acted and directed and did choreography. A
singer, radio narrator and interviewer, Harries also played t.v. roles in Police Surgeon in 1974.

618   *Anansi and Mission to Happiness.* Folk drama, produced by the Black Theatre Canada, 1978/79.

619   *Anansi in the Ant Kingdom.* Folk drama, produced by the Black Theatre Canada, 1980.

620   *Anansi and Pains to Freedom.* Toronto, 1980. Folk drama.

EGYPTIAN

INDIVIDUAL AUTHORS

LATIF-GHATTAS, Mona (1946-   )
Born in Cairo, Egypt, emigrated to Canada in 1966. She studied theatre at l'Université du Québec à Montréal
and received a Maîtrise en Création Dramatique from l'Université de Montréal. She is a stage manager in
Montréal, publishing poems in periodicals.

621   *Les chants du Karawane.* Cairo: Elias Modern Publishing House, c1985. 95 pp. Poèmes.

622   *Nicolas le fils du Nil.* Cairo: Elias Modern Publishing House, 1985. 95 pp. Roman.

623   *Quarante voiles pour un exil: récits et fragment, poétiques.* Laval: Editions Trois, 1986. 105 pp.
      Poèmes.

ZOLA, Meguido (1939-   )
Children's writer. Born in Cairo, Egypt. Educated at the University of Leeds and Bristol University. Author of biographical books on Karen Kain, Terry Fox, and Wayne Gretzky. Associate Professor of Education at Simon Fraser University, Burnaby, B.C.

624   *Le loup blanc.* Toronto: Holt, Rinehart and Winston, 1973. Story for children.

625   *A Dream of Promise: A Jewish Folktale.* Toronto: Kids Can Press, 1980. Folktale.

626   *Only the Best.* London: Franklin Watts, 1981. Story for children.

627   *Moving.* London: Julia McRae Books, 1983. Story for children.

628   *Nobody.* Winnipeg: Pemmican Publications, 1983. Story for children.

629   *My Kind of Pup.* Winnipeg: Pemmican Publications, 1985. Story for children.

EAST-INDIAN

BIBLIOGRAPHY

630 BASRAN, G.S.
"East-Indian-Canadian Periodical Publications: A Preliminary Check List." CAN ETH STUD 5, no. 1-2 (1973): 43-45.
[A list of 10 periodical titles in Panjabi and English.]

INDIVIDUAL AUTHORS

BANNERJI, Himani
Born in India. Teaches part-time at York University and does research on feminism, sociology and socialism. Her poems, short stories and literary reviews have appeared in *The Asianadian, Rikka, The Toronto South Asian Review* and in anthologies.

631 *The Two Sisters*, as told by Himani Bannerji, translated from Bengali. Illustrated by Khaletun Majumder. Toronto: Kids Can Press, 1978. 32 pp. Children's story.

632 *A Separate Sky.* Toronto: Domestic Bliss Press, 1983. 48 pp. Poems.

CHAHAL, Amarjit

633 *Baharon Āiā Ādāmī [The Alian Returning].* Amritsar, India: Nanak Singh Pustakmala, 1980. Novel, Panjabi.

CHAMAN, Kashmir Singh

634 *Kankang Rang Vatiae [Wheat has Changed Colour].* Amritsar, India: Nanak Singh Pustakmala, 1974. Poems, Panjabi.

635 *Angmarit Bundag [Nectar Drops].* Amritsar, India: Nanak Singh Pustakmala, 1975. Poems, Panjabi.

636 *Nal Piare Nehu [In Love with the Beloved].* Punjab, India: Chaman Publications, 1975. Poems, Panjabi.

637 *Tshanang Kanian [Light Rays].* Amritsar, India: Nanak Singh, 1975. Poems, Panjabi.

638 *Sūraja [The Sun].* Prīta Nagara: Nanak Singh Pustakmala, 1977. Poems, Panjabi.

CHHINA, Santokh

639 *Man di Jhuggi [A Hut of Heart].* Chandigarh, India: DES Punjab Publications, 1979. Poems, Panjabi.

CHOPRA, Shiv
Born in India, came to Canada in 1960. Studied science at McGill University. Published plays, verse drama, poems, scholarly papers on philosophy, mythology and science. Works as scientific adviser for National Health and Welfare in Ottawa.

640   *Riata and Gita.* Presented at Carleton University, Ottawa, 1981. Verse drama.

641   *In Praise of Women.* Winnipeg: Natyangali Group, 1982-84. Verse drama.

642   *The Wondrous Virgin.* Cornwall, Ont.: Vesta, 1983. 48 pp. Poems.

COWASJEE, Saros (1931-   )
Novelist, story writer, editor. Born at Hyderabad, India, educated at Agra University, India (M.A.), Leeds University, England (Ph.D.). Came to Canada in 1963. Teaches English at the University of Regina. Published in the *Journal of Canadian Fiction, Indian Literature* and in other journals. He has published several books of essays, anthologies and biographies.

643   *Stories and Sketches.* Calcutta: Writers Workshop, 1970. xi, 85 pp. Short stories.

644   *Goodbye to Elsa.* Don Mills, Ont.: New Press, 1974. 152 pp. Novel.

645   *Nude Therapy and other Stories.* Ottawa: Borealis, 1980. 119 pp. Short stories.

646   *Maharajas.* Calcutta: Writers Workshop, 1980. Screen play.

647   *Suffer Little Children.* New Delhi: Allied Publishers, 1982 162 pp. Novel.

GILL, Darshan

648   *Aapre Sanmukh [Facing Myself].* Amritsar, India: Ravi Sahit Parkashan, 1980. Poems, Panjabi.

649   *Jangala dī Agga [The Wild Fire].* Amritsar: Ravi Sahit Parkashan, 1976. Poems, Panjabi.

650   *Khaleej [The Bay].* Amritsar, India: Ravi Sahit Parkashan, 1978. Poems, Panjabi.

651   *Man and Mirror.* Surrey, B.C.: Indo-Canadian Publishers, 1980. Poems.
       [Translated from Panjabi.]

652   *Rūpa Arūpa [The Concrete and the Abstract].* Jullundur, India: Drishatī Pàrkhashan, 1976, Panjabi.

GILL, Stephen
Novelist, poet, editor, publisher. Born in India and came to settle in Cornwall, Ont. Co-editor of *Poets of the Capital*, editor of *Seaway Valley Poets, Tales from Canada* and *Green Snow.* Past president of the Cornwall Branch of Canadian Authors' Association.

653   *Reflections: A Collection of Poems.* Cornwall, Ont.: Kyte's, 1972. 48 pp. Poems.

654   *Life's Vagaries: Fourteen Short Stories.* Rexdale, Ont.: John Wiley and Sons of Canada, 1974. 104 pp. Short stories.

655   *Wounds: A Collection of Poems.* Cornwall, Ont.: Vesta, 1974. 44 pp. Poems.

656   *Why?: A Novel.* Cornwall, Ont.: Vesta, 1976. 154 pp. Novel.

657   *Immigrant: A Novel.* Cornwall, Ont.: Vesta, 1978. 121 pp. Novel.

658   *Reflections and Wounds (Poems).* Cornwall, Ont.: Vesta, 1978. 97 pp. Poems.

659   *The Loyalist City: A Novel.* Cornwall, Ont.: Vesta, 1979. 119 pp. Novel. 2d ed. 1988.

660   *Sketches of India.* Cornwall, Ont.: Vesta, 1980.

661   *Zakhamiṃ Parachāveṃ [Wounded Reflections].* New Delhi: Suchindana Prakāshana, 1980. Poems. [In Panjabi and English.]

662   *Moans and Waves.* Cornwall, Ont.: Vesta, 1982. 78 pp. 2nd enl. ed. 1988. Poems.

663   *Simon and the Snow King.* Cornwall, Ont.: Vesta, 1982.

Writings about:

664   Barr, Arlee. Review of *Wounds.* ALIVE No. 35.

665   Davy, J.D. Review of *Why?* ONTARIAN (Sept. 5, 1978): 59.

666   Dewar, Russ. "Gill Writes Novel." STAND FREEH (Feb. 24, 1977): 4.

667   Durell, Robert. Review of *Immigrant.* NUGGET FOCUS (Feb. 13, 1978): 2.

668   Hines, George. *Stephen Gill and His Works; An Evaluation.* Cornwall, Ont.: Vesta, 1982.

669   Leitao, Lino. Review of *Reflections and Wounds.* CAN WORLD FED (March 1979): 3.

670   Linder, Norma West. "Stephen Gill's Poems Depict Worldwide Themes." SARNIA OBS (Nov. 30, 1972)

671   Parakot, Manjula. "Why, Why?" CAN IND TIMES (May 5, 1975): 5. [Review of *Why?*]

672   Phillips, Bluebell S. Review of *Wounds.* CAN IND TIMES (Sept. 19, 1974): 5.

673   Pyke, Linda Annesley. Review of *Wounds.* Q & Q (June 1974): 12.

674   Sarkar, Suprovat. "Poems by Stephen Gill." LINK (Feb. 15, March 1, 1975): 5.

675   Sharma, D.R. "Indo-English Fiction." TRIBUNE (Chandīgarh, India) (March 17, 1979): 4.

676   Tierney, Frank M. "Reflections of an Indian Poet." CAN IND TIMES (Nov. 15, 1973): 5.

677   Walsh, Philip. Review of *Why?* CAN BOOK REV ANN 1976: 145-46.

678   Wilson, O.N. Review of *Why?* SARNIA OBS (Feb. 18, 1977): 4.

GILL, Tarlochan Singh

679   *Panjabi Goonj [Panjabi Echoes].* Toronto: Asia Publications, 1976. Poems, Panjabi.

680   *Tun Mun [Body and Mind].* Toronto: Asia Publications, 1978. Poems, Panjabi.

681   *Baal Avastha [Childhood].* Toronto: Asia Publications, 1979. Poems, Panjabi.

682   *Sile Lochan.* Toronto: Asia Publications, 1979. Poems, Panjabi.

683 *Bara Maha Tukhari [Drawings and Poems]*. Toronto: Centre for Contemporary Art, 1980. Poems, Panjabi.

684 *Ashok [Ashoka the King]*. Toronto: Asia Publications, 1983. Play, Panjabi.

GILLA, Morānwālī

685 *Āra Canaṇa, pāra Cānaṇa [Light on this Side, Light on that Side]*. Delhi, India: ARSI, 1973. Poems, Panjabi.

686 *Cambe dī Dālī [A Branch of Chhambra]*. Delhi, India: ARSI, 1975. Poems, Panjabi.

687 *Banjara Dharatī [Barren Land]*. Jullundur, India: Sīma Parkashan, 1976. Poems, Panjabi.

688 *Jind Bale Adhmoi [Half-dead Life is Burning]*. Jullundur, India: Gill Parkashan, 1976. Poems.

689 *Miṭṭi dī Sugandha [Fragrance of Soil]*. Delhi: Ārasī, 1978. Poems, Panjabi.

HARDEV SINGH

690 *Folk Tales and Proverbs of Panjabi People*. [N.pl.]: Ontario Khalsa Darban, 1979. Tales.

691 *Doodles and Scribbles*. London, Ont.: Shabd Publications, 1978. Stories, articles.

HAYER, Tara Singh

692 *... Te Siwa Balda Riha [And the Pyre Kept on Burning]*. Amritsar, India: Ravi Sahit Parkashan, 1976. Stories, Panjabi.

KALSEY, Surjeet Singh
(Also Singh, Surjeet Kalsey) Born in the Punjab, India, came to Canada in 1974. Educated at the Punjab University and the University of British Columbia. She has translated Panjabi writing and edited an anthology of modern Panjabi poetry. Her short stories have appeared in *The Watno Dur, Eclipse, Canadian Fiction Magazine* and *The Toronto South Asian Review*. She lives in Vancouver.

693 *Paunang Nal Guftagoo [Speaking to the Winds]*. Chandigarh, India: Raghbir Rachana Parkashan, 1979. Poems, Panjabi.

694 *Siha Ridhe Sawait Raat [Black Hearts, White Blood]*. Chandigarh, India: Raghbir Rachna, 1980. Short stories, Panjabi.

695 Speaking to the Winds: Poems. London, Ont.: Third Eye Publishing, 1982. 51 pp. illus. Poems.

696 *Foot Prints of Silence: Poems*. London, Ont.: Third Eye Publications, 1988. Poems.

KANWAL, Gurdial Singh

697 *Kuch Kangkarang [The Shards of Glass]*. Amritsar, India: Ravi Sahit, 1980. Poems, Panjabi.

698 *Meel Pathar [Milestone]*. Jullundur, India: Deepak, 1978. Poems, Panjabi.

KESARA, Singha

699 *Lahira Wadhadī Gaī [The Movement Marched on]*. Lahore: Singh Brothers, 1947. Play.

700 *Jangi Kaidī [Prisoners of War]*. Delhi: Navayuga Publications, 1969. Play.

701 *Bābā Harī Singha Usamāna [Baba Hari Sing Usman]*. Amritsar: Singh Brothers, 1975. Play.

702 *Amara Shahīda Madana Lāla Dhiṇgarā [Martyr Mewa Singh Lapoke]*. Amritsar: Singh Brothers, 1978. Play.

703 *Shahīda Ūdhama Singha [Martyr Udham Singh]*. Delhi: National Press of India, 1973. Play.

LEITAO, Lino
A Goan by birth, he was educated in India and Canada. His short stories are based on fables and have appeared in *Writer's Lifeline*, *The Toronto South Asian Review*, and *The Journal of South Asian Literature*.

704 *Collected Short Tales*. New York: Carlton, 1972. Tales.

705 *Goan Tales*. Cornwall, Ont.: Vesta, 1977. 113 pp. Short stories

706 *Six Tales*. Cornwall, Ont.: Vesta, 1980. Tales.

MENDIS, Tyrell

707 *The Canned Think*. Winnipeg: Joel Matthews, 1980. Poems.

MISTRY, Rohinton
Born in India, came to Canada in 1975. After winning three literary prizes, he began full-time writing in 1985.

708 *Tales from Firozsha Baag*. Markham, Ont.: Penguin Books Canada, 1987. 250 pp. Short stories.

MUKHERJEE, Bharati
Novelist. Born in India. Attended the University of Iowa (Ph.D.) and taught for a number of years at McGill University. Left Canada for the USA, because, as she wrote in *Days and Nights in Calcutta*, Calcutta equipped her to survive theft or even assault; it didn't equip her to accept proof of her unworthiness. Author of *The Sorrow and the Terror: The Haunting Legacy of the Air India Tragedy*, 1987.

709 *Tiger's Daughter*. Don Mills, Ont.: Thomas Allan, 1972. 213 pp. Novel.

710 *Wife*. Scarborough, Ont.: Nelson Canada, 1975. 213 pp. Novel.

711 *Days and Nights in Calcutta*, with Clark Blaise. New York: Double Day, 1977. Revised and enl. ed. Markham, Ont.: Viking-Penguin, 1986. Travel.

712 *Darkness*. Markham, Ont.: Penguin Books, 1985. 199 pp. Short stories.

713 *The Middle Man and other Stories*. Markham, Ont.: 1988. 197 pp. Short stories.

Writings about:

714 Hancock, Geoff. "An Interview with Bharati Mukherjee." CAN FIC MAG 59 (1987): 30-44.

715 Heward, Burt. "Let's Keep Mukherjee a Canadian." OTTAWA CIT (July 30, 1988) C3

716 Mandel, Ann. "Bharati Mukherjee." In *Canadian Writers since 1960.* (Detroit: Gale, 1987) pp. 266-69. port.

717 McGrawth, Joan. Review of *Darkness.* CAN BOOK REV ANN 1985: 215.

718 Parameswaran, Uma. Review of *Darkness.* CAN ETH STUD 18, no. 3 (1986): 157-60.

719 Porter, Helen. "Out of the Many." BKS CAN 17, no. 6 (1988): 25.
[Review of *The Middle Man and other Stories.*]

720 Review of *Wife.* BKS CAN 4, no. 8 (1975): 10.

721 Rule, Jane. "Failure of U.S. Melting Pot." OTTAWA CIT (July 30, 1988) C3 port.

722 Sabiston, Elizabeth. Review of *Darkness.* CAN WOMAN STUD 7 (1986): 224-26.

723 Woodcock, George. "Mulberry Brush." CAN LIT No. 107 (1985): 149-52.
[Review of *Days and Nights in Calcutta.*]

NAMJOSHI, Suniti (1941-   )
Born in Bombay, India, educated at the Universities of Poona, Missouri and McGill (Ph.D.). Her poems and fables have appeared in *The Antigonish Review, Descant, Applegarth's Folly, Canadian Forum, Canadian Ethnic Studies* and in other journals. She teaches at Scarborough College.

724 *Poems.* Calcutta: Writers Workshop, 1967. Poems.

725 *Poems of Govindagraj,* translated from the Marathi into English by the author with Sarojini Namjoshi. Calcutta: Writers Workshop, 1968. Poems.

726 *More Poems.* Calcutta: Writers Workshop, 1971. 36 pp. Poems.

727 *Cyclone in Pakistan.* Calcutta: Writers Workshop, 1971. 20 pp. Poems.

728 *The Jackass and the Lady.* Calcutta: Writers Workshop, 1980. Also by the League of Canadian Poets, 1980. 1 folded sheet (8 pp). Fable.

729 *Feminist Fables.* London: Sheba Feminist Publications, 1981. Fables.

730 *The Authentic Lie.* Fredericton, N.B.: Fiddlehead Poetry Books, 1982. 70 pp. Poems.

731 *From the Bedside Book of Nightmares.* Fredericton, N.B.: Fiddlehead Poetry Books & Goose Lane Editions, 1984. 70 pp. Fables, poems.

732 *Adili and the One-eyed Monkey.* London: Sheba Feminist Publishers, 1986. Fables.

733 *Flesh and Paper,* with Gillian Hanscombe. Charlottetown, P.E.I.: Ragweed Press, 1986. 64 pp. Poems.

734 *The Conversations of a Cow.* London: Women's Press, 1986. Fables.

735 *Middleman and other Stories.* Toronto: Penguin, 1987. 136 pp. Stories.

Writings about:

736 Brennan, Anthony. Review of *From the Bedside Book of Nightmares.* FIDDLEHEAD 145 (1985): 94-100.

737 Pilon, Ellen. Review of *Flesh and Paper.* CAN BOOK REV ANN 1986: 106.

738 Review of *From the Bedside Book of Nightmares.* ANTIG REV 60 (1985): 105-09.

739 York, Lorraine. "Fluent Shadows." CAN LIT No. 116 (1988): 185-87.
[Review of *Flesh and Paper.*]

740 York, Lorraine M. "Monsters within." CAN LIT No. 105 (1985): 190-92.

PADMANAB, S. (1938-   )

Born in Bangalore, India. A physician by profession, he has published poems in *Quest, Miscellany, The West Coast Review, CVII,* and has given readings of his work in Montreal, Winnipeg and Saskatoon. He lives in Saskatoon.

741 *A Separate Life.* Calcutta: Writers Workshop, 1974. 64 pp. Poems.

742 *Age of Birds.* Calcutta: Writers Workshop, 1976. 54 pp. Poems.

743 *Songs of the Slave: Collected Poems.* Cornwall, Ont.: Vesta, 1977. 71 pp. Poems.

PARAMESWARAN, Uma

A professor of English at the University of Winnipeg, she was born in India, and received her education there and in the USA. As a playwright, she has done work on cablevision t.v. in Winnipeg.

744 *Cyclic Hope, Cyclic Pain.* Calcutta: Writers Workshop, 1974. 23 pp. Poems.

745 *Rootless but Green are the Boulevard Trees.* The Toronto South Asian Review 4, 1 (1985): 62-103. Play.

PARANAVITANA, Senarat

746 *Sigiri Graffiti.* Oxford: Oxford University Press, 1956. 2 vols.

RAJAN, Balachandra (1920-   )

747 *Too Long in the West.* London: Heinemann, 1966. Biography.

748 *The Prison and the Pinnacle,* edited by Balachandra Rajan. Toronto: University of Toronto Press, 1973. x, 163 pp.
[Writings presented to the University of Western Ontario.]

RĀMAPŪRI, Guracarana

749 *Annhī Galī [Blind Alley].* Delhi: Navayuga, 1972. In Panjabi.

750 *Kirnan da Ahlanan [Nest of Rays].* [N.p., n.p.] Panjabi.

751 *Cheers for Muktananda,* with Robert Sward. Victoria, B.C.: Soft Press, 1976. Poems.

752 *Kancanī* Amritsar, India: New Age Book Centre, 1980. Poems, Panjabi.

RAMUWALIA, Iqbal

753   *Tin Kon [Triangle].* Vancouver: Watno Dur, 1979. Novel, Panjabi.

RASHA, Mittar

754   *Aakasma [Murmurs].* Amritsar: Ravī Sahit Prakāshana, 1976. Poems, Panjabi.

755   *Murmurs,* translated from the Panjabi by S. Virdy. Cornwall, Ont.: Vesta, c1979. 71 pp. Poems.

RODE, Ajmer (1940-   )
Born in Punjab, India. Some of his plays and poems had been translated from Panjabi into English by his wife, Surjeet Kalsey. Three of his plays have been produced in Vancouver.

756   *Dooja Pasa [The Other Side].* Chandigarh, India: Raghbir Rachana, 1977. Play.

757   *Soorti [Consciousness].* Chandigarh, India: Raghbir Rachana, 1979. Poems, Panjabi.

758   *One Girl, One Dream.* Toronto: The Toronto South Asian Review (Spring 1983) One-act play.

759   *Blue Meditations.* London, Ont.: Third Eye Publishing, 1984. Poems.

760   *Komagata Maru.* London, Ont.: Third Eye Publishing, 1986.

SADHU

761   *Sonerangi Sarak [The Gold-coloured Road].* Punjab: Chawala, 1976. Poems, Panjabi.

762   *Musa Bhajia Maut Ton [Fell from the Sky, Tumbled on a Tree].* Short stories, in press.

SAHGAL, Nayantara (Pandit) (1927-   )

763   *Prison and Chocolate Cake..* New York: Knopf, 1954. Novel.

764   *From Fear Set Free.* New York: Norton, 1963. Novel.

765   *Time to be Happy.* Bombay: Jaico, 1963. Novel.

766   *This Time of Morning.* London: Gollancz, 1965. Novel.

767   *Storm in Chandigarh.* New York: Norton, 1969. Novel.

768   *Sunlight Surround You: A Birthday Bouquet from Chandralekha Mehta,* with Rita Dar. [New Delhi: Orient Longmans, 1970]. viii, 176 pp. illus.

769   *The Day in Shadow; A Novel.* Delhi: Vikas Publications, 1971. Novel.

770   *Plans for Departure, A Novel.* New York: Norton, 1985. Novel

771   *Rich Like Us.* London: Heinemann, 1985. Novel.

SHAH, Ramanik

772   *Samaru Sathi Jamane [I Think of You, Sathi Jamane].* Amadavad, India: Gurjara Granth Karyalaya, 1976. Guj.

SINGH, Kashmir

773   *Kankan Rang Vitae [Wheat Has Changed Colour].* Amritsar: Nanak Singh Pustakmala, 1974. Poems, Panjabi.

774   *Angmarit Bundag [Nectar Drops].* Amritsar: Nanak Singh Pustakmala, 1975. Poems, Panjabi.

775   *Nal Piare Nehu [In Love with the Beloved].* Panjab: Chaman Publications, 1975. Poems, Panjabi.

776   *Tshanang Kanian [Light Drops].* Amritsar: Nanak Singh, 1975. Poems, Panjabi.

777   *Sūraja [The Sun].* Prīta Nagara: Nanak Singh Pustakmala, 1977. Poems, Panjabi.

SINGH, Nirmala

778   *The Shiva Dance.* Cornwall, Ont.: Vesta, c1979. 51 pp. Poems.

SUBRAMANIAM, V.
Born in India and received his early education in a Dikshita family of traditional Sanskrit scholarship and his Ph.D. in Australia, where also taught. He has composed several dance dramas on Buddhist themes, some of them have been choreographed and staged by leading classical dancers in India and abroad. He is a professor of political science at Carleton University, Ottawa, Ont.

779   *Pancha Kanya Tarangini.* New Delhi: Ashish Publishing House, 1975. Dance dramas. [Five dance dramas in Sanskrit with English translations.]

780   *Veera Kanya Vahini.* New Delhi: Ashish Publishing House, 1981. Dance dramas. [Four dance dramas in Sanskrit with English translations.]

781   *Kinkini Mala.* New Delhi: Ashish Publishing House, 1983. Dance dramas. [Four dance dramas in Sanskrit with English translations.]

782   *Dima Panchakam.* New Delhi: Ashish Publishing House, 1985. Dance dramas. [Five dance dramas with English translations.]

SUKHINDARA

783   *Lakkara Dīaṃ Macchīaṃ [Word Fishes].* Delhi: Ikattī Pharanarī, 1979. Poems, Panjabi.

VAIDYA, Ashwin

784   *Ladhi Tuthi Jindagini Kavita Tema Cha Mara Rasa [A Collection of Fifty Poems].* Regina: Nalini Vaidya, 1964. Poems, Guj.

ESTONIAN

BIBLIOGRAPHIES

785 **AER, Elvi**
Baltic Material in the University of Toronto Library. Toronto: University of Toronto Press, 1972. 125 pp.
[Printed for the Association for the Advancement of Baltic Studies and the University of Toronto Library. Contains 1,569 titles, with a chapter on Estonian, Latvian and Lithuanian literature, including the works of Baltic-Canadian authors, pp. 47-78. 2nd edition published by same in 1978.]

786 **EERME, Karl**
Eesti Raamatu Aupäev [A Day of Honour for the Estonian Book]. Toronto: Eesti Kultuurikogu Kanadas, 1970.
[Includes Estonian-Canadian authors.]

787 **KANGRO, Bernard**
Eesti Raamat Vabas Maailmas: Bibliograafiline Ülevaade 1944-1970. [Estonian Books in the Free World: A Bibliography, 1944-1970]. Lund, Sweden: Eesti Kirjanike Kooperatiiv AB, 1971. 40 pp.
[A compilation of Estonian books published in the Western world.]

788 **OLVET, Joan**
"Estonian-Canadian Creative Literature: A Preliminary Check List of Authors and Pseudonyms." CAN ETH STUD 2, no. 1 (1970): 41-43.
[Contains 45 names and pseudonyms, compiled from the files held by the Estonian Central Archives in Canada, Toronto.]

789 **OLVET, Joan**
"Estonian-Canadian Periodical Publications: A Preliminary Check List." CAN ETH STUD 2, no. 1 (1970): 35-40.
[Includes 44 titles with geographic index.]

BOOKS

790 *Eestlased Kanadas: Ajalooline Koguteos [The Estonians in Canada: An Historical Symposium],* edited by Alfred Kurlents. Toronto: Kanada Eestlaste Ajaloo Komisjon, 1975. 670 pp.
[Covers a diversity of topics from Estonian communities in Canada to architecture, religious life, youth activities, and literature.]

791 *Eestlased Kanadas II,* edited by Valdu Lillakas. Toronto: Kanada Eestlaste Ajaloo Komisjon, 1985. 499 pp. Photos, tables.
[Individual authors included are Arved Viirlaid, Salme Ekbaum, Arvi Kork and Urve Karuks, pp. 295-98.]

792 **MÄGI, Arvo**
Estonian Literature: An Outline. Stockholm: The Baltic Humanitarian Association, 1968. 109 pp.
[Includes an extensive list of publications in Estonian and works translated from Estonian into other languages.]

793 **ORAS, Ants**

Estonian Literature in Exile, with a biographical appendix by Bernard Kangro. Lund, Sweden: Eesti Kirjanike Kooperatiiv AB, 1967. 88 pp.
[Based on an essay by the author.]

794 ZIEDONIS, Arvids, Jr.; PUHVEL, *Joan*; SILBAJORIS, Rimvydas; VALGEMÄE, Mardi, eds.
Baltic Literature and Linguistics. Columbus, Ohio: Association for the Advancement of Baltic Studies Inc., 1973. 251 pp.
[Part of the *Proceedings of the Third Conference on Baltic Studies*, held in Toronto, May 1972.]

795 ZIPLANS, Emilija; MOCKUS, Vida; McKINSTRY; AER, Elvi
Baltic Material in the University of Toronto Library, 2nd. ed. Toronto: University of Toronto Press, 1978.

RESEARCH PAPERS

796 ARRO, Karl
"Balti rahvad võitsid juurde uusi sõpru" [The Baltic Nations Won New Friends]. VABA EEST 17, no. 2083 (March 2, 1973): 1-2, 5.

797 AUN, Karl
"Cultural Exchange." In his *The Political Refugees: A History of the Estonians in Canada*. (Toronto: McClelland & Stewart, 1985) pp. 147-52.
[Reference is made to the handicaps experienced by Estonian Canadian authors, due to linguistic isolation.]

798 d'AMFREVILLE, Henri
"Les intellectuels et le nationalisme". COMBAT No. 5708 (Nov. 1, 1962)

799 "Estonian-Canadian Literature" In *Eestlased Kanadas: Ajalooline Koguteos*. [Toronto: Kanada Eestlaste Ajaloo Komisjon, 1975] pp. 446-67.

800 "Estonian-Canadian Literature." In *The Canadian Family Tree*. (Ottawa: Canadian Citizenship Branch, 1967) p. 111.

801 GAUDY, Georges
"Aux mains des Russes." ASPECTS FRANCE (May 2, 1963)

802 GUISSARD, Lucien
"Deux romanciers devant le drame de deux peuples." La CROIX No. 24153 (May 28, 1962)

803 MÄGI, Arvo
"Soomepoisid eesti kirjandusloos " [Finnish Boys in the History of Estonian Literature]. PÕH TÄH No. 11 (1968): 18-22.

804 OJA, Hannes
"Eesti probleemid prantsuse ajakirjas" [Estonian Problems in a French Journal]. VABA EEST (Feb. 5, 1966)

805 OJA, Hannes
"Laureaadid vestlevad kirjandusprobleemidest" [Laureates Discuss Literary Problems]. VABA EEST 51, no. 1730 (July 8, 1969): 7.

806 ORAS, Ants

"A Look at Baltic Letters Today and World Literature in Review." BKS ABR 47 (1973): 623-30.

ANTHOLOGY

807 *Minu noorusmaa* [*The Land of My Youth*]. Lund, Sweden: Eesti Kirjanike Kooperatiiv AB, 1964. 307 pp.
[Includes short stories by Estonian-Canadian authors]

INDIVIDUAL AUTHORS

EKBAUM, Salme (1912-   )

808 *Valge maja* [*The White House*]. Toronto: Orto, Estonian Publishing House, 1946. 336 pp. Novel.

809 *Ilmapõllu inimesed* [*The Folks of Ilmapõllu*]. Lund, Sweden: Eesti Kirjanike Kooperatiiv, 1948. 261 pp.
[Translated into English and published by Orto, under the title *Farm in the Forest* (1949).]

810 *Indiaani suvel* [*Indian Summer*]. Toronto: The Author, 1951. 73 pp. Poems.

811 *Lindprii talu* [*The Outlawed Farm*]. Toronto: Orto, Estonian Publishing Company, 1951. 230 pp. Novel.

812 *Kärestik: Romaan* [*Rapids: Novel*]. Lund, Sweden: Eesti Kirjanike Kooperatiiv AB, 1955. 259 pp. Novel.

813 *Süteoja: Romaan* [*Emberbrook: Novel*]. Lund, Sweden: Eesti Kirjanike Kooperatiiv AB, 1957. 286 pp. Novel.

814 *Varjude maja* [*House of Shadows*]. Lund, Sweden: Eesti Kirjanike Kooperatiiv AB, 1959. 294 pp. Novel.

815 *Õigusenõudja: Romaan* [*To Claim One's Right: Novel*]. Lund, Sweden: Eesti Kirjanike Kooperatiiv AB, 1962. 302 pp. Novel.

816 *Veimevakk* [*The Dowry Chest*]. Lund, Sweden: Eesti Kirjanike Kooperatiiv AB, 1964. 295 pp. Novel.

817 *Laenatud laulatussõrmus* [*The Borrowed Wedding Ring*]. Produced in Toronto, 1965. Play.

818 *Kontvõõras* [*Gate-crasher*]. Lund, Sweden: Eesti Kirjanike Kooperatiiv AB, 1966. 287 pp. Novel.

819 *Maja Karineemel* [*House on the Reef*]. Produced in Sydney, Australia, 1966. Play.

820 *Ristitants* [*Dance of the Cross*]. Lund, Sweden: Eesti Kirjanike Kooperatiiv AB, 1966. 240 pp. Novel.

821 *Kivi kiljatas aknasse* [*Stone Crashing Through the Window*]. Stockholm: Free Estonia, 1967. 91 pp. Poems.

822 *Võerasema* [*Stepmother*]. Produced in Stockholm, 1969, and in Sydney, Australia, 1970. Play.

823 *Suitsupääsuke* [*The Swallow*]. Produced in Sydney, Australia, 1971. Play.

824 *Arm ja ahnus...* [*Love and Ambition...*]. Lund, Sweden: Eesti Kirjanike Kooperatiiv AB, 1972. 232 pp. Novel.

825 *Ajatar* [*Time*]. Toronto: Estoprint, 1974. 74 pp. Poems.

826 *Kiiktool* [*The Rocking Chair*]. Produced in Sydney, Australia, 1974. Play.

827 *Vang kes põgenes* [*The Prisoner Who Got Away*]. Lund, Sweden: Eesti Kirjanike Kooperatiiv AB, 1975. 250 pp. Novel.

Writings about:

828 ˜Ekbaum, Salme.˜ In *The Canadian Family Tree*. (Ottawa: Canadian Citizenship Branch, 1967) p. 111.

829 ˜Ekbaum, Salme.˜ In *International Who's Who in Poetry*. 4th ed. (Cambridge: IWWIP, 1974) p. 133.

830 ˜Ekbaum, Salme.˜ In *World Who's Who of Authors*.

HUBEL, Eduard see **METSANURK, Mait**

JÄRVALANE, Joan, pseud. (Real name: LÖVI, Oskar)

831 *Kiriku ehitajad; romaan* [*The Church Builders; Novel*]. Toronto: Orto, 1970. 352 pp. Novel.

KARUKS, Urve

832 *Kodakondur.* Toronto: Mana, 1976. 63 pp. Poems.

KORK, Arvi, pseud. (Real name: TINITS, Arvi E.) (1927-   )
Novelist, radio reporter and retired policeman, Arvi Tinits was born in Tallin, Estonia. Received part of his education there, as well as in Munich and Toronto. He served for 26 years on the Toronto Metropolitan Police Force. After his retirement, he worked for the Voice of America and is now editor of *Vaba eestlane*, a Toronto-based newspaper.

833 *Neli musketäri* [*Four Musketeers*]. Lund, Sweden: Eesti Kirjanike Kooperatiiv AB, 1957. 320 pp. Novel.

834 *Cetri Musketieri* [*Four Musketeers*]. Translated from the Estonian into Latvian by Zane Zemdega. Minneapolis: Tilts, 1958. Novel.
[Translation of *Neli musketäri.*]

835 *Sirel püssirauas* [*Lilacs in Riflebarrels*]. Published serially in VABA EEST SÕNA, Literary Supplement, 1959-1960. Novel.

836 *Ungari rapsoodia* [*The Hungarian Rhapsody*]. Published serially in MEIE KODU, Literary Supplement, 1959. Novel.

837 *Läti Kütid* [*The Latvian Riflemen*]. Published serially in MEIE KODU, Literary Supplement, 1959. Novel.

838 *Tänavakuningad* [*The Kings of the Street*]. Lund, Sweden: Eesti Kirjanike Kooperatiiv AB, 1963. 296 pp. Novel.

839 *Mängumaa ja Relvad* [*Playland and Weaponry*]. In *Minu noorusmaa* [Land of My Youth]. (Lund, Sweden: Eesti Kirjanike Kooperatiiv AB, 1964) Novelette.

840 *Tammiraiujad* [*The Dam Builders*]. Lund, Sweden: Eesti Kirjanike Kooperatiiv AB, 1966. Novel.

841 *Armud läinud, armud jäänud* [*Loves Gone, Loves Forgotten*]. Lund, Sweden: Eesti Kirjanike Kooperatiiv AB, 1968. 254 pp. Novel.

842 *Relvalood: Sõjasulaste seiklusi mitmel mandril* [*Gun Stories*]. Lund, Sweden: Eesti Kirjanike Kooperatiiv AB, 1971. 287 pp. Short stories.

843 *Suusamägedel* [*On Ski Hills*]. Toronto: Vaba Eestlane, 1972. A novelette published in seven parts.

844 *Sulid ja võmmid* [*Cops and Robbers*]. Lund, Sweden: Eesti Kirjanike Kooperatiiv AB, 1973. 236 pp. Novel.
[Bilingual, Estonian and English.]

845 *Röövlijahil* [*The Robberhunt*]. Lund, Sweden: Eesti Kirjanike Kooperatiiv, 1975. 239 pp. Novel.

846 *Mehhiko teel* [*Down Mexico Way*]. Published serially in *Viba Eestlane, Literary Supplement*, 1976.

847 *Välgumärgi kasvandikud* [*The Words of the Lightning-runes*]. 1982. Novel.

Writings about:

848 Adson, A. Review of *Sulid ja võmmid*. EEST PÄEV (May 30, 1973)

849 Eller, Helmi. Review of *Armud läinud, armud jäänud*. PÄEVALEHT (Aug. 14, 1968)

850 Grabbi, Hellar. "Arvi Kork" [Arvi Kork]. MANA No. 40(1974)

851 L.D.S. Review of *Neli Musketäri*. MEIE KODU (Sept. 8, 1958)

852 Mikiver, Ilmar. "Kas eesti esimene pikaresk-romaan? " [Is This the First Estonian Picaresque Novel?]. TULIMULD No. 1(1958)

853 Parlo, Olev. Review of *Tammiraiujad*. VABA EEST SÕNA (June 29, 1967)

854 "Patrol Sgt. Tinits Writes Books and Speaks Nine Languages." TOR TEL (March 16, 1970)

855 Reinans, Alur. "Olukirjeldus väikestest gangsteritest" [Milieu-description Involving Small-time Gangsterism]. EEST PÄEV (Apr. 11, 1963)

856 Voitk, Evald J. Review of *Tänavakuningad*. MEIE ELU (Apr. 25, 1963)

857 Zemdega, Zane. Review of *Cetri Musketieri*. TILTS (1958)

KRAAV, Fred (1923-   )

858 *Risttules: romaan* [*Crossfire: A Novel*]. Toronto: Eesti Kirjastus Kanadas, 1958. 298 pp. Novel.

METSANURK, Mait, pseud. (Real name: HUBEL, Eduard) (1879-1957)

859 *Kutsutud ja seatud; ühe hingekarjase päevik* [*Called and Arranged; Diary of a Minister*]. Toronto: Orto, 1969. 270 pp. Biographical novel.

860 *Ümera jõel* [*On the Ümera River*]. Toronto: Orto, 1974.
[An earlier version was published in Tallin by Eesti Riiklik Kirjastus, 1961. 330 pp.]

OJA, Hannes (1919-)
Poet, editor. Born in Martna, Estonia. Received his education in agricultural sciences. Editor of *Vaba Eestlane.* Member of P.E.N., Estonian Authors Association in Exile and Institute for Estonian Language and Literature. His poems have appeared in *Mana, Tulimuld, Põhjala Tähistel,* and other journals. Recipient of Estonian Literary Prize (for *Tunnete purdel,*1968).

861 *Koputused eneses: luultusi* [*Inner Pulsating: Poems*]. Helsinki, 1955. 62 pp. Poems.

862 *Märgid mõtteliival* [*Marks in the Sands of Thought*]. Stockholm: Vaba Eesti, 1964. Poems.

863 *Tunnete purdel: kolmas kogu luuletusi* [*Footbridge of Feelings*]. Stockholm: Vaba Eesti, 1967. 76 pp. Poems.

Writings about:

864 Adson, Artur. Review of *Märgid mõtteliival.* EEST PÄEV (1965)

865 Eller, H. Review of *Märgid mõtteliival.* TULIMULD (1965)

866 Eller, H. Review of *Tunnete purdel.* EEST PÄEV (1967)

867 Grabbi, H. Review of *Märgid mõtteliival.* MANA (1965)

868 Grünthal, I. Review of *Märgid mõtteliival.* TEATAJA (1965)

869 Kolk, R. Review of *Koputused eneses.* TEATAJA (1965)

870 Krants, E. Review of *Tunnete purdel.* VABA EEST (1967); Reprinted in MANA (1969)

871 Külvet, I. Review of *Märgid mõtteliival.* VABA EEST (1965)

872 Lumiste, L. Review of *Koputused eneses.* EEST POST (Oct. 1955)

873 Review of *Märgid mõtteliival.* MEIE ELU (1965) Signed: Lte.

874 Review of *Märgid mõtteliival.* VABA EEST SÕNA (1966) Signed: M.J.

875 Review of *Tunnete purdel.* MEIE KODU (1968) Signed: Lte.

876 Review of *Tunnete purdel.* TEATAJA (1968) Signed: Ar-gi.

877 Travas, R. Review of *Koputused eneses.* EEST HÄÄL (1955)

PIHLA, Magda (1908-)

878 *Emakese kirjulilleline põll* [*Mommy's Apron in Floral Design*]. Tallin: Tarvik, 1940. 36 pp. [A play for children in 2 acts.]

879 *Teed ja käijad* [*Walks and Walkers*]. Lund, Sweden: Eesti Kirjanike Kooperatiiv AB, 1958. 288 pp. Novel.

880 *Rõõmuraasuke* [*Little Joy*]. Illustrated by Endel Kõks. Geislingen, Germany: Kauge Kodu, 1947. 44 pp. Translated into Latvian and published in Toronto by Druva Publishers, 1959.

881 *Õnnerätsepp* [*Prescriptions for Happiness*]. Illustrated by Ernö Koch. Lund, Sweden: Eesti Kirjanike Kooperatiiv AB, 1952. 64 pp. Children's book.

882 Ristunud saatused [*Crossed Destinies*]. Toronto: Estonian Publishing Company, 1952. 244 pp. Short stories.

883 *Rõõmuraasukese kirjad* [*Letters by Rõõmuraasuke*]. Lund, Sweden: Eesti Kirjanike Kooperatiiv AB, 1952. 64 pp. [Also published in Latvian translation.]

884 *Eide tütar, taadi tütar* [*Mommy's Daughter, Daddy's Daughter*], illustrated by Ellen Uustalu-Wishik. New York: Estonian Board of Education, 1961. 32 pp. [Publisher's prize-winning book.]

885 *Küll on hea elada* [*Delighted to be Alive*], illustrated by Ellen Uustalu-Wishik. New York: Estonian Board of Education, 1961. 34 pp. Children's book.

886 *Naanu ema tütred* [*Mother Nanu's Daughters*] . Lund, Sweden: Eesti Kirjanike Kooperatiiv AB, 1963. 304 pp. Novel.

Writings about:

887 ˝Inimesed ja saatused; Magda Pihla: *Ristunud saatused*˝ [Men and Destinies; Magda Pihla: *Crossed Destinies*]. STOCK TID (Sept. 10, 1955) Signed: H.E.

888 Jürma, Mall. ˝Jälgimas ristunud saatusi; Magda Pihla: *Ristunud saatused*˝ [Tracing Crossed Destinies; Magda Pihla: *Crossed Destinies*]. VABA EEST SÕNA (Sept. 22, 1955)

889 Jürma, Mall. Review of *Teed ja käijad*. VABA EEST SÕNA (Dec. 18, 1958)

890 Jürma, Mall. ˝Kahest Noorsookirjanduse laureaadist˝ [Prize-winning Books]. VABA EEST SÕNA (December 1961)

891 Jürma, Mall. Review of *Naanu ema tütred*. VABA EEST SÕNA (1963)

892 K., V. ˝Naine uues ühiskonnas˝ [Woman in New Environment]. EESTI HÄÄL No. 596(Jan. 30, 1959)

893 ˝Kirjanduskroonika; Ilmus M. Pihla romaan *Naanu ema tütred*˝ [Literary Chronicle; Announcement and Introduction of M. Pihla's Novel *Mother Nanu's Daughters*]. MEIE ELU [July 6, 1963)

894 Lumiste, Leho. ˝Kodumaa ja maapagu˝ [Homeland and Exile]. STOCK TID (Nov. 25, 1955)

895 Lumiste, Leho. ˝Mineviku tunnelis; M. Pihla: *Naanu ema tütred* ˝ [Through the Tunnel of the Past; M. Pihla: *Mother Nanu's Daughters*]. MEIE KODU (Sept. 25, 1963)

896 Mägi, Arvo. ˝See oli nii... ˝[This is How It Was...]. TULIMULD No. 6 (1952) [Review of *Rõõmurasukese kirjad..]*

897 Mägi, Arvo. ˝Risti-rästi; Magda Pihla: *Ristunud saatused* ˝ [Criss-Cross; Magda Pihla: *Crossed Destinies*]. VÄLIS-EESTI No. 14 (July 24, 1955)

898 ˝Meie raamaturiiul; Romaan kanada eestlaste elust ˝ [Our Book Shelf; A Novel About Estonians in Canada]. STOCK TID (Oct. 17, 1958) Review of *Ristunud saatused.*

899 Oja, Hannes. ˝Ilusa naise südamelood; M. Pihla: Naanu ema tütred˝ [The Love Story of a Beautiful Woman; M. Pihla: *Naanu Mother's Daughters*]. MEIE ELU (Sept. 19, 1963)

900 Oja, Hannes. ˝Kaks kaunist lasteraamatut; Magda Pihla: *Eide tütar, taadi tütar* ja *Küll on hea elada* ˝ [Two Beautiful Children's Books; Magda Pihla: *Mommy's Daughter, Daddy's Daughter* and *Delighted to be Alive*]. MEIE ELU (Jan. 11, 1962)

901 Oja, Hannes. ˝Kullatud servadega perekonnapilt ˝ [Family Portrait with Gilded Rimming]. MEIE ELU (July 20, 1963) Interview with Magda Pihla.

902 Parlo, Olev. ˝Karikatäis puhast rõõmu eesti lastele ˝ [Pure Delight for Estonian Children]. VABA EEST SÕNA 30, 4 (1953)

903 Pihlakas, pseud. ˝Raamat ristunud saatustest ˝ [A Book About Crossed Destinies]. VABA EEST 4, 4 (1955) Review of *Ristunud saatused.*

904 Raud, M. ˝Kirjanduslikke uudiseid; Magda Pihla: *Teed ja käijad* ˝ [Literary News: Magda Pihla: *Walks and Walkers*]. POST No. 1 (1959)

905 Ristikivi, Karl. ˝Lapsepõlve ja muinasjutumaalt ˝ [From Childhood and Fairyland]. VÄLIS-EESTI (1952) Review of Rõõmuraasukese kirjad.

THOEN, Aino (1913-   )

906 *Hallide mägede maa: romaan* [*Gray Mountain Country: Novel*]. Lund, Sweden: Eesti Kirjanike Kooperativ AB, 1954. 295 pp. Novel.

VIIRLAID, Arved (1922-   )

Novelist, poet. Born in Estonia. Educated at Kloostri and at Tallin State College of Fine Arts. After serving as an officer in the Finnish Army, he moved to Sweden in 1945, to England in 1946, and then to Canada in 1954. He has published books of poetry and novels, some of them translated into Latvian, Finnish, Ukrainian, Chinese and English. He has lived in Toronto since his arrival in Canada.

907 *Hulkuri evangeelium* [*A Vagabond's Gospel*]. London: The Author, 1948. 96 pp. Poems.

908 *Tormiaasta* [*Year of Storms*]. Vadstena, Sweden: Orto, Estonian Publishing House, 1949. 2 v. 366 pp. and 442 pp. respectively. Novel.

909 *Üks suveõhtune naeratus* [*A Summer Night's Smile*]. London: The Author, 1949. 96 pp. Poems.

910 *Ristideta hauad* [*Graves without Crosses*]. Lund, Sweden: Eesti Kirjanike Kooperatiiv AB, 1952. 2 v., 368 pp. and 360 pp. respectively. Translated into English and French.

911 *Seitse kohtupäeva* [*Seven Days of Judgement*]. Lund, Sweden: Eesti Kirjanike Kooperatiiv AB, 1957. 276 pp. Novel.

912 *Vaim ja ahelad* [*Spirit and Shackles*]. Lund, Sweden: Eesti Kirjanike Kooperatiiv AB, 1961. 344 pp. Novel.

913 *Jäätanud peegel* [*Frosted Mirror*]. Lund, Sweden: Eesti Kirjanike Kooperatiiv AB, 1962. 96 pp. Poems.

914 *Tombeaux sans croix*. Paris: Ed. Albin Michel, 1962. 444 pp. Roman. [Translation of *Ristideta hauad*.]

915 *Kustuvad tuled* [*Fading Flames*]. Lund, Sweden: Eesti Kirjanike Kooperatiiv AB, 1965. 276 pp. Novel.

916 *Sadu jõkke* [*Rain for the River*]. Lund, Sweden: Eesti Kirjanike Kooperatiiv AB, 1965. 260 pp. Novel.

917 *Hõllalaulud; Neljas kogu luuletusi* [*Songs of Longing*]. Lund, Sweden: Eesti Kirjanike Kooperatiiv AB, 1967. 96 pp. Poems.

918 *Bambuskardina ees* [*At the Bamboo Curtain*]. Toronto: *Vaba Eestlane*, 1970. Published in series in Nos. 61-71. [Translated into Finnish and published in series in *Vapaa Sana*, 1971, Nos. 19-39.]

919 *Graves without Crosses*, translated from the Estonian by Ilse Lehiste, with a preface by the Rt. Hon. John Diefenbaker. Toronto: Clark, Irwin, 1972. 428 pp. Novel. [Other translations: Latvian - Minneapolis: Tilta Apgāds, 1956; Swedish - Stockholm: Andromeda Förlag, 1959; French - Paris: Éd. Albin Michel, 1962; Spanish - Barcelona: Luis de Caralt, 1966; Finnish - Hämeenlinna: A.A. Karisto Ov, 1968.]

920 *Kes tappis Eerik Hormi?: Roman* [*Who Killed Eerik Hormi?: Novel*]. Lund: Sweden: Eesti Kirjanike Kooperatiiv AB, 1974. 285 pp. Novel.

921 *Surnud ei loe* [*The Dead Don't Matter*]. Lund, Sweden: Eesti Kirjanike Kooperatiiv AB, 1975. 276 pp. Novel.

922 *Käsikäes* [*Hand in Hand*]. Lund, Sweden: Eesti Kirjanike Kooperatiiv AB, 1978. 96 pp. Poems.

923 *Märgitud* [*The Branded*]. Lund, Sweden: Eesti Kirjanike Kooperatiiv AB, 1980. 220 pp. Novel.

924 *Igaviku silmapilgutus* [*The Work of Eternity*]. Lund, Sweden: Eesti Kirjanike Kooperatiiv AB, 1982. 112 pp. Poems.

Writings about:

925 Adson, Artur. "Paguluse südametunnistuse äratus" [The Awakening of Conscience in Exile]. EESTI POST (1953)

926 ˝Arved Viirlaid.˝ In *The Canadian Family Tree*. [Ottawa: Canadian Citizenship Branch, 1967] p. 111.

927 Doyon, René-Louis. Review of *Tombeaux sans croix*. ICI PARIS (Aug. 14, 1962): 9.

928 Eller, Helmi. ˝Suur aine˝ [A Large Subject]. TULIMULD No. 2 (1966): 116-8.

929 ˝Estonian Canadian Does Excellent Novel About Freedom Fight.˝ EXPOSITOR (Aug. 19, 1972): 6.
[Review of *Graves without Crosses.*]

930 Gardner, Marilyn. ˝Estonian Reign of Terror.˝ SEATTLE POST-INT (May 19, 1974): H9.
[Review of *Graves without Crosses.*]

931 Grabbi Hellar. "Arved Viirlaid: Hõllalaulud" [Arved Viirlaid: *Songs of Longing*]. MANA 35 (1969): 102

932 Helbemäe, Gert. "A. Viirlaid romaan inglise keeles" [A. Viirlaid's Novel in English]. EEST HÄÄL (Jan. 15, 1965): 2.
[Review of *Graves without Crosses.*]

933 Holt, Kare. "Graver uten kors" *[Graves without Crosses]*. ARBEIDERBLADET (June 27, 1960)
[In Norwegian.]

934 Jürma, Mall. "Ahelad ja vaim" [Shackles and Spirit]. TULIMULD No. 4 (1961): 311-2.

935 Jürma, Mall. "Arved Viirlaid: Hõllalaulud" [Arved Viirlaid: Songs of Longing]. VABA EEST SÕNA (July 18, 1968) Signed: M.J.

936 Jürma, Mall. Review of *Seitse kohtupäeva*. VABA EEST SÕNA (Apr. 11, 1957)

937 Jürma, Mall. "Viirlaid prantsuse keeles˝ [Viirlaid in French]. TULIMULD No. 1 (1963): 66-68.

938 Kangro, Bernard. "Reedetud generatsiooni nägu" [The Face of the Betrayed Generation]. TULIMULD No. 2 (1972): 89-96.

939 Kaup, Johannes. "Esitleme uudisteose autorit" [Introducing the Author of a New Work]. MEIE ELU 14, no. 368 (1957)

940 Kaup, Johannes. ˝Kes oled sina, väljavalitu?" [Who Are You? The Chosen One?]. TULIMULD No. 1 (1953): 54-6.

941 Kim, Yang-shik. "Arved Viirlaid." READ WEEK (Sept. 11, 1977): 20.
[In Korean.]

942 Krants, Eduard. "Luule on tarbeaine; A. Viirlaid: *Hõllalaulud* " [Poetry is a Necessity: A. Viirlaid: *Songs of Longing*]. MEIE ELU 15, 951 (1968)

943 Lumiste, Leho. "Neljas kogu luuletusi. A. Viirlaid: *Hõllalaulud* " [Fourth Volume of Verse. A. Viirlaid: *Songs of Longing*]. MEIE ELU 15, 951 (1968)

944 Oja, Hannes. ˝Eesti probleemid prantsuse ajakirjas" [Estonian Problems in a French Journal]. VABA EEST (Febr. 5, 1966)

945 Oja, Hannes. "Kuidas valmis Heine trilogia" [How Did Heine's Trilogy Develop]. MEIE ELU 19, 821 (1966)

946   Oras, Ants. "Uus luuletaja. Arved Viirlaid: *Hulkuri evangeelium*" [A New Poet. Arved Viirlaid: *A Vagabond's Gospel*]. EESTI HÄÄL 25 (June 11, 1948)

947   Parrest, Harald. Review of *Tormiaasta*. TULIMULD No. 1 (1950): 58-63.

948   Pekomäe, Vello. Review of *Ristideta hauad*. STOCK TID (Dec. 3, 1952) Signed: V.P.

949   Pierre, Françoise. Review of *Tombeaux sans croix*. FEMME (June 1962)

950   Ristikivi, Karl. "Õuduste aasta. A. Viirlaid: *Ristideta hauad*" [A Year of Terror. A. Viirlaid: *Graves without Crosses*]. VÄLIS-EESTI 5 (Febr. 1, 1953) Signed: K. Rx.

951   Sorestad, Glen A. Review of *Tombeaux sans croix*. TRIB GENÈVE (Apr. 19, 1963)

952   Sorestad, Glen A. Review of *Tombeaux sans croix*. FIGARO LITT (Apr. 27, 1963)

953   Sorestad, Glen A. Review of *Graves without Crosses*. SKYLARK (Winter 1973)

954   Tretjakevits, L. Review of *Ristideta hauad I*. MEIE KODU 11, 180 (1953)

955   Viidang, Juhan. "Tõeotsija Toonela kaldal" [Searcher of Truth at the Shore of Toonela]. TULIMULD 3 (1975): 159-62.

VOMM, Ants (1931-   )

956   *Minu hing: pagulasluulet, 1948-1971* [*My Soul: Songs, 1948-1971*]. Toronto: Oma Press, 1971. 240 pp. Poems.

957   *Maa rahva ristsõnad.* [Crosswords]. [N.p., n.p.] 1973.

958   *Varjud, 1948-1978.* Toronto: Oma Press, 1979. 72 pp. Poems.

959   *Miki-hiir: olümpia 1.* [*Mickey Mouse: Olympia 1*]. Toronto: The Author, 1980. 18 leaves.

FINNISH

BIBLIOGRAPHIES

960 **BOHM, W.D.**
"Finnish-Canadian Periodical Publications: Preliminary Check List." CAN ETH STUD 1, no. 1 (1969): 5-7.
[Includes index of geographic distribution.]

961 **KORVELA, Aino**
"Finnish-Canadian Periodical Publications: First Supplement." CAN ETH STUD 5, no. 1-2 (1973): 59-62.
[Includes references to Finnish newspapers and periodicals.]

GENERAL STUDY

962 **PILLI, Arja**
The Finnish-Language Press in Canada, 1901-1939: A Study in the History of Ethnic Journalism. Helsinki: Soumalainem Tiedeakatemia, 1982. 328 pp.
[Contents: History, sources, communications among the immigrants (pp. 9-24); The emergence of the first Finnish-Canadian papers (pp. 25-132); The Finnish-Canadian press between the wars (pp. 133-263); Content analysis of the Finnish-Canadian press (pp. 264-293); Bibliography (pp. 294-314).]

ANTHOLOGIES

963 *Finnish-Canadian Play and Operetta Manuscript Collection on Microfiche.* Toronto: McLaren Micropublishing, 1974. 76 sheets.
[Photographed from original manuscripts of the Finnish Organization of Canada.]

964 *Finnish Fairy Tales and Stories for Children,* with an introduction by Irina Ilmokari. Ottawa: Borealis Press, 1981. ix, 46 pp. illus.
[Prepared by the Finnish Canadian Cultural Federation. Contains several fairy tales translated into English by Finnish-Canadian translators.]

GAELIC

BIBLIOGRAPHIES

965 **MACLEOID, Calum Iain M.**
"Bibliography." In his *Sgialachdan a Albainn Nuaidh.* (Glaschu: Gairm, 1966) pp. 149-50.

966 **SINCLAIR, Donald MacLean**
"Gaelic Newspapers and Prose Writings in Nova Scotia." In *Collections of the Nova Scotia Historical Society.* Vol. 27 (1945) pp. 105-13.
[The best collections of North American Gaelic literature are to be found in the Harvard College Library, Cambridge, Mass., in the St. Francis Xavier College Library, Antigonish, N.S., and in the private collection of the Rev. Alexander MacLean Sinclair, now in the possession of his son, Donald MacLean Sinclair, Hopewell, N.S.]

RESEARCH PAPERS

967   CAMPBELL, John Lorne
"Scottish Gaelic in Canada." GÁIDHEAL (March 1948): 69-71.

968   DUNN, Charles W.
Highland Settler. Toronto: University of Toronto Press, 1953.

969   MACNAIL, James
"Gaelic Stories, Songs, Periodicals, Personal Correspondence." Unpublished manuscript collected and compiled by Seumas Eóghainn. Available from C.I.M. Macleoid, 12 Fairview St., Antigonish, N.S.

970   SINCLAIR, Donald MacLean
"Gaelic in Nova Scotia." Paper presented to a meeting of the Humanities Conference, Halifax, June 10, 1949.

ANTHOLOGIES

971   *The Emigrant Experience: Songs of Highland Emigrants in North America.* Toronto: University of Toronto Press, 1982. 228 pp.
[A bilingual anthology of Gaelic poetry. Canadian authors represented are Domhnall Gobha, Bàrd Thighearna Chola (John Maclean), John MacDonald (Iain Sealgair), Allan MacDonald, John McQueen, Kenneth MacDonald, Duncan Black Blair, Calum Bàn MacMhannain, Rory Roy MacKenzie, A. MacLean Bàrd from Raasay, Iain Sinclair, Anna Gillis, Hugh MacCorkindale, and Angus MacIntosh. Includes bibliography (pp. 195-96).]

972   *Gaelic Bards,* edited by Alexander Maclean Sinclair. Charlottetown, P.E.I. and Sydney, N.S., 1892, 1896, 1904. 3 vols.
[Contents: Vol. 1: *The Gaelic Bards from 1715 to 1765.* Charlottetown, 1892. Vol. 2: *The Gaelic Bards from 1765 to 1825.* Sydney, N.S., 1896. Vol. 3: *The Gaelic Bards from 1825 to 1875.* Sydney, N.S., 1904.]

973   *Gaelic Songs in Nova Scotia,* edited by Helen Creighton and Calum Iain M. Macleod. Ottawa: Department of the Secretary of State, 1964. 308 pp. (National Museum of Canada, Bull. No. 198. Anthropological Series 66.)
[Words in Gaelic with English translations.]

974   *Sgialachdan a Albainn Nuaidh: air an cruinneachadh [Tales from Nova Scotia in Gaelic],* edited by Calum Iain N. Macleod. Glaschu: Gairm, 1969. 150 pp.

INDIVIDUAL AUTHORS

BLAIR, Duncan   (1815-1893)

975   Eas Niagara [On the Niagara]. [N.p.] Poems.

MACLEOID, Calum Iain Nicholson (1913-   )

976   *An t-eilthireach [The Stranger].* Sydney, N.S., 1953. 43 pp. Poems.

977   *Bardachd a Albainn Nuaidh.* Glaschu: Gairm, 1970. 108 pp. Poems.

GERMAN

BIBLIOGRAPHIES

978 CARDINAL, Clive H.
"A Preliminary Check List of Studies on German-Canadian Creative Literature. Part I. General Studies." CAN ETH STUD 1, no. 1 (1969): 38-39.
[Contains 12 names compiled from the sources of the Research Centre for Canadian Ethnic Studies.]

979 CARDINAL, Clive H.
"A Preliminary Check List of Studies on German-Canadian Creative Literature. Part II. Specific Studies." CAN ETH STUD 2, no. 1 (1970): 63-67.
[Includes 67 names as a complement to the previous citation.]

980 CARDINAL, Clive H.; MALYCKY, Alexander
"German-Canadian Creative Literature: A Preliminary Check List of Authors and Pseudonyms." CAN ETH STUD 1, no. 1 (1969): 31-37.
[Represents 141 authors. Biographical data, various literary genre and language of publication are also provided.]

981 FROESCHLE, Hartmut
"Deutschkanadische Bibliographie. Eine Auswahl." DEUTSCHKAN JAHRB 1 (1973): 327-44.
[The section on German-Canadian literature and bibliographies include 24 references.]

982 FROESCHLE, Hartmut; ZIMMERMANN, Lothar
"The Germans in Ontario. A Bibliography." DEUTSCHKAN JAHRB 8 (1984): 243-79.
[Includes 746 citations, some related to literature.]

983 GILBY, W.R.
"Imprints of German-Canadian Creative Literature. First Supplement." CAN ETH STUD 5, no. 1-2 (1973): 85-90.
[Supplement to Rolf Windthorst's compilation: CAN ETH STUD 2, no. 1 (1970): 56-62. Contains extensive chronological and genre indexes.]

984 LIDDELL, Peter G., comp.
A Bibliography of the Germans in British Columbia. Vancouver: CAUTG, 1982. 89 pp.
[Contains 293 references to monographic publications, as well as a selected list of British Columbia newspaper references from 1900 to date. Also includes a subject index.]

985 MALYCKY, Alexander
"German-Albertans: A Bibliography. Part 1." DEUTSCHKAN JAHRB 6 (1981): 311-44.
[Includes 742 citations on general publications and writings on churches and religious organizations.]

986 MALYCKY, Alexander; CARDINAL, Clive H.
"German-Canadian Periodical Publications: A Preliminary Check List." CAN ETH STUD 1, no. 1 (1969): 13-30.
[Contains 152 titles and indexes of non-German titles and geographic distribution.]

987 MALYCKY, Alexander; CARDINAL, Clive H.

"German-Canadian Periodical Publications. First Supplement." CAN ETH STUD 2, no. 1 (1970): 47-54.
[This is a continuation of the list published in CAN ETH STUD 1, no. 1 (1969): 13-30. Indexes of non-German titles and geographic distribution are also given.]

988 MALYCKY, Alexander; GOERTZ, R.O.W.
"German-Canadian Periodical Publications. Second Supplement." CAN ETH STUD 5, no. 1-2 (1973): 67-86.
[This is a continuation of the lists published in CAN ETH STUD 1, no. 1 (1969): 13-30, and 2, no. 1 (1970): 47-54. All three lists contain a total of 318 titles and indexes of non-German titles and geographic distribution.]

989 RIEDEL, Walter E.
"A Checklist of Literature Translated from the German and Published in Canada." DEUTSCHKAN JAHRB 5 (1979): 283-99.
[Includes citations relating to Walter Bauer and Arnold Dyck.]

990 WINDTHORST, Rolf E.B.
"German-Canadian Creative Literature: A Preliminary Check List of Imprints." CAN ETH STUD 2, no. 1 (1970): 55-62.

BOOKS, ANNALS

991 *Annalen 1. Symposium, 1976; Das Erste Montrealer Symposium Deutschkanadische Studien/ The First Montreal Symposium on German-Canadian Studies*, edited by Karin Gürttler and Friedhelm Lach. Montréal: Deutschkanadische Studien, 1976. 85 pp.
[Includes an extensive study by Hartmut Froeschle on German-Canadian literature, pp. 18-30.]

992 *Annalen 2. Tradition, Integration, Rezeption: Zweites Montrealer Symposium Deutschkanadische Studien/ Second Montreal Symposium on German-Canadian Studies/ Deuxiéme Symposium Montréalais Études Allemandes-Canadiennes.* Montreal, March 9-11, 1978. Montreal: Deutschkanadische Studien, 1978.
[Includes a paper by Hartmut Froeschle on German-Canadian poetry, poems by Andreas Schroeder and Henry Beissel, and a short story by Henry Kreisel.]

993 *Annalen 4/ Annals 4/ Annales 4: German-Canadian Studies in the 1980s; Symposium 1983*, edited by Michael S. Batts, Walter Riedel, and Rodney Symington. Vancouver: CAUTG, 1983.
[Includes papers on German-Canadian literature by Al Reimer, Victor Doerksen, Manfred Kuxdorf, Harry Loewen, and Walter Riedel.]

994 *Deutsch als Muttersprache in Kanada; Berichte zur Gegenwartslage* [*German as Mother Tongue; Reports on the Current Situation*]. Wiesbaden: Franz Steiner Verlag, 1977. 175 pp.
[Contents: 1. The German language in various parts of Canada, pp. 1-49; 2. The German language in various aspects of public life. Includes papers on German-Canadian literature by C.H. Cardinal, pp. 69-76, and by Fritz Wieden, pp. 77-82.]

995 *Deutschkanadisches Jahrbuch/ German-Canadian Yearbook*, edited by Hartmut Froeschle. Toronto: Historical Society of Mecklenburg Upper Canada Inc. Vol. 1 -   ; 1973 -
[Nine volumes to date. vol. 1: includes papers by Clive Cardinal and Hartmut Froeschle; vol. 2: contains poems by Almuth Lütkenhaus, Ewald Schaefer, Erwin Pottit, and Rolf Windhorst; vol. 3: papers by Hartmut Froeschle, Rodney Symington, Michael Hadley, Jack Thiessen, and poems by Walter Roome, Nicolai Unruh, Walter Bauer, Jakob Janzen, Valentin Sawatzky, Anton Frisch, and Else Seel; vol. 4: paper by Peter Erb, and poems by Wolfgang Heyde, Helga Kleer, Rüdiger Krause, Josef Mohl, Gertrude Nusenow, Ewald Schaefer, Marie Weisz; vol. 5: papers by Hartmut

Froeschle, Frank Jakobsh, Walter Pache, Walter Riedel; vol. 6: papers by Gerhard Friesen and Georg Epp, and a bibliography of Germans in Alberta by Alexander Malycky; vol. 7: includes book reviews of Hartmut Froeschle: *Drei frühe deutschkanadische Dichter*; Hermann Boeschenstein: *Heiteres und Satirisches aus der deutschkanadischen Literatur...*; Valentin Sawatzky: *Lindenblätter*. Vol. 8: Hartmut Froeschle and Lothar Zimmermann: The Germans in Ontario. A Bibliography. Vol. 9: Includes papers and book reviews on German-Canadian authors by Terrance Craig (on F.P. Grove), Walter Riedel, Gerhard Friesen and Hans-Martin Plesske (on Walter Bauer).

996　*Heiteres und satirisches aus der deutschkanadischen Literatur: John Adam Rittinger, Walter Roome, Ernst Loeb, Rolf Max Kully [Humour and Satire in German-Canadian Literature: John Adam Rittinger Walter Roome, Ernst Loeb, Rolf Max Kully]*, edited with introductions in German and English by Hermann Boeschenstein.　Toronto: German-Canadian Historical Association,　1980. 117 pp.
[Includes some text in English.]

997　*The Old World and the New: Literary Perspectives of German-speaking Canadians*, edited by Walter E. Riedel.　Toronto: University of Toronto Press, 1984.　191 pp.
[Includes papers by Walter Riedel, Rodney Symington, Anthony Riley, Günter Hess, Harry Loewen, Karin Gürttler, Helfried Seliger, Peter Liddell, and Armin Arnold.]

RESEARCH PAPERS

998　BOESCHENSTEIN, Hermann
"Betrachtungen zur deutschkanadischen Literatur" [Review of German-Canadian Literature]. ANNALEN 1 (1976): 1-17.

999　CARDINAL, Clive H.
"Begegnung mit dem deutschen Gedicht" [Encounter with the German Poem].　In *Deutsch als Muttersprache in Kanada*. (Wiesbaden: Franz Steiner Verlag, 1977) pp. 77-82.
[An analysis of the poetry of E. Hager, Erwin Pottit, V. Morrow, U. Zandmer, M. Weisz, H. Schultheis, W. Harth, G. Cardinal, I. Morf, Karl Maurer, Walter Bauer, P.V. Morstein, Ulrich Schaffer.]

1000　CARDINAL, Clive H.
"Das kulturelle Leben der Kanadier deutscher und ukrainischer Herkunft" [The Cultural Life of Canadians of German and Ukrainian Origin]. DEUTSCHKAN JAHRB 1 (1973): 53-56.
[Describes social and cultural aspects of assimilation with special reference to Ukrainian, German and some Icelandic poetry in Canada.]

1001　CARDINAL, Clive　H.
"Some German Cultural Contributions to Canada's West." DEUTSCHKAN JAHRB 1 (1973): 47-51.
[Individual creators referred to include poets Else Seel and Ulrich Schaffer, as well as several German-speaking painters such as Eric Bergman, Fritz Brandtner R. Gross and others. The work of Ukrainian-Canadian author Illîa Kyrîâk is also discussed.]

1002　DOERKSEN, Victor G.
"The Divine Plowman and the Mennonite Clod: A Reading of 'Hinterm Pflug/ Stimmungen,' by Fritz Senn." ANNALEN 4 (1983): 208-229.

1003　EPP, Georg
"Der mennonitische Beitrag zur deutsch-kanadischen Literatur" [The Mennonite Contribution to Canadian Literature]. DEUTSCHKAN JAHRB 6 (1981): 140-48.

[A study of the poems of Anton Frisch, Walter Bauer, Jacob Goerzen, and Ulrich Schaffer. Special attention is paid to Mennonite poets Arnold Dyck, Fritz Senn, Georg de Brecht, J.H. Janzen, and others.]

1004 FRIESEN, Gerhard K.
"German-Canadian Poetry under the Star-Spangled Banner." DEUTSCHKAN JAHRB 6 (1981): 103-14.
[Gives an analysis of Hermann Weigand, Johannes Maass, Otto F. Mordhorst, and Johannes Hensen.]

1005 FRIESEN, Gerhard K.
" 'Yankeische Eigenheiten': Anti-Americanism in a 19th-century German-Canadian Poem." DEUTSCHKAN JAHRB 6 (1981): 115-29.
[The poem, by Franz Joseph Egenter, first published in Texas, represents the poet's dislike for the American way of life. The paper gives a study of the 48-stanza writing.]

1006 FROESCHLE, Hartmut
"Die deutschkanadische Literatur. Umfang und Problemkreis" [The German-Canadian Literature. Range and Problems]. ANNALEN 1 (1976): 18-30.
[An analysis of the poetry of Funcken, Rembe and Querner. Also an introduction to the work of the leading Mennonite poets: Fritz Senn, Arnold Dyck, J.H. Janzen and Else Seel, and of the achievements of Walter Bauer, Ulrich Schaffer, W. Roome, and Anton Frisch.]

1007 FROESCHLE, Hartmut
"Eugen Funcken, Heinrich Rembe, Emil Querner: drei frühe deutschkanadische Dichter" [Eugen Funcken, Heinrich Rembe, Emil Querner: Three Early German-Canadian Poets]. ANNALEN 2 (1978): 47-62.
[Includes poems and evaluations.]

1008 FROESCHLE, Hartmut
"Gibt es eine deutschkanadische Literatur?" [Is There a German-Canadian Literature?] DEUTSCHKAN JAHRB 3 (1973): 174-87.

1009 GUNDY, Jeff
"Essays: Being Mennonite and Writing Mennonite." MENN LIFE 41, no. 4 (1986): 11-13.

1010 GUNDY, Jeff
"Separation and Transformation: Tradition and Audience for Three Mennonite Poets." J MENN STUD 4 (1986): 53-69.

1011 JAKOBSH, Frank K.
"German and German-Canadian Literature as Contained in the 'Berliner Journal'." DEUTSCHKAN JAHRB 5 (1979): 108-20. illus.
[The Berliner Journal, a weekly publication (1859-1918) in Kitchener, Ont., contains valuable information on German literature in Canada and abroad. This paper offers an analysis of the content and aesthetic value of poetry and fiction represented in the newspaper.]

1012 JANZEN, J.H.
"Die Belletristik der kanadischen russlanddeutschen Mennoniten" [The Belles-lettres of Canadian Mennonites from Russia]. In 47. Christlicher Gemeinde-Kalender für das Jahr 1938 (Iberstein bei Worms).

1013 KLEIN, Karl Kurt

"Literaturgeschichte des Deutschtums im Ausland" [The History of German Literature Abroad].
(Leipzig, 1939) pp. 278-87.

1014 **KLOSS, Heinz**
"Randbemerkungen zur deutschkanadischen Literatur" [Notes on German-Canadian Literature]. In
Mitteilungen des I f A 3 (1975): 191-94.

1015 **KRAHN, Cornelius**
"Literary Efforts among the Mennonites of Russian Background." MENN LIFE 24, 4 (1969):
166-68.

1016 **KÜHN, Volker**
"Farblose Ahornblätter. Gibt es eine deutschkanadische Dichtung?" [Colourless Maple Leaves. Is
There a German-Canadian Poetry?] DER NORDWESTEN (Oct. 3, 1961)

1017 **KÜHN, Volker**
"Gibt es eine deutschkanadische Dichtung?" [Is There a German-Canadian Poetry?] GERM CAN
BUS REV 7, no. 4 (1961): 27.

1018 **KUXDORF, Manfred**
"Emigrant Lyrics: A View from the other Side." ANNALEN 4 (1983): 230-39.

1019 **LEHMANN, Heinz**
"The Beginnings of a Canadian German Literature and other Artistic Activity." In his *The German
Canadians* 1750-1937. (St. John's, Newfoundland: Jesperson Press, 1986) pp. 293-94.
[A summary of the Mennonite literature with emphasis on the work of G.A. Peters, Gerhard Toews,
Johann Peter Klassen, H. Görtz, Fritz Senn, N. Unruh and J. Peetasch (Peters).]

1020 **LOEWEN, Harry**
"Canadian-Mennonite Literature: Longing for a Lost Homeland." In *The Old World and the
New....*,edited by Walter E. Riedel. (Toronto: University of Toronto Press, 1984) pp. 73-93.
[Individual authors included are Peter B. Harder, Gerhard Loewen, Jacob H. Janzen, Dietrich Neufeld,
Hans Harder, Arnold Dyck, Fritz Senn (real name: Gerhard Friesen), Valentin Sawatzky, Rudy
Wiebe, etc. The material is arranged chronologically.]

1021 **LOEWEN, Harry**
"The Linguistic Medium is the Message: The Low German, High German, and English
Languages..." ANNALEN 4 (1983): 240-53.

1022 **REIMER, Al**
"Translating Ethnic: The Translator as Critic, Editor, and Collaborator. ANNALEN 4 (1983):
197-207.

1023 **RIEDEL, Walter E.**
"Canada's Cultural Mosaic and the Literature of the German-speaking Canadians." In *The Old World
and the New...*, edited by Walter E. Riedel. (Toronto: University of Toronto Press, 1984) pp. 3-
13.
[Offers an overview of the literary accomplishments of German-speaking Canadians, including
Austrians, German-speaking Swiss authors and Mennonites.]

1024 **RIEDEL, Walter E.**
"German Writing." In *The Canadian Encyclopedia* (Edmonton: Hurtig Publishers, 1985) vol. 2, pp.
737-38.

[A summary of the pioneer Mennonite era (Eugen Funcken, Dietrich Neufeld, Arnold Dyck, Fritz Senn) and the modern era (F.P. Grove, Carl Weiselberger, Henry Kreisel, Walter Bauer, Henry Beissel, Andreas Schroeder, Ulrich Schaffer, etc.). Includes Austrian, Swiss and German-Canadian literature.]

1025 **RIEDEL, Walter E.**
"The Study of the Literature of German-speaking Canadians: A Thematic Approach. ANNALEN 4 (1983): 254-263.

1026 **THIESSEN, Jack**
"Plattdeutsch in Kanada" [Low German in Canada]. DEUTSCHKAN JAHRB 3 (1976): 211-19.
[This article deals with the past and the present of the Low German Dialect spoken by the Mennonites in Western Canada. The works of Arnold Dyck, Fritz Senn, Reuben Epp, Nikolai Unruh and Elisabeth Peters are discussed.]

1027 **THIESSEN, Jack**
"Canadian Mennonite Literature." CAN LIT No. 51 (1972): 65-72.

1028 **WIEDEN, Fritz**
"Deutschkanadische Literatur: ein Überblick" [German-Canadian Literature: A Review]. In *Deutsch als Muttersprache in Kanada: Berichte zur Gegenwartslage*. (Wiesbaden: Franz Steiner Verlag, 1977) pp. 69-76.

ANTHOLOGIES

1029 *Ahornblätter: Deutsche Dichtung aus Kanada [Maple Leaves: German Poetry from Canada]*, edited by Heinz Kloss and Arnold B. Dyck. Würzburg: Holzner-Verlag und Institut für Auslandsbeziehungen in Stuttgart, 1961. 115 pp.

1030 *Drei frühe deutschkanadische Dichter [Three Early German-Canadian Authors*: Eugen Funcken, Heinrich Rembe, Emil Querner], Herausgegeben von Hartmut Froeschle. Toronto: German-Canadian Historical Association, 1978. 112 pp. (Deutschkanadische Schriften A. Belletristik. Band 1)
[Includes poems by Eugen Funcken (pp. 26-53), Heinrich Rembe (pp. 54-88), and Emil Querner (pp. 89-112).]

1031 *Harvest: Anthology of Mennonite Writing in Canada, 1874-1974*, compiled and edited by William de Fehr, Gerhard Ens, George Epp, Helen Janzen, Peter Klassen, Lloyd Siemens, and Jack Thiessen. Winnipeg: Centennial Committee of the Mennonite Historical Society of Manitoba, 1974. 182 pp.
[Contains: Poems by Gerhard Ens, A.J. Friesen, I.P. Friesen, Heinrich Görz, J.H. Janzen, G.H. Peters, Fritz Senn, and N.H. Unruh. Stories and prose excerpts by Arnold Dyck, Gerhard Lohrenz, and Elisabeth Peters. Poems in Low German by Kornelius Epp, Reuben Epp, Wilhelm Pauls, and Gerhard Wiens. Stories in Low German by Arnold Dyck, Jack Thiessen, and P.D. Zacharias.]

1032 *Heiteres und Satirisches aus der deutschkanadischen Literatur [Cheerful and Satirical Pieces from German-Canadian Literature*: John Adam Rittinger, Walter Roome, Ernst Loeb, Rolf Max Kully], herausgegeben von Hermann Boeschenstein. Toronto: German-Canadian Historical Association, 1980. (Deutsch-Kanadische Schriften, A. Belletristik. Band 4)
[Includes excerpts from "Briefe vun Joe Klotzkopp" by John A. Rittinger (pp. 21-73), several poems in German by Walter Roome (pp. 74-91); poems by Ernst Loeb and excerpts from the writings of Rolf Max Kully (pp. 107-116).]

1033   *Hier laßt uns Hütten bauen: Deutsche Gedichte lutherischer Pfarrer in Ontario, 1869-1930 [Let's Build Our Dwelling Place Here: German Poetry by Lutheran Pastors in Ontario, 1869-1930]*, edited by Gerhard Friesen. Toronto: German-Canadian Historical Association, 1984.
[Includes a bibliography and poems by J.N. Münzinger, Carl Rudolf Gerndt, C.F. Spring, J. Schneider, W. Rein, Ernst Genzmer, Jürgen Sander, Herman A.F.L. Weigand, Heinrich Rembe, Carl C.J. Maaß, Otto Fred Mordhorst, Johannes Hensen, Hermann R. Mosig, and Reinhard Martin Sauberzweig. Provides an extensive introduction in English to Lutheran poetry in Canada (pp. xxix-xliii). Biographical sketches are given.]

1034   *Nachrichten aus Ontario: Deutschsprachige Literatur in Kanada [News from Ontario: German Literature in Canada]*, edited by Hartmut Froeschle. New York: Olms Press, 1981. xiv, 290 pp.
[Contents: Einleitung (pp. vii-xiv); Hartmut Froeschle: Literaturkritik. Die deutschkanadische Literatur: Umfang und Problemstellungen (pp. 1-12). Lyrik: includes poems by Walter Bauer, Mario von Brentani, and 40 other poets. Prosa: includes prose fiction by 18 authors. Essay: includes biographies of authors.]

1035   *A Sackful of Plautdietsch: A Collection of Mennonite Low German Stories and Poems*, edited by Al Reimer, Anne Reimer, and Jack Thiessen. Winnipeg: Hyperion Press, 1983. x, 190 pp.
[Includes poems and stories in low German, and critical texts in English and German. Some of the authors included are: H.F.W. Raabe, Jack Thiessen, Elisabeth Peters, Jacob H. Janzen, Arnold Dyck, Gerhard Ens, Reuben Epp, Gerhard Loewen, Fritz Senn. Also includes biographical notes.]

1036   *Unter dem Nordlicht: Anthologie des deutschen Schrifttums der Mennoniten in Kanada [Under the Northern Lights: Anthology of German Mennonite Writing in Canada]*, edited by G. K. Epp and Heinrich Wiebe. Winnipeg: Mennonite German Society of Canada, 1977. 292 pp.
[Contains poems by J.H. Janzen, Gerhard Friesen, P.J. Klassen, Heinrich Görz, Gerhard Loewen, G.A. Peters, A.J. Friesen, Nikolaus Unruh, Harry Loewen, J.W. Dyck, Valentin Sawatzky, Hans Enns, Hedwig Dyck, Georg Epp, Gerhard Ens, H.D. Friesen. Prose G.G. Toews, P.J. Klassen, A.J. Friesen, Hans Enns, Maria Penner, Arnold Dyck, and Reuben Epp.]

1037   *Vom Lande des Sternenbanners [From the Land of the Star-Star-Banner]*, edited by Gotthold August Neeff. 1906.
[An anthology; includes some Canadian contributors, e.g. Johannes Haass.]

INDIVIDUAL AUTHORS

BAUER, Walter (1904-1976)

Born in Merseburg, Germany, he graduated from the teachers' college there. He was a widely published author when the Nazis came to power and banned his books. Came to Toronto in 1952 and attended the University of Toronto and taught there in the German department. He published more than seventy books in German - novels, story collections, biographies, poetry, essays, and children's books. In the last years of his life he wrote his poems in English..

1038   *Der Lichtstrahl: Geschichte einer Jugend: Roman [The Lightbeam: A Story of a Youngster: Novel]*. Berlin: Deutsche Buch-Gemeinschaft, 1953. 279 pp. Novel.

1039   *Mein blaues Oktavheft: Gedichte [My Blue Octavo Notebook: Poems]*. Hamburg: Ernst Tessloff Verlag, 1954. 92 pp. Poems.

1040   *Nachtwachen des Tellerwäschers: Gedichte [Night Hours of a Dishwasher: Poems]*. Vienna: Verlag K. Desch [1957]. 99 pp. Poems.

1041   *Die Tränen eines Mannes: Erzählungen [A Man's Tears: Stories]*. Munich: Nymphenburger Verlagshandlung, 1958. 157 pp. 2nd edition published in 1966.

1042 *Über die Grenzen [Beyond the Borders]*, edited by Ivar Ljungerud. Malmö, Sweden: Gleerup Bokförlag, 1958. Stories and radioplays.

1043 *Die Familie Fritsche: Eine Erzählung für Kinder [The Fritsche Family: A Story for Children]*. Köln: H. Schaffstein, 1960. 71 pp. Children's story.

1044 *Die Stimme: Geschichte einer Liebe [The Voice: Story of a Love]*. Vienna: Verlag K. Desch, 1961. 109 pp. Novel.

1045 *Klopfzeichen: Gedichte [The Sound of Knocking: Poems]*. Hamburg: Ernst Tessloff Verlag, 1962. 84 pp. Poems.

1046 *Tagebuchblätter und drei Erzählungen [Pages of a Diary and Three Stories]*. Lübeck: Matthiesen, 1962. 31 pp. Stories.

1047 *Fremd in Toronto: Erzählung Prosastücke [As a Stranger in Toronto: Stories and Prose Selections]*. Hattingen, Germany: Hundt Verlag, 1963. 228 pp.

1048 *Der Weg zählt, nicht die Herberge: Prosa und Verse: 1928-1964 [The Road is Important, Not the Inn: Prose and Verse: 1928-1964]*, edited by Ernst Tessloff. Hamburg: Ernst Tessloff Verlag, 1964. 477 pp. Poems and stories.

1049 *Fragment vom Hahnenschrei: Gedichte [Fragment of a Rooster's Crow: Poems]*. Hamburg: Merlin Verlag, 1966. 118 pp. Poems.

1050 *Ein Jahr: Tagebuchblätter aus Kanada [A Year: Pages of a Diary from Canada]*. Hamburg: Merlin-Verlag [1967]. 248 pp. Stories.

1051 *The Price of Morning: Selected Poems.*, translated from the German, edited and with an introduction by Henry Beissel. Vancouver: Prism International in association with Morriss Print Co., 1968. 147 pp. Poems.

1052 *A Different Sun*, translated from the German by Henry Beissel. Ottawa: Oberon Press, 1976. 118 pp. Poems.

1053 *Blau und rot im Regenbogen: ein Liebesspiel [Blue and Red in the Rainbow: A Love Play]*. München: Münchener Laienspiel-Verlag [n.d.]. 53 pp. Play.

1054 *Die Erzählung des letzten Hirten: ein Weihnachtsspiel [The Story of the Last Shepherd: A Christmas Play]*. Weinheim: Deutscher Laienspiel-Verlag [n.d.]. 51 pp. (Münchener Laienspiele Heft 191) Play.

1055 *Testament: ein Stück, ein Requiem [Testament: A Play, a Requiem]*. Hamburg: Merlin Verlag [n.d.]. 45 pp. Play.

Writings about:

1056 Amprimoz, Alexandre. "Mostly a Migration of Metaphors." BRICK 2 (1978): 20-22.
[Review of *A Different Sun.*]

1057 Amprimoz, Alexandre. "Walter Bauer." Q & Q. 42, no. 8 (1976): 35-36.
[Review of *A Different Sun.*]

1058   Barbour, Douglas. "Poetry Chronicle IV." DAL REV 57 (1977): 368.
[Review of *A Different Sun.*]

1059   Beissel, Henry. "A Few Words of Farewell to a Friend." TAM REV 77-78 (1979): 5-13.

1060   Beissel, Henry. "Tribute to Walter Bauer." TAM REV 64 (November 1974): 5-8.

1061   Bickmore, G.L. "Walter Bauer." QUARRY 22, no.2 (1977): 64-66.

1062   Dabydeen, Cyril. "Will to Live." CAN LIT No. 75 (1977): 103-04.
[Review of *A Different Sun.*]

1063   Froeschle, Hartmut. "Eine hohe Ehrung für Walter Bauer: Zur Verleihung des Albert-Schweizer-Preises" [A High Honour for Walter Bauer: On the Granting of the Albert Schweizer Prize]. DER NORDWESTEN (April 12, 1956): 11.

1064   Froeschle, Hartmut. "Walter Bauer: Sein dichterisches Werk mit besonderer Berücksichtigung seines Kanada-Erlebnisses" [Walter Bauer: His Creative Work with Special Emphasis on His Experience in Canada]. DEUTSCHKAN JAHRB 5 (1979): 77-100.

1065   Hess, G.H.W. "Die Lyrik Walter Bauers" [The Lyric Poetry of Walter Bauer]. M.A. Thesis, University of Toronto, 1967.

1066   MacCallum, Hugh. "Poetry." UNIV TOR Q 38 (1968-69): 350.
[Review of *The Price of Morning.*]

1067   Maurer, Karl W. "A Particular Genius: Observations on Bauer and Translation." CONT VERSE II 2, no. 4 (1976): 34-35.
[Review of *A Different Sun.*]

1068   McNab, Ute. Review of *A Different Sun.* CAN BOOK REV ANN 1976: 132.

1069   Obst, Brigitte U. "Die Landschaft in Ausgewählten Werken Walter Bauers" [The Landscape in Selected Works by Walter Bauer]. M.A. Thesis, University of Victoria, 1984.

1070   Plesske, Hans-Martin. "Vortrag über Leben und Werk von Walter Bauer." DEUTSCHKAN JAHRB 9 (1986): 174-82.
[Compares the image of Canada found in selected works by Walter Bauer and Henry Beissel.]

1071   Review of *Nachtwachen des Tellerwäschers: Gedichte.* GERM CAN BUS REV 11 (Spring, 1958): 21-23. Signed: H. Sch.

1072   Riedel, Walter E. Review of *A Different Sun.* CRIT REV CAN LIT 4 (1977): 384-86.

1073   Stewart, Monica Renate. "Walter Bauer in Kanada: der Konflikt zwischen dort und hier im Leben und Werk des Dichters" [Walter Bauer in Canada: The Conflict between There and Here in the Life and Work of the Poet]. M.A. Thesis, Queen's University, 1981.

1074   Thorpe, Michael. "Lebensraum at Last." BKS CAN 5, no. 9 (1976): 34.
[Review of *A Different Sun.*]

1075   Vennewitz, Leila. "Everyman's Poems." CAN LIT No. 43 (1970): 94-95.
[Review of *The Price of Morning.*]

1076   Watt, F.W. "*A Different Sun:* Walter Bauer's Canadian Poetry." CAN FORUM 59 (September 1979): 20-24.

1077   Werneth, Josef. "Walter Bauer - Leben und Werk" [Walter Bauer - Life and Work]. In *Nordwesten Jahrbuch 1960* (Winnipeg: National Publishers Ltd. [n.d.]) p. 104.

BEISSEL, Henry (1929-   )

A poet, playwright, editor and translator. Born in Cologne, Germany. Professor of English literature at Concordia University in Montreal, and editor of *Edge* (1963-1970). His play, *Inook and the Sun*, was premiered at the Stratford Festival in 1973 and has been translated into many languages. Recipient of Epstein Award (1958), Davidson Award (1959), Canada Council Senior Arts Grant (1979).

1078   *The Curve.* 1963. Adaptation of a play by Tancred Dorst. Produced in Edmonton.

1079   *Witness the Heart.* Toronto: Willow Green Press, 1963. Poems.

1080   *New Wings for Icarus; A Poem in Four Parts*, illustrated by Norman Yates. Toronto: Coach House Press, 1966. 44 pp. Poems.
        [Limited edition of 500 copies.]

1081   *The World is a Rainbow*, music by W. Bottenberg. Toronto: Canadian Music Centre, 1969. Children's play.

1082   *Mister Skinflint: A Marionette Play.* Produced in Montreal, 1969, London, 1971. Play.

1083   *Face in the Dark; Poems.* Toronto: New Press, 1970. Poems.

1084   *A Trumpet for Nap*, adaptation of a play by Tancred Dorst. Toronto: Playwrights Co-op, 1973. Produced in London, 1970. Play.

1085   *Inook and the Sun.* Toronto: Playwrights Co-op, 1973. 35 leaves. 2nd ed.: Agincourt, Ont: Gage, 1980. 76 pp. Drama.

1086   *Quays of Sadness.* Montreal: Delta Press, 1973.

1087   *Trumpet for Nap* [Tancred Dorst], translated and adapted by Henry Beissel. Toronto: Playwrights Co-op, 1973. 51 leaves. Play.

1088   *The Salt I Taste: Poems.* Montreal: DC Books, 1975. 54 pp. Poems.

1089   *Grand Tirade at the Town Hall.* In *Three Plays* by Tancred Dorst. Toronto: Playwrights Co-op, 1976. Playscript.

1090   *For Crying out Loud.* Toronto: Gage Educational Publishing, 1977. Play.

1091   *Goya: A Play.* Toronto: Playwrights Co-op, 1978. 77 pp. Playscript.

1092   *Under Coyote's Eye: A Play about Ishi.* Dunvegan, Ont.: Quadrant Editions, 1980. 83 pp. Playscript.

1093   *Three Poems.* League of Canadian Poets, 1980. 1 unfolded sheet [8 pp].

1094   *Kanada, Romantik und Wirklichkeit* [Canada, Romanticism and Reality], text by Henry Beissel, photos by J.A. Kraulis. Innsbruck: Pinguin, c1981. 175 pp. illus., maps.

1095 *Cantos North*, with lithographs by Friedhelm Lach. Alexandria, Ont.: Ayorama Editions, 1981. Moonbeam, Ont.: Penumbra Press, c1982. Poems.

1096 *Hedda Gabler*. Toronto: Playwrights Canada, 1983. Play.
[A new rendering of the Ibsen play.]

1097 *Season of Blood: A Suite of Poems*. Oakville, Ont.: Mosaic Press, 1984. 45 pp. Poems.

1098 *Poems New and Selected*, edited by Gary Geddes. Oakville, Ont.: Mosaic Press, 1987. 140 pp. Poems.

Writings about:

1099 Amprimoz, Alexandre. Review of *The Salt I Taste*. CAN LIT No. 80 (1979): 72-74.

1100 Aubert, Rosemary. Review of *Cantos North*. Q & Q 48, no. 10 (1982): 33.

1101 Barbour, Douglas. Review of *New Wings for Icarus*. CAN FORUM 47 (January 1968): 239-40.

1102 Beissel, Henry. "Betting the Book Banners." Q & Q 46, no. 2 (1979): 6, 13.

1103 Cogswell, Fred. "Lensmen and Madmen." CAN LIT No. 50 (1971): 97-98.
[Review of *Face on the Dark*.]

1104 Gnarowski, Michael. "Beissel, Henry (Eric)." In *Contemporary Poets*, 2nd ed. (New York: St. Martin's Press, 1975) pp. 73-75.

1105 Harrison, Keith. "The Sense of the Word." CAN LIT No. 34 (1967): 78-79.
[Review of *New Wings for Icarus*.]

1106 MacCallum, Hugh. "Poetry." UNIV TOR Q 36 (1966-67): 368-69.
[Review of *New Wings for Icarus*.]

1107 McIlwraith, David. Review of *Inook and the Sun*. TAM REV 66 (1975): 104-05.

1108 Morton, Anne. Review of *Cantos North*. QUARRY 33, 3 (1984): 72-75.

1109 Oughton, John. "New Voices Old Ballads." BKS CAN 17, no. 2 (1988): 33-34.
[Review of *Poems New and Selected*.]

1110 Welch, Liliane. "The Canadian Song." FIDDLEHEAD 136 (1983): 91-94.
[Review of *Cantos North*.]

1111 Woodcock, George. "Heraclitean Knowledge." CAN LIT No. 97 (1983): 163-66.
[Review of *Cantos North*.]

DYCK, Arnold (1889-1970)
Born in Hochfeld, Ukraine, studied fine arts in Munich, Stuttgart, and St. Petersburg (now Leningrad). He came to Canada in 1923 and became editor of the *Steinbach Post*. He also edited *Die Mennonitische Warte* (1935-1944).

1112 *Verloren in der Steppe [Lost in the Steppe].* Parts 1, 2 and 3. Steinbach, Man.: The Author, 1944-1946. 127 pp., 122 pp. and 119 pp. respectively. Parts 4 and 5 published in North Kildonan, Man.: The Author, 1947-1948. 99 pp. and 103 pp. Novel.

1113 *Dee Fria: Plattdeutsches Lustspiel in einem Aufzug [The Suitor: Low German Comedy in One Act].* Steinbach, Man.: The Author, 1947. 2nd edition: North Kildonan, Man.: The Author, 1948. 70 pp. Play.

1114 *Koop enn Bua faore nao Toronto [Koop and Bua Travel to Toronto].* Parts 1 and 2. North Kildonan, Man.: The Author, 1948-1949. 99 pp. and 102 pp. respectively. Story.

1115 *Meine Deutschlandfahrt [My Trip to Germany].* North Kildonan, Man.: The Author, 1950. 143 pp. Travel.

1116 *"Wellkaom op'e Forstei": Szenen aus dem mennonitischen Forsteileben in Russland in plattdeutscher Sprache ["Welcome to the Forestry Service !": Scenes from the Mennonite Forestry Service in Russia in the Low German Language].* North Kildonan, Man.: The Author, 1950. 66pp. Play.

1117 *De Opnaom: 2 Akt von Wellkaom op'e Forstei: Szenen aus dem mennonitischen Forsteileben in Russland in plattdeutscher Sprache [The Reception: 2nd Act of Welcome to the Forestry Service: Mennonite Life Scenes from Russia's Forestry Service in the Low German Language].* Steinbach, Man.: The Author, 1951. 60 pp. Play.

1118 *Onse lied en ola Tiet: Waut tôm Vaalase - Waut tômVäastalle [Our Song in Olden Days: Something to Read - Something to Present].* Steinbach, Man.: The Author, 1952. 62 pp. Stories and plays.

1119 *Koop enn Bua op Reise [Koop and Bua on the Journey].* Parts 1 and 2. Steinbach, Man.: Derksen Printers Ltd., 1954. 100 pp. and 104 pp. respectively. Story.

1120 *Koop enn Bua en Dietschlaund [Koop and Bua in Germany].* Steinbach, Man.: Derksen Printers Ltd., 1960. 86 pp. Story.

1121 *Dee Millionäa von Kosefeld [The Millionaire from Kosefeld].* Steinbach, Man.: The Author, [n.d.]. 94 pp. Short Stories.

Writings about:

1122 "Arnold Dyck in Brief." MENN LIFE 24 (April 1971): 69

1123 "Arnold Dyck Publications." MENN LIFE 14 (April 1959): 95.

1124 Cornies, Martha. "Ein Arnold-Dyck-Abend" [An Evening for Arnold Dyck]. DER BOTE (Dec. 29, 1970): 6.

1125 Dyck, Henry D. Review of *Verloren in der Steppe.* CAN ETH STUD 2, no. 2 (1970): 161-68.

1126 Hadley, Michael L. "Arnold Dyck's *Verloren in der Steppe,* a Mennonite 'Bildungsroman'." CAN ETH STUD 1 (December 1969): 21-33.

1127 Hadley, Michael L. "Education and Alienation in Dyck's *Verloren in der Steppe:* A Novel of Cultural Crisis." DEUTSCHKAN JAHRB 3 (1976): 199-206.

1128 Kauenhoven, Kurt. "Arnold Dyck, ein Blick auf sein Schaffen" [Arnold Dyck, A Glance at His Work]. MENN LIFE (August 18, 1970): 3, 5.

1129 Klassen, N.J. "Arnold Dyck - An Appreciation." MENN LIFE 26 (April 1971): 59.

1130 Klassen, N.J. "Seine Lebensarbeit galt seinen Mennoniten" [His Life's Work was Devoted to His Mennonites]. DER BOTE (September 1, 1970): 5.

1131 Klassen, P. J. Review of *Dee Millionäa von Kosefeld*. MENN LIFE 2 (January 1947): 47.

1132 Kliewer, Warren. "Arnold Dyck as a Literary Artist." MENN LIFE 14 (April 1959): 85-87.

1133 Kliewer, Warren. Review of *Koop enn Bua en Dietschlaund*. MENN LIFE 15 (July 1960): 140.

1134 Knoop, Hedwig. "Arnold Dyck - At the End of the Road." MENN LIFE 26 (April 1971): 56-58.

1135 Krahn, Cornelius. "Recent Low-German Literature." Review of *Dee Fria: Plattdeutsches Lustspiel in einem Aufzug, "Wellkaom op'e Forstei": Szenen aus dem mennonitischen Forsteileben in Russland in plattdeutscher Sprache, De Opnaom: 2 Akt von Wellkaom op'e Forstei: Szenen aus dem mennonitischen Forsteileben in Russland in plattdeutscher Sprache*, and *Onse Lied en ola Tiet: Waut tôm Vaalase-Waut tôm Väastalle*. MENN LIFE 9 (January 1954): 46.

1136 Lohrenz, Gerhard. "Arnold Dyck Novel Now in English Translation." MENN REP 4, no. 24 (November 25, 1974): 17.
[Review of *Lost in the Steppe*, English version of *Verloren in der Steppe*.]

1137 Peters, Elisabeth. "Arnold Dyck - Our Last Visit." MENN LIFE 26 (April 1971): 54-59.

1138 Peters, Elisabeth. "Gedanken zum Tode Arnold Dycks" [Thoughts on the Death of Arnold Dyck]. DER BOTE (August 4, 1970): 1-2.

1139 Peters, Elisabeth. "Der Mennonitendichter Arnold Dyck in seinen Werken" [The Mennonite Poet Arnold Dyck in His Works]. M.A. Thesis, The University of Manitoba, 1968.

1140 Peters, Elisabeth. "The Popularity of Dyck's Writings." MENN LIFE 14 (April 1959): 87-88.

1141 Peters, Elisabeth. "A Tribute to Arnold Dyck." MENN LIFE 24 (January 1969): 3-5.

1142 Peters, Elisabeth. "With 'Koop enn Bua' on a Journey." MENN LIFE 14 (April 1959): 88.

1143 Reimer, Al. "The Creation of Arnold Dyck's 'Koop enn Bua' Characters." In *Mennonite Images: Historical, Cultural, and Literary Essays Dealing with Mennonite Issues*, edited by Harry Loewen. (Winnipeg: Hyperion Press, 1980)

1144 Reimer, Al. "Innocents Abroad: The Comic Odyssey of 'Koop Enn Bua op Reise'." J MENN STUD 4 (1986): 31-45.

1145 Schmiedehaus, Walter. "Der Schriftsteller Arnold Dyck" [The Author Arnold Dyck]. MENN WELT 5, no. 1 (1952): 8.

1146 Suderman, Elmer F. "Arnold Dyck Explains the Origin of Low German." MENN LIFE 24 (January 1969): 5-7.

1147   Suderman, Elmer F. "The Comic Spirit of Arnold Dyck." MENN LIFE 24 (October 1969): 169-70.

1148   Thiessen, Jack. "Arnold Dyck - the Mennonite Artist." MENN LIFE 24 (April 1969): 77-83.

1149   Wiens, Gerhard. "Arnold Dyck at Seventy." MENN LIFE 14 (April 1959): 80-84.

ENS, Gerhard (1922 -)

Born in Gnadenthal, Ukraine, emigrated to Canada in 1923. Attended the University of Manitoba, also studied at the Mennonite Biblical Seminary in Elkhart, Ind. In 1977 he became editor of *Der Bote*. Co-editor of *Harvest*, an anthology, and conducted a half-hour Low-German program on CFAM radio in Manitoba.

1150   *Dee easchte Wiehnachten enn Kanada: 1875, 1926, 1949: Drei Kurzerzählungen aus der Mennonitengeschichte [Our First Christmas in Canada: 1875, 1926, 1949: Three Short Stories from the History of the Mennonites].* [Gretna, Man.: The Author, 1974]. 32 pp.
[In Low German. Mimeographed.]

1151   *Dee Kjoaschenhatj.* A play staged in Gretna, Man.

Writing about:

1152   Dyck, Gerhard. Review of *Dee easchte Wiehnachten enn Kanada ....* CAN ETH STUD 9, no. 1 (1977): 138-39.

EPP, Peter Sr.

1153   *Gelegenheitsgedichte [Occasional Poems].* Altona, Man.: The Author, 1932.

EPP, Reuben (1922 -)

Born in Langham, Sask. Interested in English, German and Low German literature. He teaches at Northern Lights College, Dawson Creek, B.C.

1154   *Plautdietsche Schreftsteckja: Jedichta: Jeschichte: Leeda: Spelkjes/ Low-German Writings: Poems: Stories: Lyrics: Skits.* [Steinbach, Man.: Derksen Printers, 1972]. 116 pp. Poems.

Writings about:

1155   Harms, Alvin. Review of *Plautdietsche Schreftsteckja.....* CAN ETH STUD 4, no. 1-2 (1972): 67-68.

1156   "Neues plattdeutsches Buch veröffentlicht" [Publication of a New Low-German Book]. DER BOTE (June 13, 1972): 12.
[Review of *Plautdietsche Schreftsteckja.....*]

FAST, Karl (1921 -)

Born in Klubnikowo, Russia and graduated from a teachers' college there. Migrated to Germany in 1944 and from there to Canada in 1949. He worked as a printer, and was a teacher from 1972 to his retirement..

1157   *Gebt der Wahrheit die Ehre [Honour the Truth].* North Kildonan, Man., 1950-1952. 3 Vols.
Novel.
[Translated into English and published in *The Canadian Mennonite*.]

FILIP, Raymond (1950 -)

Born in Lübeck, Germany. He became a Canadian citizen in 1965. Educated at McGill University. Lives in Montreal and runs the multicultural reading series Pluriel.

1158   *Jaws in a Fishbowl: Olympic Fiction Games.* [N.p.: Ecowy Press, 1976] 82 pp. Poems and a play.

1159   *Somebody Told Me I Look Like Everyman.* Vancouver: Pulp Press, 1978. 61 pp. Poems.

1160   *St. Gabriel Farm.* Montreal: The Word Bookstore, 1979. Poems.

1161   *Hope's Half-Life: Nuclear Poems.* Montreal: Véhicule Press, 1983. 62 pp. Poems.

1162   *A Telling Silence.* Montreal: Guernice Press, 1986. Short stories.

1163   *Playing the Poet.* (casette), 1987. Play.

FRANKE, Wolfgang E. (1915-   )
Born in Horstmar, Germany, came to Canada in 1951. Received a B.A. from the University of Toronto and an M.Sc. from the University of Ottawa.

1164   *Goldenrod.* Toronto: Trans-Canada, 1983. 263 pp. Novel.

1165   *The Baltimore Connection.* Toronto: Williams-Wallace, 1984. 165 pp. Novel.

FRIESEN, Abraham Johann (1919 -   )
Born in Schönfeld, Ukraine, immigrated to Canada in 1926. He studied German, English, and American literature in Goettingen and Mainz (Dr. Phil.). At present, he is professor of German at the University of New Brunswick.

1166   *Prost Mahlzeit! [To Your Health!].* Grünthal, Man.: The Author, 1949. 89 pp. Short story.

1167   *Gott grüsse dich! [May the Lord Be With You!].* Grünthal, Man.: The Author, 1952. 67 pp. Play.

Writing about:

1168   Krahn, Cornelius. "A New Mennonite Writer." MENN LIFE 8 (October 1953): 190.

FRIESEN, Gerhard, pseud. (Real name: SENN, Fritz) (1894 - 1983)
Born in Halbstadt, Ukraine. Emigrated to Canada in 1924, where he became a farmer. He moved to Germany and lived there until his death.

1169   *Das Dorf im Abendgrauen. Gedichte von Fritz Senn,* zusammengestellt und bearbeitet von Elisabeth Peters [*The Village in the Dusk. Poems by Fritz Senn,* arranged and edited by Elisabeth Peters]. Winnipeg: Verein zur Pflege der deutschen Sprache, 1974. 98 pp.
[Includes 79 poems.]

Writings about:

1170   Doerksen, Victor G.   "The Divine Plowman and the Mennonite Clod: A Reading of Hinterm Pflug/Stimmungen by Fritz Senn." In *Annalen 4: German Canadian Studies in the Eighties* (Vancouver: CAUTG, 1983) pp. 208-29.

1171   Dueck, G.G. "Fritz Senn" [Fritz Senn]. DER BOTE (Sept. 18, 1973): 5-6.

1172   Harms, Alvin. Review of *Das Dorf im Abendgrauen.* CAN ETH STUD 10, no. 1 (1978): 175-77.

1173   Peters, Viktor. "Der mennonitische Dichter Fritz Senn" [The Mennonite Poet Fritz Senn]. MENN WELT 3 (September 1950): 2.

1174   Thiessen, Jack. Review of *Das Dorf im Abendgrauen.* MENN MIRR 5, no. 1 (October 1975)

FRIESEN, H.D.

1175   *Gedichte verschiedenen Inhalts [Poems on Various Themes].* Coaldale, Alta.: The Author, 1947. 16 pp. Poems.

1176   *Gedichti "Ut de Depresschen Tit": Muttagedichti on aundri [Poems "from the Depression Time": Mother Tongue Poems and others].* Coaldale, Alta.: The Author, 1953. 16 pp. Poems.

FRIESEN, Isaac P. (1873-1952)
Born in Ukraine. He came to North America with his parents in 1875. Settled in Rosthern, Sask. in 1952. His poems have appeared in Mennonite newspapers.

1177   *Im Dienste des Meisters [In the Service of the Master].* 1930. 2 v. Vol. 1: Konstanz: Buch und Kunstverlag Carl Hirsch. 144 pp. Vol. 2: Christliche Verlagsanstalt. 184 pp.

Writing about:

1178   Rempel, J.G. "Isaac P. Friesen." In *The Mennonite Encyclopedia.* 1956. Vol. 2, p. 405.

FRISCH, Anton (1921-   )

1179   *Though I Speak Poems.* Montreal: Ivy Publishing Company, 1949. 31 pp. Poems.

1180   *The House. New Poems in English, French, German.* Hull, Qué.: Ivy Publishing Company, 1950. 32 pp. Poems.

1181   *Third Poems.* Hull, Qué.: Ivy Publishing Company, 1951. 28 pp. Poems.

1182   *Steine aus Kanada; deutsche Gedichte [Stones from Canada: German Poems].* Wien: Verlag Kuno Hoynig, 1952. 47 pp. Poems.

1183   *Poems.* Toronto: Ryerson Press, 1954. [2], 22 pp. (Ryerson Poetry Chap Books, 1954) Poems.

FRÖHLICH, Christine (1930-   )
Born von Bergen in Hamburg, attended high school in Germany. In 1953 she came to Toronto, and has lived there since. Some of her plays were published by the German-Canadian Historical Association.

1184   *Rotkäppchen [Little Red Riding Hood]. Es begab sich aber zu der Zeit... [In Those Days a Decree Went out...].* Toronto: German-Canadian Historical Association, 1978. Two plays.

1185   *Zwei weihnachtliche Spiele für Schulbühnen [Two Christmas Plays for School Stages].* Toronto: German-Canadian Historical Association, 1978. 29 pp., 24 pp. (Deutschkanadische Schriften A. Belletristik. Band 2)

FUNCKEN, Eugen   (1831-1888)

1186   *Gedichte [Poems].* New York: Druck und Commissions-Verlag von Gebr. Karl und Nickolaus Benzinger, 1868. Poems.

1187   *Bernard von Menthon [Bernard von Menthon].* [N.p., n.p.] 1870. Play.

Writing about:

1188   Erb, Peter. "The Canadian Poems of Eugen Funcken, C.R." DEUTSCHKAN JAHRB 4 (1978): 225-31.

GOERZEN, Jacob Warkentin (1916)

1189   *Germanischet Oafgoot - Germanisches Erbe: Germanic Heritage: English: Low German: German: Canadian Lyrics in Three Languages.* 2nd ed. Edmonton: The Author, 1967. 336 pp. Poems and prose.

Writing about:

1190   Cardinal, Clive H. Review of *Germanischet Oagfoot....* CAN ETH STUD 1 (December 1969): 124-25.

GÖRZ, Heinrich (1890-1972)

Born in Schönsee, Ukraine. Emigrated to Canada in 1926. He was a teacher and preacher. Published several historical monographs.

1191   *Gedichte [Poems].* North Kildonan, Man., 1944. Poems.

GROVE, Frederick Philip (1871-1948)

Born Felix Paul Greve in Radomno, Prussia, and grew up in Hamburg. Educated there, also at Bonn and Munich. He went to the U.S.A. in 1909, then moved to Canada and became a schoolteacher in Manitoba. In 1923 Grove retired to devote himself to writing. His first book in English, *Over Prairie Trails*, was published in 1922.

1192   *Settlers of the Marsh.* New York: Doran, 1925. 341 pp. Also Toronto: McClelland & Stewart, 1965. 222 pp. (New Canadian Library No. 50) Novel.

1193   *A Search for America.* Ottawa: Graphic Press, 1927. 448 pp. Also Toronto: McClelland & Stewart, 1975. 392 pp. (New Canadian Library No. 76) Novel.

1194   *The Yoke of Life.* New York: Smith, 1930. 355 pp. Novel.

1195   *Fruits of the Earth.* Toronto: Dent, 1933. 335 pp. Also Toronto: McClelland & Stewart, 1965. 267 pp. (New Canadian Library No. 49) Novel.

1196   *Two Generations. A Story of Present Day Ontario.* Author's limited edition. Also Toronto: Ryerson Press, 1939. 261 pp. Novel.

1197   *The Master of the Mill.* Author's limited edition, 1944. 393 pp. Also Toronto: Macmillan, 1944. 393 pp., and, with an introduction by R.E. Watters, McClelland & Stewart, 1967. 335 pp. (New Canadian Library No. 19) Novel.

1198   *Tales from the Margin: The Selected Short Stories of Frederick Philip Grove,* edited by Desmond Pacey. Toronto: Ryerson Press, 1971. x, 319 pp. Short stories.

1199 *Our Daily Bread: A Novel.* New York: Macmillan, 1928. 390 pp. Also Toronto: McClelland & Stewart, 1975. 390 pp. Novel.

1200 *The Master of the Mason's House.*, translation from German. Ottawa: Oberon Press, 1976. 243 pp. Novel.

1201 *Consider Her Ways.* Toronto: Macmillan, 1947. 298 pp. Also Toronto: McClelland & Stewart, 1977. (NCL No. 132) Novel.

1202 *Fanny Essler,* translated from the German by Christine Helmers, A.W. Riley, and Douglas O. Spettigue. Edited and introduced by A.W. Riley and Douglas O. Spettigue. Toronto: Oberon Press, 1984. 2 v. Novel.

Writings about:

Monographs, Bibliographies

1203 Hjartarson, Paul, ed.
Stranger to My Time: Essays by and about Frederick Philip Grove. Edmonton: NewWest Press, 1986. 356 pp.
[Includes twenty-six papers by and about F.P. Grove. A selected bibliography is also provided.]

1204 Miska, John
Frederick Philip Grove: A Bibliography of Primary and Secondary Material. Ottawa: Microform Biblios, 1984. 32 pp. (CANLIT Bibliographic Series No. 3)
[Includes primary publications, writings about Grove, and archival material on the author held by the University of Manitoba Libraries.]

1205 Pacey, Desmond, ed.
Frederick Philip Grove. Toronto: Ryerson Press, 1945. 150 pp. (Critical Reviews on Canadian Writers No. 5)

1206 Spettigue, Douglas Odell
F.P.G.: The European Years. Ottawa: Oberon Press, 1973. 254 pp.

1207 Spettigue, Douglas Odell
Frederick Philip Grove. Toronto: Copp Clark, 1969. viii, 175 pp. (Studies in Canadian Literature No. 3)

1208 Stobie, M.R.
Frederick Philip Grove. New York: Twayne, 1973. 206 pp. (Twayne's World Author Series, 246)

1209 Sutherland, Ronald
Frederick Philip Grove. Toronto: McClelland & Stewart, 1969. 64 pp. (Canadian Writers No. 4)

Research Papers, Theses, Review Articles

1210 Arthur, Constance J. "Frederick Philip Grove as a Naturalist Novelist." Ph.D. Thesis. Fredericton: University of New Brunswick, 1968.

1211 Arthur, Constance J. "Naturalism in the Novels of Frederick Philip Grove." M.A. Thesis. Fredericton: University of New Brunswick,

1212 Ayre, Robert. "Canadian Writers of Today: Frederick Philip Grove." CAN FORUM 12 (1932): 255-57.

1213 Ayre, Robert. "Frederick Philip Grove." In *Frederick Philip Grove*, edited by Desmond Pacey. (Toronto: Ryerson Press, 1970) pp. 17-24.

1214 Bailey, N.I. "F.P.G. and the Empty House." CAN FIC MAG No. 31-32 (1981): 177-93.

1215 Bie, O. "Die Ästhetik der Lüge" [The Aesthetics of Lying]. N DEUT RUND 14 (1903): 670-72.

1216 Bierbaum, Otto J. Review of *Wanderungen*, a novel written by Grove under the name Felix Paul Greve, 1902. INSEL 3 (1901-1902): 195-96.

1217 Birbalsingh, Frank. "Grove and Existentialism." CAN LIT No. 43 (1970): 67-76.
Reprinted in *Writers of the Prairies*, edited by Donald G. Stephens. (Vancouver: University of British Columbia Press, 1973) pp. 57-66.

1218 Böckel, Fritz. Review of *Maurermeister Ihles Haus.* LIT ECHO 10 (1907-1908): 210.

1219 Braun, Albert. "Frederick Philip Grove and Catherine Wiens: Cosmopolitan Author and Mennonite Schoolmarm." A research paper presented to the Department of Bible, Bethel College, Kansas, 1957.

1220 Brown, E.K. "The Causerie." WINN FREE PRESS (Aug. 28, 1948)

1221 Brown, E.K. "The Immediate Present in Canadian Literature." SEWANEE REV 41 (1930): 430-32.

1222 Brümmer, Franz, comp. [F.P. Greve.] In *Lexikon der deutschen Dichter und Prosaisten von Beginn des 19. Jahrhunderts bis zur Gegenwart.* (Leipzig: Reclam, 1910) pp. 11, 439.

1223 CBC Symposium. "In Search of Frederick Philip Grove." 1962.

1224 Chamberlain. Review of *A Search for America.* N Y TIMES (Dec. 30, 1928): 8.

1225 Clarke, G.H. "A Canadian Novelist and His Critics." QUEEN'S Q 53 (1945): 254-55.

1226 Collin, W.E. "La tragique ironie de Frederick Philip Grove." GÉANTS DU CIEL 4 (Winter 1946): 15-40.

1227 Collins, A. "Audience in Mind When I Speak: Grove's *In Search of Myself.*" STUD CAN LIT 8, no. 2 (1983): 181-93.

1228 Craig, Terrence. "F.P. Grove and the 'Alien' Immigrant in the West." J CAN STUD 20, no. 2 (1985): 92-100.

1229 Craig, Terrence. "Frederick Philip Grove und der 'fremde' Einwanderer im kanadischen Westen." DEUTSCHKAN JAHRB 9 (1986): 141-51.

1230 Daniells, Roy. "Landscape with Figures." CAN LIT No. 51 (1972): 84-87.
[Review of *Tales from the Margin.*]

1231 Dewar, Kenneth C. "Technology and the Pastoral Ideal in Frederick Philip Grove." J CAN STUD 8 (February 1973): 19-28.

1232 Dudek, Louis. "The Literary Significance of Grove's Search." Address delivered to the Grove Symposium, Ottawa, May 6, 1973.

1233 Dunphy, John W. "The Craftsmanship of Grove's Novels." M.A. Thesis. Halifax: Dalhousie University, 1968.

1234 Dyck, Henry. "Frederick Philip Grove: His Life, His Writing, and His Place in Canadian Literature." M.A. Thesis. Minneapolis: University of Minnesota, 1955.

1235 Eaton, Charles Ernest. "The Life and Works of Frederick Philip Grove." M.A. Thesis. Wolfville: Acadia University, 1940.

1236 Eggleston, Wilfrid. "Frederick Philip Grove." In *Our Living Tradition*. 1st Ser., edited by C.T. Bissell. (Toronto: University of Toronto Press, 1957) pp. 105-27. Reprinted in *Frederick Philip Grove*, edited by Desmond Pacey. (Toronto: Ryerson Press, 1970) pp. 77-88.

1237 Eggleston, Wilfrid. "F.P. Grove's Origins Finally Disclosed." OTTAWA J (May 27, 1972): 23.

1238 Ettlinger, J. "Der Fall Hofmannswaldau" [The Hofmanswaldau Case]. LIT ECHO 10 (1907-1908): 19-23.

1239 Fairley, Barker. "Philip Grove." CAN FORUM 19 (October 1939): 225.
[Review of *Two Generations*.]

1240 Fee, Margery. "The Wild Side." CAN LIT No. 105 (1985): 161-63.
[Review of F.P. Greve: *Oscar Wilde*.]

1241 Ferguson, Mildred. "A Study of the Tragic Element in the Novels of Frederick Philip Grove." M.A. Thesis. Winnipeg: University of Manitoba, 1947.

1242 Fränchel, L. "Stoffgeschichte." JAHRESB NEUE DEUT LIT 21 (1908): 935.

1243 "Frederick Philip Grove." In *Literary History of Canada: Canadian Literature in English*, edited by Carl F. Klinck and others. (Toronto: University of Toronto Press, 1965) pp. 370, 471, 472, 621, 623, 679-83.

1244 "Frederick Philip Grove." In *Notes on the Canadian Family Tree*. (Ottawa: Citizenship Branch, 1960) p. 124.

1245 French, William. "Grove Exposed." GLOBE MAIL (Apr. 18, 1972): 16.

1246 George, Stefan. "Frederick Philip Grove." In *Stefan George - Friderich Gundolf: Briefwechsel*, edited by Robert Boehringer and Peter Laudmann. (Munich: Helmut Küpper, 1962) pp. 115, 120.

1247 Gide, André. "Conversation avec un Allemand." Dans *Oeuvres complétes d'André Gide*. Éditions augmentées de textes inédits établie par L. Martin Chauffer. Paris: NOUV REV FRANÇ (1935): 133-43.

1248 Gide, André. "Frederick Philip Grove." In *The Journals of André Gide*. Vol. 1 (1889-1913), translated from the French, with an introduction and notes, by Justin O'Brien. (New York: Knopf, 1947) pp. 136, 150, 156, 206; Vol. 2 and 3 (1924-49) p. 214.

1249 Giltrow, J. "Grove in Search of an Audience." CAN LIT No. 90 (1981): 92-107.

1250   Grant, Gwendolen Margaret. "Frederick Philip Grove: Birth of the Canadian Novel." M.A. Thesis. Halifax: Dalhousie University, 1946.

1251   Grove, Frederick Philip. "Apologia pro Vita et Opera Sua." CAN FORUM 11 (1931): 420-22.

1252   Grove, Frederick Philip. "Grove's Letters from the Mennonite Reserve." CAN LIT No. 69 (1974): 67-80. (Introduced by Margaret Stobie.)

1253   Grove, Frederick Philip. "In Search of Myself." UNIV TOR Q 10 (1940): 60-67. Reprinted in *Masks of Fiction*, edited by A.J.M. Smith. (Toronto: McClelland & Stewart, 1961) pp. 14-22.

1254   Healy, J.J. "Grove and the Matter of Germany. The Warkentin Letters and the Art of Liminal Disengagement." STUD CAN LIT 6, no. 2 (1981): 170-81.

1255   Heidenreich, Rosmarin. "The Search for FPG." CAN LIT No. 80 (1979): 63-70.

1256   Hjartarson, P. "Design and Truth in Grove's 'In Search of Myself'." CAN LIT No. 90 (1981): 73-90.

1257   Holliday, W.B. "Frederick Philip Grove: An Impression." CAN LIT No. 3 (1960): 17-22.

1258   Keith, W.J. "The Art of Frederick Philip Grove: *The Settlers of the Marsh* as an Example." J CAN STUD 9 (August 1974): 26-36.

1259   Keith, W.J. "F.P. Gove's 'Difficult' Novel: *The Master of the Mill*." ARIEL 4, no. 2 (1973): 34-48.

1260   Keith, W.J. "Grove's 'Magnificent Failure': *The Yoke of Life* Reconsidered." CAN LIT No. 89 (1981): 104-17.

1261   Keith, W.J. "Grove's *Over Prairie Trails*: A Re-examination." LIT HALF-YEARLY 13, no. 2 (1972): 76-85.

1262   Keith, W.J. "Grove's Search for America." CAN LIT No. 59 (1974): 57-66.

1263   Knister, Raymond. "Frederick Philip Grove." ONT LIB REV 13 (November 1928): 60-62.

1264   Kroetsch, Robert. "Grammar of Silence: Narrative Pattern in Ethnic Writing." CAN LIT No. 106 (1985): 65-74.

1265   La Bossièr, C.R. "Of Words and Understanding in Grove's *Settlers of the Marsh*." UNIV TOR Q 54 (1984-85): 148-62.

1266   MacDonald, R.D. "Grove's *The Master of the Mill*." MOSAIC 7 (1974): 89-100.

1267   Makow, Henry. "'Ellen Lindstedt': The Underpublished Sequel to Grove's *Settlers of the March* [sic]." STUD CAN LIT 8, no. 2 (1983): 270-76.

1268   Makow, Henry. "Grove's 'The Canyon'." CAN LIT No. 82 (1979): 141-48.

1269   Makow, Henry. "Grove's Treatment of Sex: Platonic Love in *The Yoke of Life*." DAL REV 58 (1978): 528-40.

1270 Makow, Henry. "Letters from Eden: Grove's Creative Rebirth, edited by Henry Makow." UNIV TOR Q 49 (1979-80): 48-64.

1271 Markin, Allan. Review of *Consider Her Ways*. CAN BOOK REV ANN 1977: 96.

1272 Mathews, R. "F.P. Grove: An Important Version of *The Master of the Mill* Discovered." STUD CAN LIT 7, no. 2 (1981): 187-91.

1273 McCourt, Robert. "Recent Paperbacks." TAM REV No. 6 (1958): 97-101.

1274 McCourt, Robert. "Spokesman of a Race?" In *The Canadian West in Fiction*. (Toronto: Ryerson Press, 1949) pp. 55-70. Reprinted in *Frederick Philip Grove*, edited by Desmond Pacey. (Toronto: Ryerson Press, 1970) pp. 59-73.

1275 McGillivray, J.R. "F.P. Grove." UNIV TOR Q 9 (1940): 291-92.

1276 McLeod, G. Duncan. "The Primeval Elements in the Prairie Novels of Frederick Philip Grove." M.A. Thesis. Winnipeg: The University of Manitoba, 1966.

1277 McMullen, Lorraine. "Women in Grove." Address delivered to the Grove Symposium, Ottawa, May 6, 1973.

1278 McMullin, Stanley Edward. "Evolution vs. Revolution." Address delivered to the Grove Symposium, Ottawa, May 6, 1973.

1279 McMullin, Stanley Edward. "Grove and the Promised Land." CAN LIT No. 49 (1971): 10-19.

1280 McMullin, Stanley Edward. "Grove in Canada." CAN LIT No. 60 (1974): 107-09.

1281 McMullin, Stanley Edward. "Introduction." In *A Search for America*. (Toronto: McClelland & Stewart, 1975) pp. ix-xv.

1282 McMullin, Stanley Edward. "The Promised Land Motif in the Works of Frederick Philip Grove." M.A. Thesis. Ottawa: Carleton University, 1968.

1283 Michael, Friedrich. "Verschollene der frühen Insel" [The Lost Ones of the Early Island]. BÖRSENBLATT DEUTSCH BHD 28, no. 17 (1972): A79-A82.

1284 Middleboro', T. "Animals, Darwin, and Science Fiction: Some Thoughts on Grove's *Consider Her Ways*." CAN FIC MAG No. 7 (1972): 55-57.

1285 Middleton, J.E. "In Search of Myself." SAT N 61 (Oct. 19, 1946): 24.
[Review of *In Search of Myself*.]

1286 Middleton, J.E. "The Machine as a Frankenstein." SAT N 60 (Jan. 20, 1945): 19.
[Review of *The Master of the Mill*.]

1287 Milne, W.S. "Fictional Findings." SAT N 54 (Aug. 5, 1939): 9.
[Review of *Two Generations*.]

1288 Mitchell, Beverley. "The 'Message' and the 'Inevitable Form' in *The Master of the Mill*." J CAN FIC 3, no. 3 (1974): 74-79.

1289   Moss, John. "Frederick Philip Grove." In his *Patterns of Isolation in English Canadian Fiction*. (Toronto: McClelland & Stewart, 1974) pp. 199-209.

1290   Myles, Eugene Louise. "The Self as Theme in Grove's Novels." M.A. Thesis. Edmonton: University of Alberta, 1965.

1291   Nesbitt, Bruce H. "Grove's Poetry." Address delivered to the Grove Symposium, Ottawa, May 6, 1973.

1292   Nesbitt, Bruce H. "The Seasons: Grove's Unfinished Novel." CAN LIT No. 18 (1963): 47-51.

1293   Noel-Bentley, Peter. "The Position of the Unpublished 'Jane Atkinson' and 'The Weatherhead Fortunes', and Grove's 'Prairie Series'." Address delivered to the Grove Symposium, Ottawa, May 5, 1973.

1294   Pacey, Desmond. "Excerpts from 'Selected Reviews'." In *Frederick Philip Grove*, edited by Desmond Pacey. (Toronto: Ryerson Press, 1970) pp. 97-184.

1295   Pacey, Desmond. "Frederick Philip Grove." In *Literary History of Canada: Canadian Literature in English*, edited by Carl F. Klinck and others. (Toronto: University of Toronto Press, 1965) pp. 679-83.

1296   Pacey, Desmond. "Frederick Philip Grove." MAN ARTS REV 3, no. 3 (1943): 28-41.

1297   Pacey, Desmond. "Frederick Philip Grove: A Group of Letters." CAN LIT No. 11 (1962): 28-38.

1298   Pacey, Desmond. "Grove's Tragic Vision." In his *Frederick Philip Grove*. (Toronto: Ryerson Press, 1944) pp. 123-34. Reprinted in *Frederick Philip Grove*, edited by Desmond Pacey. (Toronto: Ryerson Press, 1970) pp. 45-55.

1299   Pacey, Desmond. "In Search of Grove in Sweden: A Progress Report." J CAN FIC 1, no. 1 (1972): 69-73.

1300   Pacey, Desmond. "On Editing the Grove Letters." Address delivered to the University of Toronto, November 1972.

1301   Pacey, Desmond. Review of *Consider Her Ways*. CAN FORUM 26 (1947): 283-84.

1302   Pache, Walter. "Dilettante in Exile: Grove at the Centenary of His Birth." CAN LIT No. 90 (1981): 187-91.

1303   Pache, Walter. "Der Fall Grove - Vorleben und Nachleben des Schriftstellers Felix Paul Greve" [The Grove Case - The Beforelife and the Afterlife of the Author Felix Paul Greve]. In German-Canadian Yearbook 5 (Toronto: Historical Society of Mecklenburg Upper Canada Inc., 1979) pp. 121-36.

1304   Pache, Walter. "Frederick Philip Grove's Loneliness - Comparative Perspectives." ANNALEN 4: German-Canadian Studies in the Eighties. (Vancouver: CAUTG, 1983) pp. 185-219.

1305   Parks, M.G. "Introduction." In *Fruits of the Earth*. (Toronto: McClelland & Stewart, 1965) pp. vii-xiii.

1306   Pearce, W.G. "Grove Remembered." WINN FREE PRESS (Sept. 26, 1962)

1307   Perry, Anne Anderson. "Who's Who in Canadian Literature: Frederick Philip Grove." CAN AUTH BKMN 12 (March 1930): 51-53.

1308   Peters, Victor. "Frederick Philip Grove." MAN SCHOOL J (October 1946)

1309   Phelps, Arthur Leonard. "Frederick Philip Grove." In his *Canadian Writers*. (Toronto: McClelland & Stewart, 1951) pp. 36-42. Reprinted in *Frederick Philip Grove*, edited by Desmond Pacey. (Toronto: Ryerson Press, 1970) pp. 74-77.

1310   Pierce, Lorne A. "Frederick Philip Grove." In his *Outline of Canadian Literature*. (Toronto: Ryerson Press, 1927) pp. 39-43, 136.

1311   Pierce, Lorne A. "Frederick Philip Grove (1871-1948)." PROC TRANS ROY SOC CAN 3rd Ser. 43 (1949): 113-19. Reprinted in *Frederick Philip Grove*, edited by Desmond Pacey. (Toronto: Ryerson Press, 1970) pp. 188-94.

1312   Plamondon, Louis C. S.J. "Nature in Frederick Philip Grove." Ph.D. Thesis. Montreal: University of Montreal, 1956.

1313   Potvin, Elizabeth. " 'The External Feminine' and the Clothing Motif in Grove's Fiction." STUD CAN LIT 12, no. 2 (1987): 222-38.

1314   Pratt, A.M. "By the Way." MAN SCHOOL J 16, no. 2-3 (1954): 12-17.

1315   Ranna, H.O. "Notable Canadian Author." BOOKMAN (London) 80 (April 1931): 9.

1316   Raudsepp, E. "Grove and the Wellspring of Fantasy." CAN LIT No. 84 (1980): 131-37.

1317   Ricou, Laurence R. "The Implacable Prairie: The Fiction of Frederick Philip Grove." In his *Vertical Man/Horizontal World...* (Vancouver: University of British Columbia Press, 1973) pp. 38-64.

1318   Ricou, Laurence R. "Marginalia." BKS CAN 1, no. 2 (1971): 21.
[Review of *Tales from the Margin*....]

1319   Rideout, Elliott. "The Women in Grove's Novels." M.A. Thesis. Edmonton: University of Alberta, 1968.

1320   Riley, A.W. "Grove's German Novels." Address delivered to the Grove Symposium, Ottawa, May 5, 1973.

1321   Riley, A.W.; Spettigue, Douglas O. "Introduction to *Fanny Essler*." UNIV TOR Q 54 (1984-85): 440-42.

1322   Roedder, Kartsen. Review of *A Search for America*. N.Y. HERALD TRIB (May 12, 1929): 12.

1323   Ross, Malcolm. "Introduction." In *Over Prairie Trails*. (Toronto: McClelland & Stewart, 1957) pp. v-x.

1324   Rowe, Kay M. "Here He Lies Where He Longed." MAN ARTS REV 6, no. 2-3 (1949): 62-64. Reprinted in *Frederick Philip Grove*, edited by Desmond Pacey. (Toronto: Ryerson Press, 1970) pp. 195-99.

1325   Rubio, Mary, ed. *The Genesis of Grove's "The Adventures of Leonard Broadhus": A Text and Commentary.* Toronto: Canadian Children's Press, 1984.

1326   Sandwell, B.K. "Ants as Seen by Ants." SAT N 63 (Apr. 26, 1947): 12.

1327   Sandwell, B.K. "Frederick Philip Grove and the Culture of Contemporary Canada." SAT N 61 (Nov. 24, 1945): 18. Reprinted in *Frederick Philip Grove,* edited by Desmond Pacey. (Toronto: Ryerson Press, 1970) pp. 56-59.

1328   Sandwell, B.K. "Grove's Autobiography." UNIV TOR Q 16 (1947): 202-06.

1329   Sarkowski, Heinz. "Frederick Philip Grove." In *Der Insel Verlag, Eine Bibliographie 1899-1969.* (Frankfurt: Insel Verlag, 1971) pp. 1, 14-16, 44, 84, 173, 188, 246, 259, 348, 350-54, 393, 395.

1330   Saunders, Doris B. "The Grove Collection of Papers in the University of Manitoba: A Tentative Evaluation." In *Papers of the Bibliographical Society of Canada/Cahiers de la Société Bibliographique du Canada 2* (Toronto: The Society, 1963) pp. 7-20.

1331   Saunders, Thomas. "The Grove Papers." QUEEN'S Q 70 (1963): 22-29.

1332   Saunders, Thomas. "Introduction." In *The Settlers of the Marsh.* (Toronto: McClelland & Stewart, 1965) pp. vii-xiii.

1333   Saunders, Thomas. "A Novelist as Poet: Frederick Philip Grove." DAL REV 43 (1963): 235-41. Reprinted in *Frederick Philip Grove,* edited by Desmond Pacey. (Toronto: Ryerson Press, 1970) pp. 88-96.

1334   Sherwood, C.B. Review of *Our Daily Bread.* N.Y. HERALD TRIB (Oct. 14, 1928): 7.

1335   Sirois, Antoine. "Grove et Ringuet: témoins d'une époque." CAN LIT No. 49 (1971): 20-27.

1336   Skelton, Isobel. "Frederick Philip Grove." DAL REV 19 (1939): 147-63. Reprinted in *Frederick Philip Grove,* edited by Desmond Pacey. (Toronto: Ryerson Press, 1970) pp. 24-44.

1337   Smith, Marion B. "Period Pieces." CAN LIT No. 10 (1961): 72-77.
[Review of *The Master of the Mill.*]

1338   Smith, Mary Ainslie. "Canadian Content: The Amish Conversion of W.W. Campbell and the Americanization of Frederick Philip Grove." BKS CAN 12 (August-September 1983): 34-36.
[Review of *The Adventure of Leonard Broadhus.*]

1339   Spettigue, Douglas O. "Forschungen über den Schiftsteller Felix Paul Greve" [Research on the Author Felix Paul Greve]. DER ARCHIVAR 25 (Mai 1972): 240.

1340   Spettigue, Douglas O. "Frederick Philip Grove." In *The Oxford Companion to Canadian Literature,* edited by William Toye. (Toronto: Oxford University Press, 1983) pp. 324-327.

1341   Spettigue, Douglas O. "Frederick Philip Grove." QUEEN'S Q 78 (1971): 614-15.

1342   Spettigue, Douglas O. "The Grove Enigma Resolved." QUEEN'S Q 79 (1972): 1-2.

1343   Spettigue, Douglas O. Review of *Frederick Philip Grove,* by M.R. Stobie. QUEEN'S Q 78 (1971): 614-15.

1344 Spettigue, Douglas; Riley, A.W. "Felix Paul Greve redivivus: zum frühen Leben des kanadischen Schriftstellers Frederick Philip Grove" [Felix Paul Greve redivivus: On the Early Life of the Canadian Author Frederick Philip Grove]. SEMINAR J GERM STUD 9, no. 2 (1973): 148-55.

1345 Sproxton, B.E. "Grove's Essay on Man." Address delivered to the Grove Symposium. Ottawa, May 5, 1973.

1346 Stanley, C. "Frederick Philip Grove." DAL REV 25 (1946): 433-41.

1347 Stanley, C. "Voice in the Wilderness." DAL REV 25 (1946): 173-81.

1348 Stephens, D.G. "New Criticism." CAN LIT No. 43 (1970): 79-82.
[Review of *Frederick Philip Grove* by Ronald Sutherland.]

1349 Stich, K.P. "Extravagant Expression of Travel and Growth: Grove's Quest for America." STUD CAN LIT 6, no. 2 (1981): 155-69.

1350 Stich, K.P. "Grove's New World Bluff." STUD CAN LIT (1981): 111-23.

1351 Stobie, M.R. "Frederick Philip Grove and the Canadianism Movement." STUD NOVEL 4, no. 2 (1972): 173-85.

1352 Stobie, M.R. "Grove and the Ants." DAL REV 58 (1978): 418-33.

1353 Stobie, M.R. "Grove's Letters from the Mennonite Reserve." CAN LIT No. 59 (1974): 67-80.

1354 Sutherland, Ronald. "Nationalism in the Works of Grove." Address delivered to the Grove Symposium, Ottawa, May 5, 1973.

1355 Thomas, C.; Lennox, J. "Grove's Maps." ESSAYS CAN WRIT 26 (1983): 74-79.

1356 Thompson, Joyce Lesley. "In Search of Order: The Structure of Grove's *Settlers of the Marsh*." J CAN FIC 3, no. 3 (1974): 65-73.

1357 Thompson, Joyce Lesley. "Structural Techniques in the Fiction of Frederick Philip Grove." M.A. Thesis. Winnipeg: University of Manitoba, 1968.

1358 Verwey, A. "Frederick Philip Grove." In *De Documenten van hun vriendschap. Bijeengebracht en toegelicht door Mea Nijland-Verwey, Albert Verey, en Stefan George.* (Amsterdam: Polak & van Gennep, 1965) pp. 111, 114-15.

1359 Watters, Reginald Eyre. "Introduction." In *The Master of the Mill.* (Toronto: Mcclelland & Stewart, 1961) pp. vii-xiii.

1360 Webber, Bernard. "Grove and Politics." CAN LIT No. 63 (1975): 126-27.

1361 Wiebe, Rudy. "A Novelist Looks at Grove." Address delivered to the Grove Symposium, Ottawa, May 6, 1973.

1362 Wilson, Jennie M. "A Comparative Study of the Novels of Frederick Philip Grove and Theodore Dreiser." M.A. Thesis. Fredericton: University of New Brunswick, 1962.

1363   Wolfskehl, Carl. "Frederick Philip Grove." In *Wolfskehl und Verwey. Die Dokumente ihrer Freundschaft, 1897–1946*, edited by Mea Nijland-Verwey. (Heidelberg: Verlag Lambert Schneider, 1968) pp. 26–27.

ISAAK, P.

1364   *Dem Leben abgelauscht [True Life].* Waldheim, Sask.: The Author, 1946. 200 pp. Poems.

JANZEN, Jacob H. (1878–1950)

Born in Steinbach, Ukraine and obtained a teacher's certificate in that country. In 1924 he emigrated to Canada, after having lost his position as a teacher in Tiege, Ukraine. He has lived in Guelph and Vancouver. Received an honorary doctorate degree from Bethel College, Kansas.

1365   *Durch Wind und Wellen: Gedichte [Through Wind and Waves: Poems].* Waterloo, Ont.: The Author, 1928. 93 pp. Poems.

1366   *Abraham: Innere Wandlung zur Zeit der Geschichte des Alten Bundes, zum Vortrag auf Jugendvereinsfesten in 15 Gesängen dargestellt [Abraham: Inner Change at the Time of the Old Covenant, Presented in 15 Songs for Recitation at Youth Association Festivals].* 1931. 28 pp. Poems.

1367   *Utwaundre: Stimmungsbild in zwei Aufzuegen [It's Time to Emigrate: Sketch in Two Acts].* Waterloo, Ont.: The Author, 1931. 95 pp. Play.

1368   *Im Frauenverein [At the Women's Club].* Waterloo, Ont.: The Author, 1938. 17 pp. Mimeographed. Play.

1369   *Zu Weihnachten 1938: Ein Gedicht und drei Gespräche [Christmas 1938: A Poem and Three Discourses].* Waterloo, Ont.: The Author, 1938. 9 pp. Mimeographed. Poem.

1370   *Eltern und Kinder [Parents and Children].* Play in 2 acts. Waterloo, Ont.: The Author, 1939. Mimeographed. Play.

1371   *Das Sexuelle Problem [Sexual Problem].* Waterloo, Ont.: The Author, 1942. 32 pp. Mimeographed. Play.

1372   *Leben und Tod [Life and Death].* Waterloo, Ont.: The Author, 1942. Mimeographed. Play.

1373   *Erzählungen aus der Mennonitgeschichte [Tales from Mennonite History].* Waterloo, Ont.: The Author, 1943. 72 pp. Stories.

1374   *Tales from Mennonite History.* Waterloo, Ont.: The Author, 1945. 96 pp. Stories.

1375   *Wanderndes Volk: Die Geschichte einer Familie von der Ansiedlung des Dorfes Petershagen bis in unsere Tage [People on the Move: The Story of a Family from the Time of the Settlement of Petershagen until Present Days].* Waterloo, Ont.: The Author, 1945, 1946, 1947. 3 v. 100 pp., 96 pp., 120 pp. respectively. Volume 1 appeared in a separate edition in 1946.

1376   *Altes und Neues zu Weihnachten und Neujahr [Something Old and Something New at Christmas and the New Year].* (Waterloo, Ont.: The Author) 1947. 92 pp. Poems, plays, short stories.

1377   *Erfahrungen, Gedanken und Träume [Experiences, Thoughts, and Dreams].* Waterloo, Ont.: The Author, 1947. 120 pp. Stories.

1378 *Mein Felsengarten [My Rock Garden].* Waterloo, Ont.: The Author, 1949. 128 pp. Stories.

Writings about:

1379 "Books by Jacob H. Janzen." MENN LIFE 6 (July 1951): 42.

1380 Driedger, N.N. "Janzen, Jacob H." In *The Mennonite Encyclopedia.* Vol. 3 (1957) pp. 95-96.

1381 Driedger, N.N. "Zum Gedenken an Aeltesten Jacob H. Janzen" [In Memory of Elder Jacob H. Janzen]. DER BOTE (Feb. 10, 1970): 1-2.

1382 Dyck, Arnold. "Jacob H. Janzen - Writer." MENN LIFE 6 (July 1951): 33-34, 43.

1383 Janzen, Heinz. "Jacob H. Janzen - at Home." MENN LIFE 6 (July 1951): 35-37, 43.

1384 Janzen, Jacob H. *Aus meinem Leben: Erinnerungen [From My Life: Recollections].* Rosthern, Sask., 1929. Autobiography.

1385 Sachs, Hilde. "Zum Tode des Schriftstellers Jacob H. Janzen" [On Jacob H. Janzen's Death]. MENN AUSL 1, no. 1 (1951): 11.

JANZEN, Johannes Heinrich

1386 *Das Märchen vom Weihnachtsmann [The Fairytale of Santa Claus],* with Waldemar Janzen. Winnipeg: CMBC Publications, 1975. 35 pp. Story.

JEWINSKI, Ed.
Born in Oberammergau, Germany. He is now professor of English and creative writing at Wilfrid Laurier University, Waterloo, Ont. He is poetry editor of *The New Quarterly.*

1387 *The Cage in the Open Air.* Windsor, Ont.: Black Moss Press, 1979. Poems.

1388 *Any Morning may Start the Revolution.* Toronto: Gabro Press, 1983. Poems.

1389 *No Place to Go.* Toronto: Gabro Press, 1983. Poems.

KLASSEN, Is. P.

1390 *Licht und Schatten [Light and Shadow].* [Steinbach, Man.: Derksen Printers, 1981.] 49 pp. Play.

KLASSEN, Johann Peter   (1889-1947)

1391 *Dunkle Tage [Dark Days].* Scottdale, Pa., 1924. 32 pp. Poems.

1392 *Krümlein [Bits and Pieces].* Scottdale, Pa., 1924. 43 pp. Poems.

1393 *Wegeblumen [Roadside Flowers].* Scottdale, Pa., 1924? 52 pp. Poems.

1394 *Brocken [Fragments].* Winnipeg, 1932. 32 pp. Poems.

1395 *Ährenlese [Gleanings].* Winnipeg, 1944. 73 pp. Poems.

1396 *Nohoaksel [Bits and Pieces Left Over].* Yarrow, B.C., 1946. 87 pp. Poems.

1397   *Roggenbrot [Ryebread]*. Vancouver, 1946. 134 pp.

1398   *Der Zwillingsbruder von "Meine Garbe" [The Twin Brother of "My Sheaf of Grain"]*. Vancouver: The Author, 1946. 100 pp. Story.

1399   *Meine Garbe [My Sheaf of Grain]*. Vancouver [n.d.] 102 pp. Story.

Writings about:

1400   Bender, H.S. "Klassen, Johann Peter." In *The Mennonite Encyclopedia*. Vol. 3 (1957) p. 192

1401   Krahn, Cornelius. "Klassen, Johann Peter." In *The Mennonite Encyclopedia*. Vol. 3 (1957) pp. 192-93.

KLASSEN, PETER

1402   *Beim uns alten Russland [With Us in Old Russia]*. Winnipeg: Echo-Verlag, 1959. 96 pp. Story.

KLASSEN, Peter Johann (1889-1953)
Born in Ohrloff, Ukraine, came to Canada in 1925. He took up farming and preaching near Superb, Sask. His plays and articles were published in *Der Kinderbote* and *Warte*.

1403   *Dee Gaofajäajasch [Gopher-hunters]*. MENN WART (January 1930) Dialogue in Low German.

1404   *Bei Weihnachtsmanns am Nordpol [At Santa Claus's at the North Pole]*. MENN RUND (November 1935) Christmas play.

1405   *Tue desgleichen [You Do the Same]*. MENN RUND (December 1935) Christmas play.

1406   *Zwei Wege [Two Roads]*. In One Act. DER BOTE (November 1935) Play.

1407   *Dee Pojsen-Steiasch [Poison-strewers]*. MENN WART (August 1936) Story.

1408   *In Ontarios SchwarzemTann [In the Black Forest of Ontario]*. Published in series in DER COURIER, 1937. Story.

1409   *Grossmutters Schatz und andere Geschichten, Gedichte und Fabeln [Grandmother's Treasure and other Stories, Poems and Fables]*. Superb, Sask., 1939. Stories.

1410   *Wenn eine Mutter betet fuer ihr Kind [If a Mother Prays for Her Child]*. Published in series in DER BOTE and COURIER, 1941. Story.

1411   *Wie einer wieder beten lernte [How a Man Learned to Pray Again]*. Published in series in DER BOTE and COURIER. Story.

1412   *Die Heimfahrt [The Journey Home]*. Superb, Sask., 1943. 104 pp. Story. Mimeographed.

1413   *Der Peet: Geschichten vom Peet und seinen Kameraden [Peet: Stories about Peet and His Pals]*. Superb, Sask.: The Author, 1943-45. Yarrow, B.C., 1949. 4 v. Vol. 1, 2 and 3 (1943-45), vol. 4 (1949).

1414   *Fünfunddreissig Fabeln [Thirty-five Fables]*. Superb, Sask., 1944. 74 pp. Fables.

1415   *Die Geschichte des Ohm Klass [The Story of Uncle Klass].* Regina: Western Printers, 1947. 130 pp. Stories.

1416   *Verlorene Söhne [Lost Sons].* Yarrow, B.C.: The Author, 1952. 110 pp. Stories.

1417   *Als die Heimat zur Fremde geworden, wurde die Fremde zur Heimat [Alienated in the Homeland, at Home in a Foreign Country].* Winnipeg [n.d.] Story.

1418   *Heimat einmal: Eine Erzählung aus Russlands jüngster Vergangenheit [In a Country Once a Homeland: A Story from Russia's Most Recent Past].* [Yarrow, B.C.: Columbia Press, n.d.] 2 v. Novel.

LAPP, Claudia
Born in Stuttgart, Germany, emigrated to the USA and graduated from Bennington College, Baltimore. Came to Québec in 1968.

1419   *Honey.* Montreal: Véhicule Press, 1973. 57 pp. port. Poems.

1420   *Dakini.* Montreal: Davinci Press, 1974. [n.p.]

   Writing about:

1421   Holland, Patrick. Review of *Honey.* CAN BOOK REV ANN 1977: 147.

LOEB, Ernst (1914-1987)
Born in Andernach am Rhein. Emigrated to the United States in 1936, received a Ph.D. degree at the University of Washington. He has been a professor at Queen's University, Kingston. Author of two books of essays, one on Goethe, the other on Heine.

1422   *Löbliches [To Praise].* Kingston, Ont.: The Author, 1974. 60 pp. Poems.

LOEWEN, A.J.

1423   *Am Christabend [On Christmas Eve].* DER BOTE (1938) Play.

1424   *Freuden und Leiden [Joy and Suffering].* DER BOTE (1938) Play.

LOEWEN, Gerhard (1868-1946)
Born in Ukraine and taught at various schools and private homes there. In 1925 he emigrated to Canada. Contributed articles to *Warte.*

1425   *Feldblumen: Gedichte [Flowers of the Field: Poems].* Steinbach, Man.: Arnold Dyck, 1946. 136 pp. Poems.

   Writings about:

1426   Dyck, Arnold. "Der Dichter Gerhard Loewen" [The Poet Gerhard Loewen]. In *Mennonitisches Jahrbuch 1948.* Vol. 42 (Newton, Kans.: Mennonite Publications Office, 1948) pp. 46-47.

1427   Dyck, Arnold. "Loewen, Gerhard." In *Mennonite Encyclopedia.* Vol. 3 (1957) p. 386.

1428   Dyck, Arnold. "The Poet Gerhard Loewen." MENN LIFE 3 (January 1948): 22-23.

LOHRENZ, Gerhard (1899-   )

Born in Sagradowka, Ukraine. Came to Canada in 1925 and took up farming at Gilroy, Sask. Received his education at the University Manitoba (B.A.). Taught in Manitoba schools between 1931 and 1952 and in the Canadian Mennonite Bible College in Winnipeg. He was also Pastor of the Sargent Avenue Mennonite Church in Winnipeg.

1429 *Storm Tossed.* Winnipeg [n.d.] Novel.

1430 *Lose Blätter [Loose Leaves].* Winnipeg, 1974-1976. 3 v. Stories.

MAAS, Carl Coelestin Johannes (1862-1940)

Born in Bergen, Germany, emigrated to Canada and served in various towns in Ontario as a Pastor of the Lutheran Church. In 1915 he became editor of *Berliner*, a periodical in English, published.

1431 *Gedichte [Poems].* Putbus, Germany, 1900. Poems.

1432 *Moos-je-Keen [o. O. vor 1931].* A verse story distributed in manuscript form.

1433 *Hilda the Saxon Maid.* Boston, 1932. Story in verse.

Writing about:

1434 "Obituary. Rev. C.C.J. Maas." KITCHENER-WATERLOO RECORD (Dec. 3, 1940)

MORSTEIN, Petra von

Born in Germany. Studied philosophy at the University of Manitoba. Author of *Fachaufsätze*, a book of essays.

1435 *An alle: Gedichte [To Each and All: Poems].* Frankfurt am Main: S. Fischer Verlag, 1969. 46 pp. Poems.

Writing about:

1436 Cardinal, Clive H. Review of *An Alle: Gedichte.* CAN ETH STUD 1 (December 1969): 123.

NEUENDORFF, Gert (1930-   )

Born in Tallin, Estonia, arrived in Canada in 1948. Published poems in German newspapers. Since 1954 he has been active in the Winnipeg-based theatre group of the First Mennonite Church, which also produced his play *Und keiner hoert hin.*

1437 *Und keiner hoert hin [And Nobody Listens].* Winnipeg, 1972. Play.
[Performed by the Winnipeg Mennonite Theatre, Winnipeg, Nov. 17 and 18, 1972. A modern drama in English and German about a German-Canadian immigrant family at the time of the Vietnam war.]

Writings about:

1438 Eldring, Werner. "Worte zur Wahrheit gratulieren Gert Neuendorff" [Words of Truth Compliment Gert Neuendorff]. MAN COUR NORD (Dec. 7, 1972)

1439 Jaeger, Manfred. "A Plea for Understanding." WINN FREE PRESS (Nov. 9, 1972)

1440 Rehwald, E. "Menschen wie Du und ich" [People like You and Me]. MAN COUR NORD (Nov. 23, 1972)

1441   Reimer, Al. "The Stage as a Mirror of Our Secret Selves." MENN MIRROR (December 1972)

1442   Wolf, Dietrich E. "Hoert wirklich keiner hin?" [Does Really Nobody Listen?] MAN COUR NORD (Dec. 7, 1972)

1443   Woloski, Rosalie. "Mennonite Theatre Offers Premiere of City Author's Play." WINN TRIB (Nov. 11, 1972)
[Review with photos.]

NEUFELD, Dietrich (1886-1958)   (Pseud.: NOVOCAMPUS)

1444   *Kanadische Mennoniten [Canadian Mennonites].* Winnipeg, 1924. Play.

Writings about:

1445   Kloss, Heinz. Review of *Kanadische Mennoniten.* DIE LITERATUR 30 (November 1928)

1446   Krahn, Cornelius. "Neufeld, Dietrich." In *The Mennonite Encyclopedia.* Vol. 4 (1959) pp. 1111-12.

NUSENOW, Gertrude (1889-1968)
Born in Leipzig, came to settle in Montreal. Her poems appeared in the *Montrealer Nachrichten.*

Writings about:

1447   Cardinal, Clive H. "Drei deutsche Dichter in Kanada" [Three German Poets in Canada]. DER NORDWESTEN (Jan. 1, 1963): 9.
[About Gertrude Nusenow, Erwin Potitt, and G.-I. von Cardinal.]

1448   Cardinal, Clive H. "Über deutsche Dichtung in Kanada" [On German Poetry in Canada]. MONT NACH (Apr. 3, 17, May 1, 1975): 9. of each issue.
[A review of the work of Gertrude Nusenow, Erwin Potitt and H. Schultheis.]

PAULS, Wilhelm

1449   *Gedichte verschiedenen Inhalts in Hoch-und Plattdeutscher Sprache [Poems on Various Subjects in High and Low German].* Calgary: The Author, 1984. iii, 52 pp. Poems.

PETERS, Gerhard Abraham (1880-1935)
Born in Ladekop, Ukraine, taught in Mennonite schools there and in Germany. In 1923 he emigrated to Canada and was active as a teacher, preacher and writer.

1450   *Gedichte [Poems].* Scottdale, Pa.: Rundschau, 1923. Poems.

1451   *Menschenlos in schwere Zeit [Man's Fate in Troubled Times].* Scottdale, Pa., 1924. Poems.

1452   *Wehrlos? [Defenceless?].* Scottdale, Pa., 1924. Poems.

1453   *Blumen am Wegrand: Gedichte [Wayside Flowers: Poems].* Gretna, Man., 1946. Poems.

PETERS, Isaak

1454   *Um Glaube und Freiheit [For Faith and Freedom].* Play in three acts. DER BOTE (1940) Play.

QUERNER, Emil (1827-1884)

1455   *Wilde Blüthen [Wild Flowers].* Philadelphia, 1874. Poems.

RABL, Hans

1456   *Der grosse Zug [The Great Trek]..* Published in series in *Der Courier,* 1939. Novel.

REMBE, Heinrich (1858-1927)
Born in Eisleben, Germany. Emigrated to Hamilton, Ont., in 1927 via New York and Mount Vernon. He served as a Pastor of the Lutheran Church in Montreal, Arnprior, Ont., Hamilton, and elsewhere.

1457   *Aus der Einsamkeit einer kanadischen Landpfarre [About a Canadian Country Parish's Solitude].* Halle, 1901. Poems.

1458   *Herz und Natur [Heart and Nature].* [N.p.] 1906. Poems.

   Writing about:

1459   Friesen, Gerhard K. "Heinrich Rembe's 'Gethsemane': Text and Context." DEUTSCHKAN JAHRB 6 (1981): 130-39.

REMPEL, Olga

1460   *Wer nimmt uns auf [Who'll Take Us In?]* Winnipeg: CMBC Publications, 1977. 29 pp. Play. [A story of Mennonite migrations.]

ROSS, Veronica (1946-   )
Born in Hanover, Germany, came to Canada as a child with her parents and grew up in Montreal. Moved to the Maritimes and now lives in Kitchener, Ont. Received a Benson & Hedges Magazine Writing Award for 1977, and a Periodical Distributors of Canada Award for 1980 and 1984.

1461   *Goodbye Summer: Stories.* [Ottawa]: Oberon Press, 1980. 143 pp. Short stories.

1462   *Dark Secrets: New Stories.* Ottawa: Oberon Press, 1983. Short stories.

1463   *Fisherwoman: A Novel.* Porter's Lake: Pottsfield, 1984. Novel.

1464   *Homecoming.* Ottawa: Oberon Press, 1987. Novel.

SAUBERZWEIG, Reinhard Martin (1900-   )
Born in Königsdorf, Germany, received part of his education there. He came to Waterloo, Ont., in 1927, and continued his education in Canada. He is a Pastor of the Lutheran Church.

1465   *Im Schatten des Ewigen [In Eternity's Shadow].* Herford and Leipzig, 1929. Poems.

1466   *Der Heimat entgegen [Via the Fatherland].* Herford and Leipzig, 1930. Poems.

SAUDER, Benjamin (1899-1978)
Born in Hesson, Ont., farmed near St. Jacobs, Ont.

1467   *Der Nachbar an der Schtroas [The Neighbour in Our Street].* Pennsylvania German Folklore Society of Ontario, 1955. Poems.

SAWATZKY, Heinrich

1468   *Templer mennonitischer Herkunft [Templars of Mennonite Stock]*. Winnipeg: Echo-Verlag and Karl Fast, 1956. 69 pp. Biographical stories.

SAWATZKY, Valentin (1914-)
Born in Chorlitza-Rosental, Ukraine, migrated to Germany in 1943 and in 1948 to Canada, where he settled in Waterloo, Ont. Received vocational training and graduated from a technological school as an engineer. His poems have appeared in various Mennonite papers and textbooks.

1469   *Lindenblatter: Ausgewaehlte Gedichte [Linden Leaves: Selected Poems]*. Virgil, Ont.: Niagara Press, 1958. 84 pp. 2nd ed. 1962. 90 pp. Poems.

1470   *Heimatglocken: Lyrik und Balladen [Call of the Homeland: Lyrics and Ballads]*. Virgil, Ont.: Niagara Press, 1962. 97 pp. Poems.

1471   *Friendenskläge Gedichte [Sounds of Peace: Poems]*. Waterloo, Ont.: National Publishers, 1971. Poems.

1472   *Abendlicht, Gedichte und Märchen [Twilight, Poems and Fairy Tales]*. Waterloo, Ont.: The Author, 1977. Poems and stories.

1473   *Eichenlaub: Gedichte und Märchen [Laurel: Poems and Fairy Tales]*. [Waterloo, Ont.: The Author, 1981] 141 pp. Poems and tales.

1474   *Glockenlaeuten. Gedichte [Bells Ringing. Poems]*. Waterloo, Ont.:The Author, 1982. Poems.

1475   *Einkehr: Gedichte und Märchen [Contemplation Poems and Fairy Tales]*. [Waterloo, Ont.: The Author, 1983. 158 pp. Poems and tales.

SCHAFFER, Ulrich (1942-)
Born in Pommern, Germany. In 1945 he escaped to West Germany and settled in Bremen. Came to Canada in 1953, completed his university studies at the University of British Columbia. Since 1970 he has been teaching at Douglas College, Vancouver.

1476   *Im Gegenwind. Gedichte [Facing the Headwind. Poems]*, with illustrations by the author. [Karlsruhe]: Kurt Rüdiger, 1964. [73] pp. Poems.

1477   *Gurluana. Gedichte und Graphiken [Gurluana: Poems and Drawings]*. [Karlsruhe]: Kurt Rüdiger, 1965. 45 pp. Poems.

1478   *Überrascht vom Licht [Surprised by Light]*. Wuppertal: Oncken, 1975.
[Translated into English.] Poems.

1479   *Kreise schlagen. Gedanken, Gebete, Gedichte [Making Circles. Thoughts, Prayers, Poems]*. Wuppertal: Oncken, 1973. 5th ed. 1978. Poems.

1480   *Umkehrungen. Gedanken, Gebete, Gedichte [Return. Thoughts, Prayers, Poems]*. Wuppertal: Oncken, 1975. 4th ed. 1978. Poems.

1481   *Searching for You*. San Francisco: Harper & Row, 1978. Poems.
[Translation of *Im Aufwind.*]

1482   *Im Aufwind [In the Upcurrent]*. 3rd ed. Wuppertal: Oncken, 1979.
[Translated into English.]

SCHROEDER, Andreas (1946-   )

Born in Hoheneggelsen, Germany. Came to Canada with his parents in 1951. Studied creative writing at the University of British Columbia (B.A., M.A.). Founder and editor of the journal of *Contemporary Literature in Translation*. He was a columnist for the Vancouver paper *Province*. Taught creative writing for the University of Victoria, and was chairman of the Writers' Union of Canada (1976-77).

1483   *Immobile.* 1969. Screenplay.

1484   *The Plastic Mile.* 1969. Screenplay.

1485   *The Ozone Minotaur.* Vancouver: Sono Nis Press, 1969. xii, 15-58. Poems.

1486   *The Pub.* 1970. Screenplay.

1487   *File of Uncertainties.* Surrey, B.C.: Sono Nis Press, 1971. Poems.

1488   *The Late Man.* Port Clements, B.C.: Sono Nis Press, 1971. 118 pp. Novel.
[Also in screenplay, 1972.]

1489   *uniVerse*, with David Frith. Vancouver: MASSage Press, 1971. Poems.

1490   *Shaking it Rough: A Prison Memoir.* Toronto: Doubleday Canada; Garden City, N.Y.: Doubleday, 1976. xii, 214 pp. Autobiographical novel.

1491   *Toccata in "D": A Micro-novel.* Lantzville, B.C.: Olichan Books, 1985. 57 pp. Novelette.

1492   *Dustship Glory.* Toronto: Doubleday, 1986. 224 pp. Novel.

Writings about:

1493   Amiel, Barbara. "Crime, Punishment and Making the Best of It." MACLEAN'S 89 (Sept. 20, 1976): 64.
[Review of *Shaking it Rough.*]

1494   Cogswell, Frederick William. Review of *The Ozone Minotaur.* FIDDLEHEAD 83 (1970): 76-78.

1495   Gibbs, Robert. Review of *File of Uncertainties.* FIDDLEHEAD 90 (1971): 112.

1496   Glover, Douglas. "Rewriting History." BKS CAN 15 ((June-July 1986): 34.
[Review of *Dustship Glory.*]

1497   Green, P. Review of *The Late Man.* CAN FIC MAG 6 (1972): 83-84.

1498   Hancock, Geoff. "Interview with Andreas Schroeder." CAN FIC MAG 27 (1977): 47-69.

1499   Hancock, Geoff. "A Monument to Folly." CAN FORUM 66, no. 766 (1987): 34-40.
[Review of *Dustship Glory.*]

1500   MacSkimming, Roy. "A B.C. Poet's Rough Time in Prison." SAT N 91 (October 1976): 69-70.
[Review of *Shaking it Rough.*]

1501   Peters, Joanne. Review of *Dustship Glory.* CM 14 (1986): 221-22.

1502 Rosengarten, Herbert J. "Writer and Subject." CAN LIT No. 55 (1973): 111-13.
      [Review of *The Late Man*.]

1503 Sherrin, Robert G. Review of *Shaking it Rough*. CAN FIC MAG 24-25 (1977): 160-62.

1504 Staton, Eleanor. "WUC Makes Waves in Canada." Q & Q 42, no. 8 (1976): 1, 24.

1505 Stuewe, Paul. Review of *Shaking it Rough*. Q & Q 42, no. 13 (1976): 45. photo.

1506 Suchard, Alan. "The O-Zone and other Places." CAN LIT No. 48 (1971): 80-82.
      [Review of *The Ozone Minotaur*.]

1507 Van Mil, Patrick. Review of *Toccata in 'D'*. CAN BOOK REV ANN 1986: 85.

1508 Watmough, David. "Calm Sense on Prisons." CAN LIT No. 73 (1977): 120-22.
      [Review of *Shaking it Rough*.]

1510 Woodcock, George. "Andreas Schroeder (Peter)." In *Contemporary Poets*. 2nd ed. (New York: St. Martin's Press, 1975) pp. 1351-53.

1509 Woodcock, George. "The Great Inside." CAN FORUM 56 (November 1976): 47-48.
      [Review of *Shaking it Rough*.]

SEEL (LÜBCKE), Else (1894-1974)

Born in Schivelbein, Pomerania, Germany, emigrated to Vancouver in 1927. She lived in British Columbia as a trapper. Her poems appeared in yearbooks.

1511 *Haus im Urwald: Deutsch-Kanadische Gedichte [House in a Virgin Forest: German-Canadian Poems]*. Vancouver [1956] 26 pp. Poems.

1512 *Kanadisches Tagebuch [Canadian Diary]*. Tübingen: Horst Erdmann Verlag [1964]. 246 pp. (Schriftenreihe des Instituts für Auslandsbeziehungen Stuttgart. Literarisch-künstlerische Reihe, vol. 12) 2nd ed. 1966.

1513 *Ausgewählte Werke, Lyrik und Prosa [Selected Works. Poems and Prose]*. Herausgegeben von Rodney T.K. Symington. Toronto: German-Canadian Historical Association, 1979. iv, 211 pp. (Deutschkanadische Schriften A. Belletristik Band 3)

Writings about:

1514 Boeschenstein, Hermann. "Else Seel, eine deutsch-kanadische Dichterin" [Else Seel, A German-Canadian Poetess]. GERM CAN BUS REV 10 (Spring 1957): 17-19.

1515 Boeschenstein, Hermann. "Else Seel, A German-Canadian Poetess." CAN ETH STUD 1 (December 1969): 51-55.

1516 Dolman, Dick. "And Now All This." THE UBYSSEY (Oct. 21, 1955): 2.

1517 Hoeter, Bernhard W. "Deutschkanadische Pionierdichterin: Ein Interview mit Else Seel" [A German-Canadian Pioneer Poetess: An Interview with Else Seel]. DER NORDWESTEN (Apr. 5, 1956): 15.

1518 "Leben im kanadischen Busch" [Life in the Canadian Bush]. In *Kürschners Deutscher Literatur Kalender*. Vol. 55 (Berlin, 1967)

[Review of *Haus im Urwald*.]

1519 Maurer, K.W. "*Haus im Urwald*: Zu den Gedichten einer deutschkanadischen Frau" [*House in a Virgin Forest*: On the Poems of a German-Canadian Woman]. DER NORDWESTEN (July 14, 1954)

1520 Review of *Haus im Urwald*. AMER-GERM REV 23 (1957)

1521 Symington, Rodney T.K. "Else Seel: Eine Biographie im Nachlass [Else Seel: A Biography]. DEUTSCHKAN JAHRB 3 (1976): 193-98.

SIBUM, Norman (1947-   )
Born at Oberammergau, Germany. Lived in the U.S. until relocating in Vancouver in 1968.

1522 *Banjo*. Vancouver, 1972. Poems.

1523 *Loyal and Unholy Hours*. Madeira Park: Harbour Publishing Co., 1980. 40 pp. Poems.

1524 *Other Howls in the Storm*. Vancouver: Pulp Press, 1982. 46 pp. Poems.

SPRING, Christian Friederick (1825-1888)
Born in Neuffen, Württemberg, Germany. Came to Canada in 1865 via Ohio and Michigan. Served as a Pastor of the Lutheran Church in various towns in Ontario.

1525 *Lehrreiche und erbauliche Lieder* [*Educational and Devotional Songs*]. New York, 1958. Songs.

1526 *Gedichte und Dialoge* [*Poems and Dialogues*]. Reading, Pa., 1878. 2nd ed. 1892.

1527 *Der treue Hirte* [*The Faithful Shepherd*]. 1878. Versified stories.

TOEWS, Gerhard G. (1897-   )
Born in Wiesenheim, Ukraine. Graduated from the School of Commerce in Molotschna. Studied at the University of Kharkow. Came to Canada in 1923 and settled in St. Catharines, Ont.

1528 *Die Heimat in Flammen* [*The Homeland in Flames*]. Regina, 1933. Novel.

1529 *Die Heimat in Trümmern: Deutsche Schicksale im Russland der Anarchie* [*The Homeland in Ruins: The Germans and Their Fate in Russia under Anarchy*]. Steinbach, Man.: Warte-Verlag, 1936. 316 pp. Novel.

Writing about:

1530 Dyck, Jacob. "Georg de Brecht und Quidam" [Georg de Brecht (i.e. Gerhard Toews) and Quidam (i.e. Peter Johann Klassen)]. DER BOTE (Jan. 12, 1971): 5-6.

TSCHETTER, Lorenz R.

1531 *Weihnachts- und Neujahrs-Gedichte* [*Christmas and New Year Poems*]. Macleod, Alta.: The Author, 1949. 19 pp. Poems.

UNRUH, Nicolai H. (1897-   )
Born in Muntau, Ukraine. In 1924 he emigrated to Canada and settled on a farm near Ste. Elizabeth, Man. For forty years he served his church as a Sunday school teacher and preacher.

1532   *Gedichte und plattdeutsche Gespräche: De Dartja Joare: De scheene Geläajenheit: Onse scheenste Wiehnachte [Poems and Low-German Conversations: The Thirties: Good Opportunity: Our Most Wonderful Christmas].* [Steinbach, Man.: Derksen Printers] 1973. 64 pp. Poems in German and plays in Low-German.

1533   *Kaunst du di noch dentje? Eine dramatische Auffuehrung in drei Akten: 1924-1974 [Can You still Remember? A Dramatic Performance in Three Acts: 1924-1974].* Ste. Elizabeth, Man., 1974. 50 pp. In Low-German. Play.

1534   *Aufscheed von de Heimstäd [Farewell to the Homestead].* [Steinbach, Man., n.d.] 54 pp. Story.

Writing about:

1535   Dyck, Arnold. " 'Aufscheed von de Heimstaed' in Clearbrook" ['Farewell to the Homestead' in Clearbrook]. DER BOTE (May 1, 1973): 6.

1536   Harms, Alvin. Review of *Gedichte und plattdeutsche Gespräche.* CAN ETH STUD 4, no. 1-2 (1972): 66-67.

1537   Lohrenz, Gerhard. Review of *Gedichte und plattdeutsche Gespräche.* DER BOTE (Feb. 20, 1973): 12.

WALL, J.J.

1538   *Eine freie Aussprache [Freely Stated]..* DER BOTE (1939) Play.

WEISZ, Marie

1539   *Stürme und Stille: Gedichte [Storms and Tranquility: Poems].* Vancouver: Continental Book Centre, 1956. 68 pp. Poems.

Writing about:

1540   Cardinal, Clive H. "Ergriffenes Dasein" [Enchanted Existence]. GERM CAN BUS REV 11 (Summer 1965): 13-14.
        [About Marie Weisz and Mario von Brentani.]

WERNER, Hans (1946-   )
Playwright, translator. Born in Germany. His writings have appeared in *Canadian Forum, Weed, Books in Canada, Saturday Night, Jewish Dialogue, Vanguard, Forum: 50 Years of Canadian Life and Letters.*

1541   *Blessed Art Thou among Women.* Toronto: Playwrights Canada, 1982. 47 pp. Play.

WIENS, Johann

1542   *Eine Hilfe in den grossen Nöten [Help Given in Dire Need].* 1925. Story.

WIENS, J.B.

1543   *Taunty Wellmschy [Aunt Wellmsch].* Winnipeg, 1965. 75 pp. Story.

WINTER-LOEWEN, Maria

1544   *Höhen und Tiefen [Highs and Lows].* Steinbach, Man.: Derksen Printers [?] 2 v.

GREEK

BIBLIOGRAPHIES

1545 BOMBAS, Leonidas C.
The Greek Community Media of Today. Montreal: McGill University, Faculty of Education, 1981.
[Includes sections on the various sectors of the media: newspapers, periodicals, radio, t.v.]

1546 BOMBAS, Leonidas C.
Greeks in Canada (An Annotated Bibliography). [Montreal: Hellenic Psychological and Pedagogical Institute of Montreal, 1982] 139 leaves. Mimeographed.
[Contains 70 entries with extensive annotations, titles on social studies, education, religion and history.]

1547 BOUCHARD, Jacques
"Les débuts de l'imprimerie en langue grecque au Québec." ÉTUDES HELLÉNIQUES/HELLENIC STUDIES 1, no. 1 (1983): 53-59.

1548 JOBLING, J. Keith
"University Research on Greek-Canadians: A Preliminary Check List of Theses." CAN ETH STUD 5, no. 1-2 (1973): 125-26.
[Includes titles retrieved from Canadian and American dissertation sources.]

1549 KAKABELAKIS, Helen
"Greek-Canadian Periodical Publications: A Preliminary Check List." CAN ETH STUD 2, no. 1 (1970): 71-74.
[Contains 20 citations with an index of non-Greek titles and a geographical distribution index.]

BOOKS, MONOGRAPHS

1550 BOMBAS, Leonidas C., ed.
O Ellēnismos toy Montreal 1843-1985/Montreal's Hellenism 1883-1985. Montreal: Hellenic Psychological & Pedagogical Institute of Montreal, 1985. 164 pp. illus.
[Includes 12 papers on integration, social life and organizations, education, the Greek media, Greek cultural activities and youth participation in community life. Reference is made to the Greek Writers' Association of Montreal, by Lydia Skalkou (pp. 135-41).]

1551 CHIMBOS, Peter
A History of Canada's Peoples. The Canadian Odyssey. The Greek Experience in Canada. Toronto: McClelland & Stewart, 1980. viii, 176 pp.

1552 CONSTANTINIDES, Thalia
La communauté grecque à Montréal. Montréal, 1979. 21 pp. Texte ronéotype.

1553 GAVAKI, Efrosini
The Integration of Greeks in Canada. San Francisco: R and E Research Associates, 1977. 117 pp.
[A general study of the Greek presence in Canada, with an extensive bibliography (pp. 107-17).]

1554 IOANNOU, Tina
La communauté grecqe du Québec. Québec: Institut Québécois de Recherche sur la Culture, 1983. 333 pp. Illus., photos.

[Table des matières: L'histoire des Grecs du Québec; Aspects démographiques (pp. 13-62); Conditions économiques (63-74); La structure familiale; La vie culturelle (pp. 75-98); L'intégration des Grecs dans la société d'accueil (pp. 99-108). Bibliographies (pp. 325-333).]

1555   **VLASSIS, George Demetrios**
The Greeks in Canada. Ottawa, 1942. 364 pp. illus. 2nd ed. 1953. Photos.
[Includes chapters on history, education, social and religious organizations in the provinces. A chapter entitled "Modern Hellenic Poetry in Canada" includes poems by George Vlassis, Miltiades Malacassis, Dionysios Solomos and Lambros Porphyras (pp. 37-39). Biographical sketches (pp. 255-96).]

ANTHOLOGIES

1556   *Dhiakrotima [Sound Variations].* Toronto, 1976. 124 pp.
[Includes poems by A. Mastoras, X. Gounaropoulos, George Thaniel, Kaliopoulos, George Stoubos and Xp. Ziatos.]

1557   *Katamartyria: Poiemata.* [Toronto, 1978] [32] pp. Poems.

INDIVIDUAL AUTHORS

ATHANASIADIS, A.A.

1558   *Mas enose o thanatos stē maurē zenēteia [Death Joined Us in the Foreign Land].* Montreal: Knossos Publishing House, 1960. Novel.

1559   *Poiemata [Poems].* Montreal: The Author, 1979. 22 pp. Poems.

AULONITOU, Lyntia

1560   *Galazia Kampylē. [Skyblue Curve].* Athens, 1955. 47 pp. Poems.

1561   *Paramythi [Fairy Tales].* Montreal, 1975. 31 pp. Fairy tales.

1562   *Stēn aichmē tēs vrontes [At Thunder's Spear-point].* Montreal, 1975. 68 pp. Poems.

1563   *Rogmes sto choma [Cracks in the Soil].* Montreal, 1979. 44 pp. Poems.

1564   *Ena leivadi diattontes* Montreal [L. Aulōnitou] 1977. 46 pp. illus. Poems.

1565   *Sphragidolithoi. [Pebbles].* Montreal, 1980. 68 pp. illus. Poems.

Writings about:

1566   Petritis, Takis. Review of *Paramythi.* ATLANTIS 2, no. 11 (1976): 2.

1567   Raezes, Byron. "Lyntia Aulonitou." NAT HERALD TRIB 63, no. 21.712 (1978): 1.

BELEGRI, P.K.

1568   *[A Concert for Target Shooting]* Athens: Dorikos, 1983. Poems.

BOMBAS, Leonidas C.

1569   [*Steps in the Light*] Nice, 1969. Poems.

1570   [*E and Then*] Montreal, 1980. Poems.

1571   [*In Short and Slowly*] Montreal, 1985. Poems.

CHARALAMBIDOU-PAPADOPOULOU, Eleni

1572   [*When Adventures Become Blessings*] 1981. Novel.

DALAS, Dimitris

1573   *Skepseis eirēnēs* [*Thoughts on Peace*]. Montreal: The Author, 1978. 52 pp. Poems.

HATZEGEORGIOU, Kyprou

1574   *Elegeiakh symphonia* [*Elegiac Symphony*]. Montreal: The Author, 1961. 61 pp. Poems.

HATZIDAVID, Vissarionas

1575   [*Wide Groves on Dry Land*] Montreal, 1983. Poems.

IOANNOU, Paulos L.

1576   *Epymartyria* [*Tears for Cyprus*]. Cyprus: Stavrinidis [n.d.] Poems.

KACHTITSIS, Nikos   (1926-1970)

1577   [*The Terrace*] Athens: Prote Yle, 1964. 123 pp. Novel.

1578   *To enupnio* [*The Dream*]. Thessalonika, 1960. 40 pp. Short stories.

1579   *I peripetia enos Vivliou* [*The Trials of a Book*]. Montreal: Lotofaghos, 1965. 116 pp. Autobiographical novel.

1580   *Poioi oi philoi – ē "Omorphasxēmē" – to enupnio* [*Who Were the Friends – The "Omorphaschimi" – The Dream*]. Athens: Kedros Publishing Co., 1976. 127 pp. Novel.

1581   *O ērōas tēs ghandēs: muthistorēma* [*The Hero of Gandes: Novel*]. Montreal: Lotofaghos, 1967. 351 pp. Novel.

Writing about

1582   Thaniel, George. "The Prefaces of Nikos Kachtitsis. "   HELLENIC STUDIES/ÉTUDES HELLÉNIQUES 2, no. 1 (1984): 63-68.

KLISOURA, Sofia

1583   *Ta pikrotragouda tou xenētemou* [*The Bitter Songs of Immigration*]. Montreal, 1977. 40 pp. Poems.

1584   *E taxē ton pragmaton* [*The Order of Things*]. Montreal, 1977. Poems.

LINGAS, Helen

1585   *My Centennial Torch for World Peace.* Edmonton, 1967. 144 pp. Autobiographical novel.

1586   *My Olympic Torch for World Justice, Unity and Peace.* Edmonton: Co-op Press, 1980. 309 pp. Autobiographical novel.

MASTORAS, A.

1587   *He Mache [Struggle].* Athens, 1971. Poems.

MAVRIDES, Lambis (1926-   )

Born in Crete, Greece. Received his education in chemistry in Athens (B.Sc.) and in biochemistry at the University of Ottawa (Ph.D.). Spent two years doing post-doctoral studies at New York University. He taught biochemistry at the University of Ottawa until his retirement in 1986.

1588   *Anachoriseis [Departures].* Athens: Diogenis, 1975. 48 pp. Poems.

1589   *Penthos ghia tin Alkisti [Mourning for Alcestis].* Athens: Diogenis, 1982. 43 pp. Poems.

1590   *I strophes tou kairou [The Turns of Time].* Athens: Diogenis, 1982. 38 pp. Poems.

1591   *Rachel [Rachel].* Athens: Diogenis, 1983. 56 pp. Poems.

1592   *Ena telos kalokairiou [An End of Summer].* Athens: Diogenis, 1985. 50 pp. Poems.

1593   *Anepisimos Desmos [Unofficial Relation].* Athens: Diogenis, 1988. 68 pp. Poems.

NTALAS, Demetris

1594   *[Thoughts of Peace.]* Montreal, 1978. Poems.

1595   *[Poetry of Montreal.]* Montreal, 1980. Poems.

1596   *[Beginning and End.]* Montreal, 1984. Poems.

PAPADATOS, G.

1597   *Ho Kautos Helios tes Mesogeiou: Theatriko ergo se pente tēraxeis [Hot Sun over the Mediterranean: A Theatrical Play in Five Acts].* Montreal: The Author, 1980. 124 pp. Play.

1598   *Mia megalē nikē [The Great Victory].* Montreal: Marathon Publishing Co., 1975. 49 pp. Play.

SKALKOU, Lyndia

1599   *[One Voice Uphill.]* Montreal, 1982. Poems.

SMERAEDES, Elias

1600   *Xenēgemos [Immigration].* Montreal, 1977. 158 pp. Poems.

STAMIRIS, GIANNES E.

1601   *O xopapas [The Part-time Priest].* Montreal: Éd. Nouvelle Frontiére, 1971. 302 pp. Novel. [Winner of the "Markos Avgeris" award issued by the Greek Canadian Society.]

STATHOS, John

1602   *Astartē [Astarti].* Montreal: The Author, 1967. 17 pp. Poems.

STOUBOS, George

1603   *To stadhia [The Street].* Toronto: Desmos, 1975. 64 pp. Poems.

THANIEL, George (1938-   )
A native of Greece, he has been in Canada since 1964 and presently teaching Greek at the University of Toronto. He has published a number of books and papers on scholarly subjects and book reviews. His poems in English translation have appeared in *The Charioteer, Grove, Vergilius, Canadian Forum, Anthos* and such monographic sources as *The Linchpin, Poems in English, Beyond the Moment,* and *Seawave and Snowfall.* . His other interests include photography.

1604   *I prokes [The Nails].* Montreal: Lotofaghos, 1968. 62 pp. Poems.

1605   *To dhohio [The Vessel].* Toronto: The Author, 1974. 32 pp. Poems.

1606   *Poems in English. I. Villa Vergiliana. II. You Bet.* Toronto: Amaranth Editions, 1979. 55 pp. illus., port. Poems.

1607   *Seawave & Snowfall; Selected Poems 1960-1982,* translated from the Greek by Edward Phinney. Toronto: Amaranth Editions, 1984. 120 pp. Poems.

   Writings about:

1608   Martindale, Sheila. Review of *Beyond the Moment.* CAN AUTH BKMN 60, no. 1 (1984): 24.

1609   Review of *I prokes.* BKS ABR 43 (1969)

1610   Review of *I prokes.* BULL ANALYT BIBLIO HELLEN (1968)

1611   Review of George Thaniel's poetry. NAT HERALD TRIB (Nov. 14, 1976)

TROGADIS, Pantelis

1612   *Sto pandoxeio ton trion anemon [At the Hotel of Three Hills].* Athens, 1960. 73 pp. Poems.

1613   *E sugxonē salinikē tragodia [The Modern Greek Tragedy].* Montreal: Kouros Publishing House, 1967. 64 pp. Short novel.

TSIMACILIS, Stavros (1950-   )
Born in Skoura, Greece, emigrated to Canada in 1963. His poems have appeared in *The Eyeopener, The Whitewall Review* and other journals. He lives in Toronto.

1614   *Anticipation.* Ottawa: Borealis Press, 1978. 50 pp. Poems.

1615   *Exiled, the Myth Needles Deeper.* Erin, Ont.: Porcupine's Quill, 1981. Poems.

1616   *Liturgy of Light.* Toronto: Aya Press, 1986. Poems.
       [Text in Greek and English.]

VLASSIS, George (1892-1964)

1617 *Roda kai violettes [Roses and Violets].* Ottawa, 1924. Poems.

1618 *Phylla apo tēn Kanadikē poiēsē [Pages from Canadian Poetry].* Ottawa, 1936. Poems.

Writing about:

1619 Petritis, Takis. "Treis axioi korinthioi protometanastes ston Kanada" [Three Corinthian Immigrants in Canada]. KORINTHIAKA 2, no. 5 (1978): 196-200.
[Provides a summary of George Vlassis' poetry.]

ZEI, Martha

1620 *Elpida ghia leuteria-ē sklēpē zoē mias Ellēnidas metanastrias [Hope for Freedom - The Hard Life of a Greek Immigrant Woman].* Athens: Nicos Agas Publisher, 1975. 78 pp. Autobiographical novel.

Writing about:

1621 Petritis, Takis. Review of *Elpida gia leuteria-ē sklēpē.* ATLANTIS 2, no. 11 (1976): 2.

ZIATOS, Christos.(1937-   )

1622 [Without Appearance.] Thessalonica, 1971. Poems.

1623 *Cheironomies [Gestures].* Toronto: Toxotēs, 1975. Poems.

1624 *To syneches paron: Poiemata [The Continuous Present: Poems].* Toronto: Greek Publications, 1980. 32 pp. Poems.

1625 [Thirty Four and One Absurdities for Love.] Athens: Odesseas, 1980. Poems.

GUYANESE

CAMBRIDGE, Vibert C. (1942-   )
Born in Guayana and lived in the U.K. and the U.S.A. before coming to Canada in the mid-1970s. In addition to being a poet, he is also an actor and a painter.

1626   *Excuse Me! May I Offer Some Interpretations: Poems.* Toronto: Wacacro Production, 1975. vi, 66 leaves. Poems.

1627   *Historical Perspectives.* Toronto: Wacacro [n.d.] Poems.

DABYDEEN, Cyril (1945-   )
Born in Berbicé, Guyana, emigrated to Canada in 1970. Educated at Queen's University, Kingston (M.A. English, Master of Public Administration) and taught English at Algonquin College, Ottawa and at the University of Ottawa. His poems and short stories have appeared in *Canadian Fiction Magazine, Nebula, Quarry, Canadian Literature, Fiddlehead, Grain, Prism International, Waves* and other journals. Recipient of the S. Parker Gold Medal for Poetry (1964); A.J. Seymour Lyric Poetry Prize; Louise Plumb Poetry Prize, Okanagan Fiction Prize, etc. Poet Laureate of Ottawa (1984-1987). He is an activist in race relations.

1628   *Poems in Recession.* Georgetown: Sadeek Press, 1972. Poems.

1629   *Distances.* Vancouver: Fiddlehead Poetry Books, 1977. Poems.

1630   Goatsong. [Cover and illustration by Sharon Katz.] Oakville/Ottawa: Mosaic Press/Valley Editions, 1977. vi, 34 pp. Poems.

1631   *Heart's Frame: Poems.* Cornwall, Ont.: Vesta, 1979. 73 pp. Poems.

1632   *This Planet Earth.* Ottawa: Borealis Press, 1979. 81 pp. Poems.

1633   *River in Me.* Ottawa: League of Canadian Poets [1980] 1 folded sheet. Poems.

1634   *Still Close to the Island.* Ottawa: Commoner's Publishing, 1980. 111 pp. Short stories.

1635   *Elephants Make Good Stepladders.* London, Ont.: Third Eye Publications, 1982. 52 pp. Poems.

1636   *The Wizard Swami.* Calcutta: Writers Workshop, 1985. 115 pp. Novel.
[Revised edition published in U.K. in 1988.]

1637   *Islands Lovelier than a Vision.* Leeds, U.K.: Peepal Tree Press, 1986. 85 pp. Poems.

1638   *To Monkey Jungle.* London, Ont.: Third Eye Publications, 1988 120 pp. Short stories.

Writings about:

1639   Hurley, Michael. "Elusive Surfaces." CAN LIT No. 89 (1981): 166-68.
[Review of *This Planet Earth.*]

1640   Itwaru, Arnold. "A First with a Promise of More." SPEAR (December 1977)

[Review of *Distances.*]

1641 Miller, J. "City Poet Sees Himself as Model for Ethnic Kids." OTTAWA CIT (June 18, 1984)

1642 Milles, Ron. "Boxed Set." CAN LIT No. 81 (1979): 138-39.
[Review of *Goatsong.*]

1643 Morley, Patricia. "New Visions from Caribbean." OTTAWA CIT (July 16, 1988) C3.
[Review of *A Shapely Fire.*]

1644 Morley, Patricia. "Sensitive Poetry in Ottawa..." OTTAWA J (March 8, 1978)
[Review of *Goatsong.*]

1645 Mukherjee, Arun. "The Poetry of Michael Ondaatje and Cyril Dabydeen: Two Views of Others." J COMMONW LIT (1985)

1646 Nazareth, Peter. Review of *The Wizard Swami.* WORLD LIT TODAY 60, no. 4 (1986)

1647 Peacock, D. "Heart/Body/Harmony." CAN LIT No. 87 (1980): 142-44.
[Review of *Heart's Frame.*]

1648 Tibbet, Ron. "Young Poet Leaps into Light with Collection." OTTAWA J (July 26, 1980)
[Review of *This Planet Earth.*]

1649 Van Steen, Marcus. "A Poet Worth Nurturing." OTTAWA CIT (Sept. 10, 1977)
[Review of *Distances.*]

1650 West Linder, Norma. "Come to My World." CAN AUTH BKMN 55 (February 1980): 2.
[Review of *Goatsong.*]

1651 West Linder, Norma. "Know Thyself - Through Poetry." CAN AUTH BKMN 55 (May 1980): 23.
[Review of *Heart's Frame.*]

DOWNIE, Jill
Born in Georgetown, Guyana and educated in Great Britain and the Channel Islands. Emigrated to Canada in 1966 and settled in Burlington, Ont.

1652 *Turn of the Century.* New York: Avon, 1982. 395 pp. Novel.

1653 *Angel in Babylon.* Toronto: PaperJacks, 1984. 350 pp. Novel.

1654 *Dark Liaisons.* Toronto: PaperJacks, 1985. Novel.

1655 *Mistress of Moon Hill.* Toronto: PaperJacks, 1985. 320 pp. Novel.

EDONEY, Haile Telatra
Born in Guyana, now lives in Toronto. Her short stories are based on her own experience in Canada.

1656 *Cry of the Illegal Immigrants.* Toronto: Third World Books and Crafts, 1979. Short stories.

ITWARU, Arnold (1942-   )
Born in Berbicé, Guyana, emigrated to Canada in 1969. Teaches sociology at York University. His poems have appeared in *Quarry, Balloon, Nebula* and other periodicals.

1657   *Shattered Songs.* (*A Journey from Somewhere to Somewhere*).   Toronto: Aya Press, 1982. 45 pp. Poems.

SINGH, Nirmala

Born in Demerara, Guyana, came to Canada in 1974. She was educated at Algonquin College, Ottawa. She works for the Federal Government.

1658   *The Shiva Dance.* Cornwall, Ont.: Vesta, 1979. Poems.

HAITIAN

MONOGRAPHS, RESEARCH PAPERS

1659 DEJEAN, Paul
Les Haïtiens au Québec. Montréal: Les Presses de l'Université du Québec, 1979. 189 pp.

1660 JEAN-BAPTISTE
Haitians in Canada/Aysisyin nan Kanada 1957. Hull, Qué.: Minister of Supply and Services Canada, 1979. 44 pp.
[A list of authors with their publications is provided on pp. 31-34.]

1661 JONASSAINT, Jean
La Déchirure du (corps) texte et autres brèches. Montréal: Nouvelle Optique, 1984.
[Décrit la complexité des conditions de vie des noirs dans un monde de blancs et plus particulièrement au Canada français.]

1662 JONASSAINT, Jean
Le Pouvoir des mots, les maux du pouvoir – Des romanciers haïtiens en exil. Montréal: Presses de l'Université de Montréal, 1986.
[Comprend de longues entrevues avec les écrivains canadiens d'origine haïtienne suivants: Lilianne Dévieux, Gérard Étienne, Émile Ollivier et Anthony Phelps.]

1663 LAROCHE, Maximilien
La Littérature haïtienne: identité, langue, réalité. Montréal: Leméac, 1981. 127 pp.
[Table des matières: Littérature et identité (pp. 17-40); Littérature et langue (pp. 41-104); Littérature et réalité (pp. 105-123).

1664 LAROCHE, Maximilien
Le Miracle et la métamorphose: Essai sur les littératures du Québec et Haïti. Montréal: Éds. du Jour, 1970. 239 pp.

1665 VANASSE, André
"Haïti, Haïti, de Anthony Phelps et Gary Klang." LETTR QUÉB 39 (1985): 73.
[Compte rendu de ce roman québécois.]

1666 VANASSE, André
"Le syndrome professoral." VOIX IMAG 10, no. 1 (1984): 163-67.
[Critique de deux romans écrits par des Haïtiens vivant au Canada depuis longtemps: *Mère-solitude*, d'Émile Ollivier, et *Une femme muette*, de Gérard Étienne.]

INDIVIDUAL AUTHORS

ADAM, Michel

1667 *Vers-de-terre: anté-poésie.* Montréal: Dérive, 1975. 28 pp. Poèmes.

ANTOINE, Yves

1668 *Les sabots de la nuit.* Hull, Qué.: Gasparo, 1974. 76 pp. Poèmes.

130

1669   *Alliage, poésie et prose.* Sherbrooke, Qué.: Naaman, 1979. 59 pp. Poèmes et prose.

BERROUËT-ORIOL, Robert (1951-   )
Né à Port-au-Prince, Haïti. Arrive au Québec en 1968. Étudie la linguistique à l'Université de Montréal. Ses poèmes ont paru dans des revues.

1670   *Lettres urbaines: poèmes, suivi de Le dire-à-Soi [du rapport à la langue].* Montréal: Triptyque, 1968. 87 pp. Poèmes.

BLACKSNOWGOAT, Ruben Francois, pseud. (Vrai nom: RUBEN, François) (1945-1974)
Né à Haïti. Émigré au Canada à la fin des années 60. Meurt tragiquement à Montréal.

1671   *Confessions One: Blues and Rapp-sodies of a Black Immigrant.* Montreal [n.p., n.d.] Poems.

1672   *My Soul in Tears: A Book of Poems.* Montreal [n.p., n.d.] Poems.

1673   *The Scavangers and Other Poems.* Montreal [n.p., n.d.] Poems.

CASSÉUS, Maurice

1674   *Viejo.* Montréal: Édition La Presse, Kraus Reprint, 1970. Roman.

CASTERA, Georges, fils.

1675   *Kónbèlann.* Montréal: Nouvelle Optique, 1974. 225 pp. Poèmes créoles.

CHAM, Serge

1676   *Plaidoirie pour les hommes.* Ottawa, 1974. 48 pp. Poèmes.

CHARLES, Jean-Claude

1677   *Ste-Dérive des cochons.* Montréal: Nouvelle Optique, 1977. 104 pp. Roman.

CHASSAGNE, Raymond

1678   *Mots de passe.* Sherbrooke, Qué.: Naaman, 1976. 65 pp. Poèmes.

    Writings about:

1679   Cimon, Renée. Critique: *Mots de passe.* NOS LIVR 9, no. 110 (1978)

1680   Laroche, Maximilien. Critique: *Mots de passe.* LIVR AUTR QUÉB 1976: 142-43.

CIVIL, Salvadore Jean (1932-   )
Né à Jaemel, Haïti. Reçoit son éducation à Port-au-Prince. Vient au Canada en 1967. Il enseigne dans une école secondaire à Sherbrooke et est directeur littéraire de l'Association des auteurs des Cantons de l'est. Récipiendaire de prix littéraires pour sa poésie.

1681   *Entre deux pays: poésie.* Sherbrooke, Qué.: Éds. Sherbrooke, 1979. Poèmes.

1682   *Au bout l'abîme: poésie.* Sherbrooke, Qué.: Éds. la Margelle, 1985. Poèmes.

Writings about:

1683 Bélanger, Christian. Critique: *Entre deux pays.* LIVR AUTR QUÉB 1979: 107-08.

1684 Bonenfant, Joseph. "Notes sur la poésie." VOIX IMAG 6, no. 3 (1981): 482.

1685 Critique: *Entre deux pays.* CAHIERS HIBOU 1, no. 4-5 (1980): 115.

1686 Gagnon, Daniel. Critique: *Entre deux pays.* GRIMOIRE 3, no. 8 (1980): 7.

1687 Giguère, Richard. "S.J. Civil." LETTR QUÉB No. 17 (1980): 30-33.

1688 Giguère, Richard. "Salvadore Jean Civil." Dans *Petit album des auteurs des Cantons de l'est.* (Saint-Élie d'Orford, 1980) pp. 31-32. portr.

1689 Gonzalo-Francoli, Yvette. Critique: *Entre deux pays.* VOIX IMAG 5, no. 3 (1980): 599-601.

1690 Janoël, André. Critique: *Entre deux pays.* NOS LIVR 12 (avr. 1981) no. 182.

1691 Pierre-Gilles, Élie. Review of *Entre deux pays.* GRIMOIRE 3, no. 1 (1980): 5-7.

COLAS, Justin

1692 *Mosaïques.* Chicoutimi, Qué.: Éditions le Progrès du Saguenay, 1969. Poèmes.

1693 *Port ensablé.* Desbiens: Éditions du Phare, 1970. 127 pp. Roman.

DELPHIN, Jacques

1694 *Une robe au destin.* Québec: Éditions Garneau, 1970. 83 pp.

DÉPESTRE, René

1695 *Alleluia pour une femme-jardin.* Montréal: Leméac, 1973. 148 pp. [Collection francophonie vivante.]

DÉVIEUX DEHOUX, Lilianne (1942-)
Née à Port-au-Prince, Haïti. Vient à Montréal en 1965. Reçoit un certificat d'études littéraires à la Sorbonne et une maîtrise ès lettres à l'Université de Montréal où elle fait présentement de la recherche. Ses nouvelles ont été publiées dans *Contes et Nouvelles* de langue française et ailleurs.

1696 *L'amour oui, la mort non: roman haïtien* Sherbrooke, Qué.: Naaman, 1976. 134 pp. Roman. [Prix littéraire des Caraïbes.]

Writings about:

1697 Bergeron, Henri-Paul. Critique: *L'amour oui, la mort non.* NOS LIVR 8, no. 7 (1977)

1698 Laroche, Maximilien. Critique: *L'amour oui, la mort non.* LIVR AUTR QUÉB 1976: 66-67.

ÉTIENNE, Gérard (1936-)
Né à Cap-Haïtien, Haïti. A terminé son doctorat ès lettres à Strasbourg en France. Vient à Montréal en 1964. Il est professeur au département de français de l'Université de Moncton (N.B.). Il a publié des recueils de poèmes, des nouvelles et des essais qui sont encore réprimés en Haïti.

1699   *Lettre à Montréal*. Montréal: Éds. de l'Estérel [1966] 32 pp. Poèmes.

1700   *Dialogue avec mon ombre*. Montréal: Éds. francophones du Canada, 1972. 135 pp. Poèmes.

1701   *Le Nègre crucifié: récit*. Montréal: Nouvelle Optique, 1974. 150 pp.

1702   *Un ambassadeur macoute à Montréal*. Montréal: Nouvelle Optique, 1979. 233 pp. Roman.

1703   *Cri pour ne pas crever de honte*. Montréal: Nouvelle Optique, 1983. 64 pp.

1704   *Une femme muette*. Montréal: Nouvelle Optique, 1983.

Writings about:

1705   Laroche, Maximilien. Critique: *Lettre à Montréal*. LIVR AUTR QUÉB 1966: 99-101.

1706   Paratte, Henri-Dominique. "*Un ambassadeur macoute à Montréal*." PRÉSENCE FRANCOPHONE No. 20 (1980): 188-92.

1707   Régnier, Claude. "*Une femme muette*." NUIT BLANCHE No. 16 (décembre 1984-janvier 1985): 5.

1708   Royer, Jean. Critique: *Lettre à Montréal*. L'ACTION 22 (juil. 1960): 21.

1709   Simon, Sherry. "De l'exil à l'appartenance." SPIRALE No. 43 (mai 1984): 6.
[Critique: *Une femme muette*.]

1710   Valiquette, Bernard. "À la page. *Lettre à Montréal*." ÉCHOS-VEDETTES 27 (août 1966): 25.

1711   Vanasse, André. "Le syndrome professoral." VOIX IMAG 10, no. 1 (1984): 164-67.
[Critique: *Une femme muette*.]

FOUCHÉ, Franck

1712   *Bouqui au paradis*. Montréal: Leméac, 1968. Théâtre.

1713   *Trou de dieu*. Montréal: Leméac, 1968. Théâtre.

1714   *Général Baron Lacroix: ou le silence masqué*. Montréal: Leméac, 1974. 124 pp. Théâtre.

Writing about:

1715   Beausoleil, Claude. "Vaudou et théâtre." JEU No. 5 (1977): 145-46.

JACQUES, Maurice (1939-   )
Né à Verreltes, Haïti. Vient au Québec en 1969. Il enseigne à Loretteville, Qué.

1716   *Le miroir: poésie*, postface de Jean Cau Parisien, illus. de M. Bonaparte. Sherbrooke, Qué.: Naaman [1977] 77 pp. Poèmes.

1717   *L'Ange du diable: conte haïtien*. Sherbrooke, Qué.: Naaman, 1979. 58 pp.

1718   *Les Voix closes: poésie* Sherbrooke, Qué.: Naaman, 1980. 77 pp. Poèmes.

Writings about:

1719   Bayard, Caroline. Critique: *Les Voix closes.* UNIV TOR Q 50 (1980-81): 51.

1720   Bonenfant, Joseph. "Notes sur la poésie." VOIX IMAG 6, no. 3 (1981): 484.
[Critique: *Les Voix closes.*]

1721   Janoël, André. Critique: *Les Voix closes.* NOS LIVR 12 no. 141 (mars 1981)

LAFERRIÈRE, Dany

1722   *Comment faire l'amour avec un nègre sans se fatiguer.* Montréal: VLB Editeur, 1986. Roman.

1723   *How to Make Love to a Negro*, translated from the French by David Homel. Toronto: Coach House Press, 1988. 117 pp. Novel.

Writings about:

1724   Beaudoin, Réjean. "Les mouches du plafond." LIBERTÉ 165 (juin 1986): 126-31.
[Critique: *Comment faire l'amour avec un nègre sans se fatiguer.*]

1725   Frank, Steve. "How to Make Love to a Negro without Tiring." OTTAWA CIT (July 2, 1988)
[Review of *How to Make Love to a Negro.*]

1726   Grady, Wayne. "Black and White in Colour." BKS CAN 17, no. 2 (1988): 38-39.
[Review of *How to Make Love to a Negro.*]

1727   Lamy, Suzanne. "Enfin de l'humour noir." SPIRALE 58 (fév. 1986): 6.
[Critique: *Comment faire l'amour avec un nègre sans se fatiguer.*]

1728   Marcotte, Gilles. Critique: *Comment faire l'amour avec un nègre sans se fatiguer.* L'ACTUALITÉ 11, no. 2 (1986): 126.

LAGAGNEUR, Serge (1937-   )
Né à Jérémie, Haïti. Ses écrits ont paru dans des anthologies (*Manuel illustré de la littérature haïtienne, Histoire de la littérature haïtienne, Poésie vivante d'Haïti, Poésie québécoise des origines à nos jours*).

1729   *Textes interdits: poésie* Montréal: Estérel, 1965. 140 pp. Poèmes.

1730   *Textes en croix.* Montréal: Nouvelle Optique, 1978. 148 pp. Poèmes.

1731   *Le crabe.* Montréal: Estérel, 1981. Poèmes.

1732   *Inaltérable.* Montréal: Éditions Noroît, 1983. Poèmes.

1733   *Textes muets.* Montréal: Éd. Noroît/La table rase, 1987. Poèmes.

MORRISSEAU, Roland (1933-   )
Né à Port-au-Prince, Haïti. A commencé à publier en 1960.

1734   *Germination d'espoir.* Port-au-Prince, 1961. 48 pp. Poèmes.

1735   *Clef du soleil.* Port-au-Prince, 1963. Poèmes.

1736   *La Chanson de Roland.* Montréal: Nouvelle Optique, 1979. 100 pp. Poèmes.

Writing about:

1737   Critique: *La Chanson de Roland.* LIVR AUTR QUÉB 1980: 130-31.

OLLIVIER, Émile (1940-   )

Né à Port-au-Prince, Haïti. Émigré au Canada en 1965. Pendant qu'il terminait une maîtrise en pédagogie à l'Université d'Ottawa, il entreprend une maîtrise et un doctorat en sociologie à l'Université de Montréal. Il est professeur à la faculté de l'éducation de l'Université de Montréal.

1738   *Paysage de l'aveugle.* Montréal: Pierre Tisseyre, 1977. 142 pp. Roman.

1739   *Mère-solitude: roman.* Paris: Albin Michel, 1986. 209 pp. Roman.

1740   *La Discorde aux cent voix.* Paris: Albin Michel, 1986. Roman.

Writing about:

1741   Cossette, Gilles. "*Mère-solitude* de Émile Ollivier. Avec des mots." LETTR QUÉB No. 33 (1984): 37-38.

1742   Kröller, Eva-Marie. Critique: *Mère-solitude.* CAN LIT No. 103 (1984): 131.

1743   Marcotte, Gilles. Critique: *Mère-solitude.* L'ACTUALITÉ 9, no. 1 (1984): 77.

1744   Minot, René. Critique: *Mère-solitude.* NOS LIVR 15 (décembre 1984): 30-31.

1745   Simon, Sherry. Critique: *Mère-solitude.* SPIRALE No. 39 (1983): 9.

PAUL, Cauvin

1746   *Nuit sans fond.* Montréal: Presses Solidaires, 1976. 56 pp. Roman.

PEREIRA, Roger

1747   *Les Galops de Dune,* illus. Dicky Pereira. Sherbrooke, Qué.: Naaman, 1976. 100 pp. Poèmes.

PHELPS, Anthony (1928-   )

Né à Port-au-Prince, Haïti. Étudie aux Etats-Unis et au Canada et retourne dans son pays natal pour travailler comme journaliste et reporter à la radio. Revient au Canada en 1964 et travaille à Radio-Canada International jusqu'à sa retraite au Mexique en 1985. Connu comme romancier, dramaturge et essayiste, Phelps est l'un des auteurs canadiens d'origine haïtienne les plus importants.

1748   *Éclats de silence: poèmes.* [Port-au-Prince, 1962] [50] pp. Poèmes.

1749   *Points cardinaux: poésie* Dans THÉÂTRE VIVANT No. 4 (1968): 4-44. Également Montréal: Holt, Rinehart & Winston, 1966. 60 pp. Poèmes.

1750   *Le Conditionnel.* Montréal: Holt, Rinehart & Winston, 1968. 40 pp. Théâtre.

1751   *Mon pays que voici.* Paris: J.P. Oswald, 1968. 142 pp. Poèmes.

1752   *Moins l'infini: roman haïtien.* Paris: Éditeurs français réunis, 1972. 217 pp. Roman.

1753 *Et moi, je suis une île/As for Myself, I am an Island.* Montréal: Leméac, 1973. 93 pp. Contes.

1754 *Mémoires en colin-maillard: roman.* Montréal: Nouvelle Optique, 1976. 153 pp. Roman.

1755 *Motifs pour le temps saisonnier.* Paris: J.P. Oswald, 1976. Poèmes.

1756 *La bélière caraïbe.* Montréal: Nouvelle Optique, 1980. 132 pp. Poèmes, nouvelle.

Writings about:

1757 Allante-Lima, Willy. "Les livres." PRÉSENCE AFRICAINE 71 (1969): 109-11.

1758 Bellemare, Madeleine. Critique: *La bélière caraïbe.* NOS LIVR 12, no. 150 (1981)

1759 Burlet, Françoise Laure. Critique: *Moins l'infini.* Dans *Dictionnaire des oeuvres littéraires du Québec* (Montréal: Fides, 1970-1975) vol. 5, pp. 558-59.

1760 Darry, Bernard. "Chronique des livres." JEUNE AFRIQUE 442 (juin 23-29, 1969): 15.

1761 Gladu, Paul. "Un album d'images qui a de l'originalité, de la gueule." PETIT J 41, no. 4 (1966): 61.

1762 Hamel, Louis-Paul. "*Points cardinaux.*" SOLEIL 70, no. 45 (févr. 18, 1967): 30.

1763 Image et verbe à la Mousse-spatêgue." PRESSE 82, no. 260 (1966): 65.

1764 Laroche, Maximilien. "*Et moi je suis une île* d'Anthony Phelps." LIVR AUTR QUÉB (1973): 41.

1765 Laroche, Maximilien. "*Le Conditionnel* d'Anthony Phelps." LIVR AUTR QUÉB (1968): 77-78.

1766 Laroche, Maximilien. Critique: *Mémoires en colin-maillard.* LIVR AUTR QUÉB 1977: 73-74.

1767 Marchand, Olivier. "Micheline Gagnon et Anthony Phelps: sobre plainte et large chant." PR 83, no. 57 (1967): 5.

1768 *Moins l'infini* d'Anthony Phelps." Dans le *Bulletin critique du livre français* 284-285 (août-sept. 1969): 727.

1769 Pallascio-Morin, Ernest. "Entre le feu qui fait l'acier, entre la mer et la toundra, un qui veut aimer." L'ACTION 60, no. 17 (1967): 17.

1770 "Parution du premier volume de la collection 'Le chant du monde'." L'ACTION 60, no. 17 (1967): 14.

1771 Piazza, François. "*Points cardinaux.*" ÉCHOS-VEDETTES 31, no. 14 (1967): 21.

1772 Poisson, Roch. "De bons collages, et une mauvaise fugue." PHOTO-JOURNAL 30, no. 32 (1966): 86.

1773 Poisson, Roch. "Phelps et Saint-Aubin: invitations au voyage." PHOTO-JOURNAL 30, no. 42 (1967): 70.

1774 Rioux, Gilles. "Lu pour vous: *Moins l'infini..*" Dans *Croissance des jeunes nations* 149-150 (1974): 42.

1775 Rioux, Gilles. Critique: *Points cardinaux.* SEPT-JOURS 1, no. 23 (1967): 46.

1776 Robert, Guy. "*Points cardinaux* d'Anthony Phelps." LIVR AUTR QUÉB (L967): 103.

1777 Savard, Michel. Critique: *La Bélière caraïbe.* LIVR AUTR QUÉB 1980: 129-30.

1778 Tard, Louis Martin. "Où le verbe s'allie à la poésie de l'image." PATRIE 87, no. 45 (1966): 63.

1779 Théberge, Jean-Yves. "Un poète haïtien parmi nous." CAN FRANÇ 107, no. 39 (1967): 26.

1780 Thériault, Jacques. "Image et verbe d'Irène Chiasson... Elle creuse l'imaginaire." DEVOIR 57, no. 286 (1966): 8.

PIERRE, Claude (1941-   )
Né à Corail, Haïti. Il reçoit son éducation à l'Université d'Haïti. Il vient au Canada et étudie à l'Université Laval et à l'Université d'Ottawa. Il donne des cours en littérature française à l'Université d'Ottawa.

1781 *Coucou rouge.* Québec: Abeille, 1972. Poèmes.

1782 *Coïncidence.* Ottawa: Presses université d'Ottawa, 1973. Poèmes.

1783 *Tourne ma toupie, suivi de Oeil*, postface de L. Berthaud. Sherbrooke, Qué.: Naaman, 1974. 79 pp. Poèmes.

1784 *Huit poèmes infiniment*; textes, Stéfane-Albert Boulais. Le groupe 7-1, 1983. 1 portf.

1785 *D'Encens et de Soufre.* Montréal: Vermillon, 1986. Poèmes.

1786 *Crues: Klod Pyè*; encres, Francine Houle. Ottawa: Vermillon, 1986. 1 portf. illus.

RENAUD, Alix (1945-   )

1787 *Carême.* Paris: Éds. St-Germain des Prés, 1972. 57 pp. Poèmes.

1788 *Extase exacte.* Paris: La Pensée universelle, 1976. Poèmes.

1789 *Grâces: Poème de chevet*, illustré d'une aquarelle de Marie Leberge. [Lévis: Éds. de l'Erbruar, 1979.] 1 feuillet double. illus.

1790 *Le Mari.* Sherbrooke, Qué.: Naaman, 1980. 91 pp. Nouvelles.

1791 *Dix secondes de sursis: nouvelles.* Québec: Laliberté, 1983. 135 pp. portr. Nouvelles.

1792 *Merdiland.* Marseille: Le Temps, 1983.

1793 *À corps joie: roman.* Montréal: Nouvelle Optique, 1985. 253 pp. Roman.

Writings about:

1794 Cantin, Léonce. Critique: *Le Mari.* LIVR AUTR QUÉB 1980: 64-65.

1795 Janelle, Claude. "Alix Renaud, écrivain éclectique." SOLARIS 10, no. 3 (1984): 10-11.

1796 Janoël, André. Critique: *Extase exacte.* NOS LIVR 12 no 211 (avril 1981)

1797 Laroche, Maximilien. Critique: *Extase exacte.* LIVR AUTR QUÉB 1976: 141-42.

1798 Vandendorpe, Christian. Critique: *Le Mari.* QUÉB FRANÇ No. 40 (1980): 14.

HUNGARIAN

BIBLIOGRAPHIES, DIRECTORIES

1799 BISZTRAY, George
"Biographical Bibliography of Hungarian-Canadian Authors since World War II." In his *Hungarian-Canadian Literature.* (Toronto: University of Toronto Press, 1987) pp. 95-113.
[A complete list of literary publications with biographical notes. Some secondary materials are also included.]

1800 BOGNÁR, Desi K.; SZENTPÁLY, Katalin, eds.
Hungarians in America; A Biographical Directory of Professionals of Hungarian Origin in the Americas. 3rd. ed. Mt. Vernon, N.Y., 1971. 238 pp.
[Provides biographical sketches and lists of publications. Several Hungarian-Canadian authors are included. 2nd edition was edited by Tibor Szi, published by the Hungarian University Association, 1963.]

1801 DUSKA, László; MALYCKY, Alexander
"Hungarian-Canadian Periodical Publications: A Preliminary Check List." CAN ETH STUD 2, no. 1 (1970): 75-81.
[Contains references to Hungarian newspapers and periodicals published in Canada.]

1802 HALÁSZ de BÉKY, Iván L.
The Hungarians in Canada: A Bibliography. Toronto: The Author, 1977. 15 pp.
[Includes 127 citations under the following headings: Bibliographies, Biographies, Directories; General history; Local history; Church history; Integration; Refugees of 1956; Statistics; and Travelogues.]

1803 MISKA, John (i.e. János)
Canadian Studies on Hungarians 1886-1986: An Annotated Bibliography of Primary and Secondary Sources. Regina: Canadian Plains Research Center, University of Regina, 1987. 245 pp.
[Contains references to Canadian writing related to Hungarians. Part II includes 664 entries on Hungarian literature in Canada (pp. 105-58), listed under Poetry, Prose and Plays.]

1804 MISKA, John (i.e. János)
"Hungarian-Canadian Creative Literature: A Preliminary Check List of Imprints." CAN ETH STUD 5, nos. 1-2 (1973): 131-37.
[Arranged alphabetically by author-title, includes references to books of poetry, prose and drama.]

1805 NÁDAS, János; SOMOGYI, Ferenc, eds.
A Magyar Találkozó Krónikája/Proceedings of the Hungarian Annual Congress. Cleveland, OH: Árpád Publishing Co., 1961-   .
[Contains biographical notes on members, with bibliographic data relating to their publications. Several Hungarian-Canadian authors are represented. The first volumes, e.g. 1961-62, were edited by Béla Béldy.]

1806 PAULSON, Ildikó; DUSKA, László
"Hungarian-Canadian Creative Literature: A Preliminary Check List of Authors and Pseudonyms." CAN ETH STUD 2, no. 1 (1970): 83-84.
[Provides a list of creative literature.]

1807 SZÉPLAKI, Joseph

The Hungarians in America 1583-1974: A Chronology & Fact Book. New York: Oceana Publications, 1975. 152 pp. (Ethnic Chronology Series, no. 8)
[Several Hungarian-Canadian authors are represented.]

1808 SZÉPLAKI, Joseph
Hungarians in the United States and Canada: A Bibliography. Holdings of the Immigration History Research Center of the University of Minnesota. Minneapolis: Immigration History Research Center, University of Minnesota, 1977. 113 pp.
[Includes bibliographic data arranged by subject. The sections under Textbooks (p. 30) and Literature (pp. 31-45) contain books of poetry and fiction by Ferenc Fáy, László Kemenes Géfin, János Miska, Tamás Tűz, György Vitéz and others.]

BOOKS, RESEARCH PAPERS

1809 BÉLÁDI, Miklós; POMOGÁTS, Béla; RÓNAY, László
A nyugati magyar irodalom 1945 után [Hungarian Literature in the Western World since 1945]. Budapest: Gondolat, 1986. 327 pp.
[Canadian poets included are János Bebek, Iván Béky-Halász, György Faludy, Ferenc Fáy, Tamás Hajós, László Kemenes Géfin, Ilona Szitha, Tamás Tűz, György Vitéz and others.]

1810 BISZTRAY, George
Canadian-Hungarian Literature: A Preliminary Survey, edited by Michael Batts. [Ottawa: Multiculturalism, Department of the Secretary of State, 1988.] 48 pp.
[A survey of Hungarian-Canadian literature written in Hungarian. Provides an analysis of the various genres, a comprehensive list of bio-bibliographies of authors, a select list of studies and periodicals cited.]

1811 BISZTRAY, George
"Canadian Hungarian Literature: Values Lost and Found." In *Identifications: Ethnicity and the Writer in Canada,* edited by Jars Balan. (Edmonton: Canadian Institute of Ukrainian Studies, 1982) pp. 22-35.
[An analytical study of Hungarian literature in Canada from the 1930s to date. Major authors included are Iván Béky-Halász, György Faludy, Ferenc Fáy, Tamás Hajós, László Kemenes Géfin, Ödön Kiss, János Miska, Ernő Németh, Éva Sárvári, Tamás Tűz, György Vitéz, Magda Zalán.]

1812 BISZTRAY, George
Hungarian-Canadian Literature. Toronto: University of Toronto Press, 1987. 113 pp. ports.
[A comprehensive study of the following aspects: Canadian literature in the non-official languages (pp. 3-8); Hungarian-Canadian literature (pp. 9-16); Stages of Hungarian-Canadian literature (pp. 17-64); Sociopsychological profile of the Hungarian-Canadian author (pp. 65-73); The future (pp. 74-78); Bibliography (pp. 94-113). Authors included are László Kemenes Géfin, György Faludy, Ferenc Fáy, János Miska, Éva Sárvári, Tamás Tűz, György Vitéz, Tamás Hajós, and many others.]

1813 BISZTRAY, George, ed.
"Hungarian Poetry in the Diaspora: A Symposium." HUNG STUD REV 8, no. 1 (1981): 127-35.
[Includes presentations by, and biographical notes on, György Faludy, László Kemenes Géfin, Tamás Tűz, and György Vitéz. The papers, originally presented in Hungarian to the Hungarian Studies Conference held at the University of Toronto in 1981, were translated into English by George Bisztray.]

1814 BISZTRAY, George
"A kanadai magyar irodalom: interjú" [Hungarian-Canadian Literature: An Interview]. MAGY HÍR 37, no. 20 (1984): 11. port.
[An interview given in Budapest, dealing with the main stream of Hungarian-Canadian literature.]

1815   BISZTRAY, George

"Külhonban – nemzettudattal" [Abroad – Retaining National Identity]. MOZGÓ VILÁG no. 4 (1982): 22-31.

[In spite of their daily contact with life in Canada, Hungarian authors in this country have managed to preserve their national heritage through their writing. Individual authors discussed are Ferenc Fáy, László Kemenes Géfin, György Vitéz, János Miska, Éva Sárvári and others.]

1816   BORBÁNDI, Gyula

"A kanadai magyar írókról" [On Hungarian Canadian Authors]. In his *A magyar emigráció életrajza 1945-1985*. (Munich: The Author, 1985.)

[This 510-page study provides a comprehensive analysis of the social, political, literary, organizational, and religious aspects of Hungarians in the Western world. Hungarian-Canadian authors included are Iván Béky-Halász, György Faludy, Ferenc Fáy, László Kemenes Géfin, János Miska, Tamás Tűz, and Magda Zalán.]

1817   CZIGÁNY, Lóránt

The Oxford History of Hungarian Literature: From the Earliest Times to the Present. Oxford: Clarendon, 1984. x, 582 pp.

[Canadian authors included are György Faludy, Ferenc Fáy, László Kemenes Géfin, Tamás Tűz, and György Vitéz.]

1818   FEJŐS, Zoltán

"A kanadai hungarológia eredményei" [The Accomplishments of Hungarian Studies in Canada]. ÉLET IROD 33, no. 11 (1988): 10.

[Review of John Miska's *Canadian Studies on Hungarians*. Reprinted in AMERIKAI MAGYAR SZÓ (July 7, 1988): 7.]

1819   KOVÁCS, Martin L.

"Early Hungarian-Canadian Culture." CAN-AMER REV HUNG STUD 7, no. 1 (1980): 55-76.

[Contents: A folk community (Békevár) (pp. 55-57); The Békevár culture: music, poetry (pp. 57-67); Early experiences depicted by Hungarian pioneer poets (pp. 67-71); Poetical creativity at Békevár (pp. 71-72).]

1820   KOVÁCS, Martin L.

"Some Early Hungarian Canadian Literary Gems of Saskatchewan: Hungarian Canadians in Saskatchewan. In *Second Banff Conference on Central and East European Studies. Banff, Alta., March 2-5, 1978*, edited by Metro Gulutsan. (Edmonton: CEESA, 1978) vol. 1, pp. 55-85.

[Provides an analysis of Hungarian poetry in Saskatchewan, with extensive excerpts from the works of Beny Szakács, Steve Tóth, Kálmán Kováchi and others.]

1821   KÜRTÖSI, Katalin

"Könyv a kanadai magyar irodalomról" [A Book about Hungarian-Canadian Literature]. ÉLET IROD 33, no. 11 (1988): 10.

[Review of George Bisztray's *Hungarian-CanadianLiterature*.]

1822   MISKA, János

"Hungarian Poetry in Canada." In *Second Banff Conference on Central and East European Studies. Banff, Alta., March 2-5, 1978*, edited by Metro Gulutsan. (Edmonton: CEESA, 1978) vol. 1, pp. 140-48.

[An introductory survey of Hungarian poetry in Canada. Poets represented are Ferenc Fáy, Tamás Tűz, László Kemenes Géfin, and György Vitéz.]

1823   MISKA, János

Kanadából szeretettel: Válogatott írások 1975–1985 [From Canada with Self-respect: Selected Essays] 1975–1985]. Ottawa: Kanadai Magyar Írók, 1989. 121 pp. port.
[A collection of literary essays, reports and book reviews pertaining to Hungarian literary and scholarly activities in Canada.]

1824 MISKA, János
"A kanadai magyar irodalom" [Hungarian-Canadian Literature]. In his *A magunk portáján...* (Lethbridge: Kanadai Magyar Írók, 1974) pp. 80-84.
[Describes various aspects of Hungarian-Canadian literature including the literary experiments of Ferenc Fáy, Tamás Tűz, György Vitéz, Kemenes Géfin László and historical novels by Sándor Domokos and Lajos Simon. The difficulties in finding publishers and distributors are also discussed.]

1825 MISKA, János
"A kanadai magyar irodalom két dimenziója" [On the Two Dimensions of Hungarian-Canadian Literature.] KRÓNIKA 2, no. 11 (1976): 7-9. Reprinted in his *Kanadából szeretettel* (Ottawa: Kanadai Magyar Írók, 1987) pp. 29-33.
[Hungarian literature in Canada falls into two categories. Authors belonging to the first group are Ferenc Fáy, Tamás Tűz, György Vitéz, Sándor Domokos, László Kemenes Géfin, who write in Hungarian. John Marlyn, Gabriel Szohner, George Páyerle and some others who write in English form the second dimension. The latter group is introduced to Hungarian readers.]

1826 MISKA, János
"A kanadai magyar prózaírásról" [On Hungarian-Canadian Fiction]. NYELVÜNK KULTÚRÁNK 49 (1982): 21-26.
[Hungarian prose writing in Canada is explored, including historical background, literary genres and themes. Authors analyzed include Sándor Domokos, József Juhász, János Miska, István Nagy, Imre Naphegyi, Lajos Simon, László Szilvássy, Éva Sárvári, and Tamás Tűz.]

1827 MISKA, János
A magunk portáján: Válogatott írások 1963-1973/Mending Our Fences: Selected Papers 1963-1973. Lethbridge: A Kanadai Magyar Írók, 1974. 119 pp.
[Includes several essays on Hungarian literature in Canada. Some of the relevant studies are listed under separate titles in this compilation. Received silver medal from the Árpád Akadémia, Cleveland, Oh.]

1828 MISKA, János
"Magyar forrásaink felmérése [A Survey of Hungarian Literary Sources in Canada." In his *Kanadából szeretettel...* (Ottawa: Kanadai Magyar Írók, 1989) pp. 108-121.
[A survey of Hungarian literary and scholarly material in Canada. Areas covered: Statistical survey, thematic analysis, bibliographic sources, archival and private collections, texts and official publications, and bibliographic techniques as research tools.]

1829 MISKA, János
"Magyar költészet Kanadában" [Hungarian Poetry in Canada]. KRÓNIKA 4, no. 3 (1978): 20-22.
[Hungarian version of a paper printed in the *Second Banff Conference on Central and East European Studies Association of Canada*, with additional paragraphs on sociological aspects of authors.]

1830 MISKA, János
"Modern Hungarian Poetry in Canada." CAN-AMER REV HUNG STUD 7, no. 1 (1980): 77-83.
[An analysis of the poetry of Ferenc Fáy, Tamás Tűz, László Kemenes Géfin and György Vitéz. The author maintains that it is quite courageous to pledge loyalty to one's mother tongue in an alien land due to the possibility of intellectual isolation from both Canadian and Hungarian social and cultural contacts.]

1831 MISKA, János
"Notes on Hungarian Poetry." CONT VERSE II, no. 4 (1976): 48.
[Introduces Ferenc Fáy, Tamás Tűz and some members of the younger generation.]

1832 PAPP de CARRINGTON, Ildikó
"From 'Hunky' to Don Juan: The Changing Hungarian Identity in Canadian Fiction." CAN LIT No. 89 (1981): 33-44.
[Describes the changing image of Hungarian-Canadians as explored in the works of John Marlyn, Marika Robert, Stephen Vizinczey, János Miska, István Nagy, and László Szilvássy. English-Canadian authors represented are Robert Kroetsch and Robert Fulford.]

1833 POMOGÁTS, Béla
"Magyar költők nyugaton" [Hungarian Poets in the West]. NYELVÜNK KULTÚRÁNK 55 (1984): 7-11.
[Includes Iván Halász-Béky, György Faludy, Ferenc Fáy, László Kemenes Géfin, Tamás Tűz, György Vitéz and many others.]

1834 RÁDICS, Károly
"Van-e kanadai magyar irodalom?; Interjú Miska Jánossal" [Is There a Hungarian-Canadian Literature? An Interview with János Miska]. A KÖNYV No. 1 (1988): 117-24.
[An interview relating to the present state of Hungarian poetry, fiction, drama in Canada. Miska gives an analysis of the work of Ferenc Fáy, György Faludy, László Kemenes Géfin, John Marlyn, Éva Sárváry, Tamás Tűz, György Vitéz, and many others. He reaches the conclusion that, in spite of some of the specific techniques used by the younger generation of poets, the literature under review tends to be an integral part of Hungarian literature in general, rather than being an independent entity of its own.]

1835 RUZSA, Jenő
"Irodalmunk" [Our Literature]. In his *A kanadai magyarság története*. (Toronto: The Author, 1940) pp. 400-29.
[Gives a brief summary of early literary achievements with emphasis upon poetry. Includes poems by Kálmán Kováchi, Ilona Hordósy, I. Karnai, Ernő Csók, Gyula Izsák, Béla Jagicza, and Lajos Berta.]

1836 SCHROEDER, Andreas
"Next Year in Lethbridge." CAN LIT No. 65 (1975): 95-98.
[A review of *The Sound of Time*... The author questions the usefulness of literary anthologies of general contents.]

1837 SZAKOLCZAY, Lajos
Dunának, Oltnak [Of the Rivers Danube and Olt (e.g. the sound of)]. Budapest: Szépirodalmi Kiadó, 1984. 443 pp.
[A book of essays, includes Tamás Tűz and György Vitéz.]

1838 THACKER, Robert
"Foreigner: The Immigrant Voice in *The Sacrifice* and *Under the Ribs of Death*. CAN ETH STUD 14, no. 1 (1982): 25-35. Special issue.
[The two novels under review depict the ethnic and immigrant experience in Canada, indicating the presence of "invisible" ghettos.]

1839 TŰZ, Tamás
"Magyar irodalom Kanadában" [Hungarian Literature in Canada]. ÚJ LÁTÓH 23, no. 1 (1972): 76-7.
[A study of the works of contemporary Hungarian authors in Canada, including the poems of

Sándor Domokos, Sándor Kristóf, Ernő Németh, Frigyes Schwilgin and the short stories of Lajos Kasza-Marton, Lajos Simon, and Ödön Kiss.]

1840 **VITÉZ, György**
"Magyar Író Amerikában" [Hungarian Author in America]. TANÚ (September 1978): 2-3.
[An analysis of three generations: the generation of Ferenc Molnár, the middle generation of Lajos Zilahy and his contemporaries, and the newer generation whose members are being established as Hungarian authors in the Americas. The problems of publishing and distribution and the welfare of authors in the minority languages are also discussed. By and large, an author writing in a language other than English or French has virtually insurmountable obstacles to tackle.]

ANTHOLOGIES

1841 *Antolológia 1: A Kanadai magyar írók könyve/Anthology 1: A Book of Canadian-Hungarian Authors,* edited by János Miska. Ottawa: Kanadai Magyar Írók Köre, 1969. 146 pp.
[This volume contains poems by Sándor Domokos, Ferenc Fáy, Ödön Kiss, Sándor Kristóf, Ernő Németh, and Frigyes Schwilgin and prose by Sándor Domokos, Lajos Kulcsár, János Miska, István Nagy, Imre Naphegyi, Lajos Simon, and László Szilvássy.]

1842 *Antológia 2: A kanadai magyar írók könyve/Anthology 2: A Book of Canadian-Hungarian Authors,* edited by János Miska. Ottawa: Kanadai Magyar Írók Köre, 1970. 101 pp.
[Includes poetry by László Boldisár, Lajos Kasza Marton, Ödön Kiss, Sándor Kristóf, István Nagy, Imre Naphegyi, Ernő Németh, and Frigyes Schwilgin and prose by Sándor Domokos, Lajos Kulcsár, Veronika Mikó, János Miska, István Nagy, Imre Naphegyi, Lajos Simon, and László Szilvássy.]

1843 *Antológia 3: A kanadai magyar írók könyve/Anthology 3: A Book of Canadian-Hungarian Authors,* edited by János Miska. Ottawa: Kanadai Magyar Írók Köre, 1972. 122 pp.
[Contains poetry by Sándor Domokos, Ferenc Fáy, Lajos Kasza Marton, Sándor Kristóf, Mayora Lee, Ernő Németh, Lukács Tapolczay, and György Vitéz, prose by István Balatoni, Ödön Kiss, Veronika Mikó, István Nagy, Imre Naphegyi, and Lajos Simon and a play by Sándor Bordás. Biographical notes on the authors are provided.]

1844 *Crossroads: An Anthology of Hungarian-Canadian Authors,* edited by János Miska, with an introduction by George Bisztray. Winnipeg: Queenston House Publishing, 1988. 210 pp. (Anthology no. 10)
[Parts 1 and 4 include poetry by Ferenc Fáy, Ödön Kiss, Miklós Tamási, Iván Béky-Halász, Tamás Tűz, Sándor Kristóf, György Faludy, Csaba Dósa, József Seres, Szabolcs Sajgó, Endre Farkas, Tamás Hajós, Tom Könyves, Tihamér Tóth, Jim Tallosi, Nancy Tóth, Éva Tihanyi, Robert Zend, and György Vitéz.
[Parts 2 and 3 contain short stories by Maria Green, John Marlyn, Sándor Domokos, Marina Mezey-McDougall, Magda Zalán, János Miska, László Kemenes Géfin, Gabriel Szohner, Éva Sárvári, Karl Sándor, George Payerle, and Robert Zend. Biographical sketches of authors, and a select list of publications on Hungarian-Canadian literature are also given.]

1845 *Éledő őrtűz: Válogatás a Kanadai Magyar Írók Szövetsége tagjainak munkáiból... [Reviving Flames: Selections from the Works of the Members of the Hungarian -Canadian Authors Association...],* edited by József Juhász. Toronto: The Association, 1980. (Anthology no. 7)
[Includes poetry and short stories by István Balatoni, Anna Baráth, Sándor Domokos, Gyula Erdélyi, Zsuzsanna Gurdonyi, Endre Haraszti, József Juhász, Olga Kertész, Viktor Kiss, Sándor Kostya, Sándor Kristóf, Lajos Kulcsár, Ferenc Mózsi, Imre Naphegyi, Ernő Németh, József Seres, Lajos Simon, Zoltán Simon, László Spanyol, Ilona Szitha, Attila Takács, Lukács Tapolczay, and Péter Tamás Vajk.]

1846   *Határok nélkül: Válogatás a Kanadai Magyar Írók Szövetsége utóbbi irodalmi pályázatán díjazott és kitüntetett legjobb alkotásaiból/Without Borders: Selections from the Prize-winning and Distinguished Writings of the Latest Literary Contest of the Canadian-Hungarian Authors' Association*, edited by József Juhász. Toronto: Kanadai Magyar Írók Szövetsége, 1979. 192 pp. (Anthology no. 6.)
[Includes poetry by Tamás Tűz, János Bebek, Ferenc Mózsi, Anna Baráth, Maxim Tábory, Sándor Kristóf, József Seres, Péter Tamás Vajk, Endre Haraszti, and Viktor Kiss and prose by Lajos Makkó (real name for Tamás Tűz), József Csernyi, László Spanyol, Sándor Domokos, Endre Haraszti, Viktor Kiss, Imre Naphegyi, and Gyula Erdélyi.]

1847   *Hungarian Helicon*, edited and translated by Watson Kirkconnell. Calgary: Széchenyi Society [1986]. xxxix, 763 pp.
[Hungarian-Canadian poets included are Sándor Domokos, György Faludy, Ferenc Fáy, László Kemenes Géfin, Tamás Tűz, György Vitéz.]

1848   *Kanadai Magyar Újság Képes Nagy Naptára [An Almanac of the Hungarian Canadian News]*, edited by Gusztáv Nemes. Winnipeg: Kanadai Magyar Újság, 1930-1975.
[Published annually up to 1975. Contents included fiction, poetry and journalistic writings, as well as writings about Hungary and Canada by authors of Hungarian and Canadian descent.]

1849   *Két dióhéj: A nyugat-európai és tengerentúli magyar prózaírók [Two Nutshells: Western-European and Overseas Hungarian Authors]*, edited by Erzsébet Berkes and László Rónay. Budapest: Szépirodalmi Könyvkiadó, 1987. 333 pp.
[Includes a short story by Tamás Tűz.]

1850   *Kézfogás: Válogatás a Kanadai Magyar Írók Szövetsége tagjainak munkáiból / Handshake: Selections from the Works of Members of the Canadian-Hungarian Authors' Association*, edited by József Juhász. Toronto: Kanadai Magyar Írók Szövetsége, 1977. 100 pp. ports. (Anthology no. 5)
[Contents include poetry by József Juhász, Sándor Kristóf, Ernő Németh and József Seres, short stories by József Juhász and Lajos Kulcsár, and a play by Lajos Simon.]

1851   *Magyar irodalom: Versek és elbeszélések [Hungarian Literature: Poems and Short Stories]*, edited by Mrs. József Ormay. [Toronto]: Hungarian Helicon Committee [n.d.] 200 pp.
[A textbook edition; some of text is translated into English.]

1852   *Maréknyi föld: A Kanadai Magyar Írók Szövetsége 9. antológiája [A Handful of Soil : Anthology 9 of the Hungarian Canadian Authors' Association]*. Toronto: The Association, 1983. 248 pp. (Anthology no. 9)
[Contents include poetry by Anna Baráth, András Doma, Sándor Domokos, Lajos Kasza Marton, Sándor Kristóf, Ernő Németh, Miklós Tamási, and Lukács Tapolczay and short stories by István Balatoni, András Doma, Sándor Domokos, Gyula Gyimesi, Endre Haraszti, Lajos Kulcsár, Gyula Lemke, Lajos Simon, Zoltán Simon, and László Spanyol.]

1853   *Új égtájak [New Horizons]*, edited by György Gömöri and V. Juhász. Washington, DC: Occidental Press, 1969.
[Includes poems by László Kemenes Géfin and György Vitéz.]

1854   *Nyugati magyar költők antológiája [An Anthology of Hungarian Poets in the Western World]*, edited by László Kemenes Géfin. Bern: Európai Protestáns Magyar Szabadegyetem, 1980. 391 pp.
[Includes the following Hungarian-Canadian poets: János Bebek, György Faludy, Ferenc Fáy, László Kemenes Géfin, Tamás Tűz, György Vitéz, and Robert Zend. Biographical notes are also provided.]

1855   *The Sound of Time: Anthology of Canadian-Hungarian Authors*, edited by János Miska. Lethbridge:Canadian-Hungarian Authors' Association, 1974. 208 pp. (Anthology no. 4)
[Includes poems and short stories translated into English or written in English. Biographical sketches of authors and lists of their publications are provided. Contains poetry by Sándor Domokos, György Faludy, George Jónás, Lajos Kasza-Marton, László Kemenes Géfin, Ödön Kiss, Sándor Kristóf, Tamás Tűz, György Vitéz and Robert Zend and short stories by Maria Green,Tamás Kabdebó, Lajos Kasza Marton, Márton Kerecsendi Kiss, Veronika Mikó, Márta Leszlei-Dósa, John Marlyn, János Miska, István Nagy, George Payerle, Karl Sándor, Lajos Simon, János Szanyi, Stephen Vizinczey, and Robert Zend.]

1856   *Szabadon - Living Free; Válogatás a Kanadai Magyar Írók Szövetsége tagjainak műveiből az ötvenhatos magyar forradalom negyedszázados évfordulója alkalmából - Selections from the Writings of the Members of the Hungarian-Canadian Authors' Association on the Occasion of the 25th Anniversary of the 1956 Revolution*, edited by József Juhász. Toronto: Kanadai Magyar Írók Szövetsége, 1981. 184 pp. (Anthology no. 8)
[This anthology contains poetry by József Seres, Ernő Németh, Lukács Tapolczay, Ferenc Mózsi, Péter Tamás Vajk, Lajos Kasza Marton, Kálmán Váthy, and Károly Bálint and prose by László Spanyol, Lajos Simon, Gyula Erdélyi, Lajos Kulcsár, Sándor Domokos, József Juhász, Sándor Kristóf, József Csernyi, Peter Vincent, István Balatoni, and essays by Endre Haraszti and Zoltán Simon.]

1857   *A Winnipegi Magyar Irodalmi Kör Antológiája [An Anthology of the Hungarian Literary Association of Winnipeg]*, edited by Sándor Domokos. Winnipeg: The Association, 1986. 112 pp.
[Includes poems and short stories by Sándor Domokos, Endre Haraszti, Sándor Kristóf, Lajos Kulcsár, Kálmán László, János Miska, István Nagy, Imre Naphegyi, Zsigmond Pikó, László Szegedi. Biographies are included.]

Anthologies - writings about

1858   Ferdinandy, György. "Felelőtlenül" [Irresponsible Work] SZIVÁRVÁNY 2, no. 7 (1982): 107-09.
[A review of *Szabadon - Living Free*, describing the editing of the work as an irresponsible undertaking.]

1859   Grantham, Ronald. "Canadian-Hungarians: Prose and Poetry in First Anthology." OTTAWA CIT (July 6, 1974)
[Review of *The Sound of Time*.]

1860   Határ, Győző. "Bevezető őszinte beszéd" [Candid Introduction]. In *Új égtájak...* (Washington, D.C.: Occidental Press, 1969)
[Canadian authors analyzed are László Kemenes Géfin and György Vitéz.]

1861   Juhász József. "Ezévi antológia" [Anthology of the Present Year]. MAGY ÉLET (June 14, 1973)
[Review of *Antológia 3.]*

1862   Kovács, Martin L. Review of *The Sound of Time*. CAN ETH STUD 9, no. 1 (1977): 132-33.
[Provides a sociological analysis of Hungarian writing in Canada.]

1863   Máté, Imre. "Táguló kör: *Antológia 2* " [Expanding Horizon: Anthology 2]. NEMZETŐR 15 (March 1972)
[Describes Hungarian creative writing in Canada as one of distinctive style and theme.]

1864   Miska, János. "Élni jó: a kanadai magyar írók könyve" [Life's Good: A Book of Hungarian-Canadian Authors]. MAGY ÉLET (Nov. 16, 1971).
[This review of *Antológia 2* describes the collection as a volume of optimistic short stories and

poems.]

1865   Miska, János. "Könyvekről Kanadában" [Of Hungarian Books in Canada]. NEMEZTŐR (November 20, 1977).
[Review of *Kézfogás;* finds the short stories of poor quality, the poems original and of good quality.]

INDIVIDUAL AUTHORS

ÁGOSTON-ADLER, Jenő   (1898-1979)

1866   *Költemények. Összeállította Vadnay Zsuzsa [Poems: Compiled by Zsuzsa Vadnay].* Montreal: Three Star Printing, 1982. 103 pp. Poems.

BALATONI, István (1914-   )
Born in Győr, Hungary, emigrated to Canada in 1951. He lived in Toronto until his retirement in 1967, when he relocated in Florida. He has published in *Krónika, Magyar Élet* and *Sun Valley.*

1867   *Rábaparti mennyegző: Válogatott novellák és versek [Wedding at Rábapart: Selected Short Stories and Poems].* Toronto: Pátria, 1974. 84 pp. Short stories, poems.

1868   *Mi muzsikus lelkek... [We Musical Souls].*   Toronto: Pátria, 1983. 122 pp. Short stories, poems.

   Writing about:

1869   Wass, Albert. "Magyar szemmel" [Through Hungarian Eyes]. MAGY ÉLET (1975)

BARANYAI, Tibor (1925-   )
Born in Apagy, Hungary. He was an activist in the Social Democratic Youth Movement and served as a Parliamentary Deputy after the war. Left Hungary in 1948, arrived in Canada during the fifties. Resides in Montreal.

1870   *Útszéli virágok: Versek, novellák, fordítások [Roadside Flowers: Poems, Short Stories, Translations].* Montréal: The Author, 1956. 111 pp. Poems, short stories.

1871   *Break-through.* Montreal: Pallas Printing, 1962. 47 pp. Poems.

   Writing about

1872   Dudek, Louis. "Hungarian Poet in Canada." DELTA 20 (1963): 20.

BARTHA, Kálmán

1873   *Trianoni átok [The Curse of Trianon].* Hamilton: The Author, 1959. 118 pp. Poems.

BEBEK, János (1948-   )
Born in Budapest and received his education in that city. An Engineer by profession, he emigrated to Canada in 1974. He has published in *Tanú, Szivárvány* and other periodicals. Also as János BENEDEK.

1874   *32ASA [32ASA].* [Mississauga: The Author, 1968] 102 pp. Poems.

   Writing about:

1875   Miska, János. "Fiatal kanadai magyar írók: Bebek János" [Young Hungarian-Canadian Authors: János Bebek]. NYUG MAGY (Calgary) 1, no. 8 (1982): 5.

BÉKY-HALÁSZ, Iván (1919-   ) Also: HALÁSZ de BÉKY, I.L.
Born in Hungary and attended the University of Budapest. Came to Toronto in 1956, where he obtained a B.L.S. degree from the University of Toronto and worked in the John Robarts Research Library until his retirement in 1975. His poems, articles and translations in English and Hungarian languages have appeared in several periodicals and anthologies. He returned to Hungary in 1985. His bibliographies have appeared under the name Ivan L. HALÁSZ de Béky.

1876   *Arccal a falnak: Válogatott versek [Facing the Wall: Selected Poems]*. Toronto: Amerikai Magyar Írók, 1972. 47 pp. Poems.

1877   *Rab és börtönőr [Prisoner and Guard]*. Toronto: Amerikai Magyar Írók, 1975. 96 pp. Poems.

1878   *20 Poems*, translated into English by the author. Toronto, 1978. Poems.

1879   Áldott kikötők [Blessed Harbours]. Toronto: Amerikai Magyar Írók, 1979. Poems.

1880   *Tomiban már virágoznak a fák: Válogatott versek, 1975-78 [In Tomi the Trees are Already in Bloom: Selected Poems, 1975-78]*. Toronto: The Author, 1979. Poems.

1881   *Indián nyár [Indian Summer]*. Toronto: Amerikai Magyar Írók, 1981. Poems.

1882   *Korai dér [Early Frost]*. Toronto: Amerikai Magyar Írók, 1981. 28 pp. Poems.

Writings about:

1883   Béládi, Miklós. "Béky-Halász Iván" [Iván Béky-Halász]. In *A magyar irodalom története, 1945-1975. IV: A határon túli magyar irodalom*. (Budapest: Akadémiai Kiadó, 1982) pp. 337, 345, 392.

1884   Béládi, Miklós; Pomogáts, Béla; Rónay, László. "Béky-Halász Iván" [Iván Halász-Béky]. In their *A nyugati magyar irodalom 1945 után*. (Budapest: Gondolat, 1986) pp. 31, 43, 168-69, 302.

1885   Borbándi, Gyula. "Béky-Halász Iván" [Iván Béky-Halász]. In his *A magyar emigráció életrajza...* (Bern: Az Európai Protestáns Magyar Szabadegyetem, 1985) pp. 375, 382, 466.

1886   S. Koósa, Antal. Review of *Rab és börtönőr [Prisoner and Guard]*. DETR MAGY ÚJS (Nov. 14, 1975)

1887   Széplaki, József. Review of *Arccal a falnak [Facing the Wall]*. DETR MAGY ÚJS (March 9, 1973)

1888   Török, József. "Forrásmunkák a magyar múlthoz Kanadában" [Source Material Relating to the Hungarian Past in Canada]. KAT MAGY VAS (Sept. 18, 1977): 8.
        [Review of Béky-Halász's bibliographies.]

1889   Tűz, Tamás. Review of *Arccal a falnak [Facing the Wall]*. IROD ÚJS (January-February 1973): 4.

BÉLA DEÁK, pseud. (Real name: IRSA, Béla) (1911-   )
A former officer of the Royal Hungarian Army, Irsa came to Canada at the end of World War II. Settled in Calgary, where he has lived ever since his arrival in this country. His poems and short stories have appeared in various newspapers and periodicals outside of Hungary.

1890   *Hulló vércseppek: Az utolsó tatárjárás balladái [Drops of Blood: Ballads of the Last Tartar Incursion].* Calgary: The Author, 1952. 93 pp. Poems.

1891   *Csízió [Calendar].* Calgary: Corvin, 1982. 304 pp. Poems.

1892   *Tán igaz sem volt [It May Not Have Been True].* Toronto: Apolló Press [n.d.] 238 pp. Short stories.

BENTEFY, Kálmán   (1900-1985)
Born in Hódoscsépány, Hungary, studied agricultural management, followed by years of clerical work. Enlisted in the Hungarian Army during World War II, came to Canada at the end of the war.

1893   *Lángokban Hunnia [Hungary Aflame].* Calgary: Corvin, 1982. 256 pp. Poems.

BERECZ, Tibor
Born in Hungary and came to Canada after the 1956 uprising. His satirical poems have appeared in Hungarian newspapers in Canada.

1894   *Erős János: Költői elbeszélés [John, the Strong One: An Epic Story].* Toronto: The Author, 1966. 58 pp. Poem.

1895   *Társtalan utakon [Along Lonely Roads].* Toronto: The Author, 1966. Poems.

BODROGHKÖZY, Zoltán

1896   *A világ tetején [On Top of the World].* Toronto: Pátria, 1971. 295 pp. port. Novel

1897   Ezredévi nemzedék [Milleneal Generation]. Toronto: Patria, 1972. Novel.

BOLDISÁR, László   (1908-1977)
Born in Ungvár, now USSR, emigrated to London, Ont. in 1962. His poems have appeared in the anthology series of the Hungarian-Canadian Authors' Association, in *Krónika* and in newspapers.

1898   *Csurranó színes pohár: Versek [Clinking Coloured Glass: Poems].* Toronto: Weller, 1971. 156 pp. Poems.

1899   *Hószobor a téren: elbeszélések, vidám írások [Snow Sculpture on the Square: Short Stories, Humorous Writings].* London, Ont.: Kanadai Magyar Írók, 1974. 231 pp. Short stories.

1900   *Karikó furcsa esete: Prózai írások múltból és jelenből [The Strange Case of Karikó: Prose-writings from Past and Present].* London, Ont.: Kanadai Magyar Írók, 1976. 160 pp. Short stories.

1901   *A kor számadása: Válogatott versek [Summing Up the Age: Selected Poems].* London, Ont.: Kanadai Magyar Írók, 1977. 184 pp. Poems.

Writings about:

1902   Juhász, József. Review of *Hószobor a téren [Snow Sculpture on the Square].* MAGY ÉLET (Apr. 19, 1975)

1903   Seres, József. "Hullatja levelét az idő vén fája" [Time's Old Tree Sheds Its Leaves]. KRÓNIKA 3, no. 12 (1977): 34. port.

1904   Seres, József. Obituary. MAGY ÉLET (Nov. 19, 1977)

BORDÁS, Sándor (1889-)
Born in Budapest, left Hungary after World War II, came to Toronto in 1960, after a stay in France. His plays have been performed by various groups in Canada and France.

1905 *A megoldás [The Solution].* Produced in Paris and Toronto. Also published in *Antológia 3* (Ottawa: Kanadai Magyar Írók Köre, 1972) pp. 15-29. Play.

DEÁK, István (1938-)
Born in Barcs, Hungary, completed his higher education in Innsbruck, Munich and Taiwan. He came to Canada in 1968, received an M.A. in Religious Studies at the University of Toronto, where he works at present as a librarian.

1906 *Ismert ismeretlen [Known, Unknown].* Toronto: The Author, 1975. 100 pp. Poems.

DOBOG, Béla

1907 *Hazátkiáltok [Naming One's Country].* Toronto: Canadian Stage and Arts Publications, 1987.

DOMA, István (1920-)
Born in Hungary and completed his university education in that country. He was arrested in 1954 under political pretext, was liberated by the revolution of 1956, the year he left for Canada. Graduated from the University of Montreal and taught science in various high schools in four provinces.

1908 *Nagybotú Lőrinc: Történelmi regény [Lawrence Bigstick: Historical Novel].* Toronto: Duna Publisher, 1961. Novel.

DOMOKOS, Sándor (1921-)
Born and educated in Hungary, former officer of the Royal Hungarian Gendarmery, spent seven years in prison camps in USSR. Came to Canada in 1956 and has lived in Winnipeg ever since. Received several literary awards including the gold medal of the Árpád Academy.

1909 *Útikalandok az ígéret földjén [Adventures in the Promised Land].* Winnipeg: Kanadai Magyar Újság, 1960. 50 pp. Satirical novelette.

1910 *Ha nem is születtem volna magyarnak [Even if I wasn't Born a Hungarian].* Winnpeg, 1965. Drama in one act, produced in Winnipeg, 1965.

1911 *Bolondgomba [Toadstool].* Winnipeg, 1966. Comedy in three acts.

1912 *Vajk és Vazul: Történelmi regény [Vajk and Vazul: Historical Novel].* Winnipeg: Kanadai Magyar Újság, 1968. 43 pp. Historical novelette.

1913 *Megbűnhődte már e nép...[This People Has Made Atonement]..* Winnipeg: Kanadai Magyar Újság, 1969. 121 pp. Novel.

1914 *Sasok és keselyűk [Eagles and Vultures].* Winnipeg: Kanadai Magyar Újság, 1970. 55 pp. Historical novelette.

1915 *Ajándék [A Gift].* Winnipeg: The Author, 1970. Drama in three acts.

1916 *Két kő között [Between Two Millstones].* Winnipeg: Kanadai Magyar Újság, 1971. 75 pp. Novel.

1917 *The Birth of a Book.* Winnipeg: The Author, 1973. A play in three acts, about Paul Bang Jansen.

1918   *Gyertyaláng (Versek) [Candlelight (Poems)].* [Winnipeg: The Author, 1980] 100 pp. illus. Poems.

1919   *Prisoners, Refugees, Citizens.* Winnipeg: The Author, 1980. 169 pp. illus. Autobiographical novel.

1920   *Forbidden Fruits: Short Stories and Essays.* Winnipeg: The Author, 1981. 118 pp. Short stories.

1921   *The Lonely Nation.* [Winnipeg: The Author, 1981]. 213 pp. illus. Mimeographed.

1922   *Ego Sum Via: A Drama about the Resurrection.* Winnipeg: The Author, 1982. 52 pp. Drama in two acts.

1923   *The Chosen One.* [Winnipeg: The Author, 1983]. 62 pp. Novelette.

1924   *Prometheus: Fiction beyond the Future.* Winnipeg: The Author, 1986. 243 pp. Novel.

Writings about:

1925   Miska, János. Review of *Két kő között.* NYUG MAGY 3 (1983): 5.

1926   Somogyi, Ferenc. "Domokos Sándor" [Sándor Domokos]. In *Az Árpád Akadémia tagjainak tevékenysége* (Cleveland: Árpád Publishing Co., 1982) pp. 72-73.

EGRI, György

Former editor of Menorah, a Toronto-based newspaper for Jewish-Hungarians, and author of many articles and satirical writings. He has lived in Toronto since 1956, the time he came to Canada.

1927   *Én különben jól érzem magam ... [Otherwise I'm Fine...].* Toronto: The Author, 1981. 336 pp. Articles, satirical stories.

EGYEDI, Béla (1913-1985)

Former professor of Modern Languages, he was born in Budapest. After several years of service in forced labour camps he left Hungary for France in 1948, and emigrated to Canada in 1951. He lived in Montreal until his death.

1928   *3 x 7 (-) = .* Montreal: The Author [n.d.] Poems.
       [Includes poems in English, French, German and Hungarian.]

1929   *Mushi-no-koe [Voice of Insects].* Montreal: Swamp Press, 1978. 1 portfolio, 24 leaves. illus., some col. Poems.

1930   *Haiku-no-hiroba. [Haiku Plaza].* Montreal: Distributors, Mansfield Book Mart, c1980. 46 pp. illus.

FALUDY, György (1910-)

Born in Budapest, escaped Hungary in 1930, served in the U.S. Army during World War II. Returned to Hungary after the war, arrested on false charges and spent several years in forced labour camps. Left Hungary for the second time in 1956, came to Canada via England and France, where he edited *Irodalmi Ujság* and wrote *My Happy Days in Hell, Karoton, Erasmus of Rotterdam.* Recipient of two honorary doctorate degrees and nominated for the Nobel Prize for Literature twice.

1931   *Levelek az utókorhoz [Letters to Posterity].* Toronto: Institut Marcile Ficin, 1975. 206 pp. Poems.

[Includes an autobiographical writing.]

1932   *East and West: Selected Poems of George Faludy*, edited by John Robert Colombo. Toronto: Hounslow Press, 1978. 160 pp. Poems.

1933   *Villon balladái [Villon's Ballads].* New Brunswick, N.J.: I.H. Printing, 1978. 88 pp. Poems. [Transliterations of the ballads of François Villon. Orginally published in Budapest in 1937.]

1934   *Összegyűjtött versei [Collected Poems].* New York: Püski, 1980. 635 pp. Poems.

1935   *Learn this Poem of Mine by Heart: Sixty Poems and One Speech by George Faludy*, edited by John Robert Colombo. Toronto: Hounslow Press, 1983. 127 pp. Poems.

1936   *Twelve Sonnets*, translated by Robin Skelton. Victoria: Pharos Press, 1983. 20 pp. Poems.

1937   *Börtönversek 1949-52 [Prison Poems 1949-52].* Munich: Recski Szövetség, Európa, 1983. Poems.

1938   *Ballad for Isabelle*, translated by Robin Skelton. White Rock, B.C.: White Rhino Press, 1984. Poems.

1939   *Selected Poems 1933-1980*, translated by Robin Skelton. Toronto: McClelland & Stewart, 1985. 232 pp. Poems.

1940   *Corpses, Brats, and Cricket Music*, translated from the Hungarian Hullák, kamaszok, tücsökzene by Robin Skelton. Vancouver: Tanks, 1987. Poems.

Writings about:

1941   Amiel, Barbara. "You Should Know Something about George Faludy." SAT N 88 (December 1973): 23-26, 27.

1942   Aubert, Rosemary. Review of *East and West*. Q & Q. 44, no. 10 (1978): 12.

1943   Béládi, Miklós. "Faludy György" [György Faludy]. In *A magyar irodalom története, 1945-1975.* IV: *A határon túli magyar irodalom* (Budapest: Akadémiai Kiadó, 1982) pp. 342, 345, 405-07.

1944   Béládi, Miklós; Pomogáts, Béla; Rónay, László. "Faludy György" [György Faludy]. In their *A nyugati magyar irodalom 1945 után.* (Budapest: Gondolat, 1986) pp. 7, 39, 43, 47, 59, 87, 144, 150-56, 303.

1945   Borbándi, Gyula. "Faludy György" [György Faludy]. In his *A magyar emigráció életrajza.* (Bern: Európai Protestáns Magyar Szabadegyetem, 1985) pp. 276-79, 285, 306, 364, 368, 378, 381, 473.

1946   Brooks, Andrew. Review of *Learn this Poem of Mine...* CAN BOOK REV ANN 1984: 224.

1947   Czigány, Lóránt. "Igricek utóda" [A Descendent of Minstrels]. ÚJ LÁTÓH (1981): 534-37.

1948   D'Evelyn, Thomas. "The Odyssey of George Faludy." CHRIST SCI MON (Sept. 3, 1986): 2, 3. [Review of *Selected Poems.*]

1949   Dobbs, Kildare. "The Police Chief and the Poet." SAT N 93, no. 6 (1978): 66-67. [Review of *East and West.*]

1950 Drache, Sharon. "Twelve Birds on Hand to Remind a Poet of Freedom." OTTAWA CIT (Oct. 24, 1987) port.

1951 Egri, György. "Faludy György új verseskötetéről" [Of György Faludy's New Book of Poetry]. IROD ÚJS (November-December 1980): 13.

1952 Ferdinandy, György. "Levelek és tükrök" [Letters and Mirrors]. ÚJ LÁTÓH (1977): 524-28.

1953 Filip, Ray. "Pillars and Eye-cons." BKS CAN 15, no. 3 (1986): 30-31.
      [Review of *Selected Poems* by György Faludy and *Oāb* by Robert Zend.]

1954 Fletcher, Peggy. "Humour and Sadness." CAN AUTH BKMN 54, no. 1 (1978): 36-37.
      [Review of *East and West.]*

1955 Fulford, Robert. "The Poet and the Commercial." SAT N 91, no. 6 (1976): 11.

1956 Havelda, John. "Co-translators." CAN LIT No. 103 (1984): 98-101.
      [Review of *Learn this Poem of Mine...*]

1957 Kinczyk, Bohdan. "George Faludy." CM 14 (186): 139.
      [Review of *My Happy Days in Hell.*]

1958 Kreisel, Henry. "Columns of Dark." CAN LIT No. 115 (1987): 272-75.
      [Review of *Selected Poems.*]

1959 Kreisel, Henry. "The Humanism in Faludy." CAN FORUM 58 (March 1979): 27-29.
      [Review of *East and West.*]

1960 Lane, M. Travis. "George Faludy: Master of Peeps." FIDDLEHEAD 120 (1979): 136-39.
      [Review of *East and West.*]

1961 Levenson, Christopher. "A Meeting of the Twain." BKS CAN 7, no. 11 (1978) 14-15.
      [Review of *East and West.]*

1962 Martindale, Sheila. Review of *Learn this Poem of Mine...* CAN AUTH BKMN 60, no. 1 (1984): 2.

1963 Matyas, Cathy. "Bett-er to Reid Faludy." ESSAYS CAN WRIT 30 (1984/85): 352-58.
      [Review of *Learn this Poem of Mine by Heart.*]

1964 Merrett, Robert James. Review of *Selected Poems.* CAN BOOK REV ANN 1986: 95-96.

1965 Nagy, Csaba. "Énem nem illett semmi sorba" [I've Never Fitted in]. IROD ÚJS No. 11-13 (1980): 13.

1966 Stuewe, Paul. "Grace under Pressure..." BKS CAN 13, no. 3 (1984): 31.
      [Review of *Learn this Poem of Mine...*]

1967 Szakolczay, Lajos. "Faludy György látomásai" [The Visions of György Faludy]. MOZGÓ VILÁG 9 (1982): 75-79.

1968 Zalán, Magda. "Ének a betonból" [Song from the Pavement]. ÚJ LÁTÓH Nos. 1-2 (1977): 67-71.

FARKAS, André (1948-   )
Born in Hajdúnánás, Hungary. Came to Canada in 1956. He has lived in Montreal since. Edited three anthologies. His poems have appeared in anthologies and periodicals.

1969   *Szervusz.* M.A. Thesis, Concordia University, 1976. 70 leaves. Poem.

1970   *Murders in the Welcome Café.* Montreal: Véhicule Press, 1977. 18 pp. Poems.

1971   *Romantic at Heart and Other Faults.* Montreal: Cross Country Press, 1979. 72 pp. Poems.

1972   *The Véhicule Poets.* Montreal: Maker Press, 1979. Poems.

1973   *From Here to Here.* Montreal: The Muse's Co., 1982. 32 pp. Poems.

1974   *How to....* Montreal, 1988. 96 pp. Poems.

Writings about:

1975   Barker, Edna. Review of *Murders in the Welcome Café.* CAN BOOK REV ANN 1977: 171.

1976   Bartlett, Brian. "Crumbs in a Plastic Bag." BKS CAN 8 no. 2 (1979): 24.
[Review of *Montreal English Poetry of the Seventies.*]

1977   Carpenter, David. "Where Poetry Is." CAN LIT No. 80 (1979): 101-03.
[Review of *Montreal English Poetry of the Seventies.*]

1978   David, Jack. "Three Poets from Montreal." CONT VERSE II 3, no. 3 (1978): 23-24.
[Review of *Murders in the Welcome Café.*]

1979   Davies, Gwendolyn. "Something's Happening in Montreal." ESSAYS CAN WRIT 10 (1978): 82-87.
[Review of *Murders in the Welcome Café.*]

1980   Daymond, Douglas. "In Minor Key." CAN LIT No. 97 (1983): 140-43.
[Review of *From Here to Here.*]

1981   Fee, Margery. Review of *English Montreal Poetry of the Seventies.* CAN BOOK REV ANN 1977: 156-57.

1982   Garebian, Keith. "Sub-camp." CAN LIT No. 81 (1979): 126-28.
[Review of *Murders in the Welcome Café.*]

1983   Review of *Szerbusz.* IN REVIEW 9, no. 1 (1975): 27.

FÁY, Ferenc   (1921-1981)
A former officer of the Royal Hungarian Army, born in Pécel, Hungary. He came to Toronto in 1948 and lived there until his death. One of the leading Hungarian poets, his works have appeared in the major periodicals, anthologies and newspapers.

1984   *Jeremiás siralmai [The Lamentations of Jeremiah].* Toronto: Magyar Helicon Társaság, 1956. 32 pp. Poems.

1985   *Az írást egyszer megtalálják [They are Going to Find the Writing One Day].* Toronto: Magyar Kultúra, 1959. 126 pp. Poems.

1986   *Törlesztő ének [Penitent Song].* Toronto: Magyar Figyelő, 1963. 107 pp. Poems.

1987   *Magamsirató [Self-lamentation]* . Toronto: Magyar Helicon Társaság, 1967. 96 pp. Poems.

1988   *Áradás [Flood]*. Toronto: The Author, 1972. 98 pp. Poems.

1989   *Kövület: Versek [Petrification: Poems]*. Toronto: Vörösváry Publishing Co., 1977. 131 pp. Poems. [Dust jacket includes excerpts from letters written by Győző Határ, Pál Ignótus and György Rónay.]

1990   *Összegyűjtött versek [Collected Poems]*, sajtó alá rendezte [edited by] Fáy István. Előszót írta [With an introduction by] Határ Győző. Toronto: Vörösváry Publishing Co., 1982. 668 pp. Poems.

Writings about:

1991   Abafy, László. "Pécel és Torontó között" [Between Pécel and Toronto]. ÚJ LÁTÓH 20 (1969): 176-78.
[Review of *Magamsirató*.]

1992   Béládi, Miklós. "Fáy Ferenc" [Ferenc Fáy]. In *A magyar irodalom története, 1945-1975, IV: A határon túli magyar irodalom*. (Budapest: Akadémiai Kiadó, 1982) pp. 340, 393-95.

1993   Béládi, Miklós; Pomogáts, Béla; Rónay, László. "Fáy Ferenc" [Ferenc Fáy]. In their *A nyugati magyar irodalom 1945 után*. (Budapest: Gondolat, 1986) pp. 34, 166, 170-75, 197, 304, 315.

1994   Bisztray, George. "Ferenc Fáy." In his *Hungarian-Canadian Literature*. (Toronto: University of Toronto Press, 1987) pp. 23, 25-28, 29, 31, 32, 38, 43, 47, 52, 64, 70, 72, 76.

1995   Botond, István. "Könyvszemle - Fáy Ferenc: *Magamsirató*" [Book Review - Ferenc Fáy: *Self-lamentation*]. AUSZT MAGY (May 1969)

1996   Buday, László. "Fáy Ferenc új verseskötetéről" [Of Ferenc Fáy's New Book of Poetry]. KRÓNIKA 4, no. 1 (1978): 12-13.
[Review of *Kövület.*]

1997   Csiky, Ágnes Mária. "Magyar Jeremiás" [Hungarian Jeremiah]. KAT SZEM (1957): 95.

1998   Dénes Tibor. Review of *Törlesztő ének*. KAT SZEM (1963): 153-54.

1999   Hegyi, Béla. "Fáy Ferenc" [Ferenc Fáy]. In his *Alkotó időszak* (Budapest, 1982) pp. 464-501.

2000   Ignótus Pál. "Miért szép? Sárga villogás: Sainte-Beuve, van Gogh, Fáy Ferenc" [What Makes it Beautiful? Yellow Blinking: Sainte-Beuve, van Gogh and Ferenc Fáy]. IROD ÚJS (1969)

2001   Kabdebó, Tamás. "Haza a tudatban, Fáy Ferenc: *Magamsirató*" [Homeland in the Mind, Ferenc Fáy: *Self-lamentation*]. IROD ÚJS (Jul. 1, 1968)

2002   Kemenes Géfin, László. "Perlekedés a kertért" [Quarrels for the Garden]. IROD ÚJS 25, no. 3-4 (1974)
[Review of *Áradás.*]

2003   Nehéz Ferenc. "Messzelátás a körtefa csúcsáról; Fáy Ferenc verseskönyve: *Magamsirató*" [Long View from the Pear Tree; Ferenc Fáy's New Poems: *Self-lamentation*]. KAN MAGY (1969)

2004   Rónay, László. "Magyar költők Nyugaton" [Hungarian Poets in the West]. VIGILIA (1982): 38-43.

2005   S. Koósa, Antal. "Fáy Ferenchez" [To Ferenc Fáy]. DETR MAGY ÚJS (1969)

[Review of *Magamsirató (Self-lamentation).]*

2006 Tábory, Maxim. "A kőbe dermedt őshal" [The Petrified Ancestral Fish]. ÚJ EUR 18, no. 6. (1979)
[Review of *Kövület.]*

2007 Tábory, Maxim. "Kövület" [Petrification]. CAN-AMER REV HUNG STUD 6, no. 2 (1979): 118-21.
[Review of *Kövület. (Petrification).]*

2008 Tóth, László. "Fáy Ferenc újabb versei" [Ferenc Fáy's New Poems]. KAT SZEM (1969): 91-92.
[Review of *Magamsirató.]*

2009 Tóth, László. Review of *Törlesztőének.* KAT SZEM (1981) 281-84.

2010 Vásárhelyi, Vera. "Búcsú Fáy Ferenctől" [Farewell to Ferenc Fáy]. KAT SZEM (1981): 281-84.

FINTA, Imre

2011 *Így éreztem: Versek [The Way I Felt: Poems].* Toronto: The Author, 1978. 47 pp. Poems.

FODOR, András

2012 *Forr a dalom [Heated Songs].* Montreal: Very Fast Print. Co., 1976. 120 pp. Poems.

GERŐ, Sándor (1922-1981)
Born in Érmihályfalva (now Valea lui Mihai, Romania). He was a Professor of Theology at the Baptist Theological Seminary, Budapest. Received a Master of Divinity degree from McMaster University. From 1977 to 1981 he was minister of the Toronto Hungarian Baptist community.

2013 *Harangláb [Bell-cote].* Toronto: The Author, 1981. Poems.

GOTTLIEB, Paul
Born in Budapest, Hungary, and came to Montreal in 1957. Received a B.A. and an M.A. from Sir George Williams University. Taught at Concordia University and Ryerson. Now head of media writing program at Sheridan College, Oakville, Ont. He wrote the filmscript of Vizinczey's *In Praise of Older Women..*

2014 *Agency: A Novel.* Don Mills, Ont.: Musson, 1974. 221 pp. Mystery novel.

Writing about:

2015 Review of *Agency.* J CAN FIC 3, no. 4 (1975): 99-100.

HAJÓS, Tamás (1953)
Born in Budapest. Came to Canada as a graduate student. He is taking graduate studies in Literature at the University of Toronto. He has published poetry and translations in his native country, as well as in Canada. His poems in English translation have appeared in WRIT/FOR 1982 *Translations.*

2016 *Szárítókötélen [On the Clothesline].* Toronto: Amerikai Magyar Írók, 1982. 72 pp. Poems.

Writings about:

2017 Béládi, Miklós; Pomogáts, Béla; Rónay, László. "Hajós Tamás" [Tamás Hajós]. In their *A nyugati magyar irodalom 1945 után.* (Budapest: Gondolat, 1986) pp. 31, 250-51.

2018   Tűz, Tamás. Review of *Szárítókötélen.* NYUG MAGY (Calgary) (1982)

IZSÁK, Gyula (1884-1960)

Born in Bótrágy, Hungary, came to Canada in 1901. He settled in Kipling- Békevár, Sask., where he operated a grocery store. Later he moved to Toronto. His poems have appeared in newspapers and calendars.

2019   *Mezei virágok, költemények [Prairie Flowers: Poems].* Kipling, Sask.: Kanadai Magyar Farmer, 1919. 202 pp. Poems.

2020   *A samaritánus: Igaz történet az első telepesek korából; Történelmi korrajz [The Samaritan: A True Story from the Times of the First Settlers; A Historical Case Study].* Toronto: The Author, 1954. 109 pp. A collection of narratives.

JÓNÁS, George (1935-   )

Poet, novelist, playwright, director of television drama at CBC. Born in Budapest and received his education in his native land. He came to Canada in 1956 and settled in Toronto. His work has appeared in numerous English-language and Hungarian periodicals and anthologies. His television and radio plays have been broadcast by CBC TV and Radio. Co-author of books dealing with Canadian legal cases and systems, e.g. *By Persons Unknown.* (in collaboration with Barbara Amiel, 1977), *The Scales of Justice* (with Edward Greenspan), *Vengeance.* He has also written the librettos to two operas by Tibor Polgár: *The European Lover* (1966) and *The Glove* (1973). He is recipient of the Edgar Allan Poe Award for *Best Fast Crime Book.*

Poems

2021   *The Absolute Smile.* Toronto: House of Anansi, 1967. 61 pp. Poems.

2022   *The Happy Hungary Man.* Toronto: House of Anansi, 1970. 56 pp. Poems.

2023   *Cities.* Toronto: House of Anansi, 1973. 73 pp. Poems.

2024   *Final Decree.* Toronto: Macmillan, 1981. 224 pp. Novel.

Plays:

2025   *Fasting Fryar.* Toronto, 1967.

2026   *Master and Man.* Toronto, 1967.

2027   *Mr. Pym Passes by.* Toronto, 1967.

2028   *First and Vital Candle.* Toronto, 1967.

2029   *Catullus.* Toronto, 1967.

2030   *Tell His Majesty.* Toronto, 1968.

2031   *Ave Luna, Morituri Te Salutant.* Toronto, 1970.
[Based on György Faludy's poem by the same title, translated into English by G. Jónás.]

2032   *The Sinking of the Mary Palmer.* Toronto, 1972.

2033   *Pushkin.* Toronto, 1978.

2034   *Crocodile in the Bathtub and other Perils.* Toronto: Totem, 1987.

Television plays:

2035   *The Major.* Toronto, 1964.

2036   *The Family Man.* Toronto, 1972.

2037   *Ave Luna, Morituri Te Salutant.* Toronto, 1973.
       [Based on George Faludy's poem by the same title.]

Radio plays,   librettos:

2038   *Of Mice and Men.* Toronto, 1963. Radio play.

2039   *To Cross a Bridge.* Toronto, 1964. Radio play.

2040   *The Agent Provocateur.* Toronto, 1966. Radio Play.

2041   *The European Lover.* Toronto, 1966. Libretto.

2042   *The Redl Affair.* Toronto, 1966. Radio play.

2043   *The Glove.* Toronto, 1974. Libretto.
       [Music by Tibor Polgár.]

2044   *Scales of Justice.* Toronto, 1983.

Writings about:

2045   Annesley, P. "I Interview a Poet" TOR TEL (March 31, 1970)

2046   Atwood, Margaret. Review of *The Absolute Smile.* POET CHIC (1969)

2047   Bilan, R.P. "Fiction, Letters in Canada 1981." UNIV TOR Q 51 (1981-82): 316.
       [Review of *Final Decree.*]

2048   Bowering, George. "To Share the World or Despair of It." GLOBE MAIL (May 2, 1970): 16.
       [Review of *The Happy Hungry Man.*]

2049   Buitenhuis, P. Review of *The Happy Hungry Man.* McGILL DAILY (Oct. 23, 1970)

2050   Carruth, Hayden. "George Jonas." TAM REV 47 (1968): 104.

2051   Chambers, D.D.C. "George Jonas." In *Contemporary Poetry.* 2nd ed. (New York: St. Martin's Press, 1975) pp. 789-90.

2052   Coleman, T. "George Jonas." LOND GUARD (June 1969)

2053   Colombo, John Robert. "Attempting to Remake Civilization." GLOBE MAIL (Sept. 10, 1966): 19.

2054   Ditsky, J. Review of *The Happy Hungry Man.* CAN FORUM 49 (August 1970)

2055   Dobbs, Kildare. "A Glory Murder, a High-minded Tone." SAT N 92 (June 1977): 61-62.

[Review of *By Persons Unknown.*]

2056   Doyle, Mike. "Where Prufrock Was." CAN LIT No. 45 (1970): 85-86.
[Review of *The Happy Hungry Man.*]

2057   Engel, H. Review of *Cities.* TOR STAR (Feb. 9, 1974)

2058   Fefferman, S. Review of *The Absolute Smile.* TOR TEL (Oct. 21, 1967)

2059   Freedman, A. "Beyond Scandal: The Demeter Trial." Q & Q 43, no. 7 (1977): 33.
[Review of *By Persons Unknown.*]

2060   Fulford, Robert. "Conversations with George Jonas." Televised 1968.

2061   Garnet, E. Review of *The Happy Hungry Man.* TOR TEL (March 22, 1970)

2062   Hayne, D.M. Review of *The Absolute Smile.* UNIV TOR Q 37 (1967-68): 375-76.

2063   Hill, Douglas. "Ethnic Fiction..." BKS CAN 10, no. 10 (1981): 31-32.
[Review of *The Final Decree.*]

2064   Kretzer, Jon. Review of *The Final Decree.* FIDDLEHEAD 135 (1983): 126-27.

2065   MacCallum, Hugh. Review of *The Absolute Smile.* UNIV TOR Q 37 (1967-68)

2066   Owen, I.M. "A Hit-the-Missis Saga." BKS CAN 6, no. 5 (1977): 22-23.
[Review of *By Persons Unknown.*]

2067   Purdy, Al. Review of *The Absolute Smile.* CAN FORUM 47, no. 566 (1968): 284.

2068   Purdy, Al. "George Jonas." TAM REV 47 (1968): 82.
[Being part of a review article "Aiming Low."]

2069   Rapaport, Janis. "The Mask of Jonas Slips Ever so Slightly." GLOBE MAIL (Dec. 23, 1973): 25.
[Review of *Cities.*]

2070   Roberts, Paul. Review of *Final Decree.* Q & Q 47, no. 10 (1981): 34-35.

2071   Rogers, Linda. "Sour Grapes." CAN LIT No. 93 (1982): 156-57.
[Review of *Final Decree.*]

2072   Sandler, Linda. "George Jonas." CAN LIT No. 73 (1977): 25-38.
[Interview with George Jonas.]

2073   Schroeder, Andreas. "The Poetry of George Jonas: A Critical Map." CAN LIT No. 48 (1971): 37-50.

2074   Škvorecký, Josef. "Pride and Prejudice." SAT N 97 (Jan. 19, 1982): 54-55.
[Review of *Final Decree.*]

2075   Stuewe, Paul. "Tales of Multicultural Mystery..." BKS CAN 7 (Aug/Sept., 1978): 38.
[Review of *By Persons Unknown.*]

2076   Surguy, Phil. "Stranger than Fiction." BKS CAN 13 (Aug/Sept.,1984): 11-12.
[Review of *Vengeance....*]

2077   Sypnowich, Peter. "Poetry and Public Relations." TOR STAR (March 14, 1970): 85.

2078   Thompson, Kent. Review of *The Absolute Smile*. FIDDLEHEAD (Winter, 1968): 82-83.

2079   Thompson, Kent. "Sensibility of Quality." FIDDLEHEAD (Spring, 1974): 79-81.
       [Review of *Cities*.]

2080   Watt, F.N. "Why Poetry? Eleven Answers." CAN FORUM 55 (June 1975/76)
       [Review of *Cities*.]

2081   Woodcock, George. "Recent Canadian Novels." QUEEN'S Q 89 (1982): 758.
       [Review of *Final Decree*.]

JUHÁSZ, József (1920-   )
Born in Szentistván, Hungary. Came to Toronto in 1956, where he has lived ever since. A student of the Hungarian Populist movement, his writings have appeared in Hungarian newspapers and anthologies in Canada. Former president of the Hungarian-Canadian Authors' Association and editor of several volumes of its anthologies.

2082   *Idegen partok között; Elbeszélések [Facing the Unknown Shores; Short Stories]*. Toronto: The Author, 1971. 158 pp. Short stories.

2083   *Ablaknyitás: Elbeszélések [On Opening the Window: Short Stories]*. Toronto: Kanadai Magyar Írók, 1974. 158 pp. Short stories.
       [Some of the stories are in English translation.]

       Writings about:

2084   Boldisár, László. "Nemzetség és kétnyelvűség" [Nationality and Bilingualism]. VAGYUNK 4, no. 3 (1975): 18-19.
       [Review of *Ablaknyitás*.]

2085   Csathó, Imre. "Könyvújdonságok Kanadában" [Of New Books in Canada]. AUSZT MAGY (Apr. 14, 1973): 6.
       [Review of *Ablaknyitás*.]

2086   Fényes, Mária. Review of *Ablaknyitás*. KALIF MAGY (Nov. 15, 1974): 4.

2087   Major, Tamás. Review of *Idegen partok között*. SZITTYAKÜRT (January 1972): 6.

2088   Miska, János. Review of *Ablaknyitás*. MAGY ÉLET (Jan. 4, 1975)

2089   Nehéz, Ferenc. Review of *Idegen partok között*. NAPNYUGAT (Oct. 20, 1972)

2090   Nehéz, Ferenc. "Juhász József első szántása" [József Juhász's First Ploughing]. MAGY ÉLET (Dec. 2, 1972)

2091   Németh, Ernő. "Juhász József új könyve" [A New Book by József Juhász]. KAN MAGY ÚJS (Dec. 13, 1974)
       [Review of *Ablaknyitás*.]

2092   Tűz, Tamás. Review of *Idegen partok között*. KAN MAGY (Jun. 17, 1972).

2093   Tűz, Tamás. "Új Ábel Amerikában" [A New Ábel in America]. ÚJ EUR (Apr. 1973).

2094   Zsigmond, András. "Tizennégyévi hallgatás után" [In the Wake of Fourteen Years of Silence]. MAGY ÉLET (Apr. 15, 1972)
[Review of *Idegen partok között.*]

KASZA MARTON, Lajos (1939-)

Born in Salgótarján, Hungary. Received part of his education in his native land. He came to Canada in 1956 and continued his education in Toronto. He is vice-president of the Hungarian-Canadian Authors' Association. His poems have appeared in periodicals and anthologies. He lives in Pickering, Ont.

2095   *Ostor és vallomás: Versek [Whip and Confessions*: Poems].   Toronto: Kanadai Magyar Írók Szövetsége, 1988. 160 pp. Poems.

KEMENES GÉFIN, László (1937-)

Poet, educator, translator, editor. Born in Szombathely, Hungary, arrived in Canada in 1956. Educated in Hungary and at Sir George Williams (now Concordia) University, Montreal (Ph.D., in English Literature). Translated Ezra Pound's Cantos into Hungarian. His experimental poems have appeared in periodicals and anthologies. Edited the anthology *Nyugati magyar költők antológiája (An Anthology of Hungarian Poets of the Western World)*, and is co-editor of *Arkánum*, a periodical for avant garde literature. He teaches English Literature at Concordia University.

2096   *Jégvirág [Ice Flower].* Paris: Magyar Műhely, 1966. 43 pp. Poems.

2097   *Zenit [Zenith].* Münich: Auróra Könyvek, 1969. 62 pp. Poems.

2098   *Pogány diaszpóra [Pagan Diaspora].* Montreal: Amerikai Magyar Írók, 1975. 80 pp. Poems.

2099   *Fehérlófia [Son of the White Horse].* Montreal: Amerikai Magyar Írók, 1978. 111 pp. Poems.

2100   *Fehérlófia második könyve [Second Book of the Son of the White Horse].* Montreal: Arkánum, 1981. 69 pp. Poems.

Writings about:

2101   Balázs, Attila. "Ezra Pound költészete, Cantók, és legújabb magyar nyelvű fordításuk" [The Poetry of Ezra Pound, Cantos, and its Most Recent Translations into Hungarian]. ÚJ SYMP 12, no. 133 (1966): 150-56.

2102   Béládi, Miklós. "Kemenes Géfin László" [László Kemenes Géfin]. In *A magyar irodalom története, 1945-1975: IV. A határon túli magyar irodalom.* (Budapest: Akadémiai Kiadó, 1982) pp. 337, 346, 368, 393-94, 414, 421-22, 445.

2103   Béládi, Miklós; Pomogáts, Béla; Rónay, László. In their *A nyugati magyar irodalom 1945 után.* (Budapest: Gondolat, 1986) pp. 24, 31, 44, 56, 224, 228, 246-48, 300, 304, 308, 313, 315.

2104   Bisztray, George. "László Kemenes Géfin." In his *Hungarian-Canadian Literature.* (Toronto: University of Toronto Press, 1987) pp. 40-46.

2105   Borbándi, Gyula. "Kemenes Géfin László" [László Kemenes Géfin]. In his *A magyar emigráció életrajza, 1945-1985.* (Bern: Európai Protestáns Magyar Szabadegyetem, 1985) pp. 357, 369, 374, 382.

2106   Határ, Győző. "A költészet kísérlete" [Poetry's Experiment]. ÚJ LÁTÓH 20 (1969): 561-64.

[Review of *Zenit.]*

2107 Kabdebó, Tamás. "Cinkosok közt vétkes aki él " [He Who Lives Amongst Accomplices is Guilty]. KAT SZEM 27 (1985): 285-86.

2108 Kucka, Péter. "A költészet menedéke" [Poetry's Refuge]. LÁTÓHATÁR 18 (1968): 553-58. [Review of *Jégvirág.]*

2109 Lőkkös, Antal. "Egy költő bemutatkozása" [The Introduction of a Poet]. KAT SZEM (1967): 286-87.

2110 Márton, László. "Három költő" [Three Poets]. MAGY MŰH 6, no. 21 (1967): 51-54.

2111 Monoszlói, Rezső. "Pogány hetykeség" [Pagan Insolence]. ÚJ LÁTÓH 27 (1976): 364-66. [Review of *Pogány diaszpóra.]*

2112 Pomogáts, Béla. "A montreali végvárban" [In a Montreal Fortress]. MŰHELY 1 (1981): 68-70.

2113 Review of Ezra Pound's Poetry *The Cantos*, translated into Hungarian by László Kemenes Géfin. VIGILIA 41, no. 7 (1976): 502.

2114 Review of *Halálos szójáték*, a monograph by László Kemenes Géfin on Tamás Tűz's poetry. VIGILIA 41, no. 4 (1976)

2115 Szanyi, János. "Pogány diaszpóra, vagy meddig juhász a juhász?" [Pagan Diaspora, or to What Extent Is a Shepherd a Sheperd?]. IROD ÚJS 26 (1975)

2116 Szente, Imre. "A zenit fele" [Half of the Zenith]. ÚJ LÁTÓH 20 (1969): 558-60. [Review of *Zenit.]*

2117 Tóth, László. "Többsíkú költészet" [Many-layered Poetry]. KAT SZEM (1980): 382-83.

2118 Tűz, Tamás. "A bizarr költő" [The Bizarre Poet]. NYUG MAGY ÉLET (Jan. 9, 1970) [Review of *Jégvirág.]*

2119 Tűz, Tamás. "A halál rokonai" [The Relatives of Death]. In his *Angyal, mondd ki csak félig.* (Toronto: Amerikai Magyar Írók, 1974) pp. 105-11. [Review of *Jégvirág.]*

2120 Tűz, Tamás. Review of *Pogány diaszpóra*. KRÓNIKA 4, no. 8 (1978): 20-21.

2121 Vitéz, György. "Mester és a tolmácsa" [The Master and His Interpreter]. IROD ÚJS 27, no. 11-12 (1976): 2-3. [Review of Ezra Pound's Poetry, The Cantos, translated into Hungarian by László Kemenes Géfin.]

2122 Vitéz, György. "Minden kezdet nehéz" [Every Beginning is Hard]. ÚJ LÁTÓH 18 (1967): 285-86. [Review of *Jégvirág.]*

2123 "A Zenit olvasása közben" [While Reading the Zenith]. KRÓNIKA 2, no. 10 (1976): 16-17.

KENDERESSY, Lajos
Novelist, born in Transylvania and moved to Hungary after World War II, then to Canada in 1956. His short stories and novels have appeared in periodicals and in book form. He now lives in the USA.

2124   *Harc az örökségért : Regény. [Fight for a Heritage, Novel].* Toronto: Apolló Press, 1959. 150 pp. Novel.

2125   *Házasság négyesben [Wedding for Four].* Niagara Falls, Ont.: Victoria Press, 1960. 159 pp. Novel.

KENESEI, László

2126   *Járatlan utakon: regény [On Untrodden Roads].* Toronto: Kanadai Magyarság, 1960. 183 pp. Novel.

KENÉZ, Zsuzsa

2127   *Irsai Kartársnő [Ms Irsai].* Toronto: Pátria, 1970. 187 pp. Novel.

KENT, Valerie (1947-)
Born in Tokaj, Hungary, educated at Sir George Williams (now Concordia) University, Montreal and the University of Iowa. Taught Creative Writing at Concordia University, McGill University and Dawson College, Montreal. Director of the Canadian Language Institute.

2128   "Polly Wants a Cracker." In *The Story So Far.* Toronto: Coach House, 1971. Story.

2129   *Wheelchair Sonata.* Toronto: Coach House, 1974. 86 pp. Novel.

2130   *A Thousand Days in the Attic.* Toronto: Coach House, 1976. 211 pp. Novel.

Writing about:

2131   Review of *Thousand Days in the Attic.* Q & Q 43, 6 (1977): 40-41.

2132   Review of *Wheelchair Sonata.* BKS CAN 4, no. 5 (1975): 14-15.

KERECSENDI KISS, Márton (1917-)
Born in Kerecsend, Hungary, came to Canada after World War II. His filmscripts were produced in Budapest during the war. Former editor of two newspapers, *Magyar Harangok* and *Magyar Utak.* His short stories and reports have appeared in *Magyar Élet.* He now lives in the U.S.A.

2133   *Hetedhétország: Mesejáték [Beyond the Seven Seas: Fairy Tale].* Cleveland: Orpheus, 1963. 160 pp. Play.

2134   *Emlékkönyv [Album].* Cleveland: Orpheus, 1972. 302 pp. Short stories, reports.

Writings about:

2135   Béládi, Miklós. "Kerecsendi Kiss Márton" [Márton Kerecsendi Kiss]. In *A magyar irodalom története: IV. A határon túli magyar irodalom...* (Budapest: Akadémiai Kiadó, 1982) pp. 357, 362.

2136   Béládi, Miklós; Pomogáts, Béla; Rónay, László. "Kerecsendi Kiss Márton" [Márton Kerecsendi Kiss]. In their *A nyugati magyar irodalom 1945 után.* (Budapest: Gondolat, 1986) pp. 36, 58, 68-69.

KISS, Ödön   (also: VISEGRÁDI, Aladár) (1921-1972)
Poet, born in Maglód, Hungary, arrived in Canada in 1956 and worked for Queen's University, Kingston, Ont. His poems have appeared in newspapers, periodicals and anthologies. His translations of English poems into Hungarian were published posthumously in a book entitled *Bimbóban, rügyben visszatérek.*

2137 *Emlékezzetek Magyarországra!* [Remember Hungary!] Toronto: Weller Publishing Co., 1966. 101 pp. Poems.
[Published under the pen name Aladár Visegrádi.]

2138 *Átutazóban a városomon: versek* [Passing through My Town: Poems]. Toronto: Weller Publishing Co., 1970. 93 pp. Poems.

2139 *A sziget nincs többé (kingstoni temetés)* [The Island Is No Longer (Funeral at Kingston]. Oakville, Ont.: Sovereign Press, 1972. 46 pp.

2140 *Bimbóban, rügyben visszatérek* [I shall Return with Spring], edited by Lajos Simon. Toronto, 1975. 127 pp. Poems.
[Translations into Hungarian. Some of Kiss's own early poems are also included.]

Writings about:

2141 Bisztray, George. "Ödön Kiss." In his *Hungarian-Canadian Literature.* (Toronto: University of Toronto Press, 1987) pp. 32-33.

2142 Fáy, Ferenc. "Búcsú és üzenet" [Farewell and a Message]. In *A sziget nincs többé...* (Oakville, Ont.: Sovereign Press, 1972) pp. i-iii.

2143 Miska, János. Obituary. NEMZETŐR (July 1972)

2144 Seres, József. "Valóság és reménység" [Reality and Hope]. KRÓNIKA 3, no. 6 (1977): 18.

2145 Tűz, Tamás. "Utóhang helyett requiem - Kiss Ödön emlékezete" [For Postscript, a Requiem - Ödön Kiss, in memoriam]. In *A sziget nincs többé....* (Oakville, Ont.: Sovereign Press, 1972) pp. 45-46.

KÖNYVES, Tom
An avant-garde poet, editor of *Hh* (Hobbyhorse) and director of Poetry Véhicule. His poems have appeared in *Anthol, CrossCountry, Mouse Eggs, CV II, MPIE Sampler.* His videopoems have been exhibited in England, Montreal, Winnipeg, Rome and Vancouver, where he resides.

2146 *Love Poems.* Montreal: Asylum, 1974. 40 pp. Poems.

2147 *Proverbsi,* in collaboration with Ken Norris. Montreal: Asylum, 1977. Poems.

2148 *No Parking.* Montreal: Véhicule Press, 1978. 59 pp. Poems.

2149 *Poetry in Performance.* Ste-Anne de Bellevue, Que.: The Muse's Co., 1982. 174 pp. Poems.

2150 *Ex Perimeter.* Vancouver: Caitlin Press, 1988. Poems.

Writings about:

2151 Biesenthal, Linda. Review of *No Parking.* CAN BOOK REV ANN 1978: 111-12.

2152 Fletcher, Peggy. "Véhicules Expression." CAN AUTH BKMN 55 (November 1979): 24.
[Review of *No Parking.*]

KORONDI, András

2153 *Őrzöm a házat [Guarding the House].* Toronto: Magyar Élet, 1961. 107 pp.

KRISTÓF, Sándor (1919-)

Poet, physician. Born in Mezőtúr, Hungary, and received his education in internal medicine at the University of Budapest. Came to Canada in 1957 and practised medicine at the St. Boniface Clinic, Winnipeg, until his retirement in 1985. Founding member of the Hungarian Literary Society of Winnipeg and contributor to newspapers and anthologies. He lives in Toronto.

2154 *Koncert versben [Concert in Poems]. Tétel I and II [Movements I and II].* Winnipeg: The Author, 1983. 126 pp. *Tétel II (Movement III).* 73 pp. Poems.

2155 *Twelve Sonnets and Selected Poems,* translated from the Hungarian by the Author, in collaboration with David Cunningham and Charles Corbet. [Winnipeg: The Author, 1985] 47 pp. Poems.

KULCSÁR, Lajos (1914-)

Born in Győr, Hungary. Came to Canada in 1956 and lived in Winnipeg until his retirement. Some of his early poems were set to music in Hungary and became popular songs there. His poems and short stories have appeared in newspapers and anthologies. He resides in Vancouver.

2156 *A nagy kérdés: Mikor lesz az emberből ember? és rövid elbeszélések [The Great Puzzle: When will Man Become Man? and Other Stories].* [Vancouver]: The Author, 1987. 149 pp. Short stories.

LING, Gyula

Born in Rakamaz, Hungary. Left for Australia in 1956 and came to Canada a decade later. He did not take up writing until late in life, but produced two novels in about as many years. He lives in Ottawa.

2157 *Várni és remélni: Regény [Waiting in Hope: Novel].* Toronto: The Author, 1983. 253 pp. Novel. [Winner of a bronze medal issued by the Árpád Academy, Cleveland.]

2158 *Ilyen kicsi a világ! Regény [What a Small World! Novel].* Toronto: The Author, 1984. 272 pp. Novel.

MÁNYOKY-NÉMETH, Károly

Born in Hungary, where he was a school teacher. He came to Canada in 1957. Edited the newspaper *Számadás,* now defunct. He lives in Toronto.

2159 *1956 október 23 (October 23, 1956].* Toronto: The Author, 1972. 108 pp. Poems.

2160 *Örvénylő sodrásban [Swept away in a Maelstrom].* Toronto: The Author, 1973. 109 pp. Poems.

2161 *Bújdosó: Regény [The Fugitive: Novel].* Toronto: The Author, 1973. 135 pp. Novel.

2162 *The Hunted: A Novel,* translated from Hungarian by Alex Falconer. Hicksville, N.Y.: Exposition Press, 1979. 96 pp.
[Translation of the novel *Bújdosó*.].

MARLYN, John (1912-)

Novelist and playwright, born in Nagybecskerek, Hungary. Came to Canada as a child with his parents. He spent his formative years in Winnipeg, the source of his novels. Received the Beta Sigma Phi First Novel Award (1958), a Canada Foundation Award (1958), Canada Council Senior Arts Award (1969 and 1976) and an Ontario Arts Council Award (1975). His short stories have appeared in periodicals and anthologies.

2163 *Under the Ribs of Death.* Toronto: McClelland & Stewart, 1957. 2nd ed. 1961. 288 pp. (New

Canadian Library No. 41) Novel.

2164 *Putzi, I Love You, You Little Square.* Toronto: Coach House, 1982. 90 pp. Novel.

Writings about:

2165 Adachi, Ken. "Fast-talking Fetus Becomes a Comic Hero." TOR STAR (July 31, 1982)
[Review of *Putzi, I Love You.*]

2166 Atwood, Margaret. "John Marlyn." In her *Survival.* (Toronto: House of Anansi, 1972) pp. 34, 152-54, 156, 207.

2167 Dafoe, Christopher. Review of *Under the Ribs of Death.* WINN FREE PRESS (Jan. 20, 1958)

2168 Mandel, Eli. "Introduction." In *Under the Ribs of Death.* (Toronto: McClelland & Stewart, 1961) pp. vii-xiv.

2169 Miska, János. "A kanadai magyar irodalom két dimenziója" [Two Dimensions of Hungarian-Canadian Literature]. KRÓNIKA 2, no. 11 (1976): 7-9.

2170 Miska, János. Review of *Putzi, I Love You...* NYUG MAGY (Calgary) 1, no. 7 (1982): 5.

2171 Moulton-Barrett, Donalee. Review of *Putzi, I Love You.* Q & Q 48, no. 7 (1982): 61-62.

2172 Rasporich, Beverly. "An Interview with John Marlyn." CAN ETH STUD 14, no. 1 (1982): 36-40.

2173 Roberts, John. "Irony in an Immigrant Novel: John Marlyn's *Under the Ribs of Death.*" CAN ETH STUD 14, no. 1 (1982): 41-48.

2174 Rose, Marylin. "John Marlyn." In *The Oxford Companion to Canadian Literature.* (Toronto: Oxford University Press, 1983) p. 517.

2175 Story, Norah. "John Marlyn." In her *Oxford Companion to Canadian History and Literature.* (Toronto: Oxford University Press, 1967) p. 263.

2176 Waddington, Miriam. Review of *Under the Ribs of Death.* QUEEN'S Q (1958): 627.

McDOUGALL (MEZEY), Marina (1945-   )
Born in Budapest, came to Canada with her parents in 1956. Attended McGill University, served as Program Coordinator for OECD in Paris and was official translator for various companies in Zurich and Toronto. Recipient of the Vicky Metcalf Short Story Award.

2177 *A kiskakas gyémántfélkrajcárja /Little Rooster's Diamond Half-penny,* as told by Marina (Mezey) McDougall, illustrated by Yüksel Hassan. Toronto: Kids Press, 1978. 32 pp. Children's story. [Text in Hungarian and English.]

Writing about:

2178 "Vicky Metcalf Awards Winners." APLA BULL 43 (January 1980): 1.

MATYAS, Cathy

2179 *Solstice.* London, Ont.: New Poetry, South Western Ontario Poetry, 1983. 24 pp. Poems.

2180   *Inside Out.* Willowdale, Ont.: Piraeus Press, 1983. [n.p.] Poems.

Writing about:

2181   Bastien, Mark. Review of *Inside Out.* CAN BOOK REV ANN 1983: 239.

MESTER, János

2182   *Fekete hó [Black Snow]* Toronto: The Author, 1973. 67 pp. Poems.

MISKA, János (1932-   )
Librarian, bibliographer, author, translator, editor. Born in Nyírbéltek, came to Canada in 1957. Attended the University of Budapest, McMaster University and the University of Toronto. Founding president of the Hungarian-Canadian Authors' Association and editor of its anthologies. Recipient of several grants and awards including the Queen's Jubilee Silver Medal (1977), and the Alberta Achievement Award for Excellence in Literature (1978). His translations of short stories have appeared in a book entitled *Legjobb elbeszélések angolból [Best Short Stories from English].*

2183   *Egy bögre tej: Elbeszélések [A Mug of Milk: Short Stories]* Ottawa-Munich: Mikes Kelemen Kiadó, 1969. 141 pp. illus., port. Short stories.

2184   *A magunk portáján: Válogatott írások 1963-1973 [Mending Our Fences: Selected Writings 1963-1973].* Lethbridge, Alta.: Kanadai Magyar Írók, 1974. 119 pp Stories and essays.

2185   *Kanadából szeretettel: Válogatott írások 1975-1985 [From Canada with Self-respect: Selected Writings 1975-1985] .* Ottawa: Kanadai Magyar Írók, 1989. 121 pp. Stories and essays.

Writings about:

2186   Bisztray, George. "John Miska." In his *Hungarian-Canadian Literature.* (Toronto: University of Toronto Press: 1987) pp. 60-63. port.

2187   Domokos, Sándor. "Köszönő levél" [Letter of Gratitude]. KAN MAGY ÚJS (Apr. 18, 1975)

2188   Fehér, Ferenc. "Szerzői est Ottawában" [Authors' Evening in Ottawa]. MAGY ÉLET (Feb. 20, 1968)

2189   Juhász, József. Review of *A magunk portáján.* NEMZETŐR (May 1974)

2190   Ludányi, András. "Barátaink a hírekben" [Newsmaking Friends]. ITT-OTT 8, no. 3 (1975): 31.

2191   Máté, Imre. "Elbeszélések Kanadából: Miska János: *Egy bögre tej*" [Short Stories from Canada: János Miska: *A Mug of Milk*]. NEMZETŐR (July 1969)

2192   Máté, Imre. Review of *A magunk portáján.* VAGYUNK (February 1976): 19.

2193   Naphegyi, Imre. "Miska János új könyve" [János Miska's New Book]. KAN MAGY ÚJS (Aug. 15, 1974)
        [Review of *A magunk portáján.*]

2194   Simon, Lajos. "A kanadai magyar irodalom; beszélgetés Miska Jánossal" [Hungarian-Canadian Literature; Interview with János Miska]. In *A magunk portáján .* (Lethbridge: Kanadai Magyar Írók, 1974) pp. 80-84.

2195　Somogyi, Ferenc. "Magyar álom valóraválása Kanadában" [Hungarian Dream Turns to Reality in Canada]. MAGY ÚJS 66, no. 47 (1976): 5.

2196　Somogyi, Ferenc. "Miska János" [János Miska]. In his *Az Árpád Akadémia tagjainak tevékenysége.* (Cleveland: Árpád Kiadó, 1982) pp. 235-36.

2197　Wass, Albert. Review of *Egy bögre tej.* AMER MAGY SZÉPM CZÉH NEGYED ÉRT (1966): 12.

MISKOLCI PANULICS, Lajos
Born in Miskolc, Hungary, emigrated to Canada after World War II. He has published poems and short stories in Hungarian newspapers in Canada. Two of his monographs on the Hungarian community of southern Alberta have appeared in Hungarian and English.

2198　*Vihartól sodortan: Próza és vers [Swept about by the Elements: Prose and Poetry].* Stirling, Alta.: The Author. 60 pp. Poems and short stories.

MUZSI, Jenő
Born in Hungary, where he received his university education. Emigrated to Canada in 1956. A novel relating to his experience in Canada is in manuscript. He lives in Toronto.

2199　*Öt könnycsepp: elbeszélések [Five Tears: Short stories].* Toronto: Weller, 1966. Short stories.

NÁDASY, Stephen

2200　Hotel Canada: Szatíra [Hotel Canada: Satire]. Toronto: Canadian Printing Service, 1959. 125 pp. Novel.

NAGY, István　(1890-1974)
Former Minister of the Hungarian United Church and Principal of the Institute of Diaconates of Debrecen, was born in Nagykároly (now in Romania). He was editor of the church periodical *Új Élet.* His short stories have appeared in that magazine, as well as in anthologies and newspapers in Canada and the USA.

2201　*A fenségtől a hallja kendig: Hazai emlékek [From the Bishop to the Bell Ringer: Memoirs].* Winnipeg: Új Élet, 1965. 222 pp. Short stories.

Writings about:

2202　Aday-Keresztúry, Lajos. "In Memoriam, Nagytiszteletű Nagy István, 1890-1974" [In Memoriam, the Rev. István Nagy, 1890-1974]. KAN MAGY ÚJS (Nov. 29, 1974)

2203　Domokos, Sándor. "Búcsúzás Pista bácsitól" [Farewell to Uncle Steve]. KAN MAGY ÚJS (Nov. 29, 1974)

2204　Miska, János. "Hazai emlékek" [Memories from Home]. ÚJ ÉLET (October 1966)
[Review of *Fenségtől a hallja kendig.*]

2205　Naphegyi, Imre. "Búcsú Nt. Nagy István lelkésztől" [Farewell to Reverend István Nagy]. KAN MAGY ÚJS (Nov. 22, 1974)

2206　Tamási, Miklós. "Több, mint kenyér – beszámoló helyett vallomás" [More than Bread – Confessions in Place of a Report]. KAN MAGY ÚJS KÉPES NAGY NAPT: 1975.

NAPHEGYI, Imre (1912-　)
Sculptor, poet, prose writer, born in Kolozsvár (now Romania), former officer of the Royal Hungarian

Army. He came to Canada after World War II and settled in Winnipeg. Founding member of the Hungarian Canadian Authors's Association. His writings have appeared in newspapers, periodicals and anthologies.

2207 *Irka-firka [Doodle and Scrawl]*. Winnipeg: The Author, 1970. 108 pp. Short stories.

2208 *Csalánba nem üt a ménkü: Tréfás elbeszélések [Lightning doesn't Hit the Nettle: Humorous Short Stories]*. Winnipeg: The Author, 1983. Short stories.

2209 *Fiókból [From My Drawers]*. Winnipeg: The Author, 1985. 108 pp. illus. Short stories.

2210 *Plébános úr [Father Nyírő]*. Winnipeg: The Author, 1987. 101 pp. Novel.

Writing about:

2211 Tábory, Maxim. "Kincs a fiókban" [Treasure in the Drawer]. NEMZETŐR (Apr. 15, 1988): 6. [Review of *Fiókból*.]

NÉMETH, Ernő (1903-1987)
Born in Kecskeméth, Hungary, educated at the University of Szeged. A former officer of the National Bank of Hungary, he came to Canada after the 1956 uprising. His poems have appeared in Hungarian newspapers, periodicals and anthologies.

2212 *Októberi árnyak [October Shadows]*. Toronto: Pátria, 1966. 64 pp. Poems.

Writings about:

2213 Bisztray, George. "Ernő Németh." In his *Hungarian-Canadian Literature*. (Toronto: University of Toronto Press, 1987) pp. 29, 33-34.

2214 Csepi, Béla. Review of *Októberi árnyak*. A HÉT (Nov. 3, 1967)

2215 Eszterhás, István. "Versek" [Poems]. KAT MAGY VAS (Jun. 25, 1972)

2216 Kecsi, A. Review of *Októberi árnyak*. FÁKLYA 16 (November-December 1967)

2217 Mérő, Ferenc. "Németh Ernő" [Ernő Németh] In *Az emigrációs magyar irodalom lexikona*. (Cologne: Amerikai Magyar Kiadó, 1966)

2218 Somogyi, Ferenc. "Németh Ernő" [Ernő Németh]. In his *Az Árpád Akadémia tagjainak tevékenysége*. (Cleveland: Árpád Kiadó, 1982) pp. 263-64.

PALLAY, István (1930-   )
Born in Budapest, received diplomas in Library Science from the University of Budapest and the University of Toronto. He came to Canada in 1956 and works as a Librarian in the Music Library of the University of Toronto.

2219 *Csak felnőtteknek: Még egy marék vicc a javából [For Adults Only: Another Fistful of Risqué Jokes]* Toronto: Forum Press, 1975. 207 pp. Stories, anecdotes.

2220 *Abszolut sikamlós: Összeállitotta Pallay István [Absolutely Risqué Things: Collected by István Pallay]*. Toronto: Neptune Press, 1979. 238 pp. Stories, anecdotes.

PIKÓ, Zsigmond (1903-   )
Born in Füzesgyarmat, Hungary, educated at the University of Debrecen. Served as a lawyer in his own company in Füzesgyarmat. He was a P.O.W. in the USSR. Emigrated to Canada in 1966 and settled in

Winnipeg.

2221 *Könnyező rímek [Tearful Rhymes].* [Winnipeg: The Author, n.d.] 120 pp. port.

PORTER, Anna

Born in Hungary, emigrated with her parents to New Zealand and then to Canada. She first worked for McClelland and Stewart, now controls Key Porter Books, Seal Books, and Doubleday Canada. Author of two successful novels.

2222 *Hidden Agenda.* Toronto: Irwin Publishing, 1985. 280 pp. Novel

2223 *Mortal Sins.* Toronto: Irwin Publishing, 1987. 274 pp. Novel.

Writings about:

2224 Cowan, Bert. Review of *Mortal Sins.* BKS CAN 17, no. 1 (1988): 27.

2225 Currie, Rod. "Easy-going Publisher Laughs at 'Great White Shark' Label." OTTAWA CIT (Dec. 12, 1987): H3.

2226 Heward, Ber. "Publisher Who Can Write." OTTAWA CIT (Jan. 19, 1987): C2.
      [Review of *Mortal Sins.*]

2227 Money, Darlene. Review of *Hidden Agenda.* CAN BOOK REV ANN 1985: 153-54.

2228 North, John. Review of *Mortal Sins.* Q & Q 53, no. 10 (1987): 22.

RÁBA, Margit

Born in Hungary, escaped to Canada after the October Revolution. Settled in Thunder Bay. Her writings on the revolution have appeared in the *Kanadai Magyar Újság* and other papers outside Hungary.

2229 *A rettenet évei: 1956 október 23 [Years of Horror: October 23, 1956].* Winnipeg: Kanadai Magyar Újság, 1957. 243 pp. Novel.

RÉKAI, Kati (1921-   )

Author of children's books and playwright. Born in Budapest and came to Toronto in 1956. She worked as public relations officer in the Central Hospital, Toronto, and director of *Performing Arts Magazine.* All her books have been transcribed into Braille and talking books by the Canadian National Institute for the Blind. Member of the Multicultural Advisory Board of the Toronto Historical Board. Her awards include Knighthood of St. Ladislaus, Certificate of Honour for contribution to Canadian unity, etc.

Children's Books:

2230 *The Adventures of Mickey, Taggy, Puppo and Cica, and How They Discover Toronto.* Toronto: Canadian Stage and Arts Publications, 1974. 142 pp. French translation in 1976, 118 pp. Hungarian in 1980, Polish 1983, 142 pp.

2231 *The Adventures of Mickey, Taggy, Puppo and Cica, and How They Discover Ottawa.* Toronto: Canadian Stage and Arts Publications, 1976. 108 pp. French translation 1979, 118 pp.

2232 *The Adventures of Mickey, Taggy, Puppo and Cica, and How They Discover Budapest.* Toronto: Canadian Stage and Arts Publications, 1979. 148 pp.

2233 *The Adventures of Mickey, Taggy, Puppo and Cica, and How They Discover Montreal.* Toronto: Canadian Stage and Arts Publications, 1979. 102 pp. French translation 1982, 120 pp.

2234 *The Adventures of Mickey, Taggy, Puppo and Cica, and How They Discover the Thousand Islands.* Toronto: Canadian Stage and Arts Publications, 1979. 58 pp. French translation 1980.

2235 *The Adventures of Mickey, Taggy, Puppo and Cica, and How They Discover Vienna.* Toronto: Canadian Stage and Arts Publications, 1980. 120 pp.

2236 *The Adventures of Mickey, Taggy, Puppo and Cica, and How They Discover the Netherlands.* Toronto: Canadian Stage and Arts Publications, 1981. 126 pp.

2237 *The Adventures of Mickey, Taggy, Puppo and Cica, and How They Discover Switzerland.* Toronto: Canadian Stage and Arts Publications, 1982. 120 pp.

2238 *The Adventures of Mickey, Taggy, Puppo and Cica, and How They Discover France.* Toronto: Canadian Stage and Arts Publications, 1984. 140 pp.

Plays:

2239 *The Great Totem Pole Caper* [Starring Mickey, Taggy, Puppo and Cica], with Marika Elek. Toronto, 1979.

2240 *The Tale of Tutankhamen* [Starring Mickey, Taggy, Puppo and Cica], with Marika Elek. Toronto, 1979.

2241 *The Boy Who Forgot*, with Alan Edmonds. Toronto, 1980.

Writings about:

2242 Pape, Gordon. "Painted into a Corner." FIN POST MAG (June 1, 1984): 65, 70-71.

2243 Review of the Adventure of *Mickey, Taggy, Puppo and Cica and How They Discover Toronto.* IN REVIEW 9, no. 1 (1975): 33.

REYTO, Martin (1948-   )
Born in Budapest, came to Toronto in 1956. Attended the University of Toronto and Dalhousie University. He is a technical writer, living in Montreal.

2244 *The Cloned Mammoth.* Dunvegan, Que.: Quadrant Editions, 1981. Poems.

SAJGÓ, Szabolcs (1951-   )
Clergyman, poet, born in Budapest, received his education at the Seminary of Esztergom and the Theological Academy of Budapest. He was ordained to the priesthood in 1974. Came to Canada in 1982 and continued his studies at the University of Toronto. Coeditor of *A Szív Magazin.* He has published in periodicals and anthologies.

2245 *Elárult látomás [Betrayed Apparition].*, with an introduction by Tamás Tűz. Illustrated by Katalin Rohonczy and Tibor Nyilasi. Toronto: Amerikai Magyar Írók, 1987. 136 pp. Poems.

SÁRVÁRI, Éva (1931-   )
Novelist, short story writer, born in Budapest, left Hungary in 1956 for Denmark, then moved to Australia and to Canada in 1966. Most of her writings depict the Hungarian experience in Canada and Australia. Some of her books have been translated into English and await publication. She has lived in Toronto since her

arrival in this country.

2246   *Kigyúlt a fény: Regény [The Light Goes On Again: Novel]*, with postscript by János Miska. Toronto: Kanadai Magyar Írók, 1972. 134 pp. Novel.

2247   *Féluton [Halfway Through]*. Toronto: Magyar Élet, 1975. 157 pp. Novel.

2248   *Messze délen: Regény [Faraway in the South: Novel]*. Munich: Vagyunk Kiadó, 1976. 167 pp. Novel.

Writings about:

2249   Bisztray, George. "Éva Sárvári." In his *Hungarian-Canadian Literature*. (Toronto: University of Toronto Press, 1987) pp. 56-60.

2250   Dohnányiné, Z. Ilona. "Álljunk meg egy pillanatra" [Let's Stop for a Moment]. AMER MAGY VIL (1973): 14.
        [Review of *Kigyúlt a fény*.]

2251   Juhász, József. Review of *Kigyúlt a fény*. KAN MAGY (Oct. 14, 1972)

2252   Kasza-Marton, Lajos. "Könyvekről" [Of Books]. KÉPES MAGY VIL (December 1972): 12.
        [Review of *Kigyúlt a fény*.]

2253   Miska, János. "Útravaló egy regényhez" [Introducing a Novel]. KAN MAGY ÚJS (July 21, 1972)
        [Review of *Kigyúlt a Fény*.]

2254   Nyisztor, Zoltán. Review of *Kigyúlt a fény*. ÚJ EUR (July-August 1973)

2255   Sz. Kanyó Leona. "Másfél óra regénye" [A Novel of One-and-a-Half Hours]. VAGYUNK (March 1973)
        [Review of *Kigyúlt a fény*.]

2256   Tűz, Tamás. Review of *Kigyúlt a fény*. MAGY ÉLET (Dec. 23, 1972)

2257   Tűz, Tamás. Review of *Messze délen*. KRÓNIKA 3, no. 1 (1977): 8-9.

SCHWILGIN, Frigyes   (1926-1984)
Born in Dunaharaszti, graduate of the Technical University of Budapest and The University of Manitoba (M.S.). He came to Canada in 1956 and worked as Chief of the Urban Planning Section of the Department of Public Works.

2258   *Tiéd csupán [Yours Only]*. Ottawa: The Author, 1973. Poems.

2259   *Töredékek: Versek [Fragments: Poems]*. [Ottawa: The Author, 1975]. 62 leaves. illus. Poems.

2260   *Versek, 1962-1971 [Poems, 1962-1971]*, with an introduction by Tamás Tűz. Ottawa: The Author, 1972. 156 pp. Poems.
        [Contents: *Tiéd csupán [Yours Only]. Visszanézés előre [Reminiscences]*.

Writings about:

2261   Máté, Imre. "Schwilgin Frigyes, költő" [Frigyes Schwilgin, Poet]. NEMZETŐR 13, 6 (1970).

2262   Németh, Ernő. "Versek" [Poems]. NEMZETŐR 16, no. 5 (1973)

SERES, József (1942-   )

Sculptor, poet, born in Szerencs, Hungary. Came to Canada in 1972. Graduated from the Ontario College of Art in 1979. His poems have appeared in Hungarian language periodicals and anthologies.

2263   *Évszakok nélkül: Versek [Without Seasons: Poems]*. Toronto: The Author, 1978. 120 pp. illus. Poems.

Writings about:

2264   Juhász, József. "Ábrázolás és kifejezés, Évszakok nélkül című irodalmi est bevezetője" [Poetic Images and Expressions: Introduction to a Literary Evening: Without Seasons]. KRÓNIKA 4, no. 3 (1978): 26.

2265   Seres, József. "Évszakok nélkül" [Without Seasons]. KRÓNIKA 4, no. 3 (1978): 26.

SIMON, Lajos (1925-   )

Born in Balatonszentgyörgy, Hungary, came to Canada in 1956. Published in newspapers and anthologies. He lives in Toronto.

2266   *Mindig árnyékban [Always in the Shadow]*. Calgary: The Author, 1968. 91 pp. Short stories.

2267   *Fáklyafény [Torchlight]*. Toronto: The Author, 1976. 98 pp. illus. Historical novel.

2268   *Kárthágó lánya [Daughter of Carthage]*. In *Kézfogás....* (Toronto: Kanadai Magyar Írók Szövetsége, 1977) pp. 89-100. Play in one act.

SZÉKELY MOLNÁR, Imre   (1903-1980)

Journalist and short story writer, he was born in Transylvania and emigrated to Canada after World War II. Contributed to *Kanadai Magyar Újság* and several other newspapers and anthologies.

2269   *Hallod-e, Zsófi? [Zsófi, Do You Hear?]*. Toronto: Apolló Press, 1962. 225 pp. Novel.

2270   *Föltisztul az ég [The Sky Clears Up]*. Toronto: Herkules Print, 1965. 255 pp. Short stories.

2271   *Az apostol és a paradicsommadár: Regény és elbeszélések [The Apostle and the Tomato-bird: Novel and Short Stories]* Toronto: Sovereign Press, 1971. 318 pp. Novel and short stories.

2272   *Forgó komédia [A Whirlwind of Comedy]*. Toronto: Y & G Studio, 1979. Short stories.

SZILVÁSSY, László   (1910-1964)

Former editor of the periodical *Képes Világhíradó*, now defunct. He was born in Budapest and served as an officer in the Royal Hungarian Army. Came to Canada in 1951 and lived in Toronto. His satirical short stories are related to the immigrant experience in Canada.

2273   *Mesék a brianszki erdőből [Tales from the Briansk Forest]*. Toronto: Pátria, 1958. 2 v. Novel.

2274   *Minden csak illúzió... [Everything is but an Illusion...]*. Toronto: Képes Világhíradó Kiadása, 1966. 237 pp. Short stories.

SZITHA, Ilona (1946-   )

Born Éva Tomasovszky in Budapest. She came to Canada with her parents after the 1956 uprising. Her poems have appeared in newspapers and anthologies. She lives in Toronto.

2275   *Sötétben vadászó nap [The Sun in Dark Hunting Ground].* Munich: HERP Kiadó, with Amerikai Magyar Írók, 1982. 92 pp. Poems.

Writings about:

2276   Béládi, Miklós. "Szitha Ilona" [Ilona Szitha]. In *A magyar irodalom története, 1945–1975: IV. A határon túli magyar irodalom.* (Budapest: Akadémiai Kiadó, 1982) p. 337.

2277   Béládi, Miklós; Pomogáts, Béla; Rónay, László. "Szitha Ilona" [Ilona Szitha]. In their *A Nyugati magyar irodalom 1945 után.* (Budapest: Gondolat, 1986) pp. 31, 266, 315.

2278   Tűz, Tamás. "Fiatal kanadai magyar írók" [Young Hungarian-Canadian Authors]. NYUG MAGY 1, no. 6 (1982): 5.
        [Review of *Sötétben vadászó nap.*]

SZOHNER, Gabriel (1936-   )

Novelist, short story writer, painter. Born in Hungary, came to Canada in 1956. Received a grant from the Canada Council for *The Immigrant,* a novel. Published short stories in *Western News, Canadian Fiction Magazine* and other periodicals. He has two completed novels in manuscript: "The Anti-Semite" and the "Red Danube". He lives in Ottawa.

2279   *The Immigrant.* Vancouver: Intermedia Press, 1977. 194 pp. Novel.

Writings about:

2280   Miska, János. Review of *The Immigrant.* KRÓNIKA 4, no. 6 (1978): 33.

2281   Miska, János. Review of *The Immigrant.* CAN ETH STUD 10, no. 2 (1978): 202-203.

2282   Smith, Michael. "Refuse from a Teaming Shore." BKS CAN 7, no. 3 (1978): 14.
        [Review of *The Immigrant.*]

TAKÁCS, Attila, pseud. (Real name: Kovács, Ottó Attila) (1934-   )

Born in Pécs, Hungary. He came to Canada in 1957. He is a member of the Hungarian-Canadian Authors' Association. His poems have appeared in anthologies, newspapers and periodicals.

2283   *Valami néha visszahív [Something Sometimes Calls Me Back],* introduction by Tamás Tűz. Toronto: The Author, 1988. 52 pp. port.

TALLOSI, Jim (1947-   )

Born in Dunakeszi, Hungary, he came to Canada with his parents in 1956. A graduate of the University of Winnipeg, currently in the employ of Parks Canada. He lives in Winnipeg.

2284   *The Trapper and the Fur-faced Spirits.* Drawings by Réal Bérard. Winnipeg: Queenston House Publishing, 1981. 107 pp. illus., port. Poems.

2285   *Talking Water, Talking Fire.* Drawings by Réal Bérard. Winnipeg: Queenston House Publishing, 1985. 87 pp. illus., port. Poems.

Writings about:

2286   Davis, Richard. "Looking North." CAN LIT No. 94 (1982): 134-36.
        [Review of *The Trapper and the Fur-faced Spirits.*]

2287   Keith, W.J. Review of *Talking Water*.... CAN BOOK REV ANN 1985: 199.

2288   Mesman, Leslie. "James Tallosi." In *Connections Two: Writers and the Land*. (Winnipeg: Manitoba School Libraries Association, 1983) pp. 101-02. port.

TAMÁSI, Miklós

Born in Hungary, came to Canada as a student with the Sopron Forestry group. President of the Hungarian Cultural Centre, Vancouver, and editor of its monthly magazine *Tárogató*.

2289   *Eszkimó szerelem: Versek 1958-69 [Eszkimo Love Affair: Poems 1958-69]* with an introduction by Márton Kerecsendi Kiss. Toronto: Vörösváry Kiadó, 1977. 151 pp. Poems.

TAPOLCZAY, Lukács, pseud.

Born in Miskolc, Hungary. Came to Canada after World War II. His poems have appeared in newspapers and anthologies. He lives in Toronto.

2290   *Lombhullás előtt [Before Autumn]* with a foreword by Ferenc Fáy. Toronto: The Author, 1973. 56 pp. Poems. port.

TIHANYI, Éva (1956-   )

Born in Budapest and came to Canada with her parents after the revolution. Attended the University of Windsor. She taught at Humber College, George Brown College, Seneca College and the University of Windsor. Her poems have appeared in *Canadian Literature, Prism International, Quarry, The Antigonish Review*, etc.

2291   *A Sequence of Blood*. Toronto: Aya Press, 1982. 72 pp. Poems.

2292   *Prophecies Near the Speed of Light*, illustrated by Martin McCarney. Saskatoon: Thistledown Press, 1984. 80 pp. Poems.

Writings about:

2293   Matyas, Cathy. Review of *Prophecies Near the Speed of Light*. POET CAN REV 6, no. 4 (1985)

2294   Pilon, Ellen. Review of *Prophecies Near the Speed of Light*. CAN BOOK REV ANN 1983: 256-57.

TOLDY, Endre

2295   *Az öreg csatár [The Old Fighter]*. Toronto: Pátria, 1971. 105 pp. Novel.

TÓTH, Tihamér (1940-   )

Born in Bény, Hungary. He came to Canada in 1956. Attended the University of Montreal, the University of Ottawa and York University. He works as a social worker at the Queen Elizabeth Hospital in Toronto. He is editor of *Earth and You*, a literary magazine appearing since 1970.

2296   *Test Your Freedom: A Discourse of Man's Role in the Universe*. New York: Exposition Press, [1969] 144 pp. Poems.

2297   *My Heart's Thorns to Moira: A Collection of Unusual Love Poems*. Toronto: Earth and You, 1974. 128 pp. Poems.

2298   *Golden Heart.* Toronto: Earth and You, 1979. 3 vols. (167 pp.) illus. Poems.

2299   *But Joy.* Toronto: Earth and You, 1980. 3 vols. (242 pp.) Poems.

2300   *Your Money, Your Life.* Toronto: Earth and You, 1983. 140 pp. Poems.

2301   *Glooscap.* Toronto: Earth and You, 1987. 75 pp. Poems.

2302   *Haleric Master Leper.* Toronto: Earth and You, 1987. 67 pp. illus. Poems.

TŰZ, Tamás, pseud. (Real name: MAKKÓ, Lajos) (1916-   )
Poet, novelist, essayist, one of the most accomplished authors of contemporary Hungarian literature. Born in Győr, Hungary, and ordained a priest of the Roman Catholic Church. He served as a chaplain in the Hungarian Army during World War II and spent several years in prisoner of war camps in the USSR. He came to Canada after the 1956 uprising. An editor of anthologies, his poems have also appeared in periodicals and newspapers on both sides of the Hungarian border. He lives in Toronto.

2303   *Nyugtalan szárnyakon [On Restless Wings].* Cologne: Amerikai Magyar Kiadó, 1959. 152 pp. Poems.

2304   *Egy ország küszöbén [On the Threshold of a Country].* Los Angeles: Amerikai Magyar Írók, 1966. 160 pp. Poems.

2305   *On Restless Wings.* San Diego: The Author, 1966. port.
(A small collection of poems translated by the author in collaboration with other poets.]

2306   *Elraboltam Európát [I Have Stolen Europe].* Los Angeles: Amerikai Magyar Írók, 1967. Poems.

2307   *Tükörben játszik a kéz [Playful Hands in the Mirror].* Toronto: Amerikai Magyar Írók, 1970. 222 pp. Poems.

2308   *Válogatott versek [Selected Poems].* Toronto: Amerikai Magyar Írók, 1972. 319 pp. port. Poems.

2309   *Harmincnapos nászút [Thirty-day Honeymoon].* Toronto: Amerikai Magyar Írók, 1973. 156 pp. Novel.

2310   *Angyal, mondd ki csak félig [Angel, Reveal Only Half of It].* Toronto: Amerikai Magyar Írók, 1975. 256 pp. Poems.

2311   *Hova tűntek a szitakötők? [Where have the Dragonflies Gone?]* Toronto: Amerikai Magyar Írók, 1977. 314 pp. Essays, autobiography, poems.

2312   *Jelen voltam [I was There].* Toronto: Amerikai Magyar Írók, 1977. 192 pp. Poems.

2313   *Aranyrét utca: Versek az ifjúságnak [Aranyrét Street: Poems for the Young]* Toronto: Amerikai Magyar Írók, 1978. 96 pp. Poems.

2314   *Égve felejtett álmok [Flaming Dreams].* Munich: Amerikai Magyar Kiadó, 1980. 192 pp. Poems.

2315   *Szemünktől kék az ég [Our Eyes Tint the Sky Blue].* Munich: HERP, 1982. 189 pp. Poems.

2316   *Leheletnyi öröklét [A Breathful of Eternity].* Munich: HERP, 1983. 184 pp. Poems.

2317   *Hét sóhaj a hegyen [Seven Sighs on the Mountain].* Toronto: Amerikai Magyar Írók, 1987.

Poems.

Writings about

2318   Béládi, Miklós. "Tűz Tamás" [Tamás Tűz]. In *A magyar irodalom története, 1945-1975: 4. A határon túli magyar irodalom*. (Budapest: Akadémiai Kiadó, 1982) pp. 337, 342, 367-69, 445.

2319   Béládi, Miklós; Pomogáts, Béla; Rónay, László. "Tűz Tamás" [Tamás Tűz]. In their *A Nyugati magyar irodalom 1945 után*. (Budapest: Gondolat, 1986) pp. 6, 31, 39, 59, 77, 166, 195-201, 246, 297, 302, 304, 308, 315-16.

2320   Bisztray, George. "Tamás Tűz" In his *Hungarian-Canadian Literature*. (Toronto: University of Toronto Press, 1987) pp. 28-32.

2321   Borbándi, Gyula. "Tűz Tamás" [Tamás Tűz]. In his *A magyar emigráció életrajza 1945-1985*. (Bern: Az Európai Protestáns Magyar Szabadegyetem, 1985) pp. 368, 373, 382, 474.

2322   Csiky, Ágnes Mária. "Istenkereső nyugtalanság" [A Restless Search for God]. IROD ÚJS (May-June 1981): 11.
[Review of *Égve felejtett álmok*.]

2323   Csiky, Ágnes Mária. "Szimultán látomás" [Simultaneous Vision]. ÚJ LÁTÓH 24 (1973): 463-64.
[Review of *Válogatott versek*.]

2324   Fenyő, Miksa. "Tűz Tamás versei" [Tamás Tűz's Poems]. ÚJ LÁTÓH 17 (1966): 285-87.
[Review of *Egy ország küszöbén*.]

2325   Garai, István. Review of *Égve felejtett álmok*. SOMOGY 3 (May-June 1981): 100-102.

2326   Hegedűs, Géza. "Egy magyar költő a hontalanságban" [A Hungarian Poet in Exile]. KORTÁRS 4 (1971)

2327   Hegedűs, Géza. "Egy napnyugati magyar költő" [A Hungarian Poet of the West]. ÉLET IROD (March 19, 1982): 10.
[Review of *Szemünktől kék az ég*.]

2328   Kemenes Géfin, László. *Halálos szójáték: Bevezetés Tűz Tamás költészetébe [Deadly Play with Words: Introduction to Tamás Tűz's Poetry]*. Montreal: Amerikai Magyar Írók, 1976. 66 pp.

2329   Kemenes Géfin, László. "Játék az utolsó leheletig" [Play to the Last Breath]. IROD ÚJS 25, no. 1-2 (1974): 11-12.
[Review of *Válogatott versek*.]

2330   Lőkkös, Antal. "Tűz Tamás két verseskötete" [Two Collections of Poetry by Tamás Tűz]. KAT SZEM No. 2 (1984): 193-96.

2331   Makay, Gusztáv. "Korszerűtlen gondolatok a líráról" [Outmoded Reflections on Lyric Poetry]. VIGILIA 5 (1976)
[Review of *Angyal, mondd ki csak félig*.]

2332   Nehéz, Ferenc. "Az angyali költő" [Angelic Poet...]. KAN MAGY ÚJS (Dec. 12, 1975)
[Review of *Angyal, mondd ki csak félig*.]

2333   Parancs, János. Review of *Szemünktől kék az ég*. MŰHELY 2 (1982): 94-96.

2334   Reményi, József Tamás. Review of *Hova tűntek a szitakötők?* KRITIKA No. 5 (1979)

2335   Rónay, László. "Magyar költők nyugaton" [Hungarian Poets in the West]. VIGILIA (August 1981): 546-51.

2336   Rónay, László. Review of *Égve felejtett álmok.* KRITIKA No. 3 (1981)

2337   Rónay, László. "Tűz Tamás versei" [Tamás Tűz's Poems]. MŰHELY 2 (1980): 43-47.

2338   Szakolczay, Lajos. "Tűz Tamás költészete" [The Poetry of Tamás Tűz]. In his *Dunának, Oltnak.* (Budapest: Szépirodalmi, 1984) pp. 415-24.

2339   Szakolczay, Lajos. "Tűz Tamás Versei" [Tamás Tűz's Poems]. JELENKOR (March 1982): 242-47.

2340   Szigethy, Gábor. Review of *Angyal, mondd ki csak félig.* VALÓSÁG 11 (1974)

2341   Szigethy, Gábor. "Tűz Tamás költészetéről [Of Tamás Tűz's Poetry]. KORTÁRS (June 1981): 942-48.
       [Review of *Jelen voltam.*]

2342   Szitha, Ilona. "Egy költő álmai" [The Dreams of a Poet]. KAT MAGY VAS (Nov. 9, 1980): 6.
       [Review of *Égve felejtett álmok.*]

2343   Szitha, Ilona. Review of *Égve felejtett álmok.* KAT SZEML 2 (1982): 179-83.

2344   Tűz, Tamás. "Magamról és verseimről" [About Myself and My Poems]. ÚJ LÁTÓH 27 (1976): 230.

2345   "Tűz Tamás" [Tamás Tűz]. ÚJ LÁTÓH 23 (1972): 184; 24 (1973): 88; 25 (1974): 183.

VAJK, Péter Tamás

Born in Budapest and received a degree in Mining Engineering at the University of Sopron. He came to Canada in 1967 and is working for the Ontario Ministry of Transport as Chief of Material Inspection. He started writing poetry at an early age, his writing appearing in *Pesti Napló* and *Magyar Hírlap*, and recently in *Krónika* and anthologies.

2346   *Ha elmegyek: Válogatott versek [If I Leave: Selected Poems].* Toronto: Rákóczi Press, 1986.
       Poems.

VÁTHY, Kálmán (1927-   ).

Born in Nagykanizsa, Hungary. He left his country for Germany at the end of the war, then moved to Austria, England and, in 1952, to Canada. A mathematician and computer scientist by profession, he took up poetry quite late in life.

2347   *Alkonyati ébredés: Versek [Awakening at Dusk: Poems].* Toronto: The Author, 1982.] 161 pp.
       Poems.

VERKOCZY, Elizabeth

Born in Budapest, educated in her native land, and in England. Joined the Hungarian National Children's Newspaper at the age of 15. Went to England in 1956 and emigrated to Canada in 1966.

2348   *White Tulips for Lena.* Toronto: Simon & Pierre, 1983. Novel.

VITÉZ, György, pseud. (Real name: NÉMETH, György) (1933-   )
Born in Budapest and completed his university education there. Came to Canada following the Hungarian uprising of 1956. Continued his university education at Sir George Williams (now Concordia) University and McGill University. Teaches psychology at Concordia and has his own practice in clinical psychology, in which he holds a doctoral degree. Translated into Hungarian Ginsberg's *Howl*. Co-editor of *Arkánum*.

2349   *Amerikai történet [An American Story]*. Paris: Magyar Műhely, 1977. Poems.

2350   *Missa agnostica [Agnostic Mass]*. Paris: Magyar Műhely, 1979. 47 pp. Poems.

2351   *Jel beszéd [Sign Language]*. Paris: Magyar Műhely, 1982. 77 pp. Poems.

Writings about:

2352   Béládi, Miklós. "Vitéz György" [György Vitéz]. In *A magyar irodalom története 1945-1975: IV. A határon túli magyar irodalom*. (Budapest: Akadémiai Kiadó, 1982) pp. 346, 414, 417, 421, 444.

2353   Béládi, Miklós; Pomogáts, Béla; Rónay, László. "Vitéz György" [György Vitéz] In their *A nyugati magyar irodalom 1945 után*. (Budapest: Gondolat, 1986) pp. 23, 44, 224, 228, 243-45, 296, 308, 312, 316.

2354   Bisztray, George. "Vitéz György" [György Vitéz]. In his *Hungarian-Canadian Literature*. (Toronto: University of Toronto Press, 1987) pp. 46-49.

2355   Gömöri, György. "Játékos, bizarr realizmus" [Playful, Bizarre Realism]. ÚJ LÁTÓH (1977): 536-37.

2356   Molnár, Miklós. "Közeledés a lehetséges szöveghez" [Approacing a Probable Text]. ÉLETÜNK 1 (1980): 93-96.

2357   Pomogáts, Béla. "Az emigráció második költőnemzedéke: Vázlat" [Second Generation of Poets in Exile: An Outline]. ÉLETÜNK 6 (1981): 555-67.

2358   Pomogáts, Béla. "Magyar költők Nyugaton" [Hungarian Poets in the West]. JELENKOR No. 1 (1981): 91-96.

2359   Pomogáts, Béla. "A szótól a szövegig" [From the Word to the Text]. JELENÜNK No. 6 (1979): 553-59.

2360   Szakolczay, Lajos."Magyar Költő Kanadában" [Hungarian Poet in Canada]. MAGY NEMZET (Aug. 9, 1979): 4.

2361   Szakolczay, Lajos. "Vitéz György és a Missa Agnostica" [György Vitéz and His Missa Agnostica] In his *Dunának, Oltnak*. (Budapest: Szépirodalmi, 1984) pp. 415-24.

2362   Tűz, Tamás. Review of *Amerikai történet*. KRÓNIKA 4, no. 1 (1978): 9.

2363   Zalán, Tibor. "Külföldi magyar könyvek" [Hungarian Books Abroad]. ÉLETÜNK No. 9 (1982): 862-64.

VIZINCZEY, Stephen (1932-   )
Novelist, essay writer, born in Budapest, where he began his literary career as a poet and playwright. In Canada he wrote scripts for the National Film Board and was a writer and producer for CBC in Toronto, a job he held until the mid-sixties, when he turned to writing on a full-time basis. He has published two

books of essays and book reviews (*Rules of Chaos* and *Truth and Lies in Literature*).

2364   *In Praise of Older Women: The Amorous Recollections of András Vajda.* Toronto: The Author, 1965. American edition by Ballantine Books, New York, 1967. 224 pp. Novel. [Made into a film.]

2365   *The Innocent Millionaire.* Toronto: McClelland & Stewart, 1983. 388 pp. Novel.

Writings about:

2366   Bannerman, James. "Who Says Sex Can't be Wrong?" MACLEAN'S 78 (Sept. 4, 1965): 46.

2367   Conklin, Jamie. Review of *The Innocent Millionaire.* Q & Q 49, no. 11 (1983): 20.

2368   Dobbs, Kildare. "Hungarian Loves." SAT N (September 1965): 29-31. [Review of *In Praise of Older Women.*]

2369   Hoy, Helen. "Ficton. Letters in Canada." UNIV TOR Q 53 (1983-84): 332. [Review of *The Innocent Millionaire.*]

2370   "Outstanding Canadian of 1975." MACLEAN'S 79 (Jan. 1, 1976): 13. ports.

2371   Owen, I.M. "In Appraisal of Older Writers." BKS CAN 15, no. 6 (1986): 21. [Review of *Truth and Lies in Literature.*]

2372   Sutherland, Fraser. "Rhinestones in the Rough." BKS CAN 12, no. 12 (1983): 24. [Review of *The Innocent Millionaire.*]

2373   Zalán, Magda. "In Praise of Innocent Millionaires". In her *Stubborn People.* (Toronto: Stage and Art Productions, 1985) pp. 58-66. port.

ZALÁN, Magda

Born in Medgyes (now in Romania), grew up in Budapest. She started her literary career in Hungary as a radio broadcaster. She spent a number of years in Italy prior to coming to Canada. Author of *Stubborn People*, a collection of biographies about notable Hungarians. She lives in Washington, D.C.

2374   *In a Big Ugly House Far from Here*, translated by Rosella Calnan and John Sömjén, illustrated by Julius Varga. Toronto: Press Porcépic, 1982. 87 pp. Short stories.

ZEND, Robert   (1929-1985)

Born in Budapest, graduated from Pázmány University and worked as a journalist, poet and translator. He came to Toronto in 1957 and lived there until his death. Zend had a long career with CBC as a librarian, film editor and radio producer. He published extensively in Hungarian and English and gave readings in both languages across the country.

2375   *From Zero to One.* Vancouver: Sono Nis Press, 1973. 110 pp. Poems.

2376   *Arbor Mundi; 15 Selected* Typescapes. Vancouver: Blewointment Press, 1982.

2377   *Beyond Labels.* Toronto: Hounslow Press, 1982. 158 pp. Poems. [Includes poems translated into English with John Robert Colombo, as well as poems written in English.]

2378   *Oāb..* Vol. 1. Toronto: Exile, 1983. Poems.

2379   *The Three Roberts: Premiere Performance.* Montreal: HMS Press, 1985. Poems.

2380   *Oāb.* Vol. 2. Toronto: Exile Editions, 1985. Poems.

2381   *The Three Roberts: On Childhood,* with Robert Priest and Robert Sward. St. Catharines, Ont.: Moonstone Press, 1985. 55 pp. Poems.

2382   *The Three Roberts: On Love.* Dreadnought, 1984. Poems.

Writings about:

2383   Barbour, Douglas. "Canadian Poetry Chronicle: VI." DAL REV 58 (1978): 555-78.
[Review of *From Zero to One.*]

2384   Béládi, Miklós; Pomogáts, Béla; Rónay, László. "Zend Róbert" [Robert Zend]. In their *A nyugati magyar irodalom 1945 után.* (Budapest: Gondolat, 1986) pp. 224, 239-41, 316.

2385   Bisztray, George. "Robert Zend." In his *Hungarian-Canadian Literature.* (Toronto: University of Toronto Press, 1987) pp. 39-40.

2386   Buckley, Paul. "Robert Zend, 1929-1985." BKS CAN 14, no. 8 (1985): 18.

2387   Douglas, Charles. "Poetry: Presence and Presentation." LAUR UNIV REV 7, no. 1-2 (1976): 74-85.
[Review of *From Zero to One* and *Oāb.*]

2388   Galt, George. "Prisoner of Zend." BKS CAN 12, no. 3 (1983): 20-21.
[Review of *Beyond Labels.*]

2389   Levenson, Christopher. "Tragedy Viewed from a Distance." SAT N 89 (February. 1974): 33-34.
[Review of *From Zero to One.*]

2390   MacLulich, T.D. "All Trad not Bad." ESSAYS CAN WRIT 2 (1975): 62-64.
[Review of *From Zero to One.*]

2391   Priest, Robert. "Robert Zend." Q & Q 51, no. 10 (1985): 31.

2392   Querengesser, Neil. Review of *The Three Roberts.* . CAN BOOK REV ANN 1985: 200.

2393   Singleton, Martin. Review of *Oāb.* CAN BOOK REV ANN 1985: 204.

2394   Tapping, Craig. "Free Words." CAN LIT No. 101 (1984): 161.
[Review of *Beyond Labels.*]

2395   Wynand, Derk. Review of *From Zero to One.* MAL REV 3 (1974): 168-69.

ZIMÁNYI, Rudolf

2396   *Szomjúság [Thirst].* Oakville, Ont.: Sovereign Press, 1973. Poems.

ICELANDIC

BIBLIOGRAPHIES

2397 LINDAL, Walter J.
"Icelandic-Canadian Creative Literature: A Preliminary Check List of Authors and Pseudonyms."
CAN ETH STUD 2, no. 1 (1970): 91-94.
[A list of 73 authors.]

2398 LINDAL, Walter J.
"Icelandic-Canadian Periodical Publications: A Preliminary Check List." CAN ETH STUD 2, no. 1
(1970): 85-90.
[Includes references to 54 titles and indexes.]

2399 SIGVALDADÓTTIR-GEPPERT, Margrét
"Icelandic-Canadian Creative Literature: A Preliminary Check List." CAN ETH STUD 5, no. 1-2
(1973): 139-51.
[Provides bibliographic data on 97 books: poetry, short stories and novels.]

BOOKS, MONOGRAPHS

2400 BECK, Richard
History of Icelandic Poets, 1800-1940. Ithaca, N.Y.: Cornell University Press, 1950. 247 pp.
(Islandica 34)
[Includes a chapter on Icelandic-American, and mainly Canadian, poets (pp. 199-242). Individual
poets discussed are Stephan G. Stephansson, Kristinn Stefánsson, Jón Runólfsson, Magnús
Markússon, Kristján Níels Július, Jónas A. Sigurðsson, Gísli Jónsson, Guttormur J. Guttormsson,
Vigfús Guttormsson, Þ. Þorsteinn Þorsteinsson, Einar Páll Jónsson, Jónas Stefánsson frá Kaldbak,
Páll S. Pálsson, and Bjarni Þorsteinsson.]

2401 BECK, Richard
Yrkisefni Vestur-íslenzkra skálda [Poem-subjects of North American Icelandic Poets]. Offprint
from *Skírnir.* Reykjavík, 1956. 23 pp.

2402 EINARSSON, Stefán
History of Icelandic Literature. Baltimore: The Johns Hopkins Press for the American-
Scandinavian Foundation, 1957. 409 pp.
[Includes a chapter on American and Canadian authors of Icelandic descent, pp. 340-54.
Bibliography: 355-62.]

2403 EINARSSON, Stefán
History of Icelandic Prose Writers 1800-1940. Ithaca, N.Y.: Cornell University Press, 1948. 269
pp. (Islandica 32 and 33) Reprinted by Kraus Reprint Corp., 1966.
[Includes a chapter on American-Canadian Icelandic writers (pp. 233-54). Icelandic-Canadian authors
included are Gunnsteinn Eyjólfsson, Johann Magnús Bjarnason, Stephan G. Stephansson,
Guttormur J. Guttormsson, Jóhannes P. Pálsson, Þ. Þorsteinn Þorsteinsson, Guðrún H. Finnsdóttir.]

2404 HERMANNSON, Halldór
Icelandic People of Today. New York: Kraus Reprint Corp., 1966. 69 pp.

2405 KRISTJANSON, W.

Icelandic People in Manitoba: A Manitoba Saga. Winnipeg: Wallingford Press, 1965. 557 pp.
[Includes a chapter on literature and journalism (pp. 483-501). Describes the works of Stephan G. Stephansson, Kristinn Stefánsson, Jón Runólfsson, Kristján Níels Júlíus, Johann Magnús Bjarnason, S.J. Jóhannesson, Guttormur J. Guttormsson, Þ. Þorsteinn Þorsteinsson, Einar Páll Jónsson, and L. Goodman Salverson.]

2406 KRISTJÁNSSON, Benjamín
      Vestur-íslenzkar æviskrár I [Biographies of Icelanders in America I]. Akureyri: Bókaforlag Odds Björnssonar [1961-   ].
      [Published annually.]

2407 SIMUNDSSON, Elva
      Icelandic Settlers in America. Winnipeg: Queenston House Publishing, 1981.
      [Provides a historical account of migration, settlement, community developments and cultural aspects.]

RESEARCH PAPERS

2408 ARNASON, David
      "Icelandic Canadian Literature." In *Identifications: Ethnicity and the Writer in Canada,* edited by Jars Balan. (Edmonton: The Canadian Institute of Ukrainian Studies, The University of Alberta, 1982) pp. 53-66.
      [A survey of the various generations of Icelandic-Canadian authors. Individual authors included are Þorsteinn Þorsteinsson, Sigurbjörn Jóhannsson (first generation), Guttormur Guttormsson (second generation), Laura Goodman Salverson (third) and W.D. Valgardson and Kristjana Gunnars (younger generation authors).]

2409 BARBOUR, Douglas
      "Canadian Poetry Chronicle: X." WEST COAST REV 16, no. 1 (1981): 80-84.
      [A review of books of poetry published during 1980. Ethnic authors reviewed are Kristjana Gunnars and David Arnason.]

2410 EINARSSON, Magnús
      "Oral Traditions and Ethnic Boundaries: West Icelandic Verses and Anecdotes." CAN ETH STUD 7, no. 2 (1975): 19-32.
      [Contents: The West Icelandic historical tradition (pp. 18-21); Biographically oriented folklore (pp. 21-22);Verses (pp. 22-27); Anecdotes (pp. 27-31).]

2411 EINARSSON, Stefán
      "Emigrants I: American-Icelandic Writers." In his *History of Icelandic Prose Writers, 1800-1940.* (New York: Kraus Reprint Corp., 1966) pp. 235-55.

2412 EINARSSON, Stefán
      "Vestur-íslenzkir " [Icelandic Authors in America]. In his *Íslenzk bókmenntasaga, 874-1960.* (Reykjavík: Oddi H.F., 1961) pp. 454-73.

2413 "Icelandic Poetry and Prose." In *The Canadian Family Tree.* (Ottawa: Canadian Citizenship Branch, 1967) pp. 164-65.

2414 JOHNSON, Sigrid
      "Icelandic Collection at the University of Manitoba: A Source for Genealogical Research." ICELAND-CAN (Spring 1984): 41-42.

[The collection is described to include more than 20,500 volumes, being the largest of its kind in Canada.]

2415   LINDAL, Walter J.
"The Contribution of Icelanders to Manitoba's Poetry." MOSAIC 3, no. 3 (1970): 48-57.
[Describes the Icelandic literary traditions and how they became diffused into the Canadian scene through the poetry of Stephan G. Stephansson, Guttormur J. Guttormsson, Jóhannes. P. Pálsson, Einar Páll Jónsson, Kristín Hansdóttir and Sigurður Júlíus Jóhannesson.]

2416   LINDAL, Walter J.
"Cultural Pursuits of the First Generation of Icelanders in Canada." CAN ETH STUD 1, no. 2 (1969): 1-9.
[Authors studied are Stephan G. Stephansson, Vilhjalmur Stefansson, Guttormur J. Guttormsson, and Paul Sigurdson. Bibliography: p. 9.]

2417   LINDAL, Walter J.
"Icelandic Prose Writers." In his *The Icelanders in Canada*. (Ottawa/Winnipeg: National Publishers and Viking Press, 1967) pp. 268-75.

2418   OLESON, Tryggvi J.
"Saga Íslendinga í Vesturheimi" [History of Icelanders in America]. (Reykjavík, 1951) vol. 5, pp. 48-56.

ANTHOLOGIES

2419   *Vestan um haf: Ljóð, leikrit, sögur og ritgerðir eftir Íslendinga í Vesturheimi [From West of the Ocean: Poems, Plays, Stories, and Essays by Icelanders in America*, edited by Einar H[jörleifsson] Kvaran and Guð[mundur] Finnbogason. Reykjavík: Bókadeild Menningarsjóðs, 1930. 736 pp.
[Contains: **Poems** by Jóhann Magnús Bjarnason, Páll Guðmundsson, Guttormur J. Guttormsson, Sigurður Júlíus Jóhannesson, Sigurbjörn Jóhannsson, Jakobína Johnson, Einar Páll Jónsson, Gísli Jónsson, Magnús Markússon, Jón Runólfsson, Jónas A. Sigurðsson, Jónas Stefánsson frá Kaldbak, Kristinn Stefánsson, Stephan G. Stephansson, E.E. Wíum, and Þorsteinn Þorsteinsson. **Stories** by F.J. Bergmann, Johann Magnús Bjarnason, Gunnsteinn Eyjólfsson, Guðrún H. Finnsdóttir, Grímur Grímsson, B.E. Johnson, Magnús Jónsson, Kveldúlfur (pseud., real name unknown), Örn (i.e. Kristinn Pétursson), Jóhannes P. Pálsson, Lára Goodman Salverson, Stephan G. Stephansson, and Þorsteinn Þorsteinsson. **Plays** by Guttormur J. Guttormsson, and Jóhannes P. Pálsson.]

2420   *Redhead the Whale and other Icelandic Folktales*, edited by Kristjana Gunnars. Winnipeg: Queenston House, 1985.
[Originally compiled by Helga Miller.]

INDIVIDUAL AUTHORS

BENEDICTSSON, Sigfús B.   (1865-1951)
Born in Iceland, a long-time resident of Manitoba, he has published poetry, fiction and scholarly papers.

2421   *Ljóðmæli [Lyric Poems]*. Winnipeg, 1905. Poems.

BENEDIKTSSON, Kristján Ásgeir

2422   *Valið [The Chalice]* Winnipeg, 1898. Novelette.

BJARNASON, Jóhann Magnús   (1886-1945)

Novelist, poet, teacher, born in Iceland, long-time resident of Manitoba and Saskatchewan.

2423   *Sögur og kvæði [Stories and Poems]*. Winnipeg, 1892. Stories, poems.

2424   *Ljóðmæli [Lyric Poems]*. Ísafjörður, Iceland, 1898. Poems.

2425   *Þráin [The Longing]*. Geysir, Man., 1902. 152 pp. Novel.

2426   *Eiríkur Hansson: Skáldsaga frá Nýja Skotlandi [Eiríkur Hansson: A Novel of Nova Scotia]*.
        Copenhagen and Akureyri, 1899-1903.   Also published in Akureyri, 1973.   503 pp.
        Autobiographical novel.

2427   *Brasilíufararnir [Immigrants to Brazil]*. Winnipeg, 1905. 2nd ed. Reykjavík, 1908. Novel.

2428   *Vornæur á Elgsheiðum: Sögur frá Nýja Skotlandi [Spring Nights on Mooselands Hights. Stories
        from Nova Scotia]*. Reykjavík, 1910. Short stories.

2429   *Haustkvöld við hafið [Autumn Nights by the Ocean]*. Reykjavík, 1928. Stories.

2430   *Karl litli: Saga frá draumamörk [Little Carl: A Story from the Dream Forest]*. Reykjavík, 1935.
        224 pp. Story.

2431   *Æintýri [Adventures]*. Reykjavík, 1946. Stories.

2432   *Í Rauðárdalnum [In the Red River Valley]*. Akureyri, 1942. Novel.

2433   *Ritsafn [Collected Works]*, edited by Árni Bjarnason. Akureyri: Edda, 1942-1950. 4 vols. Poetry and
        prose.

BJARNASON, Páll   (1881-1967)
Poet and translator, born in North Dakota, long-time resident of Saskatchewan.

2434   *Fleygar [Wedges]*. Winnipeg: Columbia Press, 1953. 270 pp. Poems.

2435   *Odes and Echoes*. Vancouver: The Author, 1954. 186 pp. Poems.

2436   *Flísar: Nokkur kvæði þýdd og frumsamin [Chips: A Few Translated and Original Poems]*.
        Vancouver: The Author, 1964. 72 pp. Poems.

    Writing about:

2437   Stubles, Roy St. George. "Paul Bjarnason, Poet and Apostle of a Brave New World." ICELAND
        CAN   45, no. 1 (1986): 9-21.

BJÖRNSSON, David   (1890-1980)
Born in Iceland, long-time resident of Manitoba. Poet and bookstore owner.

2438   *Rósviðir: ljóðmaeli [Rosewoods: Poems]*. Winnipeg: Columbia Press, 1952. 83 pp. Poems.

BJÖRNSSON, Sveinn E.   (1885-1970)
Born in Iceland, he was a medical doctor in rural Manitoba.

2439   *Á heiðarbrún [On a Heaths Edge]*. Vol. 1. Winnipeg: Viking Press, 1945. 231 pp. Vol. 2:
        Reykjavík, 1971. Poems.

ERLENDSSON, Gunnar
Born in Iceland, resident of Manitoba. Music teacher, pianist and poet.

2440   *Minningar um Dolores Victoria Johnson [In Memory of Dolores Victoria Johnson].* Winnipeg, 1960. Poems.

EYJÓLFSSON, Gunnsteinn   (1866-1910)
Born in Iceland, resident of Riverton, Man. Novelist, poet and music composer.

2441   *Elenóra [Eleanora].* Reykjavík, 1894. Novelette.

2442   *Tíund [Tithe].* Winnipeg, 1905. Story.

2443   *Jón á Strympu og fleiri sögur [Jón of Strympa and More Stories],* edited by Gísli Jónsson. Winnipeg: Columbia Press for Vilborg Eyjólfsson, 1952. 229 pp. Short stories.

FINNSDÓTTIR, Guðrún Helga   (1884-1946)
Born in East Iceland, came to Canada in 1904 and settled in Winnipeg. Her short stories were published in *Tímarit.*

2444   *Hillingalönd [Land of Mirage].* Reykjavík: Félagsprentsmiðjan, 1938. 224 pp. Short stories.

2445   *Dagshríðarspor: Tólf sögur [Tracks of a Day's Journey: Twelve Short Stories].* Akureyri: Árni Bjarnason, 1946. 230 pp. Short stories.

2446   *Ferðalok [Journey's End].* Winnipeg: Columbia Press, 1950. 194 pp. Poems.

Writing about:

2447   Einarsson, Stefán. "Guðrún Helga Finnsdóttir." In his *History of Icelandic Prose Writers, 1800-1940.* (Ithaca, N.Y.: Cornell University Press, 1948) pp. 248-50.

GUNNARS, Kristjana (1948-   )
Born in Reykjavík, Iceland, immigrated to Canada in 1969. Educated at the Universities of Oregon, Saskatchewan and Manitoba. She has worked as a freelance translator and as a university instructor and high school teacher. Editor of *Crossing the River: Essays in Honour of Margaret Laurence.* Her poems have appeared in *Draft, The Oxford Book of Canadian Verse, Sundogs* and other anthologies and periodicals.

2448   *One-eyed Moon Maps.* Victoria: Press Porcépic, 1980. 73 pp. Poems.

2449   *Settlement Poems I.* Winnipeg: Turnstone Press, 1980. 55 pp. Poems.

2450   *Settlement Poems 2.* Winnipeg: Turnstone Press, 1980. 49 pp. Poems.

2451   *Wake-pick Poems.* Toronto: Anansi, 1981. 96 pp. Poems.

2452   *The Axe's Edge.* Toronto: Press Porcépic, 1983. 93 pp. Short stories.

2453   *The Night Workers of Ragnarök.* Toronto: Press Porcépic, c1985. 104 pp. Poems.

Writings about:

2454 Haverstick, Sylvia. "Kristjana Gunnars." In *Connections Two*. (Winnipeg: Manitoba School Library Association, 1983) pp. 39-40. port.

2455 Lane, M. Travis. "Ground of Being." CAN LIT No. 111 (1986): 180-82.
[Review of *The Night Workers of Ragnarök*.]
Lane, M. Travis. "Kristjana Gunnars." In *Canadian Writers Since 1960*. [Detroit: Gale, 1987) pp. 96-100. port.

2456 MacKinley-Hay, Linda. Review of *The Axe's Edge*. CAN BOOK REV ANN 1985: 268.

GUTTORMSSON, Guttormur Jónsson (1878-1966)

Born near Riverton, Man. He wrote his poems in Icelandic, some of them translated into English by Watson Kirkconnell, and others.

2457 *Jón Austfirðingur og nokkur smákvæði [Jón from the Eastfjords and a Few Poems]*. Winnipeg, 1909. 76 pp. Story and Poems.

2458 *Bóndadóttir [A Farmer's Daughter]*. Winnipeg: Hecla Press, 1920. 92 pp. Poems.

2459 *Gaman og alvara [Jest and Earnest]*. Winnipeg: Columbia Press, 1930. Poems.

2460 *Tíu leikrit [Ten Plays]*. Reykjavík, 1930. Plays.

2461 *Byltingin [The Revolution]*. In one act. ÓÐINN, 1936. Play.

2462 *Líkblæjan [Wind-sheet]*. In one act. ÓÐINN, 1937. Play.

2463 *Hunangsflugur [Honey Bees]*. Winnipeg, 1944. 128 pp. Poems.

2464 *Kvæðasafn [Collected Poems]*, edited by Arnór Sigurjónsson. Reykjavík: Iðunn, 1947. 383 pp. Poems.

2465 *Kanadaþistill [Canada Thistle]*. Reykjavík: Helgafell, 1958. 117 pp. Poems.

Writings about:

2466 Beck, Richard. "Guttormur J. Guttormsson." In his *History of Icelandic Poets 1800-1940*. (Ithaca, N.Y.: Cornell University Press, 1966) pp. 226-29.

2467 Beck, Richard. *Guttormur J. Guttormsson, áttræður [Guttormur J. Guttormsson at Eighty]*. Offprint from *Tímarit*. Reykjavík, 1959.

2468 Beck, Richard. *Guttormur J. Guttormsson skáld [Guttormur J. Guttormsson, Poet]*. Offprint from *Skírnir*. Reykjavík, 1948. 21 pp. Reprinted by Columbia Press, Winnipeg, 1949. 24 pp.

2469 Jónsson, Jón frá Sleðbrjót. "Guttormur J. Guttormsson skáld í Nýja Íslandi" [Guttormur J. Guttormsson, a Poet of New Iceland]. ÓÐINN 14 (1978): 17-18.

2470 Kirkconnell, Watson. "A Skald in Canada." TRANS ROY SOC CAN 33 (1939): 107-21.

2471 Sigurbjörnsson, Lárus. "Guttormur J. Guttormsson: Tíu leikrit" [Guttormur J. Guttormsson: Ten Plays]. LÖGRÉTTA 30 (1935): 37-42.

GUTTORMSSON, Vigfús J. (1875-1964)

Born in Iceland, came to Canada with his parents as a child. He was a farmer and a merchant at Lundar, Man.

2472   *Eldflugur [Fireflies].* Winnipeg: Columbia Press, 1947. 199 pp. Poems.
[Published in 100 copies, numbered.]

HALLDORSON, Albert H.

2473   *Wings of the Wind.* Winnipeg: Columbia Press, 1948. Poems.

HANSDÓTTIR, Kristín (1855-1928)
Spent most of her adult life in Winnipeg as a devoted religious person. Her poems and articles have appeared in Icelandic-Canadian newspapers.

2474   *Kristínar fró: Ljóðmæli [Kristin's Comfort: Poems].* Winnipeg, 1927. 148 pp. Poems.

HÓLM, Torfhildur (1845-1918)
Born in Iceland, received her education in Reykjavík and Copenhagen. She came to Canada in 1877 and became the first teacher in the Icelandic settlements in Manitoba in 1876. Her short stories have appeared in newspapers. Returned to Iceland in 1890.

2475   *Brynjólfur Sveinsson biskup [Bishop Brynjólfur Sveinsson].* Reykjavík, 1882. 2nd ed. Reykjavík, 1912. Novel.
[Biographical novel about Bishop B. Sveinsson, an 18th century religious leader.]

2476   *Sögur og ævintýri [Stories and Fairy Tales].* Reykjavík, 1884. Stories.

2477   *Smásögur handa börnum og unglingum [Short Stories for Children and Young Adults].* Reykjavík, 1885. Children's stories.

2478   *Elding [Lightning].* Reykjavík, 1889. Novel.

2479   *Högni og Ingibjörg [Högni and Ingibjörg].* Reykjavík, 1889. Novel.

2480   *Barnasögur [Stories for Children].* Reykjavík, 1890. Children's stories.

HÚNFJÖRD, Jón

2481   *Ómar [Strains].* Winnipeg: Viking Press, 1947. 147 pp. Poems.

JÓHANNESSON, Sigurður Jón (1850-1933)
Born in Western Iceland, emigrated to Canada in 1892. Published several volumes of poetry.

2482   *Ljóðmæli [Lyric Poems].* Winnipeg, 1899. Poems.

2483   *Kvæði [Poems].* Winnipeg, 1905. Poems.

2484   *Fornmenjar [Antiquities].* Winnipeg, 1909. Poems.

2485   *Nokkur ljóðmæli forn og ný [Some Lyric Poems Old and New].* Winnipeg, 1915. Poems.

JÓHANNESSON, Sigurður Júlíus (1868-1956)
Born in Iceland. Came to Canada as an adult. Some of his collections of poetry have been published in Iceland. He was a medical doctor in several Manitoba communities and editor of the Icelandic-Canadian weeklies *Lögberg* and *Voröld*.

2486 *Sögur og kvæði [Stories and Poems]*. Winnipeg, 1900, 1903. Poems and stories. 2 vols.

2487 *Kvistir [Twigs]*. Reykjavík, 1910. 262 pp. Poems.

2488 *Nokkur ljóðmæli [Lyric Poems]*. Winnipeg, 1915. 160 pp. Poems.

2489 *Ljóð [Poems]*, edited by Steingrímur Arason. Reykjavík: B. Aeskan, 1950. 147 pp. Poems.

2490 *Our Heritage*. Winnipeg: Icelandic Canadian, 1950. 9 pp. Poems.

2491 *Úrvalsljóð [Selected Poems]*, edited by Richard Beck. Reykjavík: Prentsmiðjan Oddi H.F., 1968. 87 pp. Poems.

Writings about:

2492 Beck, Richard. "Sigurður Júlíus Jóhannesson." In his *History of Icelandic Poets 1800-1940*. (Ithaca, N.Y.: Cornell University Press, 1966) pp. 221-24.

2493 Beck, Richard. "Sigurður Júlíus Jóhannesson skáld" [Sigurður Júlíus Jóhanneson Poet]. ALMANAK Ó.S. THORGEIRS 54 (1948): 21-28.

2494 Ólafsson, Jón. "Sigurður Júlíus Johannesson." ÓÐINN 6 (1910): 5-6.

2495 Stubles, Roy St. George. "Dr. Sigurður Júlíus Johannesson." ICELAND-CAN 45, no. 4 (1987): 18-30.

JÓHANNESSON, Þorsteinn (1837-1918)

2496 *Ljóðmæli [Lyric Poems]*, edited by Þorsteinn Jónsson and Björn Walterson. Winnipeg: Prentsmiðja Lögbergs, 1902. 350 pp. Poems.

2497 *Dalurinn minn [My Valley]*. Winnipeg, 1905. Novel.

JOHANNSSON, Sigurbjörn

2498 *Ljóðmæli [Poetry]*. Winnipeg: Logberg Press, 1902. 350 pp. Poems.

JOHNSON, Andres

2499 *Nýgrædingur; Kvæði [New Growth Poems]*. Winnipeg, 1906. Poems.

JOHNSON, Jakobína (1883-   )
Born in northern Iceland, came to Canada in 1889. She was a teacher in Manitoba and published poems and articles in newspapers and magazines.

2500 *Kertaljós: Úrvalsljóð [Candlelights: Selected Poems]*. Reykjavík Ísafoldarprentsmiðja, 1938. 95 pp. Poems.

2501 *Sá ég svani [I Saw Swans]*, edited by Þórhallur Bjarnason. Reykjavík: Prentsmiðjan Hólar, 1942. 39 pp. Poems.

2502 *Kertaljós: Ljóðasafn [Candlelights: Collected Poems]*. Reykjavík: Leiftur H.F., 1956. 164 pp. Poems.

2503   *Northern Lights.* Reykjavík, Bókaútgáfa Menningarsjóðs, 1959. 91 pp. Poems.

Writings about:

2504   Beck, Richard. "Jakobína Johnson." In his *History of Icelandic Poets 1800-1940.* (Ithaca, N.Y.: Cornell University Press, 1966) pp. 236-38.

2505   Friðriksson, Friðrik A. "Skáldkonan Jakobína Johnson" [The Poet Jakobína Johnson]. LESBÓK MORGUNBLAÐSINS 10 (1935): 2-3.

2506   Sigurðsson, Sveinn. "Góður gestur" [A Fine Guest]. EIMREIÐIN 41 (1935): 257-60.

JÓNATANSSON, G.K.

2507   *Fjallablóm [Mountain Flowers].* Winnipeg: Maple Leaf Press, 1927. 183 pp. Poems.

JÓNSDÓTTIR, Júlíana

2508   *Hagalagðar [Tufts of the Wool from Pasture].* Winnipeg, 1916. Poems.

JÓNSSON, Einar Páll   (1880-1958)
Born in Iceland, emigrated to Canada in 1913. He was editor of *Lögberg*, an Icelandic-Canadian weekly.

2509   *Öræfaljóð [Poems of the Wilderness].* Winnipeg: Thorgeirsson Press, 1915. Poems.

2510   *Sólheimar [Sun-worlds].* Reykjavík: Menningarsjóður, 1944. 2nd ed. 1969. 238 pp. Poems.

Writings about:

2511   Beck, Richard. *Aettjarðaljóð Einars Pálls Jónssonar [Patriotic Poetry of Einar Páll Jónsson].* Winnipeg: Lögberg-Heimskringla Press, 1963. 10 pp.

2512   Beck, Richard. "Einar Páll Jónsson." In his *History of Icelandic Poets 1800-1940.* (Ithaca, N.Y.: Cornell University Press, 1966) pp. 231-34.

2513   Beck, Richard. "Einar Páll Jónsson skáld" [Einar Páll Jónsson, Poet]. EIMREIÐIN 48 (1942): 211-22.

JÓNSSON, Gísli   (1876-1974)
Born at Háreksstaðir, Iceland. Graduated from high school in 1896 and emigrated to Winnipeg in 1903. He was for years a manager of a printing shop, and founder of a periodical: *Heimir.* His poems and articles have appeared in newspapers and journals.

2514   *Farfuglar [Birds of Passage].* Winnipeg, 1919. 244 pp. Poems.

2515   *Fardagar [Days of Departure].* Winnipeg: Columbia Press, 1956. 175 pp. Poems.

Writing about:

2516   Beck, Richard. "Gísli Jónsson." In his *History of Icelandic Poets 1800-1940.* (Ithaca, N.Y.: Cornell University Press, 1966) pp. 224-26.

JÚLÍUS, Kristján N.

Born in Iceland; humorist. His short poems appeared in *Lögberg* and *Heimskríngla*, two Icelandic newspapers published in Winnipeg.

2517　*Kviðlingar og Kvæði [Short Poetry]*.　Winnipeg: Columbia Press, 1920.　172 pp. Reprinted in Reykjavík: Bókfellsútgáfan H.F., 1945.　Poems.

KRISTJÁNSSON, Aðalsteinn

2518　*In the West (Prose and Poetry)*.　California: Schauer Printing Studio, 1936.　Poems and short stories.

KRISTJÁNSSON, Luðvík

Born in Eastern Iceland, immigrated to Canada and settled in Winnipeg, where he is a plasterer by trade.

2519　Ljóðakorn [Poems].　Winnipeg: Lögberg-Heimskringla, 1983.　Poems.

KRISTOFFERSON, Kristine Benson

Teacher, resided at Gimli, Man.

2520　*Tanya, Novel.*　Toronto: Ryerson, 1951.　Novel.
　　　[Novel takes place in Icelandic-Canadian communities near Gimli, Man.]

KVARAN, Einar Hjörleifsson　(1859-1938)

Born in Iceland, educated in Copenhagen. Published poetry in his native land prior to immigrating to Canada in 1885. Author of several short stories and novels, Kvaran was co-founder of two weekly Icelandic papers in Winnipeg.

2521　*Vonir [Hopes]*.　Winnipeg, 1890.　Novelette.

2522　*Ljóðmæli [Lyric Poems]*.　Reykjavík, 1893.

2523　*Smælingjar [Little People]*.　Winnipeg: Thorgeirsson Press, 1908.　Short stories

LÍNDAL, Jakob H.　(1850-1920)

2524　*Misskilningur [Misunderstanding]*.　Winnipeg, 1919.　Autobiography.

LYNGHOLT, Bjarni

2525　*Fölvar rósir [Pale Roses]*.　Winnipeg, 1913.　Poems.

MAGNÚSSON, H.E.

2526　*Lykkuföll [Dropped Stitches]*.　Wynyard, Sask.: Wynyard Advance Press, 1923.　70 pp.　Poems.

MARKÚSSON, Magnús　(1858-1948)

Born in Hafsteinsstaðir, Iceland, immigrated to the USA in 1886 and then to Canada, where he served for years in the Canadian Immigration Service.

2527　*Ljóðmæli [Lyric Poems]*.　Winnipeg, 1907.　Poems.

2528　*Hljómbrot [Fragments of Melody]*.　Winnipeg: City Printing and Publishing Co., 1924.　266 pp. Poems.

Writings about:

2529   Beck, Richard. "Magnús Markússon skáld" [Magnús Markússon, Poet]. ALMAN Ó.S. THORGEIR 40 (1949): 21-27.

2530   Jónsson, Einar P. "Aldursforseti íslenzkra skálda vestan hafs" [The Elder Statesman of Icelandic Poets in North America]. TÍM ÞJOÐ ISL VEST 27 (1946): 32-33.

ÓLAFSSON, Guðmundur

2531   *Nokkur ljóðmæli [Lyric Poems]*. Winnipeg, 1916. 100 pp. Poems.

OTTENSON, Nikulás   (1867-1955)
Born in Iceland, emigrated to Canada and resided in Winnipeg.

2532   *Minni Nýja Íslands [A Toast to New Iceland]*. Winnipeg, 1934. 104 pp. Rhymes and poems.

PÁLSSON, Jóhannes P. (1881-   )
Born in Manitoba, he was a medical doctor practising in Manitoba and Saskatchewan.

2533   *Hnausaför mín [My Trip to Hnausa]*. 1928. Story.

2534   *Hún iðrast [She Repents]*. Winnipeg [n.d.] Play.
[Produced locally.]

2535   *Gunnbjarnarskér [Gunnbjörn's Shoals]*. Reykjavík: Vestan um Haf [n.d.]   Play.

Writing about:

2536   Einarsson, Stefán. "Jóhannes P. Pálsson." In his *History of Icelandic Prose Writers, 1800–1940.* (Ithaca, N.Y.: Cornell University Press, 1940) pp. 245-46.

PÁLSSON, Kristján S.   (1886-1947)
Born in Iceland, resident of Selkirk, Man.

2537   *Kvæðabók [A Book of Poems]*, edited by Ingibjörg Pálsson. Winnipeg: Columbia Press, 1949. 298 pp. Poems.

PÁLSSON, Páll S.   (1892-1963)
Born in Reykjavík, Iceland, emigrated to Canada and settled in Winnipeg. He sang in choirs and acted in plays.

2538   *Norður-Reykir [North-Reykir]*. Winnipeg: Viking Press, 1936. 176 pp. Poems.

2539   *Skilarétt: Kvæði [The Sorting-fold: Poems]*. Winnipeg: Viking Press, 1947. 223 pp. Poems.

2540   *Eftirleit: Kvæði [Final Roundup of Sheep: Poems]*. Reykjavík: Ísafoldarprentsmiðja, 1954. 92 pp. Poems.

2541   *Minningar frá Íslandsferðinni 1954 [Reminiscences from a Trip to Iceland 1954]*. Reykjavík: Prentsmiðjan Leiftur, 1959. 91 pp. Stories.

RUNÓLFSSON, Jón   (1856-1930)

Born in Gilsárteigur, Iceland. He went to Minnesota in 1879. Four years later he moved to Winnipeg and taught in public schools in the Icelandic communities.

2542 *Þögul leiftur [Silent Flashes]*. Winnipeg, 1924. 270 pp. Poems.

Writings about:

2543 Beck, Richard. "Skáldið Jón Runólfsson" [The Poet Jón Runólfsson]. TÍM ÞJOÐ ISL VEST 20 (1938): 92-100.

2544 Bjarnason, J. Magnús. "Jón Runólfsson skáld" [Jón Runólfsson Poet]. ÓÐINN 25 (1929): 23-26.

SIGURDJÖRNSSON, Rannveig K.

2545 *Þradarspottar [Bits of Yarn]*. Reykjavík: Ísafold Publishing Co., 1937. Short stories.

SIGURDSSON, Friðrik Pétur
Born in Iceland, emigrated to Manitoba, where he became a farmer in Riverton.

2546 *Kvæði [Poems]*. Winnipeg: Columbia Press, 1946. 317 pp. Poems.

2547 *Römm er Sú Taug [Strong are The Bonds]*. Reykjavík: Prentsmiðja Austurlands H/F, 1950. Poems.

SIGURDSSON, Gus

2548 *Peneilstub Stanzas*. Vancouver, 1950. Poems.

2549 *Dreams and Driftwood*. Vancouver, 1951. Poems.

2550 *Roses for Stephanie*. Vancouver, 1966. Poems.

SIGURÐSSON, Jónas Ari   (1865-1937)

2551 *Ljóðmæli [Lyric Poems]*, edited by Richard Beck. Winnipeg: Columbia Press, 1946. 317 pp. Poems.

STEFÁNSSON, Jónas   (1882-1952)

2552 *Ljóðmæli [Lyric Poems]*. Víðir, Man.: Northern Press, 1939. 175 pp. Poems.

STEFÁNSSON, Kristinn   (1856-1916)
Born in Egilsá, Iceland, emigrated to Canada in 1873 and settled in Winnipeg in 1881. All his poems were written in this country.

2553 *Vestan hafs [West over the Ocean]*. Reykjavík, 1900. Poems.

2554 *Út um vötn og velli [On Sea and Land]*. Winnipeg, 1916. 300 pp. Poems.

STEPHANSSON, Stephan G.   (1853-1927)
Born in Iceland, emigrated to the USA in 1873, and came to Alberta in 1889. He was a poet of international stature.

2555 *Út á víðavangi [In the Open Air]*. Winnipeg, 1894. Poems.

2556   *Á ferð og flugi [Faring and Flying].* Reykjavík, 1900. Poems.

2557   *Andvökur [Sleepless Nights].* Reykjavík: Prentsmiðjan Gutenberg, 1909-1910. 3 v. 309 pp., 312 pp., 231 pp. respectively. Vols 4 and 5 in Winnipeg: Heimskringla Press, 1938. 290 pp., 314 pp. respectively. Vol. 6 in Reykjavík: Menningarsjóður, 1953-1958. Poems.

2558   *Kolbeinslag: Gamanríma [The Lay of Kolbeinn: Comic Rhyme].* Winnipeg: Viking Press, 1914. Poems.
[Kolbeinn was an Icelandic poet and legendary figure.]

2559   *Heimleiðis [Homeward].* Reykjavík, 1917. Poems.

2560   *Vígslóði [A Section on Homicides].* Reykjavík, 1920. Poems.
[The title refers to "Grágás," the Nordic collection of laws.]

2561   *Úrval [Selected Poems],* edited by S. Nordal. Reykjavík: Mál og menning, 1939. Poems.

2562   *Úrvalsljóð [Selected Poems],* edited by Unnur Benediktsdóttir Bjarklind. Reykjavík: Ísafoldarprentsmiðja, 1945. 188 pp. Poems.

2563   *Bréf til Stephans G. Stephanssonar: Úrval [Selections].* Reykjavík: Bókaútgáfa Menningarsjóðs og Þjóðvinafélagsins, 1971-1975. 3 v.

Writings about:

2564   Beck, Richard. "Stephan G. Stephansson." In his *History of Icelandic Poets 1800-1940.* (Ithaca, N.Y.: Cornell University Press, 1966) pp. 201-10.

2565   Bjarnason, Ágúst H. "Skáldið Stephan G. Stephansson" [The Poet Stephan G. Stephansson]. IÐUNN 2 (1916-17): 356-78.

2566   Cawley, F. Stanton. "The Greatest Poet of the Western World: Stephan G. Stephansson." SCAND STUD NOTES 15 (1938): 99-109.

2567   Friðjónsson, Guðmundur. "Stephan G. Stephansson." SKÍRNIR 81 (1907): 193-209, 289-314.

2568   "Heimför Stephans G. Stephanssonar skálds" [The Poet Stephan G. Stephansson's Journey Home]. ALMAN Ó.S. THORGEIR (1918): 21-59.

2569   Kirkconnell, Watson. "Canada's Leading Poet; Stephan G. Stephansson: 1853-1927." UNIV TOR Q 5 (1935-36): 264-65.

2570   "Lífsskoðun Stephans G. Stephanssonar" [Stephan G. Stephansson's Philosophy of Life]. SKÍRNIR 86 (1912): 44-63.

2571   Magnússon, Jón. "Andvökur hinar nýju" [The New 'Sleepless Nights' Poems]. EIMREIÐIN 46 (1940): 212-24.

2572   McCracken, Jane W. *Stephan G. Stephansson: The Poet of the Rocky Mountains.* Edmonton: Alberta Culture, 1982. 120 pp. (Alberta Culture Historical Resources Division, Occasional Paper No. 9)

2573 Nordal, Sigurður. "En isländsk bondeskáld: Stephan G. Stephansson." [An Icelandic Farmer-poet: Stephan G. Staphansson]. BYGD OCH FOLK 2 (1929)
[Translation of *Alþýðuskáldið* into Swedish by Benjamín Kristjánsson, published in TÍM ÞJOD ISL VEST 13 (1931): 52-58.

2574 Pálsson, Johannes P. "Stephan G. Stephansson: Nokkur orð um skáldið og manninn" [Stephan G. Stephansson: A Few Words about the Poet and the Man]. TÍM ÞJOD ISL VEST 9 (1927): 37-45.

2575 "Stephan G. Stephansson: Drög til ævisögu" [Stephan G. Stephansson: Notes for a Biography]. ANDVARI 72 (1947): 3-25.

2576 Sveinsson, Baldur. "Stephan G. Stephansson sjötugur" [Stephan G. Stephansson's 70th Birthday]. IÐUNN 8 (1923): 4-21.

2577 Wood, Kerry. *Tribute*. Red Deer, Alta.: The Author [1974?] [12] pp.
[On cover: The Icelandic-Canadian Poet, Stephan Guðmundsson Stephansson, 1853-1927. Includes a three-page biography by Kerry Wood, and two poems in English by Stephansson.]

2578 Þorbergsson, Jónas. "Stephan G. Stephansson." IÐUNN 8 (1934): 161-77.

ÞORSTEINSSON, Bjarni (1868-1943) (Bjarni frá Höfn, pseud.)
Born in Iceland, emigrated to Canada in 1903. Resided for a long time in Selkirk, Man. He was a photographer, poet and a translator of Icelandic poems.]

2579 *Kvæði [Poems]*, with an introduction by Gísli Jónsson. Winnipeg, 1948.

ÞORSTEINSSON, Þ. Þorsteinn (1879-1955)
Born in Uppsalir, Iceland, came to Canada in 1901. He was one of the most versatile of the Icelandic-Canadian writers, having publishing short stories, essays and sketches as well as poetry.]

2580 *Þættir: Ljóð [Strands: Poems]*. Winnipeg, 1918. Poems.

2581 *Heimhugi: Ljóð [Nostalgia: Poems]*. Reykjavík: Gutenberg, 1921. 94 pp. Poems.

2582 *Kossar [Kisses]*. Reykjavík: The Author, 1934. Short stories.

2583 *Björninn frá Bjarmalandi [The Bear from the Glowing Land]*. Winnipeg, 1945. 183 pp. Poems.

2584 *Ljóðmæli [Lyric Poems]*, edited by Gísli Jónsson. Akureyri, 1959. 2 v. Poems

2585 *V ljóðasafn [Collected Poems]*. Reykjavík: Bókaforlag Odds Björnssonar, 1959. 2 v. 591 pp. Poems.

INDIAN

BIBLIOGRAPHIES

2586 ABLER, T.S.; SANDERS, D.E.; WEAVER, S.M.
A Canadian Indian Bibliography, 1960-70. Toronto: University of Toronto Press, 1974. xii, 732 pp.

2587 *About Indians: A Listing of Books.* 2nd ed. rev. and enl. Ottawa: Indian and Northern Affairs, 1973. 135 pp.

2588 *Books by Native Authors.* Toronto: Canadian Association in Support of the Native Peoples, 1977. 7 leaves.
[Includes books by 100 Canadian Indian scholars, artists and authors.]

2589 *Books in Native Languages in the Rare Books Collection of the National Library of Canada.* Ottawa: Canadian Government Publishing Centre, Supply and Services Canada, 1986.
[Contains more than 500 titles published before 1958, representing 58 languages and comprising hymnals, dictionaries and grammars.]

2590 BUSH, Alfred; FRASER, Roberts
American Indian Periodicals in the Princeton University Library: A Preliminary List. Princeton: Princeton University Library, 1970. 78 pp.

2591 BYLER, Mary Gloyne
American Indian Authors for Young Readers: A Selected Bibliography. New York: Association on American Indian Affairs, 1973. 26 pp.

2592 HIRSCHFELDER, Arlene B., comp.
American Indian and Eskimo Authors: A Comprehensive Bibliography. New York: Association on American Indian Affairs, 1973. 99 pp.
[This is an enlarged edition of the original list published by the association in 1970.]

2593 *Index to Literature on the American Indian.* San Francisco: The Indian Historian Press, 1970-
[Published annually, includes references to authors, serial publications and monographs.]

2594 *Indian-Inuit Authors: An Annotated Bibliography/Auteurs indiens et inuit: bibliographie annotée.* Ottawa: Department of Indian Affairs and Northern Development, 1974. 108 pp.

2595 OGLE, Robert; MALYCKY, Alexander
"Periodical Publications of Canada's Indian and Métis: A Preliminary Check List." CAN ETH STUD 2, no. 1 (1970): 109-15.

2596 STENSLAND, Anna Lee
Literature by and about the American Indian: An Annotated Bibliography for Junior and Senior High School Students. Urbana, Ill.: National Council of Teachers of English, 1973. x, 208 pp.

BOOKS, RESEARCH PAPERS

2597 BEAUMONT, Ronald C.

She Shashishalhem, the Sechelt Language: Language, Stories and Sayings of the Sechelt Indian People of British Columbia. Penticton, B.C.: Theytus Books, 1985. xx, 305 pp.

2598 BROTHERSTON, Gordon
Image of the New World: The American Continent Portrayed in Native Texts. London: Thames and Hudson, 1979. 324 pp.
[Includes chapters on invasion from the old world, defence of traditional values and forms, ritual, cosmogony, hunting and planting, conquest, healing, and cultural aspects, e.g. literature. Bibliography (pp. 305-19).]

2599 BYLER, Mary Gloyne
"Introduction." In her *American Indian Authors for Young People....* (New York: Association on American Indian Affairs, 1973) pp. 5-11.

2600 FORSYTH, Christine
"Quotes from Raven." BKS CAN 4, 10 (1975): 24.
[Review of Gail Robinson and Douglas Hill: *Coyote the Trickster*; Patricia Robins: *Star Maiden*; Christine Harris: *Sky Man on the Totem Pole*; and Tamar Griggs: *There's Sound in the Sea....*]

2601 GIBSON, Michael
The North American Indian. Maidenhead, England: Sampson Low, c1978. 48 pp.

2602 GOULD, Sheila Arlene
"Dream and Reality among North American Indian Peoples: An Examination of the Literature." M.A. Thesis, University of British Columbia, 1978. v, 180 leaves.

2603 KROEBER, Karl
Traditional Literatures of the American Indian: Texts and Interpretations. Lincoln: University of Nebraska Press, c1981. 162 pp.
[Includes chapters on mythic and fictive writing, the spoken word and poetic translation.]

2604 PETRONE, Penny
"Indian Literature." In *The Oxford Companion to Canadian Literature*, edited by William Toye. (Toronto: Oxford University Press, 1983) pp. 383-88.
[A summary of historical background with emphasis upon nineteenth-century literature and that of the modern period. Individual Indian authors studied are George Copway, Rev. Peter Jones, George Henry, Pauline Johnson, John Brant-Sero, and Basil Johnston.]

2605 PURDY, Susan; SANDAK, Cass R.; FRENCK, Hal; GUZZI, George
North American Indians. Toronto: F. Watts, 1982. 32 pp.
["A Civilisation Project Book."]

ANTHOLOGIES

2606 *First People, First Voices.* Toronto: University of Toronto Press, 1983. ix, 221 pp. *Aboriginal, Pre-twentieth Century Canadian Literary Materials*, edited by Penny Petrone. [Thunder Bay, n.p.], 1983. iii, 507 pp.

2607 *Achimoona.* Saskatoon: Fifth House, 1985. 98 pp. Includes children's stories.

2608 *The Adventures of Nanabush: Ojibway Indian Stories by Sam Snake, Emerson S. Coatsworth, and Francis Kagige.* Toronto: Doubleday, c1979. 85 pp.

2609 *American Indian Prose and Poetry.* New York: John Day, 1946. Reprinted by Capricon, 1962.

2610   *Bella Bella Tales*, compiled by Franz Boas. New York: American Folk-lore Society, 1932. 178 pp.
(American Folk-lore Society, Memoirs, vol. 25.)

2611   *Close to the Rising Sun: Algonquian Legends*, edited by Virginia Frances. Champaign, Ill.: Garrad
Publishing Co., 1972. 63 pp.

2612   *The Elders Wrote: An Anthology of Early Prose by North American Indians 1768-1931*, edited by
Bernd Peyer. Berlin: D. Reimer Verlag, c1982. 196 pp.

2613   *I am an Indian*, edited by Kent Gooderham. Toronto: Dent, 1969. xv, 196 pp.
[A collection of legends, poetry and biographical writings.]

2614   *Indian Stories from James Bay*, edited by Lillian Small. Cobalt, Ont.: Highway Book Shop, 1972.
22 pp.
[Lillian Small recorded and translated into English the stories included in this collection.]

2615   *Legends of a Lost Tribe: Folk Tales of the Beothuck Indians of Newfoundland*, compiled by Paul
O'Neill. Toronto: McClelland & Stewart, c1976. 94 pp.

2616   *Legends of Nanabush*, compiled by Daphne ("Odjig") Beavon. Toronto: Ginn, 1971.
[Comprises ten booklets, 16 pages each, intended as supplementary reading for children.]

2617   *Legends of My People, the Great Ojibway*, by Norval Morrisseau, edited by Selwyn Dewdney.
Toronto: Ryerson Press, 1965. 130 pp.

2618   *The Long-Tailed Bear and other Indian Legends*, by Natalia Maree Belting. Indianapolis: Bobbs-
Merrill, c1961. 96 pp.

2619   *Malecite Tales*, edited by W.H. Mechling. Ottawa: King's Printer, 1914. 133 pp. (Canada.
Geological Survey. Memoirs, no. 49)

2620   *Many Voices: An Anthology of Contemporary Canadian Indian Poetry*, edited by David Day and
Marilyn Bowering. Vancouver: J.J. Douglas, 1977. 98 pp.

2621   *Medzi Indianmi.* Cambridge, Ont.: Slovenski Jezuiti, 1984. 169 pp.
[Includes children's stories in Slovak based on Indian legends]

2622   *The Moons of Winter and other Stories* by Norman Quill and Charles E. Fiero. Red Lake, Ont.:
NLGM, 1965. 47 pp.
[Text in Ojibwa and English, based on Chippewa legends.]

2623   *Myths and Folk-lore of the Timiskaming Algonquin and Timagami Ojibwa*, edited by Frank G.
Speck. Ottawa: King's Printer, 1915. 87 pp. (Canada. Geological Survey. Memoirs no. 71)

2624   *The Only Good Indian: Essays by Canadian Indians*, edited by [Harvey McCue] Waubageshig.
Toronto: New Press, 1970. 188 pp.
[Includes some poems.]

2625   "The Oral Literature of Native North America: A Critical Anthology," prepared by Andrew O.
Wiget. Ph.D. Thesis, University of Utah, 1977. xvi, 657 leaves.

2626   *Red Earth, Tales of the Micmacs, with an Introduction to the Customs and Beliefs of the Micmac
Indians*, compiled by Marion Robertson. Halifax: Nova Scotia Museum, 1969. 98 pp.

2627 *Sacred Legends of the Sandy Lake Cree*, edited by James R. Stevens. Toronto: McClelland & Stewart, 1971. 144 pp.

2628 *Sacred Stories of the Sweet Grass Cree*, edited by L. Bloomfield. Ottawa: King's Printer, 1930. 346 pp. (Canada. National Museum. Bull. 60)

2629 *Shaking the Pumpkin: Traditional Poetry of the Indian of North Americas*, edited by Jerome Rothenberg. Garden City, N.Y.: Double Day, 1972. xxvi, 475 pp.

2630 *Son of Raven, Son of Deer: Fables of the Tse-shaht People*, edited by George Clutesi. Sidney, B.C.: Gray's Publishing, 1967. 126 pp.
      [School text used in an English course at the University of British Columbia.]

2631 *Songs of the Dream People: Chants and Images from the Indians and Eskimos of North America*, edited and illustrated by James Houston. New York: Atheneum, 1972. 83 pp.

2632 *Songs of the Indians*, edited by John Robert Colombo. Ottawa: Oberon Press, c1983. 2 vols. (124pp., 100 pp. respectively.)
      [Translations from Indian tribes into English. Vol. 1: Beothukan, Algonquin, Iroquian, Athapascan, Siouan, Kootenayan. Vol. 2: Salishan, Wakashan, Tsimshian, Haidan, Koluscan and Chinookan. Bibliography: pp. 87-100.]

2633 *Spirits, Heroes and Hunters from North American Indian Mythology*, by Marion Wood and John Sibbick. Vancouver: Douglas & McIntyre, 1983.
      [Originally published in London by P. Lowe, 1981.]

2634 *Sweetgrass: An Anthology of Indian Poetry*, by Wayne Keon, Orville Keon, and Ronald Keon. Elliot Lake, Ont.: W.O.K. Books, 1972. 156 pp.

2635 *Tales of Nokomis*, by Patronella Johnston. Toronto: Musson, 1970. 64 pp.
      [Contains Ojibwan legends.]

2636 *Teepee Tales of the American Indian*. 1st American edition, edited by Dee Brown. New York: Holt, Rinehart and Winston, 1979. 174 pp.

2637 *The Trees Stand Shining: Poetry of the North American Indians*, selected by Hettig Jones, paintings by Robert Andrew Parker. New York: Dial Press, 1971. 32 pp.

2638 *Ts'oodunne hik'uyalhduk-I [Children's Stories: Book One]*, edited by Ileen Austin and Nellie Prince. Fort Saint James, B.C.: Carrier Linguistic Committee, 1977. ii, 38 pp. Children's stories.

2639 *What They Used to Tell about: Indian Legends from Labrador*, edited by Peter Desbarats. Toronto: McClelland & Stewart, 1969. 92 pp.
      [Translated from the Indian as recorded on tape.]

2640 *Wild Drums. Tales and Legends of the Plains Indians, as Told by Alex Grisdale to Nan Shipley*, illustrated by Jim Ellis. Winnipeg: Peguis, 1972. 78 pp.
      [Most of the tales included in this collection relate to life among Indians prior to the coming of the white man.]

2641 *Windigo and other Tales of the Ojibways*, edited by Herbert T. Schwarz, illustrated by Norval Morrisseau. Toronto: McClelland & Stewart, 1979. 40 pp.

INDIVIDUAL AUTHORS

BRUCE, Skyros (1950-   )
A Salishan poet, her poems have appeared in *Blackfish*, *Form*, *40 Women Poets of Canada*, *Tamarack Review* and other periodicals.

2642   *Kalala Poems.* Vancouver: Daylight Press [n.d.]. 54 pp. Poems.

CLUTESI, George (1905-   )
An eminent Tse-Shaht artist and author, a former pupil of Emily Carr, Clutesi is a spokesman for the traditional fables and stories of his people.

2643   *Potlatch*, illustrated by the author. Sidney, B.C.: Gray's Publishing, c1969. 188 pp. illus. Stories.

2644   *Son of Raven, Son of Deer: Fables of the Tse-Shaht People*, illustrated by the author. Sidney, B.C.: Gray's Publishing, 1975. 126 pp. illus. Fables.

COPWAY, George

2645   *The Ojibway Conquest, a Tale of the Northwest.* New York: Putnam, 1850. 91 pp. Epic story.
[An epic of the last battle between the Sioux and the Ojibway.]

ERICKSON, Sheila
Editor of *Tawow*, a Canadian Indian cultural magazine, she is of Ojibway descent. Her poems and prose writings have appeared in *Tawow*.

2646   *Notice: This is an Indian Reserve*, photos by Frederick Stevenson. Toronto: Griffin House, 1972. Poems.

HUBERT, Cam
Poet, playwright, scriptwriter, published poems in *A Room of One's Own*, *Branching Out*, *The Malahat Review* and other periodicals.

2647   *Twin Sinks of Allan Sammy.* Toronto: Playrights Co-op, 1973. 27 leaves. Play.

2648   *We're All Here Except Mike Casey's Horse.* Toronto: Playrights Co-op, 1974. 30, 20 leaves. Play.

2649   *Dreamspeaker and Tem Eyos Ki and the Land Claims Questions.* Toronto: Clarke, Irwin, 1978. 137 pp. 85, 89-137 pp. Novel.

JOHNSON, Emily Pauline (Tekahionwake) (1861-1913)
Daughter of a hereditary chief of the Mohawks and an English mother, she was born on the Six Nations Reserve near Brantford, Ont. Her poems appeared in magazines and anthologies in Canada and the USA, including *Gems of Poetry* and *The Week*. Her stories were published posthumously in two small collections: *The Shagganappi* (1913), and *The Moccassin Maker* (1913).

2650   *The White Wampum.* Toronto: Copp Clark, 1895. 87 pp. Poems.

2651   *In the Shadows.* Gouverneur, N.Y.: The Author, 1898. 4 pp. Poems.

2652   *Legends of Vancouver.* Vancouver: The Author, 1911. 89 pp. Short stories.
[Originally published in the Vancouver *Province*.]

2653 *Flint and Feather: The Complete Poems of E. Pauline Johnson*, with an introduction by Theodor Watts-Dunton. Toronto: Musson, 1917. 176 pp. Poems.

Writings about:

2654 Devorski, Lorraine. *Pauline: The Indian Poet.* London, Ont.: Operation Literacy, London Council for Adult Education, 1980. 22 pp.

2655 Hartley, Lucie. *Pauline Johnson.* Minneapolis: Dillon Press, c1978. 61 pp.

2656 Jackel, David. "Johnson, Pauline." In *The Oxford Companion to Canadian Literature*, edited by William Toye. (Toronto: Oxford University Press, 1983) pp. 398-99.

2657 Keller, Betty. *Pauline; A Biography of Pauline Johnson.* Vancouver: Douglas & McIntyre, 1981. 317 pp. illus.
[Includes 16 pages of plates.]

2658 Shrive, Norma. "What Happened to Pauline?" CAN LIT No. 13 (1962)

McLEOD, Joseph (1929-   )
Of Micmac and Scottish ancestry, he has published poems in *Alive, Canadian Forum, Dalhousie Review, Quarry.* Author of *The Teacher, Wa-Sha-Quon: Grey Owl* and other plays. He lives in Ontario.

2661 *Sam Slick's Surprise: A Farce in One Act.* Chicago: Dramatic Publications, c1973. 16 pp. Play.

2662 *Conversations with Maria.* Guelph, Ont.: Alive Press, c1974. 51 pp. Poems.

2659 *Collected Citizen.* Fredericton, N.B.: Fiddlehead Poetry Books, 1976. Poems.

2660 *Cleaning the Bones.* Erin, Ont.: Press Porcépic, 1977. 62 pp. illus., phots. Poems.

2663 *Protect My House.* Ottawa: Borealis Press, 1977. x, 54 pp. Poems.

SEPASS, K'HHalserten

2664 *The Songs of Y-Ail-Mihth*, recorded and translated into English by Eloise Street. New York: Vantage, 1963. 110 pp. Poems.

STUMP, Sarain (1945-1975)
Born of Cree and Shoshone parents, made his home in Alberta, died in Mexico. His illustrated poems have been published in many magazines.

2665 *And There is My People*, illustrated by the author. Sidney, B.C.: Gray's Publishing, (?)

2666 *There is My People Sleeping: The Ethnic Poem;* drawing of Sarain Stump. Sidney, B.C.: Gray's Publishing, 1974., c1971. 150 pp., illus. Poem.

TAPPAGE, Mary Augusta (1888-   )
Born at Soda Creeek, B.C., spent her entire life in the Cariboo.

2667 *The Days of Augusta*, edited by Jean E. Speare. Vancouver: J.J. Douglas, (?) Oral poems.

INUIT

BIBLIOGRAPHIES, RESEARCH PAPERS

2668 **GEDALOF, Robin**
An Annotated Bibliography of Canadian Inuit Literature. (A Preliminary Listing). [N.p., np.] 1978. [108] pp.

2669 **LEWIS, Richard**
"Bibliography." In *I Breathe a New Song,* edited by Richard Lewis. (New York: Simon and Schuster, 1971) pp. 126-28.

2670 **McGRATH, Robin Gedalof**
"Inuit Literature." In *The Oxford Companion to Canadian Literature,* edited by William Toye. (Toronto: Oxford University Press, 1983) pp. 390-91.
[Gives an outline of the major sources of Inuit literature, poetry and fiction.]

ANTHOLOGIES

2671 *Anerca,* edited by Edmund Carpenter. Toronto: Dent, 1959. [Unpaged.]

2672 *Beyond the High Hills: A Book of Eskimo Poems,* edited by Knud Rasmussen. Cleveland: Word Publishing, 1961. 32 pp. Poems.

2673 *Chants de la tundra: Poèmes eskimos du Canada,* ed. Pierre R. Leon. Sherbrooke, Qué.: Editions Naaman, 1985. 143 pp. Poèmes.

2674 *The Day Tuk Became a Hunter and other Eskimo Stories,* edited by Ronald Melzack. Toronto: McClelland & Stewart, 1967. 92 pp.
[Includes ten stories recorded by anthropologists and explorers.]

2675 *Eskimo Poems from Canada and Greenland,* translated by Tom Lowenstein from material originally collected by Knud Rasmussen. London: Allison & Busby, 1973. xxiii, 149 pp. Poems.

2676 *Eskimo Songs and Stories,* edited by Edward Field. New York: Delacorte Press, 1975. 102 pp. Poems.
[Retold from the literal English renderings in the official records of Rasmussen's *Voyages* published by the Royal Danish Archives.]

2677 *Fifth Thule Expedition (1921-1924). Report,* Knud Rasmussen. Copenhagen: Gyldendal, 1929. Vol. 9.
[Includes songs, spirituals and folktales.]

2678 *Harpoon of the Hunter,* Markoosie, illustrated by Germaine Arnaktauyok. Montreal: McGill-Queen's University Press, 1970. 81 pp. Stories.

2679 *I Breathe a New Song Poems of the Eskimo,* edited by Richard Lewis, with an introduction by Edmund Carpenter. New York: Simon and Schuster, 1971. 128 pp. Poems.
[Includes ninety poems.]

2680   *Iliqusituqarnit unikkaqtuat/Tales of Heritage*, edited by H.A. Bouraoui, Saul Field and Ceci Heinrichs. Willowdale, Ont.: Upstairs Gallery [1983]. Poems and tales.
[Texts in two Inuktitut dialects and other languages.]

2681   *Inuit Legends.* La Macaza, Que.: Thunderbird Press, 197(?) 15 pp. Legends.
[Cover title: For Use in Schools.]

2682   *More Tales from the Igloo*, by Agnes Nanogak. Edmonton: Hurtig, 1986. xii, 116 pp. Tales.

2683   *Northern Voices: Inuit Writing in English*, edited by Penny Petrone. Toronto: University of Toronto Press, 1988. xvii, 314 pp. port.

2684   *Paper Stays Put: A Collection of Inuit Writing*, edited by Robin Gedalof. Edmonton: Hurtig, 1980. 172 pp. Tales, legends.
[Tales and legends included were translated from the Inuit.]

2685   *Poems of the Inuit*, edited by John Robert Colombo. Ottawa: Oberon Press, 1981. 117 pp. Poems.
[Originally songs transcribed and translated from Danish and Inuktitut into English.]

2686   *Raven, Creator of the World: Eskimo Legends Retold*, edited by Ronald Melzack. Toronto: McClelland & Stewart, 1970. 91 pp. Stories.
[Includes ten stories.]

2687   *Tales from the Igloo*, edited and translated by Maurice Metayer. Illustrated by Agnes Nanogak, foreword by Al Purdy. Edmonton: Hurtig, 1972. 127 pp. Tales.
[Includes tales told by Copper Eskimos.]

2688   *Unikkaatuat sanaugarngnik atyingnaliit Puvirgni turngmit/Eskimo Stories from Povungniyuk, Quebec*, edited by Zabedee Nungak and Eugene Arima. Ottawa: Queen's Printer, 1969. 139 pp. illus. Stories.
[Includes 68 carvings and 46 myths and legends which they illustrate.]

2689   *Why the Man in the Moon is Happy and other Eskimo Creation Stories*, edited by Ronald Melzack, illustrated by László Gál. London: Good Reading, 1977. 61 pp. Also Toronto: McClelland & Stewart, 1977. Stories.

IRAQI

INDIVIDUAL AUTHOR

KATTAN, Naïm (1928-   )

Born in Bagdad, Iraq, to a Jewish family. Studied law at the University of Bagdad, then went to France and completed a doctorate at the Sorbonne. Came to Canada in 1954 and worked as an editor and as a lecturer at l'Université Laval. He is also a critic and radio commentator and long-time head of Canada Council's Writing and Publication Section. Published novels, short stories, review papers and three books of essays: *Le réal et le théatral*, 1970, *La Mémoire et la promesse* (c1978), and *Le Désir et le pouvoir*, 1983.

2690 *La Discrétion et autres pièces.* Montréal: Leméac, 1974. 141 pp. Théâtre.

2691 *Dans le désert (nouvelles).* Montréal: Leméac, 1974. 153 pp. Nouvelles.

2692 *Adieu, Babylone: roman.* Montréal: La Presse, 1975. 238 pp. Roman.

2693 *Farewell, Babylon*, translated from the French by Sheila Fischman. Toronto: McClelland & Stewart, 1976. 191 pp. Novel.

2694 *La Traversée* Montréal: Hurtubise HMH, 1976. Nouvelles.

2695 *Écrivains des Amériques.* Tome 1: *Les États-Unis;* Tome 2: *Le Canada anglais;* Tome 3: *L'Amérique latine.* Montréal: Hurtubise HMH, 1972-80.

2696 *Les Fruits arrachés: roman.* Montréal: Hurtubise HMH, 1977. 222 pp. Roman.

2697 *Le Rivage: nouvelles.* Montréal: Hurtubise HMH, 1979. 179 pp. Nouvelles.

2698 *Paris Interlude*, translated from the French by Sheila Fischman. Toronto: McClelland & Stewart, 1979. 208 pp. Novel.

2699 *Le Sable de l'île (nouvelles].* Montréal: Hurtubise HMH, 1981. Nouvelles.

2700 *The Neighbour and other Stories*, translated from the French by Judith Madley and Patricia Claxton. Toronto: McClelland & Stewart, 1982. Short stories.
[Includes stories selected from his *Dans le désert* and *La Traversée*.]

2701 *La Fiancée promise: roman.* Montréal: Hurtubise HMH, 1983. Roman.

2702 *La Reprise: nouvelles.* Montréal: L'Arbre HMH, 1985. Nouvelles.

Writings about:

2703 Allard, Jacques; Simard, Sylvain; Robert, Lucie. "Naïm Kattan." VOIX IMAG 11, no. 1 (1985): 6-54.

2704 Amprimoz, Alexandre. "La Solitude dans l'œuvre de Naïm Kattan." TAM REV 72 (1977): 79-87.

2705 Appenzell, Anthony. "The Modes of Maturity." CAN LIT No. 72 (1977): 72-73.
[Review of *Farewell, Babylon*.]

2706   Arés, Raymond. Critique: *Les Fruits arrachés.* LIVR AUTR QUÉB 1977: 78-79.

2707   Beaulieu, Benoît. Critique: *Le Rivage.* LIVR AUTR QUÉB 1979: 54-55.

2708   Benazon, Michael. "An Iraqi in Paris." CAN FORUM 50 (December 1979-January 1980): 40-41.
[Review of *Paris Interlude.*]

2709   Boivin, Aurélien. Critique: *Le Sable de l'île.* QUÉB FRANÇ No. 43 (1981): 12-13.

2710   Boivin, Aurélien. Critique: *Le Sable de l'île.* LIVR AUTR QUÉB 1981: 54-55.

2711   Bush, B.J. Review of *Farewell, Babylon.* CAN BOOK REV ANN 1976: 133.

2712   Bush, B.J. Review of *Farewell, Babylon.* CAN READER 17, no. 12 (1976): 12.

2713   Czarnecki, Mark. "Baguettes and Love Affairs in Paris." MACLEAN'S 92 (Oct. 22, 1979): 58.
[Review of *ParisInterlude.*]

2714   Desjardins, Normand. Critique: *La Fiancée promise.* NOS LIVR 14 (nov. 83): 32-33.

2715   Dey, Olga. "Naïm Kattan: Writer; Interview." CAN AUTH BKMN 55, no. 4, 56, no. 1 (1980): 24-25.

2716   Dorsinville, Max. "Ideologies." CAN LIT No. 84 (1980): 87-89.
[Review of *Les Fruits arrachés.*]

2717   Drolet, Gill. Critique: *Les Fruits arrachés.* Q & Q 44, no. 10 (1978): 13.

2718   Freedman, Adele. Review of *Farewell, Babylon.* MACLEAN'S 89, no. 16 (1976):

2719   Fulford, Robert. "The Canada Council at Twenty-five." SAT N 97 (March 1982): 34-45. port.

2720   Garebian, Keith. Review of *Paris Interlude.* Q & Q 48, no. 4 (1982): 28.

2721   Godbout, Jacques. Critique: *Adieu Babylone* et *Dans le désert.* MACLEAN'S 16, no. 4 (1976): 12.

2722   Grady, W. "Other Canadian." BKS CAN 11, no. 5 (1982): 9-11. Port.

2723   Greenstein, M. "Desert, The River & the Island: Naïm Kattan's Short Stories." CAN LIT No. 103 (1984): 42-48.

2724   Grosskurth, Phyllis. "The Young Man Who Wanted to Love." SAT N 95 (January-February 1980): 50.
[Review of *Paris Interlude.*]

2725   Hodgson, Richard. "Analyst." CAN LIT No. 90 (1981): 151-53.
[Review of *Le Rivage* and *Écrivains des Amériques.*]

2726   Hornbeck, Paul. Review of *Farewell, Babylon.* Q & Q 42, no. 14 (1976): 7-8.

2727   Jacques, André. Critique: *Écrivains des Amériques,* t. 3: *L'Amérique latine.* LIVR AUTR QUÉB 1980: 197-99.

2728   Janoël, André. "Le Désir et le pouvoir." NOS LIVR 14 (octobre 1983): 25-26.

2729   LaRue, Monique. "Une chevauchée planétaire. *Le Désir et le pouvoir.*" SPIRALE No. 39 (décembre 1983): 12.

2730   Mantz, Douglas. Review of *Farewell, Babylon.* CAN FIC MAG No. 24/25 (1977): 179-81.

2731   Marshall, Fred. "Government Role." CAN AUTH BKMN 57 (Fall 1981): 21.

2732   Mélançon, Robert. Critique: *Écrivains des Amériques,* II." LIVR AUTR QUÉB 1976: 233-34.

2733   Mezei, Kathy. Review of *The Neighbour.* UNIV TOR Q 52 (1982-83): 392-93.

2734   Moreau, Jean-Marie. Critique: *Écrivains des Amériques,* tome 1: *Les États-Unis*; tome 2: *Le Canada anglais* NOS LIVR 8 (juin-juillet 1977) no. 218.

2735   Moreau, Jean-Marie. Critique: *La Traversée.* NOS LIVR 8 (mars 1977) no. 93.

2736   Moreau, Jean-Marie. Critique: *Le Rivage.* NOS LIVR 10 (aou-septembre 1979)

2737   O'Connor, John J. Review of *Paris Interlude.* UNIV TOR Q 49 (1979-80): 386.

2738   Ouellette-Michalska, Madeleine. Critique: *Le Rivage.* CHÂTELAINE 20, no. 11 (1979): 10.

2739   "Our Only Arab-Jewish-French-Canadian Writer." SAT N 94 (January-February 1979): 9.

2740   Page, Raymond. Review of *Adieu, Babylone.* CHELSEA J 3, no. 2 (1977): 96.

2741   Piette, Alain. Critique: *La Traversée.* LIVR AUTR QUÉB 1976: 83.

2742   Scobie, Stephen. "Far from Eyes of Night." BKS CAN 8 no. 10 (1979): 8.
        [Review of *Paris Interlude.*]

2743   Simpson, Leo. "Conversation with Naïm Kattan." Q & Q 42, no. 17 (1976): 9-10, 36.

2744   Spettigue, D.O. Review of *Farewell, Babylon.* QUEEN'S Q 84 (1977): 510-11.

2745   Sutherland, Ronald. "Mind Broadening." CAN FORUM 56, no. 669 (1977): 36.
        [Review of *Farewell, Babylone.*]

2746   Vanasse, André. "La Traversée... de Babylone." LETTR QUÉB No. 5 (1977): 8-10.

2747   Vigneault, Robert. "L'Essai cette passion du sens. *Le Désir et le pouvir.*" LETTR QUÉB No. 3 (1983): 67-68.

2748   Wayne, Joyce. "Canada Deals with its Contradiction by Expressing Them Loudly. An Interview with Naïm Kattan." Q & Q 47, no. 5 (1981): 9-10.

ITALIAN

BIBLIOGRAPHIES

2749   PIVATO, Joseph

"Documenting Italian-Canadian Writing: A Bibliography." ITAL CAN 1 (1985): 28-37.
[Although Italian-Canadian authors have been active for a number decades, it wasn't until 1978 that Italian creative writing in Canada began to flourish. The late seventies witnessed the publication of the anthology *Roman Candles* and such novels as Paci's *The Italians*. This introductory paper provides an overall summary of accomplishments and suggestions for methodology to be used in bibliographic and scholarly work.]

2750   PIVATO, Joseph

Italian-Canadian Writers: A Preliminary Survey, edited by Michael S. Batts. Ottawa: Multiculturalism, Secretary of State, 1988. 53 pp.
[This bio-bibliography was prepared for the Multiculturalism Program as part of a series on ethnic Canadian literature. The author places emphasis upon socio-cultural aspects. The manuscript contains an outline of modern trends in Italian-Canadian poetry, fiction and drama, with biographical notes and bibliographic data on individual authors and their publications. Bibliographical list: pp. 25-52]

2751   PIVATO, Joseph

"Selected Bibliography." In *Contrasts: Comparative Essays on Italian-Canadian Writing*, edited by Joseph Pivato. (Montreal: Guernica Editions, 1985) pp. 231-46.
[Includes data on bibliographic sources and individual titles of poetry, prose and drama.]

MONOGRAPHS, RESEARCH PAPERS

2752   AMPRIMOZ, Alexandre L.; ESSAR, Dennis F.

"La Poétique de la mort: La Poésie italo-canadienne et italo-québécoise aujourd'hui." STUD CAN LIT 12 (1988): 161-76.
[Critique: Saro D'Agostino, Pier Giorgio Di Cicco, Pasquale Verdicchio, Len Gasparini, et al.]

2753   AMPRIMOZ, Alexandre L.; VISELLI, S.A.

"Death between the Two Cultures: Italian-Canadian Poetry." In *Contrasts...*, edited by Joseph Pivato. (Montreal: Guernica, 1985) pp. 101-20.
[The image of death is a dominant concept of Italian literature in general. Italian-Canadian poets, including Saro D'Agostino, Pier Giorgio Di Cicco, Mary Melfi and Mary di Michele, attempt to combine in their work the Mediterranean and Nordic cultures.]

2754   ANSELMI, William

"A Survey of Italian-Canadian Literature: A Paradoxical Panorama Unresolved." VICE VERSA No. 16 (1986): 41-43.
[This study is based on the anthologies *Roman Candles, La Poesia Italiana nel Quebec, Qêtes* and *Italian Canadian Voices.*]

2755   CACCIA, Fulvio

"The Italian Writer and Language," translated by Martine Leprince. In *Contrasts...*, edited by Joseph Pivato. (Montreal: Guernica, 1985) pp. 153-68.

[A study of the conditions under which immigrant literature is created and an examination of existing political and linguistic conflicts that influence the creative work of Italian authors in Quebec and Canada in general.]

2756   CACCIA, Fulvio
"Les poètes italo-montréalais: sous le signe du phénix." CAN LIT No. 106 (1985): 19.
[Critique: T. Caticchio, Augusto Tomasini, Filippo Salvatore, Antonino D'Alfonso, Marco Fraticelli, Mary Melfi, Mario Campo, et al.]

2757   CACCIA, Fulvio
Sous le signe du phénix: Entretiens avec quinze créateurs italo-québécois. Montréal: Guernica Editions, 1985.
[Des entretiens intelligents avec Francesco Iacurto, Guido Molinari, Mario Merola, Tonino Caticchio, Camillo Carli, Vittorio Fiorucci, Marco Micone, Paul Tana, Mary Melfi, Marco Fraticelli, Dominique De Pasquale, Mario Campo, Antonino D'Alfonso, Filippo Salvatore et Lamberto Tassinari.]

2758   CANADIAN LITERATURE No. 106 (1985). 191 pp.
[Special issue dedicated to Italian-Canadian literature. Contents include an interview with F.G. Paci, papers on Italian-Canadian writing in Québec and Montreal, a study of Marco Mico's plays and book reviews of individual collections of Italian-Canadian literature. For annotated papers see under various authors in this section.]

2759   COMENSOLI, Viviana
"Transculture." CAN LIT No. 112 (1987): 120-23.
[Critique: Filippo Salvatore: *La Fresque de Mussolini*; Fulvio Caccia: *Sous le signe du phénix*; et Fulvio Caccia: *Scirocco: poèmes*.]

2760   COSETTE, Gilles
Critique: *Quêtes, textes d'auteurs italo-québécois.* LETTR QUÉB No. 3 (1984): 79.

2761   D'ALFONSO, Antonino
"The Road Between: Essentialism. For an Italian Culture in Quebec and Canada." In *Contrasts...*, edited by Joseph Pivato. (Montreal: Guernica, 1985) pp. 207-30.
[Describes the process through which the author has managed to become an Italian in Canada and how such processes lead to the flourishing of minority literatures in Canada.]

2762   Di MICHELE, Mary
"We Came to Eat..." BKS CAN 15, no. 8 (1986): 3.
[Describes the events and contents of The First Conference of the Italian-Canadian Authors, held in Vancouver in 1986. Also offers a review of Marco Micone's play: *Gens du silence*.]

2763   HUTCHEON, Linda
"Voices of Displacement." CAN FORUM (June-July 1985): 33-39.

2764   KOWALICZKO, Béatrice.
"Vitalité de la production littéraire italo-québécoise." ACS NEWSL/BULL AEC 6, no. 4 (1984): 7.
[Critique: *Quêtes.*]

2765   LONGO, Louise
"The Italian Connection." BKS CAN 15, no. 9 (1986): 36-37.
[Review of *Contrasts....*]

2766   MANGANIELLO, Dominic

"Graze." CAN LIT No. 116 (1988): 220-21.

[Review article on the work of Vincenzo Albanese, Dorina Michelutti, and Pier Giorgio Di Cicco.]

2767   MICONE, Marco

"Immigrant Culture or the Identity of the Voiceless People." VICE VERSA (May-June 1985): 14-15.

2768   MINNI, C.D.

"The Short Story as an Ethnic Genre." In *Contrasts...*, edited by Joseph Pivato. (Montreal: Guernica, 1985) pp. 66-76.

[Short story, by and large, deals with outside figures, called marginal people. They are isolated characters, because their emotional terms of reference are different. Ethnic short story, according to the author, is a good example of this thesis. Individual authors examined are Caterina Edwards, F.G. Paci, John Metcalf, Alice Munro, Anne Hébert, Monique Bosco, Alexandre Amprimoz and others.]

2769   NATIONAL CONFERENCE OF ITALIAN-CANADIAN WRITERS. 1st, Vancouver, 1986.

Writers in Transition: Proceedings of the First National Conference of Italian-Canadian Writers, edited by C.D. Minni and Anna Foschi Ciampolini. Montreal: Guernica, 1988. (Essay series: 6)

2770   PACI, Frank G.

"Tasks of the Canadian Novelist Writing on Immigrant Themes." In *Contrasts...*, edited by Joseph Pivato. (Montreal: Guernica, 1985) pp. 35-60.

[The author maintains that a novel has to be good, enjoyable and meaningful to the reader. Minority authors referred to are John Marlyn, Henry Kreisel, Mordecai Richler and several Italian-Canadian novelists.]

2771   PADOLSKI, Enoch

"The Place of Italian-Canadian Writing." J CAN STUD 21, no. 4 (1986/87): 138-52.

[Provides a critical and conceptual framework in which Italian-Canadian, and in a broader sense, all Canadian writing, may be placed. The author raises a number of important issues such as the nature, scope and limits of ethnic literature, the concept of ethnicity and Canadian "mainstream" literature, the desirability of using "minority" (as opposed to the term "ethnic") as a key critical term.]

2772   PALMER, Tamara

Review of *Contrasts....* CAN ETH STUD 18, 1 (1986): 141-42.

2773   PIVATO, Joseph

'The Arrival of Italian-Canadian Writing." CAN ETH STUD 14, no. 1 (1982): 127-37.

[This essay examines recent developments in Italian-Canadian literature. Authors studied include Frank Paci, C.D. Minni, Giorgio Di Cicco, Filippo Salvatore, Mary di Michele, and Alexandre Amprimoz. Includes bibliographies.]

2774   PIVATO, Joseph

"Constantly Translating: The Challenge for Italian-Canadian Writing." CAN REV COMP LIT 14, no. 1 (1987): 60-76.

2775   PIVATO, Joseph, ed.

Contrasts: Comparative Essays on Italian Canadian Writing. Montreal: Guernica Editions, 1985. 246 pp.

[Includes papers by Joseph Pivato, F.G. Paci, Roberta Sciff-Zamaro, Alexandre Amprimoz and S.A. Viselli, Robert Billings, Fulvio Caccia, Filippo Salvatore, and Antonino D'Alfonso. For annotated papers see entries under the individual authors.]

2776   PIVATO, Joseph
"Ethnic Writing and Comparative Literature." In *Contrasts...*, edited by Joseph Pivato. (Montreal: Guernica, 1985) pp. 15-34.
[Offers a summary of traditional literary trends in the official languages and the earlier approaches to treating minority literatures. Specific works referred to include several anthologies such as *Canadian Overtones, Volvox.* Individual authors analysed are Walter Bauer, Josef Škvorecky, Rachel Korn, Naím Nómez, John Marlyn, Joy Kogawa, Frank G. Paci, Filippo Salvatore, Alexandre Amprimoz, Mario Duliani and many others.]

2777   PIVATO, Joseph
"Interview." VICE VERSA 1, no 5-6 (1984): 22.

2778   PIVATO, Joseph
"Italian-Canadian Women Writers Recall History." CAN ETH STUD 18, no. 1 (1986): 78-79.
[Examines selected works by Italian-Canadian authors writing in English, French and Italian on the early history of Italian immigration to Canada. Authors analysed are Mario Duliani, Mary di Michele, Maria Ardizzi, Elena Albani, Mary Melfi, Caterina Edwards, and Dorina Michelutti.]

2779   PIVATO, Joseph
"Italian Identity in Canadian Literature." CAFFE (October-November 1981): 1-2.

2780   PIVATO, Joseph
"Literature of Exile: Italian Language Writing in Canada." In *Contrasts...*, edited by Joseph Pivato. (Montreal: Guernica, 1985) pp. 169-87.
[The concept of exile has been prominent in Italian literature. The concepts of death/exile/emigration that can be traced back to the work of Virgil, Dante, Moravia, and Bassani are examined in the literary output of Mario Duliani, F.G. Paci, Romano Perticarini, Maria Ardizzi and others.]

2781   PIVATO, Joseph
"The Return Journey in Italian-Canadian Literature." CAN LIT No. 106 (1985): 169-76.

2782   PIVATO, Joseph
"Shock of Recognition: Italian-Canadian Writers." VICE VERSA 2, no. 3 (1985): 29-30.
[Defines the term: 'Italo-Canadian writing' based on the work of Pier Giorgio Di Cicco, Marco Micone, Frank Paci, Maria Ardizzi, Romano Perticarini, and Mary di Michele.]

2783   SALVATORE, Filippo
"The Italian Writers of Quebec: Language, Culture and Politics," translated by David Homel. In *Contrasts...*, edited by Joseph Pivato. (Montreal: Guernica, 1985) pp. 189-206.
[Contents: Quebec in the 1980s: A host of interpretations; Escaping the third solitude; Cultural specificity and political role of Italian writers in Quebec.]

2784   SCIFF-ZAMARO, Roberta
"Black Madonna: A Search for the Great Mother." In *Contrasts...*, edited by Joseph Pivato. (Montreal: Guernica, 1985) pp. 77-100.
[The complex cluster of meanings associated with the Italian mamma has been demonstrated in countless works of literature. An analysis of the concept of woman/mother/lover is examined through comparative references to such Canadian novels as Margaret Atwood's *Lady Oracle* and Anne Hébert's *Kamouraska*.]

ANTHOLOGIES

2785 *Italian Canadian Voices: An Anthology of Poetry and Prose (1946-1983)*, edited by Caroline Morgan Di Giovanni. Oakville: Mosaic Press, co-published with the Canadian Centre for Italian Culture and Education, 1984. 205 pp.
[Includes poetry, short stories and excerpts from novels under the following headings: First Voices (Mario Duliani, Gianni Grohovaz, Guiseppe Ricci); Roman Candles: The First Anthology (reprint of the anthology by the same title); A Mosaic: Selected Short Stories (C.D. Minni, Alexandre Amprimoz, Gianni Bartocci, Caterina Edwards); Identities: Excerpts from Novels (Maria Ardizzi, Caterina Edwards, Frank Paci, Matilde Torres); Presence Poetry 1979-1983 (George Amabile, Alexandre Amprimoz, Antonio D'Alfonzo, Celestino De Iuliis, Pier Giorgio Di Cicco, Mary di Michele, Len Gasparini, Antonino Mazza, Mary Melfi, Romano Perticarini, Joseph Pivato, and Filippo Salvatore). Bibliography: pp. 193-98.]

2786 *La Poesia Italiana nel Québec [Italian Poetry from Quebec]*, edited by Tonino Caticchio. Montreal: Centre de Culturelle Populaire Italien, 1983. 139 pp.
[Contains poems by Italian authors residing in Quebec.]

2787 *Quêtes: Textes d'auteurs italo-québécois*, présentés par Antonino D'Alfonso et Fulvio Caccia. Montréal: Guernica Editions, 1983. 280 pp.
[Includes poems, prose and plays by 18 authors: Dominique de Pasquale, Marco Micone, Ken Norris, Paul Tana, Marco Fraticelli, Mary Melfi, Mario Campo, Nicola Zavaglia, Filippo Salvatore, François d'Apollonia, Fulvio Caccia, Jacques Mascotto, Vincenzo Albanese, Antonino d'Alfonso, Laurent Gagliardi, Francis Catalano, Lamberto Tassinari and Carole David. Biographical notes are provided.]

2788 *Ricordi: Things Remembered*, edited by Dino C. Minni. Montreal: Guernica, 1987. 300 pp.
[An anthology of short stories on the Italian immigration experience.]

2789 *Roman Candles: An Anthology of Poems by Seventeen Italo-Canadian Poets*, edited by Pier Giorgio Di Cicco. [Toronto: Hounslow Press, 1978.] 85 pp.
[Includes poems by Filippo Salvatore, Len Gasparini, C. Cantasano, Pier Giorgio Di Cicco, Antonio Mazza, A. Iacovino, E. Prato, T. Pignattaro, M. Zizis, Mary Melfi, J. Ranallo, V. Albanese, Mary di Michele, J. Melfi, S. d'Agostino, Alexandre Amprimoz, Joseph Pivato. Biographical notes: pp. 83-85.]

INDIVIDUAL AUTHORS

ALBANESE, Vincenzo (1952-   )
Born in Mammola, Italy. His poems have appeared in *Quêtes* and *Roman Candles*. Unpublished manuscripts include "The Bells Toll for the Rain, Poems," and "The Trains that Leave: Novel."

2790 *Dead Loves and Tall Angels.* Montreal: Concordia University, 1976. Poems.

2791 *The Night Is a Beautiful Woman.* Ottawa: National Library, 1981. 72 fr. (Microfiche) Poems.

2792 *Slow Mist.* Dunvegan, Ont.: Cormorant, 1988. Poems.

ALBANI, Elena, pseud. (Real name: RANDACCIO, Elena) (1921- 1987)
Born in Bologna, Italy. Her writings depict the experiences of an Italian woman who moved to Canada in 1940.

2793 *Canada; mia seconda patria [Canada: My Second Home].* Bologna: Edizioni Sirio, 1958. Novel.

AMPRIMOZ, Alexandre L. (1948-   )

Poet, short story writer, critic, translator. Born in Rome, educated at the Université Aix-Marseille, Prytanée, and the universities of Ottawa, Toronto, Windsor and Western Ontario. At the latter he received a Ph.D. He is professor at Brock University and recipient of Pierian Spring, an editor's prize for best poem. He has published in *Salt, Quarry, Descant, The Tamarack Review, Waves,* and other periodicals.

2794 *Jiva and Other Poems.* Lakemont: C.S.A. Press, 1971. 47 pp. Poems.

2795 *Re and Other Poems.* New York: Vantage Press, 1972. xi, 81 pp. Poems.

2796 *Visions.* Lakemont: Tarnhelm Press, 1973. 64 pp. Poems.

2797 *An Island in the Heart and Other Dialogues.* Lakemont: Tarnhelm Press, 1973. 47 pp. Poems.

2798 *Studies in Grey.* London, Ont.: Killaly Press, 1976. 18 pp. Poems.

2799 *Chant solaire suivi de Vers ce logocentre.* Sherbrooke, Qué.: Éditions Naaman, 1978. 80 pp. Poèmes.

2800 *Against the Cold.* Fredericton, N.B.: Fiddlehead Poetry Books, 1978. 40 pp. Poems.

2801 *Selected Poems.* Toronto: Hounslow Press, 1979. 80 pp. Poems.

2802 *10/11.* Sudbury, Ont.: Prise de Parole, 1979. 40 pp. Poèmes.

2803 *In Rome.* Toronto: Three Trees Press, 1980. Short stories.

2804 *Other Realities.* Toronto: Three Trees Press, 1980. 90 pp. Poems.

2805 *Odes for Sterilized Streets.* Cornwall, Ont.: Vesta Publications, 1980. 55 pp. Poems.

2806 *Ice Sculptures.* Toronto: Three Trees Press, 1981. 50 pp. Poems.

2807 *Changements de ton.* St. Boniface, Man.: Éditions des Plaines, 1981. 60 pp. Poèmes.

2808 *Conseils aux suicidés.* Paris: Éditions Saint Germain des prés, 1982. 60 pp. Poèmes.

2809 *Fragments of Dreams.* Toronto: Three Trees Press, 1982. 48 pp. Poems.

2810 *Selected Writings.* Winnipeg: Turnstone Press, 1982.

2811 *Sur le damier des tombes: Poésie.* St. Boniface, Man.: Les Éditions du Blé, 1983. 70 pp. Poèmes.

2812 *Dix plus un demi: Poésie.* St. Boniface, Man.: Les Éditions du Blé, 1983. Poèmes.

2813 *For a Warm Country.* Brandon, Man.: Penion Press, 1984. 12 pp. Poems.

2814 *Dix plus un demi.* St. Boniface, Man.: Les Éditions du Blé, 1984. 54 pp. Poèmes.

2815 *Bouquet des signes.* Sudbury, Ont.: Prise de Parole, 1986. 96 pp. Poèmes.

2816 *Hard Confessions.* Winnipeg: Turnstone Press, 1987. 87 pp. Stories.

Writings about:

2817 Bell, John. Review of *Other Realities*. QUARRY 30, no. 2 (1981): 65-66.

2818 Billings, Robert. "Hounslow's Poetry List: Quality and Diversity." WAVES 8, no. 1 (1977): 75.
[Review of *Selected Poems*.]

2819 Billings, Robert. "The Poet as Critic." POETRY TORONTO No. 67-68 (1981): 19-20.
[Review of *Other Realities*.]

2820 Brodeur, Léo-A. Critique: *Chant solaire*. REV UNIV MONCTON 14, no. 1 (1981): 113-16.

2821 Clément, Michel. Critique: *Changements de tons*. LIVR AUTR QUÉB 1981: 118-19.

2822 Fletcher, Peggy. "Vision and the Personal Ark." CAN AUTH BKMN 54, no. 4 (1979): 26-27.
[Review of *Selected Poems*.]

2823 Giguère, Richard. "En d'autres lieux (de poésie)." LETTR QUÉB No. 17 (1980): 30-34.

2824 Hutchman, Laurence. "Different Journeys." CONT VERSE II 7, no. 3 (1983): 15-16.
[Review of *Other Realities*.]

2825 Janoël, André. Critique: *Sur le damier des tombes*. NOS LIVR 15 (juin-juillet 1984): 18.

2826 Kidd, Marylin E. "Other Francophones." CAN LIT No. 96 (1983): 141-43.
[Review of *Changements de tons*.]

2827 Meadwell, Kenneth. "Langue et parole dans l'œuvre poétique d'Alexandre Amprimoz." CAN LIT No. 106 (1985)

2828 Moisan, Clément. Critique: *10/11*. LIVR AUTR QUÉB 1979: 92.

2829 Ricou, Henriette. Critique: *Changements de tons*. BULL CENTRE ÉTUD FRANCO-CAN OUEST No. 8 (1981): 35-37.

2830 Russell, D.W. Review of *Dix plus un demi*. QUEEN'S Q 93 (1986): 178-79.

2831 Saunders, Leslie. Review of *Against the Cold*. QUARRY 27, no. 4 (1978): 74-75.

2832 Soudeyns, Maurice. "Du Manitoba..." LETTR QUÉB No. 35 (1984): 85.
[Critique: *Sur le damier des tombes*.]

ARDIZZI, Maria J. De Dominics (1931-)
Born in Leognano, Italy, emigrated to Canada in 1954. Her novel, *Made in Italy*, won the Ontario Arts Council award for a novel written in a language other than English or French. She lives in Toronto.

2833 *Made in Italy: Romanzo [Made in Italy: Novel]*. Toronto: Toma, 1982. 216 pp. Novel.
[Published simultaneously in Italian and English. English translation with same imprint, by Anna Maria Castrilli. Part 1 of the author's trilogy: *Il Ciclo Degli Emigranti [The Emigrant Cycle]*.

2834 *Il Sapore Agro della Mia Terra: Romazo [The Acrid Taste of My Country: Novel]*. Toronto: Toma, 1984. 259 pp. Novel.
[This novel is second in the trilogy.]

2835 *Conversation with My Son/Conversazione col figlio*, translated from the Italian by Celestino de Iuliis. Toronto: Toma, 1985. 101 pp. port. Poems.

2836   *La Buona America.* Toronto: Toma, 1987. 157 pp. Novel.

BARTOCCI, Gianni (1925-   )
Born at Fiuminata, studied law and medicine for several years at the University of Rome, where he took his doctorate in philosophy and history. He teaches Italian literature at the University of Guelph.

2837   *I Volsci a Dublino. Romanzo [In Dublin. A Novel].* Parma: Intelisano, 1968. Novel.

2838   *Equinozo ad Armanderiz [Equinox in Armanderiz].* Firenze: Kursaal, 1968. 130 pp. Novel.

2839   *Stars and Solitude.* Philadelphia: Dorrance, 1969. 49 pp. Poems.

2840   *Viaggio agli Antipodi [Travel to the Antipodes].* Firenze: Kursaal, 1967. 35 pp. Poems.

2841   *In Margine a Gaugin: Poesia del Pacifico [In Gaugin's Footsteps: Poetry of the Pacific].* Padova: Rebellato, 1970. 37 pp. Poems.

2842   *Biography of Love.* Parma: C.E.M., 1976.

2843   *La Riabilitazione di Galileo [Galileo's Rehabilitation].* Firenze: Luciano Landi Editore, 1980. Short stories.

BEDON, Elettna (1944-   )
Born in Padova, Italy.

2844   *Ma l'estate verra Ancora.* Brescia Ed. la Scuola, 1985. 105 pp. Short stories.

BERTELLI, Mariella (1951-   )
Born in Alexandria, Egypt. Translated several plays into Italian including *Tua per Sempre, Marilu,* by M. Tremblay, *Solange,* by Jean Barbeau, and *Open Marriage - Wide Open,* by Dario Fo and Franca Rame.

2845   *The Shirt of the Happy Man./La Camicia dell' Uomo Felice,* illustration by László Gál. Toronto: Kids Can Press, 1977. 28 pp. Italian folktale.
       [Bilingual edition.]

CACCIA, Fulvio (1952-   )
Author, playwright, poet, scholar. His plays have been performed on stage and radio.

2846   *Irpinia.* Montréal: Guernica, 1983. 57 pp. Poems in French.

2847   *Sous le signe du Phénix. Entretiens avec quinze créateurs italo-québecois* Montréal: Guernica, 1985. 305 pp.

2848   *Scirocco: Poèmes.* Montréal: Triptyque, 1985. 64 pp. Poèmes.

Writings about:

2849   Beaulieu, Michel. "*Quêtes* de Fulvio Caccia et Antonino D'Alfonso." LIVR D'ICI 9, no. 9 (1984): 22.

2850   Cosette, Gilles. Critique: *Quêtes...* LETTR QUÉB No. 35 (1984): 79.

2851   D'Alfonso, Antonio. "*Quêtes...*" POET CAN REV 5, no. 4 (1984): 12.

2852　Simon, Sherry. "La Quêtes commee mode d'invention." SPIRALE (avril 1984): 4.
[Critique: *Quêtes...*]

2853　Trudel, Serge. Critique: *Irpinia.* NOS LIVR 15 (mars 1984): 26-27.

CARLI, Camillo, pseud. (Real name: ANTELMINELLI, Coreglia) (1920-　)
Born in Italy, emigrated to Montreal, where he was editor of *La Tribuna Italiana* in the 1960s and 1970s.

2854　*Razzola Amore Mio... [Razzola, My Love...].* Poggibonsi: Lalli, 1977. Novel.

2855　*La Giornata di Fabio [One Day in Fabio's Life].* Poggibonsi: Lalli, 1984. Novel.

CASTRUCCI, Anello (1930-　)
Born in Monti Lepini. He lives in Ottawa.

2856　*I Miei Lontani Pascoli: Ricordi di Emigrante [My Far-away Grassland: An Immigrant's Notes].* Montreal: Riviera, 1984. Novel.

CATICCHIO, Tonino　(1930-1984)

2857　*La Storia de Roma: Ariccontata in Sonetti da Nonno Pippa [The Story of Rome: An Account in Sonnet Form].* Montreal: Er Core de Roma Editore, 1981. Novel.
[A story of Rome in Roman dialect.]

2858　*La Scoperta de Canada [The Story of Canada].* Montreal: Edizioni Romana, 1981. Story in sonnet form.

2859　*Rugantino [Roman Masquerade].* Montreal: Er Core de Roma Editore, 1982. Novel.

CONTE, Vittoria Ruma

2860　*Raccolta di Poesie [A Collection of Poetry].* Toronto: The Author, 1977. Poems.

COREA, Antonio Filippo (1941-　)
Born in Alpi. His poetry is stemming from the immigrant experience in Canada. Most of his poems are unpublished.

2861　*I Passi [The Steps].* Catanzaro: Rubbettino Editore, 1981. 116 pp. Poems.

2862　*Per non finire [In Order not to Finish].* Catanzaro: Calabria Letteraria Editice, 1986. 57 pp. Poems.

CUGGIA, Gérard (1951-　)
Born in Morocco.

2863　*Ciel de Novembre. Receuil [November Sky].* Laval, 1973. 93 pp. Poèmes.

2864　*Roue libre. Roman [Oper Road].* Montréal: The Author, 1974. Roman.

De FRANCESCHI, Marisa (1946-　)
Born in Udine, Italy. Also writes under the name Marisa De Monte. Her stories are based on situations encountered by immigrants. Published in Canadian Author and Bookman.

2865 *Stories about Real People; A Graded Reader for Students of English.* Windsor, Ont.: Mardan, 1982. Stories.

De IULIIS, Celestino (1946-   )
Born in Campotosto. Educated at the University of Toronto, B.A., M.A., and taught Italian language and literature at Syracuse University. Returned to Toronto in 1976. Translated into English *Open Marriage - Wide Open*, by Dario Fo and Franca Rame, published in Toronto in 1985. His poems relate to immigrant experience in Canada.

2866 *Love's Sinning Song and Other Poems.*   Toronto: Canadian Centre for Italian Culture and Education, 1981. ix, 60 pp. Poems.

Di CICCO, Pier Giorgio (1949-   )
Born in Arezzo, Italy, emigrated to Canada with his parents and has lived in Montreal, Baltimore and Toronto. His poems have appeared in anthologies and Canadian periodicals. Edited the anthology *Roman Candles.*

2867 *We are the Light Turning.* Scarborough, Ont.: Missing Link, 1975.   Also in Birmingham, AL: Thunder City Press, 1976. 40 pp. Poems.

2868 *The Sad Facts.* Fredericton, N.B.: Fiddlehead, 1977. 28 pp. Poems.

2869 *The Circular Dark.* Ottawa: Borealis, 1977. 65 pp. Poems.

2870 *Dancing in the House of Cards.* Toronto: Three Trees Press, 1978. 63 pp. Poems.

2871 *A Burning Patience.* Ottawa: Borealis, 1978. 82 pp. Poems.

2872 *Dolce-Amaro.* Alabama, N.Y.: Papavero, 1979. Poems.

2873 *The Tough Romance.* Toronto: McClelland & Stewart, 1979. 96 pp. Also by Guernica, 1988. Poems.

2874 *A Straw Hat for Everything.* Angelstone, 1981. Poems.

2875 *Dark to Light: Reasons for Humanness.* Vancouver: Intermedia, 1981. 48 pp. Poems.

2876 *Flying Deeper into the Century.* Toronto: McClelland & Stewart, 1982. 96 pp. Poems.

2877 *Women We Never See Again.* Ottawa: Borealis, 1984. 54 pp. Poems.

2878 *Post Sixties Nocturne.* Fredericton, N.B.: Fiddlehead Poetry Books, 1985. 49 pp. Poems.

2879 *Virgin Science.* Toronto: McClelland & Stewart, 1986. 183 pp. Poems.

Writings about:

2880 Barbour, Douglas. "Review Article on Canadian Poetry." DAL REV 58 (1978/79): 556. [Review of *Circular Dark.*]

2881 Daniel, Lorne. Review of *Dancing in the House of Cards.* Q & Q 44, no. 10 (1978): 11-12.

2882 Davis, Richard C. Review of *The Tough Romance.* CAN ETH STUD 14, no. 1 (1982): 174.

2883 Hatch, R.B. "Time's Motion." CAN LIT No. 81 (1979): 129-32.
[Review of *Circular Dark*.]

2884 Jewinski, Hans. "Poetic Contracts Bid..." BKS CAN 7, no. 5 (1978): 42.
[Review of *Circular Dark*.]

2885 King-Edwards, L. "Lists and Incantations." BKS CAN 11, (December 1982): 22.
[Review of *Flying Deeper into the Century*.]

2886 Lincoln, Bob. Review of *Post Sixties Nocturne*. CAN BOOK REV ANN 1985: 171.

2887 Nicol, Eric. "A Vulgarian View." CAN LIT No. 87 (1980): 108-10.
[Review of *The Tough Romance*.]

2888 Pratt, Larry. Review of *We Are the Light Turning*. Q & Q 43, no. 1 (1977): 32.

2889 St. Pierre, Paul M. "Pier Giorgio Di Cicco." In *Canadian Writers since 1960*. (Detroit: Gale, 1987) pp. 47-53.

2890 Singleton, Martin. Review of *Women We Never See Again*. CAN BOOK REV ANN 1984: 222.

2891 Wolfe, Morris. "Sasquatch and Sauerkraut, with Senate Salad, Italian Dressing...." BKS CAN 7 (October 1978): 33.
[Review of *Roman Candles*.]

DIDONE, Angelo

2892 *Come into a Heart of Sharing*. Cobalt, Ont.: Highway Bookshop, 1977. 56 pp. Poems.

Di LULLO, Giovanni (1950-   )
Born in Agnone. He has published scholarly papers in *Il Cittadino Canadese*, poems in *Antologia Discografica* and in periodicals.

2893 *Il fuoco della pira* [The Fire of the Pyre]. Montreal: Simposium, 1976. Poems.

Di MICHELE, Mary (1949-   )
Born in Italy, emigrated to Canada in 1955. Educated at the University of Toronto and the University of Windsor. She won the silver medal in the Du Maurier Award for poetry in 1983. Edited *Anything is Possible*.

2894 *Tree of August*. Toronto: Three Trees Press, 1978. 47 pp. Poems.

2895 *Bread and Chocolate*. Ottawa: Oberon, 1980. 85 pp. Poems.

2896 *There's Sky above My Sky*. Toronto: League of Canadian Poets, 1980. 1 folded sheet (8 pp.) Poems.

2897 *Mimosa and other Poems*. Oakville, Ont.: Mosaic Press, 1981. 46 pp. Poems.

2898 *Necessary Sugar: Poems*. Ottawa: Oberon, 1983. 64 pp. Poems.

2899 *Immune to Gravity*. Toronto: McCelland & Stewart, 1986. 119 pp. Poems.

Writings about:

2900 Billings, Robert. "Contemporary Influences on the Poetry of Mary di Michele." In *Contrasts...*, edited by Joseph Pivato. (Montreal: Guernica, 1985) pp. 121-52.

2901 Billings, Robert. "Discovering the Sizes of the Heart: The Poems of Mary di Michele." ESSAYS CAN WRIT No. 27 (1983-84): 95-115.

2902 Brown, Russell. "New Poems and Old Stories." CAN FORUM 61 (February 1982): 37-39. [Review of *Bread and Chocolate.*]

2903 Daurio, Bev. Review of *Immune to Gravity.* CAN BOOK REV ANN 1986: 90.

2904 Dudek, Louis. "Poetry at the End of Things." CAN FORUM 65 (April 1985): 29-30. [Review of *Anything is Possible.*]

2905 Helwig, Maggie. Review of *Necessary Sugar.* Q & Q 50, no. 6 (1984): 35.

2906 Kertzer, Jon. "Perplexing Love." CAN FORUM 64 (June-July 1984): 41-42.

2907 Longo, Louis. Review of *Immune to Gravity.* BKS CAN 15, no. 6 (1986): 25.

2908 McKinney, Louise. Review of *Immune to Gravity.* Q & Q 52, no. 5 (1986): 28.

2909 Miles, Ron. "Fine Lines and Fractures." CAN LIT No. 112 (1987): 183-85. [Review of *Immune to Gravity.*]

2910 Pivato, Joseph. "An Immigrant Daughter and a Female Writer: Mary di Michele." VICE VERSA No. 5-6 (1984): 21-22.

2911 Robinson, Judy. Review of *Bread and Chocolate.* Q & Q 47, no. 1 (1981): 28-29.

2912 Wainwright, J.A. "To Revelations." CAN LIT No. 91 (1981): 148-51. [Review of *Bread and Chocolate.*]

2913 Whiteman, Bruce. Review of *Bread and Chocolate.* QUEEN'S Q 89 (1982): 223-24.

DULIANI, Mario (1885-1964)
A prolific playwright and author of scholarly work, Duliani was interned in 1940, when Italy entered the war on the side of Germany. After the war he emigrated to Canada. He was editor of *La Verità*, a weekly newspaper published in Montreal. His writings have appeared in *La Presse*.

2914 *La Ville sans femmes.* Montréal: Pascal, 1945. Novel.

2915 *Citta Senza Donne [City Without Women].* Montréal: Gustavo D'Errico Editore, 1946. Novel. [Italian translation of *La Ville sans femmes.*]

2916 *Deux heures de fou rire.* Montréal: Éditions Serge, 1944, 1947, 1948. Short stories.

2917 *La fortune vient en parlant.* Montréal: Fernand Pilon, 1946. Short stories.

FELICIANO, Margarita (1938-   )
Author, translator, teacher. Born in Sicilia, Italy. Her poems and translations in English and Spanish have appeared in *Waves, Fireweed, Existere, Nouvelle Europe, Landscape, Ventana Sobre el Mar/Window on the Sea,* etc.

2918 *Circadian Nuvolitatis. [Everyday Feelings].* Luxembourg: Elvoeditor, 1986. 75 pp. Poems.

FERRARI, Leo (1927-   )

2919 *The Worm's Revenge,* foreword by Al Pittman. 1968.

2920 *Over the Edge ! Poems in Grateful Celebration of Fifty Years of Life, Love and Laughter.* Fredericton, N.B.: Owl & Pussycat, 1977. 61 pp. Poems.

FRANGEL, Bepo, pseud. (Real name: BULTON, Ermanno) (1942-1985)
Born in Udine, Italy, emigrated to Toronto, where he died prematurely.

2921 *Un Friûl vivût in Canada [Friuli Lived in Canada].* Udine, Italy: Ente Friûli and Mando, 1911. 75 pp. Poems in Friulano.

FRUCHI, Dino (1919-   )
Born in Laterina. In addition to writing stories, he has also written an Italian grammar for French-Canadians. At work on "Romanzo sociale d'un immigrante italiano," a social novel on an Italian immigrant in Canada.

2922 *L'Arno Racconta; la Guerra, l'Amore, la Vita [The Arno Recalls: War, Love and Live].* Poggibonsi: Antonio Lalli, 1979. Stories about Tuscany.

GIAMBAGNO, *Domenica* (1942-   )
Born in Molise. Her poems have appeared in newspapers.

2923 *Risveglio e Trionfo; Poesie d'Amore e Storie Vere. [Revival and Triumph: Love Poetry and True Stories].* Toronto: The Author, 1976.

GROHOVAZ, Gianni A. (1926-1988)
Born in Fiume, emigrated to Canada in 1950. Former editor of *La Settimana, Corriere Canadese, Il Giornale di Toronto,* and other newspapers. Received several awards for his contributions to Italian culture in Canada. His biographical novel, *La Strada Bianca,* will be published shortly.

2924 *Per Ricordar le Cose che Ricordo [Remembering Things I Recall].* Toronto: Dufferin, 1974. Poems in Fiuman.

2925 *From Flanders Fields to Italian Alps.* Toronto: Coro Santa Cecilia, 1975. One act play.

2926 *Parole, Parole e Granelli di Sabbia [Words, Words and Grains of Sand].* Toronto: The Author, 1980. Poems.

IANORA, Claudio (1945-   )

2927 *Sint Stephen Canada, Polyphemus' Cave and the Boobieland Express.* Don Mills, Ont.: New Press, 1970. 124 pp. Satirical novel.

IERFINO, Giuseppe (1936-   )
Born in Italy.

2928 *L'ortana di Cassino. [The Orphan Girl of Cassino].* Toronto: The Author, 1987. 238 pp. Novel.

La RICCIA, Ermanno (1928-   )

2929   *Terra Mia, Storie di Emigrazione [My Land: Story of Emigration].* Padova: Graf. Messagero di S. Antonio, 1984. 236 pp. Short stories.

MASTROPASQUA, Corrado (1929-   )
Born in Cimitile, published poems in Neapolitan in newspapers and periodicals.

2930   *'Na Lacrema e 'na Risa [No Tears and no Smiles].* Napoli: D'Alessandro, 1969. Poems.

MAZZA, Antonio (1949-   )
Born in Italy, came to Canada in 1961. Educated at Carleton University and the University of Toronto. He taught at the University of Ottawa, 1978-1981. Published translations of Montale and Pasolini. Associate editor of *Anthos.*

2931   *Structures of Chaos:* Poems. Hull: The Author, 1979. Poems.

2932   *Infinite Hope.* Ottawa: Mosaic Press, 1984. Poems.

McRAN, E., pseud. (Real name: RANDACCIO, Elena) (1921-   )
See also Albani, Elena

2933   *The Sound of a Harp.* Philadelphia: Dorrance, 1976. 279 pp. Novel.

2934   *Diario di una Emigrante [Diary of an Immigrant].* Bologna: Tamari, 1979. Autobiographical novel.

MELE, Jim (1950-   )

2935   *An Oracle of Love.* Montreal: Cross Country Press, 1976. 24 pp. Poems.

2936   *The Sunday Habit.* Montreal: Cross Country Press, 1978. 54 pp. Poems.

MELFI, Mary (1951-   )
Born in Cascalenda, Italy, emigrated to Canada in 1956. She is a graduate of Loyola College and McGill University. Her poems have appeared in *Exile, Matrix, Waves, Antigonish Review,* etc.

2937   *The Dance, the Cage and the Horse.* Montreal: D. Press, 1976. 90 pp. Poems.

2938   *A Queen is Holding a Mummified Cat.* Montreal: Guernica, 1982. 87 pp. Poems.

2939   *A Bride in Three Acts.* Montreal: Guernica, 1983. 96 pp. Poems.

2940   *A Dialogue with Masks.* Toronto: Mosaic Press, 1986. 114 pp.

2941   *The O Canada Poems.* Brandon, Man.: Dollarpoems, 1986. 12 pp. Poems.

Writings about:

2942   Daymond, Douglas. "In Minor Key." CAN LIT No. 97 (1983): 140-43.
[Review of *A Queen is Holding a Mummified Cat.*]

2943   Weiss, Allan. Review of *A Dialogue with Masks.* BKS CAN 15, no. 5 (1986): 40.

MICHELUTTI, Dorina (1952-   )

Born in Friuli, Italy, and emigrated to Canada in 1958. She returned to Italy in 1972 and re-immigrated to Canada in 1980. She studied at the University of Florence and the University of Toronto. She lives in Toronto.

2944 *Loyalty to the Hunt.* Montreal: Guernica, 1986. illus. 54 pp. (Essential Poets: 29) Prose-poems.

MICONE, Marco (1945-   )

2945 *Gens du silence.* Montréal: Éditions Québec/Amérique, 1982. 140 pp. Théâtre.

2946 *Voiceless People: A Play,* translated from French by Maurizia Binda. Montreal: Guernica, 1984. 92 pp. Play.
[Translation of *Gens du silence.*]

2947 *Addolorata.* Montréal: Guernica, 1984. 101 pp. (Drama series no. 2) Play.
[Published in French and English.]

2948 *Gens du silence,* 2d éd. rev., corr. Montréal: Guernica, 1988. Théâtre.

2949 *Two Plays: Voiceless People and Addolorata.* Montreal: Guernica, 1988.
[Translation of *Gens du silence* and *Addolorata.*]

Writings about:

2950 Comensoli, Viviana. "Voice Registers." CAN LIT No. 106 (1985): 84-85.
[Review of *Italian Voices*; Micone: *Voiceless Poeple*; Melfi: *A Bride in Three Acts.]*

2951 Forni, Lorenza. "Emigration." CAN LIT No. 106 (1985): 822-84.
[Review of *Addolorata.*]

2952 Mezei, Kathy. Review of *Voiceless People.* UNIV TOR Q 54 (1984-85): 397-98.
[Review of *Voiceless People.*]

2953 Plant, Richard. "Opening Lines." BKS CAN 14, no. 4 (1985): 22.
[Review of *Voiceless People.*]

2954 Simon, Sherry. "Speaking with Authority: The Theatre of Marco Micone." CAN LIT No. 106 (1985): 57-64.

MINNI, Constantino Dino (C.D.) (1942-   )
Born in Bagnoli del Trigno, Isernia, emigrated to Canada as a child, grew up in Vancouver. His short stories have appeared in anthologies, textbooks and periodicals, and on CBC Radio. Served as critic-at-large for *The Canadian Author and Bookman* in 1977-1980.

2955 *Other Selves: A Collection of Short Stories.* Montreal: Guernica, 1985. 98 pp. Short stories.

Writings about:

2956 Sciff-Zamaro, Roberta. Review of *Other Selves.* CAN ETH STUD 18, no. 3 (1986): 155-56.

2957 Van Mill, Patrick. Review of *Other Selves.* CAN BOOK REV ANN 1985: 214-15.

NARDI, Tony (1958-   )
Born in Cosenza. His writings are related to the Italian immigrant experience in Canada.

2958   *La Storia dell' emigrante [The Story of an Immigrant].* Montreal, 1982. Play.

PACI, Frank G. (1948-   )
Born in Pesaro, Italy, emigrated to Canada in 1952 and grew up in Sault Ste. Marie, Ont. He was educated at the University of Toronto (B.A.) and Carleton University (M.A.).

2959   *The Italians: A Novel.* Ottawa: Oberon, 1978.   205 pp. Toronto: New American Library, 1980. 185 pp. Novel.

2960   *Black Madonna: A Novel.* Ottawa: Oberon, 1982. 198 pp. Novel.

2961   *The Father.* Ottawa: Oberon, 1984. Novel.

Writings about:

2962   Bonanno, Giovanni. "Italian Identity." CAN LIT No. 106 (1985): 80.
[Review of The Father.]

2963   Bonanno, Giovanni. "The Search for Identity: An Analysis of Frank Pacci's Novels." In *Canada: The Verbal Creation*, edited by A. Pizzardi. (Abano Terme, Italy: Piovon Editore, 1985) pp. 167-82.

2964   Brennan, Anthony. Review of *The Italians.* FIDDLEHEAD 119 (1978): 128-29.

2965   Brown, Barry. "Our Lady of Sorrows." BKS CAN 11, no. 6 (1982): 26.
[Review of *Black Madonna.*]

2966   Colalillo, Giuliana. Review of *Black Madonna.* CAN ETH STUD 14, no. 3 (1982): 131-32.

2967   DiGiovanni, Caroline. Review of *The Italians.* CAN ETH STUD 10, no. 2 (1978): 204-05.

2968   Fogan, Cary. Review of *Black Madonna.* Q & Q 48, no. 6 (1982): 32.

2969   Hill, Douglas. Review of *Black Madonna.* UNIV TOR Q 52 (1982-83): 325-26.

2970   Hlus, Carolyn. Review of *The Father.* CAN ETH STUD 18, no. 1 (1986): 139-40.

2971   Johnson, Lorraine. Review of *The Father.* BKS CAN 14, no. 5 (1985): 25.

2972   Ortenzi, Stephanie. Review of *The Father.* Q & Q 50, no. 7 (1984): 73.

2973   Ruddell, Simon. "Skirmishes with the Past." CAN LIT No. 99 (1983): 87-89.
[Review of *Black Madonna.*]

2974   Ryder, Carolyn. Review of *The Father.* CAN BOOK REV ANN 1983: 197.

PAPA, Vito (1905-   )
Born in Simbaro, Italy. Published poems in newspapers.

2975   *Poesie del Carpentiere.* Toronto: The Author, 1976. Poems.

PERTICARINI, Romano (1934-   )

Born in Fermo, Italy, emigrated to Canada with his family in 1967. His writings have appeared in *L'Eco d'Italia* (Vancouver) and *Il Cittadino Canadese* (Montreal). Recipient of the City of Pompeii Prize (Italy) and other awards.

2976 *Quelli della Fionda/The Sling-shot Kids.* Vancouver: Azzi, 1981. Bilingual poems.

2977 *Il Mio Quaderno di Novembre/From My November Record Book.* Vancouver: Scala, 1983. 165 pp. Bilingual poems.

PIRONE, Michele
Born in Molise. One of her short stories appeared in *Canadian Fiction Magazine*, 20A, 1976.

2978 *'N'uochhio e 'na Lacrema [Nuts and a Tear].* Montreal: The Author, 1974. 126 pp. Short stories.

PISAPIA, Roberto (1891-)
Born in Napoli, Italy.

2979 *Tiempo ca nun Torneno [Time doesn't Return].* Toronto: Villa Colombo, 1977. Poems in Neopolitan and Italian.

POLLO, Evasio (1928-)
Born in Borgovercelli, Italy. Editor of the newspaper *La Parola*.

2980 *Antonio Santo e Profeta [St. Anthony the Prophet].* Toronto: St. Thomas Press, 1979. Prose play.

RANIERI, Joseph (1947-)
Born in San Vito Iono. Several of his short stories, mainly for educating children, are still in manuscript.

2981 *December/Dicembre.* Toronto, 1983. Children's stories.

2982 *Giovedi/Thursday.* Toronto: Easter Educational Publications, 1985. Children's stories.

RIMANELLI, Giose (1926-)
Author of *Italian Literature: Roots and Branches: Essays.* In addition to novels, he has also published poetry.

2983 *Tiro al Piccione [A Shot at a Pigeon].* Milano: Mondadori, 1948. Novel.

2984 *Peccato Originale [The Original Sin].* Milano: Mondadori, 1954. Novel.

2985 *Fall of Night (The Day of the Lion): A Novel,* translated from the Italian by Ben Johnson. Toronto: Popular Library, 1955. 189 pp. Novel.

2986 *Biglietto di Terza [Third-class Ticket].* Milano: Mondadori, 1958. Novel.

2987 *Una Posizione Soziale [A Social Position].* Firenze: Vallechi, 1959. Novel.

2988 *Il Mestiere del Furbo [The Work of the Cunning].* Milano: Sugar, 1959. Essays.

2989 *Tragica America [American Tragedy].* Genova: Immordino, 1968. Novel.

2990 *Molise, Molise [Molise, Molise].* Isernia: Marinelli, 1979. Novel.

ROMANO, John (1950-)
Born in Limosano, came to Canada in 1956.

2991   *Time and Chance.* Toronto: Lantern Theatre Company, Poor Alex Theatre, 1980. Two-act play.

2992   *The Process.* Toronto: Toronto Centre for the Arts, 1981. One-act play.

2993   *A Story.* Toronto: Perforum Co., 1981. One-act play.

ROMEO, Luigi

2994   *Battesimo [The Christening].* Toronto: Dante Society, 1963. Poems.

SALVATORE, Filippo (1947-   )
Born in Guglionesi, Italy, came to Canada in 1964. Educated at McGill University and Harvard (Ph.D.) Teaches contemporary Italian literature and cinema at Concordia University.

2995   *Tufo e Gramigna [Necrosis and Weeds].* Montreal: Symposium, 1977. Poems.

2996   *Suns of Darkness.* Montreal: Guernica, 1980. Poems, bilingual edition.

2997   *La Fresque de Mussolini [Mussolini's Fresco].* Montreal: Guernica, 1985. 85 pp. Play.

SAVONA, Baldassare

2998   *Tristezza: Raccolta di Poesie [Sorrow: A Collection of Poetry].* Toronto: Grizzi, 1961. Poems.

SUCCORO, Giovanna Maria (1949-   )
Born in San Giovanni in Fiore.

2999   *Un Povera Famiglia [The Poor Family].* Windsor, Ont.: La Gazetta, 1984. Novel. [Published serially.]

TACCOLA, Umberto (1922-   )

3000   *Una Scatola di Sole: Raccolta de Liriche e Disegni di Viaggio [A Boxfull of Sun: A Collection of Lyric Poetry and Descriptions].* Montreal, 1978. Poems.

3001   *Una Scatola di Passi: Liriche e Disegni [A Boxful of Steps: Lyric Poems and Descriptions].* Iserbia, 1983. Poems.

3002   *Terra Mia: Abruzzo, Friuli, Vinchiaturo [My Land: Abruzzo, Friuli, Vinchiaturo].* Montreal, 1978. Poems.

TANZI, Gaetano (1940-   )
Born in Genoa.
3003   *Non Rompete i Coglioni al Colonello [Don't Disturb the Colonel].* Roma: Trevi, 1981. Novel.

TASSINARI, Lamberto (1945-   )
Born in Castelfiorentino, Italy, came to Canada in 1980. Published short stories in *Quêtes.* A novel, "L'ordre établi," is in manuscript.

3004   *Durante la Partenza [During Departure].* Montreal: Guernica, 1985. 118 pp. Novel.

TORRES-GENTILE, Matilde (1950-   )

Born in Tagliacozzo, Italy. Studied medicine at the University of Rome. Emigrated to Canada in 1977 and practises medicine in Toronto. Her novel is about a woman doctor's visit to Canada and eventual immigration to this country.

3005   *La Dottoressa di Cappadocia [Cappadocio's Doctor].* Roma Edizione della Urbe, 1982. Novel.

VERDICCHIO, Pasquale (1954-)
Born in Naples, Italy, emigrated to Canada as a teenager. Educated at the University of Victoria, University of Alberta and University of California. His poems, translations and photography have appeared in Canadian, American and Italian periodicals. He is editor of *Carte Italiane: A Journal of Italian Studies,* and *The Raddle Moon Review.*

3006   *Moving Landscape.* Montreal: Guernica, 1985. 46 pp. Poems.

3007   *Ipsissima Verba [The Ultimate Word].* Vancouver: Parenthesis Writing, 1986. 16 pp. Poems.

Writings about:

3008   Di Cicco, Pier Giorgio. "A Man without Borders: An Interview." FROM AN ISLAND (February 1979)

3009   McKinney, Louise. "Roman Heartbeat." CAN LIT No. 115 (1987): 232-33.
[Review of *Moving Landscape.*]

3010   Minni, Dino. "A Poet in a Moving Landscape: An Interview with Pasquale Verdicchio." VICE VERSA No. 16 (1986): 39-40.

ZAGOLIN, Bianca (1945-)
Author, teacher. Born in Friuli, Italy.

3011   *Une femme à la Fenêtre.* Montréal-Paris: Rohart Laffont, 1988. 201 pp. Roman.

ZAMARO, Silvano (1949-)
Born in Cormons, Italy. His poems and translations have appeared in *Caffe, Gateway, Today's Greatest Poems, American Poetry Anthology.*

3012   *Autostrada per la luna [Highway to the Moon].* Montréal: Guernica, 1987. 60 pp. Poems.

ZIOLKOWSKI, Carmen A.
Born Carmen Laurenza, in Italy, came to Canada in 1956. Educated in journalism at Port Huron Junior College and Wayne State University, Detroit. She lives in Sarnia, Ont.

3013   *Roses Bloom at Dusk:Poems.* Cornwall, Ont.: Vesta, 1976. 50 pp. Poems.

3014   *The House of Four Winds.* Sarnia, Ont.: River City Press, 1987. iii, 126 pp. port. Novel.

JAMAICAN

INDIVIDUAL AUTHORS

ALLEN, Lillian
Born in Spanish Town, Jamaica, came to North America in 1969 and settled in Toronto. She has a B.A. in literature from York University. An exponent of dub poetry, she received a Juno Award, 1987, for *Revolutionary Tea Part.*

3015   *Rhythm an' Hardtimes.* Frontline, 1983. Poems.

3016   *De Dub Poets.* E.p. record. 1984. Poems.

3017   *Revolutionary Tea Party.* Album. 1986. Poems.

3018   *If You See the Truth.* Frontline, 1987. Poems.

3019   *Let the Heart See.* Casette. 1987. Poems.

3020   *Conditions Critical.* Album. 1988. Poems.

ANDERSON, Abbot
Born and educated in Jamaica, Anderson came to Canada in 1963 and continued his studies in music. He also directed and acted in such plays as *Behind God's Back, The Mercenaries,* and *The Case of the Undecided Molecule* for CBC TV, and *Roman Life - The House* for ETV.

3021   *Psalms of Babylon.* Toronto: Advent, 1972.

ANDERSON, Hope(ton)
Born in Montreal, but he was raised in Jamaica. After his return to Montreal he attended Sir George Williams University. Co-editor of the anthology *The Body.* He now lives in Vancouver.

3022   *Back Mount.* Montreal: Mondiale, 1974. Poems.

ARTHURS, Patrick
Born in Jamaica. He lives in Toronto.

3023   *Soul Revolution.* New York: Exposition, 1975. Novel.

BLACK, Ayanna
Born in Jamaica and lived in England before she emigrated to Canada. A writer and freelance publicist, she is also active in the women's community in Toronto.

3024   *No Contingencies.* Toronto: Williams-Wallace, 1986. Poems.

COOPER, Afua
Born in Jamaica. Gave numerous readings throughout Canada and abroad. Published articles in magazines.

3025   *Breaking Chains.* Weelas Publications, 1983. Poems.

3026   *Red Caterpillar on College Street.* sisterVision Press, 1988. Poems.

D'OYLEY, Enid Frederica

Born in Jamaica. Educated at the University of Toronto. She has travelled in Europe and Latin America. Now works as a bibliographer for Spanish and Portuguese and Latin American studies at the University of Toronto Library.

3027 *Between Sea and Sky.* Toronto: Wacarco Productions, 1979. Novel.

3028 *Animal Fables and other Tales Retold.* Toronto: Williams-Wallace, 1982. Stories.

PALMER, Everard C.

Born in Kendal, Jamaica and received his education there and at the Lakehead University, Thunder Bay, Ont.

3029 *A Broken Vessel.* Kingston, Jamaica: Pioneer Press, 1960. Novel

3030 *The Cloud with the Silver Lining.* London: Deutsch, 1966. Novel.

3031 *The Sun Salutes You.* London: Deutsch, 1970. Novel.

3032 *A Cow Called Boy.* New York: Bobbs Merill, 1972. Novel.

3033 *The Wooing of Beppo Tate.* London: Deutsch, 1972. Novel.

3034 *The Hummingbird People.* London: Deutsch, 1974. Novel.

3035 *Baba and Mr. Big.* New York: Bobbs Merrill, 1974. Novel.

3036 *My Father Sun Sun Johnson.* London: Deutsch, 1974. Novel.

3037 *Big Dog Bitteroot.* London: Deutsch, 1974. Novel.

3038 *A Dog Called Houdini.* London: Deutsch, 1978. Novel

WATSON, Edward

Born in Jamaica. Attended Kingston College. Received his M.A. from the University of Chicago and his Ph.D. from the University of Toronto. He teaches practical criticism and critical theory at the University of Windsor. Received two Canada Council grants, one in 1968 and and another in 1971.

3039 *Out of the Silent Stone and other Poems.* Red Hills, Jamaica: Bruckings House [n.d.] Poems.

ZHINA, Andri

A playwright and poet.

Writing about:

3040 Bell, Gay. "An Interview with Andri Zhina." FUSE 10, no. 1-2 (1986): 58-63.

JAPANESE

RESEARCH PAPER

3041 **SHIKATANI, Gerry**
"Introduction." In *Paper Doors: An Anthology of Japanese-Canadian Poetry*, edited by Gerry Shikatani and David Aylward. (Toronto: Coach House Press, 1981) pp. 7-13.
[Traces the history of Japanese-Canadian poetry, haiku and tanka, written in Japanese over several decades, and other poems of an inward-facing nature, centered around church and social clubs and the development of the more recent writings of younger poets.]

ANTHOLOGIES

3042 *Maple: Tanka Poems by Japanese Canadians*, edited by Tomi Nishimura, with translations by Toyoshi Hiramatsu. Toronto: The Centennial Times, 1975. xiv, 222 pp.
[Includes poems in Japanese and English by more than 50 poets. Provides a portrait and biographical sketch of each author.]

3043 *Minazuki: An Anthology*, edited by Chusaburō Koshū [n.d.]
[Includes poetry in Japanese by Japanese-Canadian authors.]

3044 *Paper Doors: An Anthology of Japanese-Canadian Poetry*. 2nd ed., edited by Gerry Shikatani and David Aylward, with translations by David Aylward. Toronto: Coach House Press, 1981. 194 pp.
[Includes poems by Chōichi Handō Sumi, Minoru Furusho, David Fujino, Hidetarō Shūzan Nishi, Kevin Irie, Takeo Ujō Nakano, Roy Kiyooka, Tomi Nishimura, Gerry Shikatani, Midori Iwasaki, Joy Kogawa, Chūsaburō Koshū Itō, Sukeo Mokujin Sameshima..]

INDIVIDUAL AUTHORS

NAKAMURA, Michiko

3045 *Gonbei's Magic Kettle.* Toronto: Kids Can Press, 1980. Children's story.
[Text in Japanese and English.]

NAKANO, Takeo (1903-)
Born in Fukuoka-ken, came to Canada in 1929. In 1964 he was one of twelve authors to win a prize in the Imperial Poetry Contest sponsored by the Emperor and Empress in Tokyo. His poems were included in *Reniya no Yuki (The Snows of Mount Rainier)*, an anthology published in Seattle in 1956.

3046 *Sensei: Nakano Ujo kabum shu [Oath of Citizenship].* Tokyo: Kashiva Soin, Showa 44, 1969. Poems.

3047 *Within the Barbed Wire Fence: A Japanese Man's Account of His Internment in Canada*, with Leatrice Nakano. Toronto: University of Toronto Press, 1980. Autobiographical novel.

NAKAYAMA, Gordon G.

3048 *ISSEI: Stories of Japanese Canadian Pioneers.* Vancouver: The Author, 1983. 217 pp. ports. Biographical stories.
[Includes 26 "stories" about pioneer Japanese Canadian immigrants, one of them, Denbei Kobayshi, being a poet (pp. 71-79).]

TANAKA, Shelley

3049   *Michi's New Year*, translated from the Japanese by Ron Berg. Toronto: PMA Books, 1980. 29 pp.
Juvenile fiction.

JEWISH

BIBLIOGRAPHIES, BIO-BIBLIOGRAPHIES

3050   BENJAMIN, Louis M.
"Some Canadian Jewish Writers." CAN JEWISH YEARB 2 (1940-44): 152-65.
[Includes the following authors: A.B. Bennett, Ida Bension, Vera Black, Maurice Eisendrath, M.Z. Frank, A.M. Klein, and Bertha Meyer.]

3051   DAVIES, Raymond Arthur
Printed Jewish Canadiana, 1685-1900: Tentative Check List of Books, Pamphlets, Pictures, Magazine and Newspaper Articles and Currency, Written by or Relating to the Jews of Canada. Montreal: L. Davies, 1955. 56 pp.
[Includes books of poetry, fiction and plays by leading Jewish Canadian authors.]

3052   DECHENE, Verona M., comp.
Literary Works by Jewish Writers in Canada in the Elizabeth Dafoe Library. Winnipeg: The University of Manitoba Libraries, 1972. 21 pp. (Reference Series No. 4).
[Includes novels, books of short stories and poems.]

3053   GOERTZ, R.O.
"University Research on Jewish-Canadians: Second Supplement." CAN ETH STUD 5, no. 1-2 (1973): 207-12.
[Some of the 89 theses contained in this list are related to Jewish-Canadian poets, e.g. Leonard Cohen, Irving Layton, A.M. Klein.]

3054   MALYCKY, Alexander; PEARLMAN, Rowena
"Jewish-Canadian Periodical Publications: First Supplement." CAN ETH STUD 2, no. 1 (1970): 131-49.
[Contains 242 references, a supplemental index of non-Hebrew, non-Yiddish titles in English with translations of Hebrew and Yiddish titles. A supplemental list of Jewish-Canadian periodical publications is also provided.]

3055   NADEL, Ira Bruce
Jewish Writers of North America. A Guide to Information Sources. Detroit: Gale, 1981. 493 pp. (The American Studies Information Guide Series, no. 8)
[Contains references to 3,291 literary publications. Several Jewish-Canadian authors are represented, with their works listed in chronological order.]

3056   PEARLMAN, Rowena
"Jewish-Canadian Creative Literature: A Preliminary Check List of Authors and Pseudonyms." CAN ETH STUD 1, no. 1 (1969): 50-53.
[Includes 64 authors with biographical data.]

3057   PEARLMAN, Rowena
"Jewish-Canadian Periodical Publications: A Preliminary Check List." CAN ETH STUD 1, no. 1 (1969): 44-49.
[A list of 38 citations. Also provides 38 non-Yiddish, non-Hebrew titles and English translations of Hebrew and Yiddish titles.]

3058   ROME, David

The Early Jewish Presence in Canada: A Book Lover's Ramble through Jewish Canadiana, introduction by J.B. Lightman. Montreal: Bronfman Collection of Jewish Canadiana, 1971. 102 leaves.
[A bio-bibliography of Jewish-Canadians between 1445-1910.]

3059　ROME, David
Jews in Canadian Literature: A Bibliography to 1964. Montreal: Canadian Jewish Congress and Jewish Public Library, 1962. 218 pp. Revised edition, 1964.
[Includes some works by early Jewish-Canadian authors.]

3060　ROME, David
Recent Jewish Authors and la language française, with preface by Joseph Kage. Montreal: Bronfman Collection of Jewish Canadiana at the Jewish Public Library, 1970. Various pagination.
[Supplement to *Jews in Canadian Literature*, rev. ed. 1964.]

3061　ROME, David
A Selected Bibliography of Jewish Canadiana. Montreal: Canadian Jewish Congress and Jewish Public Library, 1959.
[Mimeographed. Includes a list of Jewish-Canadian literary publications put out in English and Hebrew.]

BOOKS, COLLECTIONS

3062　FOX, Hayyim Leib, ed.
100 Yor Yidishe un Hebrishe Literatur in Kanade [100 Years of Yiddish and Hebrew Literature in Canada]. Montreal: H.L. Fuks Bukh Fond Komitet, 1980. 326 pp.
[Includes analytical notes on authors, excerpts from their work and biographical sketches.]

3063　GOLDKORN, Isaac
Heymishe un Fremde: Literarishe etyudn [Literary Etudes]. Buenos Aires: Sviva, 1973. 260 pp.

3064　PARIS, Erna
Jews. An Account of their Experience in Canada. Toronto: Macmillan, 1980. 304 pp.

3065　ROME, David; NEFSKY, Judith; OBERMEIR, Paule
Les Juifs du Québec. Bibliographie rétrospective annotée. Québec: IQRC, 1981. 317 pp.

3066　TEBOUL, Victor
Mythe et images du Juif au Québec. Montréal: Éds. de Legrave. 1977.

3067　WEINFELD, Morton; SHAFFIR, William; COTLER, Irwin, eds.
The Canadian Jewish Mosaic. Toronto: John Wiley and Son, 1981. 511 pp.

RESEARCH PAPERS

3068　AGES, Arnold
"Canadian Jewish Writing." CHRON REV (December 1972): 15-19.

3069　AGES, Arnold
"Canadian Jewish Writing." CONG BIWEEKLY, AMER JEWISH CONG 40 (Feb. 23, 1973): 19-22.

3070　AGES, Arnold
"David Rome on Canadian Jewish Literature." CHRON REV (November 1975): 19, 21.

3071 GOULD, Alan M.
"A Portrait of the Canadian Writer as a Young Jew: The Historical and Religious Influences in the Lives and Works of Klein, Layton, Richler and Cohen." Ph.D. Thesis, York University, 1972.

3072 HAYES, Saul
"Canadian Jewish Culture: Some Observations." QUEEN'S Q 84 (1977): 80-88.

3073 HOROWITZ, A.
"The Hebrew Language and Culture in Canada and the Jewish State." Montreal: Canadian Hebrew Cultural Organization [n.d.] 8 leaves.

3074 KAYFETZ, B.G.
"The Immigrant Reaction as Reflected in Jewish Literature." CONG BULL (1962): 4-5.

3075 KAYFETZ, B.G.
"Jewish-Canadian Literature." In *Polonia for Tomorrow*, edited by T. Kott and J.A. Wojciechowski. (Toronto: Canadian Polish Congress, 1977) pp. 226-29.

3076 KEMELMAN, Arthur
"The Montreal School of Jewish Poets." JERUS POST MAG LIT SUPPL (Aug. 28, 1970): 11

3077 LEVITAN, Seymour
"An Introduction to Canadian Yiddish Writers." In *Identifications...*, edited by Jars Balan. (Edmonton: The Canadian Institute of Ukrainian Studies, University of Alberta, 1982) pp. 116-34. [Introduces Rochl Korn as a poet.]

3078 LISTER, Rota Herzberg
"Out of the Silence: Canadian Testaments." CAN FORUM 45, no. 753 (1985): 30-34. [The importance of writing about the holocaust is emphasized.]

3079 MANDEL, Eli
"Ethnic Voices in Canadian Writing." In his *Another Time*. (Erin, Ont.: Press Porcépic, 1977) pp. 91-102. [Analyses the problem of identity in ethnic literature. The focus is on Mordecai Richler, Leonard Cohen and Irving Layton.]

3080 MELAMET, Max
"The Anglo-Jewish Press." VIEWPOINTS IV, 4 (1969-70): 50-57.

3081 NADEL, Ira Bruce
"The Absent Prophet in Canadian Jewish Fiction." ENG Q 5 (1972): 83-92. [A study of A.M. Klein: *The Second Scroll* and Mordecai Richler: *St. Urbain's Horseman*.]

3082 ORENSTEIN, Eugene V.
"Publications in Other Languages." UNIV TOR Q 47 (1977-78): 501-03. [A review of Rochl Korn, M.M. Shaffir and Sholem Shtern, all writing in Yiddish.]

3083 ORENSTEIN, Eugene V.
"Publications in Yiddish." UNIV TOR Q 46 (1976-77): 500-06. [A critical appraisal of Jewish-Canadian writing in Yiddish.]

3084 ORENSTEIN, Eugene V.

"Yiddish Culture in Canada: Yesterday and Today." In his *The Canadian Jewish Mosaic*. (Toronto: John Wiley, 1981) pp. 293-313.
[Provides an analysis of the work of J.I. Segal, Sholem Shtern, Melech Ravitch, and Rochl Korn.]

3085 RABINOVITCH, Israel
"Yiddish Theatre in Canada." In *Canadian Jewish Yearbook*. (Montreal: Canadian Jewish Yearbook Registered 1940-41) vol. 2, pp. 166-71.
[An historical summary of Jewish theatre life in Canada.]

3086 RABINOVITCH, Israel
"Yiddishe Literatur un Literarishe Tetikeitn in Kanada [Yiddish Literature and Literary Activities in Canada]. KEN ADL (Oct. 30-Nov. 6, 1950)

3087 ROME, David
"Literature of Jewish Canadiana." JEWISH BOOK ANN 18 (1960): 44-53.

3088 ROME, David
"The Remarkable Literature of Canadian Jews." JEWISH CULT AFFAIRS, WORLD JEWISH CONG 14: 4.

3089 SACK, Benjamin G.
"Literature." In his *History of the Jews in Canada from the Earliest Beginnings to the Present Day*. (Montreal: Canadian Jewish Congress, 1945) pp. 116, 225.
[The author traces the first Canadian literary work of Jewish authorship to Toronto in 1844, a review article on William Miller's teachings and chronology. Authors discussed are Abraham de Sola, Gerald E. Hart, and Jules Helbroner. None of them were creative writers in the true sense.]

3090 SHAFFIR-SCHACTER, M.M.
"Literarishe Groosn foon Roomanye" [Literary Greetings from Romania]. KEN ADL (Jan. 2, 1960)

3091 SHAFFIR-SCHACTER, M.M.
"Vegn Shprach Inyonim" [On Matters of Language]. OIFN SHVEL (May-June 1968)

3092 STEINBERG, M.W.
"Jewish Canadiana." CAN LIT 23 (1965): 80.
[Review of David Rome's compilations of and books on Jewish-Canadian literature.]

3093 WADDINGTON, Miriam
"Yiddish Literature." In *The Oxford Companion to Canadian Literature*, edited by William Toye. (Toronto: Oxford University Press, 1983) pp. 840-41.
[Individual authors described include Yakov Segal, Esther Segal, Ada Maze, Shlomo Weissman, Melech Ravitch, Chaveh Rosenfarb, Rochl Korn, etc.]

3094 WEINFELD, Morton; SHAFFIR, William; COTLER, Irwin
"Jewish Culture and Canadian Culture: An Interview with Ruth Wisse, Mervin Butovsky, Howard Roiter. In *The Canadian Jewish Mosaic*. (Toronto: John Wiley, 1981) pp. 315-42.
[Contents: Defining Jewish culture; The Immigrants and Canadian culture; Varieties of Canadian Jewish cultures; The shaping of modern Jewish society; The Canadian Jew in French and English; Jewish culture - past, present and future; Intellectual life and ideology. Individual authors referred to: Mordecai Richler, A.M. Klein, Adele Wiseman, Seymour Mayne, Saul Bellow, Naïm Kattan, Leonard Cohen.]

ANTHOLOGIES

3095   *Canadian Jewish Anthology, English, French, Yiddish/Anthologie juive du Canada, anglais, français, yiddish*, edited by Chaim Spilberg and Yaacov Zipper. Montreal: National Committee on Yiddish-Canadian Jewish Congress, 1982.
[The English section contains papers on the Canadian Jewish Congress and the Montreal Jewish community, and an interview with Irving Layton. The French section includes a drama, *Jacob et Esaú* by Naïm Kattan, and poems by Rochl Korn, Melech Ravitch, J.I. Segal and Sholom Shtern. The Yiddish section of 500 pages includes writings by the above authors. Biographical notes are provided throughout the volume.]

3096   *Canadian Yiddish Writings*, edited by Abraham Boyarsky and Lazar Sarna. Montreal: Harvest House, 1976. 149 pp.
[Includes poems and short stories by Yaacov Zipper, Chava Rosenfarb, Rochl Korn, J.I. Segal, Melech Ravitch, and Sholom Shtern. Biographical notes are given.]

3097   *Essential Words: An Anthology of Jewish Canadian Poetry*, edited by Moyshe Abraham. Ottawa: Oberon, 1985. 182 pp.
[A collection of poems selected from the work of 34 authors including George Jonas, A.M. Klein, Irving Layton and others.]

3098   *Kanadish, the Yiddish Literature of Canada*, edited by Samuel Rollansky. Buenos Aires: Ateneo Literario en el Iwo, 1974. 448 pp. (Masterworks of Yiddish Literature, vol. 62)
[Includes excerpts from the works of Canadian Jewish authors writing in Yiddish.]

3099   *Le miroir d'un peuple: anthologie de la poésie Yidich 1870-1970*, textes choisis traduits et presentes par Charles Dobzynsky. Paris: Gallimard, 1971. 529 pp.
[Includes poems by Melech Ravitch, J.I. Segal, Rochl Korn, Sholom Shtern, etc.]

3100   *Mirror of a People: Canadian Jewish Experience in Poetry and Prose*, edited by Sheldom Oberman and Elaine Newton. Winnipeg: Jewish Educational Publishers of Canada, 1985. 250 pp.
[Represents thirty authors, four of them: Rochl Korn, Henry Kreisel, Irving Layton and J.I. Segal, of ethnic origin.]

3101   *Pinkes Tishevits [Tiszowic-Book]*, edited by Jaacov Zipper. Tel Aviv: Organization of Tiszowic Exiles in Israel, 1970. 326 pp.
[A memorial collection dedicated to the victims of the holocaust: Tiszowic, Lublin, Poland. Includes poems by Jewish-Canadian poets.]

3102   *The Spice Box: An Anthology of Jewish Canadian Writing*, selected by Gerri Sinclair and Morris Wolfe. Toronto: Lester & Orpen, Dennys, 1981. 310 pp.
[Represents 36 authors, six of minority literature: Solomon Ary, Abraham Boyarsky, A.M. Klein, Henry Kreisel, J.I. Segal, and Helen Weinzweg.]

3103   Yidishe Dikhter in Kanade [Yiddish Poets in Canada], edited by H.M. Caiserman-Vital. Montreal, 1934. 221 pp.
[Includes poems by J.I. Segal, A. Sh. Shkolnokoff, E. Segal, Ida Massey, G. Pomerantz, S. Pearl, J.L. Zlotnik, Sholem Shtern, H. Edelstein, A.M. Klein, A. Katzenelenbogen, and M. Erdberg-Shatan.]

INDIVIDUAL AUTHORS

BLACK, Vera

3104   *Poems*. Montreal: Twentieth Century Impress, 1954. 47 pp. Poems.

3105   *Poems.* Montreal: The Author, 1956. 40 pp. Poems.

BOYARSKY, Abraham (1946-   )
Born in Poland and came to Canada in 1951. He grew up in Montreal. Published a collection of short stories and a novel. Boyarsky is professor of mathematics at Concordia University in Montreal.

3106   *A Pyramid of Time.* Erin, Ont.: Porkupine's Quill, 1978. Short stories.

3107   Shreiber. Novel.

ELBERG, Jehude (1912-   )
Born in Poland, ordained a Rabbi there. Educated in textile engineering. Participated in the Warsaw-ghetto underground movement. Came to Canada via the U.S. in 1956. His writings depict life in Jewish ghettos in Poland. Received several literary prizes (the I.I. Segal, the Mangel and the Wisenger prize).

3108   *Unter kuperne himlen: Dertseilunge [Under Copper Skies].* Buenos Aires: Unión Central Israelita Polaca en la Argentina, 1951. 252 pp. Short stories.
        [These stories are about ghetto life in Warsaw.]

3109   *Oyfn shpits fun a mast: Roman [On Top of a Mast: Novel].* New York: Shulsinger Brothers, 1974.
        393 pp. Novel.
        [Describes the Jews' attempt to escape the "final solution".]

3110   *Tzevorfenne zangen [Scattered Stalks].* Montreal: Shula Publications, 1976. 356 pp. Novelettes, stories.

3111   *Belev Yam.* Tel Aviv: Eked, 1978.

3112   *Be-lev yam: Roman.* New York: Shlusinger, 1979. 339 pp. Novel.

3113   *Mayses.* Tel Aviv: Farlag Y.L. Perets, 1980. 159 pp.

3114   *Tales.* Tel Aviv: World Council for Jewish Culture, 1980. Tales.

3115   *Kalman Kali kes imperye [The Empire of Kalman the Cripple.].* Tel Aviv: Farlag Yisroel Buh, 1983. 417 pp. Novel.

3116   *In leimene hayzer: Roman [In Clay Houses.: Novel]* Tel Aviv: Israel Book, 1985. Stories.

FOX, Chaim Laib (1897-   )

3117   *Sho fum lid [The Hour of Poesie].* Paris: Pen Club, 1951. 136 pp. Poems.

3118   *Die teg neigen die kep [The Days Bow their Heads].* New York: Cyco, 1969. 96 pp. Poems.

3119   *Zunfergang [Sundown].* Haifa: Yiddish Writers' Press, 1972. 72 pp. Poems.

3120   *Der achter himmel [The Eighth Heaven].* New York: Cyco, 1975. 128 pp. Poems.

GOLDKORN, Isaac (1911-   )
Critic, poet, essayist. Born in Szydlowiec, Poland, came to Canada after World War II. He was awarded the 1976 Jacob Glatstein Prize by the World Congress for Jewish Culture in New York. Former writer and book reviewer for *Daily Forward*, a Jewish weekly. He lives in Willowdale, Ont.

3121 *Epigramatish [Epigrams]*. Montreal: City Printing, 1954. 83 pp. Poems.

3122 *Fun welt-kwal [On the Pain of the World]*. Tel Aviv, 1963. 280 pp. Prose.

3123 *Mesholim [Fables]*. New York: Farlag Eygns, 1975. 89 pp. Stories.

3124 *Yellow Letters, Green Memories*. Cornwall, Ont.: Vesta, 1979. 79 pp. Poems.

3125 *Kurtz un sharf: Epigram [Brief and Trenchant: Epigrams]*. Toronto, 1981. 80 pp. Poems.

3126 *Letzter shnitt [Last Harvest]*. 1984. Novel.

GOTLIB, Noah Isaac (1900-1967)

3127 *Mine land, mine liedershe [My Land, My Songs]*. Montreal: Eagle Publishing Co., 1958. 220 pp. Poems.

3128 *Zechstik*. Montreal: Old Rose Print, 1965. 276 pp. Poems.
[Includes some essays on Gotlib.]

3129 *Montreal [Montreal]*. Montreal: The Author's Book Committee, 1968. 224 pp. Poems.

Writing about:

3130 Shaffir-Schacter, M.M. "Vegn N.I. Gotlib's *Mine land, mine liedershe*" [On N.I. Gotlib's *My Land, My Songs]*. KEN ADL (Apr. 21, 1958)

HUSID, Mordecai (1909-   )

3131 *Doyres shrayen mich ariber [The Sorrows of the Generation Exceed My Cry]*. Montreal, 1969. 141 pp. Poems.

3132 *A shotn trogt mayn kroyn [A Shadow Wears My Crown]*. Montreal: M. Husid Book Fund, 1975. 149 pp. Poems.

3133 *Shtoyb un eybikeyt [Dust and Eternity]*. Montreal: Adler Printing and Lithographing, 1981. 153 pp. Poems.

Writing about:

3134 Dunsky, Shimshon. "Mordecai Husid: Poet of His People." VIEWPOINTS 4, no. 4 (1969-70): 46-48.
[Excerpts from an essay read at an assembly at which the poet was honoured with the Dvora and Hirsch Rosenfeld literary award of the J.I. Segal Fund.]

KORN, Rochl (i.e. Rachel) (1898-1982)
Born in Poland, she lived in Uzbekistan, U.S.S.R. In 1948 she came to Canada via Sweden. Her poems have appeared in periodicals in the U.S.A., Israel, Canada, and Europe. She was awarded a number of literary prizes for her contributions to Yiddish literature. Published several books of poetry before she came to Canada including *Erd [Earth*, 1935], *Roiter mon [Red Poppies*, 1937], and *Shnitt [Harvest*, 1941].

3135 *Haym un haymlozikeit [Home and Homelessness]*. Montreal, 1948. Poems.

3136 *Bashertkeit [Fatedness]*. Montreal, 1949. 116 pp. Poems.

3137   *9 erzehlungen [9 Stories].* Montreal, 1957. 326 pp. illus. Short stories.

3138   *Fun yener zeit lied [From beyond Poetry].* Montreal, 1962. Poems.

3139   *Lider un erd/Shirim V'odomeh [Songs of the Homeland],* with facing Hebrew translation by Shimshon Meltzer. Tel Aviv: Farlag Hamenorah, 1966. 103 pp. illus. Poems.

3140   *Die gnod fun vort [The Grace of Words].* Tel Aviv: Hamenorah, 1968. 94 pp. Poems.

3141   *Oyf der sharf fun a rege [In the Flash of an Instant].* Tel Aviv: Hamenorah Publishers, 1972. 111 pp. Poems.

3142   *Farbittene vor, lider [Transformed Reality, Songs].* Tel Aviv: Farlag Yisroel-Bukh, 1977. 92 pp. Poems.

3143   *Generations: Selected Poems,* translated from the Yiddish by Seymour Mayne. Oakville, Ont.: Mosaic Press, 1982. 60 pp. Poems.

3144   *Paper Roses,* bilingual with translations from the Yiddish by Seymour Levitan. Toronto: Aya Press, 1985. 115 pp. Poems.

Writings about:

3145   Fagan, Cary. Review of *Paper Roses.* BKS CAN 15, no. 3 (1986): 27.

3146   Hlus, Carolyn. Review of *Paper Roses.* CAN BOOK REV ANN 1985: 183-84.

3147   Waddington, Miriam. "Rahel Korn." In *The Oxford Companion to Canadian Literature,* edited by William Toye. (Toronto: Oxford University Press, 1983) pp. 416-17.

KWINTA, Chava

3148   *I'm still Living.* Toronto: Simon and Pierre, 1974. 279 pp. Autobiography.

Writing about:

3149   Blumstock, Robert. Review of *I'm still Living.* CAN ETH STUD 9, no. 2 (1977): 149-50.

MASSEY, Ida (i.e. MAZE, Ida) (1893-1962)

3150   *Vaksn meine kinderlech, mutter und kinder-lieder [My Children Grow, Songs of Mother and Children].* Montreal: City Printing Co., 1954. 201 pp. Poems.

3151   *Den ah; Autobiographical Novel.* Montreal: Northern Printing and Lithographing Co., 1970. 269 pp. Novel in Yiddish.

MILLER, Max

3152   *Fun shturm [Of the Storm].* Edmonton, 1936. 68 pp. Poems.

3153   *Fun'm Yiddischn kval [Gist of the Yiddish Jest],* with an introduction by Rabbi Zlotnik. Winnipeg: Israelite Press, 1937. 306 pp. Short stories, narratives.

MIRANSKY, Peretz

3154   *A likht far a groshn [Candle for a Penny].* Montreal: The Author, 1951. 107 pp. Poems.
[Includes some fables of his pre-war Vilna Period and poems written during World Warr II.]

3155   *Shures shire [Lines of Song].* Tel Aviv: I.L. Peretz Pub. House, 1974. 250 pp. Elegiac lyrics and fables.

3156   *Tsvishn shmeykhl un trer: Mesholim [Between Smile and Tears: Poems].* Toronto: The Author, 1979. 177 pp. Poems.

Writing about:

3157   "Peretz Miransky of Toronto Wins Yiddish Literature Prize." CAN JEWISH NEWS 28, no. 49. (1988): 5.

RAVITCH, Melech, pseud. (Real name: BERGNER, Zekharye Kohne) (1893-1976)
Born in Radymno, Poland. Published his first volume of poetry in 1912. He was co-founder in Warsaw of the Yiddish section of the International PEN Club. Came to Canada in 1931. Some of his early publications include *Oif der shwel [On the Threshold,* 1912], *Ruinengroz [The Wilted Grass,* 1917], *Shpinoza [Spinoza,* 1918], *Nakete lider [Naked Songs,* 1921], *Der keren fun ale meine lider [The Spiritual Joy of All My Poems,* 1922], Blut oif der fon [Blood on the Banner, 1929].

3158   *Lider un baladn fun di letzte drei-fir yor [Poems and Ballads for the Last Three-Four Years].* Mexico, 1940. 112 pp. Poems.

3159   *67 lider [67 Poems].* Buenos Aires: Unión Central Israelita Polaca en la Argentina, 1946. 164 pp. Poems.

3160   *Di kroinung fun a yungn Yiddishn dichter in Amerike [The Crowning of a Young Yiddish Poet in America.].* New York, 1953. 71 pp. Poem.

3161   *Di lider fun mayne lider [The Songs of My Songs].* Montreal: M. Ravitch Book Committee at the Jewish Public Library, 1954. 448 pp. illus.
[An anthology of poems selected from the poet's earlier collections.]

3162   *Dos ma'aseh-buch fun mein leben, 1908-1921 [The Deed-book of My Life, 1908-1921].* Buenos Aires: Unión Central Israelita Polaca en la Argentina, 1964. Vol. 1: 387 pp. Vol. 2, 1964: 525 pp. Vol. 3: Tel Aviv: I.L. Peretz Pub. House, 1975: 442 pp.

3163   *Chamishim shirim [Fifty Poems],* translated from the Yiddish into Hebrew by A.D. Shafir. Tel Aviv: Shirim, 1969. 159 pp. Poems.

3164   *Ikar shochahti, 1954-1969 [I Forgot the Main Theme, 1954-1969],* drawings by Audrey and Yosl Bergner. Montreal: M. Ravitch Book Committee at the Jewish Public Library, 1969. 170 pp. Poems.

3165   *Sefer hamasiot shel chayai [The Story-book of My Life],* translated from Yiddish into Hebrew by Moshe Youngman. Tel Aviv: American Israel Publishing Company, 1976. 564 pp. Poems.
[Hebrew translation of the original Yiddish version in three volumes.]

Writings about:

3166 Honig, Camille. "Melech Ravitch - The Poet with a Jewish Mission; Reflections upon a Tragic Theme." CALIF JEWISH VOICE (March 15, 1954)

3167 Horn, I. "Por los caminos del mundo; A proposito de la visita del poeta Malej Ravitch" [By the Roads of the World; Regarding the visit of the Poet Melech Ravitch.] JUDAICA (December 1937): 258-61.

3168 Kanfer, M. "Krew na szdandarze" [Blood on the Flag: Standard]. NOWY DZIEN (May 4, 1931.]

3169 Kreitzer, Samuel. "One's Jewish Thoughts in the Twentieth Century." CONG WEEKLY (Dec. 18, 1950)

3170 Levy, Robert. "Malej Ravitch" [Melech Ravitch]. MUND ISR (Nov. 13, 1937)

3171 Lew, S. "Les tendences naturiennes dans la littérature etrangère." NEO-NATURIEN (mai-juin 1922)

3172 Lewenstein, I. "Poezja globtrottera" [A Globe-trotter's Poems]. NOWY GŁOS (1938)

3173 Mark, Yudel. "Yiddish Literature." In The Jews: Their History, Culture and Religion. (New York, 1949) p. 893.

3174 "Melech Ravitch's Author's Evening." AUST JEWISH HER (March 11, 1937)

3175 Milabauer, Joseph. "Melech Ravitch." In Poétes Yidich d'aujour'hui. (sept. 15, 1936): 71-72.

3176 Patkin, A. "The Religious Motives in Melech Ravitch's Poetry." AUST JEWISH FOR No. 5 (1941): 19-24.

3177 Pomer, Stefan. "Poeta Zydowski wedruje przez Kontinenty i Oceany" [Jewish Poet Wanders through Continents and Oceans]. RANO (Nov. 14, 1937)

3178 Resnick, Solomon. "Las letras Judias despues de la Gran Guerra." In La Poesia. Esquema de la literatura Judia. (Buenos Aires, 1933) p. 141.

3179 Roback, A.A. "Yiddish Literature." In The Story of Yiddish Literature. (New York: Yiddish Scientific Institute, 1940) p. 347.

3180 Roback, A.A. "Yiddish Poetry. Curiosities of Yiddish Literature." In Syllabus of Yiddish Literature. (Cambridge, Mass.: Sci-Art Publishers, 1933) p. 186.

3181 Shaffir-Schacter, M.M. "Melech Ravitches Dos ma'aseh-buch fun mein leben' [Melech Ravitch's Deed Book of My Life]. OIFN SHVEL (September 1968)

3182 Shaffir-Schacter, M.M. "Vegn Melech Ravitches Ikar shochahti" [On Melech Ravitch's I Forgot the Main Theme]. ZUKUNFT (July-August 1971)

3183 Tremblay, Jean-Noël. "Homage au poète Yiddish, Melech Ravitch." Montréal: Bibliothèque Juive Publique de Montréal, 1969. [6] pp.

3184 Trunk, J.J. "Portrait of a Hebraist." COMMENTARY (1949): 477-78.

ROGEL, Joseph

3185 *Auschwitz, lieder [Auschwitz, Poems].* Montreal: City Printing Co., 1951. 94 pp. Poems.

3186 *Confessions of an Auschwitz Number.* Montreal, 1972. Poems.

3187 *Poems for My Mother,* illustrated by Sylvia Ary. Montreal: Concordia University, 1975. 91 pp. Poems.

3188 *Poèmes pour ma mère,* traduit de l'anglais et revise par Olivier Gianolta et Guy Maheux. Montréal: La société de belles-lettres Guy Maheux Inc., 1977. 64 pp. port. Poèmes.

Writings about:

3189 Ages, Arnold. "David Rome on Canadian Jewish Literature." CHRON REV (November 1975) [Reference is made to Rogel's poetry.]

3190 Callaghan, Eleanor. "Poems Help Joseph Survive Life's Terror." MONT STAR (March 17, 1978) B: 6.

3191 Fitzgerald, John. "A Lifelong Dream Realized." GAZETTE (March 6, 1976)

3192 Keeping, Patricia. "People on Parade: Joseph Rogel - From Pain to Poetry." INFORMER 5, no. 1 (1976): 4.

3193 Kerby, Jill. "Joseph Rogel: 'My Poetry Kept Me Alive'." LOYOLA NEWS (Oct. 12, 1973): 5.

3194 Lowe, Patricia. " 'Auschwitz Strengthened My Belief in God,' Says Prize-winning Poet and Author." MONT STAR (Apr. 13, 1976) C: 4.

3195 Morantz, Alan. "Gorges of Hell-fences of Death." Snowdon Press (Dec. 15, 1976): 3.

3196 Parnass, Paul. "The Holocaust Shapes Poetry." CONG BULL (September 1975): 10.

3197 Purdy, Patricia. "Joseph Rogel: A PLANT Profile." PLANT (Oct. 29, 1976): 9.

3198 Solway, Diane. "His Death-camp Legacy is Poetry, not Hatred." SUNDAY SUN (Toronto) (Jul. 30, 1978)

ROSENFARB, Chava (1923-   )
Poet, novelist, playwright. Born in Lodz, Poland, spent his childhood in the Lodz Ghetto and Auschwitz, Sasel and Bergen-Belsen concentration camps. Came to Canada after the war, educated at the Jewish Teachers' Seminary, Montreal. Received Segal Prize (1972), Nieger Prize (Argentina, 1972), Manger Prize (Tel Aviv, 1979), Atran Prize (New York, 1985).

3199 *Di balade fun nekhtikn vald un andere lider [The Ballad of Yesterday's Forest-ghetto and other Poems].* Montreal: H. Hershman, 1948. 102 pp. Poems.

3200 *Der foygl foon geto [The Bird of the Ghetto].* Montreal, 1958. Play.
[About Itsik Wittenberg, commander of the United Partisan Organization of the Vilna Ghetto. Produced by the Israeli National Theatre Habimah, 1965.]

3201 *Der boym fun lebn [The Tree of Life].* Tel Aviv: Hamenorah Publishers, 1972. 3 vols. Novel.

3202 *Eytz hachaim [The Tree of Life].* Tel Aviv, 1980. Novel.
[Translation into Hebrew of *Der boym fun lebn.*]

3203   *Bociany [Bociany].* Tel Aviv, 1983. Novel.

Writing about:

3204   Shaffir-Schachter, M.M. Review of *Der foygl foon ghetto.* KEN ADL (Nov. 24, 1958)

SEGAL, J.I.   (1896-1954)
Born in Ukraine, came to Montreal in 1911 and remained there until his death. He worked as a tailor but later became a teacher in the Jewish Day Schools. He wrote some poems in Russian and Hebrew, but the bulk of his work was written in Yiddish.

3205   *Fun mayn velt [From My World]* . Montreal: "Montreal," 1918. 67 pp. Poems.

3206   *[House of the Humble.]* Montreal, 1940. 383 pp. Poems.

3207   *Seyfer Yidish [Book of Yiddish].* Montreal: Northern Printing and Stationery Co., 1950. 584 pp. Poems.

3208   *Lider un loybn [Poems and Praises].* Montreal: J.I. Singer Committee, 1974. 507 pp. Poems.

3209   *Letste lider [Last Poems].* Montreal: J.I. Segal Foundation, 1975. 332 pp. Poems.

Writing about:

3210   Shaffir-Schacter, M.M. "J.I. Segal un mir" [J.I. Segal and We]. KEN ADL (June 12, 1955)

SELCHEN, S.M.

3211   *Agav-urcha [By the Way].* Winnipeg: Israelite Press, 1948. 291 pp. Stories.

SHAFFIR-SCHACTER, Moyshe Mordechai (1909-   )

3212   *A steshke [A Path].* Montreal: Old Rose Printing, 1940. 192 pp. Poems.

3213   *Ikh koom ahaym [Homecoming].* Montreal: Northern Printing and Lithographing Co., 1963. 210 pp. Poems.

3214   *Oif maynt feedele leed [On My Fiddle Song].* Montreal: Northern Printing and Lithographing Co., 1966. 80 pp. Poems.

3215   *Der Shtern-vogn [The Dipper].* Montreal: Northern Printing and Lithographing Co., 1968. 80 pp. Poems.

3216   *A regge dakhtenish [A Moment of Fantasy].* Montreal: Northern Printing and Lithographing Co., 1969. 69 pp. Poems.

3217   *Boiray meenay khalymes [Creator of Dreams].* Montreal: Northern Printing and Lithographing Co., 1971. 111 pp. Poems.

3218   *Mit der leeder-torbe [With My Songbag].* Montreal: Northern Printing and Lithographing Co., 1973. 111 pp. Poems.

3219   *In maynt gefalnkeyt [In My Distress].* New York: Shulsinger, 1975. 110 pp. Poems

3220 *Mit tzoogenaygte rayd [Words of Engagement]*. New York: Shulsinger, 1977. 106 pp. Poems.

3221 *De flayt foon maynt bayner [The Flute of My Bones]*. Montreal: Canadian Eagle Publishing, 1978. 96 pp. Poems.

3222 *Di lipn fun maynt troyer [The Lips of My Sadness]*. Montreal: The Author, 1979. 105 pp. Poems.

3223 *Fir eyln elntkeyt [Four Ells of Solitude: Poems]*. Montreal: The Author, 1980. 103 pp. Poems.

3224 *A rege ru gefinen [To Find a Moment of Rest: Poems]*. Montreal: The Author, 1981. 118 pp. Poems.

Writings about:

3225 Bayon, L. "In geist foon doiresdiker sheferishkayt" [In the Spirit of Generations' Creativity]. OIFN SHVEL (January-February 1969)
[Review of *Der Shtern-vogn.*]

3226 Berkovitch, B. "Portret foon a yungn dikter" [Portrait of a Young Writer]. KEN ADL (December 1945)

3227 Bikel, Shloyme. "Foon sentimentalism tzoo hartzikayt" [From Sentimentalism to Deep Feelings]. ZUKUNFT (December 1973)
[Review of *Ikh koom ahaym.*]

3228 Botoshansky, Y. "M.M. Shaffir - Folks dikter un abisl hecher" [M.M. Shaffir - Folk Writer and a Little More]. Di PRESSE (June 1963)

3229 Emyot, Y. "Poet mit shtarke folks-aktzentn" [A Poet with Strong Folk Accents]. JEWISH DAILY FORW (Aug. 22, 1971)
[Review of *Boiray meenay khalymes.*]

3230 Frankel, B. Review of *Ikh koom ahaym.* UNZER SHTIMEH (January 1964)

3231 Gladstone, J. "Zamlung leeder foon M.M. Shaffir" [M.M. Shaffir's Book of Poems]. DAY (June 1963)
[Review of *Ikh koom ahaym.*]

3232 Gotlib, Noah Isaac. "Dee ershteh trit foon a yungn dikter" [A Young Writer's First Steps]. KEN ADL (September 1940)

3233 Haas, M. "Der dikter M.M. Shaffir" [M.M. Shaffir - the Poet]. JEÜD RUND MACC (Aug. 13, (1971)

3234 Hacken, Vera. "M.M. Shaffir's Poetry." OIFN SHVEL (May-July 1974)

3235 Kantz, S. "Der koiach un kishuf tzu redn foon hartz tzu hartz" [The Magic Force of Poetry]. LAST NEWS (July 23,1971)

3236 Marmor, K. "Nayeh leeder" [New Poems]. MORG FREIH (Aug. 25, 1940)
[Review of *A steshke.*]

3237 Newman, B.G. "Moyshe Shaffir, Poet." JEWISH STAND (April 1967)

3238 Panner, Y. "Der Bukoveener in der fremd - Vegn dee leeder foon M.M. Shaffir" [The Bukovinian Poet in a Strange Land - The Poetry of M.M. Shaffir]. GOLD KEYT 69/70 (1979-70): 313-16.

3239 Ravitch, Melech. "A chaverish vort tzoom dersheinem foon M.M. Shaffir's *Oif maynt feedele leed*" [A Friendly Word about M.M. Shaffir's *On My Fiddle Song*]. KEN ADL (Dec. 25, 1966)

3240 Ravitch, Melech. "Koyl demomo dakko - a kol foon 'Shtilkayt' [A Voice of Silence - on the Poem 'Strings']. KEN ADL (Nov. 22, 1968)

3241 Sack, B.G. "Shaffir als poet" [Shaffir as a Poet]. KEN ADL (May 12, 1963)

3242 Shtern, I. "M.M. Shaffir's *Der Shtern-vogn*" [M.M. Shaffir's *The Dipper*]. KEN ADL (March 7, 1969)

3243 Zvi, Ben. "Nayeh beecher" [New Books]. UNZER AIGN VINKL (June 1971)
[Review of *Boiray meenay khalymes*.]

SHTERN, Sholem (1907-   )
Born in Poland, came to Montreal in 1927. His essays on Jewish culture and literature have appeared in Jewish publications throughout the world.

3244 *Es lichtikt [The Light Goes Up]*. Montreal: The Author, 1941. 171 pp. Poems.

3245 *In der free [In the Morning]*. Montreal: Kanader Vohenblatt Pub., 1945. 286 pp. Poems.

3246 *In Kanade [In Canada]*. Montreal: S. Shtern Book Committee, 1960-1963. 2 v. 480 pp., 232 pp. respectively. Epic novel in verse.

3247 *Dos vayse hoyz [The White House]*. New York: ICUF, 1967. 284 pp. Autobiographical verse-novel.

3248 *The White House: A Novel in Verse*, translated from the Yiddish and with a foreword by Max Rosenfeld. Montreal: Wardbrook Publishers, 1974. 202 pp. Verse novel.
[English version of *Dos vayse hoyz*. Same work was translated into French by Guy Maheux.]

3249 *Di mishpoke in Kanade un dos hoyzgezind fun Profesor Sidni Goldstin [The Family in Canada and the Household of Professor Sidney Goldstein]*. Montreal: Northern Printing and Lithographing Co., 1975. 333 pp. Novel.

Writings about:

3250 "It's a Jewish Love Story, but Better!" CONG BULL (March 1975)

3251 Levy, Stephen. "A Novel in Verse." JEWISH CURR (November 1976)
[Review of *The White House*.]

3252 Liptzin, Sol. "Poet Radiates Compassion for Fellow Men." CAN JEWISH OUTL (July-August 1976)

3253 Matenko, Percy. Review of *The White House*. JEWISH FRONT (February 1976)

3254 "Sholem Shtern." In *Yiddish Literature, 1933-1961*. (New York: Institute of Jewish Affairs, World Congress, 1962)

3255   Slomon, M.M. "*The White House: A Saga by Sholem Shtern.*" CAN ZION (April 1975)

3256   Weiss, David. "*The White House* - Viewpoints." CAN JEWISH Q 9, no. 2 (1975): 2.

3257   Zatz, S.R. Review of *The White House*. MONT JEWISH LIFE (1975-76)

TREPMAN, Paul (1916-   )

3258   *A gesl in Varshau [An Alley in Warsaw].* Montreal: Northern Printing and Stationery, 1951. 132 pp. Novel.

WOLOFSKY, H.   (1878-1949)

3259   *Journey of My Life.* Montreal: Eagle Publishing Co., 1945. 183 pp. Autobiography.

3260   *Mein lebens-reise [Journey of My Life].* Montreal: Eagle Publishing Co., 1946. 265 pp. [Yiddish version of *Journey of My Life*.]

YAIR, Ish, pseud. (Real name: SHTERN, Israel) (1914-   )

3261   *Out of the Burning Bush.* Rome: Centro Studi e Scambi Internazionali, Accademia Internazionale Leonardo da Vinci, 1968. 16 pp. Poems.

3262   *Wayehi biyemey... [It Came to Pass in the Days...].* Montreal: The Author, 1975. 176 pp. Poems. [Includes 75 Yiddish poems and a major poem in for parts, and three poems in Hebrew.]

Writings about:

3263   Baraban, Abraham. Review of *Pinkes tishevits*. YIDD TSAY (1971)

3264   Emyot, Yisroel. "Lider fun Ish Yair." [The Poetry of Ish Yair]. FORVERTS (Apr. 19, 1976)

3265   Green, Ber. "Der khurbn fun a shtetl" [The Devastation of the Town]. MORG FREIH (Dec. 26, 1971) [Review of *Pinkes tishevits*.]

3266   Luden, Yosef. "Bikher un shrayber" [Books and Authors]. PROBLEMEN No. 90 (May-June 1976): 7. [Review of *Wayehi biyemey*.]

3267   Rabinovitch, J. "In undzer Montreal" [In Our Montreal]. KEN ADL 62, no. 6 (1969): 3.

3268   Sadan, Dov. "Beyn te leyayin" [Between Tea and Wine]. MAARIV (Sept. 24, 1974): 37.

3269   Sherman, Yosef. "Protest kegn retsenzye" [A Protest against a Review]. FORVERTS (May 9, 1976) [On *Wayehi biyemey*.]

3270   Shimon, K. "Nayeh bikher - bibliografish - kristishe notisn" [New Books - Bibliographical - Critical Notes]. LETS NAY (Apr. 16, 176) [Review of *Wayehi biyemey*.]

3271　Shtok, Tsvi. "A gevagter farzukh fun Ish Yair (Dr. Yisroel Shtern" [A Daring Adventure by Ish Yair (Dr. Israel Shtern]. BNAI YIDDISH No. 42 (March-April 1976): 12-15.

3272　Tencer, L. Review of *Vayehi biyemey*. KEN ADL 70, no. 30 (Oct. 14, 1977): 9; no. 31 (Oct. 21, 1977): 10.

3273　Wind, Bernard. "Ish Yair's *Wayehi biyemey* " [Ish Yair's *It Came to Pass in the Days...*]. NAY YIDD VORT 66, no. 15 (1976): 1-2.

ZIPPER, Yaacov (1900-　)

Born in Tiszowce, Poland, where he taught in secularist schools. In 1925 he emigrated to Canada and served as principal of the Yiddish Peretz School in Winnipeg. He moved to Montreal in 1971.

3274　*Oyf yener zayt Bug [On the other Side of the River Bug]*. Montreal: J. Zipper Book Committee, 1946. 273 pp. Semi-autobiographical novel.

3275　*Tsvishn taykhn un vasern [Amidst Lakes and Waters]*. Montreal: Northern Printing and Lithographing Co., 1960. 428 pp. Novel.

3276　*Ch'bin vieder in mein chorever heim gekumen [And I Came again to My Devastated Homeland]*. Montreal: Northern Printing and Lithographing Co., 1965. 80 pp. Poem.
[Poetic elegy about the holocaust.]

3277　*Bein neharot u'nechalim [Amidst Rivers and Streams]*. Tel Aviv: Hamenora Publishing House, 1967. 352 pp. Short stories.

3278　*Be-ohole Avraham mi-sipurei bereshit [In Abraham's Tents]*. Tel Aviv: Hofsa at Milo, 1974. 115 pp. Bible stories.
[Also published in Yiddish under the title *In die getzeltn fun Avrohom*.]

3279　*Fun nechtn un heint [Of Yesterdays and Todays]*. Montreal: J. Zipper Book Committee, 1974. 352 pp. Autobiography.
[Reprinted in 1978, 347 pp.]

3280　*In die getzeltn fun Avrohom [In Abraham's Tents]*. Montreal: J. Zipper Book Committee, 1974. 156 pp. Autobiography.

3281　*The Far Side of the River: Selected Short Stories*, translated and edited by Mervin Butovsky and Ode Garfinkle. Oakville, Ont.: Mosaic Press, 1985. 101 pp. Short stories.

Writings about:

3282　Auerbach, Ephraim. "Dos shtetl is der held" [The Hamlet is the Hero]. DER TOG (May 1, 1961)
[Review of *Bein neharot u'nechalim.*]

3283　Avinur, Gita. "Me'ever L'nhar Bug" [On the other Side of the River Bug]. LAMERCHAV (1957)
[In Hebrew.]

3284　Ben-Maeir, M. Sh. "B'ikvot Habesht." HADOAR (Oct. 28, 1957)
[In Hebrew.]

3285　Botoshansky, Yaacov. "A Yiddish shtetl" [A Yiddish Town]. ZUKUNFT (September 1961)
[Reprinted in Di PRESSE (November 1961.]

3286 Brownstein, Ezekiel. "J. Zipper." In his *Impressions of a Leiner.* (Los Angeles, 1941)

3287 Brownstein, Ezekiel. "J. Zipper." In his *Pardes fun Yiddish.* (Los Angales, 1965)

3288 Brownstein, Ezekiel. "J. Zipper." In his *In fraid fun yetzire.* (Los Angeles, 1968)

3289 Dunsky, Shimshon. "Nusach, Yaacov Zipper" [Well Said, Yaacov Zipper]. KEN ADL (May 7, 1976)

3290 Elberg, Y. Review of *Tsvishn taykhn un vasern.* VIEWPOINTS 3, no. 1 (1968)

3291 Filson, Brucek. Review of *The Far Side.* CAN BOOK REV ANN 1985: 216-17.

3292 Mokdoni, A. "Vegen geven is a ments" [About 'There was a Man']. MORG J (Oct. 15, 1941)

3293 Niger, Sh. "Besht un zeine chassidim" [Besht and his Chassidim]. DER TOG (May 26, 1941) [Chassidim is an ultra-orthodox mystical sect.]

3294 Rome, David. "A Jewish Literary Family." CONG BULL 6, no. 1 (1949)

3295 Rosenberg, M. "Geven is a ments" [There was a Man]. DER VEG (1946)

3296 "Y. Zipper" [Y. Zipper]. In *Encyclopedia Judaica Yearbook 1974.* (Jerusalem, 1974) p. 273.

3297 Yungman, M. Review of *In die getzeltn fun Avrohom.* ZUKUNFT (December 1976)

LATVIAN

BIBLIOGRAPHIES, DIRECTORIES, ENCYCLOPEDIAS

3298 **AKMENTIŅŠ, Osvalds**
"Latvian-Canadian Periodical Publications: A Preliminary Check List." CAN ETH STUD 5, no. 1-2 (1973): 213-20.
[Includes 41 references.]

3299 **AKMENTIŅŠ, Osvalds**
"Latvian-Canadian Creative Literature: A Preliminary Check List of Authors and Pseudonyms." CAN ETH STUD 5, no. 1-2 (1973): 221-24.
[A list of 55 poets and prose writers with biographical data.]

3300 *Archīvs [Archives].* Vol. 8. Edgars Dunsdorf: Vēsture, Politika, Valoda, Literātūra [History, Politics, Language, Literature]. Melbourne: Latviešu apvienības Austrālijas zinātnes nozare, and Kārla Zariņa fonds, 1968.
[Includes Latvian-Canadian authors.]

3301 *Latvju enciklopēdija [Latvian Encyclopedia],* edited by Arvēds Švābe. Stockholm: Trīs Zvaigzanes, 1950-55. 3 v.
[Latvian-Canadian authors are included.]

3302 **ZELTIŅŠ, Teodors**
Pašportreti [Autobiographies]. Brooklyn: Grāmatu Draugs, 1965.

RESEARCH PAPER

3303 **LORBERGS, Modris**
"Moods in Latvian Literature 1944-1977; A Review of Themes of Latvian Poets Abroad and in Latvia." In *Second Banff Conference of Central and East European Studies, Banff, Alta., March 2-5, 1978.* (Edmonton: CEESAC, 1978) vol. 1, pp. 117-39.
[Most of the paper is devoted to literary trends in present day Latvia.]

INDIVIDUAL AUTHORS

GREBDZE, Irma, pseud. (Real name: RUBENE, Irmgarde) (1912-   )

3304 *Pazemīgā [The Humble One].* Germany: Selga Kempten, 1946. 103 pp. Novel.

3305 *Ieva [Eva].* Germany: "Sauksme" Kempten, 1948. 77 pp. Novelette.

3306 *Purva zāle [Grass in the Swamps].* Germany: Kadilis apgāds, 1948. 186 pp. Short stories.

3307 *Ragana [The Witch].* New York: Grāmatu Draugs, 1951. 172 pp. Short stories.

3308 *Ikdiena [Our Every Day].* New York: Grāmatu Draugs, 1952. 211 pp. Novel.

3309 *Inga [Inga].* New York: Grāmatu Draugs, 1952. 229 pp. Novel.

3310 *Palēkā māja [The Grey House].* New York: Grāmatu Draugs, 1954. 210 pp. Novel.

3311   *Rudens negaiss [Autumn Storm]*. New York: Grāmatu Draugs, 1954. 210 pp. Novel.

3312   *Dūda [Duda]*. New York: Grāmatu Draugs, 1958. 221 pp. Novel.

3313   *Sveicināta mana zeme [Greetings to You, My Homeland]*. New York: Grāmatu Draugs, 1960. 301 pp. Autbiography.

3314   *Ielejā sagriezās putenis [Storm in the Valley]*. New York: Grāmatu Draugs, 1963. 223 pp. Novel.

3315   *Te nu es esmu [Here I Am]*. New York: Grāmatu Draugs, 1963. 223 pp. Novel.

3316   *Māsas [The Sisters]*. New York: Grāmatu Draugs, 1965. 520 pp. Novel.

3317   *Ēnas dzeltenā stiklā [Shadows in a Yellow Glass]*. New York: Grāmatu Draugs, 1967. 192 pp. Short stories.

3318   *Tikai meitene [Just a Girl]*. New York: Grāmatu Draugs, 1968. 157 pp. Novel for children.

3319   *Vai ābele ziedēja? [Did the Apple Tree Blossom?]*. New York: Grāmatu Draugs, 1969. 271 pp. Novel.

3320   *Saule manā logā [Sunshine in My Window]*. New York: Grāmatu Draugs, 1970. 172 pp. Short stories.

3321   *Meitene un puķe [A Girl and a Flower]*. New York: Grāmatu Draugs, 1971. 288 pp. Novel.

3322   *Aizdedziet sveces [Light Your Candles]*. New York: Grāmatu Draugs, 1974. 195 pp. Short stories.

3323   *Sējējs izgāja sēt [A Sower Went to Sowing]*. New York: Grāmatu Draugs, 1976. 172 pp. Novel.

GUBIŅA, Indra (1927-   )

Author, poet, novelist, Mrs. Gubins was born in Livberze, Latvia. She left her homeland for Germany during the war, then went to England in 1947 and came to Canada in 1952. She has published a great number of art and contributed articles, short stories, book reviews to periodicals. She is recipient of the Latvian Press Association's award, and the J. Jaunsudrabina award presented in 1979. In 1987 received an award from the Latvian Fund for Culture. She lives in Toronto.

3324   *Draugam nepiemērota sieva* [An Unsuitable Wife for a Friend]. Lincoln:Vaidava, 1958. 143 pp. Short stories.

3325   *Zelta ieleja [The Golden Valley]*. Minneapolis: Tilts, 1959. 240 pp. Novel.

3326   *Par sapņiem nemaksā [No Payment for Dreams]*. New York: Grāmatu Draugs, 1962. 253 pp. Short stories.

3327   *Gandrīz karaliene [Almost a Queen]*. New York: Grāmatu Draugs, 1965. 222 pp. Novel.

3328   *Rītdiena neskaitās [Tomorrow doesn't Count]*. New York: Grāmatu Draugs, 1967. 221 pp. Short stories.

3329   *Raksts putekļos [Inscription in the Dust]*. New York: Grāmatu Draugs, 1970. 208 pp. Novel.

3330   *Ziema nāk pretim [Winter is Approaching]*. New York: Grāmatu Draugs, 1973. 189 pp. Novel.

3331 *Ar diviem punktiem teikums nebeidzas [Two Periods do not End a Sentence]*. New York: Grāmatu Draugs, 1974. 208 pp. Short stories.

3332 *Paskaties kļavā [Look at the Maple]*. New York: Grāmatu Draugs, 1974. 123 pp. [Includes poems by Gunars Janovskis.]

3333 *Iztiksim bez mēness [Let's do without the Moon]*. New York: Grāmatu Draugs, 1976. Novel.

3334 *Ir katram sava pasaula [For Each of their Own World]*. New York: Grāmatu Draugs, 1979. Novel.

3335 *Dziesma - tevī esmu [I Exist in a Song]*. New York: Grāmatu Draugs, 1979. Poems.

3336 *Sidrabkāzas [Silverwedding]*. New York: Grāmatu Draugs, 1980. Short stories.

3337 *Pār plašu jūru [Across the Wide Sea]*. Toronto: V. Ziediņē, 1982. Poems.

3338 *Uz vienpadsmito stāvu [To the Eleventh Floor]*. New York: Grāmatu Draugs, 1983. Novel.

3339 *Kaza kāpa debesis [A Goat Climed Up to Heaven]*. New York: Grāmatu Draugs, 1984. Travelogs.

3340 *Uz akmaņa stāvēdams [While Standing on a Rock]*. New York: Grāmatu Draugs, 1986. Novel.

Writings about:

3341 Aigars, P. "Anglijas latvieši romānā" [Latvians of England in Novel]. LOND AVIZ (November 1959)
[Review of *Zelta ieleja*.]

3342 Aizsila, Zīlīte. "Mūsdienu dzīves traģēdija literatūrā" [Contemporary Tragedy in Literature]. LATV AMER (Jul. 29, 1959)
[Review of *Zelta ieleja*.]

3343 Akacis, V. "Kādas nedēļas sprīdis" [Just One Week]. LATVIJA (March 1977)
[Review of *Iztiksim bez mēness*.]

3344 Akacis, V. Review of *Ziema nāk pretim*. LOND AVIZ (Nov. 9, 1973)

3345 Akacis, V. "Mīlestības motīvs" [The Motive of Love]. LATVIJA (July 5, 1980)
[Review of *Ir katram sava pasaula*.]

3346 Andrups, Jānis. "Viņas majestāte vientulība" [Her Majesty's Loneliness]. CEĻA ZĪMES 55 (1974)
[Review of *Ziema nāk pretim*.]

3347 Andrups, Jānis. "Vienkāršības valdzinājums" [The Beauty of Simplicity]. CEĻA ZĪMES 61 (1981)
[Review of *Dziesma - tevī esmu*.]

3348 Andrups, Jānis. "Latvijas vīzija Gotlande" [A Vision of Latvia in Gotland]. LOND AVIZ (Oct. 28, 1983)
[Review of *Pār plašu jūru*.]

3349 Apse, Arnolds. "Pārlaikmetīga grāmata" [An Ageless Novel]. LATVIJA (March 31, 1971)
[Review of *Raksts putekļos*.]

3350 Apse, Arnolds. "Rakstniece ar sirdi" [Author with Heart]. LATV AMER (December 1963)
[Review of *Pār sapņiem nemaksā*.]

3351 Apse, Arnolds. Review of *Ziema nāk pretim*. LATV AMER (Nov. 3, 1973)

3352 Biela, A. Review of *Dziesma, tevī esmu*. AUST LATV (June 20, 1980)

3353 Cēbere, Irma. "Cilvēki slīd kopa" [The People are Merging]. UNIVERSITAS 48, no. 4 (1981)
[Review of *Sidrabkāzas*.]

3354 Cīrule, Alide. Review of *Pār plašu jūru*. UNIVERSITAS 52, no. 2 (1983)

3355 Eglīte, Livija. Review of *Uz vienpadsmito stāvu*. LAIKS (Feb. 22, 1984)

3356 Ermanis, P. "Jauns daiļprozas talants" [A New Talent in Literature]. LATVIJA (Sept. 5, 1959)
[Review of *Zelta ieleja*.]

3357 Gāters, A. "Ģimenes dzīves romāns" [A Novel about a Family]. LAIKS (Oct. 13, 1979)
[Review of *Ir katram sava pasaule*.]

3358 Gāters, A. "Stāsti ar dramatisku un atrisinājumu [Stories with Dramatic and Explosive Solutions].
LATV AMER (May 1968)
[Review of *Ritdiena neskaitās*.]

3359 Gulbītis, J. "Liriska dokumentacija" [Document Lyrics]. LATVIJA (March 21, 1983)
[Review of *Pār plašu jūru*.]

3360 Irbe, Gunars. "Indras Gubiņas mikroklimati" [The Microclimates of Indra Gubins]. LATVIJA (May
1977)
[Review of *Iztiksim bez mēness*.]

3361 Irbe, Gunars. "Indras Gubiņas Visbija" [Visby - as Seen by Indra Gubina]. LARAS LAPA 30
(1983)
[Review of *Pār plašu jūru*.]

3362 Irbe, Gunars. "Problematiska pelnrušķīte" [Problematic Cinderella]. JAUNĀ GAITA No. 101 (1974)
[Review of *Gandrīzkaraliene*.]

3363 Irbe, Gunars. "Specificēta vientulība" [Specific Loneliness]. JAUNĀ GAITA No. 101 (1974)
[Review of *Ziema nāk pretim*.]

3364 Irbe, Gunars. Review of *Dziesma - tevī esmu* . LAIKS (June 2, 1980)

3365 Janovskis, Gunars. Review of *Raksts puteķlos*. LOND AVĪZ (Jan. 8, 1971)

3366 Janovskis, Gunars. Review of *Rītdiena neskaitās*. LOND AVĪZ (Feb. 2, 1968)

3367 Kalniņš, N. Review of *Uz vienpadsmito stāvu*. UNIVERSITAS No. 5(1983)

3368 Kalniņš, N. Review of *Pār plašu jūru*. LATV AMER (Apr. 9, 1983)

3369 Lasmanis, M. "Uz pārmaiņām gaidot" [Waiting for Changes]. JAUNĀ GAITA 154 (1983)
[Review of *Uz vienpadsmito stāvu*.]

3370 Liepa, Rita. "Kas esam, kas bijām" [Who We Are, Who We Were]. LAIKS (Nov. 29, 1981) [Review of *Sidrabkāzas.*]

3371 Liepiņš, O. "Pievilcīgas sievietes psicholoģija [An Attractive Lady's Psychology]. LAIKS (July 1973) [Review of *Ziema nāk pretim.*]

3372 Pelēcis, Valentins. Review of *Par sapņiem nemaksā.* TILTS 52/53 (1963)

3373 Plavkalns, G. Review of *Dziesme - tevī esmu.* JAUNĀ GAITA 134 (1980)

3374 Rolavs, Jānis. "Anglijas latviešu dzīve jaunas rakstnieces romānā" [The Life of Latvians in England as Described in a Novel by a Young Author]. LOND AVĪZ (Aug. 25, 1967) [Review of *Gandrīz karaliene.*]

3375 Rozentāle, M. Review of *Pār plašu jūru.* DV MĒNESRAKSTS 1 (1984)

3376 Rudzītis, Jānis. "Romāns par mūdienu pelnruškīti" [A Novel about a Contemporary Cinderella]. LATVIJA (June 12, 1965) [Review of *Gandrīz karaliene.*]

3377 Silkalns, Ed. Review of *Ir katram sava pasuale.* AUST LATV (Sept. 25, 1980)

3378 Tamuža, Austra. Review of *Gandrīz karaliene.* AUST LATV (Jan. 28, 1966)

3379 Tichovskis, H. Review of *Ar diviem punktiem teikums nebeidzas.* LATV AMER (Apr. 26, 1975)

3380 Tichovskis, H. Review of *Raksts putekļos.* LAIKS (Dec. 12, 1970)

3381 Upatnieks, K. "Divejādas mīlestības" [A Two-fold Love Story]. LAIKS (Apr. 21, 1965) [Review of *Gandrīz karaliene.*]

3382 Valtere, Nora. "Dvēseles dzīves tēlotāja" [Depicter of the Soul]. LAIKS (Jan. 15, 1975) [Review of *Ar diviem punktiem teikums nebeidzas.*]

3383 Valtere, Nora. "Indra Gubiņa" [Indra Gubins]. UNIVERSITAS No. 39 (1977)

3384 Zariņs, Guntis. "Par vietām un cilvēkiem" [Of Places and People]. LOND AVĪZ (Jan. 18, 1963) [Review of *Pār sapņiem nemaksā.*]

3385 Zuzena, Edite. "Pastāvēs, kas pārvērtīsies" [Who Transforms will Survive]. JAUNĀ GAITA No. 115 (1977) [Review of *Iztiksim bez mēness .*]

ĶIĶAUKA, Tālivaldis

3386 *Tramvajs tuksnesī [Streetcar in a Desert].* Minneapolis: Tilts, 1965. Short stories.

3387 *Leonards [Leonard].* Minneapolis: Tilts, 1967. Novel.

3388 *Zēns un pūķis [A Boy and a Dragon].* København: Imanta, 1967. Story in poem.

3389 *Putni [The Birds].* København: Imanta, 1969. Novel.

SWEDE, George (1940-   )

Poet, short story writer, children's author, critic, editor. Born in Riga, Latvia, emigrated with his parents to Canada after the war. Received his education at the University of British Columbia and Dalhousie University. His haiku poems have appeared in *Bonsai, Cicada, Haiku Journal, Poetry Nippon, Wee Giant,* etc. He has published poems in more than thirty anthologies and periodicals. He lives in Toronto.

3390   *Unwinding.* Toronto: Missing Link Press, 1974. 24 pp. Poems.

3391   *Tell-tale Feathers.* Fredericton, N.B.: Fiddlehead Poetry Books, 1978. 55 pp. Poems.

3392   *Endless Jigsaw.* Toronto: Three Trees Press, 1978. 64 pp. Poems.

3393   *A Snowman Headless.* Fredericton, N.B.: Fiddlehead Poetry Books, 1979. 44 pp. Poems.

3394   *Wingbeats.* La Cross, Wisc.: Juniper, 1979. 24 pp. Poems.

3395   *As Far as the Sea can Eye.* Toronto: York, 1979. 119 pp. Poems.

3396   *Quillby, the Porcupine Who Lost his Quills.* Toronto: Three Trees Press, 1979. 24 pp. Children's fiction with Anita Krumins.]

3397   *The Case of the Moonlit Gold Dust.* Toronto: Three Trees Press, 1979. 30 pp. Children's fiction.

3398   *This Morning's Mockingbird.* Battle Ground, Ind.: High/Coo, 1980. 16 pp. Poems.

3399   *The Case of the Missing Heirloom.* Toronto: Three Trees Press, 1980. 36 pp. Children's fiction.

3400   *Eye to Eye with a Frog.* La Cross, Wisc.: Juniper, 1981. 20 pp. Poems.

3401   *The Case of the Seaside Burglaries.* Toronto: Three Trees Press, 1981. 54 pp. Children's fiction.

3402   *Sherlock, the Bloodhound Detective (with Watson the Cat) in the Case of Seaside Burglaries,* illustrated by Danielle Jones. Toronto: Three Trees Press, 1981. 54 pp. Children's fiction.

3403   *All of Her Shadows.* Battle Ground, Ind.: High/Coo, 1982. 28 pp. Poetry.

3404   *The Case of the Downhill Theft.* Toronto: Three Trees Press, 1982. 64 pp. Children's fiction.

3405   *Undertow.* Toronto: Three Trees Press, 1982. 64 pp. Children's fiction.

3406   *Flaking Paint.* Toronto: Underwich, 1983. 48 pp. Poems.

3407   *Tick Bird: Poems for Children.* Toronto: Three Trees Press, 1983. 48 pp. Poems.

3408   *Frozen Breaths.* Glen Burnie, Md.: Wind Chimes Press, 1983. 20 pp. Poems.

3409   *Cicada Voices.* Battle Ground, Ind.: High/Coo, 1983. 64 pp. Poems.

3410   *Bifids.* Toronto: Curvd H/Z, 1984. 28 pp. Poems.

3411   *Night Tides.* London, Ont.: South Western Ontario Poetry, 1984. 28 pp. Poems.

3412   *Time is Flies: Poems for Children.* Toronto: Three Trees Press, 1984. 48 pp. Poems.

3413   *Dudley and the Birdman.* Toronto: Three Tress Press, 1985. 24 pp. Children's picture book.

3414   *High Wire Spider.* Toronto: Three Trees Press, 1986. 48 pp. Poetry for children.

3415   *The Space Between.* Glen Burnie, Md.: Wind Chimes Press, 1986. 24 pp. Poems.

Writings about:

3416   Di Cicco, Pier Giorgio. "No Man is an Island." BKS CAN 8, no. 9 (1979): 21-22.
[Review of *Tell-tale Feathers.*]

3417   Kertzer, Adrienne. "Word Games." CAN LIT 111 (1986): 178-80.
[Review of *Tick Bird* and *Time is Flies.*]

TOMA, Velta

3418   *Minējums [Indication].* Rīga: E. Kreišmanis, 1943. Poems.

3419   *Latviešu sieva [A Latvian Woman].* Hanau: Gaismas pils, 1946. Poems.

3420   *Sēlzemes sesteidna [A Saturday of Selia].* Toronto: Druva, 1953. Poems.

3421   *Vēl [Again].* København: Imanta, 1959. Poems.

3422   *Aldaune [Aldaune].* New York: Grāmatu Draugs, 1960. Novel.

3423   *Mūžigā spēle [Eternal Play].* Toronto: Daugavas Vanagi, 1960. Poems.

3424   *Dziļumā jāpārtop [To Transform Deep Down].* New York: Grāmatu Draugs, 1963. Poems.

3425   *Sērdienes spēks, 1963-1969 [An Orphan's Strength, 1963-1969].* New York: Grāmatu Draugs,
1969. Poems.

3426   *Pēc uguns [After the Fire].* New York: Grāmatu Draugs, 1975. Poems.

VĪKSNA, Ingrida, pseud. (Real name: FOGELE, Ingrida) (1920-   )

3427   *Rūgtais prieks [Bitter Joy].* Riga: Kreišmanis, 1942. 94 pp. Poems.

3428   *Mums jābrien jūrā [We must Wade in the Sea].* Cøbenhavn: Imanta, 1951. 256 pp. Novel.

3429   *Dāvana [Gift].* Toronto: Valters Ziediņš, 1953. 136 pp. Short stories.

3430   *Es saku paldies [I Say Thank You].* Toronto: Meduslācis, 1955. 136 pp. Poems.

3431   *Pilnsapulce Čučičingā [A Meeting in Couchiching].* [N.d.] Performed by various Latvian theatre
groups in Canada and the U.S.A. Play.

3432   *Un gājiens neapstājas [And the Journey does not End].* Toronto: Daugavas Vanagi, 1968. 80 pp.
Poems.

3433   *Piecas naktis [Five Nights].* Toronto: Valters Ziediņš, 1975. 150 pp. Poems.

Writings about:

3434   Ērmanis, Pēteris. Review of *Dāvana*. LATVIJA (1954): 6.

3435   Liepiņš, Oļģerts. "Stāsti par emigrantu dzīvi; Ingrida Vīksna: *Dāvana*" [Short Stories about the Lives of Immigrants; Ingrid Vīksna: *Gift*]. LAIKS (1953): 6.

3436   Veselis, Jānis. Review of *Dāvana*. LATV AMER (1953): 4.

VOITKUS, Arturs

3437   *Aproce [The Bracelet]*. Toronto: Meduslācis, 1955. Novel.

3438   *Bet es jums saku [But I'm Telling You]*. New York: Grāmatu Draugs, 1961. Novel.

3439   *Tev nebūs [Thou Shalt Not]*. New York: Grāmatu Draugs, 1964. Novel.

3440   *Aiz rožainiem mākoņiem [Beyond the Rosy Clouds]*. New York: Grāmatu Draugs, 1965. Novel.

3441   *Mēs gribam būt mājās [We Want to Be Home]*. New York: Grāmatu Draugs, 1966. Novel.

3442   *Aiz miglas aust saule [The Sun Rises beyond the Fog]*. New York: Grāmatu Draugs, 1968. Novel.

3443   *Dzīvais cilvēks [A Living Man]*. New York: Grāmatu Draugs, 1968. Novel.

3444   *Ceļi tāļi, ceļi tuvi [Roads Faraway, Roads Close-by]*. New York: Grāmatu Draugs, 1970. Novel.

3445   *Četri simti [Four Hundred]*. New York: Grāmatu Draugs, 1972. Novel.

3446   *Sudraba un zelta man nav [I Have no Silver nor Gold]*. New York: Grāmatu Draugs, 1972. Novel.

3447   *Dod man savu sirdi [Give Me Your Heart]*. New York: Grāmatu Draugs, 1975. Novel.

3448   *Svešnieki un piedsīvotāji [Strangers and Lodgers]*. New York: Grāmatu Draugs, 1977. Novel.

3449   *Ogles pelnos [Coals in Ashes]*. New York: Grāmatu Draugs, 1978. Novel.

3450   *Vēja nestas lapas [Wind-blown Leaves]*. New York: Grāmatu Draugs, 1978. Novel.

ZEMDEGA (KRUMIŅA), Aina

3451   *Basām kājām [Barefoot]*. Chicago: Alfred Kalnājs, 1963. 107 pp. Novel.

3452   *Egles istabā [Spruce Trees in the Living Room]*. Cøbenhavn: Imanata, 1968. 32 pp. Story.

3453   *Cirsma [In the Clearing]*. Västeras, Sweden: Ziemeļblāsma, 1974. 119 pp. Novel.

LEBANESE

INDIVIDUAL AUTHORS

ASFOUR, John (1945-   )
Born in Aiteneat, Lebanon, came to Canada in 1968. He teaches at Dawson College, Montreal.

3454   *Nisan.* Fredericton, N.B.: Fiddlehead Books, 1976. Poems.

3455   *Land of Flowers and Guns.* Montreal: DC Books, 1981. Poems.

BASMAJIAN, Shaunt (1950-   )
Born in Beirut, Lebanon. He came to Toronto at the age of seven. He has lived in the U.S.A., Vancouver and Edmonton and, of late, Toronto. Edited several anthologies.

3456   *The Resurrection of the Third Happening.* Toronto: Portage Press, 1976. [7] leaves. Poems.

3457   *Boundaries   Limits and Space: Concrete Poems.* [Toronto] Underwich Editions, 1980. [49] pp. Poems.

3458   *Surplus Waste and other Poems.* Toronto: Unfinished Monument Press, 1982. Poems.

3459   *8 Irrigations.* [Toronto] Curvd H / Z, 1983. 8 pp. Poems.

3460   *Poets Who don't Dance.* Toronto: Unfinished Monument Press, iv, 27 pp. Poems.

   Writing about:

3461   Pell, Barbara. "Towards Poetry." CAN LIT No. 97 (1983): 112.
        [Review of *Surplus Waste.*]

BOUYOUCAS, Pan
Novelist, playwright, short story writer, translator. Born in Beirut, Lebanon. Emigrated to Quebec in 1963. Educated at Concordia University, Montreal. Awards include first prize at the Concours d'œuvres dramatiques radiophoniques de Radio-Canada (1983), second prize at the Concours de la Communauté radiophonique des programmes de langue française (France, 1983), Screener's Award, 1986 Quebec Drama Festival (for *Kill the Music*), two Canada Council grants, etc. He lives in Montreal.

3462   *Le dernier souffle.* Montréal: Éditions du Jour, 1975. 186 pp.

3463   *Une bataille d'Amérique.* Montréal: Les Éditions Quinze, 1976. 213 pp.

3464   *Fuites et poursuites.* Montréal: Les Éditions Quinze, 1982. Stories.

KARAMÉ, Antoine

3465   *La Voix de l'immigrant: Poésies.* Sherbrooke, Qué.: Naaman, 1980. 106 pp. Poèmes.

3466   *Les Chants intérieurs: Poèmes d'autrefois et aujourd'hui.* Sherbrooke, Qué.: Naaman, 1983. 93 pp. Poèmes.

3467 *Lègendes   pharanoiques* (avec la collaboration de Léo Brodeur, Antoine Karamé, et Antoine Naaman). Sherbrooke, Qué.: Naaman. 77 pp. Nouvelles.

3468 *Le Raspoutine Egyptien et autres nouvelles.* Sherbrooke, Qué.: Naaman, 1985. 116 pp. Nouvelles.

NASRALLAH, Emily

3469 *Flight against Time*, translated from the Lebanese by Issa J. Boulatta. Charlottetown, P.E.I.: Ragweed Press, 1987. 208 pp. Novel.

SAAD, Fouad (1935-   )
Of Lebanese origin, Saad was born in Cairo, Egypt, and came to Canada in 1967. He is a professor of political science and an investment consultant in Montreal.

3470 *De Sable et de neige: poèmes.* Sherbrooke, Qué.: Naaman, 1979. 74 pp. Poèmes.

LITHUANIAN

BIBLIOGRAPHIES

3471 **BALYS, Jonas**
"Baltic Encyclopedias and Biographical Directories." Q J LIB CONG 22 (1966): 270-75.
[Includes citations of Canadian interest.]

3472 **BALYS, Jonas**
"Bibliography of Baltic Bibliographies." [Chicago, 1969-71. 52 pp.]
[Deteched from *Lituanistikos darbai* [Chicago: Lituanistikos institutas, 1969. Vol. 2, pp. 141-86, and *Naujoji viltis* (Chicago, 1969) Vol. 2, pp. 115-20. Includes Lithuanian-Canadian literature.]

3473 **GAIDA, Pr.; BALTGAILIS, P.**
"Lithuanian-Canadian Periodical Publications: A Preliminary Check List." CAN ETH STUD 2, no. 1 (1970): 151-55.
[Includes references to 38 Lithuanian periodicals and newspapers in Canada.]

3474 **GAIDA, Pr.; KAIRYS, S.; KARDELIS, J., and others**
"Selected Bibliography." In their *Lithuanians in Canada.* (Ottawa-Toronto: Lights and Time Press Litho., 1967) pp. 350-61.
[Includes publications in the social sciences and humanities.]

3475 **GAIDA, Pr.; KAIRYS, S.; KARDELIS, J., and others**
"Writers, Novelists, Poets." In their *Lithuanians in Canada.* (Ottawa-Toronto: Lights and Time Press Litho, 1967) pp. 158-168. ports.
[Provides biographical sketches of authors with titles of their publications. Poets: Marija Aukštaitė, K. Barteška, P. Kozulis, Henrikas Nagys, S. Prapuolenytė-Bunker, Birutė Pūkelevičiutė, Balys Rukša, L. Svėgždaitė. Prose writers: Pranys Alšėnas, M. Eggleston, V. Kastytis, Juozas Kralikauskas, Vytautas Tamulaitis, P. Young, and J. Žmuidzinas.]

3476 **KANTAUTAS, Adam; KANTAUTAS, Filomena**
A Lithuanian Bibliography: A Check-list of Books and Articles Held by the Major Libraries of Canada and the United States. Edmonton: The University of Alberta Press, 1975. 725 pp.
[Includes primary and secondary material by and about Lithuanian-Canadian authors.]

3477 **KANTAUTAS, Adam; KANTAUTAS, Filomena**
Supplement to A Lithuanian Bibliography... A Further Check-list of Books and Articles Held by the Major Libraries in Canada and the United States. Edmonton: University of Alberta Press, 1979. 316 pp.
[This supplement includes 4127 references.]

BOOKS, ENCYCLOPEDIAS

3478 *Encyclopedia Lituanica*, edited by Simas Sužiedėlis. Boston: J. Kapočius, Lithuanian Encyclopedia Press, 1970. 6 v.
[Contains references to Lithuanian-Canadian authors.]

3479 **GAIDA, Pr.; KAIRYS, S.; KARDELIS, J.; PUZINAS, A.; RINKŪNAS, A.; SUNGAILA, J.**

Lithuanians in Canada. Ottawa-Toronto: Lights and Time Press Litho, 1967. xx, 370 pp. illus., ports. (Canada ethnica, 5)
[Includes a section on literature, with biographical notes on authors.]

3480 *Lietuvių enciklopedija [Lithuanian Encyclopedia].* Boston: Lietuvių enciklopedijos leidykla, 1953-1969. 36 v.
[Lithuanian-Canadian authors are included.]

3481 *Lietuvių literatūra svetur, 1945-1967 [Lithuanian Literature Abroad, 1945-1967],* edited by Kazys Bradūnas. Chicago: Į. lalsvę fondas lietuvškai kultūrai ugdyti, 1968. 697 pp. (Leidinys, No. 8)

3482 ŠILBAJORIS, Rimvydas Pranas
Perfection of Exile; Fourteen Contemporary Lithuanian Writers. Norman, Oklah.: University of Oklahoma Press, 1970. 322 pp.

3483 ZIEDONIS, Arvids; PUHVEL, Joan; SILBAJORIS, Rimvydas Pranas
Baltic Literature and Linguistics. Columbus, Oh.: Association for the Advancement of Baltic Studies, 1973. ix, 251 pp.
[Includes a paper by Ivar Ivask in Part I on Baltic literature in exile.]

RESEARCH PAPERS

3484 BABRAUSKAS, Benys
"The New Lithuanian Literature." BKS ABR 29 (1955): 144-48.

3485 KAUPAS, Julius Viktoras
"Our Literature in Exile." LITUANUS 4, no. 3 (1958): 87-92.

3486 ŠILBAJORIS, Rimvydas Pranas
"Ausserhalb der Heimat entstandene litauische Literature" [Lithuanian Literature Abroad]. ACT BALT 6 (1966): 221-36.

3487 ŠILBAJORIS, Rimvydas Pranas
"Lithuanian Poets: Strangers and Children of Their Native Land." LITUANUS 17, no. 1 (1971): 5-6. Reprinted in *Second Conference on Baltic Studies: Summary of Proceedings.* (Norman, Oklah.: Association for the Advancement of Baltic Studies, 1971) pp. 128-30.
[Reference is made to Henrikas Nagys.]

3488 VAICIULAITIS, Antanas
"Lithuanian Literary Happenings 1942." BKS ABR 17 (1943): 130-31.

ANTHOLOGIES

3489 *Gabija; literatūros metraštis spaudos atgavimo penkiasdešimtmečiui ir tremties dešimtmečiui paminėti [A Literary Yearbook to Commemorate the 50th Anniversary of the Re-establishment of the Free Press and the Ten Years of Exile],* redaktoriai Jonas Aistis ir Stepas Zobarskas. New York: Gabijos leidykla, 1954. 550 pp.
[Includes writings by Lithuanian-Canadian authors.]

3490 *Lietuvių beletristikos antologija [Anthology of Lithuanian Belles-Lettres].* Chicago: Lietuviškos knygos klubas, 1957-1965. 2 v.
[Includes poetry, short fiction and essays.]

3491   *Lietuvių poezija išeivijoje, 1945-1971 [Lithuanian Poetry in Exile, 1945-1971].* Redagavo Kazys Bradūnas. Chicago: Ateitis, 1971. 671 pp. (Literatūros serija, No. 5)
[Bibliography: pp. 640-44.]

3492   *Lietuvių poezijos antologija [An Anthology of Lithuanian Poetry],* compiled by Jonas Aistis, and A. Vaičiulaitis. Chicago: Lietuviškos knygos klubas, 1951. 832 pp.
[Includes several Lithuanian-Canadian authors.]

INDIVIDUAL AUTHORS

ALŠENAS, Pranys (1911-   )
Born in Lithuania and emigrated to Canada after World War II. As a journalist, he has contributed articles to newspapers and periodicals. A collection of his journalistic works was published under the title: *Maži žodžiai apie didelius dalykus.* He lives in Toronto.

3493   *Talismanas: novelės [Talisman: Short Stories].* Bambergas, Germany: The Author, 1946. 59 pp. Short stories.

3494   *Tūkstantis šypsnių [A Thousand Smiles].* Toronto: The Author, 1962. 272 pp. Humorous sketches.

Writing about:

3495   "Worker by Nights - Journalist by Day." BLOOR W VILLAG 3, no. 27 (1974) port.

AUKŠTAITĖ, Marija (1896-   )
Born in Lithuania, received private education there. She came to Canada in 1930. Former editor of the newspaper *Nepriklausoma Lietuva .*

3496   *Rožių vasara [The Summer of Roses].* [Toronto: The Author] 1966. 760 pp. Poems.

3497   *Išeives keliu: Apysaka. [The Road of a Woman in Exile: A Novel].* Toronto: A.F. Navikevičius, 1978. 207 pp.

3498   *Išeive. [A Woman in Exile].* Toronto: A.F. Navikevičius, 1980. 265 pp.

3499   *Nubangavo kūdikystės dienos: Autobiografija. [Childhood Days are Gone with the Waves: Autobiography].* Toronto: A.F. Navikevičius, 1981. 233 pp. Autobiographical novel.

3500   *Ant Marių Krašto: Romanas [On the Seaside: Novel].* Toronto: A.F. Nevikevičius, 1981. 419 pp. Novel.

3501   *Lyrika [Lyrics].* Toronto: A.F. Navikevičius, 1983. 202 pp. Poems.

BARONAS, Aloyzas (1914-   )

3502   *Uzgeses sniegas: Romanas. [Burned Out Snow: Novel].* Toronto: Kanados Kataliku Kultūros Draūgija, 1953. 285 pp. Novel.

GAIDAMAVIČIUS, Pranas

3503   *Išblokštasis žmogus; benamio likimo perspektyvos [A Displaced Person; The Destiny of a Homeless Man].* Augsburg: Venta [1951] 278 pp. Biographical novel.

3504   *Didysis nerimas [The Great Unrest].* Putnam, Conn., 1962. 297 pp. Novel.

KRALIKAUSKAS, Juozas (1910-   )

Educator and novelist, born in Lithuania, where he began publishing novelettes. He came to Canada after World War II and settled in Toronto.

3505   *Urviniai žmonės [Cavemen].* Chicago: Lietuviškos knygos klubas, 1954. 208 pp. Novel.

3506   *Šviesa lange: romanas [Light in the Window: Novel].* London: Nida, 1960. 248 pp. (Nidos knygos klubas, No. 29) Novel.

3507   *Titnago ugnis [Flint Fire].* Chicago: Lietuviškos knygos klubas, 1962. 205 pp. Novel.

3508   *Minduago nužudymas [The Murder of Mindaugas].* Chicago: Lietuviškos knygos klubas, 1964. 246 pp. Novel.
[Awarded a Draugas literary prize of $1000.]

3509   *Vaišvilkas: romanas [Vaišvilkas: Novel].* Chicago: Lietuviškos knygos klubas, 1971. 234 pp. Novel.

3510   *Tautvila [Tautvila].* Chicago: Draugas, 1973. 205 pp. Novel.
[Winner of the Lithuanian Writers' Association Award.]

3511   *Martynas Mažvydas Vilniuje [Martinas Mažvidas in Vilnius].* Chicago: Draugas, 1976. 307 pp. Novel.
[Winner of the first literary prize of $1,500 in a US-wide literary competition for Lithuanian authors.]

Writings about:

3512   Barbauskas, B. "Juozas Kralikauskas" [Juozas Kralikauskas]. In *Lietuvių enciklopedija.* (Boston: J. Kapočius, 1957) vol. 12, p. 531.

3513   Dyvas, Vytautas. Review of *Martynas Mažvydas Vilniuje.* AIDAI No. 6 (1977)

3514   Gliauda, J. Review of *Šviesa lange.* DRAUGAS (Oct. 29, 1960)

3515   Grinius, J. "J. Kralikausko romanai apie Mindaugo epochą" [J. Kralikauskas' Novels about the Mindaugas Epoch]. AIDAI No. 6 (1964)

3516   Grinius, J. Review of *Šviesa lange.* DRAUGAS (Dec. 10, 1960)

3517   Jonynas, V.A. Review of *Tautvila.* TĖV ŽIB (July 6, 1974)

3518   "Juozas Kralikauskas" [Juozas Kralikauskas]. In *Antologia 2.* (Chicago: Lietoviškos knygos klubas, 1965) pp. 442-51.

3519   "Juozas Kralikauskas" [Juozas Kralikauskas]. In *Lietuvių literatūra svetur.* (Chicago: I.L. Fondas, 1968) pp. 113, 132-34, 159-60, 174-80, 185-86, 419.

3520   Landsbergis, Algirdas. "Juozas Kralikauskas." In *The Lithuanian Short Story, Fifty Years.* (New York: Manyland Books, 1977) pp. 302-03.

3521 Naujokaitis, Pranas. "Juozas Kralikauskas" [Juozas Kralikauskas]. In *Lietuvių literatūros istorija* 4. (Chicago, 1976) pp. 97-106.

3522 Naujokaitis, Pranas. Review of *Urviniai žmonės.* AIDAI No. 7 (1955)

3523 Vaičiulaitis, A.; Grinius, J. Review of *Vaišvilkas.* AIDAI No. 7 (1955)

LAUGALIS, Vytautas

3524 *Himnai, tau tevyne: Pro patria [Hymns to Thee, My Homeland].* Toronto: Moravia Press, 1981. 197 pp. Poems.

NAGYS, Henrikas (1920-   )
Poet, playwright. Born at Mažeikiai, Lithuania. Studied at the Universities of Kaunas, Lithuania, and Innsbruck, Austria. He is a commercial artist and a lecturer at the University of Montreal.

3525 *Eilėraščiai [Poems].* Innsbruck, Austria: Fraternity Lithuania, 1946. 78 pp. Poems.

3526 *Lapkričio naktys: Lyrika [November Nights: Lyrics].* Freiburg, Germany: P. Abelkis, 1947. 112 pp. Poems.

3527 *Saulės laikrodžiai [The Sundials].* Chicago: Lietuviškos knygos klubas, 1952. 80 pp. Poems.

3528 *Mėlynas sniegas: poezija [Blue Snow: Poems].* Boston: Lietvių enciklopedijos leidukla, 1960. 87 pp. Poems.

3529 *Broliai balti aitvarai [Brothers, White Legendary Birds].* Chicago: Algimanto Mackaus knygų leidimo fondas, 1969. 70 pp. Poems.

3530 *Prisijaukinsiu skalą [I'll Tame a Falcon].* Chicago: AM & M Publications, 1978. Poems.

Writings about:

3531 Copelius, Henriko. "Nagio eilėraščiai" [Nagys' Poems]. ŠVIESA (1946)

3532 Raginis, A. "Henriko Nagio eilėraščiai" [Henrikas Nagys' Poems]. AMERIKA (1947)

3533 Sakalas, J. "Modernioji mūsų poezija" [Our Modern Poetry]. ATEITIS 152 (1944)

NAGYS, Jacob

3534 *Dejuoja ir dainuoja. [Lamenting and Singing].* Toronto: The Author, 1977. 152 pp. Poems.

3535 *Klajoja ir galvoja: Eilėraščici: poemos, epas [Wandering and Thinking: Poems].* Toronto: The Author, 1979. 164 pp. Poems.

3536 *Meile tarp priešų: 12-kos vaizdų: Drama [Love among Enemies: 12-scene drama].* Toronto: The Author, 1980. 156 pp. Play.

PŪKELEVIČIŪTĖ, Birutė (1923-   )
Poet, novelist, director and actress. Born in Lithuania, studied drama and music at the University of Lithuania. Came to Canada in 1948. Her books of poetry and fiction have earned her several awards.

3537 *Metūgės [Year's Shoots].* Toronto: Baltija, 1952. 95 pp. Poems.

3538 *Aštuoni lapai: premijuotas romanas [Eight Sheets: Novel].* Chicago: Lietuviškos knygos klubas, 1956. 392 pp. Novel.

3539 *Aukso žąsis [Golden Goose].* Chicago: Lietuviškos knygos klubas, 1965. Comedy in 3 acts. [Winner of the World Lithuanian Community award.]

3540 *Rugsėjo šeštadienis: premijuotas romanas [A Saturday in September: Novel].* Chicago: Lietuviškos knygos klubas, 1970. 237 pp. Novel.

Writing about:

3541 Gaida, Pr. "Birutė Pūkelevičiutė." In *Lithuanians in Canada.* (Ottawa-Toronto: Lights and Time Press Litho, 1967) p. 166.

RINKŪNAS, A.

3542 *Kregždutė [The Swallow].* Toronto: Light Printing & Publishing Co., 1959. 159 pp. Novel.

RUKŠA, Balys (1920-)
Born and educated in Lithuania. Escaped to Germany during the war and attended the Wuerzburg University. Came to Canada after the war and settled in Toronto.

3543 *Žemės rankose [In Earth's Hands].* Toronto: The Author, 1950. 80 pp. Poems.

3544 *Ugnies pardavėjas [Salesman of Fire].* Toronto: Banga, 1952. 95 pp. Poems.

Writings about:

3545 Arėnas, K. "Balio Rukšos poezija" [The Poetry of Balys Rukša]. AKIRATIS (1950)

3546 Audrius, A. "Ugnies pardavėjas" [Salesman of Fire]. DRAUGAS (1952)

3547 Dovydėnas, L. "Gyvybės šauksmas" [The Voice of Life]. NEMUNAS (1950)

3548 Grinius, J. "Visumos žvilgsnis į musų egzodo literatūrą" [A Universal View of Our Literature in Exile]. LIET LIT SVET (1968)

3549 Leskūnas, A. Review of *Žemės rankose.* NEPR LIET (1950)

3550 Nagys, Henrikas. "Balio Rukšos poezija" [The Poetry of Balys Rukša]. ŽIBURIAI (1950)

3551 Skrupskelytė, V. "Balys Rukša" [Balys Rukša]. In *Lietuvių poezijos antologija.* (Chicago, 1971)

3552 Vaičiulaitis, Antanas. "Balys Rukša" [Balys Rukša]. LIET LIT SVET (1968)

SMAIZYS, Jonas

3553 *Gyvenimas ir darbai: Eileraščiai. [Life and Work: Poems].* New York: The Author, 1973. 96 pp. Poems.

TAMULAITIS, Vytautas (1913-)

Born in Lithuania and attended the Military Academy there. Emigrated to Canada in 1948. He published children's novels in his native land. Some of his short stories and children's stories have been translated into English.

3554 *Sugrižimas [The Return]*. Tübingen, Germany: Patrija, 1948. 143 pp. Novel.

3555 *Raguvos malūnininkas [The Miller of Raguva]*. Rodney, Ont.: Rūta, 1951. 60 pp. Story.

3556 *Svirplio muzikanto kelionės [The Travels of the Musician Grasshopper]*. 1960. Children's story.

3557 *Nimblefoot the Ant.* Toronto, 1965. Novel.
[Translated from his Lithuanian novel: *Skrusdelytės greitutės nuotykiai.*]

LUXEMBOURGIAN

INDIVIDUAL AUTHOR

WELCH, Liliane (1937-   )
Born in Luxembourg and received her primary education there. Received her Ph.D. at Penn State University. She is professor of French literature at Mount Allison University, Sackville, N.B. Member of League of Canadian Poets, Writers' Union of Canada, Federation of New Brunswick Writers, and Federation of Nova Scotia Writers. Received Honorary President's Prize, Writers' Federation of New Brunswick (1986). Her writings have appeared in *First Encounter, Antigonish Review, Descant, Fiddlehead, Harvest, Germination, Waves, Dalhousie Review, Quarry, Prism,* etc. Co-author of *Emergence: Baudelaire, Mallarmé, Rimbaud,* 1977, and *Address: Rimbaud, Mallarmé, Butor,* 1979.

3558   *Winter Songs.* London, Ont.: Killaly Press, 1977. 24 pp. Poems.

3559   *Syntax of Ferment.* Fredericton, N.B.: Fiddlehead Poetry Books, 1980. 79 pp. Poems.

3560   *October Winds.* Fredericton, N.B.: Fiddlehead Poetry Books, 1980. 62 pp. Poems.

3561   *Assailing Beasts.* Ottawa: Borealis Press, 1979. 70 pp. Poems.

3562   *Brush and Trunks.* Fredericton, N.B.: Fiddlehead, 1981. 61 pp. Poems.

3563   *From the Songs of the Artisans.* Fredericton, N.B.: Fiddlehead, 1983. 69 pp. Poems.

3564   *Manstorna.* Charlottetown, P.E.I.: Ragweed Press, 1985. Poems.

3565   *Unbound Rest.* Brandon, Man.: Pieran Press, 1985. Poems.

3566   *Word-house of a Grandchild.* Charlottetown, P.E.I.: Ragweed Press, 1987. Poems.

3567   *A Taste for Words.* St. John, N.B.: The Purple Wednesday Society, 1987. Poems.

MALTESE

INDIVIDUAL AUTHOR

VIRGO, Seán (1940-   )
Born in Malta, raised in South Africa, Malaya, Ireland and England. Emigrated to Canada in 1966. Recipient of several literary awards including the Du Maurier National Magazine Award for Poetry (1978), CBC Literary Competition, Short Stories (1979), BBC-3 Short Story Competition (1980), and the 1987 W.H. Smith/Books in Canada First Novel Competition.

3568   *Sea Change.* Rushden, Northamptonshire: Sceptre Press, c1971. 4 pp. Poems.

3569   *Pieces for the Old Earth Man.* Delta, B.C.: Sono Nis Press, 1973. 82 pp. Poems.

3570   *Island.* Queen Charlotte Islands: Catspaw Press, 1975. Poems.

3571   *Kiskatinaw Songs*, with Susan Musgrave.   Victoria, B.C.: Pharos Press, 1977.   Poems.

3572   *Deathwatch on Skidegate Narrows.*   Victoria, B.C.: Sono Nis Press, 1979.   142 pp.   Poems.

3573   *Vagabonds.*   St. John's, Nf.: Memorial Art Gallery, 1979.

3574   *White Lies and other Fictions.*   Toronto: Exile Editions, 1980.   150 pp.   Short stories.

3575   *Through the Eyes of a Cat: Irish Stories.*   Victoria, B.C.: Sono Nis Press, 1985.   x, 65 pp.   Short stories.

3576   *Selakhi.*   Toronto: Exile Editions, 1987.   Novel.

MARTINIQUE, GUADELOUPE

INDIVIDUAL AUTHORS

CARBET, Marie Magdeleine

3577   *Au péril de ta joie.*   Montréal: Léméac, 1972.   213 pp.   Poèmes.

3578   *D'une rive à l'autre.*   Montréal: Léméac, 1973.   Poèmes.

3579   *Comptines et chansons antillaises.*   Montréal: Léméac, 1975.   Poèmes.

3580   *Au village en temps longtemps.*   Montréal: Léméac, 1977.

3581   *Mini poèmes sur trois méridiens.*   Montréal: Léméac, 1977.   Poèmes.

DESPORTES, Georges

3582   *Cette ile quie est la nôtre.*   Montréal: Léméac, 1973.   242 pp.

JARDEL, Jean-Pierre

3583   *La conte créole.*   Montreál: Centre de recherches Carabies, Université de Montréal, 1977.

MORAND, Fleurette

3584   *Feu de brousse.*   Éditions du jour, 1967.   Poèmes.

PARILLON, Adolphe

3585   *Gustave, Je....* Sherbrooke, Qué.: Naaman, 1978.   Roman.

MÉTIS

ANTHOLOGIES

3586 *Found Poems of the Metis People*, edited by Mick Burrs. Regina: Province of Saskatchewan, Department of Youth, 1975.
[Based on interviews conducted by Carol Pearlstone with Mary Jacobson, Pierre Vandale, Rose Fleury, and Mederic McDonald, whose poems are included in this volume.]

3587 *Poems in Their Own Voices: "Going to War", World War One, World War Two: Metis Series.* Interviewer Carol Pearlstone, editor Mick Burrs. Regina: Province of Saskatchewan, Department of Culture and Youth, c1975. iv, 40 leaves, 4 leaves of plates. illus.

3588 *Three Métis Folk Songs from Saskatchewan*, arranged by Malcolm Forsyth. Willowdale, Ont.: Leeds Music, 1978. 20 pp. Songs.

INDIVIDUAL AUTHOR

CULLETON, Beatrice
Born in St. Boniface, she was raised in foster homes. She is manager of Pemmican Publications and editor of *The Pemmican Journal.*

3589 *In Search of April Raintree.* Pemmican, 1983. Story.

MONTSERRAT (W.I.)

INDIVIDUAL AUTHORS

FRANCIS, Samuel
Born in Montserrat, W.I., and came to Canada in 1941. A graduate of the Newspaper Institute of America, Francis specialized in radio and television. He is doing research in the history of blacks in Canada for the National Film Board.

3590 *Me? Who I Am?* Montreal: La Société de Belles Lettres Guy Maheux, 1977.

3591 *Long Ways to Go.* Colour film, produced by the National Film Board, 1976.

GREER, Yvonne
Born in Aruba, Dutch West Indies, but spent much of her childhood in Montserrat. She emigrated to Canada in 1954. Active in Montreal's Black community.

3592 *Malcolm, as He Lived.* One-act play, produced by the Black Theatre Workshop of Montreal, May 19, 1974.

3593 *Purged.* One-act play, 1975.

3594 *Who Keeps the Young Girls Chained?* Montreal: Association of Black Social Workers, 1988. Poems.

NETHERLANDIC

RESEARCH PAPER

3595   DEEL, T. Van
"Some Aspects of Dutch Literature." VICE VERSA 2, no. 2 (1988): 28-30.
[An analysis of contemporary Dutch literature of interest to the student of Netherlandic-Canadian writing.]

ANTHOLOGIES

3596   *Canadian Journal of Netherlandic Studies/Revue canadienne d'études Neerlandaises.* C.A.A.N.S. *Tenth Anniversary/Dixieme anniversaire de L'A.L.C.A.E.N.,* edited by Adrian van den Hoven. Windsor, Ont.: University of Windsor, 1981. iii, 99 pp.
[The entire issue is devoted to the theme of Netherlandic presence in Canada. It includes, among other writings, poems, by Adrian van den Hoven, and a paper on novelist Aritha van Herk by A. van den Hoven (pp. 64-66).]

3597   *From a Chosen Land: A Dutch-Canadian Anthology,* edited by Hendrika Ruger. Windsor, Ont.: Netherlandic Press, 1986.

INDIVIDUAL AUTHORS

BOYCE, Pleuke (1942-   )
Born, née van Dam, in Zwijndrecht, The Netherlands, came to Toronto in 1961. In 1963 she moved to Antwerp, Belgium, and returned to Canada in 1974. Her works have appeared in such journals as *Bodium, Avenue, Maatstaf, The Malahat Review.* She lives in Errington, B.C.

3598   *Dutch Medley: Poems and Stories.* Windsor, Ont.: Netherlandic Press, 1986. 71 pp. illus.

BRANDIS, Marienne (1938-   )
Born in The Netherlands. She has lived in British Columbia, Nova Scotia, and now in Ontario. Holds degrees from McMaster University. Her novels are related to young adults and adults, for which she received the Saskatchewan Library Association Award.

3599   *This Spring's Sowing.* Toronto: McClelland & Stewart, 1970. 139 pp. port. Novel.

3600   *A Sense of Dust.* Illustrated with wood engravings by G. Brender. Carlisle, Ont.: Brandstead Press, 1972. 47 pp. Story.

3601   *The Tinderbox.* Erin, Ont.: Porcupine's Quill, 1985.

BRENDER à BRANDIS, Madzi
Born in The Hague, The Netherlands and emigrated to the U.S.A. While in New York, she began writing a column for the newspaper *Het Vaderland.* Came to Canada in 1947 and settled with her family in Toronto.

3602   *Land for Our Sons.* 1958.
[The author translated this book into Dutch in 1960.]

3603   *The Scent of Spruce,* illustrated by G. Brender à Brandis. Windsor, Ont.: Netherlandic Press, 1984. Stories.

COOK, Hugh (1942-   )

Born in The Hague, The Netherlands and grew up in Vancouver. He has published short stories in periodicals. Resides in Hamilton, Ont., teaching English at Redeemer College.

3604   *Cracked Wheat and other Stories.* Oakville, Ont.: Mosaic, 1985. 122 pp. Short stories.

JACOBS, Maria, pseud. (Real name: MOENS, Marja) (1930-   )

Born in Bussum, The Netherlands, educated at York University, Toronto. Editor of *Poetry Toronto*, co-editor of *Waves* and editor of *With Other Words: A Bilingual Anthology of Contemporary Poetry by Dutch Women.* Her poems have appeared in *Canadian Verse II* and other periodicals.

3605   *Precautions against Death.* Oakville, Ont.: Mosaic Press/Valley Editions, 1983. Poems and prose. [Translated into Dutch.]

3606   *The Third Taboo.* Toronto: Wolsak and Wynn, 1983. Poems.

3607   *Vijfenvijftig Sokken [Precautions against Death],* translated into Dutch by the author. Amsterdam: De Harmonie, 1986. 116 pp. Poems and prose.

3608   *What Feathers Are for.* Toronto: Mosaic, 1986. 35 pp. Poems.

3609   *Iseult, We Are Barren.* Windsor, Ont.: Netherlandic Press, 1988. Poems.

Writings about:

3610   Adachi, Ken. "Anne Frank with a Happy Ending." SUNDAY STAR (Toronto) (July 24, 1983) G: 10.
[Review of *Precautions against Death.*]

3611   Bastien, Mark. Review of *Precautions against Death.* CAN BOOK REV ANN 1984: 181.

3612   Carey, Barbara. Review of *What Feathers Are for.* CROSS-CAN WRIT Q 9, no. 1 (1983) 23-24.

3613   Donovan, Rita. Review of *Precautions against Death.* CONT VERSE II 9, no. 1 (1985)

3614   French, William. "Poetic Courage in the Face of War." GLOBE MAIL (Aug. 6, 1983): 13.
[Review of *Precautions against Death.*]

3615   Gannes, Abraham. "In Tribute to the Righteous among the Nations." JEWISH COMM NEWS (December 1984): 15.

3616   Kalushner, Irving. "Profile." NORTH YORK ARTS COUNCIL NEWS 9, no. 6 (1986): 9. port.

3617   Lawson, Sarah. Review of *Precautions against Death.* NEW STATESMAN (July 6, 1984)

3618   Levenson, Christopher. Review of *The Third Taboo.* ARC 11 (Spring 1984)

3619   Madoff, Mark. "Personality Speaking." CAN LIT No. 104 (1985): 141-44.
[Review of *Precautions against Death.*]

3620   Martindale, Sheila. "Salute to Maria Jacobs." CAN AUTH BKMN 63, no. 2 (1988): 16-19.

3621   Schepers, Ine. "Maria Jacobs, de dichter." NEDERL COUR (Feb. 21, 1984): 6. port.

3622 Thomas, Clara. "Aging in the Works of Canadian Women Writers." CAN WOMAN STUD/CAH FEMME 5, no. 3 (1984): 45-49.
[Review of *Precautions against Death*.]

3623 Van Steen, Marcus. "Maria Jacobs schreef boek over oorlogsjaren in Nederland." HOLLANDIA NEWS (Feb. 13, 1984): 4.

VAN TOORN, Peter (1944-)
Born in The Hague, The Netherlands, and came to Montreal, where he has lived since 1954. He was educated at McGill University and teaches at Sir John Abbot College in Montreal. His poems have appeared in *Antigonish Review, Copperfield, Fiddlehead, Prism International, Vanderbilt Poetry Review*, etc. Edited *Cross/Cut: Contemporary English Quebec Poetry*.

3624 *Leeway Grass*. LaSalle, Que.: Delta Canada, 1970. Poems.

3625 *In Guildenstern Country*. LaSalle, Que.: Delta Canada, 1973. 102 pp. Poems.

3626 *Mountain Stick*. Montreal: Villeneuve Publications, 1976. Poems.

3627 *Mountain Tea and other Poems*. Toronto: McClelland & Stewart, 1984. 143 pp. Poems.

NORWEGIAN

BIBLIOGRAPHIES

3628 **MALYCKY, Aleksander**
"Norwegian-Canadian Periodical Publications: A Preliminary Check List." CAN ETH STUD 2, no. 1-2 (1973): 159-61.
[A list of 9 periodical titles.]

3629 **WITH, Peter K.**
"Norwegian-Canadian Periodical Publications: First Supplement." CAN ETH STUD 5, no. 1-2 (1973): 235-38.
[Includes 41 titles.]

INDIVIDUAL AUTHORS

KANONIKOFF, Ivan

3630 *Paa Bunden av Skagerak [On the Bottom of Skagerak]*. Published serially in NORRONA CANADIAN, 1938. Novel.

MASSEL, Dona Paul

3631 *The Vikings Who Came to Fly. Poems*. London, Ont.: Third Eye, 1983. 55 pp. Poems.

OSTENSO, Martha (1900-1963)
Born near Bergen, Norway, she came to North America with her parents and lived in various towns in Minnesota and North Dakota. Her family moved to Brandon, Man., where Ostenso attended Brandon Collegiate and then moved to Winnipeg and graduated from the University of Manitoba. She taught school

in northern Manitoba, worked as a reporter on the *Winnipeg Free Press*, and moved to the U.S.A., where she wrote twelve books of fiction, a collection of poems, *A Far Land*, and a co-authored biography of Sister Elizabeth Kenney. Her works appeared in *The Scandinavian Review* and *Poetry* (Chicago).

3632   *Wild Geese.* Toronto: McClelland, 1925. 356 pp. In England under the title *The Passionate Flight* by Hodder. Reprinted by McClelland & Stewart, 1961.

Writings about:

3633   Arnason, David.   "The Development of Prairie Realism."   Ph.D. Thesis.   University of New Brunswick, 1980.

3634   Colman, Morris.   "Martha Ostenso, Prize Novelist."   MACLEAN'S 38 (Jan. 1, 1925): 56-58.

3635   King, Carlyle.   "Introduction."   In *Wild Geese.* (Toronto: McClelland and Stewart, 1961) pp. v-x.

3636   Kuropatwa, Joy.   "Ostenso, Martha."   In *The Oxford Companion to Canadian Literature*, edited by William Toye.   (Toronto: Oxford University Press, 1983) p. 626.

3637   Lawrence, Robert G.   The Geography of Martha Ostenso's *Wild Geese.*"   J CAN FIC 16 (1976)

3638   MacLellan, W.E.   "Real 'Canadian Literature'."   DAL REV 6 (October 1926): 18-33.

3639   Mullins, Stanley G.   "Some Remarks on Theme in Martha Ostenso's *Wild Geese.*"   CULTURE 23 (1962): 359-62.

3640   Ricou, Laurence R.   "The Obsessive Prairie: Martha Ostenso's *Wild Geese.*"   In his *Vertical Man/Horizontal World; Man and Landscape in Canadian Prairie Fiction.* (Vancouver: University of British Columbia Press, 1973) pp. 74-80.

3641   Stanko, Stanley.   "Image, Theme and Pattern in the Works of Martha Ostenso."   M.A. Thesis. University of Alberta, 1968.

3642   Thomas, Clara Eileen.   "Martha Ostenso's Trial of Strength."   In *Writers of the Prairies*, edited by Donald G. Stephens.   (Vancouver: University of British Columbia Press, 1973) pp. 39-50.

PAKISTANI

RESEARCH STUDIES

3643 KALSEY, Surjeet
"Canadian Panjabi Literature." In *A Meeting of Streams*, edited by M.G. Vassarji. (Toronto: Toronto South Asian Review, 1985) pp. 109-19.
[This paper provides an outline of Punjabi poetry based on the work of Surjeet Kalsey, A. Rodé, Ravi Ravinder, Sukhinder, and short story writing as represented by the writings of A. Chahal, H. Tara Singh, Ravi Ravinder, Gurumel Singh Sidhu, and Surjeet Kalsey.]

3644 KHAN, Nuzrat Yar
"Urdu Language and Literature in Canada." In *A Meeting of Streams*, edited by M.G. Vassanji. (Toronto: TSAR, 1985) pp. 95-108.
[Poetry is the main domain of Urdu creative writing in Canada. An analysis is given of the work of Wali Alam Shaheen, Irfana Aziz, Faruq Hassan, Ashfaq Hussain, and Abrar Hassan. English translations of their poems are also included.]

3645 KHAN, Nuzrat Yar
"Urdu Literature in Canada: A Preliminary Survey."
[This manuscript was prepared for the Multiculturalism Directorate. Contents: The development of the Urdu language and its literature; Urdu language and literature and Urdu writers in Canada.]

3646 *The Toronto South Asian Review* (TSAR), edited by M.G. Vassanji. Vol. 2, no. 1, 1983. 107 pp.
[Special issue devoted to Punjabi literature in Canada.]

INDIVIDUAL AUTHORS

AZIZ, Irfana (1940-   )

3647 *Berg Rez [Autumn Leaves]*. Lahore: The Author, 1971. Poems.

3648 *Jurm-i-Isayan* AFKAR, 1968. Musical play.
[Published in the drama issue of *Afkar*, Karachi. Staged in Pakistan and has been translated into English.]

BRELVI, Ikram

3649 Aakhri Perwaz [Last Flight]. Play.

3650 Barf Ki Deewar [Wall of Ice].

3651 Khoom Unmol [Peerless Blood]. Play.
[Relates to the turbulent Russo-Afghan perspective.]

HASSAN, Faruq
Author, editor. His poems have appeared in periodicals and newspapers. Edited an anthology, *Nothing but the Truth: Pakistani Short Stories*.

3652 *Chhoti Bari Nazmen*. Lahore: Kitabiyat, 1972. Short stories.
[Includes 16 short stories.]

HUSSAIN, Ashfaq

Born in Pakistan, where he published two books of poems. Continues to write in Urdu in Canada. He is editor of *Urdu International*, published in Toronto three times a year.

3653　*That Day will Dawn.* Toronto, 1986. Poems.

Writings about:

3654　Sohail, M.K. Review of *That Day will Dawn.* URDU CAN 1, no. 2 (1986): 81-84.

3655　Voll, Linda. Review of *That Day will Dawn.* UDRU CAN 1, no. 2 (1986): 78-80.

RAWĪNDARA, Ravī

Born in Sialkot, Pakistan, and obtained his M.A. degree in Punjabi language and literature from Punjab University, India. He edited *Indian Poetry Today*, vol. 6, and co-edited two collections of poems, *The Rebel Sound*, and *The Voices of Dissent.* He lives in British Columbia and has published most of his work in Punjabi.

3656　*Shahira Wica Jangala [Forest in the City].* Jalandhara: Rāja Rūpa Prakāshana, 1969. Story.

3657　Shahira Jangalī Hai [The City is Wild]. Jalandhara: Niū Buka Kampanī, 1970.

3658　*Jala Brahama-jala [Water and Water Mirage].* Jalandhara: Ke. Lāla, 1976. Poems.

3659　*Jitthe Dīwarāṃ Nahīṃ [Where There Are no Walls].* Jalandhara: Ke. Lāla, 1978. Poems.

3660　*[Restless Soul].* Surrey, B.C.: Indo-Canadian Publishers, 1978. Poems.

3661　*Ciṭṭe Kāle Dhabbe [White and Black Patches].* Jalandhara: Ke. Lāla, 1978. Poems.

3662　*[Windsong].* Surrey, B.C.: Indo-Canadian Publishers, 1980. Poems.

SADIQ, Nazneen

Journalist, short story writer. Born in Pakistan and emigrated to Canada in 1964. Her stories are based on her personal experiences in Canada.

3663　*Camels can Make You Homesick and other Stories,* illustrated by Mary Cserepy. Toronto: Lorimer, 1985. 89 pp. Short stories.

Writing about:

3664　Kertzer, Adrienne. Review of *Camels can Make You Homesick.* CAN ETH STUD 18, no. 3 (1986): 161-64.

SHAHEEN, Wali Alam

Born in Bihar, India, but migrated at an early age to East Pakistan and later to West Pakistan. He came to Canada in 1973. Published poems in such journals as *Aaina, Aajkal, Shahrah, Dastawecz, Shair, Urdu Canada,* a journal he is editing. Recipient of the Altaf Husain Hali Aalami Award, 1988. He lives in Ottawa, working for the Federal Government as a policy adviser.

3665　*Rag-e-Saaz [Lute's Vein].* Dacca: Pak Kitab Ghar, 1967. Poems.

3666　*Baynishaan [Traceless].* Karachi: Maktaba-e-Afkar, 1984. Poems.

3667   *Dreams and Destinations: Shaheen and His Poetry*, edited by Yar Nuzrat Khan. Ottawa: Canadian-Pakistan Association, 1986.
[Includes poems in Urdu and in English translation and papers about Shaheen's poetry.]

3668   *Aangan Main Baisakh Na Sawan [Neither Sun nor Rain].*

Writings about:

3669   Ahmar, Yunus. Review of *Baynishaan.* MORNING NEWS (Aug. 17, 1984)

3670   Amjad, Rasheed. "Shaheen." In *Naya Adab.* (Mandi Baha-ud-Din, Pakistan, 1969)

3671   Fauq, Haneef. "Shaheen." URDU INT 7 (1984)

3672   Hassan, Faruq "Shaheen: A Distinctive Voice." In *Dreams and Destinations.* (Ottawa: Canadian-Pakistan Association, 1986) pp. 21-25.

3673   Hussain, Jalaluddin S. Review of *Dreams and Destinations...* NEW CAN REV 1, no. 1 (1987)

3674   Hussain, Mumtaz. "The Poetry of Shaheen." AFKAR (1984)

3675   Khan, Nuzrat Yar. "Introduction." In *Dreams and Destinations.* (Ottawa: Canadian-Pakistan Association, 1986) pp. 13-20.

3676   Mahpuri, Afsar. Review of *Baynishaan.* AFKAR (December 1984)

3677   Payami, Akhtar. "Poetry and Migrations." DAWN (July 27, 1984)

3678   Shadani, Andaleeb. "Shaheen." In *Rag-e-Saaz.* (Dacca: Pak Kitab Ghar, 1967)

3679   Siddiqui, Muhhamad Ali. "Shaheen." In *Baynishaan.* (Karachi: Maktaba-e-Afkar, 1984)

3680   Singh Verma, Rajinder. Review of *Dreams and Destinations.* URDU CAN 2, no. 1 (1988): 91-94.

SIDHU, Gurumel Singh

3681   *Dubidha [Bewilderment].* Punjab: Lahore Bookshop, 1966. Poems.

3682   Betshain Sadi [Restless Century]. Punjab: Drishti, 1975. Poems.

3683   *Aperian Watang [Unseen Footprints].* Punjab: Lahore Bookshop, 1977. Poems.

TIMURI, Neelofar

3684   Nishat

3685   Phool Muskarai [The Blossom Smiled]. Novel.

PHILIPPINE

INDIVIDUAL AUTHOR

GILL, Lakshmi

Poet. Born in the Philippines, educated at Western Washington University and the University of British Columbia (M.A.). Member of the League of Canadian Poets, recipient of First Prize in Poetry, Western Washington University (1964), and a Canada Council bursary (1972). Her poems have appeared in *Canadian Forum, Quarry, Prism International, New Wave, Face to Face.* Editor of an anthology of Asian-Canadian poetry, *Bayang Magiliw*, published in the April issue of *Asianadian.* Her pamphlet, *Portraits: Man and Hastings,* was published by the League of Canadian Poets in 1984.

3686   *Rape of the Spirit.* Manila: Colcol Press, 1962. Poems.

3687   *During Rain, I Plant Chrysanthemums.* Toronto: Ryerson Press, 1966. Poems.

3688   *Mind Walls.* Fredericton, N.B.: Fiddlehead Poetry Books, 1970. Poems.

3689   *First Clearing.* Manila: Estaniel Press, 1972. Poems.

3690   *Novena to St. Jude Thaddeus.* Fredericton, N.B.: Fiddlehead Poetry Books, 1979. Poems.

3691   *Bayang Magilv.* Toronto: Asianadian Resource Centre, 1980. Poems.

3692   *Portraits: Main and Hastings.* Toronto: League of Canadian Poets, 1980. Poems.

Writings about:

3693   Bailey, Don. "A Provincial Look at Ten Volumes of Canadian Poetry." QUEEN'S Q 79 (1972): 242-54.
[Review of *Mind Walls.*]

3694   Sundara, P.K. Review of *First Clearing* and *Mind Walls.* WEST COAST REV 8, no. 1 (1973): 62-63.

3695   Weppler, Torry L. Review of *Mind Walls.* CAN FORUM 52, no. 618-619 (1972): 4.

POLISH

BIBLIOGRAPHIES

3696 DANILEWICZ ZIELIŃSKA, Maria
Bibliografia: Kultura (1958-1973); Zeszyty Historyczne (1962-1973); Działalność Wydawnica (1959-1973). Paryż: Instytut Literacki, 1975. 430 pp.
[Includes references to Polish-Canadian authors.]

3697 KOWALIK, Jan
"Bibliografia bibliografij" [Bibliography of Bibliographies]. In *Literatura Polska na obczyźnie 1940-1960*, vol. 2, edited by Tymon Terlecki. (London: B. Świderski, 1964-65) pp. 645-80.
[Pages 647-48 include bibliographies by Polish-Canadian compilers.]

3698 KOZLOWSKI, Henryk Pavel
Union List of Polish Serials in Canadian Libraries/Inventaire des publications en série polonises dans les bibliothèques canadiennes. Ottawa: Minister of Supply and Services, 1977. 406 pp.
[Includes Polish-Canadian newspapers and periodicals.]

3699 KRYCHOWSKI, T.
"The Register of Persons of Polish Origin, Actively Engaged in Canada in Scholarly Pursuits or Scientific Research." In *Polish Canadian Scholars, Scientists, Writers and Artists.* 7th ed. (Toronto: Polish Canadian Research Institute, 1970) pp. 15-30.
[A list of Polish scholars and researchers active in Canada.]

3700 MAKOWSKI, William B.
"Polish-Canadian Creative Literature: A Preliminary Check List of Authors and Pseudonyms." CAN ETH STUD 2, no. 1 (1970): 165-67.
[Includes 38 authors.]

3701 TUREK, Victor, comp.
Polonica Canadiana: Bibliographical List of the Canadian Polish Imprints, 1848-1957. Foreword by Robert H. Blackburn. Toronto: Polish Alliance Press, 1958. 138 pp.
[Includes, among other types of publications, books of poetry, short stories, novels, plays, as well as creative writings published in newspapers and periodicals.]

3702 ZOLOBKA, V.
"Polonica Canadiana." In *Przeszłość i Teraźniejszość*, edited by Benedykt Heydenkorn. (Toronto: Canadian Polish Research Institute, 1974) pp. 143-92.
[Intended as a supplement to the Turek bibliography.]

3703 ZOLOBKA, V.
Polonica Canadiana: A Bibliographical List of the Polish Imprints, 1958-1970. Toronto: Polish Alliance Press, 1978. 414 pp. Polish title page added. (Canadian Polish Institute, Canadian Polish Congress Studies 13)
[Includes an extensive supplement, "Polonica Canadiana, 1848-1957", pp. 373-414.]

BOOKS, MONOGRAPHS

3704 CZAYKOWSKI, Bogdan

Polish Writing in Canada, edited by Michael Batts. Ottawa: Multiculturalism, Secretary of State Department, 1988. 57 pp.

[Offers an analytical survey of Polish writing in Canada from the earliest to the present. Provides a select list of secondary material and a bibliography of prose, poetry, drama and biographical works.]

3705 HEYDENKORN, Benedykt, ed.
Przeszłość i Terazniejszość [Past and Present].. Toronto: Canadian Polish Research Institute, 1974. 244 pp. (Polish Research Institute in Canada. Studies, 8) Bibliography: pp. 143-92.

3706 KOS-RABCEWICZ-ZUBKOWSKI, Ludwik
The Poles in Canada. Ottawa: Polish Alliance Press, 1968. xvi, 202 pp. (Canada Ethnica 7)
[Provides summaries of the work of Alice Poznańska-Parizeau, Wanda Malatyńska de Roussan, Jadwiga Jurkszus-Tomaszewska, Adam Tomaszewski, Aleksander Grobicki, Zygmunt Nowicki, Stanisław Michalski, Danuta Bieńkowska, Barbara Czaplicka, Bogdan Czaykowski, Zofia Bohdanowiczowa, and Wacław Iwaniuk (pp. 142-49).]

3707 KOTT, Teresa; WOJCIECHOWSKI, Jerzy, eds.
Polonia for Tomorrow: Conference Sponsored by the Polish Congress, Head Executive. Toronto, May 5-7, 1972. Toronto: The Congress, 1977. 279 pp.
[Includes papers on Polish-Canadian literature, pp. 201-04, 205-07.]

3708 MAZURKIEWICZ, Casimir; TUREK, Victor
Alfons J. Staniewski, 1879-1941, Przyczynek do prasy polskiej w Kanadzie [Alfons J. Staniewski, 1879-1941, a Chapter in the History of the Polish-language Press in Canada]. Toronto: Polish Alliance Press, 1961. 62 pp.

3709 POLISH CANADIAN RESEARCH INSTITUTE
Polish Canadian Scholars, Scientists, Writers and Artists. 7th ed. Toronto: The Institute, 1970. 31 pp.
[Part I relates to literature, arts, Part II contains a list of Polish-Canadian scholars and scientists. Individual authors introduced are: Alice Poznańska-Parizeau, Wanda Malatyńska de Roussan, Wacław Iwaniuk, Zofia Bohdanowiczowa, Andrzej Busza, Barbara Czaplicka, Bogdan Czaykowski, Florian Śmieja, Danuta Bieńkowska (poets); Franciszek Kmietowicz, Jadwiga Jurkszus-Tomaszewska, Adam Tomaszewski, Zbigniew Grabowski, Eugeniusz Żytomirski, Zygmunt Nowicki, Henryk Piekarski, J. Pawlikowski (prose writers).]

3710 RADECKI, Henry; HEYDENKORN, Benedykt
A Member of a Distinguished Family: The Polish Group in Canada. Toronto: McClelland & Stewart, 1976. 240 pp.
[Although this book has very little on Polish-Canadian literature, the student will find it useful for a comprehensive introduction to the Polish presence in Canada. Specific subjects covered are: immigration, adjustment, organizations, language, the Polish press, mobility, relationship with other immigrant groups. French translation was published in 1979.]

3711 RADECKI, Henry; HEYDENKORN, Benedykt
Un membre d'une famille distinguée: Les communautés polonaises du Canada, par Le Cercle du Livre de France, 1979. 289 pp.
[Translation of *A Member of a Distinguished Family*....]

3712 TERLECKI, Tymon, ed.
Literatura Polska na obczyźnie, 1940-1960/Polish Literature Abroad, 1940-1960. London: B. Świderski, 1964-1966. 2 v.

[A collection of studies of Polish creative writing outside Poland. Vol. 1: Poetry: pp. 23-131; Narrative Prose: pp. 133-85; Drama: pp. 187-208. Vol. 2: Documentary Literature: pp. 11-167; General evaluation of emigré literature: pp. 619-43. Includes Polish-Canadian authors.]

3713 **WOLODKOWICZ, Andrzej**
Polish Contribution to Arts and Sciences in Canada. Montreal: Polish Institute of Arts and Sciences in America, 1969. xxxii, 363 pp. [32] pp. of plates, illus.
[Contents: Preface, introduction and bibliography (pp. 7-18); Polish emigration to Canada (pp. 19-30); Polish contribution to the arts in Canada (p. 31); Polish contribution to the universities, research centres, government, engineering, etc. (pp. 31-261). Contains extensive biographies throughout the text.]

RESEARCH PAPERS

3714 **BIEŃKOWSKA, Danuta Irena**
"Anthologies of Contemporary Polish Prose in English Translation." CAN SLAVON PAPERS 8 (1966): 243-49.
[Gives an analysis of current Polish writing based on several anthologies including *The Broken Mirror, The Bitter Harvest, The Modern Polish Mind*, all published outside Poland.]

3715 **BIEŃKOWSKA, Danuta Irena**
"Polish Studies in North America." POL REV 14 (1969): 86-89.

3716 **BRZEKOWSKI, Jan**
"Poezje Adama Czerniowskiego, Bogdana Czajkowskiego i Bolesława Taborowskiego" [The Poetry of Adam Czerniowski, Bogdan Czaykowski, and Bolesław Taborowski.] KULTURA 117/118.

3717 **CARDINAL, Clive H.**
"Some Polish and German-Canadian Poetry." CAN ETH STUD 2 (1969): 67-76.

3718 **CYBULSKA, Maja E.**
"Antologia poezji polsko-kanadyjskiej" [An Anthology of Polish-Canadian Poetry]. PAMIĘTNIK LITERACKI 9 (1985): 118-22.
[Review.]

3719 **CZERNIAWSKI, Adam**
"Wiersze współczesny." (Londyn: Oficyna Poetów i Malarzy, 1977)
[A review of the work of Andrzej Busza, Bogdan Czaykowski and Wacław Iwaniuk.]

3720 **DANILEWICZ-ZIELIŃSKA, Maria**
"Szkice o literaturze emigracyjnej" [Sketches of emigré Literature]. INSTYTUT LITERACKI (1978)
[Reference is made to several Polish-Canadian authors.]

3721 **GAREBIAN, Keith**
Review of *Seven Polish Canadian Poets.* POET CAN REV 7 (1985)

3722 **GIERGIELEWICZ, Mieczysław**
"Twórczość poetycka" [Poetry]. In *Literatura Polska na obczyźnie, 1940-1960*, edited by Tymon Terlecki. (London: B. Świderski, 1964) vol. 1, pp. 23-131.

3723 **GRODECKI, J.**
"Ethnic Groups and the Future of Canadian Culture." In *Polonia for Tomorrow*, edited by Teresa Kott and J.A. Wojciechowski. (Toronto: Polish Canadian Congress, 1977) pp. 217-32.

[A panel discussion on ethnic culture, language and heritage. Participants: J. Grodecki (moderator), K. Bielski, J.S. Kalba, B.G. Kayfetz, and R. Perry (speakers).]

3724 HEYDENKORN, Benedykt
"Literatura slowieńska w Kanadzie" [Slavic Literature in Canada]. KULTURA No. 11 (1966): 134-36

3725 HEYDENKORN, Benedykt
"Polacy w kulturze Kanadyjskiej" [The Poles in Canadian Culture]. TEMATY 31-32 (1969): 463-72.
[Includes literature.]

3726 JURKSZUSZ-TOMASZEWSKA, Jadwiga
"Polish Writers in Canada." In *Polonia for Tomorrow*, edited by Teresa Kott and J.A. Wojciechoswski. (Toronto: Canadian Polish Congress, 1977) pp. 201-04.
[An outline of Polish writing in Canada.]

3727 KOERNER, Anna
"Polish Writing in Canada." Ottawa, 1985.
[Manuscript prepared for the Multiculturalism program. Provides a summary of Polish-Canadian memoirs, prose, poetry and drama. Gives analysis of the following authors: Anna Żerańska, Adam Tomaszewski, Zygmunt Nowicki, Henryk Piekarski, Wacław Liebert, Henryk Malak (authors of memoirs); Danuta Irena Bieńkowska, Zofia Bohdanowiczowa, Zbigniew Grabowski, Antoni Malatyński, Eugeniusz Żytomirski, Rafał Malczewski (prose writers); Romualda Bromke, Andrzej Busza, Bogdan Czaykowski, Artur Janusz Ihnatowicz, Wacław Iwaniuk, Jerzy Korey-Krzeczowski, Stanisław Michalski, Florian Smieja, and Stanisław Zybała (poets). Also includes an extensive bibliography of work by the above authors.]

3728 MARKIEWICZ, Zygmunt
"Proza beletrystyczna" [Narrative Prose]. In *Literatura Polska na obczyźnie, 1940-1960*, edited by Tymon Terlecki. (London: B. Świderski, 1964) vol. 1, pp. 133-73.
[An extensive study of the literary output by Polish prose writers outside Poland.]

3729 MIĄZEK, Bonifacy.
"Młoda poezja emigracji." PRZEMIANY 7 (1969)
[Includes Polish-Canadian poets.]

3730 NEMETZ, Lillian Jagna
"Polish Poets in Canada: A Comparative Study." M.A. Thesis. University of British Columbia, 1976.
[An analysis of various aspects of Polish emigré poetry in the context of English and French-Canadian poetry. Authors analyzed are Wacław Iwaniuk, Danuta Irena Bieńkowska, Zofia Bohdanowiczowa, Janusz Ihnatowicz, Frank Kwietowicz, etc.]

3731 OSTROWSKI, Jan.
"Dramatopisarstwo" [Drama]. In *Literatura Polska na obczyźnie, 1940-1960*, edited by Tymon Terlecki. (London: B. Świderski, 1964) vol. 1.

3732 SAMBOR, Michał
"Uwagi o prozie beletrystycznej" [Notes on Narrative Prose]. In *Literatura Polska na obczyźnie*, edited by Tymon Terlecki. (London: B. Świderski, 1964) vol. 1, pp. 175-85.

3733 ŚMIEJA, Florian
"Notes on Polish Canadian Creative Literature." POLYPHONY 2 (1984): 105-09.

(A summary of Polish literature in Canada. Provides an analysis of traditional and modern tendencies in poetry, prose and biographical publications.]

3734 ŚMIEJA, Florian
"Pisarze polscy w Kanadzie [Polish Writing in Canada]. ECHO TYG (October 1985) 10-16; 17-23; 24-30.
[A survey of creative literature based on the work of Polish-Canadian poets, novelists, playwrights and authors of biography.]

3735 TOMASZEWKSKI, Adam
"Polish Immigrant Writers: Publishing Opportunities." In *Polonia for Tomorrow*, edited by Teresa Kott and Jerzy Wojciechowski. (Toronto: Canadian Polish Congress, 1977) pp. 205-07.
[The author describes the limited funds and marketing possibilities available for Polish-Canadian authors. To overcome these shortcomings, he recommends that publishing funds for the promotion of Polish-Canadian books be established.]

3736 WASIUTYŃSKI, Wojciech
"Literatura Religijna" [Religious Literature]. In *Literatura Polska na obczyźnie, 1940-1960*, edited by Tymon Terlecki. (London: B. Świderski, 1964) vol. 1, pp. 438-66.
[Describes modern trends in theological and philosophical literature.]

3737 WEINTRAUB, Wiktor
"Literatura emigracyjna wczoraj i dziś" [Emigré Literature Yesterday and Today]. In *Literatura Polska na obczyźne, 1940-1960*, edited by Tymon Terlecki. (London: B. Świderski, 1964) vol. 1, pp. 15-21.
[An outline of the various literary trends from the traditional romantic movements to modern literary styles.]

3738 WIENIEWSKI, Ignacy
"Wznowienia tekstów pisarzy polskich i obcych" [New Editions of Polish and Foreign Authors]. In *Literatura Polska na obczyźnie, 1940-1960*, edited by Tymon Terlecki. (London: B. Świderski, 1964) vol. 1, pp. 445-52.
[A statistical survey of literary publications in nine countries including Palestine, Great Britain, Germany, France and Argentina.]

ANTHOLOGIES

3739 *Seven Polish Canadian Poets: An Anthology*, with introduction by Zbigniew Folejewski. Toronto: Polish Canadian Publishing Fund, 1984. 223 pp. ports.
[Includes poems in Polish and English translation by Zofia Bohdanowiczowa, Wacław Iwaniuk, Florian Śmieja, Danuta Irena Bieńkowska, Janusz Ihnatowicz, Bogdan Czaykowski, and Andrzej Busza. Biographical notes are also provided.]

3740 *Wiersze i inne okolicznościowe utwory na: 1. Dzień Matki. 2. Dzień. 3. Maja*, edited by M. Rymanowski. Toronto: Rada Edukacyjna Związku Polaków w Kanadzie, 1958. 33 leaves. (Mimeographed.)

INDIVIDUAL AUTHORS

BADOWSKI, Stanisław

3741 *W kregu wspomnien: na ojczystym szlaku [In the Circle of One's Memories: Along The Pathways of Fatherland]*. Toronto: W Drukarni Głosu Polskiego, 1983. 98 pp. Poems.

BIEŃKOWSKA, Danuta Irena (1927-1974)
Born in Toruń, spent several years in labour camps in the USSR and in refugee camps in Persia and India. She was educated at London University, University of Toronto (M.A.) and the School of Slavonic and East European Studies in London. Published short stories and poems in periodicals and anthologies. Taught at the University of Toronto. Her papers are held by the Thomas Fisher Rare Book Library, University of Toronto.

3742 *Między liniami [Between the Lines]*. Londyn: Staraniem Związku Pisarzy Polskich na Obczyźnie, B. Świderski, 1959. 31 pp. Poems.

3743 *Pieśń suchego języka [Songs of a Dry Tongue]*. Paris: IL, 1971. Poems.

3744 *Między brzegami: Poezja i proza [Between Coasts: Poems and Prose]*, edited by J. Budurowicz; introduction by Louis Iribarne. Londyn: Oficyna Poetów i Malarzy, 1978. 447 pp. Poems and short stories.

Writing about:

3745 Miązek, Bonifacy. "W kręgu uczucia: O poezji Bieńkowsjiej i Obertyńskiej." In *Teksty i komentarze*. (Londyn: Oficyna Poetów i Malarzy, 1983) pp. 138-43.

BOHDANOWICZOWA, Zofia
Born in Poland and emigrated to Canada in 1960. She wrote short stories and poems and translated American, English, French and Byelorussian poetry into Polish. She published a book of short stories, *Droga do daugiel*, in 1938, reprinted in 1955.

3746 *Ziemia miłośći* [The Land of Love]. Londyn: Nakładem Społeczności Akademickiej, 1954. Poems.

3747 *Gwiazdy i kamienie: poweść [Stones and Stars: A Story]*. Londyn: Katolicki Ośrodek Wydawniczy "Veritas", 1960. 200 pp. Novel.

3748 *Przeciwstawiając się świerszczom [Countering Crickets]*. Londyn: Katolicki Ośrodek Wydawniczy "Veritas", 1965. Poems.

Writing about:

3749 Heydenkorn, Benedykt. "Żywot prosty a złożonyi." OFICYNA POETÓW 3 (1966): 9-11.

BRODA, Joseph Walter (1906-   )

3750 *W cieniu kanadyjskiego klonu [In the Shade of the Canadian Maple Tree]*. Toronto: Biblioteczka Kieszonkowa, 1966. 116 pp. Poems and short stories.

3751 *Na ruchomej taśmie życia/On Life's Moving Assembly Line*. Toronto: The Author, 1970. 116 pp. Poems.

3752 Weterańskie listy [Letters of a War Veteran]. Toronto: The Author, 1971. Letters.

BROMKE, Romualda (?   -1962)
Born in Warsaw, came to Canada via Germany and England in 1950. Some of her early poems have appeared in the Polish underground papers.

3753 *Rymy moje [My Rhymes].* Londyn: Polskie Towarzystwo Literackie, 1964. 79 pp. Poems, published posthumously.

BRYCHT, Andrzej

3754 *Zoom: A Novel,* translated from the Polish by Kevin Windale. Toronto: Simon & Pierre, 1978. Novel.

3755 *Hubris.* Londyn: Polskie Towarzystwo Literackie, 1984. Novel.

3756 *Zmienna ogniskowa [Zoom Lens].* Londyn: Polskie Towarzystwo Literackie, 1986. Novel

Writing about:

3757 Kapolka, G.T. Review of *Zoom.* CAN BOOK REV ANN 1981

3758 Ramsey, R.H. Review of *Zoom.* CAN FORUM 59 (1979): 31.

3759 Solecki, Sam. Review of *Zoom.* UNIV TOR Q 49-50 (1979-80): 323-24.

BUCZEK, Roman

3760 *Był taki czas [There was such a Time].* Toronto: Century, 1981. Autobiography.

BUSZA, Andrzej (1938-   )
Born in Cracow, Poland. He was educated in the U.K. He teaches English at the University of British Columbia. He has published widely in Polish periodicals. He was awarded the Kościelski Foundation Prize for Literature in 1962.

3761 *Znaki wodne [Watermarks].* Paris: Instytut Literacki, 1969. 64 pp. (Biblioteka "Kultury", tome 1974) Poems.

3762 *Astrologer in the Underground,* translated from the Polish by Jagna Boraks and Michael Bullock. Athens, OH: Ohio University Press, 1970. 61 pp. Poems.
[Text in English and Polish.]

3763 *Old Men.* Vancouver: Barbarian Press, 1980. Poems.

Writings about:

3764 Bullock, Michael. "Introduction." In *Astrologer in the Underground.* (Athens, OH.: Ohio University Press, 1970)

3765 Green, P. "The Relevance of Surrealism, with some Canadian Perspectives." MOSAIC (1969): 2-4.

3766 Halikowska, Teresa. Review of *Znaki wodne.* WIADOMOŚCI (June 21, 1970)

3767 Wachowicz, Barbara. *Malwy na lewadach.* (Warszawa: Wydawnistwo Radia i Telewizji, 1983) pp. 60-68.

CHARNEY, Ann
Born in Warsaw, Poland. Educated at McGill University and the Sorbonne in Paris (M.A. in French Literature). She is a member of PEN, PWAC, columnist for *Maclean's,* and contributor to Op-Ed page of *Toronto Star.* Received several awards.

3768   *Dobryd. [Dobryd].* Don Mills, Ont.: New Press, 1973. Prose.

Writing about:

3769   "Ann Charney." In *Canada Writes!* (Toronto: Writers' Union of Canada, 1977) pp. 64-65. port.

CHCIUK, Andrzej

3770   *Trzysta mięsiecy (Dalszy ciąg Emigranckiej. Opowieści [Three Hundred Months: Ongoing Emigrant Story. Novel].* Toronto: Polski Fundusz Wydawniczy w Kanadzie, 1983. 320 pp. port. Novel.

CZARNYSZEWICZ, Florian

3771   *Nadberezyńcy; Powieść [Nadberezyńcy: A Story].* Toronto: Alliance Library, 1976. 468 pp. Novel.

CZAYKOWSKI, Bogdan (1932-   )
Born in Równe, Poland. Came to Canada after World War II via Persia, Africa and England. He was educated at the University of London. Former editor of *Kontynenty*, and compiler of the Polish issue of *Modern Poetry in Translation.* He was head of the Department of Slavonic Studies at UBC. (1974-88). Recipient of the Kościelski Foundation Literary Award.

3772   *Trzciny czcionek [Reeds of Print].* Londyn: Oficyna Poetów i Malarzy, 1957. Poems.

3773   *Reductio ad absurdum i przezwyciężenie (dialektyka wiersza) [Reductio ad absurdum and Conquest (A Dialectic Poem)].* Londyn: Nakładem autora, 1958. Poems.

3774   *Sura [Argument with Limits].* Londyn: Oficyna Poetów i Malarzy, 1961. Poems.

3775   *Spór z graniciami: poezje [Border Confrontation: Poems].* Paris: Instytut Literacki, 1964. 58 pp. (Biblioteka "Kultury", tome 98) Poems.

3776   *Point-no-point, 1953-1970.* Paris: Instytut Literacki, 1971. 96 pp. (Biblioteka "Kultury", tome 201)

Writings about:

3777   Czerniawski, Adam. "Czaykowskiego raj utracony" [Czaykowski's Lost Paradise]. In Liryka i druk. (Londyn: Oficyna Poetów i Malarzy, 1972) pp. 15-22.

3778   Czerniawski, Adam. "Pocztówka kanadyska z obrazkiem i legenda" [Canadian Postcard with a Picture and a Legend]. KULTURA 11 (1981): 110-13.

3779   Czerniawski, Adam. "Świadomość archetypiczna" [The Archetype Consciousness]. WIADOMOŚC (Oct. 3, 1971)

3780   Kunciewicz, Piotr. "Zadomowieni w kraju" [Finding Comfort at Home: The Poetry of B. Czaykowski]. PRZEG TYG 12 (1987)

3781   Marcinów, Zdzisław. "'Urodzony wiele razy'. O poezji Bogdana Czaykowskiego" [Born Many Times]. In *Wśród poetów współczesnych: Studia i szkice.* (Katowice: Universytet Sląski, 1986) pp. 142-52.

3782 Rostworowski, Jan. "Między wierszami" [Between the Lines]. WIADOMOŚCI (Dec. 6, 1964)

DZIĘCIOŁOWA, Krystyna (1914-1984)

3783 *Niedokończone strofy... Ostatni zbiór werszy [Unfinished Stanzas: The Last Collection of Poems].* Delta, B.C.: Jerzy Dzieciol, 1985. 86 pp. port. Poems.

GRABOWSKI, Zbigniew

Editor, translator, novelist, short story writer, essayist, Grabowski was editor of *Kontynenty,* a Polish literary journal, and translator of books from various languages into English. Author of two books of essays.

3784 *Anna [Anna].* Londyn: Bibliotek Autorów Polskich, 1945. Novel.

3785 *Czarny anioł [Black Angel].* Londyn: Oficyna Poetów i Malarzi, 1960. Short stories.

3786 *Nagrobek: nowele [Tombstone: Novellas].* Londyn: Oficyna Poetów i Malarzi, 1964. Short stories.

3787 *Śpiew dziewcząt [The Chant of Girls].* Londyn: Polska Fundacja Kulturalna, 1964. Memoirs.

3788 *Rosa Mystica.* [Rosa Mystica]. Londyn: Oficyna Poetów i Malarzi, 1966. Collected writings.

3789 *Rozmowy z tobą [Conversations with You].* Londyn: Oficyna Poetów i Malarzi, 1974. Essays.

GROBICKI, Aleksander

3790 *Szlakiem bojowym pradziadów. Wspomnienia o żołnierzach polskich na emigracji 1821-1878 [In the Martial Steps of Our Ancestors. Remembering Polish Emigré Soldiers 1821-1878].* Londyn: Veritas, 1956. Biographical stories.

3791 *Wojenne błyski [Flashes of the War].* Toronto: The Author, 1964. Stories.

3792 *Diamenty i aligatory [Diamonds and Alligators].* Toronto: The Author, 1966. 142 pp. Novel.

3793 *Skarby na dnie mórz [Treasures at the Bottom of the Sea].* Gdańsk: Wydawnictwo Morskie, 1974. Novel.

GROCHOWSKA, Wanda

3794 *Ciernistyn szlakiem [Along a Thorny Path].* Winnipeg: Gázeta Katolicka, 1938. Published serially. Novel.

HEINE-KOEHN, Lala (1936-   )

Born in Warsaw, Poland, spent her early years in her native land and Germany. Attended the Haendel Conservatory, Munich, the University of Munich (Law) and the University of Victoria. Her poems have appeared in *Freelance, Other Voices, Manitoba Writers' News, Malahat Review, Arc, Salt,* and *Grain,* and in anthologies. She lives in Victoria.

3795 *Portraits.* Saskatoon: Thistledown Press, 1977. Poems.

3796 *Sandpoems.* Fredericton, N.B.: Fiddlehead Poetry Books, 1979. Poems.

3797 *The Eyes of the Wind.* Winnipeg: Turnstone Press, 1981-1982. Poems.

3798   *Forest Full of Rain.* Victoria: Sono Nis Press, 1982. 104 pp. Poems.

HETMAŃSKA, Tamara

3799   *Myśli są różne [Thoughts of Various Kind].* Toronto: Polish Voice, 1976. 113 pp. Poems.

3800   *Zapomniane ścieżki [Forgotten Trails].* Toronto: W Drukarni "Głosu Polskiego", 1981. 163 pp. illus. Poems.

Writing about:

3801   Grabowski, Yvonne. Review of *Myśli są różne.* UNIV TOR Q 47 (1977/78): 500.

HEYDUK, J.R.

3802   *Śmiech ust kątów [Smiling lip-corners].* Toronto: Century, 1985. Poems.

IHNATOWICZ, Janusz Artur (1929-   )
Born in Wilno, Poland, came to Canada in 1951. In 1958 he returned to Poland, attended a seminary in Kielce and the Academy of Catholic Theology in Warsaw. After being ordained a priest in 1962, he returned to Canada. He is now teaching theology at the St. Thomas University, Houston, Texas.

3803   *Displeasure.* Londyn: Oficyna Poetów i Malarzy, 1975. Poems.

3804   *Pejzaż z postaciami [Landscape with Figures].* Londyn: Oficyna Poetów i Malarzi, 1972. Poems.

3805   *Wiersze wybrane [Selected Poems].* Kraków: Znak, 1973. Poems.

Writing about:

3806   Czerniawski, Adam. "Janusza Ihnatowicza *Wiersze wybrane*" [Janusz Ihnatowicz's *Selected Poems*]. KULTURA 11 (1973): 145-49.

IWANIUK, Wacław (1915-   )
Born in Chełm Lubelski, Poland. Following his graduation from the University of Warsaw he joined the Polish Foreign Office and was posted to Buenos Aires. In 1948 he emigrated to Canada, where he was employed as an interpreter by the City of Toronto. Some of his books of poems have been translated into English, French, German and Italian. He has received several awards and literary prizes for his poetry.

3807   *Czas Don Kichota. Poezje [Don Quixote's Time: Poems].* Londyn: Wydawnictwo Światowego Związku Polaków z Zagranicy, 1946. 31 pp. Poems.

3808   *Dni białe i dni czerwone [Red and White Days].* Bruksela: Klon, 1947. 44 pp. Poems.

3809   *Dziennik z podróży tropikalnej i wiersze o wojnie [A Diary from the Tropics and Poems about War].* Paris: Kultura, 1951. 16 pp. Poems.

3810   *Gorycze nocy: Poemat [Bitter Night: Poem].* Paris: Kultura, 1951. 10 pp. Poem.

3811   *Pieśń nad pieśniami: Poemat [Song of Songs: Poem],* with Jozef Czapski. Londyn: Oficyna Poetów i Malarzi, 1953. 43 pp. Poems.

3812   *Milczenia: wiersze, 1949-1959 [Stillness: Poems, 1949-1959].* Paris: Instytut Literacki, 1959. 41 pp. (Biblioteka Kultury, tome 49) Poems.

3813 *Wybór wierszy [Selected Poems].* Paris: Instytut Literacki, 1965. 106 pp. (Biblioteka Kultury, tome 109)
[Translated into French, German and Italian]

3814 *Ciemny czas: Poezje [Dark Times: Poems].* Paris: Instytut Literacki, 1968. 75 pp. Poems.

3815 *Lustro: Wiersze [Mirror: Poems].* Londyn: Oficyna Poetow i Malarzi, 1971. 59 pp. Poems.

3816 *Nemezis idze pustymi drogami [Nemesis Walks on Empty Paths].* Londyn: Oficyna Stanisław Gliwa, 1978. Poems.

3817 *Dark Times: Selected Poems*, translated from the Polish by Jagna Boraks, et al. Foreword by Zbigniew Folejewski. Edited by John Robert Colombo. Toronto: Hounslow Press, 1979. 109 pp. Poems.

3818 *Evenings on Lake Ontario. From My Canadian Diary.* Toronto: Hounslow Press, 1981. Poems.

3819 *Podroż do Europy. Opowidania i szkice [European Journey].* Londyn: Polska Fundacja Kulturalna, 1982.

Writings about:

3820 Baliński, Stanisław. "Światowiec i samotnik" [The Man of the World and the Recluse]. (Londyn: Dziennik Polski. Środa Literacka, 1979): 22.
[Review of *Nemezis idzie pustymi drogami.*]

3821 Bednarczyk, Czesław. "Mądre skąpstwo słów" [The Wise Persimony of Work]. KONTYNENTY - NOWY MERK 81 (1965)

3822 Bemrose, John. Review of *Evenings on Lake Ontario.* GLOBE MAIL (Nov. 23, 1981)

3823 Bird, Thomas. "Wacław Iwaniuk." In *Modern Polish Writing: Essays and Documents, Queens Slavic Papers.* (New York: Queens College Press, 1973)

3824 Boraks, Jagna. "Wacław Iwaniuk's Poetry." AMER REV (1977)

3825 Boraks, Jagna. "Translator's Note." In *Dark Times.* (Toronto: Hounslow, 1979) pp. 97-102.

3826 Brzękowski, Jan. "Awangarda" [Avantgarde]. PRZEG HUMANIST 1 (1958)

3827 Brzękowski, Jan. "Omówienie zbioru pt. Milczenia Wacława Iwaniuka" [Wacław Iwnuk's Silence]. KONTYNENTY - NOWY MERK 26 (1961)

3828 Chciuk, Andrzej. "Poezja polska na emigracji-i Iwaniuk" [Polish Poetry in Exile - and Iwaniuk]. TYG POLSK (1968)

3829 Colombo, John Robert. "Iwaniuk Ignored." BKS CAN 7, no. 6 (1978): 33.

3830 Cybulska, Maja E. "Rozmowa mistrza Iwaniuka ze śmiercią" [Iwaniuk Master's Conversation with Death]. In *Tematy i pisarze.* (Londyn: Oficyna Poetów i Malarzy, 1982)

3831 Cybulska, Maja E. " 'Sylwetka słowa' Wacława Iwaniuka" [Wacław Iwaniuk's Word Image]. In *Pamiętnik Literacki,* tome 6 (Londyn, 1983) (Związek Pisarzy Polskich na Obczyźnie.)

3832   Cybulska, Maja E. *Wacław Iwaniuk poeta: z wyborem poezji Wacława Iwaniuka [Wacław Iwaniuk the Poet: With Wacław Iwaniuk's Selections of Poems].* Londyn: Oficyna Poetów i Malarzi, 1984. 125 pp.
        [Includes poems by Iwaniuk (pp. 83-122), and writings about Iwaniuk (pp. 78-81).]

3833   Czachowski, Kazimierz. [Wacław Iwaniuk.] In *Najnowsza polska twórczość literacka 1935-1937.* (Lwów, 1938)

3834   Czerniawski, Adam. "Dwa tomiki poetickie Oficyny" [Two Volumes of poetry published by Oficyna]. (Londyn: Oficyna Poetów i Malarzi, 1973)
        [Review of *Lustro.*]

3835   Czerniawski, Adam. "Nowe wiersze Iwanuka" [Iwaniuk's New Poems]. KULTURA 6-7 (1968): 198-201
        [Review of *Ciemny czas.*]

3836   Czerniawski, Adam. "Owijając słowo w bawełnęku." OFICYNA POETÓW 2 (1966): 29-30.

3837   Czernik, Stanisław. [Wacław Iwaniuk.] In *Okolica Poetów. Wspomnienia i materialy.* (Posnań: Wydawnictwo Poznańskie, 1961)

3838   Czuchnowski, Marian. "Szelest sreba. O rzetelności *Wyboru wierszy* Wacława Iwaniuka" [Rattling of Silver. Truthful Words about Wacław Iwaniuk's *Selected Poems.]* DZIEN POLSK ŚRODA LIT 22 (1965)

3839   Danilewicz-Zielińska, Maria. [Wacław Iwaniuk.] In *Szkice o literaturze emigracyjnej.* (Paryż: Instytut Literacki, 1978)

3840   Dempster, Barry. Review of *Dark Times.* Q & Q no. 1 (1980)

3841   Dusza, Edward L. "O polskiej poezji emigracyjnej" [On Polish Poetry in Exile]. ECHO MAG 4, no. 5 (1973)

3842   Folejewski, Zbigniew. "Polish Letters 1965." BKS ABR (1966)

3843   Folejewski, Zbigniew. "Wstęp do: *Dark Times. Selected Poems* of Wacław Iwaniuk" [Introduction. In *Dark Times. Selected Poems...*]. (Toronto: Hounslow Press, 1979.

3844   Giergielewicz, Mieczysław. Review of *Ciemny zas.* BKS ABR 39 (1969)

3845   Grabowski, Yvonne. Review of *Lustro* UNIV TOR Q 47 (1977-78)

3846   Grabowski, Yvonne. Review of *Dark Times.* CAN ETH STUD 14 , no. 1 (1982): 177-78.

3847   Grabowski, Yvonne. Review of *Nemezis idze pustymi drogami.* UNIV TOR Q 48 (1978-79): 495-96.

3848   Gross, Natan. "Ocalić pamięć. Iwaniuk i epoka pieców" [Preserving Memories. Iwaniuk and the Millenarian Flames]. WIADOMOŚCI 1 (1981)

3849   Heydenkorn, Benedykt. "Poeci polsci w Toronto" [Polish Poets in Toronto]. ZWIĄZKOWIEC (1963) (Boże Narodzenie)

3850   Islam, S.M. Review of *Dark Times*. WHIG STAND MAG (July 12, 1980)

3851   Jaksiński, Józef Piotr. "Nowy tom Iwaniuka" [Iwaniuk's New Book of Poetry]. KULTURA 7-8
(1965): 204-12.
[Review of *Wybor wierszy*.]

3852   Jaworski, Kazimierz A. "W kręgu 'Kameny' " [In the 'Kameny Circle'.] Lublin: Wydawnictwo
Lubelskie (1965)

3853   Kryszak, Janusz. [Wacław Iwaniuk.] In Katastrofizm ocalający, Warszawa, Poznań, Torun, 1978,
Państwowe Wydawnictwo Naukowe.

3854   Kryszak, Janusz. "Wyobraźnia traumatyczna. Próba przybliżenia Wacława Iwaniuka" [Traumatic
Imagination. An Attempt to Get Closer to Wacław Iwaniuk]. In *Pisarz na obczyźnie*, edited by T.
Bujnicki and W. Wyskiel. (Wrocław, 1985) pp. 109, 121.

3855   Krzyżanowsky, J.R. Review of *Lustro*. BKS ABR 47 (1973): 192.

3856   Laks, Szymon. [Wacław Iwaniuk.] In *Poloniki.... Polemiki... Polityki....* (Londyn: Oficyna Poetów
i Malarzi, 1977)

3857   Lechoń, Jan. [Wacław Iwaniuk.] DZIENNIK 1 (1967); WIADOMOŚCI 2 (1970). (Nakładem
Wiadomości i Polskiej Fundacji Kulturalnej.)

3858   Lupack, Alan C. Review of *Dark Times*. POL REV 3-4 (1980)

3859   Maciuszko, Jerzy. Review of *Dark Times*. WORLD LIT TODAY 54 (1980): 455-56.

3860   Miązek, Bonifacy. Review of *Ciemny czas* and *Lustro*. In *Teksty i komentarze*. (Londyn: Oficyna
Poetów i Malarzy, 1983) pp. 97-113.

3861   Moritz, Albert. "Lessons of Catastrophe. *Dark Times* by Wacław Iwaniuk." BKS CAN 8, no. 10
(1979): 22-23.

3862   Moritz, Albert. "World of Wonders." BKS CAN no. 2 (1982): 22-23.

3863   Mrozowski, Wacław. [Wacław Iwaniuk.] In *Cyganeria*. (Lublin: Wydawnisctwo Lubelskie, 1963)

3864   Pollak, Seweryn. [Wacław Iwaniuk.] In *Spotkania z Czechowiczem. Wspomnienia i szkice (praca
zbiorowa)*. (Lublin: Wydawnictwo Lubelskie, 1971)

3865   Sułkowski, Tadeusz. "Trzej poeci" [Three Poets]. In: *Orzel Biali.* (Bruksela, 23, 1947.)

3866   Terlecki, Tymon. [Wacław Iwaniuk.] In *Literatura polska na obczyźnie 1940-1960*. (Londyn: B.
Świderski, 1964-1965) vols. 1 and 2.

3867   Tomaszewski, Adam. "Kiedy Toronto promieniowało polskością..." [When Toronto Radiated
Polish Thoughts]. WIADOMOŚCI 45 (1975)

3868   Tomaszewski, Adam. "Chłopcy z Jamy Smocy" [The Boys from Jamy Smocy]. WIADOMOŚCI
no. 4 (1976)

JANTA, Alexander

3869   *Widzenie wiary [Vision of Faith].* [Montreal] Nakładem autora, 1946. 123 pp. Poems.

JANUSZKO, Stanisław

3870   *Wyszystko przemija [Everything Passes].* Toronto: Polish Alliance Press, 1973. 101 pp. Poems.

3871   *Posiew tęsknoty i satyry [Yearning of Nostalgia and Satire].* Toronto: Polish Alliance Press, 1974. 103 pp. Poems.

3872   *Ponad horyzontem [Above the Horizon].* Toronto, 1975. 96 pp. Poems and plays.

3873   *Synowie pól [Sons of the Land].* Toronto: The Author, 1976. 92 pp. Poems.

3874   *Klęski i zwycięstwa [Victories and Defeats].* Toronto: The Author, 1977. 102 pp. Poems.

3875   *Brzask nowej ery [Sunrise over a New Era].* Toronto: w Drukarni "Głosu Polskiego", 1981. 109 pp. Poems.

JARUCKI, Jerzy

3876   *Kapusta z kaszą [Sauerkraut with Buckwheat].* Toronto: Century, 1984. Short stories.

JURKSZUS-TOMASZEWSKA, Jadwiga

3877   *Toronto, Tronto, Trana [Toronto, Tronto, Trana],* with Adam Tomaszeski. Toronto: The Author, 1967. 188 pp. Stories.

3878   *I to jest Meksyk [And this is Mexico],* with Adam Tomaszewski. Londyn: Oficyna Poetów i Malarzi, 1974. 295 pp. Stories.

3879   *Wczoraj i dzisiaj [Yesterday and Today].* Toronto: The Author, 1985. Autobiography.

Writings about:

3880   Iwanska, A. Review of *I to jest Meksyk.* KULTURA No. 4 (1975)

3881   Jacewicz, A. Review of *I to jest Meksyk.* WIADOMOŚCI No. 1519 (May 11, 1975)

3882   Nowotarska, R. Review of *Toronto, Tronto, Trana.* OST WIAD No. 4 (Apr. 30, 1967)

3883   Rusinek, Z. Review of *I to jest Meksyk.* GŁOS POLSK (March 6, 1975)

3884   Splawinski, M. Review of *Toronto, Tronto, Trana.* KULTURA No. 11 (1968)

KMIETOWICZ, Franciszek A. (pseud.: ANDREWS, Frank) (1912-   )

3885   *Kanadyjski oberek [Canadian 'Oberek'].* Toronto: Drukiem półtygodnika Związkowiec, 1960. 111 pp. Short stories.

3886   *Rejoice, We Conquer.* Toronto: New Line Fraternity, 1960. 59 pp. Stories.

3887   *City I Love.* Toronto: New Line Fraternity, 1961. 59 pp. Stories.

3888   *Bogiem sławiena: Powieśc [In God's Name: Story].* Windsor, Ont.: Towarzystwo Orkana, 1979. 171 pp. Novel.

3889   *Stars over Toronto; Dwie gwiazdy.* Windsor, Ont., 1979. Stories.

3890   *Kiedy Kraków był trzecim Rzymem [When Cracow was the Third Rome].* Detroit, 1980.

KOREY-KRZECZOWSKI, Jerzy (1921-   )

Diplomat, scholar, poet. Born in Kielce, Poland. Received an M.A. in law from the University of Cracow. Participated in the resistance in World War II. Went to Germany, where he received a Ph.D. in law from the University of Freyburg, and a Ph.D. in economics from the University of Tuebingen. Emigrated to Canada in 1951. Served as acting president of Ryerson Polytechnic Institut and chairman of the Ontario Advisory Council on Multiculturalism. He published five books of poetry before coming to Canada.

3891   *Liryki nostalgiczn [Nostalgic Lyrics].* Albany, N.Y.: Sigma Press, 1972. Poems.

3892   *Lunch w Sodomie [Lunch in Sodom].* Albany, N.Y.: Sigma Press, 1976. Poems.

3893   *Stubborn Thoughts.* Albany, N.Y.: Sigma Press, 1980. Poems.

3894   *Tree of Life: Poetic Diary: Selected Poems and Thoughts,* translated from Polish by Wojtek Stelmaszynski. Introduction by Elizabeth Sabiston. Toronto: Co-published by Mosaic Press and Canadian Society for the Comparative Study of Civilization, 1982. xiv, 116 pp. illus., port. Poems.

Writings about:

3895   Grabowski, Yvonne. Review of *Liryki nostalgiczne.* UNIV TOR Q 48 (1978-79): 496-97.

3896   Sowinski, K. Review of *Liryki nostalgiczne.* WIADOMŚĆI No. 1435 (1973): 4.

KRÓLIKOWSKI, Lucjan

3897   *Skradzione dzieciństwo. [Stolen Children].* Londyn: Veritas, 1960. 383 pp. illus. Novel.

KRYSIŃSKI, Włodzimierz

3898   *Ex occidente.* Łódz: Wydawnictwo Łódz, 1966. Poems.

3899   *Formotropie.* Montreal: Galerie Curzi, 1979. Poems.

3900   *Powroty sezonów [Returning Seasons].* Poland, 1981. Poems.

LESZCZYŃSKI, Wacław

3901   *Ostatnia przysługa latarni. Wspomnienia [The Last Service of a Lantern. Reminiscences].* Toronto: The Author, 1976. Stories.

LIEBERT, Wacław

3902   *Wrony nad Moskwa [Crows over Moscow].* Londyn: Polska Fundacja Kulturalna, 1974. 232 pp. Autobiographical novel.

3903 *Ewidencja w.16: Powieść [Presence W.16: A Story]*. Londyn: Polska Fundacja Kulturalna, 1980. 248 pp. port. Novel.

LISOWSKI, Marian
3904 *Wrócimy [We'll Return]*. Windsor, Ont.: Wyd. Ref. Osw. Dow. O.W.P. w Kanadzie, 1942. 31 leaves. Poems.

3905 *Myśli [Musings]*. Toronto: Malak, 1975. 28 pp. Poems.

MALAK, Henry

3906 *Klechy w obozach śmierci [Priests in Death Camps]*. Londyn: Veritas, 1961. Stories.

3907 *Apostołka miłosierdzia z Chicago [Apostle of Mercy in Chicago]*. Londyn: Veritas, 1962. Stories.

MALATYŃSKI, Antoni

3908 *Wielka gra, powieść raczej współczesna [Great Game, a Rather Contemporary Story]*. Toronto: The Author, 1971. Novel.

3909 *Gra toczy si wartko. Powieść raczej współczesna [The Game Progresses Briskly. Modern Novel]*. Toronto, 1973. 331 pp. (Cześć druga Wielkiej gry) Novel.

MALCZEWSKI, Rafał (1892-1965)
Born in Cracow, Poland, emigrated to Canada in 1942. He was an accomplished painter, his works shown at Venice, at the Olympic Exhibition at Los Angeles, etc. Received several medals and awards. He has published short stories in Poland.

3910 *Pepek świata, wspomnienia o Zakopenem [The Navel of the World: Memoirs of Zakopene]*. Warszawa: Czytelnik, 1960. Memoirs.

3911 *Późna jesień. Szkice i opowidania [Late Autumn. Sketches and Stories]*. Londyn: Nakładem Polskiej Fundacji Kulturalnej, 1964. 158 pp. Short stories.

MATEJCZYK, Wacław

3912 *Tristesse eternelle: Wiersze*. Londyn: Nakładem Grupy Rytm, 1953. Poems.

MICHALSKI, Stanisław (1908-)
Born and educated in Poland, he was an officer of the Polish Army and a prisoner of war. Upon release he emigrated to France, then to Costa Rica and to Canada. He obtained a diploma in physiotherapy and worked in a school on the Caughnawaga Indian Reserve near Montreal.

3913 *Wiersze wzgardzone [Verses of Disdain]*. Montreal: The Author, 1958. 82 pp. Poems.

3914 *Mord kapturowy: Ballada Bohaterska [Judicial Murder: An Heroic Ballad]*, with S.J.Z. Warnia. Toronto: Polish Alliance Press, 1959. 52 pp. Poems.

3915 *Czarna maligna [Black Malignancy]*. Montreal: Zrzeszenia Poetów Prześladowanych Im. Borysa Pasternaka, 1960. 54 pp. Poems.

3916 *Bij żyda! Poezja actualna [Smite the Jew! Poetry of the Present]*. Montreal: Zrzeszenia Poetów Prześladowanych Im. Borysa Pasternaka, 1961. 48 pp. Poems.

3917   *Garbus i garby: satyry szydercze i poezje liryczne [Hunchback and Hunches: Derisive Satires and Lyric Poems].* Montreal: Zrzeszenia Poetów Prześladowanych Im. Borysa Pasternaka, 1962. 52 pp. Poems.

3918   *Eskimoska Ewa: Poemat [Eskimo Eve: Poem].* Montreal: Zrzeszenia Poetów Prześladowanych Im. Borysa Pasternaka, 1963. 50 pp. Poems.

MNISZEK, Helena

3919   *Panicz [Young Nobleman].* Winnipeg: Czas, 1939. Novel published serially.

MRÓZ, Sylwester

3920   *Sylwanpora: Wybór utworów poetyckich [A Selection of Poems].* Londyn: Veritas, 1970. Poems.

NOWAK, Wiesław Stanisław W.

3921   *Podróze wspomnień [Memory Trips].* Londyn, 1967. Poems.

3922   *Z nocnej ciszy [From Night's Silence].* Londyn, 1976. Poems.

3923   *Technopoezja [Techno-poetry].* Mount Pearl, Nf.: Nakładem i Drukiem Firmy Hawk, 1981. [21] leaves. Poems.

NOWICKI, Zygmunt

3924   *Złota klamra [The Golden Buckle].* Toronto: Polish Alliance Press, 1963. 197 pp. Autobiography.

3925   *Długa droga [A Long Journey].* Toronto: Głos Polski-Gazeta Polska, 1965. Autobiography. [Continuation of the author's *Złota klamra*.]

3926   *Treść i forma [Content and Form].* Toronto: Głos Polski-Gazeta Polska, 1969. Novel.

ORAWSKI, Bernice (1936-)
Born in Podwilk, Poland, came to Canada with her parents in 1936. Graduated from the Mohawk College in Hamilton, Ont. She lives in Toronto.

3927   *The Little Red Car.* New York: Platt & Munk, 1978. [17] pp. illus. col. Poems for children.

PARIZEAU (POZNAŃSKA), Alice (1930-)
Journaliste, essayiste et romancière, née à Luniniec (Pologne). Libérée des camps de concentration allemands, elle la retrouve, en 1945, à Paris où elle poursuit ses études en lettres (1948), en sciences politiques (1953), en droit (1953). Elle collabore à *Châtelaine*, à *Cité libre*, à *La Presse* et à *Maclean*, rédactrice de textes à Radio-Canada. Alice Parizeau dirige les stagiaires étrangers au Département de criminologie de l'Université de Montréal. Son œuvre littéraire comprend des essais, des reportages, des romans.

3928   *Les Solitudes humaines.* Montréal: Ecrits du Canada français, 1962. Roman.

3929   *Fuir: Roman.* Montréal: Déom [1963] Roman.

3930   *Survivre.* Montréal: Pierre Tisseyre, 1964.

3931   *Une québécoise en Europe "reuge".* Montréal: Fides, 1965. 114 pp.

3932   *Rue Sherbrooke Ouest.* Montréal: Pierre Tisseyre, 1967. 188 pp.

3933   *Les Militants: roman.* Montréal: Pierre Tisseyre, 1974. 299 pp. Roman.

3934   *Les Lilas fleurissent à Varsovie.* Montréal: Pierre Tisseyre, 1981. 400 pp.

3935   *La Charge des sangliers.* Montréal: Pierre Tisseyre, 1982. 384 pp. Roman.

3936   *The Lilacs are Blooming in Warsaw,* translated from the French by A.D. Martin-Sperry. New American Library, 1985. 303 pp.

3937   *Blizzard sur Québec.* Montréal: Éditions Québec Amérique, 1987.

3938   *L'amour de Jeanne.* Montréal: Pierre Tisseyre, 1988. Roman.

Writings about:

3939   Allen, P. "Alice Parizeau, journaliste et romancière." ACT NAT 73 (mar 1984): 662-63.

3940   Alméras, Diane. "Écrivains de la liberté." RELATIONS 477-86 (1982): 336-38.
[Critique: *Les Lilas fleurissent à Varsovie.*]

3941   Barrett, Caroline; Chamberland, Roger; Bellemare, Yvon. "Alice Parizeau." QUÉB FRANÇ 61 (mar 1986): 32-40.

3942   Bernier, Yvon. " 'Ils se sont connus à Lwow', d'Alice Parizeau." LETTR QUÉB 40 (hiver 1985-86): 18-19.

3943   Cantin, Léone. "Critique: *Les Lilas fleurissent à Varsovie.*" LIVR AUTR QUÉB 1981: 72-74.

3944   Ethier-Blais, Jean. "Romans et Théâtre." UNIV TOR Q 34 (1964-65): 483.
[Critique: *Survivre.*]

3945   Ethier-Blais, Jean. "Romans et Théâtre." UNIV TOR Q 52 (1982-83): 514.
[Critique: *Fuir.*]

3946   Michon, Jaques. "Romans." UNIV TOR Q 53 (1983-84): 334.
[Critique: *Les Lilas fleurissent à Varsovie.*]

3947   Mitcham, Allison. "Alice Parizeau." In *Canadian Writers since 1960.* (Detroit: Gale, 1987) pp. 266-69.

3948   Owen, I.M. Review of *The Lilacs are Blooming in Warsaw.* BKS CAN 14 (November 1985): 24-25.

3949   "People [France's Association of French-speaking Authors' Prix d'Europe]"   col. port. MACLEAN'S 95 (Nov. 15, 1982): 50.

3950   Potvin, Elisabeth. "Passion." CAN LIT No. 117 (1988): 158-60.
[Critique: *L'amour de Jeanne.*]

3951   "Rue Sherbrooke Ouest." CULTURE 28 (décembre 1967): 428-29.

3952   Smith, Donald. "Alice Parizeau: l'histoire servie par une écriture palpitante." LETTR QUÉB 41 (1986): 44-48.

3953   Vachon, André, S.J. "Cinq romanciers." RELATIONS 281 (mai 1964): 148-49.
[Critique: *Fuir.*]

PAWLIKOWSKI, Józef

3954   *Petersburska narzeczona [A Fiancée from St. Petersburg].* Toronto: Głos Polski, 1968. 217 pp. Novel.

PIASECKI, Jan Aleksander

3955   *Uprawdopodobnienie wszechświata: Poezje i proza [Making the Universe Seem True: Poetry and Prose].* 1975. 118 pp. Poems and short stories.

PIEKARSKI, Henryk

3956   *Z nad Niemna przez Syberi do Kanady [From Niemen through Siberia to Canada].* Roma: Universita Gregoriana, 1967. 300 pp. Biographical novel.

POBÓG, Ryszard

3957   *Żołnierskie strofy [Soldiers' Poems].* Windsor, Ont.: Odsiecz-Polska walcząca w Ameryce, 1942. Poems.

POLLOCK, Harry J.
Novelist, playwright, born in Poland, received his education in journalism at Harbord Collegiate and the University of Toronto. Unpublished plays include *Yes, I will, Yes* (1965), *Night Boat from Dublin* (1967), *Giacomo Joyce* (1969), *Up from the Pedestal* (1971).

3958   *Gabriel.* Scarborough, Ont.: McGraw-Hill, Ryerson, 1975. Novel.

SIMONOVITCH, Elinore (1922-   )
Playwright. Born in Poland, educated at Brest Litovsk, Montreal and Paris (Sorbonne). Received awards from Ontario Theatre and Ottawa Little Theatre. She lives on Toronto.

3959   *Tomorrow and Tomorrow: A Play in Two Acts.* Toronto: Playwrights Canada. Act I: 37 pp., Act II: 32 pp. Play.

3960   *Big X, Little Y.* Toronto: Playwrights Canada, 1974. Play.

3961   *There are no Dragons: A Play.* Toronto: Playwrights Canada, 1981. 79 pp. Play.

3962   *A Man in the House.* Toronto: Playwrights Canada. (?) Play.

ŚMIEJA, Florian (1925-   )
Born in Kończyce, Poland, emigrated to England in 1943 and studied Spanish and English at London University (Ph.D.). Published books of poems and edited *Życie Akademickie* (1951-53), *Merkuriusz* (1957-58), and *Kontynenty* (1962-64). Presently professor of Spanish literature at the University of Western Ontario, London, Ont.

3963   *Czuwanie u drzwi: Poezje [Keeping Watch at the Door: Poems]* . Londyn: Polskie Towarzystwo Literackie, 1953. 44 pp. Poems.

3964 *Powikłane ścieżki [Twisted Paths].* Londyn: Oficyna Poetów i Malarzy, 1964. Poems.

3965 *Kopa wierszy [Threescore Poems].* Londyn, Ont.: Silcan House, 1981. 66 pp. Poems.

3966 *Wiersze [Poems].* Kraców: Wydawnictwo Literackie, 1982. Poems.

3967 *Jeszcze wiersze [More Poems].* Londyn, Ont.: Silcan House, 1984. Poems.

3968 *Not a Tourist,* foreword by Don McKay. London, Ont.: Third Eye, 1986. Poems.

Writings about:

3969 Heydenkorn, Benedykt. "Widziany przez poezje" [Seen Through Poetry]. ZWIĄZKOWIEC (Feb. 15, 1983)

3970 McKay, Don. "Foreword." In *Not a Tourist.* (London, Ont.: Third Eye, 1986) pp. 9-11.

3971 Pytasz, Marek. "O Kontynentach. Florian Śmieja: 'Gdzie nas zastanie jutro?' " [Regarding Continents. Florian Śmieja: 'Where Will the Future Find Us Tomorrow?']. In *Wśród poetów współczesnych,* edited by Ireneusz Opacki. (Katowice: Universytet Sląski, 1986) pp. 129-42. Wesołowski, Mariusz. "Głosem ściszonym." DIALOGI 4 (1985)

3972 Zyman, Edward. "Jeśli w krajobraz wchodzić masz, to z sobą." GŁOS POLSK (Apr. 16-22, 1985)

TOMASZEWSKI, Adam (1918-)

Born in Kościan, Poland, he was an officer in the Polish Army. Came to Canada in 1948, received an M.A. from the University of Ottawa. His writings have appeared in Polish newspapers and periodicals. He has also co-authored books with his wife, Jadwiga Jurkszus-Tomaszewska.

3973 *Młodość została nad Obrą [Youth Remained Near Obra].* Londyn: Polska Fundacja Kulturalna, 1969. 237 pp. Novel.

3974 *Kowboje, apasze, mormoni [Cowboys, Apaches, Mormons].* Londyn: Polska Fundacja Kulturalna, 1972. Stories.

3975 *Gorzko pachną Piołuny [Bitter Scent of Piołuny].* Toronto: Polski Fundusz Wydawniczy w Kanadzie, 1981. 228 pp. Autobiography.

Writings about:

3976 Heciak, Paweł. Review of *Młodość została nad Obra.* MYŚL POLSK (March 14, 1970)

3977 Jesman, Czesław. "Odkrywcza podróz po utartych szlakach" [Revealing Journey through the Well Known Trails]. WIADOMOŚCI No. 1405 (March 14, 1973)
[Review of *Kowboje, apasze, mormoni.*]

3978 Kowalewski, Janusz. "Rozmowa z Adamem Tomaszewskim" [Interview with Adam Tomaszewski]. TYDZ POLSK (March 7, 1970)
[In connection with *Młodość została nad Obrą.*]

3979 Nowakowski, Tadeusz. "Powrót nad Obre" [Obra Revisited]. WIADOMOŚCI No. 1256 (Apr. 26, 1970)
[Review of *Młodość została nad Obrą.*]

3980 Surynowa-Wyczółkowska, Janina. "Ameryka Tomaszewskiego" [Tomaszewski's America]. TYD POLSK (May 5, 1973)
[Review of *Kowboje, apasze, mormoni.*]

3981 Terlecki, Tymon. "Tomaszewski z Toronto" [The Tomaszewskis of Toronto]. TYD POLSK (June 19, 1976)
[An essay on the literary work of Adam Tomaszewski and Jadwiga Jurkszusz-Tomaszewska.]

3982 Tokarska, Janina. Review of *Młodość została nad Obrą.* TYD POLSK (March 21, 1970)

WANKOWICZ, Melchior

3983 *Tworzywo [Creation].* New York: Roy Publishers, 1954. 434 pp. Novel.
[Based on the life of Polish pioneer settlers in Canada.]

WEINZWEIG, Helen (1915-)
Novelist, storywriter, playwright. Born at Radom, Poland. Emigrated to Canada in 1924 and was educated in Toronto. Founding member of the Writers' Union of Canada and Playwrights' Union of Canada. Awards received: City of Toronto Fiction Award and Canada Council and Ontario Arts Council grants. Published in *Saturday Night, Toronto Life, Tamarack Review, The Spice Box, Canadian Short Stories, The Best, Fireweed,* etc. She lives in Toronto.

3984 *Ana.* Toronto: House of Anansi, 1973. 120 pp. Novel.

3985 *Passing Ceremony.* Toronto: House of Anansi, 1973. Novel.

3986 *Basic Black with Pearls.* Toronto: House of Anansi, 1980. Morrow, 1981. Novel.

Writings about:

3987 Buitenhuis, Peter. "Weinzweig, Helen." In *The Oxford Companion to Canadian Literature,* edited by William Toye. (Toronto: Oxford University Press, 1983) pp. 826.

3988 "Helen Weinzweig." In *Canada Writes!* (Toronto: Writers' Union of Canada, 1977) pp. 362-63. port.

WŁODKOWSKI, Władysław K

3989 *Metafizyczne doświadczenia [Metaphysical Experiences]..* Warszawa: Drukarnia R.S.W. Parasa [n.d.] 170 pp. Poems.
[Includes essays and some poems in Polish and English.]

3990 *Na przegiętej gałęzi [On a Bent Bough].* Londyn: Oficyna Poetów i Malarzi, 1961. 46 pp. (Odbito trzysta pięćdziesiąt pięć egzemplarzy. Egzemplarz no. 5) Poems.

3991 *Zapole duszy: Wiersze zebrane [The Afterfield of the Soul].* Toronto: Polish Alliance Press, 1965. 24 pp. Poems.

WOLIKOWSKA (LUTOWSŁAWSKA), Isabella

3992 *Małżenstwo Zazy [The Marriage of Zaza].* Poznań, 1954. Novel.

3993 *Roman Dmowski [Roman Dmowski].* Chicago, 1961. Novel.

WRZOS-WYCZYŃSKI, Paweł

3994   *W słonecznej ciemni [Sunlight in a Dark Cell]*. Ottawa: The Author, 1981. 148 pp. illus. Poems.

ZAKRZEWSKA, Helena

3995   *Białe róże [White Roses]*. Winnipeg: Gazeta Katolicka, 1939. Published serially. Novel.

ZIÓŁKOWSKA, Jadwiga

3996   *Słoneczny blask [Sun's Brightness]*. Winnipeg: Gázeta Katolicka, 1940. Published serially. Novel.

ZYBAŁA, Stanisław (1919-   )
Born in Duisburg, Poland and educated in Ostrów. He fought in the defence of Warsaw. Emigrated to Canada in 1948. He is senior adviser at the Multiculturalism Program, Secretary of State.

3997   *Resztki z kieszeni [Remnents from a Pocket]* Munich: Słowo Polskie, 1946. Poems.

ŻYTOMIRSKI, Eugeniusz (1911-   )
Novelist, poet, playwright. Born in Poland and started his literary career there. Published four novels and a several short stories before coming to Canada. He lives in London, Ont.

3998   *Ballada czarnomorska: Powieść: [Black Sea Ballad: Novel]*. Londyn: Gryf, 1970. Novel.

3999   *Chodniki się psują powoli: Utwór dramatyczny [Shattered Sidewalks: Drama]* Londyn, Ont.: The Author, 1970. 17 pp. Play.

4000   *Chopin: Poemat [Chopen: Poem]*. Londyn, Ont.: The Author, 1970. 8 pp. Poem.

4001   *Dwoje ludzi. Utwór dramatyczny [Two Persons: Dramatic Work]*. Londyn: Oficyna Poetów i Malarzi, 1970. 30 pp. Play.

4002   *Liśćie klonowe: Wiersze kanadyjskie [The Maple Leaves: Canadian Poems]*. Toronto: Głos Polski, 1971. 98 pp. Poems.

4003   *Oczy jak bursztyny [Your Amber Eyes]*. Londyn: Gryf, 1970. 192 pp. Novel.

4004   *Sonety [Sonnets]*. Londyn, Ont.: The Author, 1970. 10 pp. Poems.

4005   *Tryptyk miłosny [Love Poems]*. Londyn: Oficyna Poetów i Malarzi, 1970. 32 pp. Poems.

4006   *O noemi: rapsod pośmiertny [O Noemy: Postmortem Rhapsody]*. Toronto: The Author, 1971. 28 pp. Poem.
[Includes original title page with imprint: Warszawa, 1943.]

4007   *Życie bez snów [Life without Dreams]*. Londyn: Gryf, 1971. 162 pp. Novel.

4008   *Ballada czarnomorska: Wiersz ze zbioru Tryptyk miłosny [Black Sea Ballad: A Poem from the Collection Tryptyk miłosny]*. Toronto: Miniatura, 1972. 15 pp. Poems.
[Text in Polish with a Bulgarian translation.]

4009   *Kalina, Kalina = A Snowball, a Snowball = Une boule-de-neige, une boule-de-neige = Kalina, kalina.* Toronto, 1972. Poem.

[Text in Polish, English, French and Russian.]

4010 *Koncert na głos z towarzyszeniem młodości: Poemat ze zbioru Tryptyk miłosny [Concert for Voice: A Poem from Tryptyk miłosny]*. Toronto: Miniatura, 1972. 18 pp. Poem.

4011 *Pieśń o niebieskich oczach: Poemat ze zbioru Odebrano mi Polskę [Blue-eyed Dog: Poem from the Collection* Odebrano mi Polskę]. Toronto: Miniatura, 1972. 13 pp. Poem.

4012 *Pieś nowym świecie*. Londyn: Gryf, 1972. 29 pp. Poems.

4013 *Spowiedz [Confessions]*. Londyn: Gryf, 1973. 186 pp. Novel.

4014 *Emigracja. Liryki i satyry [Exile. Lyrics and Satires]*. Toronto, 1974. 43 pp. Poems.

PUERTO RICAN

INDIVIDUAL AUTHOR

BARRETO-RIVERA, Rafael (1944-   )

Born in San Juan, Puerto Rico. His poems have appeared in *Ganglia, Gronk, Waves, Gryphon*. He is a member of the sound poetry ensemble: Four Horsemen. He has appeared on CBC radio and television, T.V. Ontario, Global and City TV, and CBS's Camera Three. He lives in Toronto.

4015   *Canadada*. Toronto: Griffin House, 1973. Poems.
[LP recordings of poems co-authored with the Four Horsemen.]

4016   *Horse D'Oeuvres*. Toronto: General Publishing, 1975. Poems.
[LP recordings.]

4017   *Live in the West*. Toronto: Starbourne Productions, 1977. Poems.
[LP recordings.]

4018   *Here it has Rained*. Toronto: Underwhich Editions, 1978. Poems.
[Also: Toronto: Coach House, 1980. 12 pp.]

4019   *Voices, Noises*. Toronto: Coach House, 1982. Poems.

4020   *The Prose Tattoo*. Milwaukee: Membrance, 1983. Poems.

4021   *Nimrod's Tongue*. Toronto: Coach House, 1986. 109 pp. Poems.

Writings about:

4022   Ellaschuk, Lorne. Review of *Nimrod's Tongue*. BKS CAN 15, no. 6 (1986): 25.

4023   Thompson, Michael. Review of *Here it has Rained*. BKS CAN 9 (October 1980): 12.

ROMANIAN

ANTHOLOGY

4024   *Modern Romanian Poetry*, edited by Nicholas Catanoy, foreword by Irving Layton. English translations by various poets. Oakville, Ont./Ottawa: Mosaic Press/Valley Editions, 1977. 141 pp. [Includes poems in English translation by 53 Romanian poets residing in Romania and abroad. From Canada Nicholas Catanoy is represented.]

INDIVIDUAL AUTHORS

BATU, Florica

4025   *Oglinzi*. Kitchener, Ont.: Vestitorul Roman Canadian, 1975. 16 pp. Poems.

4026   *Good Friday/Vinerca Mare*. Kitchener, Ont.: Romanian-Canadian Herald, 1977. 6 leaves. Poem.

4027   *Sera Lumeasca.* Kitchener, Ont.: Vestitorul Roman Canadian, 1978. 40 pp. Poems.

4028   *Poezii pentru copii.* Kitchener, Ont.: Vestitorul Roman Canadian, 1979. 43 pp. Poems.

CATANOY, Nicholas (1925-   )

Born in Romania, where he studied medicine and philosophy. Emigrated to Canada in 1962. His poems and translations have appeared in American, French, and Canadian periodicals including *World Literature Today, Jalon, Waves, Canadian Literature* and *Quarry.*

4029   *Hic et Nunc.* 1968. Poems.

4030   *Flux Alb [Fueillets de plauches].* Fredericton, N.B.: New Brunswick Press, 1970. 52 pp. Poems. [In Romanian and French.]

4031   *The Fiddlehead Republic.* Toronto: Hounslow Press, 1979. Poems.

4032   *Around the World in Eighty Days.* Royapettah, India: Sayeeda Publications, 1983. 32 pp. Poems.

4033   *Ni debout, ni assis: Poèmes.* Paris: Dayez Editeurs, 1984. Poèmes.

ICHIM, Dumitru

4034   *Poeme Haiky [Haiku Poetry].* Kitchener, Ont.: Romanian-Canadian Herald, 1977. Poems.

4035   *Constantin Brancoveau [Constantin Brancoveau].* Kitchener, Ont.: Romanian-Canadian Herald, 1981. 16 pp. Poems.

4036   *Melcul.* Kitchener, Ont.: Romanian Canadian Herald, 1981. 20 pp. Play.

PAVEL, Thomas (1941-   )

Born in Bucharest and received his education in that city. He emigrated to Canada in 1970. He has taught at the University of Ottawa.

4037   *Inflections de voix.* Montréal: Press de l'Université de Montréal, 1976. 178 pp.

4038   *Le Miroir persan.* Montréal: Quinze, 1977. 145 pp. Nouvelles.

RUSSIAN

BIBLIOGRAPHIES

4039   **KRISZTINKOVICH, Maria**
        A Doukhobor Bibliography Based on Material Collected in the University of British Columbia Library. Vancouver: UBC Library, 1968 -   . 3 Pts. (Reference publication no. 22)
        [Includes references to monographic and periodical publications.]

4040   **KRISZTINKOVICH, Maria**
        A Doukhobor Bibliography Based on Material Collected in the University of British Columbia Library. Enl., rev. ed. of pt. 1. Vancouver: UBC Library, 1972. (Reference publication no. 22 and supplement. Its reference publication 38)

4041 **PIONTKOVSKY, Roman**
"Russian-Canadian Imprints: A Preliminary Check List." CAN ETH STUD 2, no. 1 (1970): 177-85.
[Includes 64 publications by Russian-Canadian authors, 11 entries about Russians, 4 monographs printed by Russian-Canadian publishers.]

4042 **ROSVAL, Sergei J.**
"Russian-Canadian Creative Literature: A Preliminary Check List of Authors and Pseudonyms." CAN ETH STUD 2, no. 1 (1970): 173-75.
[Provides biographical data on 37 authors.]

4043 **SAUER, Serge A.**
"Russian-Canadian Periodical Publications: A Preliminary Check List." CAN ETH STUD 1, no. 1 (1969): 61-64.
[Contains 26 titles.]

4044 **SHERRIFF, Peggy**
"The Doukhobors: A Selected Bibliography." Dipl. Lib. Thesis. University of London, 1959.

BOOK

4045 *Russian Canadians: Their Past and Present (Collected Essays)*, edited by T.F. Jeletzky with Grebenschikov, N. Gridgeman, and I. Gryndahl. Ottawa: Borealis Press, 1983.
[Includes chapters on cultural and intellectual life and a comprehensive list of newspapers and magazines (pp. 169-201).]

INDIVIDUAL AUTHORS

BOBROVA, Ella Ivanovna (1911-)
Born in Ukraine, but her creative language is Russian. She has lived in Toronto since 1950. Her Russian translations of poetry, prose, essays and review articles were published in Russian periodicals in Canada.

4046 *Kak sladko [How Sweet]*. Toronto, 1951. Poems.

4047 *Skazka o tom kak smelie snezhinki pomogli devochke Marinke [A Tale of How the Brave Snowflakes Helped Little Marinka]*. Toronto: Leonella, 1961. 8 pp. Story.

4048 *Irina Istomina: Povest' v stikhakh [Irina Istomina: A Tale in Verse]*. Toronto: Sovremennik, 1967. 87 pp. Poem.

4049 *I͡A chuda zhdu [Expecting a Miracle]*. Toronto: Sovremennik, 1970. Poem.

4050 *I͡Antarnij sok [Amber Elixir: Selected Poems]*. Toronto: Sovremennik, 1977. Poems.

4051 *Irina Istomina*. Oakville, Ont.: Mosaic Press, 1980. 93 pp. Poem.
[Translated from Russian.]

4052 *The Three Brave Snowflakes*. Oakville, Ont.: Mosaic Press, 1982. 22 pp. Story.
[Translated from the Russian *Skazka o tom....*]

4053 *Autumnal Cadenza*. Oakville, Ont.: Mosaic Press, 1985.

4054 *Die Drei Tapferen Schneeflocken*. Ottawa: Les Éditions du Vermillion, 1986. Story.
[German translation of *Three Brave Snowflakes*.]

Writing about:

4055   Grabowski, Yvonne. Review of *ĪAntarnij sok*. UNIV TOR Q 48 (1978-79): 494-95.

GAUR, Lev

4056   *Stikhi [Poems]*. Toronto: Forum, 1949. 68 pp. Poems.

GERLAKH, Vladimir

4057   *Izmennik [The Traitor]*. London: S.B.O.N.R., 1967-1969. 2 v. Novel.

GIDONI, Alexandr

Born in the USSR. Arrested for underground political activities and served several years in prison in Mordovia. He emigrated to the West.

4058   *Bez Rossiĭ - s Rossieĭ*. Toronto: Sovremennik, 1976. 145 pp. Poems.

4059   *Lira Petropolia: Stikhi [Lyra of Petropol: Poems]*. Toronto: Sovremennik, 1979. 63 pp. Poems.

4060   *Solntse idet s zapada: Kniga vospominaniĭ [The Sun Sets in the West]*. Toronto: Sovremennik, 1980. 536 pp. port. Autobiography.

ĪUREZANSKYJ, Wolodymyr

4061   *Tsarina: Istorichna povist' [Tsarina: Historical Novel]*. 2nd ed. Winnipeg: Trident Press, 1978. 171 pp. Novel.

POPOFF, Eli

4062   *Tania [Tanya]*. Grand Forks, B.C.: MIR, 1975. 276 pp. Novel.

READ, Elfreida (1920-   )

Born in Vladivostok, USSR, of Estonian parents. Came to Canada via Shanghai, China, after World War II and internment by the Japanese and settled in Vancouver. She has published in *Canadian Poetry Magazine*, *Alberta Poetry Yearbook*, *The Fiddlehead*, *The Canadian Forum*, *The Malahat Review*, etc. Received several awards including UN (International Cooperation Year) Playwriting award (1965), National Children's Short Story Award for Poetry, National Award for Poetry, CBC (1982).

4063   *The Dragon and the Jadestone*. London: Hutchinson, 1958. Juvenile.
        [German translation published by Englebert Verlag, 1971.]

4064   *The Magic of Light*. London: Hutchinson, 1959. Juvenile.

4065   *The Enchanted Egg*. London: Hutchinson, 1963. Juvenile.
        [Reissued as *The Magical Egg*. New York: Lippincott, 1965.]

4066   *The Spell of Chuchuchan*. London: Hutchinson, 1966. New York: World, 1967. Juvenile.

4067   *Magic Granny*. Toronto: Burns and MacEachern, 1967. Juvenile.

4068   *Twin Rivers*. Toronto: Burns and MacEachern, 1968. Juvenile.

4069   *No One Need Ever Know.* Boston: Ginn, 1971. Novel.

4070   *Brothers by Choice.* New York: Farrar Straus & Giroux, 1974. Novel.

4071   *The Message of the Mask.* Toronto: Gage, 1981. Juvenile.

4072   *Kristine and the Villains.* Toronto: Gage, 1982. Juvenile.

4073   *Race against the Dark.* Toronto: Gage, 1983. Juvenile.

4074   *Growing up in China.* Ottawa: Oberon, 1985. Biography.

RUBINSKA, A.F.

4075   *Nezateilivye rasskazy.* London, Ont.: Zaria Publishing, 1982. 123 pp. Short stories.

STRAKHOVSKY, Leonid   (1898-1963)

4076   *Dolg zhizni [Life's Business].* Toronto, 1953. Poems.

SERBIAN

BIBLIOGRAPHIES, BOOK

4077 GAKOVICH, Robert P.; RADOVICH, Milan M., comp.
Serbs in the United States and Canada: A Comprehensive Bibliography, foreword by M.B. Petrovich, edited by J.D. Dwyer. [Minneapolis] Immigration History Center, University of Minnesota, 1976. xii, 129 pp. (IHRC Ethnic Bibliography: 1)

4078 JURIČIĆ, Ž.B.; MALYCKY, Alexander
"Serbian-Canadian Periodical Publications: A Preliminary Check List." CAN ETH STUD 2, no. 1 (1970): 187-89.

4079 *Serbs in Ontario: A Socio-cultural Description*, edited by Sofija Skoric and George Vid Tomashevich. Islington, Ont.: Serbian Heritage Academy of Canada, 1987.
[Includes bibliography.]

ANTHOLOGY

4080 *Rodoljublje: zbirka izabranih pesama [Patriotism: Selected Poems]*, edited by Nikola P. Ivkov. Toronto, 1974.

INDIVIDUAL AUTHORS

AVRAMOVIĆ, Lazar M.

4081 *Teći će voda kud je tekla; Roman iz rata [The River Will Run Where it Aways Did]*. Windsor, Ont.: Izd. piščevo, 1959. 222 pp. Novel.
[Relating to World War II.]

BOJIČIC-KOMSKI, Milić R.

4082 *Pax: Poema marseljske tragedije [Pax: A Poem of the Marseille Tragedy]*. Toronto, 1957. 198 pp. Poem.

4083 *Ravnogorski božuri [Peonies of Ravna Gora]*. Dearborn, Mich., 1966. 197 pp. Poems.

FROTHINGHAM, Helen (Losanitch)

4084 *Mission for Serbia; Letters from America and Canada, 1915-1920*, edited by Matilda Spence Rowland. New York: Walker, 1970. xiv, 326 pp.

JAVONOVIĆ, Leposava

4085 *Mutne oči; Roman iz savremenog života [Troublesome Ages; Novel from Modern Life]*. Hamilton, Ont.: Kanadski Srbobran, 1975. Novel.

MILJEVIĆ, Vojo V.

4086 *Broken Lullabies; Dramatic Spirits*. Calgary, 1965. 175 pp. Poems.

MRKITCH, Danny D.

4087   *Death in the City.* Toronto, 1967. 47 pp. Poems.

4088   *Serpent and the Butterfly: Poems.* Windsor, Ont.: Avala, 1971. 67 pp. Poems.

PAVEĆIĆ, Mićum M.

4089   *Gorske ruže [Mountain Roses].* Chicago: Palandačić, 1909. Poems.

4090   *Krvavim poljanama; Odlomci [On the Bloody Meadows; Fragments].* Welland, Ont.: Kanadski Glasnik, 1916. 53 pp. Poems.

4091   *Pogrebna zvona; satiričke pjesme o crnogorskim upravljačima [Funeral Bells; Satiric Poems about the Montenegro Rulers].* New York, 1916. Poems.

4092   *Iz memljivih dana; Zapisi [From the Bad Times; Legacies].* Welland, Ont.: Kanadski Srbobran, 1916. 89 pp. Poems.

4093   *Od Cetinja fo Njujorka; Putopis u desetercu [From Cetinje to New York; Travel Record].* New York, 1916. Poems.

4094   *Apoteoza besmrtnicima; Poema o jugoslovenskim pobjedama [Apotheosis of Immortals; A Poem about Yugoslav Victories].* Welland, Ont.: Kanadski Glasnik, 1917. Poems.

4095   *Šta ko sanja; Satire u prozi [One's Dreams; Satires in Prose].* Welland, Ont.: Kanadski Glasnik, 1917. Stories.

4096   *Razmisljanja o Božiću; Pjesma u prozi [Thoughts about Christmas; A Poem and Prose].* Welland, Ont.: Kanadski Glasnik, 1917. Poem.

4097   *Nejski vijenac; Satira o kralju o Nikoli i njegovoj vladi [Nejski Coronet: Satire about King Nikola and His Reign].* New York, 1918. Poem.

4098   *Novi motivi [New Motives].* New York, 1918. 2 v. Poems.

PETKOVIĆ, Vlastimir

4099   *U našim ambarima bice opet žita [We'll have Grain in Our Granary].* Chicago: Srpski narodni univerzitet, 1957. 73 pp. Short stories.

4100   *Podmorničar Paja Salašev, I druge pripovetke [The Submariner Paja Salašev and other Stories].* Hamilton, Ont.: Kanadski Srbobran, 1958. Short stories.

4101   *Veliko pokoljenje; Pripovetke [Great Generation; Stories].* Melburn: Srpska Misao, 1968. Short stories.

POP-HRISTIĆ, Lena

4102   *Nekad bilo [Long ago].* Windsor, Ont.: Glas Kanadskih Srba, 1952. 106 pp. Novel.

RAJIC, Négovan (1923-   )
Born in Belgrade, Yugoslavia, and came to Canada via Austria, Italy and Germany in 1969. He taught mathematics at Collège d'enseignement général et profesionnel, Trois-Rivières. His works have appeared in

French and English periodicals. His novel *Les Hommes-taupes* was awarded the Prix Esso of the Cercle du livre de France.

4103 *Les Hommes-taupes.* Montréal: Pierre Tisseyre, 1978. 154 pp. Roman.
[Translated into English: *The Mole Man.*]

4104 *The Mole Man,* translated from the French by David Lobdell. Ottawa: Oberon Press, 1980. 95 pp. Novel.
[Translation of *Les Hommes-taupes.*]

4105 *Propos d'un vieux radoteur.* Montréal: Pierre Tisseyre, 1982. 207 pp. Nouvelle.

VELIMIROVIĆ, Nikolaj

4106 *Zemlja nedootija; Jedna moderna bajka [Neverland: A Modern Legend].* Windsor, Ont.: The Author, 1950. 67 pp. Story.

VUKČEVIC-STAVORSKI, Marko I.

4107 *Kapi bola: Pesme I [Doses of Pain: Poems].* Toronto, 1952. 94 pp. Poems.

4108 *Omladinski spomenik: Pesme [Monument to the Youth: Poems].* Detroit, 1952. 62 pp. Poems.

ŽIVKOVIĆ, Danica

4109 *Na sanatama života [On Life's Icebergs].* Toronto, 1973. 196 pp. Novel.

SLOVAK

BIBLIOGRAPHIES

4110 **KIRSCHBAUM, Joseph M.**
"Slovak-Canadian Creative Literature: A Preliminary Check List of Authors and Pseudonyms."
CAN ETH STUD 1, no. 1 (1969): 69.
[Contains references to 13 authors.]

4111 **KIRSCHBAUM, Joseph M.**
"Slovak-Canadian Periodical Publications: A Preliminary Check List." CAN ETH STUD 1, no. 1
(1969): 65-68.
[A list of 33 periodical titles, complete with places, publishers, dates and frequency of publication.]

4112 **LACKO, M.**
"Slovak Bibliography Abroad, 1945-1965." SLOVAK STUD 7 (1970)
[Contains references to general publications, publications on history, political science,
organizations and literature.]

BOOKS, RESEARCH PAPERS

4113 **GELLNER, John; SMEREK, John**
The Czechs and Slovaks in Canada. Toronto: University of Toronto Press, in association with the
Masaryk Memorial Institute [1968] x, 172 pp.
[Provides a short section on Czech and Slovak creative literature, including the work of Pavel
Javor, Jozef Čermák, Jozef Dragos-Alžbentinčan, L'udo Bešeňovský, Jozef Zvonár-Tien, and Ján
Doránski.]

4114 **KIRSCHBAUM, Joseph M.**
Slovaks in Canada. Toronto: Canadian Ethnic Press Association of Ontario, 1967. xvi, 468 pp.
[40] pp. of plates, illus., ports.
[Includes chapters on Slovak settlements in Canada, immigration patterns, Slovak organizations
and culture, and an extensive bibliography (pp. 441-55).]

4115 **KIRSCHBAUM, Joseph M.**
Slovak Language and Literature; Essays. Winnipeg: The University of Manitoba, Department of
Slavic Studies, 1975. 282 pp. (Readings in Slavic Literatures 12, edited by J.B. Rudnyćkyj.)
[Includes the following Slovak-Canadian authors: Peter Klas, Ján Doránski, L'udo Bešeňovský,
Jozef Zvonár-Tien, and M. Zlámal.]

4116 **KIRSCHBAUM, Joseph M.**
"Misconceptions of American Slavists about Slovak Literature." In *Slovakia* (Middletown, Pa.,
1961) pp. 22-24.
[The author sets out to prove the existence of a rich literature of Slovak origin.]

4117 **KIRSCHBAUM, Joseph M.**
"Misconceptions of American Slavists on Slovak Language." In *Slovakia.* (Middletown, Pa.,
1962) pp. 25-49.
[A dissertation on the specific linguistic elements making Slovak an independent language of its
own.]

ANTHOLOGIES

4118   *Spomienky pionerov [Reminiscences of Pioneers]*, edited by Imrich Stolárik. Toronto: Kanadská Slovenská Liga, 1978. 296 pp.
[A collection of stories and biographical reminiscences of Slovak-Canadian settlers about early life in Canada.]

4119   *Západ [The West]*, edited by Milo Šuchma, translated by Paul Wilson. Waterloo, Ont.: Collegium Bohemicum, 1982. 64 pp.
[A collection of writings in English translation from the periodical *Západ.]*

INDIVIDUAL AUTHORS

BEŠEŇOVSKÝ, Ľudo (1910-   )

Became an established author in his native land, published two books of poems for children. Emigrated to Canada via Austria in 1948. His poems have appeared in newspapers, periodicals and [*Nádej víťazná* and *Slovenská republika*] symposia. He has lived in Winnipeg since 1948.

4120   *V krvi ťa nosím. Verše [We Carry it out on Our Blood. Poems]*. Winnipeg: The Author, 1976. Poems.

4121   *Batôštek a slza: Verše: Rakúsko [A Bagful of Tears: Poems]*. Winnipeg, 1978. 86 pp. Poems.

Writings about:

4122   Grabowski, Yvonne. Review of *V kri ťa nosím*. UNIV TOR Q 47 (1977-78): 499-500.

4123   Kirschbaum, Joseph M. "Ľudo Bešeňovský." In his *Slovaks in Canada*. (Toronto: Canadian Ethnic Press Association, 1967) p. 350.

4124   "Ľudo Bešeňovský." In *The Canadian Family Tree*. (Ottawa: Canadian Citizenship Branch, 1967) p. 72.

BRÁZDA, Bystrík Mária

4125   *Začiatok cesty [The Beginning of a Journey]*. Vancouver, 1974. Short stories.

4126   *Na špirále života [On the Spiral of Life]*. Vancouver: Literarny Klub Zdúženia Slovák, 1977. Short stories.

Writing about:

4127   Grabowski, Yvonne. Review of *Na špirále života*. UNIV TOR Q 48 (1978-79): 494.

ČIČVÁK, Ilja (1939-   )

Born in Czechoslovakia. Attended the University of Bratislava and worked as a journalist for the *People's Voice* and the Czechoslovak Television Network. He came to Canada in 1968 and continued his postgraduate studies at the University of British Columbia and the University of London, receiving a Ph.D. degree. Dr. Čičvák has established the Society of Slovak Literature, which he manages out of Ottawa.

4128   *Vyvolávanie slnka [Raising the Sun]*. Ottawa: Spoločnosť priateľov slovenskej literatúry, 1984. 249 pp. Novel.

Writings about:

4129 "Obraz socialistického života na Slovensku [On the Socialist Way of Life in Slovakia].
KANADSKÝ SLOVÁK (Aug. 20, 1986)
[Review of *Vyvolávanie slnka.*]

4130 Review of *Vyvolávanie slnka.* NOVÝ DOMOV (Dec. 20, 1984)

4131 Review of *Vyvolávanie slnka.* SLOVAK WORLD CONG BULL 15, no. 75 (1986): 22.

DEBNÁRKIN, Ondrej M. (1919-   )
Born in Czechoslovakia, published his first book of poems in Bratislava: *Vrásnenie veku [Shrinking of Age,*
1946].

4132 *Ozveny zámoria [Echoes from Overseas].* Toronto, 1952. Poems.

4133 *Zjavným hlasom [With Manifasting Voice].* Toronto, 1952. Poems.

Writing about:

4134 Kirschbaum, Joseph M. "Ondrej Debnarkin." In his *Slovak Language and Literature.* (Winnipeg:
University of Manitoba, (1975) p. 265.

DORÁNSKI, Ján (1911- 1973)
Poet, short story writer. Left his native land in 1950, came to Montreal and lived there until his premature
death. His poems have appeared in anthologies: *Vo vyhnanste* (1974), *Zdravica Ss. Cyrilovi a Metodovi*
(1963).

4135 *Od splnu po zatmenie [From Full Moon to the Eclipse].* Rome, 1972. Poems.

4136 *Sto epigramov [Hundred Epigrams],* selected and prepared for publication by F. Vnuk. 1972.
Poems.

4137 *Stará mat' neopúšťaj nás [Grandma, don't Abandon Us].* Performed by Slovak theatrical groups
across Canada. Play.

Writings about:

4138 Kirschbaum, Joseph M. "Ján Doránski." In his *Slovak Language and Literature.* (Winnipeg: The
University of Manitoba, Department of Slavic Studies, 1975) pp. 255-57.

4139 Kirschbaum, Joseph M. "Ján Doránski." In his *Slovaks in Canada.* (Toronto: Canadian Ethnic
Press Association of Ontario, 1967) pp. 349-50.

4140 Okál, Ján. "Ján Doránski." LIT ALMAN (1972): 115-19.

4141 Okál, Ján. "Ján Doránski." MOST No. 3-4 (1973)

4142 Strmeň, K. "Ján Doránski." MOST No. 1-2 (1973)

DRAGOŠ-ALŽBENTINČAN, Józef (1909-   )

4143 *Nepoškvrnená víťazí The Immaculate is Victorious].* Toronto, 1954. Poems.

4144 *Slávme hviezdy jasné [Let's Celebrate the Bright Stars].* Middleton, PA, 1963. Poems.

KLAS, Peter, pseud. (Real name: KANDRA, L'udovit (1904-   )

4145   *Satan proti Bohu [Satan against God]*. SLOVENSKÁ OBRANA, 1951-52. Novel.
        [Published serially.]

4146   *Na strome života [On the Lifetree]*. 1959. Short stories.

4147   *Svetlo pod halenou [Light under the Sheepskin]*. 1960. Novel.

OKÁL, Ján (1915-   )
Born in Czechoslovakia and published two collections of poetry there: *Nehnem sa [I do not Move*, 1942] and
L'ubost [Love, 1944].

4148   *Kronika Slovákov [Chronicle of the Slovaks]*. 1954. Poems.

4149   *Blíženci [Twins]*. 1962. Satirical novel.

4150   *Voda a víno [Water and Wine]*. 1972. Poems.
        [Based on his experiences as an emigré in Rome.]

4151   *Nedoručené pohl'adnice [Undelivered Postcards]*. 1973. Poems.
        [Depicts his experiences in Mexico.]

Writings about:

4152   Kirschbaum, Joseph M. "Ján Okál." In his *Slovak Language and Literature*. (Winnipeg:
        University of Manitoba, 1975) pp. 254-55.

4153   "Ján Okál." LIT ALMAN (1967): 197-98.

4154   "Ján Okál." MOST (1965)

4155   "Ján Okál." SLOVAKIA 21 (1971) and 23 (1973)

ZLÁMAL, Miloslav (1922-   )
Born in Czechoslovakia and received his education there. Published two books of poems before coming to
Canada: *Mŕtvy organ [Dead Organ]* and *Preludium*.

4156   *Exile [Exile]*. 1953. Poems.

4157   *Keby sa jaro nevrátilo [If Springtime shouldn't Return]*. 1957. Poems.

4158   *Zpevy z modrých hor [Songs of the Blue Mountain]*. 1964. Poems.

4159   *The Partisan Captain*. 1970. Autobiographical novel.

Writing about:

4160   Kirschbaum, Joseph M. "Miloslav Zlámal." In his *Slovak Language and Literature*. (Winnipeg:
        University of Manitoba) pp. 265-66.

ZVONÁR-TIEN, Józef [1919-   )

Poet, short story writer, translator. Graduated from the Faculty of Law in his native land and became editor of various publications. He published versified mysteries, librettos for operas and books of poetry.

4161 *Ohne [Bonfires].* Winnipeg, 1956. Verse-drama.

Writing about:

4162 Kirschbaum, Joseph M. "Jozef Zvonár-Tien." In his *Slovak Language and Literature.* (Winnipeg: University of Manitoba, 1975) pp. 264-65.

SOMALIAN

INDIVIDUAL AUTHOR

TOGANE, Mohamud Siad (1943-   )
Born in Bawana.

4163   *The Bottle and the Bushman.* Ottawa: National Library of Canada, 1983. Microfiche. (92 fr.)
       Poems.

4164   *The Bottle and the Bushman: Poems of the Prodigal Son.* Dorion, Qué.: The Muses' Company,
       1986. 52 pp. Poems.
       [First published by NLC on microfiche.]

   Writings about:

4165   Archer, Anne. Review of *The Bottle and the Bushman.* QUEEN'S Q 94 (1987): 1042-43.

4166   Filip, Ray. "Foreign Intelligence." BKS CAN 15, no. 9 (1986): 22.
       [Review of *The Bottle and the Bushman.*]

SOUTH AFRICAN

INDIVIDUAL AUTHORS

HAVEMANN, Ernst (1918-   )
Born in Zululand, Africa and educated in Natal. He emigrated to Canada in 1978 and began taking creative
writing courses in Nelson, B.C. His short stories have appeared in *The Atlantic, Saturday Night, Grand
Street* and *Wascana Review.* He lives in Nelson, B.C.

4167   *Bloodsong and other Stories of South Africa.* Boston: Houghton Mifflin/Thomas Allen, 1987. 134
       pp. Short stories.

   Writings about:

4168   Mock, Irene. "Interview with Ernst Havemann." BKS CAN 16, no. 9 (1987): 39-40.

4169   Slopen, Beverly. "Bush League Authors... Much Depends on Visser.... Prosaic Retirement." Q & Q
       53, no. 12 (1987): 20.

HEAD, Harold
South African by birth, now resides in Toronto, where he produces Khoisan Artist books for the teaching of
Third World literature in Canadian schools.

4170   *Bushman's Brew.* Toronto: Goathair Press, 1976. Poems.

NORTJE, Arthur (?   - 1970)

Born in South Africa, he was educated at the University College of Western Cape and Jesus College, Oxford, England. In Canada he taught in British Columbia and Toronto. Died as a result of a tragic accident, after he had returned to Oxford to read for his Ph.D.

4171 *Dead Roots.* London: Heinemann, 1973. Poems.
[Published posthumously.]

SPANISH

BIBLIOGRAPHY

4172   METROPOLITAN TORONTO LIBRARY BOARD
Spanish Books/Libros en Español: A Catalogue of the Holdings of the Languages Centre, Metropolitan Toronto Central Library. Toronto: The Library Board, 1974. 299 pp.
[Contains books of poetry and prose published by Spanish-Canadian authors.]

ANTHOLOGIES

4173   *Anthology.* Madrid: Ed. Areyto, 1959. 94 pp.
[Includes works by three poets, one being Manuel Betanzos Santos, a Canadian.]

4174   *Doce jovenes poetas españoles [Twelve Young Spanish Poets],* edited by Manuel Betanzos Santos.
Barcelona: El Bardo, 1967. 208 pp.
[Includes poems by Manuel Betanzos Santos.]

4175   *Poèmes aveugles,* edited by Manuel Betanzos Santos. Nice: Profils poétiques des pays latins, 1968.

4176   *Poésie et réflexion des poètes sans frontières.*
[Issue 1977 was devoted to Manuel Betanzos Santos.]

INDIVIDUAL AUTHORS

ALLUEVA LAZARO, José (1935-   )

Born in Teruel, Spain, emigrated to Canada in 1974. Director of the Hispanic Association's theatre group in British Columbia. Works published prior to coming to Canada are *El ídolo y el gigante* (a dramatic comedy in three acts, 1957), *El campo, la paz y la justica* (tragedy in five acts, 1958), *Los irresponsables* (comedy in four acts, 1959), *Agonia* (tragedy in four acts, 1960), *La manza* (screenplay and film of *Diego y Belisa,* drama in four acts and epilogue, 1970).

4177   *Un día en la vida de Nelly [One Day in Nelly's Life].* 1977. Filmscript.

4178   *Raíz ambiciosa [Aspiring Roots].* Pt. I. 1977. Filmscript.

4179   *Canto de Alondra – Raíz ambociosa [Canto of Alondra: Aspiring Roots].* Pt. II. 1977. Filmscript.

BARÓN PALMA, Emilio (1954-   )

Born in Spain, came to Canada in 1972. Continued his education at the Université de Montréal. He is teaching Spanish at Queen's University. Published two periodicals, *Tarsis* (1974-75), and *Correo Español de Québec* (1976).

4180   *Cuénco de la soledad, 1973-1974 [Pit of Solitude...]* Madrid: Col. de Concha Lagos, 1974. Poems.

4181   *La soledad, la lluvia, los caminos [Solitude, Rain, the Road].* Madrid: Col. de Concha Lagos, 1977. Poems.

4182   *De este lado [From This Side].* 1983.

BETANZOS SANTOS, MANUEL (1933-   )

Born in Palmeira. Emigrated to Canada in 1959. He teaches Spanish at the Université du Québec. He has translated Canadian poets into Spanish, and published widely in periodicals and anthologies. A collection of Canadian poetry in his translation was published the University of San Luis Potosi in 1978. Director of Boréal, a literary review published in Montreal since 1965. For writing on Betanzos Santos see *La Region* 11 (1976), *Boreal International* 2 (1977), *Vanguardia* 2, no. 3 (1969), *La Lealtad* 8 (1972), *La Mañana* (1967, 1969, 1974, 1976), *Lanza* 2 (1969), *Vicis Lucha* 8 (1975), *El Universo* 3 (1968), and *Aturuxo* (May 1975).

4183   *Arbol amente [Loving Tree]*. Madrid: Benito Pérez Galdós, 1964. Poems.

4184   *Como piedras en la otra orilla: poesía [Like Stones on the other Shore]*. Montreal, 1964. 25 pp. Poems.

4185   *Tala, poemas de la guerra indiferente [Tala, Poems of Indifferent War]*. Bilbao: Alrededor de la mesa, Col. Communicación Poética, 1967. Poems.

4186   *Saludo a la humanidad: Poème lu à la "Soirée de Solidarité" de la Conférence pour mettre fin à la Guerre au Vietnam, a Montréal, le 30 novembre 1968*. Montreal, 1969. Poems.

4187   *Canción del niño en la ventana [Child's Song at the Window]*. Nueva York: Col. Mensaje, 1971 50 pp. Poems.

4188   *La estrella y el hombre [The Star and the Man]*. Calgary: La escuela moderna, 1972. Poems.

4189   *Conjugación irregular [Irregular Conjugation]*. Montreal: Boreal, 1973. Poems.

4190   *Pequeño tentadero [Slight Attempt]*. Calgary: La escuela moderna, 1974. Poems.

4191   *Diario de una noche de tren y ruedas [Diary of a Night on Train Wheels]*. Bilbao: Communicación Literario de Autores, 1974. Poems.

4192   *Canción en el viento: Poesias [Song into the Wind: Poems]*. Barcelona: Rondas, 1974. 45 pp. Poems.

CABAÑAS, Pablo (1967-   )

Born in Spain, taught at the universities of Nottingham and Durham. Emigrated to Canada and he teaches Spanish at the University of Victoria.

4193   *Libro de Apollonia [The Book of Pollonius]*. Madrid: Castalia, 1969. Poems.

GONZÁLEZ MARTÍN, Jerónimo Pablo (1933-   )

Born in Salamanca, Spain. He is teaching Spanish literature at Trent University. He writes in English under the name Blair McGregor. Edited a number of anthologies including *Jóvenes poetas Sevillanos* (Bilbao, 1966), *Cinco poetas franco-canadienses actuales* (Sevilla, CSIC, 1966), *Poesíá Hispánica 1929-1969* (Barcelona: Saturno, 1970).

4194   *Cayeron los negros [The Black's Fall]*. Zaragoza, 1965. Poems.

4195   *Andar a grillos [To Jump Like Crickets]*. Barcelona, 1966. Poems.

4196   *Sinceramente decidido [Sincerely Resolved]*. Barcelona, 1967. Poems.

4197 *Nuevos heraldos negros o manual del hambriento. [New Black Heralds or Manual of the Starved].* Barcelona: El Bardo, 1969. Poems.

NUÑEZ ALONSO, Alejandro (1905-)
Author of more than twenty novels. Born in Gijon, Spain, travelled to France, Mexico, Italy. He came to Canada in 1973 and has written two novels here.

4198 *La reina desnuda [The Naked Queen].* Barcelona: Planeta, 1974. Novel.

4199 *Arriba Israel [Hail Israel].* Barcelona: Planeta, 1977. Novel.

RISCO, Antonio
Born in Allariz, Spain. Emigrated to Canada in 1966. He teaches Spanish at the Université Laval. Author of several scholarly books including *La estética de Valle-Inclán en los esperpentos y en "El ruedo Ibérico"* (1966), *El demiurgo y su mondo...* (1977), *and Azor in y la ruptura con la novela tradicional* (1980).

4200 *El terrorista [The Terrorist].* Barcelona: Planeta, 1969. Novel.

ROSCOE, Patric (1962-)
Born in Spain, educated there and in Canada.

4201 *Beneath the Western Slopes.* Stoddart, 1987. 190 pp. Short stories.

Writing about:

4202 Heward, Burt. "Five Canadians Excel in Varied Fiction Form." OTTAWA CIT (Oc. 31, 1987): H4.

SRI LANKAN

ANTHOLOGY

4203 *The Toronto South Asian Review.* vol. 3, no. 2 (1984), guest edited by Suwanda Sugunasiri and A.V. Suraweera. Toronto: TSAR, 1984.

[Includes poetry and prose by, and/or writings about, the following Sri Lankan-Canadian authors: Krishantha Bhaggiyadatta, C. Kanaganayakam, Arun Mukherjee, Michael Ondaatje, and Suwanda Sugunasiri.]

INDIVIDUAL AUTHORS

BHAGGIYADATTA, Krishantha

Born in Sri Lanka and educated there and in Canada. His poems have appeared in the *Toronto South Asian Review*, *The Asianadian* and *Poems for Sale in the Street*, an anthology. He lives in Toronto.

4204 *Domestic Bliss.* Toronto: Domestic Bliss Press, 1982. Poems.

CRUSZ, Rienzi

Born in Sri Lanka, educated at the Universities of Ceylon, London and Toronto. His poems have appeared in the major Canadian periodicals and anthologies including *The Fiddlehead*, *The Malahat Review*, *The Antigonish Review*, *Waves*, *Prairie Schooner*, *and The Canadian Forum*. He is reference librarian at the University of Waterloo.

4205 *Flesh and Thorn.* Waterloo: Pasdeloup Press, 1975. Poems.

4206 *Elephant and Ice.* Erin, Ont.: Porcupine's Quill, 1980. Poems.

4207 *Singing against the Wind.* Erin, Ont.: Porcupine's Quill, 1985. 78 pp. Poems.

4208 *Time for Loving.* Toronto: Toronto South-Asian Review, 1985. Poems.

Writings about:

4209 Barbour, Douglas. Review of *Flesh and Thorn.* Q & Q 40, no. 7 (1974): 20.

4210 Barnes, W.J. Review of *Flesh and Thorn.* QUARRY 24, no. 1 (1975): 78-80.

4211 Estok, Michael. Review of Crusz' work. TOR SOUTH ASIAN REV 4, no. 2 (1985): 94-97.

4212 Gool, Reshard. "Back in Touch: Rienzi Crusz's Poetry." TOR SOUTH ASIAN REV 2 (1983): 2-13.

4213 MacLean Watt, Gladys. "Coming Home: Survival by Poetry, on the Work of Rienzi Crusz." NEW Q 1, no. 1 (19): 57-62.

4214 McKay, Don. Review of *Flesh and Thorn.* APPLEGARTH FOLLY 2 (1975): 8-9.

4215 Noonan, G. "Local Librarian's Poetry Upsets the Elephant." ARTS NOW (September-October 1985): 13.

4216 Patterson, Nancy-Lou. "Immigrant Theme has Personal Variations." KITCHENER/WATERLOO RECORD (June 8, 1985)

4217 Querengesser, Neil. Review of *Singing against the Wind*. CAN BOOK REV ANN 1985: 169-70.

4218 Sutherland, Ronald. "How Canadian is Canadian Literature?" ENG TODAY 3 (July 1985): 37-40.

4219 Tapping, Craig. "Front Lines." CAN LIT No. 117 (1988): 145-47. [Review of *A Time for Loving*.]

4220 Zachariach, Mathew. "Crusz." CAN LIT No. 112 (1987): 188-89. [Review of *Singing against the Wind*.]

ONDAATJE, Michael (1943-   )

Poet, critic, novelist, film maker, educator. Born at Colombo, Sri Lanka. Educated at St. Thomas College, Colombo, Dulwich College, London, Bishop's University, University of Toronto and Queen's University. Teacher at Glendon College, York University. Member of League of Canadian Poets and Writers' Union of Canada. His writings have appeared in the major Canadian periodicals. Received the Governor General's Award in 1970 and 1980.

4221 *The Dainty Monsters*. Toronto: Coach House Press, 1967. 77 pp. Poems.

4222 *The Man with Seven Toes*. Toronto: Coach House Press, 1969. 42 pp. Poems.

4223 *The Collected Works of Billy the Kid*. Toronto: House of Anansi, 1970. 105 pp. London: Boyars, 1980. Narrative lyric.

4224 *The Broken Ark: A Book of Beasts*. Ottawa: Oberon, 1971. Poems.

4225 *Rat Jelly*. Toronto: Coach House Press, 1973. 71 pp. Poems.

4226 *Coming through Slaughter*. Toronto: House of Anansi, 1976. 156 pp. New York: Norton, 1976; London: Boyars, 1979. Documentary fiction.

4227 *A Book of Beasts*. Ottawa: Oberon, 1979. Poems.

4228 *Elimination Dance*. Ilderton, Ont.: Nairn Coldstream, 1979. Poems.

4229 *The Long Poem Anthology*. Toronto: Coach House Press, 1979. Poems.

4230 *Claude Glass*. Toronto: Coach House Press Manuscript Editions, 1979. Poems.

4231 *There's a Trick with a Knife I'm Learning to Do*. Toronto: McClelland & Stewart, 1979. London: Boyars, 1980. Poems.

4232 *Rat Jelly and other Poems 1963-78*. London: Boyars, 1980. Poems.

4233 *Running in the Family*. Toronto: McClelland & Stewart, 1982. New York: Norton, 1982. London: Gollancz, 1983. Memoir fiction.

4234 *Tin Roof*. Lantzville, B.C.: Island Writing Series, 1982. 126 pp. Poems.

4235 *Secular Love*. Toronto: Coach House Press, 1984. Poems.

4236 *Buddy Bolden Blues: En Jazzlegend*, translated into Swedish by Buddy Bolden. Stockholm: Legenda, 1985. 170 pp. Play.
[Swedish translation of *Coming through Slaughter.*]

4237 *In the Skin of a Lion.* Toronto: McClelland & Stewart, 1987. 244 pp. London: Secker / Warburg, 1987. New York: Knopf, 1987. Novel.

Writings about:

Bibliography

4238 Brady, Judith. "Bibliography." In *Spider Blues*, pp. 344-65.

Books:

4239 Mundwiller, Leslie. *Michael Ondaatje: Word, Image, Imagination.* Vancouver: Talonbooks, 1984. 160 pp.
[Contents: *Dainty Monsters* ; *The Man with Seven Toes*: Logical Interpretation and Context in Reception; The Role of Imagination in Ondaatje's Poetry; The Poetry and the Imaginative Process; *Coming through Slaughter* and tragic bathos; The films, throes of modernism, notes, bibliographies.]

4240 *Spider Blues: Essays on Michael Ondaatje*, edited by Sam Solecki. Montreal: Véhicule Press, 1985. 369 pp.
[Includes research papers and review articles by 26 authors. A bibliography by Judy Brady is also provided. Individual papers are entered under their authors below.]

Research Papers:

4241 Abley, Mark. "Bone beneath Skin." MACLEAN'S 92, no. 17 (1979): 62-63.
[Review of *There's a Trick with a Knife....*]

4242 Abley, Mark. "Home Is Where the Hurt Is." MACLEAN'S 92 (Apr. 23, 1973): 62.

4243 Abley, Mark. "The Past Is Another Country." MACLEAN'S 95 (Oct. 11, 1982): 66.

4244 Almon, Bert. "A Bitter Aspic." BKS CAN 2, no. 2 (1973): 17.
[Review of *Rat Jelly*. Reproduced in *Spider Blues*, pp. 114-16.]

4245 Atwood, Margaret. "Introduction." In *The New Oxford Book of Canadian Verse: In English*, edited by Margaret Atwood. (Toronto: Oxford University Press, 1982) pp. xxiii, xxxviii.

4246 Atwood, Margaret. "Mathews and Misrepresentation." THIS MAG 7, no. 1 (1973): 30. Reprinted in her *Second Words...* (Toronto: House of Anansi, 1982) p. 142.

4247 Atwood, Margaret. "Michael Ondaatje." In her *Survival: A Thematic Guide to Canadian Literature.* (Toronto: House of Anansi, 1972) pp. 76, 84.

4248 Barbour, Douglas. "All that Poetry should be." CAN FORUM 59 (June-July 1979): 34-35.
[Review of *There's a Trick with a Knife...*]

4249 Barbour, Douglas. "Controlling the Jungle: Review of *The Dainty Monsters*." In *Spider Blues*, pp. 111-13.

4250   Barbour, Douglas. "Three West Coast Poets and One from the East." LAKEHEAD UNIV REV (Fall-Winter 1973): 240-45.
[Review of *Rat Jelly*.]

4251   Barbour, Douglas; Scobie, Stephen. "Conversation with Michael Ondaatje." WHITE PELICAN 1, no. 2 (1971): 6-15.

4252   Barrie, B.D. Review of *Rat Jelly*. FIDDLEHEAD 98 (1973): 119-20.

4253   Bilan, R.P. "The Poet Novelist." In *Spider Blues*, pp. 293-95.

4254   Blodgett, E.D. "The Canadian Literatures as a Literary Problem." In his *Configurations: Essays in the Canadian Literatures*. (Downsview, Ont.: ECW, 1982) pp. 34, 37n.

4255   Blott, Anne. "Michael Ondaatje." In *Canadian Poetry*, edited by Jack David and Robert Lecker. (Toronto/Downsview: General/ECW, 1982) vol. 2, pp. 317-18.

4256   Blott, Anne. "Stories to Finish." STUD CAN LIT 2 (1977): 188-202.
[Review of *The Collected Works of Billy the Kid*.]

4257   Bowering, George. "Modernism could not Last Forever." CAN FIC MAG No. 32-33 (1979-80): 5, 8. Reprinted in his *The Mask in Place: Essays on Fiction in North America*. (Winnipeg: Turnstone, 1982) pp. 78, 81-82.

4258   Bowering, George. "Ondaatje Learning to Do." In *Spider Blues*, pp. 61-69.

4259   Bowering, George. "The Painted Window: Notes on Post-realist Fiction." UNIV WINDSOR REV 13, no. 2 (1978): 28. Reprinted in his *The Mask in Place*, p. 118.

4260   Chamberlin, J.E. "Let there be Commerce between Us: The Poetry of Michael Ondaatje." In *Spider Blues*, edited by Sam Solecki. (Montreal: Véhicule Press, 1985) pp. 31-41.

4261   Cleary, Val. Review of *Rat Jelly*. BKS CAN 2, no. 2 (1973): 17.

4262   Cogswell, Fred. Review of *The Collected Works of Billy the Kid*. FIDDLEHEAD 89 (1971): 105-06.

4263   Cook, John. Review of *Secular Love*. QUEEN'S Q 93 (1986): 415-16.

4264   Cooley, Dennis. " 'I am Here on the Edge' Modern Hero/Postmodern Poetics in *The Collected Works of Billy the Kid*." In *Spider Blues*, pp. 211-39.

4265   Davey, Frank. "Michael Ondaatje." In *From There to Here: A Guide to English Canadian Literature since 1960*. (Erin, Ont.: Press Porcépic, 1974) pp. 222-27.

4266   David, Jack. "Michael Ondaatje's *The Collected Works of Billy the Kid*." CAN NOTES QUERIES 13 (1974): 111-12.

4267   Davis, Marilyn. Review of *The Collected Works of Billy the Kid*. CAN FORUM 51, 606-7 (1971): 34-35.

4268   Donnell, David. "Notes on *The Collected Works of Billy the Kid*." In *Spider Blues*, pp. 240-45.

4269 Draper, Gary. "Stranger than Fiction." BKS CAN 11 (December 1982): 19-20.
[Review of *Running in the Family*.]

4270 Duckles, Richard. "A Quick Draw." OPEN LETTER 2d ser. 1 (1971-72): 73.
[Review of *The Collected Works of Billy the Kid*.]

4271 Fetherling, Doug. "A New Way to Do it." SAT N 86, no. 2 (1971): 29, 39.

4272 Fetherling, Doug. "Poetic Journal." TAM REV 57 (1971): 80-84.
[Review of *The Collected Works of Billy the Kid*.]

4273 Galloway, Priscilla. Review of *Coming through Slaughter*. CAN BOOK REV ANN 1976: 125-26.

4274 Geddes, Garry. "Ondaatje, Michael." In *Supplement to The Oxford Companion to Canadian History and Literature*, edited by William Toye. (Toronto: Oxford University Press, 1973) pp. 238-39.

4275 Geddes, Garry; Bruce, Phyllis, eds. *15 Canadian Poets Plus 5*. (Toronto: Oxford University Press, 1978) pp. 402-03.

4276 Gilday, Katherine. Review of *Coming through Slaughter*. BKS CAN 6, no. 2 (1977): 29-30.

4277 Glickman, Susan. "From 'Philoctetes on the Island' to 'Tin Roof', The Emerging Myth of Michael Ondaatje." In *Spider Blues*, pp. 70-81.

4278 Gray, Lynn. " 'Half-said Things': An Interview with Michael Ondaatje." PRAIRIE FIRE 7, no. 4 (1986-87): 5-11.

4279 Gustafson, Ralph "Ondaatje, (Philip Michael)." In *Contemporary Poets*. (New York: St. Martin's Press, 1975) pp. 1145-46.

4280 Hatch, Ronald B. Review of *Secular Love*. UNIV TOR Q 54 (1984-85): 350.

4281 Healey, James. Review of *The Collected Works of Billy the Kid*. PRAIRIE SCHOONER 49 (1975): 88.

4282 Hicks, Lorne. Review of *There's a Trick with a Knife....* Q & Q 45, no. 6 (1979): 47.

4283 Hill, Douglas. Review of *Running in the Family*. UNIV TOR Q 52 (1982-83): 350-51.

4284 Hornyasky, Michael. Review of *The Collected Works of Billy the Kid*. UNIV TOR Q 40 (1970-71): 377-78.

4285 Hunter, Lynette. "Form and Energy in the Poems of Michael Ondaatje." J CAN POETRY 1, no. 1 (1978): 49-70.

4286 Hutcheon, Linda. "Ex-centric." CAN LIT No. 117 (1988): 132-35.
[Review of *In the Skin of the Lion*.]

4287 Hutcheon, Linda. "*Running in the Family*: The Postmodernist Challenge." In *Spider Blues*, pp. 301-14.

4288 Hutcheon, Linda. "Snow Storm of Paper: The Act of Reading in Self-reflexive Canadian Verse." DAL REV 59 (1979): 114-26.

4289   Kamboureli, Smaro. "The Poetics of Geography in Michael Ondaatje's *Coming through Slaughter*." DESCANT 42 (1983): 112-26.

4290   Kareda, U. "Immigrant's Song." SAT N 98 (December 1983): 44-51.

4291   Kertzer, Jon. "The Blurred Photo: A Review of *Coming through Slaughter*." In *Spider Blues*, pp. 296-300.

4292   Kertzer, Jon. "On Death and Dying: *The Collected Works of Billy the Kid*." STUD CAN LIT (1975): 86-89.

4293   Kertzer, Jon. "Ondaatje." CAN LIT No. 106 (1985): 163-65.
[Review of *Secular Love*.]

4294   Kertzer, Jon. Review of *Coming through Slaughter*. FIDDLEHEAD 113 (1977): 126-29.

4295   King-Edwards, Lucille. "On the Brink." BKS CAN 13 (December 1984): 16-17.
[Review of *Secular Love*.]

4296   Lane, M. Travis. "Dream as History: A Review of *The Man with Seven Toes*." In *Spider Blues*, pp. 150-55.

4297   Lee, Dennis. [Michael Ondaatje.] In his *Savage Fields: An Essay in Literature and Cosmology*. (Toronto: House of Anansi, 1977) pp. 15-60, 115-22.

4298   Lee, Dennis. "Michael Ondaatje: *The Collected Works of Billy the Kid*." In *Spider Blues*, pp. 166-84.

4299   Lee, Dennis. "Part Two: *The Collected Works of Billy the Kid*.; Part Three: Interlude." Lee (1977): 13-60.

4300   MacIntyre, Ernest. "Outside of Time: *Running in the Family*." In *Spider Blues*, pp. 315-20.

4301   MacLulich, T.C. "Ondaatje's Mechanical Boy. Portrait of the Artist as a Photographer." MOSAIC 14 (1981): 107-19.

4302   MacSkimming, Roy. "The Good Jazz." CAN LIT No. 73 (1977): 92-94.
[Review of *Coming through Slaughter*.]

4303   Mandel, Ann. "Michael Ondaatje." In *Canadian Writers since 1960*. (Detroit: Gale, 1987) pp. 273-81. port.

4304   Mandel, Eli. "The Regional Novel: Borderline Art." In *Taking Stock: The Calgary Conference on the Canadian Novel*, edited by Charles R. Steele. (Downsview, Ont.: ECW, 1982) pp. 103-04, 116.

4305   Marshall, Tom. "Canpo: A Chronicle." QUARRY 19, no. 4 (1970): 50-54.
[Review of *The Man with Seven Toes*.]

4306   Marshall, Tom. "Deeper Darkness, After Choreography: Michael Ondaatje." In his *Harsh and Lovely Land: The Major Canadian Poets...* (Vancouver: British Columbia Press, 1977) pp. 144-49.

4307   Marshall, Tom. "Layering: The Shorter Poems of Michael Ondaatje." In *Spider Blues*, pp. 82-92.

4308 Marshall, Tom. "Michael Ondaatje." In: *Harsh and Lovely Land: The Major Canadian Poets and the Making of a Canadian Tradition.* (Vancouver: University of British Columbia Press, 1979)

4309 Marshall, Tom. "Missed Connections." BKS CAN 16, no. 2 (1987): 16.
[Review of *In the Skin of a Lion.*]

4310 Mathews, Robin. "Michael Ondaatje." In *Canadian Literature: Surrender or Revolution*, edited by Gail Dexter. (Toronto: Steel Rail, 1978) pp. 158-59.

4311 Mathews, Robin. "Private Indulgence and Public Discipline: Violence in the English Canadian Novel since 1960." In *Violence in the Canadian Novel since 1960/dans le roman canadien depuis 1960*, edited by Terry Goldie and Virginia Harger-Grinling. (St. John's: Memorial University, 1981) pp. 40, 41, 42-43.

4312 Maxwell, Barry. "Surrealistic Aspects of Michael Ondaatje's *Coming through Slaughter.*" MOSAIC 18, no. 3 (1985): 101-14.

4313 McColm, Sheila Clare. "Metaphorical Style and Thought in the Poetry of Margaret Avison and Michael Ondaatje." M.A. Thesis. University of Western Ontario, 1981.

4314 McKinnon, David. Review of *Rat Jelly.* OPEN LETTER 2nd ser. 5 (1973): 122-23.

4315 McNally, Paul. Review of *There's a Trick with a Knife....* QUEEN'S Q 86 (1979): 720-21.

4316 McWhirter, George. Review of *Rat Jelly.* QUARRY 23, no. 1 (1974): 75-76.

4317 Mills, John. Review of *Coming through Slaughter.* QUEEN'S Q 84 (1977): 436-37.

4318 Moss, John. "Michael Ondaatje." In his *A Reader's Guide to the Canadian Novel.* (Toronto: McClelland & Stewart, 1981) pp. 223-24, 355, 360, 363, 365.

4319 Mukherjee, Bharati. "Ondaatje's Sri Lanka is Prospero's Land." Q & Q 48, no. 10 (1982): 30.
[Review of *Running in the Family.*]

4320 Musgrave, Susan. Review of *Rat Jelly.* MAL REV 31 (1974): 161-62.

4321 Nodelman, P. "Collected Photographs of Billy the Kid." CAN LIT No. 87 (1980): 68-69.

4322 Norris, J. "*Coming through Slaughter.* Theatre Passe Muraille, Toronto." CODA 172 (1980): 31.

4323 Oughton, John. "Sane Assasin: The Double Life of Michael Ondaatje, Mild-mannered Professor of English Literature and Risk-taking Celebrator Madman." BKS CAN (June-July, 1983): 7-10.

4324 Owens, J. " 'I Send You a Picture': Michael Ondaatje's Portrait of Billy the Kid." STUD CAN LIT 8, no. 1 (1983): 117-39.

4325 Pearce, John. "Moving to the Clear." In his *Twelve Voices: Interviews with Canadian Poets.* (Ottawa: Borealis, 1980) pp. 129-43.

4326 Pierce, Gretchen. "Canada Gives Writers 'Sense of Place'; Author of 'Billy' Keeps Low Profile." HALIF CHRON HER 10 (October 1975): 30.

4327 Ripley, John. "Drama and Theatre." In *Literary History of Canada: Canadian Literature in English.* Gen. ed. Carl F. Klink. 2nd ed. (Toronto: University of Toronto Press, 1979) vol. 3, p. 224.

[Review of the drama version of *The Collected Works of Billy the Kid.*]

4328 Rodriguez, Elizabeth. "A Report on the Poets at Festival 70. (Bishop's University)." FIDDLEHEAD 84 (1970): 124-25.

4329 Rooke, Constance. "Dog in a Grey Room: The Happy Ending of *Coming through Slaughter.*" In *Spider Blues*, pp. 268-92.

4330 Sarkar, E. "Michael Ondaatje's *Billy the Kid*; The Aesthetics of Violence." WORLD LIT WRITT ENG 12 (1973): 230-39.

4331 Schreiber, Ron. Review of *Dainty Monsters*. NEW Q 12 (1970): 43-46.

4332 Schroeder, Andreas. "The Poet as a Gunman." CAN LIT No. 51 (1972): 80-82.
[Review of *The Collected Works of Billy the Kid.*]

4333 Scobie, Stephen. "*Coming through Slaughter*: Fictional Magnets and Spider's Webs." ESSAYS CAN WRIT No. 12 (1978): 5-23.

4334 Scobie, Stephen. "His Legend a Jungle Sleep: Michael Ondaatje and Henri Rousseau." CAN LIT No. 76 (1978): 6-21. Repr. in *Spider Blues*, pp. 42-60.

4335 Scobie, Stephen. "The Lies Stay in: A Review of *There's a Trick with a Knife I'm Learning to Do.*" In *Spider Blues*, pp. 117-20.

4336 Scobie, Stephen. "Two Authors in Search of a Character: bp Nichol and Michael Ondaatje." CAN LIT No. 54 (1972): 37-55. Reprinted in *Spider Blues*, pp. 185-210.

4337 Scobie, Stephen; Barbour, Douglas. "A Conversation with Michael Ondaatje." WHITE PELICAN 1, no. 2 (1971): 6-15.

4338 Scott, Peter Dale. "Canadian Chronicle." POETRY 115 (1970): 353-64.

4339 Sharp, Daryl L. "Michael Ondaatje." COMMENTATOR 15 (March 1971): 13-14.

4340 Skelton, Robin. Review of *The Collected Works of Billy the Kid.* MAL REV 18 (1971): 127.

4341 Skelton, Robin. Review of *Secular Love.* Q & Q 51, no. 2 (1985): 39.

4342 Smith, P.K. "Michael Ondaatje: A Poet Sets the Stage." PERF ARTS CAN 17 (1980): 30-33.

4343 Solecki, Sam. "Dementia Praecox Paranoid Type." CAN FORUM 56 (December-January 1976-77): 46-47.
[Review of *Coming through Slaughter.*]

4344 Solecki, Sam. "An Interview with Michael Ondaatje." RUNE 2 (1975): 39-54.

4345 Solecki, Sam. "An Interview with Michael Ondaatje." In *Spider Blues*, pp. 321-32.

4346 Solecki, Sam. "Making and Destroying: *Coming through Slaughter* and Extremist Art." In *Spider Blues*, pp. 246-67.

4347 Solecki, Sam. "Michael Ondaatje." DESCANT 42 (Fall 1982): 77-78.

4348   Solecki, Sam.   "Michael Ondaatje: A Paper Promiscuous and out of Forme with Several Enlargements and Untutored Narrative." In *Spider Blues*, pp. 333-43.

4349   Solecki, Sam.   "Nets and Chaos: The Poetry of Michael Ondaatje." STUD CAN LIT 2 (Winter 1977): 36-48. Reprinted in *Brave New Wave*, edited by Jack David. (Windsor, Ont.: Black Moss, 1978) pp. 24-50, and in *Spider Blues*, pp. 93-110.

4350   Solecki, Sam.   "Point Blank: Narrative in *The Man with Seven Toes*." In *Spider Blues*, pp. 135-49.

4351   Solecki, Sam.   "Sharpening His Act; Like a Knife-thrower, Michael Ondaatje Hazards Great Risks with Art as His Confidence Builds. BKS CAN 8, no. 6 (1979): 11.
[Review of *There's a Trick with a Knife...*]

4352   Stevens, Peter.   "Ondaatje, Michael." In his *Modern English Canadian Poetry....* (Detroit: Gale, 1978) pp. 37, 41, 185-87. (Vol. 15 of American Literature, English Literature and World Literatures in English)

4353   Stevens, Peter.   Review of *The Collected Works of Billy the Kid*. QUEEN'S Q 78 (1971): 326-27.

4354   Stevens, Peter.   Review of *Rat Jelly*. QUEEN'S Q 80 (1973): 656-57.

4355   Surette, Leon.   Review of *Coming through Slaughter*. CAN FIC MAG 24-25 (1977): 165-67.

4356   Turner, Barbara.   "In the Skin of Michael Ondaatje: Giving Voice to a Social Conscience." Q & Q (May 1987): 21-22.
[An interview.]

4357   Wagner, Lidia.   "Four Young Poets." ONT REV 1 (1974): 89-97.

4358   Waterston, Elizabeth.   "Michael Ondaatje." In her *Survey: A Short History of Canadian Literature.* (Toronto: Methuen, 1973) pp. 88, 139. (Methuen Canadian Literature Series)

4359   Watson, Sheila.   "Michael Ondaatje: The Mechanization of Death." WHITE PELICAN 2, no. 4 (1972): 56-64. Reprinted in OPEN LETTER 2nd ser. 3, no. 1 (1974-75): 158-66, and in *Spider Blues*, pp. 156-65..
[Review of *The Collected Works of Billy the Kid.*]

4360   Witten, Murk.   "Billy, Buddy, and Michael..." BKS CAN 6 (June-July 1977): 9-10, 12-13.

WEERASINGHE, Asoka

Born in Sri Lanka. He was educated there, in the U.K., and in Canada. He emigrated to this country in 1968. His poems have appeared in *Bardic Echoes*, *The Canadian Indian Times*, *The Muse*, *Poetry Magazine*, and *Green Snow*. He lives in Ottawa.

4361   *Nine Poems for Jeannie*. [Ottawa: The Author] 1971. Poems.

4362   *Spring Quartet*. [N.p.] Breakthrough Press, 1972. Poems.

4363   *Poems for Jeannie*. Cornwall, Ont.: Vesta, 1976. 89 pp. Poems.

4364   *Poems in November*. Ottawa: Commoner's Publishing, 1977. [30] pp. Poems.

4365   *Exile, 1956-1978*. Cornwall, Ont.: Vesta, 1978. 73 pp. Poems.

4366 *Hot Tea and Cinnamon Buns: Poems.* Cornwall, Ont.: Vesta, 1980. 53 pp. Poems.

4367 *Home again, Lanka.* Ottawa: Commoner's Publishing, 1981. 70 pp. illus. Poems.

4368 *Selected Poems 1958-1983.* Cornwall, Ont.: Vesta, 1983. 160 pp. Poems.

SUDANESE

INDIVIDUAL AUTHOR

ALIANAK, Hrant (1950-   )
Television director and writer. Born at Khartoum, Sudan, and moved with his parents to Montreal in 1967. He was educated at McGill University (economics) and York University (English). Unpublished plays include *The Blues* (1976), *Lucky Strike* (1974), *Night* (1974), *Noah's Kiosk* (1973), *Titus Andronicus* (adaptation, 1975).

4369 *Return of the Big Five.* Toronto: Fineglow, 1974. Plays.
[This volume contains the author's following stage plays: *Christmas, Mathematics, Tantrums,* and *Western.*]

4370 *Passion and Sin.* In *Canadian Theatre Review* (Summer 1978) pp. 49-106.

Writings about:

4371 Leggat, Alexander. "Alianak, Hrant." In *Canadian Encyclopedia.* (Edmonton: Hurtig, 1985) vol. 2, p. 6.

4372 Leggat, Alexander. "Alianak, Hrant." In *The Oxford Companion to Canadian Literature,* edited by William Toye. (Toronto: Oxford University Press, 1983) p. 7.

SWEDISH

BIBLIOGRAPHIES

4373 **BORYS, Ann Mari**
"Swedish-Canadian Periodical Publications: A Preliminary Check List." CAN ETH STUD 2, no. 1 (1970): 191-92.

4374 **BROOK, M.; MALYCKY, Alexander**
"Swedish-Canadian Periodical Publications: First Supplement." CAN ETH STUD 5, no. 1-2 (1973): 263-67.

INDIVIDUAL AUTHORS

GÄNBERG, Selma

4375 *Tempelbyggaren [The Builder of the Temple].* Winnipeg: Canada Posten, 1940. Novel.
[Published serially.]

STRÖMBERG, Leonard

4376 *Hederns vägar [Ways of Honour].* Winnipeg: Canada Posten, 1940. Novel.
[Published serially.]

SWISS

INDIVIDUAL AUTHORS

BÖSCHENSTEIN, Hermann (1900-   )
Born in Stein am Rhein, Switzerland. Studied in Zürich, Munich, Berlin and Rostock. He came to Canada in 1928 and worked at the University of Toronto. Between 1950 and 1975 he was a visiting professor at various universities in England, the United States and Canada. Received an honorary LLD degree from Queen's University. He has written a number of essays on German literature.

4377   *Unter Schweizern Kanada [Among the Swiss in Canada].* Basel: Gute Schriften, 1974. 140 pp. Stories.

4378   *Im Roten Ochsen [In the Red Oxen].* Schaffhausen, Switzerland: Meier, 1977. 231 pp.

Writings about:

4379   Arnold, Armin. "The Fiction of Böschenstein." INT FIC REV 5, no. 1 (1978): 52-58.

4380   Arnold, Armin. "Hermann Böschenstein als Erzähler" [Hermann Böschenstein as a Storyteller]. In *Tradition - Integration - Rezeption. Annalen 2,* edited by Karin R. Gürttler and Herfried Scheer. (Montréal: Université de Montréal, 1978) pp. 82-90.

4381   Milnes, Humphrey. "Herman Böschenstein." In *Analecta Helvetica et Germanica, Eine Festschrift zu Ehren von Hermann Böschenstein,* edited by Armin Arnold, H. Eichner, E. Heier, and S. Hoefert. (Bonn: Bouvier Verlag Herbert Grundmann, 1979) pp. 387-92.

4382   Milnes, Humphrey. "Hermann Böschenstein." GERM LIFE LETTR 23, no. 1 (1969) 1-6.
       [The entire issue is dedicated to the Hermann Böschenstein anniversary.]

CARDINAL, George-Irwin von (1907-   )

Writing about:

4383   Cardinal, Clive H. "Missa sine nomine: Von deutscher Dichtung in Kanada" [Missa sine nomine: Regarding German Poetry in Canada]. DER NORDWESTEN (July 5, 1966): 15.

GLAUSER, Alfred
Né en Suisse, Alfred Glauser a fait des études universitaires à Berne et à Genève. Après quelques années d'enseignement, il émigre au Canada et s'installe à Winnipeg. Glauser fréquente ensuite l'Université du Manitoba, et celle du Wisconsin durant la Deuxième Guerre mondiale. À cette dernière, il obtient un doctorat en littérature et il enseigne.

4384   *Le vent se lève.* Montréal: Valiquette, 1942. 219 pp. Prose poétique.

LATHION, Gilbert-Bernard (1924-   )
Né à Sion, Suisse, Lathion est peintre, sculpteur, poète, romancier. Membre de la Société académique Arts-Sciences-Lettres de Paris et de la Société des Écrivains Suisses, il est détenteur de nombreuses médailles, entre autres les Palmes académiques 1980, Paris.

4385   *Le Chant de l'univers.* Paris: Éditions de l'Athanor, 1976. 60 pp. Poèmes.

4386   *La main de Satan.* Paris: Éditions de la Pensée Universelle, 1978. 64 pp.

4387   *Le soleil noir.* Sherbrooke, Qué.: Naaman, 1978. 57 pp. Poèmes et prose.

4388   *Vanda.* Paris: Éditions de l'Athanor (?)

4389   *Alpha et Oméga.* Sherbrooke, Qué.: Naaman, 1980. 104 pp. Poèmes et prose.

SYRIAN

INDIVIDUAL AUTHOR

VAROUJEAN, Vasco (1936-   )
Born in Késsab, Syria, received his education in Beirut and graduated from the University of Milan in journalism. His writings have appeared in *Le Devoir* and *Perspectives*. French language poems have been broadcast on Radio Canada.

4390   *Le Moulin du diable.* Montréal: Cercle du livre de France, 1972. 159 pp. Nouvelles.

4391   *Les Raisins verts.* Montréal: Cercle du livre de France, 1975. 130 pp. Récit.

4392   *Les Pâturages de la rancœur.* Montréal: Cercle du livre de France, 1977. 256 pp. Roman..

TANZANIAN

INDIVIDUAL AUTHOR

SENKORO, E.M.K. Fikeni
Born in Tanzania and emigrated to Edmonton. His Ph.D. dissertation is related to Caribbean and Canadian literature. He has published poetry in Africa, the U.S.A., and Canada. A book of poetry, *Reflexions,* is forthcoming.

4393　*Mzalendo [Patriot].*　Nairobi: Shungwaya Publishers, 1972.　Poems.

4394　*Upacha [Twinship].*　Nairobi: Shungwaya Publishers, 1979/80.　Poems.

TOBAGAN

INDIVIDUAL AUTHORS

ALEXANDER, Winston
Born in Tobago, attended Bishop's High School there. Studied at the University of the West Indies, Jamaica. He lives in Ottawa and works for the Department of Energy, Mines and Resources.

4395　*The Joy, the Sorrow and Denn.*　New York: Vintage, 1974.　Novel.

ELLIOTT, Lorris
Born in Tobago, came to Canada in 1959. He continued his education at the University of British Columbia (B.A., M.A.), and the University of Montreal (Ph.D.). Teaches at McGill University.

4396　*A Li'lle Bit o' Somet'ing.*　One-act play performed by the Black Theatre Workshop, Montreal, 1978.

4397　*Coming for to Carry.*　Toronto: Williams-Wallace, 1982.　Novel.

4398　*How Now Black Man.*　A Multi-media play, performed at the Centaur Theatre by the Black Theatre Workshop of Montreal.

TRINIDADIAN

INDIVIDUAL AUTHORS

BISSOONDATH, Neil

4399　*Digging Up the Mountains: Selected Stories.*　Toronto: Macmillan, 1986.　247 pp.　Short stories.

4400　*A Casual Brutality.*　Toronto: Macmillan, 1988.　376 pp.　Novel.

Writings about:

4401   Hill, Douglas. "From St. John's to Casaquemada." BKS CAN 17, no. 6 (1988): 35. port. [Review of *A Casual Brutality*.]

4402   Martin, Peter. "Literary 'Gretzky' Scores." OTTAWA CIT (March 8, 1986): C2. [Review of *Digging Up the Mountains*.]

4403   Pashley, Nicholas. Review of *Digging Up the Mountains*. CAN BOOK REV ANN 1985: 205-06.

BRAND, Dionne (1953-   )
Born in Trinidad, emigrated to Canada and studied literature and drama at the University of Toronto.

4404   *'foreday Morning: Poems*. Toronto: Khoisan Artists, 1978. 34 pp. Poems.

4405   *Earth Magic*, drawings by Roy Cross. Toronto: Kids Can Press, 1979. 61 pp. illus. Poems for children.

4406   *Primitive Offensive*. Toronto: Williams-Wallace, 1982. 59 pp. Poems.

4407   *Chronicles of the Hostile Sun*. Toronto: Williams-Wallace, 1984. 75 pp. Poems.

4408   *Winter Epigrams & Epigrams to Cardinal in Defence of Claudia*, edited by Roger McTair. Toronto: Williams-Wallace, 1984. 38 pp. Poems.

BRATHWAITE, J. Ashton
Born in Trinidad, moved to England at an early age. He served in the British Army in the Middle East. Lives in Toronto.

4409   *A Black British Soldier*, rev. ed. Toronto: 21st Century, 1969. 72 pp. Autobiography.

4410   *Bitter Soul*. Toronto: 21st Century, 1970. 20 pp.

4411   *Souls in the Wilderness*. Toronto: 21st Century, 1970.

4412   *Niggers... This is Canada*. Toronto: 21st Century, 1971. 70 pp.

4413   *Grassroot Philosopher*. Toronto: 21st Century, 1977.

CAYONNE, John Antonio
Born in Trinidad and was educated there, in the U.S.A., and Canada (B.A., M.A., at York University). Founding director of the Black Theatre Group in Montreal, and artistic director of Caribana Players and La Petite Musicale Folk Group, Toronto. Some of his poems were read by the Black Theatre Workshop in Montreal in 1966.

4414   *Calypsopora*. Montreal, 1966. Folk opera. [Performed by the Black Theatre Workshop at the Review Theatre, Montreal, 1966.]

4415   *Calypsopora II*. Montreal, 1968. Folk opera. [Performed by the Black Theatre Workshop at the Westmount H.S. Auditorium, Montreal, 1968.]

COKER, Anthony
Born in Trinidad, came to Canada in 1969. He attended Dawson College and McGill University, where he gained a B.A. in psychology. He directed several dramatic performances in Montreal.

4416   *Climax*. Montreal, 1976. Poems.

CROMWELL, Liz

Born in Trinidad, she studied at New York State University and taught English in Brooklyn, N.Y., before moving to Toronto. She is a writer and associate editor of *Contrast*. Also edited *One Out of Many*, an anthology.

4417 *Canadian Jungle Tea: Poems.* Toronto: Khoisan Artists, 1975. 47 pp. Poems.

HOSEIN, Clyde

Short story writer and former journalist. Was born in Trinidad. Currently lives in Toronto. His short stories have appeared in *The London Magazine* and *The Toronto South Asian Review*, and have been broadcast on CBC's *Anthology.*

4418 *The Killing of Nelson and other Stories.* London: London Magazine Press, 1980. 128 pp. Short stories.

LADOO, Sonny Harold (-1972)

Born in Trinidad of East Indian descent and came to Canada in 1968. He died in a tragic accident during a visit to Trinidad in 1972.

4419 *No Pain Like this Body.* Toronto: House of Anansi, 1972. 141 pp. Novel.

4420 *Yesterdays.* Toronto: House of Anansi, 1974. 110 pp. Novel.

McTAIR, Roger

Born in Trinidad; came to Toronto in 1971. He is active in documentary film making, theatre and film directing. Obtained a BAA in motion picture studies at Ryerson. Published poems in *Voices, Savacou* and *Manna.*

4421 *The Chain.* A play sponsored by the Ottawa Little Theatre, 1972-73.
[Awarded second prize in Canadian Playwrighting Competition.]

4422 *Is the Carnival Over?* Toronto, 1972-73.
[Honourable mention in Canadian Playwrighting Competition.]

4423 *One Flight Up, Two Flights Down.* Toronto, 1973.
[Honourable mention in Canadian Playwrighting Competition, 1973-74.]

ROACH, Charles

Born in Trinidad, emigrated to Canada in 1955. He is practising law in Toronto. His poems have appeared in periodicals.

4424 *Root for Ravens: Poems for Drum and Freedom*, illustrated by Hugh Williams. Toronto: N.C. Press, 1977. 95 pp. illus. Poems.

SELVON, Samuel

Born in Trinidad, emigrated to England in 1950, where he lived for 28 years. Produced several radio plays and television scripts. Received many honours and awards including two Guggenheim Fellowships and two grants from the Arts Council of Britain. Novels authored while in England are *The Brighter Sun* (1952), *The Island is a World* (1952), *The Lonely Londoners* (1956), *Ways of Sunlight* (1957), *Turn again, Tiger* (1959), *I Hear Thunder* (1963), *The Housing Lark* (1965), *The Plains of Caroni* (1970), *Those Who Eat the Cascadura* (1972), *Moses Ascending* (1975). He lives in Calgary and continues to write.

4425 *Moses Migrating.* London: Longman, 1983. 186 pp. Novel.

331

Writings about:

4426 Harber, Philip K. Review of *The Plains of Caroni.* CM 14, (1986): 222.

4427 Ramraj, Victor. "Political Commitment in the Writing of Sam Selvon." Presented to the Commonwealth in Canada Conference, Winnipeg, 1985.

SITAHAL, Errol
Born in Trinidad, came to Canada via England after studying English and theatre at the universities of Bristol and Manchester.

4428 *The Mission Begins.* Play, performed by the San Fernando Group, Trinidad, 1968.

4429 *Sea Shango.* Play, performed by Fountainhead Theatre, Toronto, 1974.

TUNISIAN

INDIVIDUAL AUTHOR

BOURAOUI, Hédi (1932-)
Poète, nouvelliste, essayiste, critique littéraire. Né à Sfax, Tunisie, détient une license ès lettres de l'Université de Toulouse, une maîtrise en littératures anglais et américaine de l'Indiana University et un doctorat en littérature comparée de l'Université Cornell. À Toronto depuis vingt ans, il enseigne la littérature comparée à l'Université York et dirige le Collège Stong. Membre fondateur de la revue *Waves*, dont il dirige la section francophone pendant quinze ans; la chronique francophone de *Poetry Canada Review* lui est aussi confiée. Membre du comité de rédaction des revues *Liaison* (Ottawa), *Créateurs* d'Univers (Toronto) et *Sindbad* (Maroc).

4430 *Musocktail.* Chicago: Tower Associates, 1965. Poems.

4431 *Tremblé.* Paris: Éditions Saint-Germain-des-Prés, 1969. Poèmes.

4432 *Éclate module.* Montréal: Éditions Cosmos, 1972. Poèmes.

4433 *Vésuviade.* Paris: Saint-Germain-des-Prés, 1976. Poèmes.

4434 *Sans frontières.* Saint Louis: Francité, 1980. Poèmes.

4435 *Haïtuvois, suivi de Antillades.* Québec: Éditions Nouvelle Optique, 1980.

4436 *Ignescent.* Paris: Éd. Silex, 1982. Poèmes.

4437 *Vers et l'Envers.* Toronto: ECW, 1982. Poèmes.

4438 *L'Icônaison.* Sherbrooke, Qué.: Naaman, 1985. Roman.

4439 *Échosmos.* Toronto: Mosaic Press, 1986. Poèmes.

4440 *Reflet pluriel.* Bordeuax: Presses universitaires de Bordeaux, 1986. Poèmes.

Writings about:

4441 Alyn, Marc. "Un français en Amérique." FIGARO LITT No. 1241 (2-8 mars 1970): 27.

4442 Baciu-Simian, Mira. Review of *Vésuviade*. FRENCH REV 51 (1977): 132.

4443 Cloutier, Cécile. Review of *Vésuviade*. WAVES 6, no. 1 (1977): 76-77.

4444 "Hédi Bouraoui. *Le Grand Meaulnes*: autobiographie romantique ou nouvelle forme romanesque?" L'OPINION (lundi 2 mai 1977): 6.

4445 La Charité, Virginia A. Review of *Éclat module*. FRENCH REV 47 (1973): 486-87.

4446 La Charité, Virginia A. Review of *Tremblé*. FRENCH REV 45 (1971): 189-90.

4447 Sabiston, Elizabeth. "Hédi Bouraoui's Quest: Poetry and Cultural Heritage." CAN LIT No. 95 (1982): 67-83.

4448 Tapping, Craig. "Front Lines." CAN LIT No 117 (1988): 145-47. [Review of *Échosmos*.]

4449 Welch, Liliane. Review of *Éclat module* DAL REV 55 (1972-73): 689-90.

4450 Welch, Liliane. Review of *Tremblé*. DAL REV 50 (1970): 416-17.

4451 Welch, Liliane. Review of *Vésuviade*. ANTIG REV 34 (1978): 104-05.

4452 Welch, Liliane. Review of *Without Boundaries* DAL REV 59 (1979): 368-70.

UKRAINIAN

BIBLIOGRAPHIES, DIRECTORIES, ENCYCLOPEDIAS

4453　GERUS-TARNAWECKA, Iraida, comp.
East Slavic Cyrillica in Canadian Repositories: Cyrillic Manuscripts and Printed Books. Winnipeg: Volyn, 1981. 186 pp.
[Includes old Ukrainian manuscripts and printed material.]

4454　GREGOROVICH, Andrew S.
"Ukrainian Canadiana: A Selected Bibliography of Scholarly Works 1970-1980." CAN ETH STUD 12, no. 2 (1980): 102-24.
[Arranged under the following headings: Bibliographies and reference works; historical, political and general works; sociological, literary, cultural and artistic writings.]

4455　HARASYMIW, E.V.; MALYCKY, Alexander
"Ukrainian-Canadian Creative Literature: A Preliminary Check List of Imprints." CAN ETH STUD 2, no. 1 (1970): 205-27.
[Includes 252 citations of poetry and fiction in Ukrainian.]

4456　KUBIJOVYCH, Volodymyr, ed.
Encyclopedia Ukraine. Vol. 1: A-F, Vol. 2: G-K. Toronto: University of Toronto Press, 1984-1988. 952, 737 pp. respectively.
[Includes entries on Ukrainian-Canadian authors.]

4457　KUBIJOVYCH, Volodymyr, ed.
Ukraine: A Concise Encyclopedia. Toronto: University of Toronto Press, 1963 and 1971. 1185 and 1394 pp.
[Includes Ukrainian authors in Canada.]

4458　LEWANSKI, Richard C.
"Ukrainian Literature." In his *Literatures of the World in English Translation.* Vol. 2: *The Slavic Literatures.* (New York: New York Public Library and Frederick Ungar, 1967) pp. 427-44.
[Includes H. Ewach and Anatol' Kurdydyk.]

4459　MAGOCSI, Paul, comp.
A Guide to Newspapers and Periodicals. Toronto: University of Toronto Press, 1983.
[Contains 175 entries.]

4460　MALYCKY, Alexander
"A Preliminary Check List of Studies on Ukrainian-Canadian Creative Literature. Pt. I: General Studies." CAN ETH STUD 1, no. 1 (1969): 161-63.
[A list of 24 references to research papers, dissertations and monographic publications.]

4461　MALYCKY, Alexander
"Studies in Ukrainian-Canadian Creative Literature. Pt. 2: General Studies. First Supplement." CAN ETH STUD 5, no. 1-2 (1973): 379-86.
[Contains 76 entries.]

4462　MALYCKY, Alexander

Ukrainian Book Imprints of Edmonton, Alberta. Edmonton: Ukrainian Bibliographical Society of Alberta, 1985. 62 pp.
[Includes books of poetry and fiction.]

4463 **MALYCKY, Alexander**
"Ukrainian-Canadian Creative Literature: First Supplement to the Listing of Authors and Pseudonyms." CAN ETH STUD 5, no. 1-2 (1973): 359-63.
[Represents 76 authors. This is a continuation of a list published in CAN ETH STUD 1, no. 1 (1969): 143-60.]

4464 **MALYCKY, Alexander**
"Ukrainian-Canadian Periodical Publications: First Supplement." CAN ETH STUD 2, no. 1 (1970): 195-203.
[Continuation of a list published in CAN ETH STUD 1, no. 1 (1969): 77-142. Also provides indexes of non-Ukrainian titles and geographic distribution.]

4465 **MALYCKY, Alexander**
"Ukrainian-Canadian Periodical Publications: A Preliminary Check List." CAN ETH STUD 1, no. 1 (1969): 77-142.
[A major compilation, includes 549 references with indexes of non-Ukrainian publications and geographic distribution.]

4466 **MALYCKY, Alexander**
"Ukrainian-Canadian Periodical Publications: Second Supplement." CAN ETH STUD 5, no. 1-2 (1973): 275-92.
[This supplement completes listings of Ukrainian-Canadian periodicals. The three compilations on the subject contain 701 titles.]

4467 **MALYCKY, Alexander; HARASYMIW, E.V.**
"A Preliminary Check List of Studies on Ukrainian-Canadian Creative Literature. Pt. 2: Specific Studies." CAN ETH STUD 2, no. 1 (1970): 229-44.
[Includes 142 references.]

4468 **MALYCKY, Alexander; MUCHIN, Ivan; ROÏK, Oleksander**
"Magisters'ki tezy, doktors'ki dysertatsiï ta inshi pratsi na ukraïns'ki temy" [Master's Theses, Doctoral Dissertations on Ukrainian Themes]. In *Zakhidn'okanads'kyĭ zbirnyk*, edited by IAr Slavutych. (Edmonton: Shevchenko Scientific Society, 1975) vol. 2, pp. 199-207.

4469 **PROKOPIW, O.L.; MALYCKY, Alexander**
"Imprints of Ukrainian-Canadian Creative Literature: First Supplement." CAN ETH STUD 5, no. 1-2 (1973): 365-78.
[A list of primary material with chronological and genre indexes.]

4470 **PROKOPIW, O.L.; ROYÏCK, Alexander; MALYCKY, Alexander**
"Ukrainian-Canadian Creative Literature: A Preliminary Check List of Authors and Pseudonyms." CAN ETH STUD 1, no. 1 (1969): 143-60.
[This list contains 416 names and pseudonyms.]

4471 **ROMANENCHUK, B.**
Azbukovnyk. Entsyklopediia ukrains'koï literatury. *[Encyclopedia of Ukrainian Literature.]* Philadelphia: Kyiw, 1969 and 1973 2 vols. 472, 535 pp.
[Includes some Ukrainian-Canadian authors.]

4472 **RUDNYĆKYJ, J.B.**

"Ukrainian-Canadian Bibliography." In *Papers of the Bibliographical Society of Canada/Cahiers de la Société Bibliographique du Canada I.* (Toronto: The Society, 1962) pp. 44-48.
[Includes titles of a scholarly and literary nature.]

4473 RUDNYĆKYJ, J.B. et al
Ukrainica Canadiana. Winnipeg: UVAN, 1953-1972.
[The set contains 20 issues, covering various aspects of scholasticism, history, social science, religion, literature. Bibliographic information on prose and poetry is provided.]

4474 RUTKOWSKI, Alan; CYNCAR, Nadia
Ukrainian Serials: A Checklist of Ukrainian Journals, Periodicals and Newspapers at The University of Alberta Library. Edmonton: Canadian Institute of Ukrainian Studies, 1983. 62 pp.
[Arranged by major subject headings, includes complete bibliographic data on creative literature.]

4475 *Scripta manent.* Winnipeg-Ottawa, 1975-1980. 4 vols.
[Bio-bibliography devoted to the work of J.B. Rudnyćkyj. A valuable source for literary studies.]

4476 SHTOHRYN, Dmytro, ed.
Ukrainians in North America: A Bibliographical Directory of Noteworthy Men and Women of Ukrainian Origin in the United States and Canada. Champaign, Ill.: Association for the Advancement of Ukrainian Studies, 1975. 424 pp.
[Includes several Ukrainian-Canadian authors.]

4477 SLAVUTYCH, Îăr
Anotovana bibliohrafiia ukraïns'koï literatury v Kanadi: Kanads'ki knyzhkovi vydannia 1908-1983 [Annotated Bibliography of Ukrainian Literature in Canada: Canadian Book Publications, 1908-1983]. Edmonton: Slavuta, 1984. 161 pp. 2nd enl. ed. 1908-1985. Ibid., 1986. 155 pp. 3rd enl. rev. ed. 1908-1986. Ibid., 1987. 167 pp.
[Contains annotations, bibliographic data and lists of primary and secondary publications. A major reference tool.]

4478 SLAVUTYCH, Îăr
Bibliohrafiia ukraïns'koï poeziï v Kanadi" [Bibliography of Ukrainian Poetry in Canada]. In his *Zakhidn'okanads'kyĭ zbirnyk* (Edmonton: Shevchenko Scientific Society, 1975) vol. 2, pp. 327-38.
[Includes primary book publications only.]

4479 SUCHOWERS'KY, Mykola, comp.
List of Periodicals and Serials in East European and Slavic Studies. Edmonton: University of Alberta Library, 1971.
[Contains 738 entries.]

4480 SUCHOWERS'KY, Mykola, comp.
Reference Materials in Slavic and East European Studies. Edmonton: University of Alberta Library, 1974. 117 pp.
[Arranged by subject, provides complete bibliographic data on source material.]

4481 SWYRIPA, Frances A.
Guide to Ukrainian Canadian Newspapers, Periodicals and Calendar-Almanacs on Microfilm, 1903-1970. Edmonton: Canadian Institute of Ukrainian Studies, 1985. 236 pp.
[A major source material for serial publications. Arranged by subject.]

4482 SWYRIPA, Frances A.; MAKUCH, Andrij
Ukrainian Canadian Content in the Newspaper Svoboda, 1893-1904. Edmonton: Canadian Institute of Ukrainian Studies, 1985. 157 pp.

[Includes creative literature.]

4483 **TARNAWS'KA, Marta**
Ukraïns'ka National'na Revolutsiâ v poeziï (1917-1967) [Ukrainian National Revolution in Poetry (1917-1967)]. Edmonton: Slavuta, 1969. 8 pp.

4484 *Ukrainian Canadiana, 1904-1979: A Bibliography of the Book Exhibit to Mark the 75th Anniversary of Ukrainian Book Publishing in Canada.* Toronto: University of Toronto Library, 1979. 40 pp.
[Literary publications are included.]

4485 *Ukraïns'ki kanads'ki pys'mennyky [Ukrainian-Canadian Writers],* edited by Petro Kravchuk. L'viv, Ukraine: Vydavnystvo "Kameniar", 1971.
[Provides biographical notes, bibliographic data and critical evaluations of individual authors.]

4486 **WERES, Roman**
Ukraine: Selected References in English Language. 2nd ed. Chicago: Ukrainian Research and Information Institute, 1974. vi, 312 pp.
[Includes references to Ukrainian-Canadian creative literature.]

BOOKS, MONOGRAPHS

4487 **BEZPECHNYĬ, Ivan**
Teoriâ literatury [Literary Theories]. Toronto: Moloda Ukraïna, 1984. 304 pp.
[Literary textbook for advanced students.]

4488 **BOROVYK, Mykhailo**
Ukraïns'ko-kanads'ka presa ta ïï znachennia dlia ukraïns'koï menshyny v Kanadi [The Ukrainian-Canadian Press and its Significant Role in the Ukrainian Minority in Canada]. München: Ukrainische Freie Universität, 1977. 341 pp. maps.
[Includes scholarly publications, covering the period between 1903 and 1967.]

4489 *First Convention of Ukrainian Artists and Writers from Canada, the United States and Western Europe, Who Met in Toronto, July 3-5, 1954.* Toronto [n.d.] 298 pp.
[Includes papers on Ukrainian writing in Canada.]

4490 **HAĬ-HOLOVKO, Oleksa**
Ukraïns'ki pys'mennyky v Kanadi: Literaturno-krytychni narysy [Ukrainian Writers in Canada: Literary-critical Sketches]. Winnipeg: Volyn', 1980. vol. 1, 191 pp.
[Includes biographical information on 20 authors, supplemented by excerpts from their writing.]

4491 **HOSHOWS'KYJ, Bohdan, ed.**
My i nashi dity. Dytiacha literatura, mystetstvo, vykhovanniâ [We and Our Children. Ukrainian Children's Literature, Art and Education]. Toronto: Association of Ukrainian Writers for Children, 1965. vol. 1, 390 pp.

4492 **HOSHOWS'KYJ, Bohdan, ed.**
Ukraïns'ka dytîacha literatura. Sproba ohlîâdu i problematyka [Outline of Ukrainian Children's Literature]. Toronto: Association of Ukrainian Writers for Children, 1966. 116 pp.

4493 *Ĩûvileinyĭ zbirnyk: Ukraïns'koï Vil'noï Akademiï Nauk v Kanadi/The Jubilee Collection of the Ukrainian Free Academy of Sciences in Canada,* edited by A. Baran, O.W. Gerus, and J. Rozumnyj. Winnipeg: UVAN, 1976. xiii, 657 pp.

[Includes a paper on Ukrainian literature in Canada by Watson Kirkconnell.]

4494 KLYNOVYĬ, ĨUriĭ
Moïm synam, moïm pryiateliam: statti i esseï [To My Sons and My Friends: Articles and Essays].
Edmonton: Slovo, 1981. 616 pp.
[Includes papers on Ivan Bodnarchuk, Viktor Kupchenko, Borys Oleksandriv, Ulas Samchuk, Vasyl' Sofroniv-Levyts'kyĭ and others.]

4495 KOZIĬ, Dmytro
Hlybynnyĭ etos: Narysy z literatury i filosofiï [Truthful Ethos: Sketches on Literature and Philosophy]. Toronto: Kursy ukraïnoznavastva, 1984. 494 pp.

4496 KRAVCHUK, Petro
Ukraïns'ka literatura v Kanadi [Ukrainian Literature in Canada]. Kiev: Dnipro, 1964. 154 pp.

4497 MANDRYKA, M.I.
History of Ukrainian Literature in Canada. Foreword by J.B. Rudnyćkyj. Winnipeg: Ukrainian Free Academy of Sciences, 1968. 247 pp.
[A comprehensive study of Ukrainian-Canadian literature. Includes historical background with a brief summary of Ukrainian literature (pp. 13-24), and the various chronological stages of Ukrainian literature in Canada from the pioneer days (pp. 29-49); the interwar era (pp. 116-31); post-World War II era and poets, literary critics, authors and researchers (pp. 173-229). A select bibliography is provided on p. 224.]

4498 MARUNCHAK, Michael (i.e. Mykhaĭlo)
The Ukrainian Canadians: A History/L'Histoire des Ukrainiens-Canadiens. Winnipeg: Ukrainian Free Academy of Sciences, 1970. 792 pp. illus., photos, maps. 2nd ed. Winnipeg: UVAN, 1982. 970 pp.
[Includes a chapter on creative literature (pp. 499-536). The second edition has two chapters on literature: "Literature of the Pioneers" (pp. 297-308), and "Literature of the Second Era" (pp. 498-536).]

4499 SLAVUTYCH, Yar (i.e. ĨAr)
Ukrainian Literature in Canada. Edmonton: Slavuta Publishers, 1966. 15 pp.
[Revised excerpt from the paper "Slavic Literature in Canada," which appeared in the *Proceedings of the First National Conference on Canadian Slavs,* published by the Edmonton Inter-University Committee on Slavs, 1966, entitled *Slavs in Canada.* The following authors are analysed: P. Kazan, Pavlo Krat, I.N. Kret, Illîa Kyrîâk, Oleksander Luhovyĭ, Ulas Samchuk, Stepan Fodchuk and others.]

4500 SLAVUTYCH, ĨAr
Ukraïns'ka poeziia v Kanadi [Ukrainian Poetry in Canada]. Edmonton: Slavuta Publishers, 1976. 103 pp.
[Individual authors analysed are Teodor Fedyk, Semen Kovbel', Vasyl' Kudryk, Panteleĭmon Bozhyk, Ivan Danyl'chuk, Pavlo Step, Oleksander Smotrych, Volodymyr Havrylîuk, Mykyta Mandryka and others. Bibliography, pp. 91-103.]

4501 SWYRIPA, Frances
Ukrainian Canadians: A Survey of Their Portrayal in English-language Works. Edmonton: The University of Alberta Press for the Canadian Institute of Ukrainian Studies, 1978. 166 pp.
[Includes chapters on literature and references.]

4502 WOYCENKO, Ol'ha

Canada's Cultural Heritage: Ukrainian Contribution. Winnipeg: Ukrainian Free Academy of Sciences, 1964. 16 pp. (Chronicle series no. 22)
[Includes references to authors.]

4503 WOYCENKO, Ol'ha
Napriamni ukraïns'koï literatury v Kanadi. Z perspectyvy mynuloho i suchasnoho [Trends in Ukrainian Literature in Canada. With Past and Future Perspectives]. Winnipeg, 1963. 7 pp.
[Reprinted from WOMAN'S WORLD No. 2 (1963)

4504 WOYCENKO, Ol'ha
Slavic Literature in Canada. I. Ukrainian Canadian Letters. Winnipeg: UVAN, 1969. 27 pp. Slavistica no. 65.

RESEARCH PAPERS, REVIEW ARTICLES

4505 ANDRUSYSHEN, C.H.
"Ukrainian Literature in Canada." In *Ukraine, A Concise Encyclopedia.* (Toronto: University of Toronto Press, 1971) vol. 2, pp. 1180-82.
[Offers a general survey of creative writing by Ukrainian authors in Eastern and Western Canada.]

4506 BALAN, Jars
"Ukrainian Writing." In *The Oxford Companion to Canadian Literature,* edited by William Toye. (Toronto: Oxford University Press, 1983) pp. 807-10.
[Describes the various stages and generations of Ukrainian Canadian literature, from the pioneer era through the inter-war years to the post-World-War II generation of authors.]

4507 BILASH, Borislav
"Kanadyzmy ta ïkh stylistychni funktsiï v movi ukraïns'ko-kanads'kykh pys'mennykiv" [Canadianisms and Their Stylistic Functions in the Language of the Ukrainian-Canadian Writers]. Ph.D. Dissertation, Ukrainian Free University, Munich, 1965.

4508 BODNARCHUK, Ivan
"Nashi paristky " [Our Budding Writers]. UKR HOLOS (Dec. 20, 1972): 7.
[Introduces some new-generation authors.]

4509 IVAKH, Onufriï
"Potreba svoieï literatury kanadiïs'kym ukraïntsiâm" [The Need of Their Own Literature for Canadian Ukrainians]. UKR HOLOS (May 18, 1921)

4510 IVAKH, Onufriï
"Ukraïns'ko-kanadiïs'ke pys'menstvo" [Ukrainian-Canadian Creative Literature]. In *Îûvileïnyï al'manakh dlia vidmichenniâ 50-littiâ pratsi "Ukraïns'koho holosu" 1910-1960.* (Winnipeg: Tryzub [n.d.]) pp. 156-65.

4511 KIRKCONNELL, Watson
"Ukrainian-Canadian Poetry." In his *Canadian Overtones: An Anthology of Canadian Poetry Written Originally in Icelandic, Swedish, Norwegian, Hungarian, Italian, Greek, Ukrainian....* (Winnipeg, 1935) pp. 76-81.
[Includes references to, and poems by, fifteen Ukrainian poets.]

4512 KIRKCONNELL, Watson
"Ukrainian Literature in Manitoba." In *The Jubilee Collection of the Ukrainian Free Academy of Sciences in Canada.* (Winnipeg: UVAN, 1976) pp. 622-31.

[Includes the following authors: Teodor Fedyk, Vasyl' Kudryk, Semen Kovbel', Stepan Doroshchuk, Onufriĭ Ivakh, Stepan Semchuk. Parts of the study deal with the pioneer group and those who received their education in Manitoba.]

4513 KIRKCONNELL, Watson
"Ukrainian Literature in Manitoba." MOSAIC 3, no. 3 (1970): 39-47.
[A summary of Ukrainian poetry from the earliest times to 1970. Of the pioneer authors, Vasyl' Kudryk and Semen Kovbel' are discussed. Other poets introduced are Stepan Doroshchuk, Semen Savchuk, Onufriĭ Ivakh, and Mykyta Mandryka.]

4514 KOVBEL', Semen
"Pochatky ukraïns'koĭ literatury v Kanadi [The Beginnings of Ukrainian Literature in Canada]. In *Propamiatna knyha Ukraïns'koho narodnoho domu u Vynypegu.* (Winnipeg, 1949) pp. 603-65.

4515 KOVBEL', Semen
"Povisti ĭ opovidannia ta ĭkh avtory" [Novels and Their Authors]. In *Propamiatna knyha Ukraïns'koho narodnoho domu u Vynypegu.* (Winnipeg, 1949) pp. 614-18.

4516 MANDRYKA, M.I.
"Kharakter i zmist ukraïns'koho pys'menstva v Kanadi" [Character and Contents in Ukrainian Literature in Canada]. In *The Jubilee Collection of the Ukrainian Free Academy of Sciences in Canada.* (Winnipeg: UVAN, 1976) pp. 632-46.

4517 MARUNCHAK, Michael (i.e. Mykhaïlo)
"Literature." In his *The Ukrainian Canadians: A History....* (Winnipeg: Ukrainian Free Academy of Sciences, 1970) pp. 499-536.
[An account of Ukrainian writing in Canada from the early 1900s to 1970. Individual authors discussed are Onufriĭ Ivakh, Mykhaïlo Petrovs'kyĭ, Vera Lysenko, I.E. Kmeta, M.I. Mandryka, Viktor Kupchenko, Stepan Semchuk and others.]

4518 MARUNCHAK, Michael (i.e. Mykhaïlo)
"Literature of the Pioneers." In his *The Ukrainian Canadians: A History....* (Winnipeg: Ukrainian Free Academy of Sciences, 1970) pp. 297-311.
[Pioneer poets were: Dmytro Rarahovs'kĭ, Pavlo Krat, Vasyl' Holovats'kyĭ, and Teodor Fedyk. Prose writers included Mykhaïlo Gowda, Sava Chernets'kyĭ, Onufriĭ Hykavyĭ, and Myroslav Stechyshyn.]

4519 MARUNCHAK, Michael (i.e. Mykhaïlo)
"Poets and Writers." In his *The Ukrainians in Canada: A History....* (Winnipeg: Ukrainian Free Academy of Sciences, 1970) pp. 664-70.
[Concerns the work of new immigrant authors such as Volodymyr Skorups'kyĭ, Danylo Struk, Levko Romen, Anatol' Kurdydyk, Ulas Samchuk, V.S. Levyts'kyĭ, Oleksa Haĭ-Holovko, Petro Volyniâk, Ivan I. Bodnarchuk, and others.]

4520 MARUNCHAK, Mykhaïlo H.
"Literatura" [Literature]. In his *Istoriia ukraïntsiv Kanady....* (Winnipeg: Ukrains'ka Vil'na Akademiiâ Nauk v Kanadi, 1968-1974) vol. 2, pp. 213-31.
[Also in vol. 3, pp. 97-204.]

4521 MARUNCHAK, Mykhaïlo H.
"Pioners'ka literatura" [Literature of the Pioneers]. In his *Istoriia ukraïntsiv Kanady....* (Winnipeg: UVAN, 1968), vol. 1, pp. 297-313.
[Includes pioneer authors.]

4522 NAZARUK, Osyp
"V spravi ukraïnskoho literaturnoho rukhu v Kanadï [Concerning the Ukrainian Literary Movement in Canada]. UKR HOLOS (March 7, and 14, 1923)

4523 PAWLIW, Orest
"Studies in Ukrainian Literature in Canada." In *Slavs in Canada; Proceedings of the Second National Conference on Canadian Slavs*. (Ottawa: Inter-University Committee on Canadian Slavs, 1968) vol. 2, pp. 235-46.

4524 PETROVS'KYJ, Michael (i.e. Mykhaïlo)
"Ukrainian-Canadian Writers." CAN AUTH BKMN 19 (March 1943): 18.

4525 RUDNYĆKYJ, J.B.
"The Case of Literary Oscillation: Tradition and Originality in Ukrainian-Canadian Literature." In *Actes du IVe congres de l'Association internationale de littérature comparée (Fribourg 1964)/Proceedings of the IVth Congress of the International Comparative Literature Association*. (The Hague-Paris: Mouton, 1966) pp. 359-62.

4526 RUDNYĆKYJ, J.B.
"Ukrainian-Canadian Letters. A Case of Literary Regionalism." MOSAIC 1, no. 3 (1968): 51-57.

4527 SKWAROK, Josaphat
"A Brief Historical Survey of Ukrainian Literature in Canada." In his M.A. Thesis entitled:"The Ukrainian Settlers and Their Schools with Reference to Government, French-Canadian, and Ukrainian Missionary Influences, 1891-1921". (The University of Alberta, 1958) pp. 159-75. [Published under the same title in book form by Basilian Press, Edmonton, 1959.]

4528 SLAVUTYCH, Yar (i.e. ÎAr)
"Expectations and Reality in Early Ukrainian Literature in Canada (1879-1905)." In *Identifications: Ethnicity and the Writer in Canada*, edited by Jars Balan. (Edmonton: The Canadian Institute of Ukrainian Studies, The University of Alberta) pp. 14-21.
[Introduces the work of such pioneer authors as Nestor Dmytriw, Sava Chernets'kyï, Myroslaw Stechishin, Symon Palamariuk, and Mychaïlo Gowda.]

4529 SLAVUTYCH, Yar (i.e. ÎAr)
"Ukrainian Literature in Canada." FORUM No. 11 (1969/70): 23.
[Review of M.I. Mandryka's *History of Ukrainian Literature in Canada*.]

4530 SLAVUTYCH, Yar (i.e. ÎAr)
"Ukrainian Poetry in Canada: A Historical Account." CAN ETH STUD 3, no. 1 (1971): 95-108.
[Included are Mykhaïlo Gowda, Teodor Fedyk, Vasyl' Kudryk, Semen Kovbel', Ivan Danyl'chuk, I.A. Kmeta-ÎEfymovych, M.I. Mandryka, Tetiana Shevchuk, Levko Romen, Volodymyr Havryliuk, Oleksa Haï-Holovko, Volodymyr Skorups'kyï, Borys Oleksandriv, Dan Mur and others. Extended version is reprinted in *Ukrainians in Alberta*. (Edmonton: Ukrainian Pioneers' Association of Alberta, 1975) pp. 229-45.]

4531 SLAVUTYCH, Yar (i.e. ÎAr)
"Ukrainian Literature in Canada." In *A Heritage in Transition: Essays in the History of Ukrainians in Canada*, edited by M.R. Lupul. (Toronto: McClelland & Stewart, 1982) pp. 296-309.
[Covers poetry, fiction and drama.]

4532 SLAVUTYCH, Yar (i.e. ÎAr)
"Ukrainian Writing in Canada." In *The Canadian Encyclopedia* (Edmonton: Hurtig, 1985) vol. 3, p. 1862.

[Introduces three eras: Pioneer (1897-1920), Modern (1920-1950) and the post-World War II era. Since the 60s there has been a revival of poetry owing to such talents as poets Borys Oleksandriv, Bohdan Mazepa, Levko Romen, Dan Mur and others.]

4533 STRUK, Danylo
"Ukrainian Emigré Literature in Canada." In *Identifications: Ethnicity and the Writer in Canada*, edited by Jars Balan. (Edmonton: The Canadian Institute of Ukrainian Studies, The University of Alberta, 1982) pp. 88-103.
[An analysis of the writings of Illi͡a Kyrii͡ak, Myroslav Irchan, Mykyta Mandryka, Ulas Samchuk, I͡Ar Slavutych, Borys Oleksandriv, and Volodymyr Skorups'kyĭ. The author recommends a thorough sifting of traditional interpretation to avoid an inflated representation of Ukrainian literature in Canada.]

4534 VOLYNETS', Stepan
"Ukraïns'ka kanadiĭs'ka literatura i ïï tvorsi (Korotkyĭ ohliad)" [Ukrainian-Canadian Literature and Its Creators (A Short Survey)]. In *I͡Uvileĭnyĭ kalendar-al'manakh Ukraïns'koho holosu prysviachenyĭ 75-littı͡u* ...Winnipeg: Tryzub [n.d.]) pp. 73-82.

4535 WOYCENKO, Ol'ha
"The Realm of Letters." In her *The Ukrainians in Canada.* 2nd enl. ed. (Ottawa-Winnipeg, 1968) pp. 125-59.
[A survey of the pre-World War I, the interwar and post-World War II eras. Individual authors discussed are Teodor Fedyk, Mykhaĭlo Gowda, Vasyl' Kudryk, Panteleĭmon Bozhyk, Ivan Danyl'chuk, Onufriĭ Ivakh, Mykola Mandryka, M.M. Babii͡enko, Illi͡a Kyrii͡ak, Ulas Samchuk, Oleksander Luhovyĭ, and others.]

4536 YUZYK, Paul
"Literary Achievements." In his *Ukrainian Canadians: Their Place and Role in Canadian Life.* (Toronto: Ukrainian Canadian Business & Professional Federation, 1967) pp. 66-70.

4537 YUZYK, Paul
"Ukrainian Literature." In his *The Ukrainians in Manitoba.* (Toronto: University of Toronto Press, 1953) pp. 127-43.

4538 ZHYLA, Volodymyr
"Zakhidnia Kanada v ukraïns'kiĭ literaturi." In *Zakhidn'okanads'kyĭ zbirnyk*, edited by I͡Ar Slavutych. (Edmonton: Shevchenko Scientific Society, 1973) vol. 1, pp. 129-48.
[Includes Illi͡a Kyrii͡ak, M.I. Mandryka, Dan Mur, I͡Ar Slavutych, and others.]

ANTHOLOGIES

4539 *Antol'ogii͡a ukraïns'koho pys'menstva v Kanadi [An Anthology of Ukrainian Literature in Canada].* Winnipeg: Canadian-Ukrainian Educational Association, 1941. 158 pp.
[Includes poems by A. Gospodyn, A. Prus'ka, A. Novak, D. Hun'kevych, I.A. Pavchuk, I. Novosad, M. Adamovs'ka, M.I. Mandryka, M. Krypiakevych, M. Kumka, M. Petrovs'kyĭ, O. Ivakh, S Kovbel', S.M. Doroschuk, T.D. Volokhatiuk, T. Fedyk, T. Kroĭter (i.e. T. Bishop), and V.D. Tulevitriv.]

4540 *Antolohii͡a ukraïns'koï poeziï v Kanadi 1898-1973/An Anthology of Ukrainian Poetry in Canada 1898-1973*, compiled and edited by I͡Ar Slavutych. Edmonton: The Ukrainian Writers' Association in Canada, 1975. 159 pp.
[Includes poems by 48 authors with biographical notes.]

4541   *Antol'ohiîã ukraïns'koï poeziï [An Anthology of Ukrainian Poetry]*, edited by C.H. Andrusyshen. Saskatoon: University of Saskatchewan Printing Services, 1967. 220 pp. Mimeographed.

4542   *Nasha spadshchyna: Zakhidnia kanads'ko-ukraïns'ka literatura ḏia molodi [Our Heritage: Western-Canadian Ukrainian Literature for Young People]*, edited by ÎÛriï Stefanyk. Edmonton: Alberta Education, 1979. 283 pp.
[Includes I. Danyl'chuk, S. Kuz'menko, B. Mazepa, B. Oleksandriv, ÎAr Slavutych, O. Zuievs'kyï and others.]

4543   *Kanadiïs'ki opovidannia [Canadian Short Stories]*. Winnipeg: ÎA. N. Kret, 1910.

4544   *Khrestomatiia ukraïns'koï literatury dlia shkil i kursiv ukraïnoznavstva*. Toronto: OUPK, 1970. 227 pp.
[Includes O. Oleksandriv, ÎAr Slavutych, O. Zuievs'kyï, and others.]

4545   *Kontrasty: Zbirka molodechnoï (Poeziia, proza, muzyka i hrafika/Contrasts: A Collection of Poetry, Prose, Music and Graphics by Young Ukrainians]*, edited by Larysa M.L. Zales'ka Onyshkevych. New York-Toronto: Holovna Plastova Bulava, 1970. 151 pp.
[Includes poems by Dariia Lada and poems and short stories by Khrystyna Velyhors'ka.]

4546   *Koordynaty: Antol'ohiîã suchasnoï ukraïns'koï poeziï na Zakhodi/Coordinates: An Anthology of Modern Ukrainian Poetry in the West*, edited by Bohdan Boïchuk and Bohdan T. Rubchak. [N.p.] "Suchasnist'" 1969. vol. 2.
[Includes poems by B. Oleksandriv, ÎAr Slavutych, I. Kovaliv, O. Zuievs'kyï, and T. Os'machka.]

4547   *Modern Ukrainian Short Stories*, edited with a preface by George N.S. Luckyj. Littleton, Col.: Ukrainian Academic Press, c1973. 228 pp.
[Text in Ukrainian with English traslations on opposite pages.]

4548   *My Songs. A Selection of Ukrainian Folksongs in English Translation*, compiled by J. Dziobko. Translated by H. Ivakh. Winnipeg: Ukrainian Canadian Pioneer Library, 1958. 102 pp.
[A collection of 86 songs/poems.]

4549   *Piesy dlîã molodi [Plays for Youth]*. Edmonton: Soiuz Ukraïnok Kanady, 1973.
[Plays by I. Bodnarchuk, O. Mak and V. Sofroniv-Levyts'kyï.]

4550   *Pivnichne siaïvo: Al'manakh [Northern Lights: Almanac]*, compiled and edited by ÎAr Slavutych. Edmonton: Slavuta Publishers, 1964-1971. 5 vols.
[Includes poetry, fiction, art, essays, literary survey of Canadian interest.]

4551   *Poety Kanady [Poets of Canada]*, edited by Petro Kravchuk. Kiev: Radians'kyï pys'mennyk, 1958. 212 pp.
[Includes poems by A. Ponur, D. Rarahovs'kyï, D. Zakharuk, ÎA. Manchurak, I. Koval'skyï, I. Mykytyn, I. Petruk, I. Shymchyshyn, M. Vakaliuk, T. Fedyk.]

4552   *Slovo. Zbirnyk*, vols. 1-11, edited by Sviatoslav Hordyns'kyï.et al. Edmonton: Ob'iednannia ukraïns'kykh pys'mennykiv u Kanadi Slovo, 1970-1987.
[Includes poetry, fiction, essays, art and documentary writings.]

4553   *Songs of Ukraina with Ruthenian Poems*, edited by Florence Randal Livesay. London-New York: Dent, 1916. 175 pp.
[Includes Canadian Paul Crath.]

4554   *Their Land: An Anthology of Ukrainian Short Stories*, translated and edited by M. Luchkovich. Jersey City, N.J.: Svoboda, 1964. 325 pp.

4555   *The Ukrainian Poets, selected and translated into English* by C.H. Andrusyshen and Watson Kirkconnell.   Toronto: Published for the Ukrainian Canadian Committee by the University of Toronto Press, 1963. 500 pp.
[Includes poems by O. Ivakh, M.I. Mandryka, S. Semchuk and Ĭar Slavutych.]

4556   *Ukrainian Songs and Lyrics. A Short Anthology of Ukrainian Poetry*, translated into English by O. Ivakh. Winnipeg: Ukrainian Pub. Co., 1933. 77 pp.

4557   *Ukraïns'ki kanads'ki pys'mennyky [Ukrainian Canadian Writers]*, edited by Petro Kravchuk. L'viv: Vydavnytstvo"Kameniar", 1971. 104 pp.
[Includes short stories by A. Ponur, D. Hun'kevych, I. Zelez, M. Popovych, M. Shatul's'kyĭ, M. Harasymchuk, and S. Pura.]

4558   *Zbirka prats chleniv molodizhnoï sektsiï spilky ukraïns'kykh zhurnalistiv Kanady/A Collection of Work of the Youth Section of the Association of Ukrainian Journalists of Canada*, edited by Iryna Makaryk. Toronto: Spilka Ukraïns'kykh ẐHurnalistiv Kanady, 1973. 73 pp.
[Includes prose by B. Duma.]

4559   *ẐHuravli [Cranes]*. Scranton, Penn.: Svoboda, 1903. 47 pp.
[Includes writings by S. Palamariuk and M. Stechyshyn.]

INDIVIDUAL AUTHORS

ADAMOVS'KA, Mariîâ   (1890-1961)
Born in Mykhalkove, Western Ukraine, emigrated to Canada in 1899. Her poems have appeared in *Ukrainian Voice*. She died in Melville, Sask.

4560   *Pochatky v Kanadi [Beginnings in Canada]*. In *ĬUvileĭnyĭ Al'manakh dlîâ vidmichennia 50-littîâ Ukraïns'koho Holosu 1910-1960*. (Winnipeg: Trydent Press, 1959) pp. 210-15. Autobiographical.

   Writing about:

4561   Lozyns'kyĭ, I.H. "Pionerka pera Mariîâ Adamovs'ka" [A Pioneer of the Pen: Mariîâ Adamovs'ka]. KAN FARM (June 17, 1974): 15.

ARAB'SKA, Anna (1901-   )

4562   *Lisovyĭ ohon' [Forest Fire]*. Winnipeg: Promin' Publishing Co., 1927. 31 pp. Story.

   Writing about:

4563   Lozyns'kyĭ, I.H. "Anna Arabs'ka: ẐHurnalistka-pys'mennytsia i pedahoh" [Anna Arabs'ka: Journalist, Author and Teacher]. KAN FARM (Nov. 20, 1972): 12-13.

BABIIENKO, Vasyl' V.

4564   *Mizh burlyvymy fylîâmy: Drama na 4 diï i 5 odmin [In the Midst of Stormy Waves: Drama in 4 Acts and 5 Scenes]*. Winnipeg, 1918. 80 pp.

BABÎUK, Andriĭ   see IRCHAN, Myroslav

BARCHUK, Iv.

4565 *Rizdviana zirka: Zbirka rizdvianykh virshiv i opovidan' [Christmas Star: Poems and Stories]*, in collaboration with Mykhaĭlo Podvorniak. Saskatoon: Doroha Pravdy, 1956. 173 pp. Poems and stories.

4566 *Velykodniĭ ranok: Zbirka velykodnikh opovidan' i virshiv [Easter Morning: Stories and Poems]*. Winnipeg: Doroha Pravdy, 1957. 256 pp. Poems and stories.

BESKYD-TARNOVYCH, I͡Uli͡an (1903-1977)

4567 *Sviata, ridna zemli͡a [The Holy Native Soil]*. Toronto: Orhanizatsiia oborony Lemkivshchyny, 1966. 88 pp. Short novel.

BODNARCHUK, Ivan Iryneĭ (1914-)

Born in the region of Pokuttia, Western Ukraine, completed his education in the Institute of Pedagogy in Kiev. After World War II he emigrated to Canada. His writings are related to experience in this country.

4568 *Na perekhresnykh shli͡akhakh [At the Crossroads]*. 1954. Short stories.

4569 *Znaĭomi oblychchi͡a: Opovidanni͡a [Familiar Faces: Short Stories]*. Winnipeg, 1961. 109 pp. Short stories.

4570 *Druzi moĭkh dniv: Noveli [Friends of My Days: Short Stories]*. Winnipeg, 1967. 96 pp. Short stories.

4571 *Kladka: Dyti͡achi novel'ky [Bridge: Children's Stories]*. Toronto: OPDL, 1967. 41 pp. Children's stories.

4572 *Daleki obriĭ [Distant Horizons]*. Toronto: The Author, 1968. 57 pp. Children's stories.

4573 *Pokolinni͡a ziĭdut'si͡a: Povist'/The Generations Will Get Together: Novel*, edited by I͡Uriĭ Klynovyĭ. Edmonton: Obiednannia ukraïns'kykh pys'mennykiv v Kanadi "Slovo", 1974. 151 pp. Novel.

4574 *Zamriacheni ranky. Opovidanni͡a, noveli, narisy [Misty Morning. Stories, Novellas, Sketches]*. Toronto: Slovo, 1978. 88 pp. Short stories.

4575 *Zaobriĭni perehuky [Echoes behind the Horizon]*. Toronto: Slovo, 1984. 60 pp. Short stories.

Writings about:

4576 "CHetwerta zbirka narysiv Iv. Bodnarchuka" [Ivan Bodnarchuk's Fourth Collection of Sketches]. UKR VISTI (May 2, 1968): 4.
[Review of *Druzi moĭkh dniv*.]

4577 "Daleki *obriĭ* I. Bodnarchuka" [I. Bodnarchuk's *Daleki obriĭ*]. UKR VISTI (July 10, 1969): 4.

4578 Klynovyĭ, I͡Uriĭ. "Deshcho pro povist' Ivan Bodnarchuka *Pokolinnia ziĭdut'sia*" [On Ivan Bodnarchuk's Novel *Pokolinni͡a ziĭdut'si͡a*]. Introduction. In *Pokolinni͡a ziĭdut'si͡a*. (Winnipeg: Obiednannia ukraïns'kykh pys'mennykiv v Kanadi "Slovo", 1974) pp. 6-10.

4579 Mandryka, I.M. "Ivan Bodnarchuk." In his *History of Ukrainian Literature in Canada*. (Winnipeg: Ukrainian Free Academy of Sciences, 1968) pp. 188-91.

4580   Romanenchuk, Bohdan. "Ivan Iryneĭ Bodnarchuk." In *Azbukovnyk: A Concise Encyclopedia of Ukrainian Literature.* (Philadelphia: Kyïv Publishing, 1966)

4581   Smoliĭ, Ivan. "Problematyka povisty Ivana Bodnarchuka *Pokolinnîâ ziĭdut'sîâ* (Do 60 richchîâ pys'mennika)" [The Problems Raised by the Story *Pokolinnîâ ziĭdut'sîâ*, by Ivan Bodnarchuk: (To Commemorate the 60th Anniversary of the Writer)]. NOV DNI 26, no. 305-306 (1975): 6-11.

4582   Soborian, M. "Nashe slovo, nasha pisnia: (Avtors'kyĭ vechir Ivana Bodnarchuka i vokal'nyĭ kontsert solistky Raïsy Sadovoï, Hamilton, Ont." [Our Word, Our Song: (A Literary Evening for Ivan Bodnarchuk and a Vocal Concert by Raïsa Sadova, Hamilton, Ont)]. UKR HOLOS (July 11, 1973): 10.

4583   Stepanîûk, S. "Avtors'kyĭ vechir Ivana Bodnarchuka" [A Literary Evening for Ivan Bodnarchuk]. VIL'N SLOVO (March 30, 1974): 4.

4584   Stepanîûk, S. "Deshcho pro povist' Ivana Bodnarchuka *Pokolinnîâ ziĭdut'sîâ*" [Some Remarks on the Novel *Pokolinnîâ   ziĭdut'sîâ*, by Ivan Bodnarchuk]. In *Pokolinnîâ   ziĭdut'sîâ: Povist.* (Edmonton: Obiednannia ukraïns'kykh pys'mennikiv v Kanadi "Slovo", 1974) pp. 6-10.

4585   Volynets', Stepan. "Nova zbirka opovidan' I. Bodnarchuka" [I. Bodnarchuk's New Collection of Stories]. UKR HOLOS (Apr. 10, 1968): 5.

BODRUG, Ivan (1874-1952)
Born in Ukraine and emigrated to Canada after World War II. He has also published under the pen name of IvanYrshchenyĭ.

4586   *Ubiĭnyky: Mel'odrama v 5 diîâkh a odynaĭtsîâty vidslonakh [Murderers: Melodrama in 5 Acts and Eleven Scenes].* Winnipeg: Ukraïns'ka Knyharnia [n.d.] 60 pp. Play.

BOROVYK, Mykhaĭlo (1909-   )

4587   *Pravda u krytytsi [Truth in Criticism].* Wilsonville, Ont.: The Author, 1971. 56 pp. Short stories.

4588   *Taiemnytsia shchastia [The Secret of Happiness].* Wilsonville, Ont.: The Author, 1973. 52 pp. Story and poems.

BORYSYK, Mykhaĭlo (1891-   )
Agronomist by profession, born in Zubrivka, Ukraine. Educated in Agricultural Science in Poland and Czechoslovakia and taught at a Ukrainian Technical School in Germany. Author of several scientific and literary papers. He lived in Winnipeg.

4589   *Diâk uchytelem [Cantor-Teacher].* Winnipeg: Promin', 1927. 24 pp. Juvenile comedy in one act.

BOZHYK, Panteleĭmon (1879-1944)
Born in Onut, Western Ukraine, emigrated to Canada in 1900. Author of stories, poems and scholarly works. His book *Tzerkov Ukraïntsiv v Kanadi* is an invaluable source of reference on Ukrainians in this country.

4590   *Kanadiïs'ka muza [Canadian Muses].* Winnipeg: The Author, 1936. Poems.

4591   *Odnosel'chany v Kanadi [The Fellow Willagers in Canada].* Edmonton: Ukraïns'ki Visti, 1941. Stories, published serially.

4592 *Kanadiĭs'ki opovidannĭa [Canadian Stories]*. [Yorkton, Sask.: Ukraïns'ke katolyts'ke vydavnytstvo, 1933.] 54 pp. Short stories.

Writings about:

4593 Slavutych, ĬAr. "Panteleĭmon Bozhyk." In his *Ukraïns'ka poeziia v Kanadi*. (Edmonton: Slavuta, 1976) pp. 24-25.

4594 "Velychavyĭ pokhoron bl. p.o. P. Bozhyka" [The Stately Funeral of the Late Rev. Canon P. Bozhyk]. HOLOS SPAS/RED VOICE 16, no. 12 (1944): 376-77.

BRATUN', Rostyslav (1927-   )

4595 *Kanads'ka knyha: Poeziï [Canadian Book: Poems]*. Kyïv: Derzh. vyd-vo Khudozh. li-ry, 1963. 132 pp. Poems.
[A book of poems by a Soviet Ukrainian poet who visited Canada.]

CHERNENKO, Oleksandra, pseud. (Real name: ĬENDYK, Oleksandra)
Born in Piotrkow, Poland, attended medical school. She came to Canada in 1949 and settled in Edmonton. Her stories and poems have appeared in *Kyïv, Pivnichne siaĭvo, Slovo*, and in other publications.

4596 *Liudyna: Poema na 18 pisen' [A Man: A Poem in 18 Songs]*. Philadelphia: Kyïv, 1960. 62 pp. Poems.

CHMIL, Ivan ... see KHMIL', Ivan

CHORNEĬKO, Mykhaĭlo

4597 *Shchob ne zabuty i denni podiï [Not to Forget]*. Saskatoon: The Author, 1964. 131 pp.

CHORNOOKA, Halĭa, pseud. (Real name: RIĬ, Martselĭa)

4598 *Potsilunok u temnoti: Komediĭa v 1 diï [A Kiss in the Dark: Comedy in 1 Act]*. Winnipeg: Ukraïns'kyĭ Holos, 1940. 32 pp. Play.

DANYL'CHUK, Ivan (1901-1942)
Born in Canora, Sask. He was a teacher and editor of the Winnipeg-based *Ukrainian Canadian Review*. His poems were written in Ukrainian and appeared in *Kameniari, Ukrainian Voice* and *Canadian Farmer*.

4599 *Svytaie den': Poeziï [Daybreak: Poems]*. Winnipeg: The Author, 1929. 56 pp. Poems.

4600 *Sumkivtsi: Kartyna na dvi diï z pionirs'koho i molodechoho zhyttĭa v Kanadi zo spivamy i tankamy [SMUK Members: A Play in Two Acts with Songs and Dances about the Life of Young People during Canada's Pioneer Days]*. Saskatoon: SUMK, 1941. 27 pp. Play.

Writings about:

4601 Evanyshen, J.W. "Jay Dee: (Reminiscences)." UKR CAN REV 8, no. 5 (1943): 9.

4602 Ivakh, Onufriĭ. Review of *Svytaie den'*. UKR HOLOS (Oct. 2, 1929).

4603 Ivakh, Onufriĭ. "Spohady pro poeta Ivana Danyl'chuka (v 15-littĭa ĭoho smerty)" [Recollections about the Poet I. Danyl'chuk (On the 15th Anniversary of His Death)]. UKR HOLOS (Nov. 6, 1957): 9-10.

4604 Lozyns'kyĭ, I.H. "70-richchīa z dnīa narodzhennīa poeta I. Danyl'chuka" [The 70th Anniversary of the Birth of the Poet I. Dany'lchuk]. KAN FARM 9 (Nov. 15, 1971): 15.

4605 "Pokhoron Bl. p. Ivana Danyl'chuka" [The Burial of the Late Ivan Danyl'chuk]. VISTNYK/THE HERALD (June 1, 1942): 6.

4606 Slavutych, ĪAr. "Ivan Danyl'chuk" [Ivan Danyl'chuk]. In his *Ukraïns'ka poeziia v Kanadi* (Edmonton: Slavuta, 1976) pp. 26-27.

4607 "Zhyttiepys Ivana Danyl'chuka" [Autobiography of Ivan Danylchuk]. In *Zakhidn'okanads'kyĭ zbirnyk.*, edited by ĪAr Slavutych. (Edmonton: Shevchenko Scientific Society, 1975) vol. 2, pp. 139-40.

DARKOVYCH, Mykhaĭlo T.

4608 *Kyïv i Rym. ĪAnychary. Chort. Poema [Kiev and Rome: The Janissaries: The Devil: A Poem].* Winnipeg: T. Zolotukha, 1929. 74 pp. Poem.

DARKOVYCH, O.T.

4609 *Olesia [Olesia].* Winnipeg: Promin', 1929. 46 pp. Children's play. (Kanadyĭs'ka Biblioteka No. 60)

4610 *Oto raz! Ditocha komediĭka [Isn't that Something! A Children's Comedy].* Winnipeg: Promin', 1929. 15 pp. (Kanadyĭs'ka Biblioteka No. 59)

DOLYNS'KYĬ, Ivan (1921-   )

4611 *Luna z preziĭ [Echo of the Prairies].* Introduction by O. Haĭ-Holovko. Winnipeg: The Author, 1983. 129 pp. Poems.

4612 *Winds of the West.* Winnipeg: The Author, 1984. 179 pp. Poems.
[Translations from Ukrainian, signed: John Dolinsky.]

DOROSHCHUK, Stepan (1894-1945)
Teacher, editor, printer, poet. Born in Boryshkivtzi, Western Ukraine, came to Canada with his parents in 1897. He taught elementary school in rural Manitoba for 12 years. He settled in Winnipeg and started a printing shop, editing *Promin'*, a popular publication for children. Also published the comic journal *Tochylo*.

4613 *Dlīa ridnykh diteĭ [For Our Children].* Winnipeg: The Author, 1925. 130 pp. Poems.

4614 *Sotnīa perlyn [A Hundred Pearls].* Winnipeg: Promin' Pub. Co. [n.d.] Poems.

4615 *Z khvylyn zhyttīa [From Life's Moments].* Winnipeg, 1929. Poems.

Writing about:

4616 Hun'kevych, Dmytro. Review of *Dlīa ridnykh diteĭ.* UKR HOLOS (Sept. 1, 1926)

FEDYK, Teodor (1873-1949)
Born in Uhryniv Horishny, Western Ukraine, emigrated to Canada in 1905. He collected Ukrainian songs and started publishing them in 1906. His poems appeared in newspapers in Winnipeg, where he lived.

4617   *Pisni pro Kanadu i Avstriîû [Songs about Canada and Austria].* Winnipeg, 1908. Poems.
       [Reprinted several times, the last edition under the title *Pisniï emigrantiv pro staryï i novyï kraï
       Songs about Old and New Countries]*

Writings about:

4618   Mandryka, M.I. ˝T. Fedyk˝ [T. Fedyk]. In his *History of Ukrainian Literature in Canada.*
       (Winnipeg: Ukrainian Free Academy of Sciences, 1968) pp. 43-45.

FODCHUK, Stepan   (1888-1967)

Author of humorous stories, his writings appeared in the form of letters of a dodger and simpleton,
illustrated by IAkiv Maïdanyk.

4619   *Dyvni pryhody ŜHtifa Tabachnîûka [The Marvelous Adventure of Steve Tabachnîûk],* with
       foreword by A. Il'nyts'kyï. Vancouver: Novyï ŜHlîâkh, 1958. 64 pp.

Writings about:

4620   ˝Biohrafîâ Stepana Fodchuka˝ [Biography of Stepan Fodchuk]. In *Dyvni pryhody ŜHtifa
       Tabachnîûka* (Vancouver: Novyï SHliakh, 1958) pp. 7-9.

4621   Fodchuk, Stepan. ˝Moï pochatky v Kanadi: Spohady novoho imigranta˝ [My Beginnings in Canada:
       Reminiscences of a New Immigrant]. KAN FARM (Oct. 5, 26, 1968): 10 of each issue.

4622   Fodchuk, Stepan. ˝ŜHtif Tabachnîûk - pioner humoryst˝ [ŜHtif Tabachnîûk - Pioneer Humorist].
       In *Kalendar Novoho ŜHlîâkhu na 1968 rik.* (Winnipeg: Novyï SHliakh, 1967) pp. 75-76.
       [Autobiography.]

4623   Il'nyts'kyï, A.˝Perednie slovo˝ [Foreword]. In *Dyvni pryhody ŜHtifa Tabachnîûka.* (Vancouver:
       Novyï ŜHlîâkh, 1958) pp. 3-5.

GOUZENKO, Igor   (1919-198)

Former member of the Soviet foreign service, he was born in Ukraine and worked at the Russian embassy
in Ottawa. He defected to the Western World, revealing a Russian spy ring operating out of Canada. Lived in
seclusion in southern Ontario until his death.

4624   *The Fall of the Titan: A Novel,* translated from the Russian by Mervyn Black. London: Cassell,
       1954. iii, 680 pp. Novel.

GOWDA, Mykhaïlo   (1874-1953)

Born in Ukraine and came to Edmonton, where he published poems in *Svoboda.* He was a school teacher
and an interpreter. Although his poems haven't appeared in book form Gowda's writings have influenced
Ukrainian authors in Canada.

Writings about:

4625   Mandryka, M.I. ˝M. Gowda.˝ In his *History of Ukrainian Literature in Canada.* (Winnipeg:
       Ukrainian Free Academy of Sciences, 1968) p. 8.

4626   Marunchak, Mykhaïlo. ˝Pryzabutyï spivets' pershykh ukraïns'kykh poselentsiv˝ [Forgotten Bard
       of the First Ukrainian Settlers]. NOV ŜHLÎAKH (Aug. 19, 26, 1967): 8-9 and 8 respectively.

HAÏ-HOLOVKO, Oleksa (1910-   )

Novelist, poet, born in Vinnytsia district, Ukraine. Emigrated to Canada and settled in Winnipeg in 1949. His stories and poems are related to his early experience in Ukraine under communist terror, and to Nazi atrocities in his native country during World War II.

4627 *Poiedynok z dyảvolom: Fil'my nashykh dniv [Duel with the Devil: A Narrative of Our Days].* Winnipeg: Ivan Tyktor, 1950. Books 1 and 2, 143 pp. and 160 pp. respectively. (Kliub pryiateliv ukraïns'koï knyzhky)

4628 *Odchaĭdnushni: Opovidannẩ [The Desperate Ones: Short Stories].* Winnipeg: Muse, 1959. 195 pp. Short stories.

4629 *Poetychni tvory v tr'okh tomakh [Poetical Works in Three Volumes].* Vol. 1 (1933-1947). Toronto: Novi Dni, 1970. 137 pp. Vol. 2 (1948-1977). Toronto: Novi Dni, 1978. 219 pp. Poems.

4630 *Smertel'noẩ dorohoẩ [Along the Death Path].* Winnipeg: Tryzub. Vol. 1 (1979) 284 pp. Vol. 2 (1983) 205 pp.

Writings about:

4631 Bezpechnyĭ, Ivan. "Oleksa Haĭ-Holovko i ioho *Smertel'na doroha* [Oleksa Haĭ-Holovko and his *Along the Death Path*]. NOVI DNI 35, no. 5 (1984): 13-15.

4632 Mulyk-Lutsyk, Ûriĭ. "Oleksa Haĭ-Holovko" [Oleksa Haĭ-Holovko]. In *Poetychni tvory v tr'okh tomakh.* (Toronto: Novi Dni, 1970) pp. vii-xli.

4633 Svaroh, Vadym. "Na vyskhidniĭ dorozi" [On the Way Out]. NOVI DNI 22, no. 3 (1971): 3-7. [Review of *Smertel'noẩ dorohoẩ.*]

HARASYMCHUK, Mykhaĭlo (1895-)
Born in Ukraine. In Canada he joined the Marxist group of Ukrainian authors. His stories, essays and articles were coloured by political tendencies and showed limited aesthetic values.

4634 *Vidhomin: zbirka opovidan' [Echo: A Collection of Stories].* 1928. Short stories.

Writing about:

4635 Tomashevs'kyĭ, Toma. "Pys'mennyk-samouk" [Self-taught Writer]. UKR PION 1 (September 1955): 6-7.

HAVRYLȊUK, Volodymyr (1904-)

4636 *Tin' i mandrivnyk/Shadow and Wanderer: Poems.* New York: Orhanizatsiia oborony chotyr'okh svobid Ukraïny, 1969. 109 pp. Poems.

Writings about:

4637 "Avtors'ki vechory ADUK: Volodymyr Havrylȋuk " [ADUK's Literary Evening: Volodymyr Havrylȋuk]. HOMIN UKR (Dec. 15, 1973): 1, 4.
[ADUK stands for Ukrainian Cultural Workers' Association.]

4638 Kerch, Oksana. Review of *Tin' i mandrivnyk.* ESTAFETA 1, no. 1 (1970): 224-25.

4639 Lasovs'kyĭ, Volodymyr. "Volodymyr Havrylȋuk: Dva rusla tvorchosty" [Volodymyr Havrylȋuk: Two Channels of Creative Activity]. ESTAFETA 1, no. 1 (1970): 153-55.

4640 "Literaturnyĭ vechir Volodymyra Havryliuka v N'iu-Iorku" [A Literary Evening for Volodymyr Havryliuk in New York]. ESTEFETA 1, no. 1 (1970): 249.

4641 Slavutych, IAr. "Peredusim - obraz" [First of All - The Image]. PIVN SIAĬV 5 (1971): 183-84. [Review of *Tin' i mandrivnyk.*]

4642 Struk, Danylo. Review of *Tin' i mandrivnyk.* CAN ETH STUD 4, no. 1-2 (1972): 73-74.

4643 "Volodymyr Havryliuk" [Volodymyr Havryliuk]. In *Tin' i mandrivnyk.* (New York: Orhanizatsiia oborony.... 1969) pp. 103-05.

HORBACHEVA, L.; KURPITA, T.; SHKRUMELIAK, Y.; MALYTS'KA, K.

4644 *Rizdviani poesiĭ dlia dytiachoho teatru [Christmas Play for the Children's Theatre].* Winnipeg: Trident Press, 1958. 28 pp. Play.

HUMENIUK, Teodor (1891-1978)

4645 *Pro shcho v Kremli pryzabuly [What Was Forgotten in the Kremlin].* Toronto: The Author, 1946. 80 pp. Versified satire.

Writing about:

4646 "Biohrafiia i ohliad hromads'koĭ diial'nosty adv. Teodora Humeniuka" [Biography and Review of Teodor Humeniuk's Public Activies]. UKR HOLOS (Nov. 26, 1969): 5.

HUMENNA, Dokiiâ (1904-   )
Born in Ukraine. Her poems appeared in periodicals in her native land. She has contributed to the Toronto-based *Novi dni.* She now lives in the U.S.A.

4647 *Dity chumats'kovo shliakhu [Children of the Milky Way].* Munich, 1948-1951. 4 vols. Novel.

4648 *Vichni vohni Al'berty [Alberta's Eternal Fires].* Edmonton: Petro Paush, 1959. 183 pp. Short sketches

HUN'KEVYCH, Dmytro (1893-1953)
Born in Lysovychi, Ukraine, came to Winnipeg, where he published plays for adults and children. He also wrote articles under the pen-names of Dmytrovych and Bursak. In 1934 he moved to Toronto.

4649 *ZHertvy temnoty: Drama na 5 diĭ zi spivamy i tantsiamy z zhyttia ukraïns'kykh pereselentsiv v Kanadi [Victims of Ignorance: Drama with Songs and Dances in 5 Acts about the Life of Ukrainian Immigrants in Canada].* Lviv: Rusalka, 1923. 44 pp. 2nd ed. 1926. Play.

4650 *Rozhdestven'ska nich: Ditocha operetka na 2 diĭ [Christmas Eve: Juvenile Operetta in 2 Acts].* Winnipeg: Mars, 1924. Play.

4651 *Kliûb sufrazhystok: Komediiâ na 5 diĭ [Suffragette Club: Comedy in 5 Acts].* Lviv: Teatral'na Biblioteka, 1925. 2nd ed. 1931. 3d ed. 1936. Play.

4652 *Krovavi perly: Robitnycha drama na 5 diĭ [Pearls of Blood: A Workers' Drama in 5 Acts].* Rusalka, 1927. 52 pp. Play.

4653 *Slavko v Tarapatakh [Slavko in Trouble].* Winnipeg: Promin', 1927. 24 pp. (Kanadyĭska Biblioteka no. 18) Play.

4654 *Ne zabuly: Kartyna na 2 diĭ [Not Forgotten: A Sketch in 2 Acts].* Winnipeg: Promin', 1928. Play.

4655 *Pan'ski prymkhy: ZHart na 1 diû [The Master's Caprices: Comedy in 1 Act].* Lviv: Rusalka, 1928. 8 pp. Play.

4656 *Potomky heroĭv abo zabava v istoriû [Heroes' Descendants or a Game in History].* Winnipeg: Promin', 1928. 32 pp. (Kanadyĭs'ka Biblioteka no. 28) Play.

4657 *Manivtsiamy: Tragikomediâ na 3 diĭ: Z kanadiĭs'koho zhyttia [Wanderings: Tragicomedy in 3 Acts: From Canadian Life].* Lviv: Teatral'na Biblioteka, 1931. 34 pp. Play.

4658 *Sered hradu kul': Tragediâ v 4-okh diâkh, v 5 vidslonakh zi spivamy [In a Hail of Bullets: A Tragedy in 4 Acts and 5 Scenes with Songs].* Winnipeg: Ukraïns'ka Knyharnia [n.d.] 135 pp. Play.

4659 *V halytskiĭ nevoli: Drama na 5 diĭ [Enslaved in Galicia: Drama in 5 Acts].* Winnipeg: Ukraïns'ka Knyharnia, 1921. 95 pp. Play.

4660 *Vytaĭ, vesno: Virshovana na 1 diiu [Welcome Spring: A Sketch in Verse in 1 Act].* Winnipeg: Promin' [n.d.] Play

Writings about:

4661 "Dmytro Hun'kevych" [Dmytro Hun'kevych]. PROMIN' 1 (1927): 22.

4662 Mandryka, M.I. "D. Hun'kevych." In his *History of Ukrainian Literature in Canada.* (Winnipeg: Ukrainian Free Academy of Sciences, 1968)

HYKAVYĬ, Onufriĭ (1886-1945)

Poet, short story writer. Born in Ukraine. His writings appeared in various newspapers including *Canadian Farmer,* of which he became editor in 1913. He made translations from English and Russian which were financed by *Pravda* in 1904. He also had educational books to his name (*Basic Laws of Canada, Short History of Canada*).

4663 *Opovidannîâ dlîâ diteĭ [Short Stories for Children].* Winnipeg: Rus'ka Knyharnia, 1910. 70 pp. Children's stories.

4664 *Zbirnyk baĭok [A Collection of Fables].* Winnipeg: Rus'ka Knyharnia, 1910. 72 pp. Stories.

ÎAKYMIV-METAN, I. see ÎAKYMOVYCH-METAN, Îosyf

ÎAKYMOVYCH-METAN, Îosyf (1884-1909)

Writings about:

4665 ÎAkymovych-Metan, Îosyf. "Miĭ spomyn" [My Recollections]. KAN FARM (Nov. 9, 1968): 9.

4666 "Literaturnyĭ vechir I. ÎAkymova-Metana" [Literary Evening for ÎAkymiv-Metan] UKR VISTI (Jul. 20, 1967): 3. Signed: T.L.

ÎANDA, Darîâ see MOHYLÎANKA, Darîâ

ÎASENCHUK, ÎOsyf (1893-1970)

4667 *Kanadyïs'kyï kobzar [Canadian Kobzar Player]*. Edmonton: Ukrainian Book Store, 1918. 64 pp. Poems.

ICHNÎANS'KYÏ, M. pseud. (Real name: Kmeta, Ivan) (1901-)
Born in Ichnia, Ukraine, educated at the Pryluky Teachers College and emigrated to Winnipeg in 1939, where he became a Pastor of the Ukrainian Evangelical Church. His poems had appeared in Kiev, Kharkiw and Winnipeg.

4668 *Zapysky rozstrilîanoho: Fragmenty [Notes of the Executed: Fragments]* Winnipeg: The Author, 1929. Sketches.

4669 *Lira emigranta [Lyrics of an Emigrant]*. Winnipeg: Ukrainian Book Store, 1936 138 pp. Poems.

4670 *The Hurricane*, translated from the Ukraine by Jessie Ostaff and Percival Cundy. Saskatoon: Bible College Press, 1939. 68 pp. Story.

4671 *Potokyï gornie: Rasskazy, stat'i, stikhi [Mountain Stream: Stories, Sketches, Articles]*. New York: Compass Press, 1965. 120 pp. Stories, papers, in Russian.

4672 *Chasha zolotá [Golden Chalisc]*. Winnipeg: Doroha Pravdy, 1964. 94 pp. Poems.

4673 *Rik dvotysiachnyï [A.D. 2000]*, introduction by Mykola Shcherbak. Winnipeg: Doroha Pravdy, 1972. Poems.

Writings about:

4674 Ivakh, Onufriï "Tvir vyznachnoho ukraïns'koho poeta v Kanadi" [Writings of a Distinguished Ukrainian Poet in Canada]. UKR HOLOS (Dec. 16, 1936): 2.
[Review of *Lira emigranta*.]

4675 Shcherbak, Mykola. "Stezhky ï pisni." [Paths and Songs]. SVOBODA (Apr. 13, 1965)
[Review of *Chasha zolotá*.]

4676 Slavutych, ÎAr. "Relihiïnyï liryk" [Religious Poet]. PIVN SIAÏV (1971): 176-77.

IENDYK, Oleksandra see CHERNENKO, Oleksandra

ILARION, Metropolitan (Real name: OHIÎENKO, Ivan) (1882-1972)
Born in Brusyliv, Ukraine, educated at the University of Kiev. He was Rector of the Ukrainian University in Kamianets' Podilsky and held other university posts in Poland and Czechoslovakia after having escaped from Ukraine. In 1940 he became a monk, then was ordained to the priesthood and took the name Ilarion. Came to Canada in 1947 and was elected to the Metropolitan of the Ukrainian Orthodox Church in Canada.

4677 *Narodzhennîa lîûdyny: Filosofs'ka misteria v p'iaty diîakh [Birth of Man: A Philosophical Mystery in Five Acts]*. Winnipeg: Nasha Kul'tura, 1948. 121 pp. Play.

4678 *Prometeï: Smerk hrets'kykh bohiv [Prometheus: Twilight of the Greek Gods]*. Winnipeg, 1948. 68 pp. (Nasha kul'tura No. 9)

4679 *Tvory [Works]*. Vol. 1: *Filosofs'ki misterii [Philosophical Mysteries]*. Winnipeg: Trident Press, 1957. Vol. 2: *Vikovi nashi rany: Dramatychni poemy [Our Eternal Wounds: Dramatic Poems]*. 272

pp. Vol. 3 and 4: *Nash biĭ za derzhavnist': Istorychna epopeĭà [Our Fight for Freedom: Historical Epic]* Parts 1 and 2. Winnipeg: Nasha kul'tura, 1960-1966. 144 pp. and 224 pp. Historical epic.

4680 *Rozpĭàtyĭ Mazepa: Istorychna drama na pĭàt' diĭ [Crucified Mazepa: Historical Drama in Five Acts]*. Winnipeg: Nasha kul'tura, 1961. 88 pp. Play.

Writings about:

4681 Mandryka, M.I. "I. Ohiyenko" [I. Ohiienko]. In his *History of Ukrainian Literature in Canada*. (Winnipeg: Ukrainian Free Academy of Sciences, 1968) pp. 158-60.

4682 Nesterenko, A. *Mytropolyt Ilarion sluzhytel' Bohovi i narodovi: Biohrafichna monohrafiĭà [Metropolitan Ilarion - Servant of God and the People: Biographical Monograph]*. [N.p.]: Metropolitan Ilarion [n.d.] 150 pp.

4683 "Okh, virshi" [Oh Poetry]. UKR VISTI (Jul. 7, 1966): 2. [Review of *Nash biĭ za derzhavnist'*.]

4684 Savchuk, S.W. *ĬUbileĭna knyha na poshanu Mytropolyta Ilariona [Jubilee Book for the Rev. Metropolitan Ilarion]*. Winnipeg: Trident Press, 1958. 320 pp.

IRAN, A. see IRCHAN, Myroslav

IRCHAN, Myroslav, pesud. (Real name: BABIĬUK, Andriĭ) (1897-1937)
Born in Ukraine, emigrated to Canada in 1923. He was a staff writer for *Robitychni visti*, a communist newspaper. Returned to Ukraine in 1929. Perished in Soviet prisons.

4685 *Bezrobitni: Drama na 3 diĭ [The Unemployed: Drama in 3 Acts]*. Winnipeg, 1923. Play.

4686 *Dvanaĭtsĭàt' [The Twelve]*. Winnipeg: Ukraïns'kyĭ robitychnĭ visti, 1923. 112 pp. Play.

4687 *Fil'my revolĭùtsiï: Narysy i novely [Narratives of the Revolution: Sketches and Short Novels]*. New York: Kultura, 1923. Short stories.

4688 *Nezhadnyĭ hist': Dramatychnyĭ etiud [The Unexpected Guest: Dramatic Study]*. Winnipeg: Ukraïns'kĭ robitychnĭ visti, 1923. Play.

4689 *Karpats'ka nich: Opovidannĭà [Carpathian Night: Short Stories]*. Winnipeg: Robitnycho-farmers'ke vydavnyche tovarystvo, 1924. 178 pp. Short stories.

4690 *Rodyna shchitkariv: Drama [The Brush-maker Family]*. 2nd ed. (N.p.): Robitnycho-Farmers'ke vydavnyche tovarystvo, 1925. 78 pp. Play.

4691 *V burĭànakh [In the Weed]*. Toronto: Ukraïns'kyĭ robitnychyĭ dim, 1925. Play.

4692 *Tovarystvo"Pshyk": Komediia v tr'okh diĭàkh [The Organization"Pffft": A Comedy in Three Acts]*. Winnipeg: Robitychno-Farmers'ke Vydavnyche Tovarystvo, 1925. 32 pp. Play. [Appeared under the name Josafat Tykhonchuk.]

4693 *Li ĬUnk-shan i Li ĬUnk-po i inshi opovidannĭà [Lee Yung-chan and Lee Yung-po and Other Stories]*. Kharkiv: DVU, 1926. Short stories.

4694 *Pidzemna Halychyna [Galicia Underground]*. Winnipeg: Robitnycho-farms'ke vydavnyche tovarstvo, 1926. Story.

4695   *Proty smerti: Zbirka opovidan' [In the Face of Death: A Collection of Short Stories].* Winnipeg: Ivan Hnyda, 1927. Short stories.

4696   *Radiĭ [Radium].* Kharkiv: Kul'trobitnyk, 1928. Play.

4697   *Vybrani tvory [Selected Works].* Kiev: Derzhvydav, 1958. 2 vols. 383 and 466 pp. respectively.

Writings about:

4698   Fashchenko, Vasyl'. "Novela Myroslava Irchana" [Short Stories of Myroslav Irchan]. In *Novela i novelisty: ZHanrovo-styl'ovi pytannia: (1917-1967).* (Kiev: Radians'kyĭ pys'mennyk, 1968) pp. 52-73.

4699   Haĭ-Holovko Oleksa. "Myroslav Irchan" [Myroslav Irchan]. UKR HOLOS (Jan. 30, Feb. 6, 1974): 5 and 2-3 respectively.

4700   Mashotas, V.V. *Myroslav Irchan: Bibliohrafichnyĭ pokazhchyk [Myroslav Irchan: Bibliographical Index].* Kiev: AN URSR, 1961. 151 pp.

4701   Novychenko, Leonid. "Myroslav Irchan." In *Vybrani tvory.* [Kiev: Derzhvydav, 1958,) vol. 1, pp. 5-48.

4702   Vlasenko, Vladen; Kravchuk, Petro. *Myroslav Irchan: ZHyttia i tvorchist' [Myroslav Irchan: Life and Works].* Kiev: Radians'kyĭ pys'mennyk, 1960. 260 pp.

IVAKH, Onufriĭ (1900-1964)   (Also **EWACH, Honore**)
Born in Pidpylypia, Western Ukraine, came to Canada with his parents in 1909. He was a lecturer at Mohyla Institute, Saskatoon, teaching Ukrainian History and Literature. His writings have appeared in various newspapers and periodicals, including *Ukrainian Voice*, of which he was a member of the editorial staff.

4703   *Boĭova surma Ukraïny: Poeziï [The Battle Trumpet of Ukraine: Poetry].* Winnipeg: The Author, 1931. 8 pp. Poems.

4704   *Toĭ koho svit lovyv, ta ne spiĭmav [He Who Was Sought by the World but was not Caught].* Winnipeg: The Author, 1932. 23 pp.

4705   *Holos zemli [The Call of the Land].* [N.p.]: Ukraïns'ka vydavnycha spilka v Kanadi, 1937. 92 pp. 2nd ed. by Tryzub, Winnipeg, 1973. Novel.

4706   *Ukraïns'kyĭ mudrets' [The Ukrainian Philosopher].* Winnipeg: Ukrainian Cultural and Educational Centre, 1945. 16 pp.

4707   *Ukraïns'ke ievshan-zillia v Kanadi: IUvileĭna zbirka tvoriv O. Ivakha v 40-littia ĭoho pratsi perom: 1920-1960 [Ukrainian Flowers in Canada: A Jubilee Edition of the Works of O. Ivakh from the Period 1920-1960].* Winnipeg: Trident Press, 1960. 31 pp.

Writings about:

4708   Ewanchuk, Michael. "Honore Ewach" [Honore Ewach]. In *Holos Zemli: Korotka povist' z zhyttia v Kanadi.* 2nd ed. (Winnipeg: Tryzub, 1973) pp. 7-10.

4709   Kirkconnell, Watson. Review of *Holos zemli.* FREE PRESS (Nov. 6, 1937) Reprinted in UKR HOLOS (Nov. 17, 1937): 2.

4710 "Onufriĭ Ivakh" [Onufriĭ Ivakh]. PROMIN' (March 1928): 86-87.

4711 Mandryka, M.I. "Onufriĭ Ivakh" In his *History of Ukrainian Literature in Canada*. (Winnipeg: Ukrainian Academy of Sciences, 1968) pp. 66-69.

4712 Slavutych, Ĭar. "Onufriĭ Ivakh" [Onufriĭ Ivakh]. In his *Ukraïns'ka poeziia v Kanadi*. (Edmonton: Slavuta, 1976) pp. 27-29.

KAZANIVS'KYĬ, Vasyl' H.

4713 *Pimsta za kryvdu: Drama v piat'okh diiakh a shesty vidslonakh zi spivamy i tantsiamy [Revenge for an Injury: Drama in Five Acts and Six Scenes with Songs and Dances].* Winnipeg, 1917. 101 pp. Play.
[Based on the novel *Mykola Dzheria*, by Ivan Nechuĭ-Levyts'kyĭ.]

4714 *'Adamovi sl'ozy' abo piana korova: ZHart na 1 diiu z zhyttia nashykh pereselentsiv v Kanadi ['Adam's Tears' or the Drunken Cow: A Comedy in 1 Act about Life of the Our New Immigrants].* Lviv: Rusalka, 1926. 13 pp. (Teatral'na Biblioteka No. 7) Play.

KEDR, Rostyslav (1905-   )

4715 *Skobyne hnizdo [The Nest Skob].* Toronto: OPDL, 1957. Children's poems.

4716 *Lisovi chorty [Forest Devils].* Toronto: Plast, 1972. Poems for children.

4717 *Poeziï. Zbirka tretia [Poems: Third Book].* Toronto: IEvshan zillia, 1983. 372 pp. Poems.
[Recipient of I. Franko's First Prize in 1986.]

Writing about:

4718 Paliĭ, Mykola. Review of *Poeziï.* SVOBODA (Aug. 18, 1984)

KEĬVAN, Mariia Adriiana (1914-   )

4719 *Karvendel': Povist [Karvendel': Novel].* Edmonton, 1971. 232 pp. Novel.

4720 *Plyve-shumyt' rika [Sounds of the Rushing River].* Edmonton: The Author, 1985. 330 pp. Novel.

Writings about:

4721 Bazhans'kyĭ, Mykhaĭlo. Review of *Karvendel'.* SVOBODA (Nov. 6, 1971): 3.

4722 Bazhans'kyĭ, Mykhaĭlo. Review of *Plyve-shumyt' rika.* SVOBODA (Aug. 24, 1985): 2.

4723 Brytan, IA. Review of *Karvendel'.* OKO No. 8 (1985): 12.

4724 Kachaluba, Mykhaĭlo. Review of *Plyve-shumyt' rika.* UKR SLOVO (Oct. 20, 1985): 3.

4725 Kedryn, Ivan, "Tsikava literaturna poiava" [An Interesting Literary Appearance]. SVOBODA (Aug. 28, 1985): 2.
[Review of *Plyve-shumit' rika.*]

4726 Kharchun, Ĭaroslav. Review of *Plyve-shumyt' rika.* UKR VISTI (Edmonton, Aug. 14, 1985): 15.

4727 Kobzeĭ, Toma. Review of *Karvendel'* UKR HOLOS (Oct. 13, 197)

4728 Kopach, Oleksandra. "Rika zhyttîa" [Life's River]. HOMIN UKR (Oct. 16, 1985). Reprinted in NASHE ZHYTTÎA (October 1985): 22.

4729 Lev, Vasyl'. "Povist' pro kruti stezhky liubovy" [A Novel about Pathos and Love]. NOV SHLIAKH (Nov. 6, 1986): 4.
[Review of *Karvendel'*.]

4730 Levyts'kyĭ, Vasyl'. "Vidvazhnyĭ krok v literaturi" [A Courageous Step in Literature]. UKR KNYHA 1, no. 4 (1971): 112-13. [Signed: M. Kh.]
[Review of *Karvendel'*.]

4731 "Povist' z pisliavoĭennoho zhyttîa v taborakh" [A Novel about Post-war Life in Refugee Camps]. UKR VISTI (Edmonton, Oct. 21, 1971): 4.

4732 Roslîak, Olena. "Avtors'kyĭ vechir d-ra Mariî-Adriiany Keĭvan"[Literary Evening for Dr. Mariîa-Adriiana Keĭvan]. UKR VISTI (Edmonton, Oct. 29, 1970): 3.

4733 Slavutych, Îar. "Oderzhymist' profesiieiu" [Possessed by Profession]. NOVI DNI No. 434 (April 1986): 26-27.
[Review of *Plyve-shumyt' rika*.]

4734 Sokil's'kyĭ, S. "Slovo do chytachiv" [A Word to the Reader]. In *Karvendel': Povist'*. (Edmonton, 1971) pp. 5-8.

4735 Stebel'skyĭ, Bohdan. "Skalichene pokolinnîa" [A Crippled Generation]. HOMIN UKR (NOV. 13, 1985): 13.

4736 Svaroh, Vadym. "Pid kholodnym pohliadom vichnosty" [Under Eternity's Cold Glance]. NOV DNI 24, no. 279 (1973): 5-7.
[Review of *Karvendel'*.]

4737 Veryha, V. Review of *Plyve-shumyt' rika*. NOV SHLIAKH (Dec. 21-28, 1985): 9.

KHMIL', Ivan pseud. (Real name: LAHODÎUK, Vasyl') (1896-1974)

4738 *Homin Polissîa (Poeziî) [The Echo of Polisîa (Poetry)]*. Winnipeg: The Author, 1960. 243 pp. Poems.

4739 *Idu z kobzoîu: Poeziî [Walking with Kobza (Poetry)]*. Chicago: The Author, 1962. 244 pp. Poems.

Writings about:

4740 "Ivan Khmil'" [Ivan Khmil']. In *Slovo i zbroîa*, edited by Leonid Poltava. (Toronto: Shevchenko Scientific Society, 1968) pp. 217-20, 388.

4741 Mar, S. "Vasyl' Lahodîuk - Ivan Khmil', poet-spivets' Polissia" [Vasyl' Lahodiuk - Ivan Khmil', Poet]. HOMIN UKR (Feb. 23, 1974): 12.

KHOMLÎAK, Petro

4742 *Na rozdorizhzhi: Komediia v tr'okh iiakh z kanadiis'ko-ukraïns'koho zhyttia* [At the Crossroads: A Comedy in Three Acts Taken from Ukrainian-Canadian Life]. Winnipeg: Kul'tura ĭ Osvita, 1946. 29 pp. Play.

KIRIAK, Elias   see   KYRIĬAK, Illia

KIVSHENKO, P.

4743 *Bezbatchenko. Drama na 4 diï* [Illegitimate: Drama in 4 Acts]. Winnipeg, 1927. Play.

KOHUS'KA, Natalka L. (1905-)
Born in Wyshnivets, Ukraine, came to Canada in 1928. Edited a monograph of the Ukrainian Women's Association and a history of the Ukrainian Youth Association. Editor-in-Chief of *Promin'*.

4744 *V poleti do voli: Istorychna povist'* [Flight to Freedom: A Historical Novel]. Winnipeg: The Author, 1938. 102 pp. Novel.

4745 *Maty: Opovidannia* [Mother: Short Stories]. Winnipeg: Ukrainian Publishing Co. of Canada, 1941. 29 pp. Short stories.

KOLIĂNKIVS'KYĬ, M.   see   TOCHYLO-KOLIĂNKIVS'KYĬ

KOLINSNYK, Dmytro (1883-1958)

4746 *Moie selo (Opovidannia)* [My Town (A Story)]. Saskatoon: Gospel Press, 1950-1955. 3 parts, 167, 159 and 223 pp. respectively. Biographical novel.

KOLOSIVS'KYĬ, Mykhaĭlo

4747 *Borys Honych: Roman* [Borys Honych: Novel]. Saskatoon: Novyĭ SHliakh, 1937-1952. 3 parts, 161, 159 and 191 pp. respectively.

KOMAR, Anton, pseud.   (Real name: VOLOKHATIUK, Taras D.)
Born in Ukraine. He participated in the struggle for Ukrainian independence. Came to Canada between the two World Wars. His writings reveal a warm appreciation for his adopted country.

4748 *Nasha valka* [Our Caravan]. Toronto, 1966. 32 pp. Narrative poem.

Writing about:

4749 Lozyns'kyĭ, I.H. "Poet o. T.D. Volokhatiuk" [The Poet Reverend T.D. Volokhatiuk]. KAN FARM (Oct. 4, 1971): 7.

KOPACH, Oleksandra (1913-)
Born in Ukraine. Came to Toronto after World War II and became head of the H. Skovoroda School, offering courses in Ukrainian at college level. Published short stories for adults and children.

4750 *Nepovtorni dni* [Never-returning Days]. Toronto: Nasha meta, 1960. 48 pp. Story.

4751 *Bohatyri starodavn'oï Ukraïny. Dlia diteĭ kozhnoho viku* [Heros of Ancient Ukraine]. Winnipeg: The Author, 1964. 109 pp. Children's story.

KOSOVYCHEVA, Mariia ĬA.

4752 *Horstka promeniv: Vybrani poeziï, 1939-1961 [A Handful of Sunbeams: Selected Poems, 1939-1961].* Winnipeg: Novyĭ SHliakh, 1962. 47 pp.

KOTYK, Stepan

4753 *Nad ozerom. Opovidannîa z amerykans'koho zhyttîa [At the Lake: Short Stories from the American Way of Life].* Winnipeg: The Author, 1946. 109 pp. Short stories.

KOVAL'SKYĬ, S. see ROMEN, Levko

KOVBEL', Semen (1877-1966)
Born in Borschiv, Western Ukraine. Came to Canada in 1909. His poems, short stories and plays have been published in newspapers and periodicals. He organized libraries, theatrical groups and choirs in Manitoba.

4754 *Divochi mriï: Tragi-komediîa v 6-okh vidminakh zi spivamy i tantsîamy [A Maiden's Dreams: A Tragi-comedy in 6 scenes with Songs and Dances].* [N.p.]: Ukraïns'kyĭ Holos, 1920. Play.

4755 *Ukraïnizatsiîa [Ukrainization].* [N.p.]: The Author, 1938. Play.

4756 *Virna sestra to zoloto [A True Sister is Worth Her Gold].* Winnipeg: The Author, 1938. One act play.

4757 *Delegatsiîa do raîu [Delegation to Paradise].* [N.p.]: The Author, 1938. Play.

4758 *Parubochi mriï (Zaklîata hora): Fantaziîa-drama v 4-okh diîakh [A Young Man's Dreams (The Enchanted Mountain): A Fantasy-drama in 4 Acts].* Winnipeg: The Author, 1942. 62 pp. Play.

4759 *Sviatyĭ Mykolaĭ v Kanadi [St. Nicholas in Canada].* Winnipeg: People's Publishing Co. [n.d.] 31 pp. Children's play.

Writings about:

4760 Mandryka, M.I. "Semen Kovbel'" [Semen Kovbel'] In his *History of Ukrainian Literature in Canada.* (Winnipeg: Ukrainian Free Academy of Sciences, 1968) pp. 50-55.

KOVSHUN, Mykola (1901-   )

4761 *Epiloh pryĭde. Zbirka dramatychnykh tvoriv.* [N.p., n.p.] 1975. 176 pp. Three plays.

Writing about:

4762 Harasevych, Mariîa. "Mykola Kovshun: Pys'mennyk zhyttîevoĭ pravdy" [Mykola Kovshun: Life's Faithful Author]. NOVI DNI 35, no. 1 (1984): 7-10; no. 2 (1984): 19-21.

KRAMAR, Osyp

4763 *Îa vernusîa: Strilets'ki opovidannîa [I Shall Return: Stories about the Ukrainian Legion].* Edmonton: The Author, 1947. 93 pp. Short stories.

KRAT, Pavlo (1882-1952)
Poet, prose writer, has written short stories, papers dealing with education, and humorous novels. His political satires have appeared under the pen names O. Prokolupiĭ and P. Ternenko. Editor of *Red Flag*, the first socialist Ukrainian newspaper in Canada. Also edited *Kadylo*, a humorous journal.

4764 *Sotsfálistychni pisni [Socialistic Songs].* Edmonton: Federatsiîâ Ukraïns'kykh Sotsfál-Demokrativ u Kanadi, 1909. 16 pp. Poems.

4765 *Krov za krov. Opovidanie z zhyttîâ Kyïvshchnyny [Blood for Blood].* Winnipeg: Robochyĭ narod, 1910. 16 pp. Story.

4766 *Sichyns'kyĭ v nevoli [Sichyns'kyĭ in Captivity].* Edmonton, 1910. 14 pp.
[Myroslav Sichyns'kyĭ was a Ukrainian revolutionary.]

4767 *Koly lekshe bude i inshi opovidannia [When Things will Get Better and Other Stories].* Winnipeg: Emil Holubovych, 1912. Short stories.

4768 *Vizyta ˆCHervonoï Druzhyny˝: Obraz z reviutsiĭnykh Poltavshchyni v liti 1906 roku [Visit of the ˆRed Guard˝: Sketches of the Poltava Revolutionaries in 1906].* Winnipeg: ĈHervonyĭ Prapor, 1912.

4769 *Za zemlîû i volîû [For Land and Freedom].* Winnipeg: Robochyĭ Narod, 1914. 64 pp. Poems.

4770 *Poslidne khozhdeniê Boha po zemliï abo na revolîûtsiï: Humorystychna povist' [The Last Pilgrimage of the Lord on Earth or God in Revolution: A Humorous Story].* Part 1: *Boh u Moskivshchyni [God in Muscovy].* Winnipeg: Robochyĭ Narod, 1915. 148 pp. Novel.

4771 *Koly ziĭshlo sontse: Opovidanîê z 2000 roku [When the Sun Rose: A Story from the Year 2000].* Toronto: Ukraïns'ka Knyharnîâ v Brantford, Ont., 1918. 72 pp. Novelette.

Writing about:

4772 Mandryka, M.I. ˆPavlo Krat˝ [Pavlo Krat]. In his *History of Ukrainian Literature in Canada.* (Winnipeg: Ukrainian Free Academy of Sciences, 1968) pp. 57-59.

KRAVTSIV, Melanîâ (d. 1961)

Novelist, short story writer. Born in Ukraine. One of the founding members of the Canadian League for Ukraine's Liberation, established in 1949. Her short stories have appeared in periodicals and book form.

4773 *Doroha: Roman [The Road: Novel].* Toronto: Homin Ukraïny, 1955. 244 pp. Novel.

4774 *Kaleĭdoskop: Opovidannîâ [Kaleidoskope: Stories].* Toronto: Homin Ukraïny, 1960. 133 pp. Short stories.

Writing about:

4775 Antonovych-Rudnyćka, M. ˆPerednîê slovo˝ [Foreword]. In *Doroha: Roman.* (Toronto: Homin Ukraïny, 1955)

KREMIN', Semen

4776 *Neporozuminnîâ [A Misunderstanding].* Winnipeg: Ukrainian Publishing Co. of Canada, 1928. 32 pp. Play.

KRET, Îâkhiv Nykola (1883-1965)

Born in Pechenizhyn, Western Ukraine. Came to Canada in 1907. Educated at the Manitoba College. His pocket-size English-Ukrainian dictionary was published in 1912. A larger edition remained unpublished at his death.

4777   *Taiemnyĭ zlochyn abo indiians'kyĭ SHerl'ok Hol'ms (Kryminal'ne opovidannie) [The Mysterious Crime or Indian Sherlock Holmes (Mystery Story)]*. Edmonton: Nash Postup, 1926. 94 pp. Story.

KROĬTOR, Tetiâna   see   SHEVCHUK, Tetiâna

KRUK-MAZEPYNETS'

4778   *Durni dity: Povist' iz povoĭennoĭ doby na Zakhidniĭ Ukraïni [Foolish Children: A Novel of the Post-war Days in Western Ukraine]*. Edmonton: Ivan Soliânych, 1932. 106 pp. Novel.

KRYPIÂKEVYCH, Mykhaĭlo   (1897-1968)
Born in Verbova, Ukraine. He was educated at Hampton and at the Peter Mohyla Institute in Saskatoon. He wrote humorous dialogues and monologues and published some comedies such as *On Vacations, The Magic Flute, Three Engagements, A Hero in the Bag*.

4779   *ĬAk kum kuma lichyv: ZHart na odnu diiû [How One Friend Cured Another: A Comedy in One Act]*. 2nd ed. Winnipeg: Populiarne vydavnytstvo, 1938. 16 pp. Play.

KUDRYK, Vasyl'   (1880-1963)
Poet, prose writer, scholar, Orthodox priest. Born Semen Sawchuk in Ukraine, came to Canada in 1903. First editor of *Ukraïns'kyĭ Holos* (1910-21). He was ordained to the priesthood in 1923.

4780   *Persha pryhoda Nychypora Dovhochkhuna [The First Adventure of Nychypir Dovhochkhun]*. Winnipeg, 1911. 62 pp. Humorous poem.

4781   *Pimsta robitnyka Opovidanie z kanadyĭs'koho zhytiâ [A Worker's Revenge: A Narrative of Canadian Life]*. Winnipeg: Ukraïns'kyĭ Holos, 1911. 63 pp. Story.

4782   *Vesna [Spring]*. Winnipeg: Ukraïns'kyĭ Holos, 1911. Poems.

4783   *CHuza ruka [A Foreign Hand]*. Winnipeg: Vistnyk, 1935. 208 pp. Religious polemics.

4784   *Prodav bat'ka i inshi opovidannia [He Sold His Father and Other Stories]*. Winnipeg: Trident Press [n.d.] 160 pp. Short stories.

4785   *Z velykodnem na voliû i inshi opovidanniâ [With Easter Day to Freedom and Other Stories]*. Winnipeg: Trident Press, [n.d.] 157 pp. Short stories.

4786   *Kvitky pry dorozi: opovidanniâ i narysy [Flowers by the Roadside: Short stories]*. Niagara Falls, Ont.: Zakhlodamy Komitetu vydan' prats' o. Vasyliâ Kudryka, 1975. 208 pp. Short stories.

Writings about:

4787   Haĭ-Holovko, Oleksa. "Vasyl' Kudryk" [Vasyl' Kudryk]. In his *Ukraïns'ki pys'mennyky v Kanadi* (Winnipeg: Volyn', 1980) vol. 1, pp. 100-05.

4788   *Muzh ideï i pratsi [A Man of Vision and Action: Commemorating Rev. V. Kudryk's 50 Years of Dedicated Service to the Ukrainian Community in Canada as a Journalist, Author, Lecturer and Clergyman]*. [N.p.]: The Jubilee Committee [n.d.] 127 pp.

4789   Samets', P. "Pamiâti o Prot. Vasyliâ Kudryka" [In Memory of the Very Reverend Father Vasyl' Kudryk]. UKR HOLOS (Nov. 1, 1967): 2.

4790 "Vasyl' Kudryk - pershyĭ redaktor Ukraïns'koho Holosu " [Vasyl' Kudryk - First Editor of Ukraïns'kyĭ Holos]. UKR HOLOS (Jul. 29, 1970): 25-28.

KUPCHENKO, Viktor (1892-1970)

4791 *Poeziĭa i proza [Poetry and Fiction].* Edmonton: Slovo, 1982. 304 pp. Poems and short stories.

Writing about:

4792 Klynovyĭ, I͡Uriĭ. "Viktor Kupchenko - zabutyĭ poet, drukar i kul'turnyĭ diĭach." In his *Moïm synam, moïm pryiatelĭam.* (Edmonton: Slovo, 1981) pp. 527-30.

KURDYDYK, Anatol', (1905-)
Born in Western Ukraine, educated in Lviv. He published novels, poems and articles prior to coming to Canada. First settled in Toronto, then moved to Winnipeg.

4793 *Zapysky z budniv. Feĭletony i narysy [Day-by-Day Notes: Short Stories and Sketches].* Winnipeg: The Author, 1977. 142 pp. Short sketches.

KURYLIV, S.

4794 *Proklin materi: Povist' [Mother's Curse: Novel].* Winnipeg: Ukraïns'ka vydavnycha spilka v Kanadi, 1936. 81 pp. Novel.

KUZ'MENKO, Svitlana (1928-)

4795 *Ivasyk i ioho abetka [Johnnie and His Alphabet].* Toronto: OPDL, 1974. Children's poems.

4796 *Novotalalaĭvs'ki reflekciï. Opovidaniĭa [Novotalalavian Reflections and Stories].* Toronto: Slovo, 1976. 109 pp. Short stories.

4797 *Vichnyĭ prorosten'. Poeziï [The Eternal Sprout. Poems].* Toronto: Slovo, 1981. 64 pp. Poems.

4798 *U siaĭvi promeniv. Poeziï [In Sunshine. Poems].* Toronto: Slovo, 1984. 64 pp. Poems.

Writing about:

4799 Harasevych, Mariĭa. "Svitlana Kuz'menko" [Svitlana Kuz'menko]. SVOBODA (Jul. 16, 1983): 2-3.

KUZ'MOVYCH-HOLOVINS'KA, Mariĭa Lĭubomyra (1904-1986)

4800 *CHuzynoĭu: Spomyny [On Alien Soil: Memoirs].* Toronto: Ukraïns'ke vyd-vo Dobra Knyzhka, 1977. 159 pp. Autobiographical novel.

4801 *Lisovyĭ holub [The Forest Dove].* Toronto, 1973. 278 pp. Novel.

4802 *Portret: Avtobiohrafiĭa [Portrait: Autobiography].* Toronto: Ukraïns'ke vyd-vo Dobra Knyzhka, 1978. 144 pp. Autobiographical novel.

Writing about:

4803 Andrusyshen, C.H. Review of *Lisovyĭ holub.* UNIV TOR Q 43 (1973-74): 458.

KYRII͡AK, Illĭa (1888-1955)

Novelist, poet. Born in Kniazhe, Ukraine. Came to Canada in 1906. His writings have appeared in various newspapers and periodicals. *Syny zemli*, Kyriiak's social novel, has been translated into English and became one of the most significant novels in Canada.

4804   *Syny zemli: povist' z ukraïns'koho zhyttîa v Kanadi [Sons of the Soil: Story of the Ukrainian Settlers in Canada].* Edmonton, 1939-1945. 3 v. 395, 351 and 348 pp. respectively. 2nd ed. Winnipeg: Tryzub, 1973-1974. Novel..

4805   *Sons of the Soil*, translated from the Ukrainian by Michael Luchkovich. Toronto: Ryerson Press, 1959. 303 pp.
[Condensed translation of *Syny zemli.*]

Writings about:

4806   Andrusyshen, C.H. "Kiryak's *Sons of the Soil...* An Epic of Western Canada." In *Ukrainian Yearbook.* Vol. 8 (Winnipeg, 1951/52) pp. 11-17.

4807   Bochkovs'kyĭ, O. "Epopeîa ukraïns'kykh pioniriv v Kanadi [An Epic of the Ukrainian Pioneers in Canada]. UKR HOLOS (Jul. 26, 1939): 3.
[Review of *Syny zemli.*]

4808   Bodnarchuk, Ivan. "Illîa Kyriâk i ïoho *Syny zemli*" [Illia Kyriiak and His *Sons of the Soil*]. UKR HOLOS (Aug. 23, 1972): 7-8.

4809   Cardinal, C.H. "Zwei kanadische Dichter islandischer und ukrainischer" [Two Canadian Authors, Icelandic and Ukrainian]. MITT INST AUSL 7 (July/September 1957): 195.

4810   Kohuska, Natalka. Review of *Syny zemli.* UKR HOLOS (Apr. 26, 1939): 2.

4811   Kyriâk, Illîa."V spravi vydannia druhoï chastyny povisty *Syny zemli*" [Regarding the Publication of the Second Part of *Sons of the Soil*]. UKR HOLOS (Jan. 29, 1941)

4812   Mandryka, M.I. "Illîa Kyriâk (1888-1955)" [Illîa Kyriâk (1888-1955)]. PIVN SIAIV 1 (164): 70-72.

4813   Mandryka, M.I. "Illîa Kyriâk." In his *History of Ukrainian Literature in Canada.* (Winnipeg: Ukrainian Free Academy of Sciences, 1968) pp. 72-77.

4814   Marunchak, Mykhaĭlo H. *Illîa Kyriâk ta ïoho tvorchist'/Illîa Kyriâk and His Works.* Winnipeg: Ukraïns'ka Vil'na Akademiîa Naukk v Kanadi, 1973. 80 pp.
[Originally published in series in UKR HOLOS (Oct. 16, Dec. 18, 1968, Jan. 8, Apr. 16, 1969): 4 of each issue.]

4815   "Nad svizhoiu mohyloiu Illi Kyriâka" [At the Recent Burial of Illîa Kyriâk]. UKR HOLOS (Jan. 2, 1956): 5.
[Signed: M.K.]

4816   Negrych, Olenka. "Illîa Kyriâk" [Illîa Kyriâk]. PROMIN' 2, no. 7 (1961): 16-17.

4817   Rudnyćkyj, J.B. "Canadian and Argentine-Brasilian Novels on Ukrainian Pioneers." UKR REV 21, no. 3 (1974): 91-97.

4818   Rudnyćkyj, J.B. "Pro pys'mennyka, shcho z usmikhom strichav smert'... (zamist' kvitiv na mohylu sl. p. I. Kyriâka)" [A Writer Who Met Death with a Smile... (In Lieu of Flowers for the Grave of I. Kyriâk)]. UKR HOLOS (Jan. 11, 1956): 4.

4819 Samiĭlenko, V. "Nezauvazhenyĭ talant" [A Talent Overlooked]. In ĪŪvileĭnyi Al'manakh dlia vidmichennia 50-littia pratsi Ukraïns'koho Holosu 1910-1096]. (Winnipeg: Trident Press [1959]. p. 172.

4820 Slavutych, ĪAr. "Illīā Kyrīāk: Vyznachnyĭ pys'mennyk na tli ukraïns'koï literatury v Kanadī" [Illīā Kyrīāk: A Distinguished Author of Ukrainian Literature in Canada]. UKR VISTI (Detroit, Feb. 14, 1979): 3, 5.

4821 Syrnyk, I.H. "Kil'ka spohadiv pro Illīū Kyrīāka" [Recollections about Illīā Kyrīāk]. UKR HOLOS (Feb. 1, 1956): 4.

4822 "Vyvchaiut' tvorchist' Illi Kyrīāka" [The Works of Illīā Kyrīāk are being Studied]. UKR VISTI (Detroit, June 20, 1968): 4.

4823 Woycenko, Ol'ha. "Illīā Kyrīāk" In her Slavic Literature in Canada. 1 Ukrainian Canadian Letters. (Winnipeg: UVAN, 1969) pp. 9, 15-16. (Slavistica No. 65)

4824 Zhyla, Volodymyr. "Zakhidnia Kanada v ukraïns'kiĭ literaturi" [Western Canada in Ukrainian Writing]. In Zakhidn'okanads'kyĭ zbirnyk, compiled and edited by ĪAr Slavutych. (Edmonton: Shevchenko Scientific Society, 1973) vol. 1, pp. 134-41.

4825 Zyla, W.T. "Genuine Sons of the Canadian Prairies." UKR WEEKLY (Jan. 20, 1962): 3. [Review of Sons of the Soil.]

LEVYTS'KYĬ-SOFRONIV, Vasyl' see SOFRONYV-LEVYTS'KYĬ, Vasyl'

LOBODA, Ivan (1918-   )

4826 Vony pryĭshly znovu: Roman z finliands'koho-bol'shevyts'koï viĭny [They Came Again: Novel Based on the Russo-Finnish War]. Winnipeg: Ivan Tyktor, 1953. 133 pp. Novel. (Ukrainian Book Club, Book 16)

LOMACHKA, Svyryd, pseud. (Real name: OLEKSANDRIV, Borys)

4827 Liubov do blyzhn'oho: Feĭletony [Love Thy Neighbour: Short stories]. New York: Moloda Ukraïna, 1961. 122 pp. Short stories.

LUHOVYĬ, Oleksander, pseud. (Real name: OVRUTS'KYĬ-SHVABE, Olexander Vasyl') (1904-1962)
Playwright, novelist, journalist. Born in East Ukraine. In Canada he edited and published The Ukrainian Family, a paper in which he recorded historical events in different countries, devoting considerable space to events relating to Ukrainian Canadians.

4828 Za narid sviĭ: Tragedīā v 5 dīākh (7 vidslonakh) z chasiv vyzvol'noï viĭny na velykiĭ Ukraïni [For One's People: A Tragedy in 5 Acts (7 Scenes) fom the Days of the Struggle for Freedom in Greater Ukraine]. Winnipeg: ĪA. Havryliuk, 1932. 50 pp. Play.

4829 Dala divchyna khustynu: Drama z chasiv vyzvol'noï viĭny na velykiĭ Ukraïni: 5 diĭ [A Girl Gave Her Handkerchief Away: A Drama in 5 Acts about the Time of the Liberation War in Greater Ukraine]. Winnipeg: Ukraïns'kyĭ Holos, 1933. 54 pp. Play.

4830 Brat na brata: Drama z chasiv revoliutsiï na skhidniĭ Ukraïni u 4-okh dīākh [Brother Against Brother: A Drama in 4 Acts from the Time of the Revolution in Eastern Ukraine]. Saskatoon: The Author, 1934. 31 pp. Play.

4831 *Syrits'ki sl'ozy: Drama z chasiv viǐny i revoliutsiǐ na skhidniǐ Ukraǐni [Orphans' Tears: A Drama of the War and Revolution in Eastern Ukraine].* Saskatoon: Novyǐ SHliakh, 1934. 27 pp. Play.

4832 *Ol'ha Basarabova: Drama v 5-okh diǐakh [Ol'ha Basarabova: A Drama in 5 Acts].* Saskatoon: Orhanizatsiia Ukraǐnok Kanady im. Ol'hy Basarabovoǐ, 1936. 46 pp. Play.

4833 *Vira Babenko [Vira Babenko].* Saskatoon: Ukrainian Women's Organization, 1936. Play. [Written with T. Pavlychenko.]

4834 *Bez vyny karani: Drama z suchasnoho kanads'koho zhyttǐa v 4-okh diǐakh [Punished without Guilt: A Drama in 4 Acts from Canadian Life].* Winnipeg: Ukraǐns'ka Knyharnia, 1938. 66 pp. Play.

4835 *V dniakh slavy: Drama v 4 diǐakh [In Days of Glory: A Drama in 4 Acts].* V lystopadovu nich: *Drama-fantaziǐa v 3 diǐakh [One November Night: A Drama-fantasy in 3 Acts].* Toronto: Ukrainian Publishing Co., 1938. 59 pp. Plays.

4836 *V lystopadovu nich: Drama-fantaziǐa v 3 diǐakh [One November Night: A Drama-fantasy in 3 Acts].* 1938. Play.

4837 *Za volǐu Ukraǐny (Vira Babenko): Istorychna povist' z chasiv revolǐutsiǐ i povstanchoǐ viǐny u Skhidniǐ Ukraǐni v dvokh chastynakh [For Ukraine's Freedom: A Novel from the Times of Revolution and Civil War in Eastern Ukraine in Two Parts].* Winnipeg: The Author, 1939. 212 pp. Novel.

4838 *Bezkhatnyǐ (Dity stepu): Povist' z zhyttǐa ukraǐntsiv v Kanadi u dvokh chastynakh [Homeless (Children of the Prairie): A Novel from Ukrainian Life in Canada in Two Parts].* Edmonton: Alberta Printing Co., 1946. 297 pp. Novel.

4839 *CHorni khmary izza Prypiaty: Istorychna povist' z chasiv KHmel'nychchyny [Dark Clouds from Beyond the Pripet River: Historical Novel from the Time of Ukrainian-Lithuanian War, 1949].* Edmonton: The Author, 1946. 163 pp. Novel.

4840 *V kihtǐakh dvoholovoho orla: Istorychna povist'-khronika z chasiv viǐny 1914-1917 [In the Claws of the Two-headed Eagle: Historical Novel from the Time of the First World War].* Vol. 1: *Zalizom i kroviu [By Iron and Blood].* . Edmonton: Aberta Printing Co., 1955. 349 pp. Novel.

4841 *Pozychena zhinka: Komediǐa u dvokh diǐakh [The Borrowed Wife: A Comedy in Two Acts].* Edmonton, 1968. 20 pp. Play.

4842 *Svatannǐa po poshti: Komediǐa u 3 diǐakh [Marriage by Mail: A Comedy in 3 Acts].* Winnipeg: Stsena [n.d.]. 20 pp. Play.

Writings about:

4843 Chopyk, Bohdan. "Litopys ukraǐns'koho poselentsǐa: *Bezkhatnyǐ* O. Luhovoho." In *Zakhidn'o-kanads'kyǐ zbirnyk*, edited by ǏAr Slavutych. (Edmonton: Shevchenko Scientific Society, 1975) vol. 2, pp. 148-56.

4844 Kaliavs'kyǐ, Danylo I. Review of *Za volǐu Ukraǐny.* UKR HOLOS (Nov. 29, 1939): 3.

4845 Kyrǐak, Illǐa. Review of *V kihtiakh dvoholovoho orla.* UKR HOLOS (Apr. 27, 1955): 3.

4846 Mandryka, M.I. "O. Luhowy." In his *History of Ukrainian Literature in Canada.* (Winnipeg: Ukrainian Free Academy of Sciences, 1968) pp. 95-97.

4847 Mazepa, Bohdan. "Oleksander Luhovyĭ i ĭoho tvorchist'" [Oleksander Luhovyĭ and His Works]. PIVN SIAĬV 1 (1964): 86-91.

4848 Oryshchuk, Myron. "Oleksander Luhovyĭ ĭak lĭûdyna." In *Zakhidn'okanads'kyĭ zbirnik,* edited by ĨAr Slavutych. (Edmonton: Shevchenko Scientific Society, 1975) vol. 2, pp. 141-47.

4849 Romanenchuk, Bohdan. Review of *Bezkhatnyi (Dity stepu).* UKR ROD 2, no. 1 (1948): 25-28.

4850 Samets', P. "Ne harno tak robyty " [What a Way to Act]. UKR HOLOS (June 11, 1941)

4851 Stechyshyn, Myroslav. Review of *Bezkhatnyi (Dity stepu).* UKR HOLOS (Sept. 11, 1946)

4852 Woycenko, Ol'ha. "Alexander Luhowyj - William Ovrutsky-Shwabe." In her *Slavic Literature in Canada. 1. Ukrainian Canadian Letters.* (Winnipeg: UVAN, 1969) pp. 9, 16.

LYSENKO, Vera   (1910-1975)

4853 *Yellow Boots.* Toronto: Ryerson Press, 1954. 314 pp. Novel.

LYSENKO-TULEVITRIV, Victor D.   see TULEVITRIV, Victor D.

MAĬDANYK, ĨAkiv (1891-   )

4854 *Manihrula. Komediĭâ [Immigrant. A Comedy].* Winnipeg: Rus'ka Knyharnia, 1915. 26 pp. Play.

4855 *Manigrula. [Immigrant].* 2nd ed. Winnipeg: Ukraïns'ka Knyharnia, 1926. 30 pp. Play.

4856 *Vuĭko SH. Tabachnĭûk i inshi novi korotki opovidannĭâ: Poverkh 100 illiustratsiĭ avtora [Uncle S. Tabachnĭûk and Other New Stories, with More than 100 Illustrations by the Author].* Winnipeg, 1959. 134 pp. Short stories.

Wrting about:

4857 Haĭ-Holovko, Oleksa. "ĨAkiv Maĭdanyk." In his *Ukraïns'ki pys'mennyky v Kanadi.* (Winnipeg: Volyn', 1980) vol. 1, pp. 79-91.

MAK, Ol'ha, pseud. (Real name: HETS, Ol'ha) (1913-   )

4858 *Proty perekonan': Roman [Against Convictions: Novel].* Toronto: Ukrainian Echo Press, 1959. 368 pp. Novel.

4859 *Kaminnĭâ pid kosoĭû: Povist'/Scythe on Stone: Novel.* Toronto: Homin Ukraïny, 1973. 158 pp. (Biblioteka vydavnytstva Homin Ukraïny No. 44) Novel.

Writings about:

4860 "Avtors'kyĭ vechir Ol'hy Mak" [Literary Evening for Ol'ha Mak]. BAT'KIVSHCHYNA (Dec. 18, 1971): 7.

4861 Havrylenko, Olia. "Literaturnyĭ vechir Ol'hy Mak " [Literary Evening for Ol'ha Mak]. NOV SHLIAKH (Oct. 25, 1973): 4.

4862 Keïvan, M.A. "Pys'mennytsia Ol'ha Mak v Edmontoni" [The Author Ol'ha Mak in Edmonton]. UKR VISTI (Oct. 25, 1973): 4.

4863 Kuz'menko, Svitlana. "Vechir pys'mennytsi Ol'ha Mak u Toronti" [Literary Evenening for the Author Ol'ha Mak in Toronto]. UKR HOLOS (Apr. 3, 1974): 8.

4864 "Pys'mennytsîa Ol'ha Mak z Toronta u Vinnipegu" [The Writer Ol'ha Mak of Toronto in Winnipeg]. UKR HOLOS (Sept. 26, 1973): 6.

4865 "Pys'mennytsîa Ol'ha Mak z Toronta vystupyt' u chytal'ni 'Prosvita' " [The Author Ol'ha Mak will Make an Appearance in the Community Reading Centre 'Prosvita']. NOV SHLIAKH (Sept. 29, 1973): 5.

4866 "Zustrich z pys'mennytseîû" [A Meeting with an Author]. HOMIN UKR (Jan. 7, 1974): 17, 24.

4867 "Zustrich z pys'mennytseîû Ol'hoîû Mak" [A Meeting with the Author Ol'ha Mak]. HOMIN UKR (Nov. 27, 1971): 11.

MANDRYKA, Mykyta Ivanovych (1886-1979)

Poet, scholar, literary historian. Born in Ukraine, came to Canada by way of Czechoslovakia. An accomplished scholar and translator, he has published on agriculture, Ukrainian cooperatives and literature. Dr. Mandryka edited literary anthologies and authored the book *History of Ukrainian Literature in Canada.*

4868 *Miï sad [My Garden].* Winnipeg: Canadian Ukrainian Educational Association, 1941. 125 pp. Poems.

4869 *Poeziï (1905-1957) [Poetry (1905-1957)].* 6 v. Vol. 1: *Zolota osin' [Golden Autumn, 1905-1957]*; Vol. 2: *Radist' [Happiness].* Winnipeg: Vydavnycha Spilka Tryzub, 1958-1959. 175 and 143 pp. respectively. Vol. 3: *Symfoniia vikiv [Symphony of Centuries].* Winnipeg: Vydavnycha Spilka Tryzub, 1961. 215 pp. Vol. 4: *Sontsetsvit [Helianthus].* Winnipeg: Trident Press, 1965. 128 pp. *Vybrane dlia vybranykh z poeziï za 1965-1969 roky [Selected from the Poems Written Between 1965-1969].* Vol. 5: *Vyno zhyttîa [Vine of Life].* Winnipeg: ARS, 1970. 176 pp. Vol. 6: *Zavershennia lita Poeziï (1970-1974).* Winnipeg: The Author, 1975. 193 pp.

4870 *Mazepa: Poema [Mazepa: A Historical Poem].* Winnipeg: Vydavychna Spilka Tryzub, 1960. 87 pp. Poems.

4871 *Kanada: Poema [Canada: A Poem].* Winnipeg: National Publishers, 1961. 40 pp. Poem.

4872 *Vik Petliury: Poema [Petliurian Age: A Poem].* Winnipeg: Trident Press, 1966. 47 pp. Poem.

4873 *Canada: A Poem,* translated from the Ukrainian with an introduction by Watson Kirkconnell. Winnipeg: Ukrainian Free Academy of Sciences in Canada, with the assistance of the Ukrainian Canadian Foundation of T. Shevchenko and the Department of the Secretary of State, 1977. 72 pp. Poem, parallel text edition.

Writings about:

4874 Andrusyshen, C.H. "Dr. M.I. Mandryka." UNIV TOR Q 45 (1975-76): 445-47.

4875 Hospodyn, Andriï. "d-r M.I. Mandryka - nevtomnyï pratsivnyk (28, 9 1886)" [Dr. M.I. Mandryka - An Untiring Labourer (Sept. 28th, 1886)]. UKR HOLOS (Sept. 22, 29, 1971): 5, 5 respectively.

4876   Ivakh, Onufriĭ. "Literaturni novyny" [Literary News]. UKR HOLOS (June 4, 1941)
       [Review of Miĭ sad.

4877   Marunchak, M.H., comp. Mykyta Ivanovych Mandryka: Ĭŭvileĭnyĭ zbirnuk u vidznachenniā 85-
       richchiā ĭoho zhyttiā ta 65-richchiā ĭoho poetychnoĭ, suspil'no-politychnoĭ i kul'turno-naukovoĭ
       diial'nosty: (1886-1971)/85th Anniversary of Mykyta I. Mandryka: Poet, Scholar, Cultural and
       Social Leader: (1886-1971): An Account of Jubilee Celebrations and Essentials of His Life and
       Works. Winnipeg: The Celebration Committee, 1973. 152 pp.
       [A symposium.]

4878   Marunchak, M.H. "85-richchiā d-ra M. Mandryky" [Dr. M. Mandryka 85 Years Old]. NOV
       SHLIAKH (Nov. 6, 1971): 7.

4879   "Nedovershenyĭ zadum" [The Unaccomplished Plan]. NOVI DNI 12 (October 1961): 15-19.
       [Review of Mazepa.]

4880   Rudnytś kyj, J.B. "Poema M.I. Mandryky Mazepa" [M.I. Mandryka's Poem Mazepa]. In Mazepa.
       (Winnipeg: Vydavnycha Spilka Tryzub, 1960) pp. 5-12.

4881   "Shana I diaka nashomu zasluzhenomu sen'ĭorovi M.I. Mandrytsi" [Honour and Gratitude to Our
       Deserving Senior M.I. Mandryka]. NOVI DNI 24, no. 281 (1973): 1-2, 29.

4882   Slavutych, ĬAr. "Metaphora v poeziĭ M.I. Mandryky" [The Metaphor in M.I. Mandryka's Poetry].
       UKR HOLOS (Dec. 1, 1971): 7. Reprinted in Mykyta Mandryka: Ĭŭvileĭnyĭ zbirnyk (Winnipeg:
       Celebration Committee, 1973) pp. 56-59.

4883   Slavutych, ĬAr. "Novyĭ osiach M. Mandryky" [A New Achievement of M. Mandryka]. UKR
       HOLOS (June 24, 1970): 3.

4884   Slavutych, ĬAr. "Patriârkh ukraïns'koĭ poeziĭ v Kanadi" [The Patriarch of Ukrainian Poetry in
       Canada]. PIVN SIAĬV 5 (1971): 172-74.
       [Review of Vyno zhyttiā.]

4885   Slavutych, ĬAr. Review of Zolota osin'. In Radist', pp. 136-40.

4886   ZHyla, Volodymyr. "Poema M. Mandryky Mazepa" [The Poem Mazepa by M. Mandryka]. UKR
       HOLOS (Dec. 1, 1971): 7-8.

4887   ZHyla, Volodymyr. "Sviĭ talant vin viddav narodovi." SVOBODA (Sept. 7-9, 1983)

MARTSINIV, T. ĬU.

4888   Sumna istoryia pro nuzhdu zaribnyka [A Gloomy History of a Worker]. Winnipeg: ĬA. Kret, 1911.
       28 pp. Story.

MATVIĬENKO,   Teodor (1924-   )

4889   Sonety [Sonnets]. Toronto, 1961. Poems.

   Writing about:

4890   Slavutych, ĬAr. "Vidhomin neokliâsyky" [Reverberations of Neoclassicism]. PIVN SIAĬV 5 (1971):
       187-88.
       [Review of Sonety.]

MAZEPA, Bohdan (1928-1978)

Born in Denysiv, Western Ukraine. Completed his secondary education in Germany, studied at the University of Alberta, after immigrating to Canada in 1948. His more recent poems depict the author's experience in Canada.

4891   *Zorîana dal': Liryka [Starlit Horizon: Lyrics]*.   Edmonton: The Author's Friends, 1956.   62 pp. Poems.

4892   *Polumîani akordy: Liryka [Flaming Accords: Lyrical Poems]*.   Edmonton: Slovo, 1976.   62 pp. Poems.

Writings about:

4893   Chopyk, Bohdan.   Review of *Polumîani akordy*.   UKR VISTI (May 5, 1977)

4894   Slavutych, Îar. "Bohdan Mazepa" [Bohdan Mazepa].   In his *Ukraïns'ka poeziîa v Kanadi* (Edmonton: Slavuta, 1976) pp. 53-55.

MOHYLÎANKA, Dariîa, pseud. (Real name: ÎANDA, Dariîa)

Born in Gimli, Man. Educated in the Ukrainian Peter Mohyla Institute, Saskatoon. She was a journalist, writing for *Ukraïns'kyĭ Holos* and published a book on Ukrainian women.

4895   *Dumky letîat' na Ukraïnu: Narodni virshi [Thoughts Flying to Ukraine: Folk Poetry]*.   Edmonton, 1962. 123 pp. Reprinted in 1980. Poems.

4896   *Pisni moho sertsîa: Druha zbirka poeziï [My Heart's Songs: Second Collection of Poetry]*. Edmonton, 1964. 126 pp. Reprinted in 1980. Poems.

4897   *Canadian Tapestry*. Winnipeg: Tryzub, 1970. 199 pp. Poems.
[Published under the name Doris Elizabeth Yanda.]

Writings about:

4898   Slavutych, Îar. "Dariîa Mohylîanka" [Dariîa Mohylîanka].. UKR HOLOS (Dec. 5, 1962): 7-8.

4899   Slavutych, Îar. "Ukraïns'ka narodna poetka v Kanadi" [A Ukrainian Folk Poet in Canada]. PI VN SI AÎV 5 (1971): 179-81.
[Review of *Dumky letîat' na Ukraïnu*).

MRYTS, Nina   see MUDRYK-MRYTS, Nina

MUDRYK-MRYTS, Nina (1927-   )

Born in Ukraine, came to Canada after World War II. She has published poetry for children and papers on education.

4900   *Namystechko [Necklace]*. 1955. Poems for children.

4901   *Svitanky i sumerky [Daybreak and Dusk]*. 1958. Poems for children.

4902   *Po îahidky [Berry Picking]*. Toronto: The Author, 1965. 20 pp. Stories.

4903   *Pryhody hordoï kytsi [The adventures of the Proud Kitten]*. 1965. Stories.

4904 *Pryhody horishka/Adventures of a Little Hazel-nut.* Toronto-New York: Obiednannîa pratsivnykh dyatîachnoï literatury, 1970. 16 pp. Poems for children.
[Awarded I. Franko's First Prize in 1973)

4905 *Vohnyk: Virshi dlîa diteï [Camp Fire: Poems for Children].* Cleveland: Plastovyï muzeï, 1971. Poems for children.

4906 *Legendy/Legends.* Toronto-Edmonton: Obiednannia Ukraïns'kykh Pys'mennykiv v Kanadi Slovo, 1973. 31 pp. Legends.

4907 *Na svitanku/At Daybreak: Nursery Tale in the Ukrainian Language.* Toronto: Obiednannîa pratsivnykiv literatury dlîa diteï i molodi, 1974. 12 [2] pp. Poems.

4908 *Dytîachyï kutok: Virshi dlîa diteï [Children's Nook: Poems for Children].* Toronto: OPLDM, 1983. 75 pp. Poems for children.

4909 *Kalynova sopilka: Poeziï [A Flute: Poems].* Toronto: Slovo, 1983. 78 pp. Poems.

Writings about:

4910 "Vertyporokh, Leonida. "Literaturnyï vechir pys'mennytsi" [A Literary Evening for a Writer]. KAN FARM (May 14, 1973): 10.

4911 "Vystup Viry Vovk i Niny Mudryk-Mryts u Vinnipegu" Vira Vovk and Nina Mudryk-Mryts Make Appearance in Winnipeg]. NOV SHLIAKH (Oct. 9, 1965): 5.

MULÎARCHYK, Ivan

4912 *ZHnyva dos'pily: Poeziï [The Ripe Harvest: Poetry].* Winnipeg, 1917. 17 pp. Poems.

4913 *Promin' zhyttîa: Poeziï [Ray of Life: Poetry].* Detroit, 1937. 15 pp. Poems.

4914 *Smikh pralisa [Laughter of the Forest].* Detroit, 1937. 25 pp. Poems.

MUR, Dan (1914-1978)

4915 *ZHal' i hniv: Poeziï [Sorrow and Wrath: Poetry].* Edmonton: Vasyl' i Natalka Dukhniï, 1966. 96 pp. Poems.

4916 *Skryzhali tuhy: Poeziï/Plates of Sorrow: Poems.* Edmonton: Vasyl' i Natalka Dukhniï, 1973. 120 pp. Poems.

4917 *Druhotsvit: Tretîa zbirka poeziï [Second Blossom: Third Book of Poems],* introduction by IAr Slavutych. Edmonton: Vasyl' i Natalka Dukhniï, 1979. 112 pp. Poems.

Writings about:

4918 Bolekhivs'kyï, Ivan. "Poet ukraïns'koï pravdy (Literaturnyï vechir poeta Dana Mura z nahody poiavy drukom îoho pershoï zbirky *ZHal' i hniv,* Edmonton, Alberta, 1966 r.)" [Poet of Ukrainian Truth (Literary Evening for Dan Mur Marking the Publication of His First Collection *Sorrow and Wrath,* Edmonton, Alberta, 1966)]. VIL'N SVIT (May 8, 1967): 9.

4919 Review of *ZHal' i hniv.* VIL'N SVIT (May 8, 1967): 9, 12.

4920 Ovechko, Ivan. "Poet zhalíu-tuhy, nizhnosty i patriotyzmu" [The Poet of Sorrow and Languish, Tenderness and Patriotism]. KAN FARM (Sept. 17, 1973): 12-13.
[Review of *ZHal' i hniv.*]

4921 Slavutych, Îar. "Hnivnyĭ zhal" [Angry Sorrow]. PIVN SIAĬV 5 (1971): 186-87.

4922 Slavutych, Îar. "Dan Mur" [Dan Mur]. In his *Ukraïns'ka poeziia v Kanadi* (Edmonton: Slavuta, 1976) pp. 69-72.

4923 Slavutych, Îar. "Vidrodzhennia barokko." HOMIN UKR (Apr. 7, 1973)

4924 Vertyporokh, Leonida. "Literaturnyĭ vechir poeta Dana Mura v Toronto" [Literary Evening for the Poet Dan Mur in Toronto]. KAN FARM (Jul. 16, 1973): 10.

4925 Zavads'kyĭ, M. "Pamiati Danyla Murynky." UKR VISTI (Edmonton, Sept. 21, 1978)

MUROVYCH, Larysa (1917-)

Poet, born in Chernivtsi. Educated in her native land and Czechoslovakia. She emigrated to Canada in 1948. Her poems have appeared in Canada and abroad since the 1960s.

4926 *Pionery sviatoï zemli: Tretîa zbirka* [Pioneers of Sacred Land: Selected Poems]. Toronto: Svitannîa, 1969. 64 pp. Poems.

4927 *ÎEvshan: Poeziï ta poemy/The Magic Herb: Poems in Ukrainian.* Toronto: Svitannîa, 1971. 64 pp. Poems.

4928 *ZHar-ptakha: Vybrani poeziï/The Fire-bird: Selected Poems in Ukrainian Language.* Toronto: Svitannia, 1971. 47 pp.

4929 *Derevo ridnoho rodu. Poeziï* [Tree of the Native Family. Poetry]. Toronto: The Author, 1984. 208 pp. Poems.

Writings about:

4930 Kyîanka, A. "Symvolika kalyny (Z pryvodu poiavy zbirky *Pionery sviatoï zemli* Larysy Murovych)" [Symbolism of the Cranberry Tree (On the Occasion of the Publication of Larysa Murovych's Collection *Pioneers of Sacred Land*)]. SVITANNÎA No. 9 (January 1970): 23-25.

4931 Mandryka, I.M. "L. Murovych." In his *History of Ukrainian Literature in Canada.* (Winnipeg: Free Ukrainian Scientific Academy, 1968) pp. 182-85.

4932 Ovechko, Ivan. "Larysa Murovych - poetesa liryky i mitolohiï" [Larysa Murovych - Poet of Lyrics and Mythology]. In *Pionery sviatoï zemli.* (Toronto: Svitannia, 1969) pp. 5-10.

4933 "Poetesa ukraïns'koho îevshanu" [The Poet of the Ukrainian ÎEvshan]. KAN FARM (Feb. 28, 1972): 12-13.
[ÎEvshan is a magic herb that, according to ancient Ukrainian chronicle, was supposed to restore one's memory of one's native land by its scent.]

4934 "Poety literaturnoï hrupy 'Svitannîa' " [The Poets of the Literary Group 'Svitannîa']. HOMIN UKR (Jan. 7, 1972):
[About Larysa Murovych and L. Romen.]

4935 Pohidnyĭ, Mykola. Review of *ÎEvshan*. KAN FARM (Nov. 20, 1972): 12-13.

4936   Slavutych, Ĩâr. "Mitsne korinnia rodu." NOVI DNI (February 1980): 30-31. [Review of *Derevo ridnoho rodu*.]

4937   Slavutych, Ĩâr. "Svidoma pratsia nad slovom" [A Conscious Work on Words]. PIVN SIAĨV 5 (1971): 178-79. Reprinted in UKR KNYHA 2, no. 1 (1972): 26-27. [Review of *Pionery sviatoï zemli*.]

4938   Vorsklo, Vira. "Literaturnyĭ vechir Larysy Murovych" [Literary Evening for Larysa Murovych]. KAN FARM (Nov. 1, 1969): 6.

MURYNKA, D.   see MUR, Dan

MUSIĨCHUK, S.

4939   *Na Krylakh v Ukraïnu [On Wings to Ukraine]*. Winnipeg: The Author, 1946. Poems.

4940   *Vichnym dusham Ukraïny [To Ukraine's Eternal Spirit]*. Winnipeg: Novyĭ S̃Hlâkh, 1948. Poems.

NOVAK, Apolinariĭ   (1885-1955)

4941   *Khan i ioho syn abo ukraïnka-branka i druhi opovidannia (Khan and His Son or Ukrainian Captive Woman and Other Stories]*. Winnipeg: Ukrainian Publishers, 1916. 64 pp. Short stories.

ODRACH, Fedir, pseud. (Real name: SHOLOMYĨS'KYĬ, Fedir) (1912-1964)
Novelist. Born in Polisia, joined the Ukrainian Insurgent Army. Some of his earlier writings are based on his experience as a freedom fighter. Came to Canada after World War II. Some of his best novels contain autobiographical material.

4942   *V dorozi/En el camino [On the Road]*. Buenos Aires: Peremoha, 1954. 151 pp. Novel.

4943   *S̃HCHebetun/The Wood Warbler*. New York: Orhanizatsiia Oborony C̃Hotyrokh Svobid Ukraïny, 1957. 291 pp. Novel.

4944   *Pivstanok za selom: Opovidannia/La Parada de Aldea: Novelas [The Stop Behind the Village: Short Stories]*. Buenos Aires: ĨUliân Seredîâk, 1959. 291 pp. Short stories.

4945   *Pokynuta oselia: Opovidannîâ [The Abandoned Home: A Story]*. Toronto: Dobra Knyzhka, 1961. 304 pp. Novel.

4946   *Na nepevnomu grunti [On Precarious Ground]*. Toronto: Dobra Knyzhka, 1962. 340 pp. Novel.

4947   *Voshchad/Incipient Dawn*. Toronto: [Komitet Vydannia Povisty 'Voshchad' u Toronto), 1972. 387 pp. Novel.

Writings about:

4948   Bodnaruk, Ivan. "Tvorchist' Fedora Odracha" [Fedor Odrach's Work]. KAN UKR No. 6 (1978): 14-16.

4949   Halan, A. "Tvorche padinnîâ" [Creative Decline]. NOVI DNI 13 (February 1962): 24-25. [Review of *Pokynuta oselia*.]

4950 Odrach, Fedir. "Miĭ literaturnyĭ vechir u Detroĭti [My Literary Evening in Detroit]. KAN FARM (Aug. 23, 1971): 9.

4951 Oleksandriv Borys. "Peredmova" [Preface]. In SHCHebetun. (New York: Orhanizatsiia Oborony CHotyr'okh Svobid Ukraïny, 1957) pp. 9-12.

4952 "Povist' Fedora Odracha *Voshchad' poĭavylasĭa* u Toronti" [Fedir Odrach's Novel *Incipient Dawn* has Appeared in Toronto]. LIT MYST (March 1973): 4.

4953 Vorsklo, Vira. "Polis'kyĭ vechir" [A Polisia Evening]. UKR HOLOS (Jul. 19, 1972): 10. [Polisia is part of Ukraine.]

OHIĬENKO, Ivan see ILARION, Metropolitan

OLEKSANDRIV, Borys (1921-1979)
Poet. He is described by M. Marunchak as an author "in whose work poetic prose and journalism stand higher than poetry...." He also wrote humorous sketches under the pseudonym of Svyryd Lomachka.

4954 *Kolokruh: Poeziĭ/Circuit: Poems.* Munich: Instytut Literary im. M. Oresta, 1972. 101 pp. Poems. [Shared the 2nd I. Franko prize in 1973.]

4955 *Kaminnyĭ bereh: Poeziĭ pro liubov, pro zhyttia i pro smert': 1972-1975/The Stone Shore: Poems about Love, about Life and about Death: 1972-1975.* Toronto-New York: Obiednannia ukraïns'kykh pys'mennykiv *Slovo*, 1975. 72 pp. Poems.

4956 *Povorot po slidu: Vybrani poeziĭ, 1939-1979 [Tracing Our Footsteps: Selected Poems, 1939-1979].* Toronto: Slovo, 1980. 303 pp. Poems.

Writings about:

4957 Harasevych, Mariia. "Borys Oleksandriv u Detroiti" [Boris Aleksandriv in Detroit]. UKR HOLOS (May 26, 1971): 10.

4958 ĬAvors'kyĭ, S. "U nas shanuiut' poetiv: Avtors'kyĭ vechir Borysa Oleksandrova z Ottavs'koho universytetu" [We Honour Poets: A Literary Evening for Borys Oleksandriv at the University of Ottawa]. NOV SHLIAKH (Dec. 19/26, 1970): 10.

4959 Il'nyts'ka, Roksoliana. "Borys Oleksandriv" [Borys Oleksandriv]. ĬUNAK 9 (March 1971): 4.

4960 ĬUrynak, Anatol'. Review of *Tuha za sontsem.* UKR VISTI (Feb. 11, 1968)

4961 Kachurovs'kyĭ, Ihor. "Nova knyha poeziĭ Borysa Oleksandrova" [A New Book of Poetry by Borys Oleksandriv]. NOVI DNI 24, no. 278 (March 1973): 8-9.

4962 Kachurovs'kyĭ, Ihor. "*Tuha za sontsem* moho pryiatelia Borysa Oleksandrova" [*Longing for the Sun*, by My Friend Borys Oleksandriv]. UKR VISTI (Dec. 17, 1967)

4963 Klynovyĭ, ĬUriĭ "Smert' Borysa Oleksandrova" [Borys Oleksandriv's Death]. In his *Moïm synam....* (Edmonton: Slovo, 1981) pp. 399-412.

4964 Lytvĭak, Tarasa H. "Tvorets' slavnoho Svyryda Lomachky" [The Author of the Famous Svyryd Lomachka]. UKR VISTI (Dec. 12, 1968)

4965 Nestorovych, V. "Literaturnyĭ vechir B. Oleksandrova u Detroiti" [A Literary Evening for B. Oleksandriv in Detroit]. NOV SHLIAKH (May 29, 1971): 10.

4966 Shelest, Volodymyr. "Borys Oleksandriv – poet i humoryst" [Borys Aleksandriv – The Poet and Humorist]. NOV SHLIAKH (Nov. 13, 1971): 8, 10.

4967 Slavutych, Îàr. "Maĭster bez vlasnoho oblychchia" [The Master without his Own Image]. PIVN SIAÏV 5 (1971): 189-90.
[Review of *Tuha za sontsem*.]

4968 Svaroh, Vadym. "Pamiat' poeta" [Recollections of a Poet]. NOVI DNI 19 (January 1968): 11, 12.

4969 Vorsklo, Vira. "Pisennyĭ kolokruh" [A Circuit of Songs]. NOV SHLIAKH (Feb. 3, 10, 24, 1973): 8-9 respectively.

ONUFRIĬCHUK, Fedir (1904-1989)

4970 *Opovidannîà [Short Stories]*. Yorkton: The Author, 1964. 16 pp. Short stories.

Writing about:

4971 "Vykaz napysanykh i vydanykh prats' F. Onufriĭchuka" [A List of Manuscripts and Published Works of F. Onufriĭchuk]. LIT VOL 10-11, no. 10/11 (1971-72): 135-36.

ORLYHORA, Lev. T., pseud. (Real name: SYLENKO, Lev. T.)
Poet, editor. Author of two collections of poetry and a book of short stories, he is better known as editor and publisher of an originally Winnipeg-based periodical: *Samobutnia Ukraïnia*.

4972 *Liûblîù: Liryka [Love: Lyrical Poems]*. Edmonton, 1958. 23 pp. Poems.

4973 *Heroï nashoho chasu: Novely [Heroes of Our Time: Short Stories]*. Yorkton, 1959. 155 pp. Short stories.

4974 *Maha vira [Great Faith]*. Winnipeg: Oriiana, 1969. 93 pp. Poems.

Writing about:

4975 "Deshcho pro tvorchist' Leva Sylenka (Orlyhory)" [Some Remarks about the Literary Works of Lev Sylenko (Orlyhora)]. KAN FARM (Aug. 15, 1970): 9.

OS'MACHKA, Teodosiĭ (1895-1962)

4976 *Iz-pid svitu [From Under the World]*. New York: Ukrainian Academy of Arts and Sciences, 1954. 317 pp. Novel.

4977 *Kytytsi chasu: 1943-1948 [Bouquets of Time: 1943-1948]*. Germany: Ukraïns'ki Visti, 1953. 131 pp. Poems.

4978 *Plan do dvoru: Povist' [Plan for the Farm: A Novel]*. Toronto: Ukrainian Canadian Legion, 1951. 184 pp. Novel.

4979 *Red Assassins*, translated from the Ukrainian. Minneapolis: T.S. Denison Co., 1959. 375 pp. Novel.

4980   *Rotonda dushohubtsiv [The Rotunda of Murderers].* Winnipeg: Trident Press, 1957. 365 pp. Novel.

Writings about:

4981   Doroshenko, Volodymyr. "Todos' Os'machka (Slovo, vyholoshene na avtors'komu vechori pys'mennyka...)" [Teodosiĭ Os'machka (An Address Given at a Literary Evening for the Author...)]. AMERYKA (May 23, 1961)

4982   Fylypovych, Oleksander. "Todos' Os'machka (Fragmenty spohadiv)" [Teodosiĭ Os'machka (Reminiscent Fragments)]. SUCHASNIST' 7 (January 1967): 64-73.

4983   Hamorak, I͡Uriĭ. "I͡Edynyĭ tvir Todosia Os'machky dli͡a diteĭ" [T. Os'machka's Only Work for Children]. PI VN SI AĬ V 1 (1964): 94-96.

4984   Hamorak, I͡Uriĭ. "Na smert' Todosia Os'machky" [On Teodosiĭ Os'machka's Death]. LYST PRYI AT 11 (January/February 1963): 15-20.

4985   Keĭvan, Mari͡a Adri͡ana. "Vyhranyĭ biĭ Todosia Os'machky" [Teodosiĭ Os'machka's Victorious Battle]. NASH ZHYTT 20 (January 1963): 7-8.

4986   Kovalenko, Liudmyla. "Todos' Os'machka (Do psycholohiĭ tvorchosty)" [Teodosiĭ Os'machka (On the Psychology of His Creativity)]. NOVI DNI 13 (December 1962): 7-14.

4987   Lavrinenko, I͡Uriĭ. "Todosiĭ Os'machka" [Teodosiĭ Os'machka]. In his *Rozstril͡ane vidrodzhenni͡a: Antolohi͡a 1917-1933.* (Paris: Instytut Literacki, 1959) pp. 220-23.

4988   Maliar, Pavlo. "Poet znemozhenoĭ dushi (Sproba kharakterystyky)" [Poet of a Weary Spirit (Attempt at a Character Sketch)]. NOVI DNI 13 (October 1962): 11-12.

4989   Sherekh, I͡Uriĭ. "Nezustrichannyĭ druh (*Kytytsi chasu* - Os'machchyna liryka)" [A Friend not Yet Encountered (*Kytytsi chasu* - Os'machka's Lyrics)]. In his *Ne dlia diteĭ.* (New York: Proloh, 1964) pp. 315-22.

4990   "T. Os'machka: *Kytytsi chasu...*" [T. Os'machka: *Kytytsi chasu...*] KYĬV 6 (July/August 1953): 213-14. Signed: Skryptor.

4991   Tarnavs'kyĭ, Ostap. "Try poety emigratsiĭ [Three Poets in Exile]. In his *Tuha za mitom* (New York: kliuchi, 1966) pp. 105-12.

OVERKOVYCH, Mykola, pseud. (Real name: BYTYNS'KYĬ, Mykola) (1893-1972)

4992   *Suziria lytsariv: Zibrani tvori [A Cluster of Knights: Collected Works].* Toronto: Nadia Bytyns'ka, 1975. 192 pp. Stories.

OVRUTS'KYĬ -SHVABE, Oleksander   see   LUHOVYĬ, Oleksander

PAVLYCHENKO, Toma K.   (1892-1958)

4993   *Dukh natsiĭ [The Spirit of a Nation].* Saskatoon: Ukraïnske Natsional'ne Obiednannia, 1940. 48 pp. Poems.

Writing about:

4994 Slavutych, Ĩar. "Toma Pavlychenko" [Toma Pavlychenko]. In his *Ukraïns'ka poeziia v Kanadi.* (Edmonton: Slavuta, 1976) pp. 34-36.

PAUSH, Stefianïã (1912-1979)

4995 *Nauchka: Narysy z pioners'koho zhyttĩã [The Lesson: Short Sketches of Ukrainian Pioneer Life in Alberta]*, with an introduction by Orest Starchuk. Edmonton: The Author, 1967. 75 pp. Short stories.

PETRIVS'KYĨ, Mykhaĩlo (1897-1982)

Born in Rozubovichi, Ukraine. Came to Canada in 1912. Attended the University of Iowa and the University of Ottawa. His poems have appeared in *Svoboda, Promin',* and *Ukraïnskyĩ Holos,* and his novel *Secret of the Silver Island* in the *Ukrainian Worker.* Short stories in English have appeared in *Canadian Forum.*

4996 *Kanadiïs'kyĩ zhenykh [A Canadian Suitor].* Winnipeg: Ukraïns'ka Knyharnia, 1922. Play.

4997 *Diakouchytel' v shkoli [Cantor-Teacher in School].* Winnipeg: Promin', 1927. (Kanadyĩs'ka Biblioteka No. 15) Play.

4998 *SHliakhotni khloptsi [Noble Boys].* Winnipeg: Promin', 1928. 19 pp. (Kanadiïs'ka Biblioteka No. 25) Short story.

4999 *Magichne misto: Novelïã z zhyttĩã ukraïns'kykh pereselentsiv v Amerytsi [The Magnificant City: A Short Story about Ukrainian Immigrant Life in America].* Winnipeg: The Author, 1929. 155 pp. Novel.

5000 *Taĩna sribnokho ozera [Silver Lake Mystery].* Toronto: Ukrainian Worker, 1936. Novel. [Published serially.]

5001 *Mriï sl'ozamy oblyti: Opovidannĩã z zhyttĩã ukraïns'kykh pioneriv i imihrantiv v Kanadi/Dreams Sprinkled with Tears: Short Stories about Ukrainian Pioneer and Immigrant Life in Canada.* Winnipeg-Toronto, 1973. 168 pp. Short stories.

5002 *Oĩ, Kanado, Kanadon'ko [Oh, Canada, Darling Canada].* Winnipeg: Trident Press, 1974. 168 pp.

Writings about:

5003 Andrusyshen, C.H. Review of *Mriï sl'ozamy oblyti.* CAN ETH STUD 4, no. 1-2 (1972): 80-82. [Also in UNIV TOR Q 43 (1973-74): 455-56.]

5004 Andrusyshen, C.H. Review of *Oĩ Kanado, Kanadon'ko.* CAN ETH STUD 9, no. 2 (1977): 147. [Also in UNIV TOR Q 45 (1975-76): 449.]

5005 "Knyha pro ukraïns'kykh pioneriv v Kanadi: Avtors'kyĩ vechir M. Petrivs'koho u Vinnipegu" [A Book about Ukrainian Pioneers in Canada: A Literary Evening for M. Petrivs'kyĩ in Winnipeg]. VIL'N SLOVO (July 28, 1973): 2.

5006 Kysilevs'kyĩ, Volodymyr ĨU. "Kil'ka sliv pro Mykhaĩla Petrivs'koho *Mriï sl'ozamy oblyti*" [A Few Words about *Mriï sl'ozamy oblyti,* by Mykhaĩlo Petrivs'kyĩ]. UKR HOLOS (Aug. 22, 1973): 2. Reprinted in VIL'N SLOVO (Sept. 1 and 8, 1973): 7 in each issue.

5007 Makaryk, Iryna. "Dvi novi knyzhky pro zhyttĩã na zakhodi Kanady" [Two New Books about Life in Western Canada]. UKR HOLOS (Apr. 10, 1974): 9. [Review of *Mriï sl'ozamy oblyti.]*

5008 "Mykhaĭlo Petrivs'kyĭ (Narys zhyttĭâ)" [Mykhaĭlo Petrivs'kyĭ (Biographical Sketch)]. In *Narodnyĭ Iliŭstrovanyĭ Kaliendar Kanadaiĭs'koho Farmera na rik 1934.* Winnipeg: Kanadiĭs'kyĭ Farmer, 1933) pp. 97-98.

5009 Vorsklo, Vira. "Do tvorchosty M. Petrivs'koho" [The Creative Talent of M. Petrivs'kyĭ]. VIL'N SLOVO (March 2, 1974): 7.

5010 Vorsklo, Vira. "Na kanads'kiĭ zemli" [On Canadian Soil]. NOV SHLIAKH (Nov. 3, 1973): 8. [Review of *Mriĭ sl'ozamy oblyti.*]

PIHICHYN, Petro

5011 *ĬAnychary: Statti i parodiĭ [The Janissaries: Articles and Parodies].* Winnipeg: Osnova, 1967. 48 pp. (Ukraïns'ka Seriĭâ No. 1) A play and humorous articles.

PODVORNĬAK, Mykhaĭlo (1908-   )
Poet, short story writer, novelist. His writings depict the sufferings of life. Christian philosophy and evangelism are the main ingredients of his work.

5012 *Na shlĭâkhu zhyttĭâ: Zbirka khrystiyans'kykh virshiv i opovidan' [On Life's Road: A Collection of Religious Poems and Short Stories].* Winnipeg: Doroha Pravdy, 1953. 126 pp. Chicago: Ukrainian Mission Bible Society, 1951. 127 pp. Poems and short stories.

5013 *Zelenyĭ haĭ [The Green Grove].* Winnipeg: Doroha Pravdy, 1959. 199 pp. Short stories.

5014 *Nebesnyi dim [Heavenly Home].* Winnipeg: Doroha Pravdy, 1965. 240 pp. (Doroha Pravdy No. 33) Novel.

5015 *Bozhyi spokiĭ: Opovidannĭâ/The Peace of God: Short Stories.* Winnipeg-Chicago: Doroha Pravdy, 1966. 207 pp. (Doroha Pravdy No. 35) Novel.

5016 *Nedospivana pisnĭâ: Povist' [The Unfinished Song: A Novel].* Winnipeg: Doroha Pravdy, 1967. 348 pp. (Doroha Pravdy No. 37) Novel.

5017 *Vidpavshi: Opovidannĭâ [The Renegade: Short Stories].* Winnipeg: Doroha Pravdy, 1968. 31 pp. (Doroha Pravdy No. 39) Story.

5018 *Zapashnist' polĭâ: Opovidannĭâ/Fragrance of the Field: Short Stories.* Winnipeg-Chicago: Doroha Pravdy, 1971. 199. pp. (Doroha Pravdy No. 45) Short stories.

5019 *Zolota osin': Opovidannia/Golden Autumn: Short Stories.* Winnipeg-Toronto: Doroha Pravdy, 1974. 145 pp. (Doroha Pravdy No. 54) Short stories.

5020 *Daleki berehy: Opovidannia [Faraway Shores: Short Stories].* Korntal, Germany: Licht in Osten, 1975. 149 pp. Short stories.

5021 *Kvity na kameni: Povist' [Flowers on Stone: Novel].* Winnipeg: Nakladom khrystians'koho vyd-va Doroha Pravdy, 1976. 262 pp. Novel.

5022 *Persha lĭûbov. Povist' [The First Love. A Novel].* Toronto: Doroha Pravdy, 1986. 179 pp. Novel.

Writing about:

377

5023   Kerch, Oksana. Review of M. Podvorniak's poetry. UKR KNYHA 2, no. 2 (1972): 53-54.

POLOWY, Hannah (1928-   )

5024   *Adam's Sons*, with Mitch Sago. Toronto: Ukrainian Canadian, 1969. 110 pp. Play.
[A stage play based on Ol'ga Kobyns'ka's *Zemlia*.]

PROKOLUPIĬ, O., pseud. (Real name: KRAT, Pavlo)

5025   *Lubens'kyĭ monastyr: Veseli opovidannîa [The Lubni Monastery: Humorous Short Stories]*. [n.p.]
1917. Short stories.
[Lubni is a town in Ukraine.]

5026   *Popadîa v zil'nytsi [A Priest's Wife in the Herb Storage]*. Toronto: Robitnyche Slovo, 1918. 32 pp.
Story.

PRYCHODKO, Nicholas (i.e. PRYKHOD'KO, Mykola) (1904-1980)

5027   *Dalekymy dorohamy: Povist' dlia doroslykh [Along Distant Paths: Novel]*. Toronto: Vil'ne Slovo,
1960-1961. 2 v. 288 and 294 pp. respectively. Novel.

5028   *Goodbye Siberia*. Markham, Ont.: Simon & Schuster of Canada, 1976. 346 pp. Novel.

PYLYPENKO, P., pseud. (Real name: OSTAPCHUK, Pylyp) (1898-1967)
An author and stage producer, he was noted for organizing and directing many plays and vocal ensembles in
Winnipeg.

5029   *C͡Hudovyĭ zîat' [The Wonderful Son-in-Law]*. Winnipeg: Promin', 1932. 18 pp. Play.

5030   *Slovo îak horobets': Tragi-komedîa na odnu diîu [A Spoken Word is Like a Bird in Flight: Tragi-
comedy in One Act]*. Winnipeg: Promin', 1932. 16 pp. Play.

5031   *Soviets'kyĭ rozvid [Soviet Divorce]*. Winnipeg: Promin', 1932. 22 pp. Play.

5032   *Svoiĭ do svoho: Komedîa na odnu diîu [To Each His Own Kind: Comedy in One Act]*. [N.p.]: The
Author, 1936. 18 pp. Play.

5033   *Smert' komisara Skrypnyka abo Holod na Ukraïni: Istorychna drama na 3 diï [The Death of
Comissar Skrypnyk or Hunger in Ukraine: An Historical Drama in 3 Acts]*. Winnipeg: Ukraïns'ka
Knyharnia [n.d.] 58 pp. Play.

5034   *Svyshchemo na krizu: Komedîa na odnu diîu: Diîet'sîa v kanadiĭs'komu misti pidchas krizy [The
Depression be Damned: Comedy in One Act about Life in a Canadian City during the Depression]*.
[N.p., n.d., n.p.] 27 pp. Play.

5035   *Za zhenykhamy: Komedîa na odnu diîu [Pursuing Suitors: A Comedy in One Act]*. [N.p.] The
Author, 1936. 21 pp. Play.

PYROHIVS'KYĬ, M.

5036   *Lev i krilyk: Kazka didusîa ĬAkyma [The Lion and the Rabbit: A Story of Grandfather ĬAkym]*.
Winnipeg: Promin', 1927. 30 pp. (Kanadyĭs'ka Biblioteka No. 17) Story.

RIĬ, Martselîa   see CHORNOOKA, Halîa

RIPETS'KYĬ, Nestor (1919-1974)
Born in Ukraine, emigrated to Canada after the war. Originally a poet, he wrote mostly prose after his arrival in Canada.

5037   *K͡Hvyli shuka͡ût berehiv [Waves Seek the Shores].* Toronto, 1954. Novel.

5038   *Sontse skhodyt' iz zakhodu [The Sun Rises from the West].* Toronto: Arka, 1954. 119 pp. Novel.

5039   *R 33: Opovidann͡ia/R 33: Short Stories.* Toronto: Homin Ukraïny, 1967. 224 pp. Short stories.

5040   *Pisnii dalekykh ostroviv: Perespivy z iapons'koï liryky [Songs of Distant Isles: Adaptations from the Japanese].* Toronto: ADUK, 1969. 45 pp. Poems.

Writing about:

5041   "Vechir v shanu N. Ripets'koho" [An Evening in Honour of N. Ripets'kyĭ]. NOVI DNI (June 8, 1974): 1.

ROĬENKO, Petro (1926-   )

5042   *Velyka Li͡udyna ta inshi tvory/Great Man and Other Writings.* Toronto: Liubystok, 1973. 144 pp. Short stories.

5043   *Znavisnili dni/Enraged Days.* Toronto: The Author, 1973. 80 pp. Story.

5044   *Homin voli [Freedom's Echo].* Toronto: Liubystok, 1975. 125 pp. Novel.
[Includes bibliography.]

Writings about:

5045   Kukhar, Roman. Review of *Znavisnili dni.* UKR KNYHA 4, no. 3 (1974): 91-92.

5046   Pazun͡iak, N. Review of *Znavisnili dni* and *Velyka Liudyna ta inshi tvory.* UKR KNYHA 3, no. 3/4 (1973): 96-97.

5047   "Pratsi Petra Roi͡enka" [The Works of Petro Roienko]. In *Znavisnili dni.* (Toronto: The Author, 1973) pp. 79-80.

ROMEN, Levko, pseud. (Real name: KOVAL'S'KYĬ, S.) (1893-1981)
Poet, novelist, playwright. In addition to creative literature, he has also published extensively in literary criticism and philology.

5048   *Peredhrimia: Poeziï [Before the Thunderstorm: Poems].* Philadelphia, 1953. 63 pp. Poems.

5049   *Poemy [Poems].* Toronto: Ĭ͡Evshan-Zilli͡a, 1956. 72 pp. Poems.

5050   *Z͡Hovtosyl: Dramatychna piesa iz diï UPA [Z͡Hovtosyl: A Dramatic Play on the Ukrainian Insurgent Army].* Edmonton: Slavuta, 1965. 35 pp. Play.

5051   *Dub-Nelyn [The Holm-oak].* London, Ont.: Svitannia, 1969. 80 pp.

5052   *Pol͡iaryzovane. Posmertne Vydann͡ia [Poldrized. Posthumous Edition].* Toronto: Ĭ͡E. Lohaza, 1981. 116 pp.

Writings about:

5053 "Avtors'kyĭ vechir pys'mennykiv Levka Romena i Larysy Murovych" [A Literary Evening for the Writers Levko Romen and Larysa Murovych]. KAN FARM (Dec. 6, 1971): 13.

5054 "Kil'ka sliv pro avtora" [A Few Words about the Author]. In *Dub-Nelyn*. (London, Ont.: Svitanni͡a, 1969) p. 79.

5055 "Levko Romen i Larysa Murovych - poety 'Svitanni͡a': Poezii͡a Levka Romena i Larysy Murovych" [Levko Romen and Larysa Murovych - Poets of 'Svitanni͡a': The Poetry of Levko Romen and Larysa Murovych]. LIT MYST (December 1971): 2.

5056 Slavutych, I͡Ar. "Levko Romen" [Levko Romen]. In *Poliaryzovane* . (Toronto: IE. Lohaza, 1981) pp. 5-13.

5057 Slavutych, I͡Ar. "Nelyniaiuchi barvy slova" [The Unfading Colours of the Word]. PIVN SIAĬV 5 (1971): 174-76.
[Review of *Dub-Nelyn*.]

SAMCHUK, Ulas (1905-1987)

One of the most influential novelists among Ukrainian authors. Born in Ukraine and came to Canada in 1948. He published several novels in his native language prior to his arrival in this country, including *Mariia, Youth of Vasyl' Sheremeta, The Hills Speak* and *Kulak.* Much of his recent writings are related to life in Canada. Received Shevchenko Gold Medal from T. Shevchenko Foundation in Winnipeg.

5058 *Temnota: Roman u 2-okh chastynakh/Darkness: A Novel.* New York: Ukraïns'ka Vil'na Akademii͡a Nauk u SSHA, 1957. 495 pp. Novel.

5059 *Na tverdiĭ zemli: Roman [On Solid Ground: A Novel].* Toronto: Ukraïns'ka Kredytova Spilka, 1963. 390 pp. Autobiographical novel.

5060 *Na bilomu koni. Spomyny i vrazhenni͡a [Riding the White Horse: Memoirs].* Winnipeg: Volyn', 1972. 249 pp. Memoirs.

5061 *Na koni voronomu: Spomyny i vrazhenni͡a [On the Black Horse: Reminiscences and Recollections].* Winnipeg: Vyd. t-va Volyn', 1975. 360 pp. Memoirs.

5062 *Pli͡aneta Di-Pi. Notatky ĭ lysty [The Planet D.P.: Sketches and Letters].* Winnipeg: Volyn', 1979. 354 pp. Stories.

5063 *Volyn'. Roman-khronika u tr'okh chastynakh.* 3rd ed. Toronto: Kyiv, 1965-1969. 3 v. 323, 398, and 395 pp. respectively.

5064 *Vtecha vid sebe [Escape from Himself].* Winnipeg: Volyn', 1982. 429 pp. Novel.

Writings about:

5065 Boĭtsun, Anna. "Tretiĭ tom *Ostu* U. Samchuka" [U. Samchuk's Third Volume *Ostu*]. AMERYKA (Dec. 13, 1983)

5066 Chub, Dmytro. "Novyĭ tvir Ulasa Samchuka" [Ulas Samchuk's New Literary Work]. NOVI DNI 31 (April 1980): 26-27.

5067 Harasevych, Mariîa "Shyrokyî pys'mennyts'kyî diîapazon U. Samchuka" [The Versatile Literary Activity of U. Samchuk]. DZVONY No. 3-4 (1978): 55-74.

5068 Horokhovych, T. "Ulas Samchuk: fenomen dukhovosty volyns'koho sela" [Ulas Samchuk, a Phenomenon of the Wolynian Villages Spirit]. NOVI DNI 31 (December 1980): 9-12.

5069 Klynovyî, IUriî. "Ulas Samchuk" [Ulas Samchuk]. In his *Moïm synam, moïm pryiateliam.* (Edmonton: Slovo, 1981): 415-30.

5070 Kopac'h, O ."Hlybynnyî strum zhyttîa" [Deep Stream of Life]. NOV SHLIAKH (Feb. 2, 1980) [Review of *Plianeta Di-Pi.*]

5071 Korovyts'kyî, I. "Chotyry roky v istoriî plîanety" SUCHASNIST' 20 (November 1980): 168-75. [Review of *Plianeta Di-Pi.*]

5072 "Obhovorennîa novoho romanu Ulasa Samchuka" [Review of Ulas Samchuk's New Novel]. UKR HOLOS (Jan. 24, 1968): 7.

5073 Shevel'ov, IUriî. "Spalakhy v temriavi, z temriavy, v temriavu: Memuary" SUCHASNIST' 20 (November 1980): 64-68.
[Review of *Plianeta Di-Pi.*]

5074 Tarnavs'kyî, Ostap. "Ulas Samchuk - prozaïk" [Ulas Samchuk - Prose Writer]. NOVI DNI 36 (March 1985): 6-9.

5075 "U 75-richchîa U. Samchuka" [On U. Samchuk's 75th Birthday]. NOV SHLIAKH (Feb. 16, 1980)

5076 Vlasenko-Boîtsun, A. "Khroniky, romany î memuary Ulasa Samchuka" [Chronicles, Novels and Memoirs of Ulas Samchuk]. SVOBODA (March 15-21, 1980)

5077 Zhyla, Volodymyr. "Chy zdobuto svitovu pozytsiiu?" [Is a Wolrd Position Achieved?] PIVN SIAÏV 2 (1965): 145-49.

SEMCHUK, Stepan (1898-1984)

Born in Lviv, West Ukraine. Emigrated to Canada in 1923 as a Roman Catholic Priest and an established author. In Canada he organized the Ukrainian Catholic Brotherhood and edited its many publications. His stories and poems depict Ukrainian life in Canada. Author of *Outline of Ukrainian Literature,* 1948.

5078 *Fanfary: Poemy [Fanfares: Poems]* Chicago, 1931. Poems.

5079 *Kanadiîs'ka rapsodiia: Poeziia i proza [Canadian Rhapsody: Poetry and Prose].* Winnipeg-Yorkton: The Author, 1959. 132 pp. Poems.

5080 *Refliekciî Poeziî knyzhka piata [Reflections: Poetry - Book Five].* Winnipeg, 1965. 52 pp. Poems.

5081 *Svitlist' dumky: Poeziî knyzhka desîata [Majesty of Thought: Poetry - Tenth Book].* Winnipeg, 1966. 49 pp. Poems.

5082 *ZHerela: Poeziî knyzhka shesta [Spring: Poetry - Book Six].* Winnipeg, 1966. 49 pp. Poems.

5083 *Poemy: Poeziî knizhka sema [Poems: Seventh Book of Poetry].* Winnipeg, 1967. 67 pp. Poems.

5084 *Sotvorennĭa: Poeziĭ knyzhka vos'ma [Creation: Poetry - Eighth Book].* Winnipeg, 1968. 75 pp. Poems.

5085 *Poezĭa i proza [Poetry and prose: Ninth Book.]* Winnipeg, 1969. 79 pp. Poems.

5086 *Navkolo svita: Liryka [Around the World: Lyrics].* Winnipeg, 1971. vol. ll, 77 pp. Poems.

5087 *Miĭ molytvennykh/My Prayerbook.* Winnipeg, 1974. 84 pp. Poems and short narratives. [Bilingual edition with Ukrainian original and English translation by I van Mel'nyk.]

Writings about:

5088 "Desĭata knyzhka virshiv Semchuka" [The Tenth Book of Verse by Semchuk]. UKR VISTI (Nov. 6, 1969): 4.
[Review of *Svitlist' dumky.*]

5089 "Zasluzhenyĭ svĭashchynyk o. Semchuk" [Honoured Priest - Father S. Semchuk]. UKR VISTI (Jan. 2, 1969): 31 Signed: P.S.

SEMENĬUK, Leonid

5090 *Kanada i my: Rozkazy [Canada and Us: Short Stories].* London, Ont.: Zaria, 1975. ll7 pp. Short stories.

SHANKOVS'KYĬ, Ihor (1931-   )

5091 *Kvitneva dan': Zbirka poeziĭ [April Tribute: A Collection of Poetry].* Munich: Dniprova Khvylia, 1958. ll4 pp. Poems.

5092 *Dysonansy [Dissonances].* Philadelphia: Kyïv, 1960. 93 pp. Poems.

5093 *Korotke lito [The Short Summer],* with a foreword by Rostyslav I Endyk. Edmonton: Ukraïns'ka Knyharnia, 1970. ll4 pp. Poems.

Writings about:

5094 Nykolyn, B. "Virshi i poeziĭ [Verses and Poetry]. UKR KNYHA 1, no. 4 (1971): 110-11.

5095 "Try poety - try poetychni zbirky" [Three Poets - Three Collections of Poetry]. UKR VISTI (Nov. 19, 1970): 2-3.
[Review of *Korotke lito.*]

SHARYK, Mykhaĭlo (1901-   )

5096 *Rozsypani perly [Scattered Pearls].* Toronto, 1965. Poems.

Writing about:

5097 Mandryka, M.I. "ZHaha pisennoho slova: (Z pryvodu dvokh zbirok virshiv" [Ardour of the Musical Word: (On Two Collections of Poetry)]. NOV SHLI AKH (Jan. 7, 1966): 29-30.
[Review of *Rozsypani perly.*]

SHEVCHUK, Tetĭana (1904-   )

Poet, teacher. Born in Sushno, Ukraine. Attended the Peter Mohyla Institute in Saskatoon and Queen's University. Published poetry in Ukrainian Canadian newspapers and periodicals since 1922. Her English writings have been published in the *Winnipeg Free Press*, *Farmer*, and *Youth of Today*. She lives in the U.S.A.

5098 *Probudz͡hennia dukha [Awakening of the Soul]*, with a foreword by Natalka Kohus'ka. Winnipeg: The Author, 1961. 124 pp. Poems.

5099 *Na prestil maĭbutnikh dniv: Poeziï [An Overture to Future Days: Poems]*. Winnipeg: The Author, 1964. 79 pp. 2nd ed. 1980.

Writings about:

5100 Slavutych, I͡Ar. "Spraha rozdumu" [The Thirst of Reason]. PI VN SI AĬV V (1971): 182.
[Review of *Na prestil maĭbutnikh dniv.*]

5101 Stechyshyn, S. "Poiava ridkisnoï knyz͡hky" [The Appearance of a Rare Book]. PROMIN' 2, no. 5 (1961): 15-16.
[Review of *Probudz͡hennia dukha.*]

SHKVAROK, I͡Urko (1887-1950)

5102 *Istorii͡a Rusy-Ukraïny virshamy [History of Rus'-Ukraine Versified]*. Winnipeg: Kanadyĭs'kyĭ Rusyn, 1918. 39 pp. Poem.

Writing about:

5103 "Shkvarok, I͡Urko" [Shkvarok, I͡Urko]. UKR VISTI (Edmonton, March 26, 1981)

SKLEPOVYCH, Vasyl' T.

5104 *Hory klychut' [The Call of the Mountains]*. Winnipeg: Trident Press, 1975. 294 pp. Short stories.

5105 *Shche vatra palai͡e: Istorychna povist' [The Bonfire is Still Alive: Historical Novel]*. Winnipeg: Tryzub, 1979. 178 pp. Novel.

Writing about:

5106 Andrushyshen, C.H. Review of *Hory klychut'*. UNIV TOR Q 45 (1975-76): 448-49.

SKORYPS'KYĬ, Volodymyr (1921-1985)

5107 *Moi͡a oseli͡a: Poeziï [My Home: Poetry]*. Edmonton, 1954. 96 pp. Poems.

5108 *U dorozi: Poeziï [Along the Road: Poems]*. Edmonton: The Author, 1957. 56 pp. Poems.

5109 *Bez ridnoho poroha: Poemy [The Homeless: Poetry]*. Edmonton: Ukrainian War Veterans' Association, 1958. 62 pp. Poems.

5110 *Iz dzherela: Poeziï [From the Source: Poetry]*. Toronto: The Author, 1961. 78 pp. Poems.

5111 *Nad mohyloi͡u: Vinok sonetiv [At the Grave: Sonnets]*. Toronto, 1963. 21 pp. Poems.

5112 *Aĭstry nevidtsvili : Poeziï [Asters still Blooming: Poetry]*. Toronto, 1972. 54 pp. Poems.

5113 *Spokonvichni luny: legendy i mity [Eternal Echoes: Legends and Myths].* Toronto: Obiednannīa ukraïns'kykh pys'mennykiv Slovo, 1977. 70 pp. Legends.

Writings about:

5114 *Kerch, Oksana.* "Osinni nastroï [Autumn Moods]. UKR KNYHA 2, no. 1 (1972): 21.
(Review of *Aīstry nevidtsvili.*]

5115 Slavutych, Ī︠A︡r. "Sproba myslyty" [An Endeavour to Reason]. PIVN SIAĪV 5 (1972): 184-85.
[Review of *Iz dzherela.*]

5116 Stepanī︠u︡k, S. Review of *Aīstry nevidtsvili.* UKR VISTI (Feb. 17, 1972): 2.

SLAVUTYCH, Ī︠A︡r (i.e. Yar) (1918-   )
Poet, educator, scholar and publisher. Born in Southern Ukraine, left his homeland during the war and came to the U.S.A. in 1949 and then to Canada in 1960. As a Professor of Slavic Studies at the University of Alberta, he has published a series of grammar books for Ukrainian students, edited anthologies, compiled bibliographies, almanacs and symposia, written numerous research papers and book reviews, and established a publishing firm: Slavuta Publishers. In 1983, he was awarded the title of Ukrainian Poet Laureate Abroad, in addition to five other literary prizes received over the years. Recipient of the Shevchenko Gold Medal and a Canada Council Scholarship Award. He lives in Edmonton.

5117 *Oasis: Selected Poems,* translated from the Ukrainian by Morse Manly in cooperation with the author. Foreword by J.B. Rudnyćkyj. New York: Vantage Press, 1959. 63 pp.
[Includes bibliography.]

5118 *Oaza: Piata zbirka poeziï [Oasis: Fifth Collection of Poetry].* Edmonton: Slavuta, 1960. 63 pp. Poems.

5119 *Maīestat: SHosta zbirka poeziï/Majesty (Ukrainian Poems).* Edmonton: Slavuta, 1962. 45 pp. Poems.
[Includes bibliography, pp. 47-48.]

5120 *Trofeï: 1938-1963 [Trophies: 1938-1963].* Edmonton: Slavuta, 1963. 320 pp. Poems.
[Includes bibliography and "Pochatok zhyttiepysu," [The Beginning of Autobiography], pp. 303-12.]

5121 *Zavoīovnyky preriï: S'oma zbirka poeziï [The Conquerors of the Prairies: Poetry].* Edmonton: Slavuta, 1968. 48 pp. Poems.
[Translated into English.]

5122 *Mudroshchi mandriv: Vos'ma zbirka poeziï [The Pilgrim's Wisdom: Ukrainian Poems].* Edmonton: Slavuta, 1972. 96 pp. Poems.
[Includes bibliography, pp. 95-96.]

5123 *The Conquerors of the Prairies,* translated from the Ukrainian by R.H. Morrison. Edmonton: Slavuta Publishers, 1974. Parallel text edition. A new, enlarged edition published in 1984. Ibid. 128 pp. Poems.

5124 *L'Oiseau de feu: poèmes choisis,* traduit et adapté par René Coulet du Card. Edmonton: Éd. Deux Mondes et Slavuta Publishers, 1976. 50 pp. Poèmes.

5125 *Zibrani tvory, 1938-1978 [Collected Works, 1938-1978].* Edmonton: Slavuta, 1978. 408 pp.

[Includes the epic poem "Moia doba," published for the first time. Bibliography, p. 408. Awarded I. Franko's first prize (1982).] Poems.

5126 *Válogatott versek [Selected Poems]*, translated into Hungarian by Sándor Domokos, with an introduction by János Miska. Edmonton: Hungarian Cultural Society, 1983 32 pp. ports.

5127 *ZHyvi smoloskypy: Deviãta zbirka poeziĭ [Living Torches: Ninth Collection of Poetry]*, introduction by Volodymyr ZHyla. Edmonton: Slavuta, 1983. 125 pp. Poems.
[Awarded I. Franko's second prize (1986).

5128 *Izbrannoe [Selected Poems]*, translated into Russian by Ûriĭ Pustovoĭtov. Jerusalem: Jewish-Ukrainian Society, 1986. 99 pp. Poems.

Writings about:

5129 Andrusyshen, C.H. "Knyhy, vydani v Kanadi" [Books in Canada]. In *Zakhidn' okanadskyĭ zbirnyk [Western Canadian Collected Papers].* (Edmonton: Shevchenko Scientific Society, 1975) vol. 2, pp. 182-83.
[Review of *Mudroshchi mandriv.*]

5130 Bodnaruk, Ivan. "Na marginesi *Zibranykh tvoriv*, 1938-1978, Îara Slavutycha" [On the Margins of I Ar Slavutych's Collected Works, 1938-1978]. DZVONY No. 1-2 (1980): 149-56.

5131 Boĭko, Ûriĭ. "Notatky na berehakh poeziĭ ÎA. Slavutycha [Notes on the Poetry of ÎAr Slavutych]. In his *Vybrane*. (Munich: Ukraïns'ke Vydavnytstvo, 1974) vol. 2, pp. 205-12.
[Review of *Trofeĭ.*]

5132 Buĭniak, Orest. "Mors'ka tematyka u tvorchosti ÎAra Slavutycha" [Naval Themes in Yar Slavutych's Poetry]. In *Tvorchist' ÎAra Slavutycha*. (Edmonton: Vydannia ÎUvileĭnovo Komitetu, 1978) pp. 116-121.

5133 Buyniak, Victor. "Living Torches." SMOLOSKYP, 7, no. 27 (1985): 10.
[Review of *ZHyvi smoloskypy.*]

5134 Chopyk, Bohdan. "Epitet u poeziĭ ÎAra Slavutycha" [Epithets in the Poetry of ÎAr Slavutych]. In *Zbirnyk na poshanu Volodymyra Ianeva*. (Munich: Ukrainian Free University, 1983) pp. 874-84.

5135 Chopyk, Dan B. "In Search of the Inspiring Past." In *Tvorchist' ÎAra Slavutycha...* (Edmonton: Vydannia ÎUvileĭnovo Komitetu, 1978) pp. 185-95.

5136 Chopyk, Dan B. "Neolohizmy ÎAra Slavutycha" [Neologism of Yar Slavutych]. In *Tvorchist' ÎAra Slavutycha....* pp. 79-88.

5137 Chub, Dmytro. "ÎAr Slavutych: Biohrafichno-literaturnyĭ portret" [ÎAr Slavutych: A Biographical-literary portrait]. In his *U dzerkali zhyttîã ĭ literatry.* (Melbourne: Lastivka, 1982) pp. 163-70.

5138 Chub, Dmytro. "Mudrist' i mystetstvo" [Wisdom and Art]. VIL'N DUM (March 4, 1962)
[Review of *Oaza.*]

5139 Derzhavyn, Volodymyr. "Poeziã ÎAra Slavutycha" [ÎAr Slavutych's Poetry]. In *Tvorchist' ÎAra Slavutycha*. (Edmonton: Vidannia ÎUvileĭnovo Komitetu, 1978) pp. 22-27.

5140 Gard, René Coulet du. "La poésie de Yar Slavutych." In *Tvorchist' ÎAra Slavutycha...* (Edmonton: Vydannia ÎUvileĭnovo Komitetu, 1978) pp. 207-11.

5141 Gard, René Coulet du. "Mazeppa de Victor Hugo et le neoromantisme de Yar Slavutych." *L'Ukraine et la France au XIXe siècle.* (Paris: Université de la Sorbonne Nouvelle, 1987) pp. 45-55.

5142 Harasevych, Mariîa. "Poetychna tvorchist' na etapakh zhyttîâ" [Poetical Creativity throughout a Lifetime]. DZVONY No. 3-4 (1980): 57-74.

5143 Holubenko, Serhiĭ. "Poetychni portrety dysydentiv" [Poetic Portraits of the Freedom Fighters]. UKR VISTI (Detroit, Feb. 10, 1985)
[Review of *ZHyvi smoloskypy.*]

5144 ÎUrchenko, Valentyna. "Tvorchyĭ darunok" [Creative Gift]. SVOBODA (June 12-13, 1984)
[Review of *The Conquerors of the Prairies.*]

5145 Keĭvan, Ivan. "Poetovi ÎArovi Slavutychevi - 50 rokiv" [50th Anniversary of the Poet ÎAr Slavutych]. UKR VISTI (Detroit, Feb. 1, 1968): 3.

5146 Keĭvan, Ivan. "V 50-richchîâ z dnia narodzhennîâ prof. ÎAra Slavutycha" [Prof. ÎAr Slavutych's 50th Birthday]. UKR HOLOS (Feb. 21, 1968): 6.

5147 Keĭvan, Ivan. "Zolotyĭ iuvileĭ ÎAra Slavutycha" [The Golden Jubilee of IAr Slavutych]. UKR DUM (Feb. 29, 1968)

5148 Kerch, Oksana. "Tryvalyĭ pamîâtnyk" [A Lasting Monument]. META (November 1983): 6.
[Review of *Zibrani tvory.*]

5149 Keywan, Zonîâ. Review of *The Conquerors of the Prairies.* CAN LIT No. 77 (1978): 113-16.

5150 Keywan, Zonîâ. "Ukrainian Poetry in Canada." In *Tvorchist' ÎAra Slavutycha....* (Edmonton: Vydannîâ ÎUvileĭnovo Komitetu, 1978) pp. 196-99.
[Review of *The Conquerors of the Prairies.*]

5151 Kovaluk, Markian. "Zasluzhena emerytura" [A Well-deserved Emeritus]. SVOBODA (Aug. 23-24, 1984)

5152 Kovshun, M. "Mistsîâmy zaporoz'kymy" [Along Zaporozhian Places]. UKR HOLOS (Aug. 7-11, 1986): 7, 2-3.

5153 Kyslytsîâ, Dmytro. "Khronika-epopeîâ pro pivstolittîâ" [Chronicles of a Half-Century]. UKR VISTI (Detroit, Sept. 24- Oct. 1, 1980)
[Review of *Moîâ doba.*]

5154 Kyslytsîâ, Dmytro. "Slavutycheva mova" [The Language of Y. Slavutych]. In *Tvorchits' ÎAra Slavutycha ....* (Edmonton: Vidannîâ ÎUvileĭnovo Komitetu, 1978): 97-104.

5155 Maliar, Pavlo. "Pidsumok tvorchosty poeta" [Achievements of a Poet]. NOVI DNI 17 (January 1966): 12-15.

5156 Malycky, Alexander. "Indiîâns'ka tematyka v poeziî ÎAra Slavutycha" [Indian Themes in ÎAr Slavutych's Poetry]. In *Tvorchist' ÎAra Slavutycha.....* (Edmonton: Vydannîâ ÎUvileĭnovo Komitetu, 1978) pp. 122-25.

5157 Mandryka, M.I. "Yar Slavutych." In his *History of Ukrainian Literature in Canada.* (Winnipeg: UVAN, 1968) pp. 163-68.

5158 Mazepa, Bohdan. "Liryka ÎAra Slavutycha: Do 25-richchia literaturnoï tvorchosty" [The Lyric Poetry of ÎAr Slavutych: To Commemorate the 25th Anniversary of his Literary Activity]. UKR VISTI (Edmonton) (Apr. 23, 1964)

5159 Miska, János. "Elószó" [Foreword]. In *Válogatott versek.* (Edmonton: Hungarian Cultural Society of Edmonton and Slavuta Publishers, 1983) pp. 5-8.

5160 Moroz, Valentyn. "Holos hlybyn" [A Voice of Depth]. UKR VISTI (Detroit, Nov. 18, 1984) [Review of *ZHyvi smoloskypy.*]

5161 Movchan, ÎUlian. "Moia doba - nova poema ÎAra Slavutycha" [My Epoch - A New Poem by ÎAr Slavutych]. SVOBODA (June 14-15, 1978)

5162 Murovych, Larysa. "Sanskryts'ka symvolika v *Mudroshchakh mandriv* ÎAra Slavutycha" [Sanskrit Symbolism in ÎAr Slavutych's *Mudroshchi mandriv*] In *Tvorchist' ÎAra Slavutycha...* (Edmonton: Vydannia ÎUvileïnovo Komitetu, 1978) pp. 126-31.

5163 Murovych, Larysa. "Shukannîa slidiv otfsîa Honcharenka" [A Search for Rev. A. Honcharenko's Traces]. SVOBODA (Oct. 22, 1985): 2-3. [Review of *The Conquerors of the Prairies.*]

5164 Murovych, Larysa. "Zhinochi portrety u zbirtsi *ZHyvi smoloskypy* ÎAra Slavutycha" [Women Portraits in the *Living Torches* by ÎAr Slavutych]. HOMIN UKR (Dec. 5, 1984)

5165 Ovechko, Ivan. "SHCHodennyk mandrivnyka-poeta" [Diary of a Wondering Poet]. KAN FARM (Apr. 23, 1973): 12. [Review of *Mudroshchi mandriv.*]

5166 Pazuniak, Nataliia. Review of *ZHyvi smoloskypy.* SAMOSTIÏNA UKRAINA 39 no. 1 (1987): 68-75.

5167 Prokopiw, Orysia. "Yar Slavutych as a Translator of Shakespeare's Sonnets." In *Tvorchist' ÎAra Slavutycha...* (Edmonton: Vydannia ÎUvileïnovo Komitetu, 1978) pp. 200-06.

5168 Rakhmannyï, Roman. "Slidamy zavoïovnykiv preriï [In the Footsteps of the Conquerors of the Prairies]. UKR HOLOS (May 27, 1970): 4.

5169 Romanenchuk, Bohdan. "Kliasytsyst chy romantyk" [Classicist or Romanticist]. In *Tvorchist' ÎAra Slavutycha...* (Edmonton: Vydannia ÎUvileïnovo Komitetu, 1978) pp. 162-66.

5170 Romanenchuk, Bohdan. "Poetychna tvorchist' ÎAra Slavutycha" [The Poetry of ÎAr Slavutych]. NOVI DNI 2 (1950): 10-13, 23. Reprinted in *Tvorchist' ÎAra Slavutycha,* pp. 155-62.

5171 Romen, Levko. "SHosta zbirka poeziï ÎAra Slavutycha" [ÎAr Slavutych's Sixth Collection of Poetry]. VYZV SHLIAKH 10 (February 1963): 233-34.

5172 Rozumnyï, ÎAroslav. "Mizh shchyroïu intymnistïu i nadumanym optymizmom" [Between a Sincere Intimacy and Invented Optimism]. SUCHASNIST" 9, no. 12 (1969): 110-11.

5173 Rubchak, Bohdan. "Liudyna diï - lîudyna nauky - poet" [A Man of Action, a Scholar, and a Poet]. OVYD 13 (May-June 1962): 55-58.

5174   Rudnyćkyj, J.B. "Stylistychni funktsiï kanadyzmiv u poeziï Ĩara Slavutycha" [Stylistic Functions of Canadianisms in the Poetry of Yar Slavutych]. In *Tvorchist' ĨAra Slavutycha...* pp. 89-92.

5175· Sass, Sviãtoslav. "Khrystyians'ki motyvy u tvorchosti ĨAra Slavutycha" [Christian Motifs in the Works of ĨAr Slavutych]. In *Ukraïns'kyĭ pravoslavnyĭ kalendar na rik 1984.* (South Bound Brook) pp. 110-14.

5176   Shĉherbak, Mykola. "Koly slovo plomeniê" [When Words Burn Like a Flame." SVOBODA (Nov. 20, 1968)

5177   Shĉherbak, Mykola; Zhyla, V.T. *Polumiane slovo: Do 50-richchĩã ĨAra Slavutycha [The Burning Word: The Poetry of ĨAr Slavutych].* London: Ukraïns'ka Vydavnycha Spilka, 1969. 40 pp.

5178   Slavutych, Vira. *Bibliohrafiã pysan' pro ĨAra Slavutycha (1978-1985) [A Bibliography of the Writings of ĨAr Slavutych (1978-1985)].* Edmonton: Slavuta, 1985. 19 pp. 2nd enl. ed. 1978-1985. Ibid., 1986. 23 pp. 3rd enl. ed. 1978-1986. Ibid. 1987. 26 pp.
[Bound together with *Anotovana bibliohrafiã.*]

5179   Svaroh, Vadym. "Slavutych rosiïs'koiu movoiu" [Slavutych in Russian Translation]. UKR VISTI (Detroit) (Feb. 2, 1986): 3.

5180   *Tvorchist' ĨAra Slavutycha: statti i retsenziï. Uporiadkyvav Volodymyr Zhyla/ The Poetry of ĨAr Slavutych: Articles and Reviews,* compiled by Volodymyr T. Zyla. Edmonton: Vydannã ĨUvileĭnovo Komitetu, 1978. 431 pp.
[A collection of more than thirty papers and one hundred reviews in Ukrainian, English, French, and German about the poetry of ĨAr Slavutych.]

5181   Vlasenko-Boĭtsun, A. "Kanada i svit ochyma ukraïntsia" [Canada and the World in the Eyes of a Ukrainian]. NOVI DNI 24, no. 284 (1973): 23-24.
[Review of *Zavoĭovnyky preriï.* Also in LIT MYST (May 1974): 3.]

5182   Vlasenko-Boĭtsun, A. "Z kruhosvitn'oï podorozhi" [From a Global Journey]. UKR HOLOS 2, no. 3 (1972): 84-85.
[Review of *Mudroshchi mandriv.*]

5183   Volyniak, Petro. "ĨAr Slavutych" [ĨAr Slavutych]. NOVI DNI (May 1954): 2-3.

5184   Vorsklo, Vira. Review of *Zhyvi smoloskypy.* NOV SHLIAKH (March 16, 1985)

5185   Zhyla, Volodymyr. "Poeziã vyzvol'noï borot'by " [The Poetry of Liberation Struggles]. SVOBODA (July 31 - Aug. 1, 1984) Also VYZV SHLIAKH 37 (November 1984): 1393-97.

5186   Zhyla, Volodymyr. "Kyïv u poeziï ĨAra Slavutycha" [Kiev in the Poetry of ĨAr Slavutych]. In *Zbirnyk na poshanu Volodymyra ĨAneva.* (Munich: Ukrainian Free University, 1983): 409-17.

5187   Zhyla, Volodymyr. "Novi poetychni obriï" [New Poetic Horizons]. UKR HOLOS (Oct. 22, 1969): 7. [Reprinted in *Tvorchist' ĨAra Slavutycha...* pp. 93-96.]

5188   Zhyla, Volodymyr. Review of *Zavoĭovnyky preriï.* UKR HOLOS 16, no. 4 (1969): 92-93.

5189   Zhyla, Volodymyr. "Yar Slavutych: A Spiritual Aristocrat." In *Tvorchist' ĨAra Slavutycha...* (Edmonton: Vydannia ĨUvileĭnovo Komitetu, 1978) pp. 173-84.

5190   Zyla, Volodymyr (i.e. Zhyla). "Yar Slavutych's 'Moja doba' A Poem of Intense Personal Involvement." WORLD LIT TODAY 55 (1981): 420-22.

SMOTRYCH, Oleksander (1922-   )

5191   *Buttia. 16 nikomu nepotribnykh opovidan' [Life: 16 Stories No One Needs]*. Toronto: Novi Dni, 1973. 123 pp. Short stories.

5192   *Uzhynok [Harvest]*. Munich: Suchasnist', 1985. 116 pp. Poems.

5193   *Virshi [Poems]*.
[Contains ten booklets, mimeographed, not paginated, not dated.]

Writing about:

5194   Korovyts'kyĭ, I. "Lirnyk spivaie pro smert'." SUCHASNIST', 19 (June 1979): 117-22.

SOFRONIV-LEVYTS'KYĬ, Vasyl' (1899-1975)

5195   *ĨUnyĭ skomorokh: Piesy dlĩa diteĭ i molodi/The Young Scaramouch: Plays for Children and Young Adults*. Toronto, 1972. (Teatral'na Biblioteka No. 1) Plays.

5196   *Lypneva otruta: Vybrane/The Poison of July: Selected Short Stories*. Toronto: Novyĭ SHliakh, 1972. xxv, 236 pp. Short stories.

5197   *Pid veselym oborohom: Pĩesa dlĩa teatriv malykh form/Under the Jolly Roof: A Collection of Plays for Variety Shows*. Toronto: Komitet za amators'kyĭ teatr, 1974. 207 pp. (Teatral'na Biblioteka No. 3). Plays.

Writings about:

5198   Barahura, Volodymyr. "Teatr iunoho hliadacha" [A Young Viewer's Theatre]. NOV SHLIAKH (Feb. 9, 1974): 8.
[Review of *ĨUnyĭ skomorokh.*]

5199   Klymovs'kyĭ, I Ar. "'U pryrodi lypnia ie iakas' hrishna otruta...' (Do poĩavy 'Lypnevoĭ otruty' Vasylĩa Sofronova-Levyts'koho)" [In July's Nature is a Sinful Poison... (On the Release of *Lypneva otruta* by Vasyl' Sofroniv-Levyts'kyĭ]. NOV SHLIAKH (Sept. 2, 1972): 8.

5200   Klynovyĭ, ĨUriĭ. "Deshcho pro pryzabutoho maĭstra ukraĩns'koĭ noveli" [Some Remarks about a Forgotten Master of the Ukrainian Short Story]. In *Lypneva otruta...* (Toronto: Novyĭ SHliakh, 1972) pp. v-xxv.

5201   Kryvoruchko, A. "Avtors'kyĭ vechir V.S. Levyts'koho" [A Literary Evening for V.S. Levyts'kyĭ]. NOV SHLIAKH (March 18, 1972): 8.

5202   Kuz'movych, O. "Vasyl' Sofroniv-Levyts'kyĭ " [Vasyl' Sofroniv-Levyts'kyĭ]. ĨUNAK 11, no. 1 (1973): 6.

5203   Stefanyk, ĨU. "Vasyl' Sofroniv-Levyts'kyĭ - Novelist " [Vasyl' Sofroniv-Levyts'kyĭ - The Novelist]. SUCHASNIST' 12, no. 1 (1972): 51-62.

5204 Tarnavs'kyĭ, Ostap. "V poshukuvanni ukraïns'koï noveli: Na marginesi tvorchosty Vasylia Sofronova-Levyts'koho" [In Search of the Ukrainian Novella: On the Margin of Vasyl' Sofroniv-Levyts'kyĭ's Creativity]. SUCHASNIST' 13, no. 2 (1973): 44-49.

SOLĬANYCH, Dmytro (1874-1941)

Born in Ustĭâ, Ukraine. Came to Canada in 1903. He was noted for his activities in organizing gymnastic societies in the western provinces. His short novels show the influence of Vasyl' Stefanyk.

5205 *KHto vynuvatyĭ ta inshi opovidannĭâ z zhyttĭâ selĭânstva na Pokuttĭû [Who is Guilty and Other Stories from Village Life of Pokuttia].* Edmonton: Ivan Solianych, 1932. 161 pp. Short stories.

STAVNYCHKA, Vasyl'.

5206 *Zavzĭâtyĭ ĬUrko abo poshana do rodychiv [Stubborn ĬUrko or Respect for Parents].* Winnipeg: Promin' [n.d.]. 140 pp. Stories.

STECHYSHYN, Mykhaĭlo (1888-1964)

Former editor of *Ukrainian Voice.* Born in Ukraine. His writings were devoted to social injustices. An author of fables and short stories, he also made translations from English into Ukrainian.

5207 *Baĭky. Chastyna I [Fables. Part I].* Winnipeg, 1959. 188 pp. Stories.

Writing about:

5208 Slavutych, ĬAr. "Stechyshyn, Mykhaĭlo" [Stechyshyn, Mykhaĭlo]. In his *Ukraïns'ka poezĭâ v Kanadi.* (Edmonton: Slavuta, 1976) pp. 44-46.

STEP, Pavlo (1893-1965)

5209 *Braty: Kazka [Brothers: A Fairy-tale].* Toronto: Bat'kivshchyna, 1960. 38 pp. Children's story.

SYLENKO, Lev. T. see ORLYHORA, Lev. T.

TARASĬUK, Ilarion (1910-)

5210 *Na krylakh viry: Poeziï [On the Wings of Faith: Poems].* Winnipeg: Christian Press, 1962. 183 pp. Poems.

TARNOVYCH, ĬUlĭân see BESKYD-TARNOVYCH, ĬUlĭân

TERNENKO, P. see KRAT, Pavlo

TOCHYLO-KOLĬANKIVS'KYĬ, M.

5211 *Ambasadory: Satyry i humoresky [Ambassadors: Satirical Short Stories].* Toronto: My i svit, 1968. 114 pp. Short stories.

5212 *Tovpa. Feĭletony, humoresky, satyry [A People's Person. Satires and Other Humorous Writings].* Niagara Falls, Ont.: My i svit, 1979. 127 pp. Short stories.

TRETĬAK, Ol'ha

5213 *Pisen' moïkh uzory: Poeziï: (Deshcho z rodynnoho al'boma/De mes chansons, les plus belles images: Poésies en langue ukrainienne.* Montreal, 1972. 98 pp. Poems.

5214   *Lada: Poeziï/Lada: Poésies en langue ukrainienne.* Montreal, 1973. 103 pp. Poems. [Lada is the name of a pagan deity.]

5215   *Zori: Poeziï dlia diteï ta molodi/Étoiles: Poésies en langue ukrainienne.* Montreal, 1973. 105 pp. Poems.

5216   *Povir! [Trust me!]* Montreal, 1974. 101 pp. Poems.

5217   *Poltavshchyno moia! [My Poltava Region!].* Montreal, 1975. 105 pp. Poems

TRUKH, Andriï Hryhoriï (1894-1959)

Born in Ukraine. In addition to writing plays, he was noted for his essays and review articles on religious life in Canada.

5218   *Apostol liubovy: Stsenichnyï obrazok u 2 diiakh [dlia] Ukr. SHkolariv [Apostle of Love: A Dramatic Sketch in Two Acts for Ukrainian School Children].* Mundare, Alta.: Basilian Fathers' Press, 1958. 12 pp. Play.

TULEVITRIV, Vasyl' (1886-)

He was an army captain in the First World War before coming to Canada by way of the United States. Published poems and anecdotes in journals and newspapers.

5219   *Dumy i pisni [Musings and Songs].* Toronto: Ukrainian Publishing Co., 1938. 100 pp. Poems.

5220   *Taka ïi dolia: Drama z chasiv vyzvol'nykh zmahan' na Karpats'kiï Ukraïni v 1939 r. v 4-okh diiakh [Such is Her Destiny: Drama in 4 Acts about the Struggle for Freedom in the Carpathian Ukraine in 1939].* Hamilton, Ont., 1941. 28 pp. Play.

UKRAÏNETS', Ivan, pseud. (Real name: OHIIENKO, Ivan)

5221   *Za Ukraïnu: Drama na try diï [For Ukraine: A Drama in Three Acts].* Winnipeg: Nasha Kul'tura, 1951. 68 pp. Play.

VASKAN, Stepan

5222   *Danylyshyn i Bilas [Danylyshyn and Bilas].* Edmonton: Ivan Solianych, 1933. 27 pp. Play.

5223   *Borot'ba za Ukraïns'ku SHkolu v Halychyni: Drama v chotyr'okh diiakh [The Struggle for a Ukrainian School in Galicia: Drama in Four Acts].* [n.p., n.p.] 1939. 28 pp. Play.

VITER, Danko, pseud. (1916-1982) (Real name: MARYNIAK, Marta)

5224   *Daleki mandry: Povist' molodi/Wayfarers from Yonder: A Novel.* Toronto: The Author, 1973. 303 pp. Novel.

VOLKOV, Vitaliï (1900-1973)

5225   *Dovbush. Roman [Dovbush. A Novel].* Winnipeg: Tryzub, 1957. 304 pp. Historical novel.

VOLOKHATIUK, Taras D.   see KOMAR, Anton

VOLYNIAK, Petro, pseud. (Real name: CHECHET, Petro) (1907-1969)

Born in Ukraine, spent several years in the White Sea-Baltic N.K.V.D. concentration camp. Escaped from the USSR during Wold War II to Germany, where he started *Novi Dni*, now published in Toronto, a literary forum to many writers and poets. He has published stories and literary reviews in such collections as *The Land Beckons*, *Pid Kizhurtom* and *Kuban The Ukrainian Land, the Land of the Cossacks*.

5226   *Pohovorymo vidverto. Vibrani, statti ĭ opovidannia [Let's Speak Openly. Selected Articles and Stories]*   Toronto: Novi Dni, 1975. 662 pp. Stories, articles.

Writings about:

5227   Konoval, Oleksiĭ. "Pomer nash redaktor i pryiatel'" [Our Editor and Friend has Passed Away]. NOVI DNI 20 (April 1969): 5-6.

5228   Oleksandriv, Borys. "Pamiati nezabutn'oho redaktora" [In Memory of an Unforgettable Editor]. NOVI DNI 2) (April 1969): 7-8.

5229   Stefanyk, I͡U. "Petro Volyni͡ak (1907-1969)" [Petro Volyniak (1907-1969)]. PIVN SIAĬV V (1971): 170-71.

5230   "Zamist' proshchal'noĭ promovy nad hrobom moho druha, vykhovnyka i doradnyka sl. p. Petra Voluni͡aka-CHeĉheta" [In Lieu of a Parting Speech at the Grave of My Friend, Teacher and Adviser - Petro Volyniak-CHeĉhet]. NOVI DNI 20 (April 1969): 9-10. Signed: Lilia 'Babusia'.

YRSHCHENYĬ, Ivan, pseud. (Real name: BODRUG, Ivan)

5231   *Svatanni͡a v ... Skachevani: Komedi͡a na chotyry dii [Courtship in ... Saskatchewan: Comedy in Four Acts].* Winnipeg: Petro SHevchuk [1926]. 61 pp. Play.

ZAKHARIĬCHUK, Andriĭ

5232   *ĈHerha: Komichna ditochna stsenka v odniĭ vidsloni [The Turn: Children's Play in One Act].* Winnipeg: Promin', 1927. 16 pp. (Kanadyĭs'ka Biblioteka No. 18) Play.

ZAKHARCHUK, Dmytro (1894-   )

5233   *Na chuzhyni [In Alien Land].* Winnipeg: Promin', 1934. 79 pp. Poems.

ZELEZ, Ivan O.

5234   *Praktychna utopiia: Teori͡a v opovidanni͡u [A Practical Utopia: Theory in the Form of a Story].* Montreal: Iv. Hnyda, 1926. 145 pp. (Biblioteka Novyĭ Svit No. 30) Story.

ZGURS'KYĬ, Fylyp (1892-1962)

5235   *Mynule i suchasne [Past and Present].* Calgary [n.d.] 4 pp. Mimeographed. Story.

URUGUAYAN

INDIVIDUAL AUTHORS

ESCOMEL, Gloria (1914-   )

Née à Montevideo, en Uruguay, elle a fait ses études dans son pays natal, à Paris, puis à Montréal, òu elle a obtenu un doctorat en études françaises. Elle est arrivée à Montréal en 1967. Ses articles ont paru dans des revues telles que *Châtelaine, l'Actualité, Gazette des femmes, Liberté* et également dans *Le Devoir.*

5236   *Ferveurs.* Paris: Éditions Saint-Germain, 1972. Poèmes.

5237   *Exorcisme du rêve.* Paris: Éditions Saint-Germain, 1974. Poèmes.

GARCIA MÉNDEZ, Javier (1945-   )

Born in Montevideo, Uruguay, came to Canada in 1973. Received a doctoral degree at l'Université du Québec à Montréal, where he has been a lecturer in literature since 1980. He has worked for Radio Canada International and Dérives, and has translated into French some poems by Latin American authors.

5238   *El Bandoneon desde el tango/Le bandonéon depuis le tango* (with Arturo Penon). Montréal: COATL, 1986. 71, 71 pp. illus.

VENEZUELAN

INDIVIDUAL AUTHOR

CAUDEIRON, Daniel

Born in Venezuela and educated in Trinidad, Dominica, and England. Professional interests: journalism, photography, music, theatre. He is theatre coordinator for Black Theatre Canada, Toronto. Some of his plays have been produced on television.

5239   *Speak, Brother, Speak.* Dominica, 1972. Play.

5240   *Poems, 1962-1973.* Dominica: Arts Council, 1973. Poems.

5241   *Dominican Short Stories.* Dominica: Arts Council, 1973. Short stories.

5242   *A Few Things about Us.* Toronto: Black Theatre of Canada, 1978. Play.

5243   *More about Me.* Toronto: Black Theatre of Canada, 1979. Play.

III. MINORITIES IN CANADIAN LITERATURE

THE IMMIGRANT IN CANADIAN LITERATURE

MONOGRAPHS, RESEARCH PAPERS

5244 **ABOUTEBOUL, Albert Victor**
"Le personnage juif dans le roman canadien-français du XXe siècle." M.A. Thesis. Montréal: McGill University, 1971. 114 pp. (Juif)

5245 **ANCTIL, Pierre; CALDWELL, Garry**
Juifs et réalités juives au Québec. Montréal: Institut québécois de recherche sur la culture, 1984. 371 pp. (Juif)
[Includes a paper on the Jewish character in the French-Canadian novel.]

5246 **ANDREW, Robert**
"The Ostracized Self: The Saga of the Japanese Canadians in Joy Kogawa's Obasan." AMERASIA 13, no. 2 (1986-87): 167-71. (Japanese)

5247 **ANDREW, Robert; MASON, Trisha**
We Are Their Children: Ethnic Portraits of British Columbia. Vancouver, 1977. 162 pp. (Inter-ethnic)

5248 **APONIUK, Natalia**
"The Problem of Identity: The Depiction of Ukrainians in Canadian Literature." CAN ETH STUD 14, no. 1 (1982): 50-61. (Ukrainian)
[Examines the image of Ukrainians through the work of Ralph Connor, Vera Lysenko, Henry Kreisel, W.O. Mitchell, Sinclair Ross, and Margaret Laurence.]

5249 **ATWOOD, Margaret**
"Failed Sacrifices; The Reluctant Immigrant." In her *Survival: A Thematic Guide to Canadian Literature.* (Toronto: The House of Anansi, 1972) pp. 145-59. (Inter-ethnic)
[An analysis based on the novels of Austin Clarke, John Marlyn, Brian Moore, Adele Wiseman, and Marika Robert.]

5250 **BENDER, Urie A.**
Stumbling Heavenward: The Extraordinary Life of an Ordinary Man: Peter Rempel. Winnipeg: Hyperion Press, 1984. 304 pp. (Mennonite, German, Russian)

5251 **CANADIAN ASSOCIATION FOR ADULT EDUCATION**
The New Canadian in Canada; A Brief Survey of the Experiences of New-comers to Canada, as Presented in the Selected Canadian Novels. Toronto: The Association with the cooperation of the Citizenship and Immigration Branch, 1960. 23 leaves.
[Describes the lives of new immigrants through the novels of John Marlyn, Hugh MacLennan, Gabrielle Roy, Adele Wiseman, Morley Callaghan, Mordecai Richler, and Ralph Connor.]

5252 **COWPERTHWAITE, Avon Elizabeth**
"Harmony and Discord: A Study of the Transition from the Old to Modern Ways of Life as Handled by a Group of Prairie Novelists." M.A. Thesis. Winnipeg: University of Manitoba, 1965. (Inter-ethnic)

5253 CRAIG, Terrence
Racial Attitudes in English Canadian Fiction, 1905-1986. Waterloo, Ont.: Wilfrid Laurier University Press, 1987. 163 pp. (Inter-ethnic)

5254 DAHLIE, Hallvard
Varieties of Exile: The Canadian Experience. Vancouver: University of British Columbia Press, 1986. 216 pp. (Inter-ethnic)
[Includes Susanna Moodie, Frederick Philip Grove, Mavis Gallant, Mordecai Richler, Brian Moore.]

5255 De FRANCESCHI, Marisa, ed.
Stories about Real People: A Graded Reader for Students of English. Windsor, Ont.: Mardan, 1982. 149 pp.
[Includes fictional stories about real situations of immigrants.]

5256 FISCH, Harold
The Dual Image: A Study of the Figure of the Jew in English Literature. London: Lincoln-Prager, 1959. 87 pp. (Jewish)

5257 FRIEZEN, J.W.
"Mennonites and Hutterites in Twentieth Century Alberta Literature with Specific Reference to Educational Implications." ALTA J EDUC RES 22, no. 2 (1976): 106-28. (Mennonites, Hutterites)

5258 GASPÉ, Philippe Aubert de, fils
Le chercher de trésor, ou l'influence d'un livre. Montréal: Réédition-Québec, 1968. 98 pp.

5259 KRAWCHUK, Peter
"The Ukrainian Image in Canadian Literature." In *Tribute to Our Ukrainian Pioneer in Canada's First Century. Proceedings: Special Convention of the Association of United Ukrainian Canadians and the Workers' Benevolent Association of Canada. March 23, 1966.* (Winnipeg: Association of the United Ukrainian Canadians and Workers' Benevolent Association of Canada) pp. 28-43. (Ukrainian)

5260 LUSSIER, Alain
"Attitudes toward the Jew in Canadian Literature in English and French." M.A. Thesis. Sherbrooke: University of Sherbrooke, 1968. (Jewish)

5261 LUSSIER, Alain
"Jewish Characters in Canadian Fiction." M.A. Thesis. Sherbrooke: University of Sherbrooke, 1973. (Jewish)

5262 McKENZIE, Ruth I.
"The Immigrant in Canadian Literature (English)." In *The Canadian in Canada....* (Toronto: Canadian Association for Adult Education, 1960) pp. 2-7.
[Describes the contents, technique and styles of interpretation of the immigrant through the novels of W.R. Bird, Ralph Connor, Mazo de la Roche, Edward McCourt, Frederick Niven, Laura Goodman Salverson, and Ethel Wilson.] (Inter-ethnic)

5263 McKENZIE, Ruth I.
"Life in a New Land: Notes on the Immigrant Theme in Canadian Fiction." CAN LIT No. 7 (1961): 24-33.
[A study of the novels of Frederick Philip Grove, Ralph Connor, Mordecai Richler, and Adele Wiseman.]

5264 MOSS, John G.
"Immigrant Exile." In his *Patterns of Isolation in English Canadian Fiction.* (Toronto: McClelland & Stewart, 1974) pp. 80-103. (Inter-ethnic)

5265 MUDDIMAN, Bernard
"The Immigrant Element in Canadian Literture." QUEEN'S Q 20 (1913): 404-15. (Inter-ethnic)

5266 NKOLO, Jean-Victor
"Les immigrants sont des poèmes: un entretien avec Gérald Godin." VICE VERSA 2, no. 4 (1985): 5-7. (Inter-ethnic)

5267 PAVLOVIC, Marianne
"L'affaire Ducharme." VOIX IMAG 6, no. 1 (1980): 75-95. (Jewish)

5268 SHEK, Ben Zion
"The Jew in the French-Canadian Novel." VIEWPOINTS 4, no. 4 (1969-70): 29-35. (Jewish)
[An analysis of the Jewish character as described in the novels of P.A. Gaspé fils, Pierre-Joseph Olivier Chauveau, Jean-Charles Harvey, Roger Lemelin, Gabrielle Roy, Yves Thériault, C. Martin, Claude Jasmin, Hubert Aquin.]

5269 SHEK, Ben Zion
"The Portrayal of Canada's Ethnic Groups in Some French Canadian Novels." In *Slavs in Canada.* Vol. 3. *Proceedings of the Third National Conference on Canadian Slavs,* edited by C.J. Jaenen. (Ottawa: Inter-University on Canadian Slavs, 1971)
[An examination of German, Jewish, Dutch, Russian, Polish, and Ukrainian immigrants as characters in French-Canadian creative writing.]

5270 SIROIS, Antoine
"L'étranger de race et d'ethnic dans le roman québécois." Dans *Imaginaire social et representations collectives. Mélanges offerts à Jean-Charles Falardeau.* Québec: Presses de l'Université Laval, 1982. (Inter-ethnic)

BIOGRAPHY, FICTION, POETRY

5271 AQUIN, Hubert
Prochain épisode. Montréal: Éditions H.M.H., 1965. 180 pp. Roman. (Juif)

5272 BEATTIE, Jessie L.
Strength for the Bridge. Toronto: McClelland & Stewart, 1966. 216 pp. (Japanese)

5273 BEAUPRÉ, Charles Henri
Les beaux jours viendront. Québec: Presses sociales, 1941. 241 pp. (Juif)

5274 BESETTE, Gérard
L'Incubation. Montréal: Librairie Déom, 1965. 180 pp. Roman. (Autrichien)

5275 BOWERING, George
Caprice. Toronto: Penguin, 1987. 266pp. Novel. (Inter-ethnic, Chinese, Hungarian, Italian)

5276 CALLAGHAN, Morley
Our Lady of the Snows. Toronto: Macmillan of Canada, 1985. 215 pp. Novel. (Hungarian)

5277 CHARBONNEAU, Robert
Ils posséderout la terre. Montréal: L'Arbre, 1941. 221 pp. (Polish)

5278 CHAUVEAU, Pierre-Joseph-Olivier
Charles Guérin, roman de mœurs canadiennes, dans L'Album littéraire et musical de *La Revue canadienne*, 1846-47. Also, Lovell, 1853. vii, 359 pp. (Allemand, Juif))

5279 CONNOR, Ralph, pseud. (Real name: GORDON, Rev. Charles Williams)
The Foreigner. A Tale of Saskatchewan. Toronto: Westminster, 1909. 384 pp. Also published by Hodder, London, under the title: *The Settler.* 1909. 307 pp. Novel. (Inter-ethnic)

5280 D'ALFONSO, Antonio
The Other Shore. Montreal: Guernica, 1986. 160 pp. Stories. (Italian)

5281 DANTIN, Louis, pseud. (Real Name: SEERS, Eugène)
Les enfances de Fanny. Montréal: Les Éditions Chantecler, 1951. 286 pp. Roman. (Inter-ethnic)

5282 DESMARCHAIS, Rex
La Chesnaie. Montréal: L'Arbre, 1942. 294 pp. Roman. (Juif)

5283 DEYGLUN, Henri
Les Amours d'un communiste. Montréal: Lévesque, 1933. Roman. (Slave)

5284 DRACHE, Sharon
The Mikveh Man and other Stories. Toronto: Aya Press, 1984. 80 pp. Short stories. (Juif)

5285 DUCHARME, Réjean
L'Avalée des avalés. Paris: Gallimard, 1966. 282 pp. Roman. (Juif)

5286 DUCHARME, Réjan
Le nez qui vogue. Paris: Gallimard, 1967. 275 pp. Roman. (Juif)

5287 EGGLESTON, Magdalena
Mountain Shadows. Toronto: British Book Service, 1955. 254 pp. Novel. (Serbo-Croatian)

5288 ENNS, Victor Jerrett
Correct in this Culture. Saskatoon, Sask.: Fifth House, 1985. 75 pp. Poems. (Mennonite)

5289 *The Ethnic Detectives: Masterpieces of Detective Fiction*, edited by Bill Pronzini and Martin H. Greenberg. Toronto: McClelland & Stewart, 1985. 360 pp. Detective stories. (Inter-ethnic)
[Includes stories whose protagonists are sleuths of ethnic origin.]

5290 FAESSLER, Shirley
A Basket of Apples. Toronto: McClelland & Stewart, 1988. 234 pp. Short stories. (Jewish)

5291 FRIESEN, Patrick
The Shunning. Winnipeg: Turnstone, 1980. Poems. (Mennonite)

5292 GARNER, Hugh
Cabbagetown. Toronto: Collins, 1950. 160 pp. Novel. (Inter-ethnic)

5293 GELDER, Willem de
A Dutch Homesteader on the Prairies. Toronto: University of Toronto Press, 1973. xv, 92 pp. Biography. (Dutch)
[Letters of Willem de Gelder, 1910-13. Translated and introduced by Herman Ganzevoort.]

5294 GODBOUT, Jacques
Le Couteau sur la table. Paris: Éditions du Seuil, 1967. 156 pp. Roman. (Juif)

5295 GODIN, Marcel
Ce maudit soleil. Paris: Laffont, 1965. 190 pp. Roman. (Inter-ethnic)

5296 HAAS, Maara
The Street where I Live, illustrated by Frank Mikuska. Toronto: McGraw-Hill Ryerson, 1976. 251 pp. Novel. (Inter-ethnic, Jewish)

5297 HARVEY, Jean-Charles
Marcel Fauvé... Montmagny: Imprimerie de Montmagny, 1922. 214 pp. Roman. (Juif)

5298 HEAPS, Leo
A Boy Called Nam; The True Story of How One Little Boy Came to Canada. Toronto: Macmillan, 1984. 95 pp. Story. (Vietnamese)

5299 JASMIN, Claude
La Corde au cou. Montréal: Le Cercle du livre de France, 1960. 233 pp. Roman. (Juif)

5300 JASMIN, Claude
Et puis tout est silence. Montréal: Éditions l'Homme, 1965. 159 pp. Roman. (Juif)

5301 JASMIN, Claude
Ethel et le terroriste. Montréal: Librairie Déom, 1964. 184 pp. Roman. (Juif)
[English translation: *Ethel and the Terrorist.*]

5302 JASMIN, Claude
Pointe-Calumet boogie-woogie. Montréal: La Presse, 1973. 131 pp. Roman. (Juif)

5303 KAPLAN, Bess
Corner Store. Winnipeg: Queenston House, 1975. 263 pp. Novel. (Jewish)

5304 KAPLAN, Bess
Malke, Malke. Winnipeg: Queenston House, 1977. 232 pp. Novel. (Jewish)

5305 KIYOOKA, Roy
Kyoto Airs. Vancouver, 1964. (Japanese)

5306 KIYOOKA, Roy
Pear Tree. Poems. Toronto: Coach House Press, 1987. 68 pp. (Japanese)

5307 KOGAWA, Joy
A Choice of Dreams. Toronto: McCelland & Stewart, 1974. Poems. (Japanese)

5308 KOGAWA, Joy
Obasan. Toronto: Lester & Orpen Dennys, 1981. 250 pp. Novel. (Japanese)

5309 KOSTASH, Myrna
All of Baba's Children. Edmonton: Hurtig, 1977. 414 pp. Biography. (Ukrainian)

5310 KROETSCH, Robert
But We Are Exiles. New York: St. Martin's Press, 1965. 145 pp. Novel. (Hungarian)

5311 LANGEVIN, André
Pousière sur la ville. Montréal: Le Cercle du livre de France, 1953. 213 pp. Roman. (Syrian)

5312 LAPLANTE, Jean de
Le petit juif. Montréal: Beauchemin, 1962. 162 pp. Roman. (Juif)

5313 LAURENCE, Margaret
A Jest of God. Toronto: McClelland & Stewart, 1966. 202 pp. Novel. (Inter-ethnic)

5314 LEGAULT, Roland
Risques d'hommes. Montréal: Fides, 1950. 247 pp. Roman. (Juif)

5315 LEMELIN, Roger
Au pied de la pente douce. Montréal: L'Arbre, 1944. 333 pp. Also: Québec: Institut littéraire de Québec, 1953. 333 pp. Roman. (Juif)

5316 LEMELIN, Roger
Les Plouffe. Québec: Bélisle, 1948. 470 pp. Also Paris: Flammarion, 1948. 313 pp. 1955. 314 pp. Traduction anglaise: *The Plouffe Family.* Toronto: 1950. 373 pp. Novel. (Juif)

5317 LEVINE, Norman
Canada Made Me. London: Putnam, 1958. 320 pp. Paperback edition, Ottawa: Deneau and Greenberg, 1979. 277 pp. Biography. (Inter-ethnic, Jewish, Hungarian, Mennonite)

5318 LIM, Singh
West Coast Chinese Boy. Montreal: Tundra Books, 1979. 64 pp. Story. (Inter-ethnic, Chinese)

5319 LING, Frieda; LAU, Mee-Shan
The Axe and the Sword; The Maiden of Wu Long. Toronto: Kids Can Press, 1978. 25 pp. illus. Story. (Chinese)

5320 LUMIÈRE, Cornel
Kalavrita: A Greek Tragedy. A Strange Love. Toronto: Simon & Pierre, 1985. 178 pp. Novel. (Greek)

5321 LYSENKO, Vera
Men in Sheepskin Coats: A Study in Assimilation. Toronto: Ryerson Press, 1947. (Ukrainian)

5322 LYSENKO, Vera
The Yellow Boots. Toronto: Ryerson Press, 1954. 314 pp. Novel. (Ukrainian)

5323 MARTIN, Claire
Dans un gant de fer, la joue gauche. Montréal: Cercle du livre de France, 1965. 235 pp. Roman. (Juif)

5324 MARTIN, Claire
Quand j'aurai payé ton visage. Montréal: Le Cercle du livre de France, 1962. 187 pp. Roman. (Juif)

5325 MONTERO, Gloria
The Summer the Whales Sang. Toronto: Lorimer, 1985. Novel. (Basque)

5326 PALUK, William

Canadian Cossacks. Essays, Articles and Stories on Ukrainian Canadian Life. Winnipeg: The Author, 1943. 143 pp. (Ukrainian)

5327 RICHLER, Mordecai
The Apprenticeship of Duddy Kravitz. London: Deutsch, 1959. 319 pp. Also, Toronto: McClelland & Stewart, 1969 and 1974. 377 pp. Novel. (Inter-ethnic, Jewish)

5328 RICHLER, Mordecai
Joshua Then and Now. Toronto: McClelland & Stewart, 1980. 435 pp. Novel. (Jewish)

5329 RICHLER, Mordecai
Son of a Smaller Hero. London: Deutsch, 1955. 223 pp. Also: Toronto: McClelland & Stewart, 1966 and 1969. 206 pp. Novel. (Jewish)

5330 RICHLER, Mordecai
St. Urbain's Horseman. Toronto: McClelland & Stewart, 1971. 467 pp. Also, London: Panther Books, 1973. 384 pp. Novel. (Jewish)

5331 RICHLER, Mordecai
The Street. Toronto: McClelland & Stewart, 1969. 128 pp. Novel. (Jewish)

5332 ROBERT, Marika
A Stranger and Afraid. Toronto: McClelland & Stewart, 1964. Novel. (Hungarian)

5333 ROY, Gabrielle
Alexandre Chénevert. Montréal: Beauchemin, Le Cercle du livre de France, 1954. 373 pp. Roman. (Hongrois, juif, russe)

5334 ROY, Gabrielle
Bonheur d'occasion. Montréal: Société des Éditions Pascal, 1945. 523 pp. Also, Paris: Flammarion, 1945. 473 pp. Traduction anglaise: *The Tin Flute,* 1947. 315 pp. Roman. (Inter-ethnic)

5335 ROY, Gabrielle
Ces enfants de ma vie. Montréal: Stanké, 1977. 212 pp. Nouvelles. (Jewish)
[Won a Governor General's Award. English translation: *Children of My Heart,* 1979.]

5336 ROY, Gabrielle
Fragile lumières du la terre. Montréal: Quinze, 1978. 240 pp. Documentary, articles, etc. (Inter-ethnic)

5337 ROY, Gabrielle
La montagne secrète. Montréal: Beauchemin, 1961. 222 pp. Traduction anglais par H. Benesse: *The Hidden Mountain.* Toronto: McClelland & Stewart, 1962. 186 pp. Roman. (Inter-ethnic)

5338 ROY, Gabrielle
La petite poule d'eau. Montréal: Beauchemin, 1950. 272 pp. Also Paris: Flammarion, 1951. Traduction anglais par H. Benesse: *Where Nests the Waterhen, A Novel.* New York: Harcourt, Brace, 1951. 251 pp. Nouvelles. (Inter-ethnic, Ukrainian, Finnish, Polish, Icelandic, Swedish, Belgian)

5339 ROY, Gabrielle
La route d'Altamont. Montréal: HMH, 1966. 263 pp. Roman. (Juif)
[English translation by Joyce Marshall: *The Road Past Altamont.*]

5340 **ROY, Gabrielle**
Rue Deschambault. Montréal: Beauchemin, 1955. 261 pp. Also Paris: Flammarion, 1955. 235 pp. Traduit en anglais par H. Benesse: *Street of Riches.* Nouvelles. (Inter-ethnic, Italian, Dutch, Mennonite, Doukhobor)
[Won the Prix Duvernay and a Governor General's Award.]

5341 **ROY, Gabrielle**
Un Jardin au bout du monde. Montréal: Beauchemin, 1975. 212 pp. (Juif)

5342 **SALVERSON, Laura Goodman**
Confessions of an Immigrant's Daughter. London: Faber, 1939. 523 pp. Autobiography. Reprinted by the University of Toronto Press, 1981. xiv, 415 pp. (Icelandic)

5343 **SALVERSON, Laura Goodman**
The Viking Heart. New York, 1923. 326 pp. Documentary. Also Toronto: McClelland & Stewart, 1975. (Icelandic)

5344 **SAPERGIA, Barbara**
Foreigners. Moose Jaw, Sask.: Thunder Creek, 1984. Novel. (Romanian)

5345 **SCANTLAND, Anna Cecile**
Resignation [Shikataganai]. Vancouver: Parallel Publishers, 1977. 340 pp. (Japanese)

5346 **SERWYLO, Ray**
Accordion Lessons. Vancouver: Arsenal Pulp Press, 1982. Novel. (Ukrainian)

5347 *Sharing through Poetry: A Multicultural Experience,* edited by Michael Zizis. Toronto: University of Toronto Press, 1980. Poems. (Inter-ethnic)

5348 **SHUBIK, Irene**
The War Guest. Toronto: W.H. Allen, 1986. 160 pp. Novel. (Jewish, Greek)

5349 **SLONIM, Reuben**
To Kill a Rabbi. Toronto: ECW Press, 1987. 354 pp. Documentary (Jewish)

5350 **STAEBLER, Edna**
Whatever Happened to Maggie? And Other People I've Known, illustrated by Helen Fox. Toronto: McClelland & Stewart, 1983. 224 pp. (Inter-ethnic)

5351 **SUKNASKI, Andrew**
In the Name of Nurid. Erin, Ont.: Porcupine's Quill, 1981. (Ukrainian)

5352 **SUKNASKI, Andrew**
Silk Trail. Toronto: Nightwood Editions, 1985. 93 pp. Poems. (Chinese)

5353 **TANAKA, Shelly**
Michi's New Year. Toronto: PMA Book, 1980. 30 pp. Children's book. (Japanese)

5354 **THÉRIAULT, Yves**
Aaron. Québec: L'Institut littéraire du Québec, 1954. 163 pp. Rev. ed. 1965. Also Paris: Grasset, 1957. 206 pp. Roman. (Jewish)
[Won the Prix de la Province de Québec.]

5355 **TORGOV, Morley**

A Good Place to Come From. Toronto: Lester and Orpen, Dennys, 1974. 186 pp. Novel. (Jewish)

5356 VALGARDSON, W.D.
Bloodflowers: Ten Stories. Ottawa: Oberon Press, 1973. 122 pp. Short stories. (Inter-ethnic)

5357 VALGARDSON, W.D.
The Carpenter of Dreams. Victoria: Skaldhús Press, 1986. 70. Poems. (Icelandic)

5358 VIAU, Roger
Au milieu la montagne. Montréal: Beauchemin, 1951. 329 pp. (Juif)

5359 VLASSIE, Katherine
Children of Byzantium. Dunvegan, Ont.: Cormorant Books, 1987. 120 pp. illus. Novel. (Greek)

5360 WAH, Fred
Waiting for Saskatchewan. Winnipeg: Turnstone Press, 1986. (Chinese, Swedish)

5361 WERBOWSKI, Tecia
Bitter Sweet Taste of Maple. Toronto: Williams-Wallace, 1984. 70 pp. (Inter-ethnic)

5362 WIEBE, Rudy
The Blue Mountains of China. Toronto: McClelland & Stewart, 1970. 227 pp. Also: Toronto: McClelland & Stewart, 1975. 227 pp. (New Canadian Library) Novel. (Mennonite)

5363 WIEBE, Rudy
Peace Shall Destroy Many. Toronto: McClelland & Stewart, 1962. 239 pp. Also Grand Rapids, Mich.: Berdmans, 1964. Toronto: McClelland & Stewart, 1972. 244 pp. Novel. (Mennonite)

5364 WISEMAN, Adele
Old Woman at Play. Toronto: Clarke Irwin, 1978. (Jewish)

5365 WISEMAN, Adele
The Sacrifice: A Novel. Toronto: Macmillan of Canada, 1956. 346 pp. (Jewish)

5366 YEE, Paul
The Curses of Third Uncle. Vancouver: Lorimer, 1986. (Chinese)

5367 YEE, Paul; LEE, Sky
Teach Me to Fly, Skyfighter; and other Stories. Toronto: Lorimer, 1983. 133 pp. (Chinese)

5368 YELIN, Shulamis
Shulamis: Stories from Montreal Childhood. Montreal: Véhicule Press, 1985. (Jewish)

5369 ZALAN, Magda
Stubborn People. Toronto: Canadian Stage and Arts Publications, 1985. 109 pp. Interviews. (Hungarian)

THE NATIVE IN CANADIAN LITERATURE

MONOGRAPHS, RESEARCH PAPERS

5370   ATWOOD, Margaret

"First People: Indians and Eskimos as Symbols." In her *Survival....* (Toronto: House of Anansi, 1972) pp. 87-106.

[A treatment of the native element in the work of Margaret Laurence, George Ryga, Emily Carr, Leonard Cohen, Yves Thériault.]

5371   CARD, Brigham Young; HIRABAYASHI, G.K.; FRENCH, C.L.

The Metis in Alberta Society, with Special Reference to Social, Economic and Cultural Factors Associated with Persistently High Tuberculosis Incidence. Edmonton: University of Alberta, 1963. viii, 414 pp. illus., maps. Document.

5372   CLAIRMONT, Donald Hayden

"Deviance among Indians and Eskimos in Aklavik." M.A. Thesis. Hamilton: McMaster University, 1963.

5373   CORBETT, Nancy J.

"Closed Circle." CAN LIT No. 61 (1974): 46-53.

5374   DAGG, Melvin Harold

"Beyond the Garrison: A Study of the Image of the Indian in Canadian Literature." Ph.D. Thesis. Fredericton: University of New Brunswick, 1983. 3 microfiches (281 fr.)

5375   FAIRCHILD, Hoxie N.

"The Plains Indians in Early Canadian Literature." M.A. Thesis. London, Ont.: University of Western Ontario, 1973.

5376   FISHER, Roger Frank

"The Plains Indians in Early Canadian Literature." M.A. Thesis. London, Ont.: University of Western Ontario, 1973.

5377   GIRAUD, Marcel

Le métis canadien: son rôle dans l'histoire des provinces de l'Ouest. Paris: Institut d'ethnologie, 1945. lvi, 1297 [3] pp. 8 planches, 4 cartes dép. Document.

5378   HAYCOCK, Ronald Graham

The Canadian Indian: As a Subject and Concept in a Sampling of Popular National Magazines Read in Canada 1900-1970. Waterloo, Ont.: Waterloo Lutheran University Monograph Series, 1971.

5379   HIRANO, Keiichi

"The Aborigine in Canadian Literature: Notes by a Japanese." CAN LIT No. 14 (1962): 43-52.

5380   LEECHMAN, Douglas

"The Popular Concept of the 'Red Indian' as Revealed in Literature." M.A. Thesis. Ottawa: University of Ottawa, 1940.

5381   LEECHMAN, Douglas

"The 'Red Indian' of Literature: A Study in the Perpetuation of Error." M.A. Thesis. Ottawa: University of Ottawa, 1941.

5382   LIVESAY, Dorothy
"Native People in Our Canadian Literature." ENG Q 4, no. 1 (1971): 21-32.

5383   MITCHAM, Allison
"Northern Mission. Priest, Parson and Prophet in the North: A Study in French and English-Canadian Contemporary Fiction." LAUR UNIV REV 7, no. 1 (1974): 24-31.
[An analysis of the concept of the Indian as revealed in the novels of H. Horwood, Gabrielle Roy, Yves Thériault and Robert Kroetsch.]

5384   MONKMAN, Leslie
A Native Heritage: Images of the Indian in English-Canadian Literature. Toronto: University of Toronto Press, 1981. xiv, 193 pp.

5385   MONKMAN, Leslie
"White and Red: Perspectives on the Indian in English-Canadian Literature." Ph.D. Thesis. Toronto: York University, 1975. viii, 416 leaves.

5386   MOWAT, Farley
People of the Deer, with drawings by Samuel Bryant. Toronto: Little, Brown, 1952. 344 pp. (Indian)

5387   MOWAT, William; MOWAT, Christine
Native Peoples in Canadian Literature. Toronto: Macmillan of Canada, 1975. 122 pp. (Themes in Canadian Literature Series)

5388   NEWBERRY, J.W.E.
"Action and the Secret (Indian Character)." LAUR UNIV REV 4, no. 2 (1972): 106-15.

5389   NEWTON, Norman
"Wilderness No Wilderness." CAN LIT No. 63 (1965): 18-34.

5390   OVERVOLD (BURGER), Joanne, ed.
A Portrayal of Our Metis Heritage, edited by Joanne Overvold (Burger), contributing editor, Allan Clovis. [Yellowknife, N.W.T.: Metis Association of the Northwest Territories, 1976] 144 pp. illus., maps, ports. Document.

5391   PORTER, Helen
"Death of a Race." J CAN FIC 3, no. 2 (1974): 93-94.

5392   RETZLEFF, Marjorie Anne Gilbart
"The Primitive, Mystique Romance and Realism in the Depiction of the Native Indian in English-Canadian Fiction." Ph.D. Thesis. Saskatoon: University of Saskatchewan, 1981. 5 microfiches (416 fr.)

5393   STEPHENSON, Lionel
"Interpreters of the Indian." In his *Appraisals of Canadian Literature.* (Toronto: Macmillan, 1926) pp. 171-85.

5394   STOBIE, Margaret
"Document in Disillusion." CAN LIT No. 17 (1963): 60-62.

5395   SULLIVAN, Sherry

"The Indian in American Fiction, 1820-1850." Ph.D. Thesis. Toronto: University of Toronto, 1979. 4 microfiches (385 fr.)

BIOGRAPHY, FICTION, POETRY, DRAMA

5396 ARMSTRONG, Jeannette C.
Neekna and Chemai, illustrated by Kenneth Lee Edwards. Penticton, B.C.: The Author, 1984. 43 pp. Story. (Indian)

5397 ARMSTRONG, Jeannette C.
Slash. Penticton, B.C.: Teytus Books, 1985. 254 pp. Novel. (Indian)

5398 AUBRY, Claude
Agouhanna. New York-Toronto: Doubleday, 1972. 95 pp. Also Toronto: McGraw-Hill, 1974. 95 pp. English translation, 1973. Roumanian translation Bucuresti: I. Creanga, 1980. 68 pp. Story. (Indian)

5399 BARBEAU, Marius.
Mountain Cloud: Novel. Toronto: Macmillan, 1944. 300 pp. French translation: *Le Rêve de Kamalmouk.* Montréal: Fides, 1948. 231 pp. Novel. (Indian)

5400 BARKHOUSE, Joyce; IRVING, Daphne
The Witch of Port Lajoye. Charlottetown, P.E.I.: Ragweed Press, 1983. 48 pp. Story. (Indian)

5401 BODSWORTH, Fred
The Sparrow's Fall. Scarborough, Ont-New York: New American Library, 1966. Also Garden City, N.Y.-Toronto: Doubleday, 1967. 255 pp. Novel. (Indian)

5402 BOULIZON, Guy
Du Tomahawk à la croix. Montréal: Éd. Variétés, 1943. 30 pp. Récit. (Indiens)

5404 BOULIZON, Guy
La Croix chez les Indiens. Montréal: Beauchemin, 1958. 136 pp. Récit. (Indiens)

5403 BOULIZON, Guy
Kateri Tekakwitha. Montréal: Éd. Variétés, 1943. 30 pp. Récit. (Indiens)

5405 CAMERON, Anne
Dzelarhons: Mythology of the Northwest Coast. Madeira Park: Harbour Pub. Co., 1987. 120 pp. Tales. (Indian)

5406 CARR, Emily
Klee Wyck, with a foreword by Ira Dilworth. Toronto: Oxford University Press, 1941. x, 155 pp. Novel. (Indian)

5407 CHEVALIER, Henri-Émile
Les Derniers Iroquois. Paris: Lécrivain et Toubon, 1863. 308 pp. 2e éd. Paris: Michel Lévy, 1867. 3e éd. 1888. 4e éd. Le Patriote. Montréal: Librairie générale canadienne, 1952. 139 pp. Éd. adaptée par E. Achard. Roman. (Indiens)

5408 CHEVALIER, Henri-Émile
La Fille des Indiens rouges. Paris: Michel Lévy, 1866. 359 pp. 2e éd. 1874. 316 pp. 3e éd. Paris: Calmann Lévy, 1882. Roman. (Indiens)

5409 CHEVALIER, Henri-Émile
La Huronne, scènes de la vie canadienne. Paris: Poulet-Malassis, 1862. viii, 357 pp. 5e éd. 1889. [Texte composé de 2 chapitres des "Mystères de Montréal", dans *La Ruche littéraire,* t. 2, 1853 et de 8 chapitres de "La Huronne de Lorette", dans *La Ruche littéraire,* t. 4-5, 1854, 1859. Roman. (Indiens)

5410 CHEVALIER, Henri-Émile
L'Iroquoise de Caughnawaga. Montréal: Lovell, 1858. 125 pp. Roman. (Indiens)

5411 CHEVALIER, Henri-Émile
Les Nez-percés. Paris: Poulet-Malassis, 1862. 318 pp. 2e éd. Paris: Michel Lévy, 1867. 320 pp. 3e éd. 1890. Roman. (Indiens)

5412 CHEVALIER, Henri-Émile
Poignet d'acier ou les chippiouais. Paris: Lécrivain et Toubon, 1863. 281 pp. 2e éd. Paris: Michel Lévy, 1867. 3e éd. 1875. Roman. (Indiens)

5413 CHEVALIER, Henri-Émile
La Tête-plate. Paris: Poulet-Malassis, 1862. 322 pp. (Drames de l'Amérique du Nord) 2e éd. Paris: Lécrivain et Toubon, 1863. 3e éd. Paris: Michel Lévy, 1867. 320 pp. 4e éd. 1867. 324 pp. Roman. (Indiens)

5414 CLARK, Joan
The Moons of Madeleine. Markham, Ont.: Puffin Books, 1988. 221 pp. Novel. (Indian)

5415 CLARK, Joan
The Victory of Geraldine Gull. Toronto: Macmillan of Canada, 1988. 288 pp. (Indian)

5416 CLARK, Joan
Wild Man of the Woods. Markham, Ont.: Penguin Books Canada, 1985. 170 pp. Novel. (indian)

5417 CLARKE, Mollie
Rabbit and Fox: A Story from Canada . London: Dragon, 1972. 64 pp. Story. (Indian)

5418 COHEN, Leonard
Beautiful Losers. Toronto: McClelland & Stewart, 1966. Also London: Jonathan Cape, 1970. 243 pp. Novel. (Indian)

5419 COLLURA, Mary-Ellen Lang
Winners. Saskatoon: Western Producer Prairie Books, 1984. Story. (Indian)

5420 COMMON, Dianne L.; KEMP, Carol A.
Little Wild Onion of the Lillooet. Winnipeg: Pemmican, 1982. 28 pp. Story. (Indian)

5421 CRAIG, John
The Last Canoe. Toronto: PMA Books, 1979. 128 pp. Novel. (Indian)

5422 CRAVEN, Margaret
I Heard the Owl Call My Name. Toronto: Clarke, Irwin, 1967. 138 pp. (Indian)

5423 CRYSLER, Dorothy; ROBINSON, Geraldine; SHARPE, Irwin
The Indian Princess: Nahneebahweequa. [N.p.] Grey County Historical Society, 1979. [52] pp. Story. (Indian)

5424 CUTLER, Ebbit
I Once Knew an Indian Woman. Montreal: Tundra Books of Montreal, 1975. 68 pp. Biography. (Indian) First published in Montreal by Tundra Books under the title *The Last Noble Savage: A Laurentian Idyll.*

5425 CUTLER, Ebbitt
La Vieille sauvage/The Last Noble Savage. Montreál: Fides, 1980. 74 pp. Biographie. (Indian)

5426 EBER, Dorothy, ed.
Pitseolak: Pictures Out of My Life. Montreal: McGill-Queen's University Press, 1971. (Inuit) [Edited from taperecorded interviews.]

5427 EWERT, Charles
A Cross of Fire. Markham, Ont.: Paperjacks, 1981. 253 pp. Novel. (Indian)

5428 FAULKNOR, Cliff
Cliff Faulknor's. Edmonton: J.M. Lebel, 1982. 103 pp. Novel. (Indian)

5429 FAULKNOR, Cliff
Johnny Eagleclaw. Edmonton: J.M. Lebel, 1982. Juvenile story. (Indian)

5430 FÉRON, Jean
La métisse: roman canadien inédit, ill. de A. Fournier, de S. LeFebvre et A.S. Brodeur. Montréal: Éditions E. Garand, 1923. 64 pp. illus. Roman. (Métis)

5431 GIRARD, Rodolphe
L'Algonquine. Montréal: La Patrie, 1910. 65 pp. Nouvelle (Indiens)

5432 GRAVELLE, Kim
Inook, the Eskimo Who Hated the Sun. Chicago: Childrens Press, 1975. 45 pp. Children's story. (Inuit)

5433 HAMILTON, Mary; PERNA, Deby
The Sky Caribou. Toronto: PMA Books, 1980. Juvenile fiction. (Indian)

5434 HARRIS, Christie; TAIT, Douglas
Mouse Woman and the Mischief-makers. London: Macmillan, 1978. 114 pp. Legend. (Indian)

5435 HARRIS, Christie; TAIT, Douglas
Mouse Woman and the Muddleheads. New York: Atheneum, 1979. 131 pp. Legend. (Indian)

5436 HARRIS, Christie; TAIT, Douglas
The Trouble with Princesses. Toronto: McClelland & Stewart, 1984. 170 pp. Folktale. (Indian)

5437 HORWOOD, Harold
White Eskimo: A Novel of Labrador. Don Mills, Ont.: Paper Jacks, 1973. 278 pp. Novel. (Eskimo)

5438 HOUSTON, James
Eagle Mask: A West Coast Indian Tale, illustrated by the author. Don Mills, Ont.: Longmans Canada, 1966. 63 pp. Folktale. (Indian)

5439 HOUSTON, James

The Falcon Bow: An Arctic Legend. Toronto: McClelland & Stewart, 1986. 94 pp. Legend. (Inuit)

5440 HOUSTON, James
Ghost Fox. New York: Avon, 1977. xii, 369 pp. Tale. (Indian)

5441 HOUSTON, James
Ghost Paddle: A Northwest Coast Indian Tale, illustrated by the author. Don Mills, Ont.: Longman Canada, 1972. 55 pp. Tale. (Indian)

5442 HOUSTON, James
Kiviok's Majic Journey: An Eskimo Legend. New York: Atheneum, 1973. 40 pp. Legend. (Inuit)

5443 HOUSTON, James
Ojibwa Summer, photos by B.A. King. Don Mills, Ont.: Longmans Canada, 1972. 96 pp. Story. (Indian)

5444 HOUSTON, James
River Runners: A Tale of Hardship and Bravery, drawings by the author. New York: Atheneum, 1979. 142 pp. Story (Indian)

5445 HOUSTON, James
Spirit Wrestler. Toronto: McClelland & Stewart, 1980. 306 pp. (Inuit)

5446 HOUSTON, James
Tiktáliktak; An Eskimo Legend, illustrated by the author. Don Mills, Ont.: Longmans Canada, 1965. Legend. (Inuit)

5447 HOUSTON, James
Tiktáliktak/Tiktáliktak. Paris: Castor Poche Flammarion, 1982. 104 pp. Legend. (Inuit)

5448 HOUSTON, James
The White Archer: An Eskimo Legend. Don Mills, Ont.: Academic Press of Canada, 1967. Legend. (Inuit)

5449 HOUSTON, James
The White Dawn: An Eskimo Saga. Toronto: Longman Canada, 1971. 275 pp. illus. Saga. [French translation: *L'Aube blanche: Roman.* Montréal: HMH, 1972. 378 pp.) Saga. (Inuit)

5450 HOWARD, Joseph Kinsey
A Strange Empire; Narrative of the Northwest. New York: Morrow, Lewis & Samuel, 1952. xii, 601 pp.
[About Louis Riel and the Métis people.]

5451 JOHNSTON, Basil H.
Indian School Days. Toronto: Key Porter, 1988. 256 pp. Autobiography. (Indian)

5452 KEENLEYSIDE, David
Where the Mountain Falls. Toronto: Nelson, Foster & Scott, 1977. 192 pp. Novel.

5453 KENNY, George
Indians Don't Cry. Toronto: NC Press, 1982. 102 pp. (Indian)

5454 KINSELLA, W.P.

Born Indian. Ottawa: Oberon Press, 1981. 163 pp. Novel. (Indian)

5455 KINSELLA, W.P.
Dance Me Outside. Ottawa: Oberon Press, 1977. 158 pp. Short stories. (Indian)
[A collection of seventeen stories from the point of view of the Indian.]

5456 KLEITSCH, Christel; STEPHENS, Paul; ENSE, Don
Dancing Feathers. Willowdale, Ont.: Annick Press, 1985. (Indian)

5457 KROETSCH, Robert
Gone Indian. Nanaimo, B.C.: Theytus Books, 1981. 158 pp. Novel. (Indian)

5458 LASNIER, Rina
Féerie indienne. St-Jean, Qué.: Éd. du Richelieu, 1939. 71 pp. Poèmes. (Indiens)

5459 LAURENCE, Margaret
A Bird in the House. Toronto: McClelland & Stewart, 1963. 207 pp. Toronto: McClelland & Stewart, 1970. 244 pp. (New Canadian Library series) Novel. (Indian)

5460 LAURENCE, Margaret
The Diviners, with an introduction by David Staines. Toronto: McClelland & Stewart, [1978] c1974. xiv, 467 pp. Novel. (Métis)

5461 LAURENCE, Margaret
The Fire-dwellers. Toronto: McClelland & Stewart, 1969. Also 1973: NCL series, 308 pp. Novel. (Indian)

5462 MacDONALD, Jake
Indian River: A Novel. Winnipeg: Queenston House, 1981. 205 pp. Novel. (Indian)

5463 MacEWEN, Gwendolyn
Noman's Land. Toronto: Coach House Press, 1987. Short stories. (Indian)

5464 MAILLET, André
Le Chant de l'Iroquoise. Montréal: Éd. du Jour, 1967. 80 pp. Poèmes. (Indiens)

5465 MAJOR, Henriette
L'Orge de Niagara. Montréal: A. Lévesque, 1933. (Indiens)

5466 MAXINE, pseud. (Real name: TASCHEREAU-FORTIER, Madame Alexandre)
La Cache aux canots, Histoire d'un Indien. Montréal: LACF, 1939. 136 pp. 2e éd. Montréal: Beauchemin, 1946. 159 pp. 3e éd. 1957. 158 pp. Roman historique. (Indiens)

5467 MAXINE, pseud. (Real name: TASCHEREAU-FORTIER, Madame Alexandre)
La Huronne. Paris: Casterman [1931] 124 pp. 2e éd. Montréal: Granger, 1946. 143 pp. Conte. (Indiens)

5468 MITCHELL, W.O.
The Alien. Toronto: serialized in *Maclean's* 1953-54. Novel. (Indian)

5469 MITCHELL, W.O.
The Vanishing Point. Toronto: Macmillan of Canada, 1973. 393 pp. Novel. (Indian)

5470 MOORE, Harold M.

The Indian Summer of Arty Bigjim and Johnny Jack. Winnipeg: Gullmasters Children's Boooks, 1981. xix, 132 pp. Story. (Indian)

5471 MOWAT, Farley
Snow Walker. 1975. Stories. (Inuit)

5472 NICHOL, James W.
Sainte-Marie among the Hurons: A Play. Vancouver: Talonbooks, 1980. 79 pp. Play. (Indian)

5473 NICOL, Clive
The White Shaman: A Novel. Toronto: Little, Brown, 1979. xvi, 234 pp. Novel. (Inuit)

5474 O'HAGAN, Howard
Tay John: A Novel. New York: Potter, 1960. 263 pp. Novel. (Indian)

5475 PORTER, Donald Clayton
The Renegade. Boston: G.K. Hall, 1983. 529 pp. Originally published Toronto: Bantam, 1980. (The Colonization of America Series 2.) (Indian)

5476 POWE, Bruce Allen
The Ice Eaters. Toronto: Lester and Orpen Dennys, 1987. 278 pp. (Indian-Inuit)

5477 PRATT, E.J.
Brébeuf and His Brethren. Toronto: Macmillan, 1940. 65 pp. Poem. (Indian)

5478 PRATT, E.J.
Selected Poems with Notes. Toronto: Macmillan, 1947. 149 pp. Poems. (Indian)

5479 RAILLET, René
Le Sergent Trois-Rivières: Aventures du Temps ou le Canada était français. Paris: Magnard, 1971. 190 pp. Roman. (Indiens)

5480 RICHARDSON, John
The Canadian Brothers; or The Prophecy Fulfilled. A Tale of the Late American War. Montreal: Armour and Ramsay, 1840. 2 v. Published in America as *Matilda Montgomerie.* New York: Dewitt & Davenport, 1851. 191 pp. Novel. (Indian)

5481 RICHARDSON, John
Wacousta; or The Profecy. A Tale of the Canadas. London: Cadell, 1832. 3 v. Also Toronto: McClelland & Stewart, 1967. 298 pp. New Canadian Library series. Novel. (Indian)

5482 RORDAM, Vita
Payuk and the Polar Bears. Ottawa: Borealis Press, 1981. Juvenile fiction. (Indian)

5483 ROUSSEAU, Guildo
The Iroquoise/L'Iroquoise. Une légende nord-américaine/A North American Legend, édition bilingue/Bilingual edition. Sherbrooke, Qué.: Naaman, 1984. 78 pp. Legend. ((Indian)

5484 RYGA, George
The Ecstasy of Rita Joe. Vancouver: Talonbooks, 1970. 90 pp. Play. (Indian)

5485 RYGA, George
The Ecstasy of Rita Joe and other Plays, edited and introduced by Brian Parker. Toronto: New Press, 1971. 236 pp. Play. (Indian)

5486 SCHULTZ-LORENTZEN, Finn
Arctic. Toronto: McClelland & Stewart, 1976. 496 pp. (Inuit)

5487 SETON, Ernest Thompson
Two Little Savages: Being the Adventures of Two Little Boys Who Lived as Indians and What They Learned. New York: Dover, 1962. 286 pp. 22 pp. of plates. Novel. (Indian)

5488 THÉRIAULT, Yves
Agoak, l'héritage d'Agaguk. Montréal: Quinze, 1975. 236 pp. Roman. (Inuit)

5489 THÉRIAULT, Yves
Ashini. Montréal: Fides, 1960. 173 pp. 2e éd. 1968. 164 pp. 3e éd. 1969. 167 pp. 4e éd. 1972. 145 pp. Roman. (Inuit)

5490 THÉRIAULT, Yves
Tayout, fils d'Agaguk. Montréal: Éd. de l'Homme, 1969. 160 pp. 2e éd. Montréal: L'Actuelle, 1972. 160 pp. Roman. (Inuit)

5491 TYPE, David
Just Us Indians. Toronto: Playwrights Canada, 1984. 55 pp. Play. (Indian)

5492 URSELL, Geoffrey
The Running of the Deer: A Play. Toronto: Playwrights Canada, 1981. 60 pp. Play. (Indian)

5493 VILLENEUVE, Jocelyne
Nanna Bijou: The Sleeping Giant. 46 pp. Moonbeam, Ont.: Penumbra Press, 1981. 46 pp. Legend. (Indian)
[Translation of *Nanna Bijou: Le Geant Endormi.*]

5494 WIEBE, Rudy
First and Vital Candle. Toronto: McClelland & Stewart, 1966. 354 pp. Novel. (Indian)

5495 WIEBE, Rudy
The Scorched-Wood People. A Novel. Toronto: McClelland & Stewart, 1977. 351 pp. Novel. (Métis)
[A portrait of Louis Riel.]

5496 WIEBE, Rudy, ed.
Stories from Western Canada. Toronto: Macmillan of Canada, 1972. xiv, 274 pp. Stories. (Indian)
[Includes F. Niven: "Indian Woman" (pp. 14-24), and H. O'Hagan: "The Tepee" (pp. 25-34).]

5497 WIEBE, Rudy
Where is the Voice Coming from? Toronto: McClelland & Stewart, 1974. 157 pp. Short stories. (Indian)

AUTHOR-SUBJECT INDEX

Guttormsson, Vigfús J., 2400, 2472
Guzzi, George, 2605
Gverino, Ruba, 454

Haas, Johannes, 1037
Haas, Maara, 79, 133-134, 3233, 5296
Hacken, Vera, 3234
Hadley, Michael L., 995, 1126-1127
Hager, E., 999
Haï-Holovko, Oleksa, 141, 4490, 4519, 4530, 4627-4633, 4699, 4787, 4857
Haiku poetry in Canada 180, 3041-3042
Haitian-Canadian literature, 115, 117, 1659-1798
Hajós, Tamás, 213, 1809, 1811-1812, 1844, 2016-2018
Halan, A., 4949
Halász de Béky, Iván see Béky-Halász, Iván
Halikowska, Teresa, 3766
Halldorson, Albert H., 2473
Hamel, Louis-Paul, 1762
Hamel, Réginald, 21
Hamel, Roland C., 204, 207
Hamilton, Mary, 5433
Hamorak, IUriĭ, 4983-4984
Hancock, Geoff, 87, 164, 179, 191, 589, 714, 1498-1499
Hansdóttir, Kristín, 2415, 2474
Harasevych, Mariia, 4762, 4799, 4957, 5067, 5142
Harasymchuk, Mykhaïlo, 4557, 4634-4635
Harasymiw, E.V., 4455, 4467
Haraszti, Endre, 1845-1846, 1852, 1856
Harber, Philip K., 4426
Harder, Peter P., 1020
Hardev Singh, 690-691
Hare, John, 21
Harms, Alvin, 1155, 1172, 1536
Harries, Amach, 618-620
Harrington, Normand, 6
Harris, Christie, 5434-5436
Harris, Claire, 203, 205
Harris, C.K., 180
Harris, Michael, 186
Harrison, Dick, 95
Harrison, Keith, 1105
Hart, Gerald E., 3089
Harth, W., 999
Hartley, Lucie, 2655
Harvey, Jean-Charles, 5268, 5297
Hassan, Abrar, 3644
Hassan, Faruq, 3644, 3652, 3672
Határ, Győző, 1860, 2106
Hatch, Ronald B., 131, 2883, 4280
Hatzegeorgiou, Kyprou, 1574

Hatzidavid, Vissarionas, 1575
Hauser, Gwen, 203
Havelda, John, 1956
Havemann, Ernst, 4167-4169
Haverstick, Sylvia, 2454
Havrylenko, Olia, 4861
Havrylïûk, Volodymyr, 4500, 4530, 4636-4643
Haycock, Ronald Graham, 5378
Hayer, Tara Singh, 692
Hayes, Saul, 3072
Hayne, D.M., 2062
Head, Harold, 177, 4170
Healey, J.J., 110, 1254, 4281
Heaps, Leo, 5298
Heath, Jeffrey M., 22, 324
Hébert, Anne, 2768, 2784
Heciak, Paweł, 3976
Hegedüs, Géza, 2326-2327
Hegyi, Béla, 1999
Heidenreich, Rosmarin, 1255
Heine-Koehn, Lala, 3795-3798
Heines, George, 668
Heinrichs, Ceci, 2680
Helbernäe, Gert, 932
Helbroner, Jules, 3089
Helwig, David, 138
Helwig, Maggie, 2905
Henden, Neil, 192
Hensen, Johannes, 1004, 1033
Hermannson, Halldór, 2404
Hess, Günter, 997, 1065
Hetmańska, Tamara, 3799-3801
Heward, Burt, 715, 2226, 4202
Heyde, Wolfgang, 995
Heydenkorn, Benedykt, 3705, 3710-3711, 3724-3725, 3749, 3849, 3969
Heyduk, J.R., 3802
Hicks, Lorne, 4282
Hiebert, Susan, 185
Hill, Douglas, 590, 2063, 2969, 4283, 4401
Hilts, Dan, 315
Hines, George, 668
Hirabayashi, G.K., 5371
Hirabayashi, Richard, 125, 132
Hiramatsu, Toyoshi, 211, 3042
Hirano, Keiichi, 5379
Hirschfelder, Arlene B., 2592
Hjartarson, Paul, 1203, 1256
Hlus, Carolyn, 269, 316, 2970, 3146
Hodgson, Richard, 2725
Hoeter, Bernhard W., 1517
Holland, Marjorie, 185
Holland, Patrick, 1421
Holliday, W.B., 1257

Iwaniuk, Wacław, 51, 149, 179, 201, 211, 3706, 3709, 3727, 3730, 3739, 3807-3868

Iwanska, A., 3880

Iwasaki, Midori, 3044

Izsák, Gyula, 1835, 2019-2020

Jacewicz, A., 3881

Jackel, David, 2656

Jacobs, Maria, 133, 3605-3623

Jacques, André, 2727

Jacques, Maurice, 1716-1721

Jacques, Ruxl-Léonel, 25

Jaeger, Manfred, 1439

Jagicza, Béla, 1835

Jahić, Mustafa, 454

Jakobsh, Frank K., 995, 1011

Jaksiński, Józef Piotr, 3851

Jamaican-Canadian literature, 3015-3040

Janelle, Claude, 1795

Jang, Charles, 418-421

Janoël, André, 1690, 1721, 1796, 2728, 2825

Janovskis, Gunars, 3365-3366

Janta, Alexander, 3869

Januszko, Stanisław, 3870-3875

Janzen, Heinz, 1383

Janzen, Helen, 1031

Janzen, Jacob H., 995, 1003, 1006, 1012, 1020, 1031, 1035-1036, 1365-1385

Janzen, Johannes Heinrich, 993, 1386

Japanese in Canadian literature, 5246, 5272, 5306-5308, 5345, 5353

Japanese-Canadian literature, 91, 165, 185, 3041-3049

Jardel, Jean-Pierre, 3583

Jarucki, Jerzy, 3876

Järvalene, Joan, 831

Jasmin, Claude, 5268, 5299-5302

Javonović, Leposava, 4085

Javor, Pavel, 30, 51, 141, 211, 473, 4113, 500-533 (also   Škvor, (Jiři) George)

Jaworski, Kazimierz A., 3852

Jaworsky, S.J., 26 (also Îaworsʹkyĭ, S.)

Jean-Baptiste, 1660

Jeletzky, T.F., 4045

Jensen, K., 617

Jensen, Leroy, 178

Jesih, Pavao, 457

Jesman, Czesław, 3977

Ještědský, Jan, 523-524

Jewinski, Ed., 1387-1389

Jewinski, Hans, 2884

Jewish-Canadian literature, 115, 117, 140, 146, 150, 152, 165, 167, 185, 3050-3292

Jews in Canadian literature, 5244-5245, 5259-5271, 5273, 5278-5279, 5282, 5284-5286, 5290, 5294, 5296-5304, 5314-5318, 5323-5324, 5327-5331, 5333-5341, 5348-5349, 5354-5356, 5358, 5368

Jirasek, Jiri, 198

Jíri, Jaroslav, 525

Jo-Hsi Chen see Chen Jo-Hsi

Jobling, J. Keith, 1548

Joe, Rita, 179

Jofré, Manuel, 356

Jóhannesson, Sigurður Jón, 2482-2485

Jóhannesson, Sigurður Júlíus, 2405, 2415, 2419, 2486-2495

Jóhannesson, Þorsteinn, 2496-2497

Jóhannsson, Sigurbjörn, 2408, 2419, 2498

Johnson, Andres, 2499

Johnson, B.E., 2419

Johnson, Emily Pauline, 51, 2650-2658

Johnson, Jakobína, 2419, 2500-2506

Johnson, Lorraine, 2971

Johnson, Sigrid, 2414

Johnston, Basil H., 5451

Johnston, Patronella, 2635

Jónás, George, 29, 41, 51, 56, 70, 100, 169, 201, 1856, 2021-2081, 3097

Jonassaint, Jean, 1661-1662

Jónatansson, G.K., 2507

Jones, Hettig, 2637

Jones, Katie, 135

Jónsdóttir, Júlíana, 2508

Jónsson, Einar Páll, 211, 2400, 2405, 2415, 2419, 2509-2513, 2530

Jónsson, Gísli, 2400, 2419, 2514-2516

Jónsson, Jón frá Sleðrjót, 2469

Jónsson, Magnús, 2419

Jonynas, V.A., 3517

Joseph, Clifton, 136

Joubert, Jean-Louis, 98

Juhász, József, 1826, 1845-1846, 1850, 1856, 1861, 1902, 2082-2094, 2189, 2251, 2264

Juhász, Vilmos, 1853

Júlíus, Kristján N., 141, 2400, 2405, 2517

Juričić, Želimir B., 89, 444-445, 450-452, 454, 4078

Jurkszus-Tomaszewska, Jadwiga, 3706, 3709, 3726, 3877-3884

Jürma, Mall, 888-891, 934-937

Kabdebó, Tamás, 2001, 2107

Kachaluba, Mykhaĭlo, 4724

Kachtitsis, Nikos, 1577-1582

Kachurovsʹkyĭ, Ihor, 4961-4962

Kagige, Francis, 2608

McMullen, Lorraine, 1277
McMullin, Stanley Edward, 1278-1282
McNab, Ute, 1068
McNally, Paul, 4315
McPherson, Hugo, 273
McQueen, John, 971
McRan, E., 2933-2934
McTair, Roger, 4421-4423
McWhirter, George, 4316
Mdago-Hogan, Simbo Mzuri, 197
Meadwell, Kenneth, 2827
Mechling, W.H., 2619
Meheš, Mirko, 455
Meikle, Duncan, 169
Melamet, Max, 3080
Melancon, Joseph, 149
Mélançon, Robert, 2732
Mele, Jim, 2935-2936
Melfi, Mary, 41, 80, 183, 186, 2753, 2756-2757,
2778, 2785, 2787, 2789, 2937-2943
Melzak, Ronald, 2674, 2686, 2689
Mendez, Rubín, 193
Mendis, Tyrell, 707
Mennonite-Canadian literature, 185, 1006, 1009-
1010, 1015, 1019-1020, 1023, 1026-1027, 1031, 1036
Mennonites in Canadian literature, 5250, 5257,
5288, 5291, 5317, 5362-5363
Mérő, Ferenc, 2217
Merola, Mario, 2757
Merrett, Robert James, 1964
Mesman, Leslie, 2288
Měšťan, Jaromír, 528
Mester, János, 2182
Metayer, Maurice, 2687
Metcalf, John, 2768
Métis in Canadian literature, 5371, 5977, 5390,
5430
Métis literature, 3586-3589
Metsanurk, Mait, 859-860
Meyer, Bertha, 3050
Mezei, Kathy, 2733, 2952
Mezey-McDougall, Marina, 1844, 2177-2178
Miązek, Bonifacy, 3729, 3745, 3860
Mibashan, David, 223-224
Michael, Friedrich, 1283
Michalski, Stanisław, 141, 3706, 3727, 3913-
3918
Michaud, Ginette, 253
Michelutti, Dorina, 2778, 2944
Michon, Jaques, 3946
Micmac tales, 2626
Micone, Marco, 2757, 2762, 2767, 2782, 2787,
2945-2954
Middleboro', T., 1284

Middleton, J.E., 1285-1286
Midžan, Feri, 461-462
Migus, Paul M., 103
Mikiver, Ilmar, 852
Mikó, Veronika, 1843, 1855
Milabauer, Joseph, 3175
Miles, Ron, 2909
Miljević, Vojo V., 4086
Millán, Gonzalo, 178, 350-351, 356, 358-359,
377-378
Miller, J., 1641
Miller, Max, 3152-3153
Milles, Ron, 1642
Mills, John, 4317
Milne, W.S., 1287
Milnes, Humphrey, 4381-4382
Milton, Norma, 35
Minni, C.D., 169, 178, 310, 2768-2769, 2773,
2785, 2788, 2955-2957, 3010
Minot, René, 1744
Miralles, Gabriela, 359
Miransky, Peretz, 3154-3157
Miska, János (i.e. John), 36-37, 89, 1204, 1803-
1804, 1811-1812, 1818, 1822-1832, 1841-1844, 1855,
1857, 1864-1865, 1875, 1925, 2088, 2143, 2169-
2170, 2183-2197, 2204, 2253, 2280-2281, 5159
Miskolci Panulics, Lajos, 2198
Mistry, Rohinton, 147, 708
Mitcham, Allison, 150, 3947, 5383
Mitchell, Beverley, 1288
Mitchell, W.O., 5248, 5468-5469
Mniszek, Helena, 3919
Mock, Irene, 4168
Mockus, Vida, 795
Mogridge, Basil, 359
Mohl, Josef, 995
Mohylânka, Dariâ, 4895-4899
Moisan, Clément, 2828
Mokdoni, A., 3292
Molinari, Guidio, 2757
Molnár, Miklós, 2356
Money, Darlene, 2227
Monkman, Leslie, 5385
Monoszlói, Rezső, 2111
Monteiro, João Lucio, 206
Montero, Gloria, 5325
Montserrat-Canadian literature, 3590-3594
Moodie, Susanna, 5254
Moore, Brian, 5249, 5259
Moore, Harold M., 5470
Moore, Mavor, 94
Morand, Fleurette, 3584
Morantz, Alan, 3195
Mordhorst, Otto F., 1004, 1033